MIND AND RIGHTS

Mind and Rights combines historical, philosophical, and legal perspectives with research from psychology and the cognitive sciences to probe the justification of human rights in ethics, politics and law. Chapters critically examine the growth of the human rights culture, its roots in history and current human rights theories. They engage with the so-called cognitive revolution and investigate the relationship between human cognition and human rights to determine how insights gained from modern theories of the mind can deepen our understanding of the foundations of human rights. *Mind and Rights* argues that the pursuit of the human rights idea, with its achievements and tragic failures, is key to understand what kind of beings humans are. Amidst ongoing debate on the universality and legitimacy of human rights, this book provides a uniquely comprehensive analysis of great practical and political importance for a culture of legal justice undergirded by rights. This title is also available as open access on Cambridge Core.

Matthias Mahlmann is University Professor, Chair of Philosophy and Theory of Law, Legal Sociology and International Public Law at the University of Zurich.

Mind and Rights

THE HISTORY, ETHICS, LAW AND PSYCHOLOGY OF HUMAN RIGHTS

MATTHIAS MAHLMANN

CAMBRIDGE
UNIVERSITY PRESS

CAMBRIDGE
UNIVERSITY PRESS

Shaftesbury Road, Cambridge CB2 8EA, United Kingdom

One Liberty Plaza, 20th Floor, New York, NY 10006, USA

477 Williamstown Road, Port Melbourne, VIC 3207, Australia

314–321, 3rd Floor, Plot 3, Splendor Forum, Jasola District Centre, New Delhi – 110025, India

103 Penang Road, #05–06/07, Visioncrest Commercial, Singapore 238467

Cambridge University Press is part of Cambridge University Press & Assessment,
a department of the University of Cambridge.

We share the University's mission to contribute to society through the pursuit of
education, learning and research at the highest international levels of excellence.

www.cambridge.org
Information on this title: www.cambridge.org/9781107184220

DOI: 10.1017/9781316875520

First published 2023

A catalogue record for this publication is available from the British Library.

A Cataloging-in-Publication data record for this book is available from the Library of Congress

ISBN 978-1-107-18422-0 Hardback
ISBN 978-1-316-63540-7 Paperback

Contents

Acknowledgments

The cover image is a reproduction of striking Paleolithic rock art in northern Africa, Gilf Kebir, painted by Elisabeth Pauli in 1933 during an anthropological expedition to that region. It was exhibited together with other such documents of prehistoric rock art at the MoMA in New York in 1937. The picture documents the common universal heritage of human beings, here displayed in a cave in northern Africa by people whose descendants were regarded as primitive brutes by European colonizers. It shows the rich, equal creative endowment of human beings that has been the basis for the cultural achievements of our species throughout the ages and across the globe, achievements that ultimately also include – which is the point of this book – the ethics and law of human rights.

Many people have helped to develop the argument of the book. I would like to thank John Mikhail for his comments on the manuscript and for the privilege of decades of intense discussions about the foundations of ethical thinking and the law. As doctoral students, we were both inspired by Noam Chomsky's work on the theory of the human mind and its deep implications for our understanding of what kind of creatures we are. I am very grateful for the input Noam Chomsky has provided about the topic this book now addresses. I owe a substantial debt to András Sajó for his critical input on the final manuscript and many (increasingly alarmed) discussions about rights and constitutionalism and the enemies both are facing. I also thank Christopher McCrudden and Mordechai Kremnitzer for very helpful critical feedback on the manuscript and the ongoing dialogue about a liberating and egalitarian project of human rights. I have profited very much from Eyal Zamir's criticism and suggestions on an initial paper and the final manuscript.

I was fortunate to profit from comments on talks and publications and from discussions on the topic, the theses of this inquiry and its wider background in ethics and law at various stages of the project. I thank Tilmann Altwicker, Shreya Atrey, Susanne Baer, Samantha Besson, Giovanni Biaggini, Andrea Büchler, Oliver Diggelmann, Catarina Donati, Marcus Düwell, Christoph Engel, Rivka Feldhay,

Thomas Gächter, Alain Griffel, Klaus Günther, Michael Hagner, Lutz Jäncke, Nadja El Kassar, Helen Keller, Tarunabh Khaitan, Anne Kühler, Philip Kunig, Christos Kypraios, George Letsas, Stefan Magen, Frank Meyer, Daniel Moeckli, Stephen Morse, Jörg-Paul Müller, Catherine O'Regan, Anne Peters, Orin Percus, Hubert Rottleuthner, Peter Schaber, M. N. S. Sellers, John Tasioulas, Ian Tattersall, Arun Thiruvengadam, Renata Uitz and Lutz Wingert for critically engaging with me on these questions in different forms. I am particularly grateful for the thoughts about the human rights project that Regina Kiener and the late Andreas Auer generously shared with me.

I have had the privilege to learn much about interdisciplinary perspectives on the foundations of law from my colleagues in the *Fachgruppe Grundlagen* at the Faculty of Law: José Louis Alonso, Ulrike Babusiaux, Wolfgang Ernst, Christoph Graber, Johannes Liebrecht, Elisabetta Fiocchi Malaspina, Marcel Senn and Andreas Thier.

I profited significantly from the detailed comments of the anonymous reviewers of the project.

I am particularly thankful to Margaret Hiley, who not only shouldered the task of language editing most professionally and with outstanding skill but also engaged substantially with the content of the text, which helped to considerably improve the clarity of the argument.

The members of my research group and affiliates of the law and philosophy discussion group in Zurich have contributed in many ways to the work on and arguments in the book. I am therefore indebted to Corina Diem, Peter Gailhofer, Levin Güver, Matthias Hächler, Frederik von Harbou, Jón Laxdal, Nicole Nickerson, Pascal Meier, Nebojsa Mijatovic, Angela Müller, Ilona Paulke, Lena Portmann, Nils Reimann, Stefano Statunato, Julia Stern, Hanna Stoll, Youlo Wujohktsang and Nadja Zink.

Corina Diem, Levin Güver, Jón Laxdal, Angelina Manhart, Nebojsa Mijatovic, Nicole Nickerson, and Stefano Statunato patiently assisted me during the final editorial phase of the project.

I had the opportunity to present and discuss the theses of the book during a research stay at the Bonavero Institute of Human Rights, University of Oxford, as a fellow at Mansfield College in 2021/22. I would like to thank Catherine O'Regan for her hospitality and Christos Kypraios and Sarah Norman for their support. I am grateful for the substantial input I received.

I was invited to teach a course on "Mind and Rights" at the University of Pennsylvania School of Law as a Bok Visiting International Professor. I am thankful for this invitation and the opportunity for scientific exchange it offered, in particular to Stephen Morse, who for several years has been teaching a law and neuroscience seminar with me in Zurich.

Special thanks to Matt Gallaway for his interest in the project and persistent, patient support throughout the writing process. Jadyn Fauconier-Herry and Joshua

Penney offered much-appreciated help. John Stewart Marr made copy editing a smooth and sometimes funny exercise.

Georgia Strati had a profound impact on the genesis of the book. Moreover, her philological expertise was of great importance for the work on ancient sources.

The book incorporates some materials from Matthias Mahlmann, "Mind and Rights: Neuroscience, Philosophy, and the Foundations of Justice," in *Law, Reason, and Emotion*, edited by M. N. S. Sellers, 80–137 (Cambridge: Cambridge University Press, 2017), included by kind permission.

I would like to thank the Frobenius-Institut für Kulturanthropologische Forschung, the Goethe-Universität Frankfurt and Dr. Richard Kuba for the permission to use the cover image.

Parts of the poem *Santorini* by Giorgos Seferis are reproduced with Anna Lontou's kind permission.

The open access publication of this book has been published with the generous support of the Swiss National Science Foundation.

Introduction

Navigating Deep Waters: The Problems of Human Rights and New Perspectives of Inquiry

The far-off blackness ahead of the ship was like another night seen through the starry night of the earth – the starless night of the immensities beyond the created universe, revealed in its appalling stillness through a low fissure in the glittering sphere of which the earth is the kernel.

"Whatever there might be about," said Jukes, "we are steaming straight into it."

Joseph Conrad, *Typhoon*

I.1 CRITIQUE AND DEFENSE

In 1945, humanity had sailed through a profoundly dark night. The victims had yet to be counted, but the lessons to be drawn already seemed to be indisputable. One important conclusion was to reassert with sober but unflinching determination an old, revolutionary idea – the idea of every human being's fundamental rights and equal intrinsic worth. The *Universal Declaration of Human Rights* is the flourish, heralding many following attempts to give these rights a new standing, to make them the mandatory standards for the treatment of humans in ethics and in law, in nation-states, regional organizations and the global community. Some of these attempts met with astonishing success, others were a tragic failure. So far, however, none have achieved the respect that human beings truly deserve.

This inquiry hopes to shed some new light on the content, history, justification and cognitive foundations of this remarkable idea. It argues that a theory of human rights has to engage with these different perspectives to do justice to its subject, in particular if it aims at understanding something meaningful about the relation between human rights, moral cognition and the law. This study intends to identify in a theoretically unconventional and perhaps illuminating way the place of human rights in the human form of life. It will outline why it is crucial to understand the meaning of human rights for humanity's mode of existence not only for the sake of analyzing the phenomenon of human rights itself more deeply, but also if we want to fathom what kind of creatures we humans really are. It attempts to rescue the idea of human rights in ethics and law from being washed away by a torrent of critique from history, philosophy, legal theory, moral psychology and neuroscience. It argues that rather than subverting the idea of human rights, the history of this idea and its traces in social practices, as well as normative theory and what is currently known (and not known) about the structure and evolutionary origin of human moral cognition, all only strengthen the case for human rights.

There is a long tradition in philosophy, science and, perhaps most importantly, art that, while devoid of any comforting illusions and bitterly honest about the sinister sides of human emotions, beliefs and actions and the suffering they cause, is driven by a deeply conceived and passionately felt respect for what it means to be human. For these thinkers and artists, humans appear as surprisingly richly endowed beings, with characteristics defying simple explanations, bringing something new and unprecedented to the natural world, radically and rapidly transforming life on Earth by ever new forms of living, insights and the astonishing pursuit of beauty. There is true awe in many voices in philosophy, science and art, expressing the perception that there is a spark of something lovely and sublime in human beings. One of the central reasons for this attitude towards humans is their capacity to act under moral laws with genuine concern for others, to submit to principles of justice, to respect others and their rights and to attempt to build social orders of decency – moved not by the commands of secular or religious superiors, the threat of sanctions, the prospect of direct or indirect personal gains or the hidden, innate machinery of selfishness, but by the autonomous exercise of their moral judgment and the intimate but powerful calls of their conscience. The many other impulses and ideas that drive humans forward, the broad trail of crime and folly in human history and what it says about us, only increase the importance of this often feeble, regularly neglected, occasionally gleefully derided and still sometimes strangely powerful, very peculiar capacity of human beings.

This inquiry will align itself with this tradition with due modesty, maintaining that the idea of human rights expresses a remarkably magnanimous and gentle side of the better parts of human thought and feeling that a human culture disregards to its own detriment. This study will try to show that this idea has deep roots in the history of ethical and legal thought and that it stands up to critical scrutiny of its claim to normative justification both in the ethical and the legal sphere. Its arguments challenge a certain cluster of assumptions about morality in some parts of philosophy, psychology and cognitive science that has become influential over the last decades in a range of different variations and that, for some, defines the hard scientific knowledge of the age. From this point of view, there is no such thing as genuinely selfless morality under principles of justice with a content that is justifiable by convincing reasons, has motivational force and includes all humans or even all sentient beings. Only a life in competing moral clans, guided by a small set of emotions that are the true core of human morality, comes naturally to human beings. One influential explanation for this is that concern for others beyond limited communities is irreconcilable with the way the human mind has been structured by the forces of evolution. The conclusions drawn from this common point of theoretical departure are diverse: some infer that the best one can hope for is some kind of prudential modification of the natural moral world of human beings to make life on this planet livable, while others are more optimistic and argue that, despite these constraints of human nature, just and caring social and political arrangements are achievable – always threatened, however, by humans' narrow natural moral concerns, which are limited to kin, moral clan members and the well-being and reputation of the agents themselves.

Such theories fail to convince on their own ground, we will argue, if one interprets the empirical evidence of moral psychology and neuroscience within convincing theoretical frameworks and draws plausible conclusions from a sufficiently complex theory of natural evolution's intricate machinery. Even if these theories do not succeed in achieving their theoretical aims, and even though one is well-advised not to draw any normative conclusions from facts of psychology or natural history, such visions can still have substantial harmful effects if sufficiently many people form their idea of the prospects of human morality according to what these theories assert. Such theories can discourage people from pursuing the idea for which a morality of human rights stands – which is not limited to one's own tribe but demands respect, liberty and equality for all human beings, therein lying its whole point and its appeal – by making them lose hope that human beings could be guided by such broader-minded, exacting and generous moral precepts. Such psychological theories may breed cynicism, docile acquiescence to power and self-righteous resignation in a time when a spirited resistance against the dismantling of human rights as an idea, moral practice and legal institution is of central importance if new forms of post-truth political authoritarianism, destructive ethno-nationalism and contempt for human worth are not to win the day. They may also provide an exceedingly and much-desired good conscience for those who have a keen interest in shaking off the shackles of moral principles and weakening the project of human rights because it challenges their power, interests and self-serving actions.[1]

A good starting point to indicate in sufficient detail the cognitive interests and the potential novelty of this study's approach is the simple question: What is the idea of human rights about? Answering this question will identify what the object of inquiry is understood to be and what the main aims of this inquiry are.

[1] As Noam Chomsky observed in his reflections about psychology and ideology, two sorts of questions need to be asked if we are presented with claims about the nature and psychology of human beings: "What is the scientific status of the claims? And, What social or ideological needs do they serve? The questions are logically independent, but those of the second sort naturally come to the fore as scientific pretensions are undermined," Noam Chomsky, *For Reasons of State* (New York: The New Press, 2003), 318.

I.2 REASON, CONSCIENCE AND RIGHTS

The *Universal Declaration of Human Rights*, which set the example for the attempts to bring the human rights idea into life in the post–World War II era, famously begins with an anthropological assumption: All human beings, it asserts, "are endowed with reason and conscience."[2] Its text does not draw any explicit conclusions from this, but it is clear that these assumed properties are taken to be relevant to the idea of human rights that the *Universal Declaration* restates so powerfully after the cataclysm of World War II. One underlying idea appears to be that *because* of these properties of human beings, alone or in conjunction with others, we justifiably can conclude that humans are endowed with certain inalienable rights. From this perspective, reason and conscience are *justificatory reasons* for the belief that human beings in fact enjoy human rights. Furthermore, all human beings share these attributes. While the meaning of these attributes may raise substantial questions, the general thrust of the statement thus seems sufficiently clear: Human rights are the birthright of thinking and moral beings.

Another dimension of the meaning of this prominent passage is that because of "reason and conscience," humans are in fact in an epistemic position to *understand* that their human rights are justified, that they are not doomed to ignorance, and consequently they should take action to protect these rights.[3] Reason and conscience are the means of identifying human rights as well-justified fundamental claims that human beings are entitled to pursue. Reasoning and moral thought are the epistemic keys that unlock the door to the cognition of human rights.[4]

[2] UN General Assembly, *Universal Declaration of Human Rights* (UDHR), Resolution 217 A (III), December 10, 1948, Art. 1.

[3] The preamble of the UDHR states, after all, that "disregard and contempt for human rights have resulted in barbarous acts which have outraged the *conscience of mankind*" (emphasis added).

[4] For a detailed account of the drafting process of the *Universal Declaration*, cf. Johannes Morsink, *The Universal Declaration of Human Rights: Origins, Drafting and Intent* (Philadelphia: University of Pennsylvania Press, 1999), 4 ff.; Mary Ann Glendon, A *World Made Anew: Eleanor Roosevelt and the Universal Declaration* (New York: Random House Publishing Group, 2001). The first draft was written by John P. Humphrey, head of the UN Human Rights Division, William Anthony Schabas, ed., *The Universal Declaration of Human Rights: The Travaux Préparatoires*, Vols. I–III (Cambridge: Cambridge University Press, 2013), 281 ff. (E/CN.4/AC.1/3). This draft formed the basis of René Cassin's new draft, printed in Marc Agi, *René Cassin (1887–1976), Prix Nobel de la Paix: Père de la Déclaration universelle des Droits de l'homme* (Paris: Perrin, 1998), 359 ff. The term "reason" was included in Cassin's draft by the working group on the *Universal Declaration*, cf. Schabas, *The Universal Declaration*, 788 f. (E/CN.4/AC.1/W.1). The term "conscience" was the end result of an initiative by the influential Chinese delegate Chang to add a Chinese term that he translated literally as "two-man mindedness," proposing that "sympathy" or "consciousness of one's fellow man" might be English equivalents, Schabas, *The Universal Declaration*, 800 f. (E/CN.4/AC.1/SR.8). The British delegate Wilson later proposed using the term "conscience," supported by Chang, among others, Schabas, *The Universal Declaration*, 853 (E/CN.4/AC.1/SR.13). In the final

Interestingly, the foundational role of reason and conscience is more than hortatory rhetoric in the text of the *Universal Declaration*. As was pointed out during a self-reflective moment in the drafting process, the reliance on reasons and arguments was constitutive of this process itself.[5] To be sure, drafting the *Universal Declaration* was a highly complex affair, embedded in the many conflicting aspirations of the most powerful political forces of the time, not all of these agents devoted to anything remotely resembling obedience to the commands of reason, let alone to a moral cause. After all, this was the time of the twilight of the falling European empires, a time when the dice of future world power were cast and the contours of a new epoch overshadowed by the threat of total nuclear destruction were slowly emerging from the political haze. Nevertheless, and perhaps oddly enough given this historical setting, arguments clearly counted in the drafting process. There is very little in the *Declaration*'s final text that mirrors only naked power politics and cannot, despite all its flaws, at least in principle be defended by something like universalizable arguments, controversial as these arguments may be in detail. Clear examples of such power politics, such as the attempt to leave scope for the nonapplication of human rights in the colonies that still existed, were even rebutted – a success that initially was not achieved in other cases such as the *European Convention on Human Rights and Fundamental Freedoms* (ECHR), where champions of this kind of exemption, like Great Britain's governments of the time, had more of a say.[6]

discussion on the matter, Chang argued for dropping "reason and conscience" again. In the discussion about retaining or deleting this clause, Charles Malik, as the clause's most outspoken defender, related it to central properties of human beings, arguing that the drafting Commission "should mention somewhere in the Declaration, perhaps in the Preamble, the qualities which essentially characterized man, since man and his rights were the Commission's main concern." Cassin had made a similar argument on the importance of clarifying the particular characteristics of human beings in relation to the earlier draft, Schabas, *The Universal Declaration*, 801 (E/CN.4/AC.1/SR.8). The Human Rights Commission voted to retain the clause, Schabas, *The Universal Declaration*, 1673 (E/CN.4/SR.50).

There is much debate about the reconstruction and translation of the meaning of concepts such as reason and conscience, especially in different cultural contexts. Equally rich is the discussion about how to interpret the meaning of a legal term after it has been included in a legal document (or, as in the case of the UDHR, a nonbinding document, albeit with clear legal significance), especially concerning the issue of whether or not any of the meaning associated with it by some of the drafters is relevant for its interpretation or not. Despite these legal hermeneutic intricacies, it seems clear that the passage refers to the rational and moral capacities of human beings, taken as central properties, foundational both for the attribution of their particular moral status and for the possibility of understanding this status and its normative consequences in the form of rights. On the debate and for a predominantly epistemological reading, cf. Morsink, *Origins*, 296 ff.

5 Cf. Schabas, *The Universal Declaration*, 1671 (E/CN.4/SR.50), where Charles Malik is quoted as saying: "Without reason, the very work they were engaged in would be impossible; what, then, more 'reasonable' than the explicit mention of the factor that constituted the basis of their work, in the very first article?"

6 Cf. on Art. 2 UDHR, Glendon, *A World Made Anew*, 149 f., 162, on Council of Europe, *European Convention for the Protection of Human Rights and Fundamental Freedoms, as amended by Protocols Nos. 11 and 14* (ECHR), ETS 5, November 4, 1950, Art. 56 (former

To the average observer, the two ideas of reason and conscience as justificatory reasons and means of normative cognition that underpin the human rights project according to this central statement by international actors may appear a truism and of no particular concern.

What else, one may be tempted to say, was to be stated in a document intended to revive human moral, legal and political life at a time when half the world and the ethical foundations of an epoch still were lying in smoking ruins? Should the *Universal Declaration* have taken the view that human beings are beastly predators driven by the irrational will to power? Protean beings,[7] *"nicht festgestellte Tiere,"* animals without a fixed nature,[8] which are the mere playthings of historical and social change? Shrewd calculators of self-interest following the sole motive of maximizing their own idiosyncratic preferences?

After the Nazi *danse macabre* of murderous folly, after the reign of their abstruse, cruel and deadly ideas about human life, its meaning and the ethical parameters that guide human beings, could one rely on anything other than reason and conscience? After this cataclysm of horrors, which washed away traditions, beliefs and centuries-old cultural assets, turning the supposedly impregnable walls of the institutions of human legal orders into meaningless rubble – at this moment, when it was absolutely necessary that humanity (for once) got it right, because human life for a few precious and awful moments was visibly naked in all its painful vulnerability, fragility and suffering greatness – what should have been endorsed other than the capacity for reasonable thinking and ideas of basic human decency provided by human moral understanding (for whatever they are worth) to lead the way into

Art. 63 ECHR) and background, Alfred William Brian Simpson, *Human Rights and the End of Empire: Britain and the Genesis of the European Convention* (Oxford: Oxford University Press, 2001), 288 ff., with the following illuminating comment on the "dogma" of Colonial Application Clauses and the policies of human rights: "The Colonial Office dogma was sometimes relaxed in special circumstances. Thus the *Universal Declaration* on Human Rights of 1948 did not contain a colonial application clause, and a Circular Dispatch from the Colonial Office of July 20, 1948 even stated that the UK could not therefore accept it unless all colonial government did so. This would have entailed the odium of abstaining in the final vote on December 10, with no later opportunity to come on board. In the event the UK did not secure agreement from the colonies before voting for the Declaration, and made it clear that it did indeed apply to all its dependencies. Since it did not bind anyone to do anything and in any event was not a treaty, this was not viewed by the Colonial Office as presenting a real problem." Britain extended the rule of the ECHR to most colonies in 1953. Official records note that "one of the main objects in inducing colonial territories to apply the convention was for publicity purposes at the United Nations in connection with the draft Convention on Human Rights," quoted in Simpson, *Human Rights*, 829, among substantial doubts about the political usefulness of this move, given the constraints that the ECHR was feared to impose on colonial rule.

7 Cf. Richard Rorty, "Human Rights, Rationality and Sentimentality," in *On Human Rights: The Oxford Amnesty Lectures*, eds. Stephen Shute and Susan Hurley (New York: Basic Books, 1993), 115.

8 Friedrich Nietzsche, *Jenseits von Gut und Böse*, in *Friedrich Nietzsche: Sämtliche Werke*, Vol. 5, eds. Giorgio Colli and Mazzino Montinari (Munich: Deutscher Taschenbuch Verlag, 1999), 81.

something resembling a bearable future? Would anything else not have fallen short of the lessons and demands of this pivotal historical moment?

The theoretical rationale underpinning these thoughts about the justification of human rights and the epistemic condition of human beings is far from clear, however, when we consider contemporary debates about rights, their justification and their epistemological foundations, as well as the many questions they raise.

1.3 THE PROBLEM OF RIGHTS

The foundations of rights are debated as much as their content or the claim that there are universal rights pertaining to every human everywhere, a conclusion that the *Universal Declaration* draws as one of its defining elements, echoing the universalistic hopes of the past. To be sure, serious questions are implied by this stance, the answers to which are far from obvious. What does it mean that they are rights that humans are supposed to enjoy *by virtue of their humanity*, as an almost canonical view puts it? If "humanity" refers just to a set of biological characteristics of a biped with a large brain that walks upright, how can rights be derived from such contingent facts? Is there a plausible concept of humanity that does something other than impose parochial views about human existence on others? And even if there is such a concept, are reason and conscience really part of what humanity means? What about emotions or the totality of our bodily existence? Do they not count as well?

Furthermore: What is the stuff that human rights are actually made of? Are human rights part of a Natural Law permeating the cosmos? Are they part of the mind-independent fabric of the world, like the Higgs boson? Or are they a tissue of beliefs woven by the hidden operations of the human mind? What are the reasons for their justification? Are they necessary preconditions of human autonomy and action and thus justified because we should not and indeed cannot give up our autonomy? Does a qualified need or interest in the objects protected by human rights give rise to these rights? Or is it an (imagined) contract or consensus? What do these approaches imply for the universality of human rights?

Other questions are no less difficult, not least concerning the precise content of human rights, the exact group of rights-holders, the duty-bearers or addressees of rights and the nature of rights. What is the final criterion that makes a right a *human* right? Not every legitimate human concern has found its way into the bills of rights that determine the current content of human rights. There was no question that the right to life should be included in the *Universal Declaration*. It was equally obvious that a right to be loved would not be included. Why?[9]

9 Cf. on the paradoxical, inalienable but unenforceable right to be loved, Theodor W. Adorno, "Minima Moralia," in *Theodor W. Adorno: Gesammelte Schriften*, Vol. 4, ed. Rolf Tiedemann (Darmstadt: Wissenschaftliche Buchgesellschaft, 1998), 187. An attempt to defend a right of

Humans are regarded as rights-holders. Does this mean every human being, or are certain groups to be excluded – infants, perhaps, because they lack certain properties that would make them fully human in the normatively relevant sense, as some argue?[10] Can groups be rights-holders? Can corporations enjoy human rights? All or just some? What about animals? Or robots? A self-learning algorithm?

The question of the addressees of human rights raises similar problems. Do the addressees of human rights also include private individuals, or are they only legal entities that exercise public power, most importantly states? What about corporations? Finally and importantly: Are human rights moral, legal or both? If the latter, do they mean the same in the moral and in the legal sphere? If not, what are the differences?

The assumption of human beings' shared capacity to understand the point of human rights that underpins the *Universal Declaration* leads us into no less troubled theoretical waters than the questions about the nature, content and justification of human rights. Reason has become a notoriously contentious concept, and conscience, as a human property of constitutive importance for moral orientation, does not necessarily fare better. To be sure, there are many references to reason in the debates about human rights. But what does reason mean in these contexts? A Platonic capacity to access ideas that exist independently of the mind? An Aristotelian understanding of forms or capacity of practical cognition? A natural light that pierces the darkness of error and ignorance, providing cognition that is distinct and clear? A Kantian capacity of principles constituting human understanding? A Hegelian spirit whose might irresistibly wrenches the last secrets from nature's grasp? Something else?

Reason was traditionally thought to be an attribute of human individuals, the epitome of a human being's ability to think and, by thinking, to arrive at conclusions that were insights, not false opinions. Should this idea of subjective reason perhaps be abandoned? Should reason be freed from its incarceration in the human individual because it is actually found somewhere else? Is thinking in fact taking place not "in the head" but in social practices, in *Lebensformen*, which change "as we go along" but whose nature we nevertheless can and must make explicit? Or is reason embedded in specific *Lebenswelten*, lifeworlds, in forms of cooperative communication, where better arguments reign rather than force?

Many people have sought and continue to seek to answer these questions. But is it really worth pursuing them at all? Has the reference to reason not proven to be a dead end? Have we not learned much about the dark side of reason, its immanent dialectic and contingent construction by social forces and narratives woven over time? Have concepts of reason not been tainted by partisan perspectives – of gender,

children to be loved is S. Matthew Liao, *The Right to Be Loved* (Oxford: Oxford University Press, 2015).

10 Cf. e.g. James Griffin, *On Human Rights* (Oxford: Oxford University Press, 2008), 95.

of social groups defined by skin color or religious outlook, for instance? Are ideas of reason not forged by hidden forces of social power that model them after their own image? What is conscience supposed to mean, apart from highly personal, historically and culturally contingent and subjective perspectives on matters of right and wrong that cannot have any possible claim to objectivity?

The seriousness of these questions and the difficulties in answering them are of some importance. The assertion that there is something about humans that entitles them to certain rights and that they are capable of insight in these matters is not an accessory part of the fundamental claims implied in the ethical and political project that the *Universal Declaration* stands for, but rather it lies at its very core.

The project presupposes that human beings are never again to be treated in the way they had been in the dire epoch preceding the *Universal Declaration*. Its starting point is that the imperative to treat human beings with respect had been well understood before and now has become common knowledge and nothing less than a matter of the very basic moral and legal self-understanding of humanity. The real task therefore is to build institutions that put these insights into practice, arduous and difficult as this may be. Fortunately, this endeavor is able to rely on a firm, normative, reflectively secured foundation that has stood the tough test of time.

Are these assumptions flawed? Are they the ephemeral offspring of a certain moment in history that now has passed? Are they only ideological machinations that should no longer occupy serious thought in a more mature age? Or are they expressions of appropriate respect for the autonomy of human thought and the well-warranted belief that the free exercise of human thinking would lead ultimately to insight into the justifiedness of human rights?

The historical record of human rights does not make the assessment of such claims much easier. Human rights have a very rich and complicated history. They are not an uncontested, self-evident companion of human practice and thought. As Thomas Paine dryly remarked after underlining the universal nature of the French Revolution and in particular of the *Déclaration des Droits de l'Homme et du Citoyen*, "but the governments of all those countries are by no means favourable to it."[11] Armies marched to quell this idea, and powerful structures of suppression were erected to counter its threat to power and material privilege. Many arguments were formulated that criticized this idea. There is no lack of countertheories to the idea of human rights, vividly summed up in Edmund Burke's attack upon rights and the idea that these rights could form the yardstick for legitimate forms of government:

[11] Thomas Paine, "The Rights of Man," in Thomas Paine, *Common Sense and Other Writings* (New York: Barnes & Noble Classics, 2005), 103.

> We have not (as I conceive) lost the generosity and dignity of thinking of the fourteenth century; nor as of yet have we subtilized ourselves into savages. . . . Atheists are not our preachers; madmen are not our lawgivers. . . . We have not been drawn and trussed, in order that we may be filled, like stuffed birds in a museum, with chaff and rags and paltry blurred shreds of paper about the rights of man. . . . We are afraid to put men to live and trade each on his own private stock of reason; because we suspect that this stock in each man is small, and that individuals would do better to avail themselves of the general bank and capital of nations, and of ages.[12]

Over time, such criticisms of human rights as an idea and political and legal practice came from different political camps, from the right and from the left, from crude ideologies and the commanding heights of philosophy. And human rights have continued to be an embattled idea, from Bentham's passionate critique of the egoistic, destructive, licentious behavior he thought they would breed[13] to the attack on abstract and general norms under the theoretical auspices of a negative dialectics[14] or post-modernity.[15] The rich array of human rights skepticism in current normative reflection will be discussed in some detail over the course of this inquiry.

Some of these theoretical attacks were backed by important social forces and religious creeds. This is hardly surprising. After all, fundamental rights have played many roles in human history, but not least among these is that of an ethical idea and legal instrument subversive to political power. Moreover, fundamental rights are inconvenient not only for those who aspire to unfettered might, because they draw limits to its exercise; they are inconvenient for others, too, not least for (often comfortably self-righteous) social majorities. Human rights draw lines that limit such majorities' capability to impose their view of what is right and proper on other people as well. Human rights are therefore a precious asset for any minority, for dissidents and outsiders or simply for the weakest members of human associations. That which is inconvenient for political power and social majorities inevitably will have its enemies, and human rights have attracted plenty of such to the present day.

Consequently, there is much to be said about the trajectory, roots, ruptures, discontinuities and tentative approximations to the idea of human rights in theory and practice through human history. What is clear, however, is that by the eighteenth century, this idea had been formulated precisely and become not only

12 Edmund Burke, *Reflections on the Revolution in France* (London: Penguin Books, 1968), 181 ff.

13 Jeremy Bentham, "Nonsense upon Stilts," in *The Collected Works of Jeremy Bentham: Rights, Representation and Reform: Nonsense upon Stilts and Other Writings on the French Revolution*, eds. Philip Schofield, Catherine Pease-Watkin and Cyprian Blamires (Oxford: Clarendon Press, 2002), 317 ff., 321, 398 ff.

14 Theodor W. Adorno, "Negative Dialektik," in *Theodor W. Adorno: Gesammelte Schriften*, Vol. 6, ed. Rolf Tiedemann (Darmstadt: Wissenschaftliche Buchgesellschaft, 1998), 281.

15 Jacques Derrida, "Force of Law: The 'Mystical Foundation of Authority'," in *Deconstruction and the Possibility of Justice*, eds. Drucilla Cornell, Michel Rosenfeld and David Gray Carlson (London and New York: Routledge, 1992), 13 ff., 59 ff.

common currency, but a powerful political force that made history, ultimately profoundly influencing the course of affairs in many parts of the world. Many saw it as a precise expression of justified normative principles, an insight finally attained after centuries of thought with a good claim to it lasting and standing further critical reflection by the generations to come.

The idea of human rights is thus not simply a given. It was not easy to get to the heart of the matter. It took a long time to formulate clearly. It is still in need of much clarification. It is contested at its very core, in theory no less than in politics. Consequently, neither the idea nor the reality of human rights has been fully fathomed theoretically, nor are human rights uncontroversial or politically secured. A theory of human rights needs to avoid any naivety in this respect. Glossing over any of the problems identified does not foster the cause of human rights. The only way ahead is their critical debate.

I.4 HUMAN RIGHTS INSTRUMENTS AND HEURISTICS OF LAW

When embarking on the project of contributing to a theory of human rights, legal instruments can serve a very useful heuristic function and help us to find our way through the maze of issues at stake.

After all, the *Universal Declaration* is, for instance, a crucial embodiment of the idea of human rights in the current era. It is not a binding legal instrument. However, major parts of it are now rightly regarded as customary international law. In addition to its direct legal effects, it constitutes an epochal element of moral and legal history, doubtlessly on a par with other legal documents of this quality, such as the *Codex Iuris Civilis*, the Hindu *Code of Manu*, the continental European medieval legal books such as the *Sachsenspiegel* and the *Magna Carta* or, in modernity, the *American Declaration of Independence*, the *US Constitution* and the French *Déclaration des Droits de l'Homme et du Citoyen*, which, for better or worse, made legal history.

This is because it attempts to formulate the conditions necessary for a human civilization[16] that respects the standards indispensable to a decent form of human life. It does so not only for one country or community, but for humanity in general and in the concrete, tangible form of a set of rights. This project mirrors a central aspiration of human beings from many countries and all walks of life that was felt to be of existential importance because of the experience of what new meanings war and crimes can acquire in a technologically advanced world even after centuries of

[16] "Civilization" is a term misused in some contexts, not least in colonialism and imperialism, including theories about higher and lower forms of human life, often with racist implications. Here it is used to mean something quite different, namely incrementally created forms of human culture that embody human achievements in all forms imaginable. It is thus an egalitarian concept of cultural development. Cf. for some comments on the concept, David Graeber and David Wengrow, *The Dawn of Everything* (London: Penguin Books, 2021), 432 f.: "[T]hings that really go to make civilization" are "mutual aid, social co-operation, civic activism, hospitality or simply caring for others," creating "extended moral communities."

cultural development.[17] It is the symbol of a particular insight into the conditions of human life and the urgent need to take action to shield human beings from at least some of the most destructive forces unleashed by none other than themselves.

The *Universal Declaration* is a recent, authoritative summary of global human rights thought and the foundational document for the postwar development of human rights. However, it is, like other legal instruments, only a part of wider historical, political and cultural movement. Taking such instruments as a central heuristic tool to grasp the core content of the idea of human rights therefore does not mean reading the idea of human rights only through the lens of any specific legal text that makes up the current form of human rights protection. It only means that it may be worth considering the tenets of such a document very closely.

I.5 THE LAW: IN SPLENDID ISOLATION FROM THE TROUBLES OF THEORY?

There are two important features of constitutive legal instruments that need to be addressed, because they may seem to speak against reading any particular theoretical stance into legal instruments, even for heuristic purposes, and particularly in the case of human rights:

Firstly, one common feature of the drafting processes of constitutive legal texts is the need to bridge the many divided perspectives that necessarily exist among the drafters, who inevitably come from very different political, religious or cultural backgrounds. This need was evident in the *Universal Declaration*'s drafting process as well, and pointedly so, given that the conflicts of the epoch between constitutional democracy and dictatorship, between capitalism and communism, between European colonial power and decolonization, between independence-seeking in the Global South and old and new hegemonic aspirations in the Global North, between racism and yearnings for equality, between patriarchy and women's liberation, between religious creeds and secularism were among the many subtexts and sources of political strategies of the deliberation.

Jacques Maritain famously reported about postwar discussions on human rights: "It is related that at one of the meetings of a UNESCO National Commission where Human Rights were being discussed, some expressed astonishment that certain champions of violently opposed ideologies had agreed on a list of those rights. 'Yes', they said, 'we agree about the rights but on condition that no one asks us why.' That 'why' is where the argument begins."[18] The perception that there was a

[17] Cf. on the process of civilization, Norbert Elias, *Über den Prozess der Zivilisation* (Frankfurt am Main: Suhrkamp, 1976). The reference to such a process should not be taken as an endorsement of Elias' particular notion of the forces driving the process.

[18] UN Educational, Social and Cultural Organization (UNESCO), *Human Rights: Comments and Interpretations, A Symposium Edited by UNESCO*, UNESCO/PHS/3(rev.), July 25, 1948, I.

consensus about the content of human rights but not about the reasons for this consensus is widely taken as a proper description in a nutshell not only of the background of the drafting process of the *Universal Declaration*, but also of an important feature of the human rights project in general: This project needs only limited consensus to get off the ground. It is sufficient if the consensus extends to the content of rights. There is no need for further background assumptions to be shared as well, in particular about the ultimate justification of the content of human rights.[19] Disengagement with deeper theoretical questions – the difficult sphere of the "why" – may thus be regarded as a piece of legal wisdom.

Secondly, constitutive legal instruments such as legal bills of rights are not political or philosophical treatises. Their point is to state a set of ideally concise, enforceable and justiciable norms, not the outline of their defense. Only texts such as preambles often elaborate in more detail on the spirit of the bare set of norms, but usually without much concrete legal effect. Consequently and unsurprisingly, no particular political, religious or philosophical standpoint – say Kantianism or Christian personalism, Confucianism, socialism or secular humanism – forms part of the *Universal Declaration*'s content. This feature of the *Universal Declaration* thus is not an astonishing oddity, but rather mirrors a common property of central legal instruments, such as national constitutions, and of laws in general.

However, these observations should not give rise to the impression that such constitutive legal texts are entirely neutral on these matters despite this healthy theoretical abstinence. A text such as the *Universal Declaration* obviously is incompatible with numerous background theories – say, a strong collectivism that negates the worth of the individual, authoritarianism with its contempt for individual liberty, a repressive theocracy, the idea that the true end of any body politic is the aggrandizement of a particular family (the Windsors or the Hohenzollerns, for example) or racism that defends an imaginary hierarchy of groups of humans. Otherwise, it would be a text devoid of meaning. The set of background theories that can be mustered in defense of a human rights bill therefore clearly is limited. The drafters of such instruments consequently have to agree on the importance of equality, liberty and the supreme, inalienable worth of human beings that such instruments are designed to protect. There is nothing self-evident about this consensus, as the bloodshed before the *Universal Declaration* and the conflicts since its creation amply illustrate.

Furthermore, it is useful in this context not to mistake what the drafters might have thought reconcilable with a human rights catalogue, with what can in fact be

19 Today, John Rawls' idea of an "overlapping consensus" may come to mind, John Rawls, *Political Liberalism* (New York: Columbia University Press, 1996), 144. Maritain, however, maintains that – in the long run – some agreement on the "scale of value" is necessary to make human rights operative, UN Educational, Social and Cultural Organization (UNESCO), *Human Rights: Comments and Interpretations, A Symposium Edited by UNESCO*, UNESCO/PHS/3(rev.), July 25, 1948, VIII f.

reconciled with such. Some of the drafters may have had unclear, perhaps even confused ideas about the idea of human rights. There are perhaps some deep psychological reasons for this, as we will see in Part III. Some of the drafters may have had an entirely tactical relation to the legal text, endorsing it not because of any conviction or theory about its deeper justification, but simply as a matter of political expediency – for example, because they lacked the power to oppose it or expected it to be practically meaningless.[20] Ultimately, what matters for legal bills of rights is the text itself, not the passing thoughts and intentions of those participating in the drafting process, not the least because of their great diversity. It is no accident that even the smallest small print of legal text is disputed so hotly: After becoming legally valid, the text gains a life on its own, one that may take a course quite different from what its drafters anticipated.

These observations lead to the following conclusion: Neither the factual diversity of opinions about the deeper reasons justifying a foundational legal text and the sources for the understanding of its normative content nor the lack of explicit endorsement of any such theory in a legal text alone means that there are no such deeper reasons for its legitimacy or that such reasons, if they exist, are irrelevant for the understanding of the legal instrument. Philosophical agnosticism is no good option for serious legal work.

1.6 HUMAN RIGHTS AND THE EMANCIPATION OF HUMAN THOUGHT

From a certain perspective, the reference to the double role of reason and conscience (which may reinforce each other) at a turning point of history strikes a traditional chord of the history of thought about human rights. The idea that exercising reason will lead to insights about rights not only was a basic tenet of the reflection about rights at the time when the *Universal Declaration* was drafted, but also echoes many ideas in the history of human thought. These ideas have very important consequences for the political standing of human beings and their role in political affairs.

Let us take just some examples of very different thinkers from another pivotal period in which the contemporary human rights project took concrete shape: the eighteenth-century reflection about rights. William Blackstone succinctly summarized the idea of natural rights, the "rights of mankind," absolute in the sense of not being created by state or society: "The absolute rights of man, considered as a free agent, endowed with discernment to know good from evil, and with power of choosing those measures which appear to him to be most desirable, are usually summed up in one general appellation, and denominated the natural liberty of mankind." The protection of these rights is nothing less than the "principal aim of

[20] Cf. for an example, the British attitude towards the UDHR, n. 6.

society."[21] Around the same time, from a republican perspective that in many ways was radically opposed, Thomas Paine made an early case against slavery because "the slave who is proper owner of his freedom, has a right to reclaim it" from the "Men-Stealers," and this revolutionary idea relied on nothing else but "the dictates of natural light, and Conscience, in a matter of common Justice and Humanity" to justify this fundamental "natural, perfect right of all mankind."[22] The conservative Blackstone came to the same conclusion – the "rights of mankind" made every slave "the moment he lands in England . . . a freeman"[23] – an interesting example for the potential of human rights to create common ground for in other respects opposed visions of the law.

For Kant, the natural right to equal freedom under a universal law was a necessary insight attained by the autonomous exercise of reason – if one escaped the fetters of self-incurred minority, he thought, sustained reflection would lead everybody to an understanding of the rights that each human being enjoys. The faculty of moral understanding, autonomy as freedom under a moral law, entitles all humans to vindicate their position as equal members of that imagined community of mutually guaranteed dignity that Kant, in one of his striking visions, called the "*Reich der Zwecke*," the realm of ends.[24]

One of Kant's most original philosophical pupils, Friedrich Schiller, honorary citizen of the French Republic and fierce critic of *la terreur*, put the matter concisely: For him, human rights were among those political issues of his age that decided the "very fate of humanity."[25] The "great legal dispute" of his time derives its outstanding importance from the fact that human beings are both the addressees and, by the power of their autonomous reasoning, the authors of these rights: "However important the substance and consequence of this great legal dispute might be to anyone calling himself a human being, the way in which it is conducted should be of especial interest to anyone who can think for himself."[26]

[21] William Blackstone, *Commentaries of the Law of England, Vol. 1: Of the Rights of Persons*, ed. David Lemmings (Oxford: Oxford University Press, 2016), 125, 121, 120. These "rights of mankind" are the right to personal security (life, limbs, body, health and reputation), the right to personal liberty and the right to property, and – in modern terminology – a social right to help if in material need, Blackstone, *Law of England, Vol. 1*, 125 ff.

[22] Thomas Paine, "African Slavery in America," in Thomas Paine, *Common Sense and Other Writings* (New York: Barnes & Noble Classics, 2005), 6 f.

[23] Blackstone, *Law of England, Vol. 1*, 123.

[24] Immanuel Kant, *Grundlegung der Metaphysik der Sitten*, *Akademie Ausgabe*, Vol. IV (Berlin: Georg Reimer, 1911), 433 f.

[25] Friedrich Schiller, *Die ästhetische Erziehung des Menschen* (Ditzingen: Reclam, 2000), 10; Friedrich Schiller, *On the Aesthetic Education of Man*, trans. Keith Tribe (London: Penguin Books, 2016), 6 (adapted from the German original).

[26] Schiller, *Ästhetische Erziehung*, 10; Schiller, *Aesthetic Education*, 6: "*So nahe dieser große Rechtshandel, seines Inhalts und seiner Folgen wegen, jeden der sich Mensch nennt, angeht, so sehr muß er, seiner Verhandlungsart wegen, jeden Selbstdenker in besondere interessieren.*"

The brutal rule of force gives way to the rule of reason, and arguments start to count, accessible to all: "A question that would otherwise be settled by the blind right of might now seems to have been brought before the tribunal of pure reason; and whoever remains capable of putting himself at the center of things, advancing from a mere individual to a representative of the human race, might equally consider himself a member of this tribunal, as he is, as human being and citizen of the world, party at the same time and more or less caught up in its outcome."[27] Reasoning beings are naturally entitled to determine the laws to be created: "It is hence not just his own interests that will be decided by this legal process; judgment will also be made according to laws which his rational mind is competent and entitled to dictate."[28] Schiller explicitly adopts a cosmopolitan perspective: The issue dealt with in France and elsewhere is a matter not only of local but of general human concern.

Mary Wollstonecraft strikes a similar note, though importantly to vindicate the rights of women: "If the abstract rights of man will bear discussion and explanation, those of woman, by a parity of reasoning, will not shrink from the same test." Reason is the source of insights about rights, but it is not for men alone to decide on these matters: "Who made man the exclusive judge, if woman partake with him of the gift of reason?"[29] For her, too, the cause of human rights, as rights of both sexes, was a human cause: It is "an affection for the whole human race that makes my pen dart rapidly along to support what I believe to be the cause of virtue."[30]

The fundamental stance on reason, conscience and rights exemplified by these diverse writers has a political consequence: It *radically empowers human beings* in a twofold manner. First, their personal understanding becomes the ultimate yardstick for determining what human beings' rights and duties are, and universally so. The epistemic Bastille, which hitherto withheld the power of insight from all but a

[27] Schiller, *Ästhetische Erziehung*, 10; Schiller, *Aesthetic Education*, 6: "*Eine Frage, welche sonst nur durch das blinde Recht des Stärkeren beantwortet wurde, ist nun, wie es scheint, vor dem Richterstuhle reiner Vernunft anhängig gemacht, und wer nur immer fähig ist, sich in das Centrum des Ganzen zu versetzen, und sein Individuum zur Gattung zu steigern, darf sich als ein Beysitzer jenes Vernunftgerichts betrachten, so wie er als Mensch und Weltbürger zugleich Parthey ist, und näher oder entfernter in den Erfolg sich verwickelt sieht.*"

[28] Schiller, *Ästhetische Erziehung*, 10; Schiller, *Aesthetic Education*, 6: "*Es ist also nicht bloß seine eigene Sache, die in diesem großen Rechtshandel zur Entscheidung kommt, es soll auch nach Gesetzen gesprochen werden, die er als vernünftiger Geist selbst zu diktiren fähig und berechtigt ist.*" Schiller does not refer explicitly to human rights in this passage. But the context shows beyond doubt that human rights are a key issue of the "great legal dispute" of his time – in particular, the French Revolution and its declaration of human rights. Human rights are a central concern in his thought about aesthetic education and are generally crucial for his theoretical writings and plays. Cf. e.g. Schiller, *Ästhetische Erziehung* (Augustenburger Briefe), the first version of his thought on the aesthetic education of human beings, or – as one of his major plays – *Don Carlos*.

[29] Mary Wollstonecraft, *A Vindication of the Rights of Woman* (London: Penguin Books, 1983), 87.

[30] Wollstonecraft, *Vindication*, 85.

privileged merry few, now strikes its flag. Everybody has the capacity to reach true understanding – there are no lords and masters in a fiefdom of knowledge about humans' proper actions and justified claims. On the contrary, everybody is an equal citizen in the republic of cognition and is able to grasp that which it is urgently important to know.

The intrinsic logic of this egalitarian epistemology makes it hard to maintain patriarchal, racist or colonial denials of the ability of women or people with certain skin colors (or indeed any other group) to think for themselves and understand the importance of human rights, although it took centuries for the subversive power of this epistemological stance to fully unfold. The door to understanding the justification of rights is wide open to everyone.

Second, the exercise of commonly shared human understanding does not lead to the conclusion that submission to others, inequality, bondage and disrespect for everyone apart from a chosen class of privileged persons are justified, as many great minds held in the history of ideas. On the contrary, critical thought free from prejudice, intimidation, superstition and stifling traditions confirms that respect for all human beings – for their lives and bodily integrity, freedom and equality – is the right of all who look in the mirror of a shared humanity, history and social practice, trust their eyes and draw sober-minded conclusions from what they see.

This is one important reason why the reference to everybody's capacity for critical thought and moral reflection as part of the properties that justify the ascription of rights to humans does not lead to the exclusion of certain groups of people from the realm of rights, such as infants or comatose patients who have not yet fully developed or have lost certain cognitive abilities. On the contrary, the *inclusion* of every human being is the consequence of a proper understanding of the very idea of human rights, as we will see in more detail,[31] even though the journey towards

[31] The concern as to whether the reference to properties such as "reason and conscience" excludes certain human beings from protection by human rights stands at the forefront of many debates about essentialist accounts of humanity, and rightly so, given the practical importance of these questions for the status of infants, people with certain disabilities or comatose patients, to name just a few pertinent examples. Unsurprisingly, in light of the barbarous historical example of the Nazi "Euthanasia" program (a main testing ground for the Holocaust), it was also raised in the drafting process when the inclusion of the clause referring to "reason and conscience" was debated, cf. Schabas, *The Universal Declaration*, 854 (E/CN.4/AC.1/SR.13). The Soviet delegate Koretsky argued that the reference to human beings endowed with reason "might have resulted in misunderstanding and have been interpreted as justification of the fascist destruction of feeble-minded people on the grounds they were not reasonable human beings."

Another important topic raised by various actors, delegates and stakeholders was gender-neutral language to underline the inclusion of women in the protection afforded by human rights, cf. for instance the early intervention of the *Commission on the Status of Women* to change the language of Art. 1 of the draft declaration, the debate and, in particular, Chairwoman Eleanor Roosevelt's response, Schabas, *The Universal Declaration*, 1669 ff. (E/CN.4/SR.50).

drawing political conclusions from this insight was at least as long and bitter as that towards the acceptance of all as the legitimate subjects of moral understanding.[32]

This stance echoes an intrinsically humanizing approach to the existential question of the origin of the normative principles that ought to rule human life. It is exemplified in its classical form in Socrates' practice of engaging the people of Athens in an open-minded inquiry about the good and the just and their meaning for human life. This practice (which ended fatally for Socrates himself) has inspired serious thought throughout the ages and made its protagonist a "person of world history."[33] This approach holds that human beings are able to answer questions not only of rights, but of morality in general, of justice and benevolence *themselves*. It believes that humans are not the victims and passive recipients of others' commands, but themselves are the subjects of the process that leads to determining what they ought to do and justly can demand. They are guided along this path – which is open to all human beings, difficult as progress along it may be – by universally accessible reasons and insights that can be shared with others, not by rude force or mindless accommodation to the patterns of the past.

The belief in the abilities of human thinking embodied in this stance does not mean entertaining comforting illusions about the obstacles that have to be overcome. One of the sobering lessons from the history of human rights is that it is possible to argue wholeheartedly for the equal rights of human beings and at the same time have one's tea served by a slave and not be able to conceive of the fact that the woman one has the tea with, loves and shares a life with may have all those rights, too. Prejudice, superstition and powerful interests fight the idea, and the ensuing ideological battles are not easy to win. In addition, even if the basic idea is established, much effort is still required to master the intricacies of the concept as it stands today, many of which remain controversial in detail.

This sober, disillusioned, skeptical trust in reason and conscience had far-reaching consequences that made history. It is an epistemology with a political bite. In the eighteenth century, it even became the midwife of revolutionary change that reshaped the political world through one of its most important political consequences: the gradual establishment of a democratic constitutional state under the rule of law based on human rights and embedded in an international legal order increasingly committed to the protection of these fundamental human entitlements. And not only that: It seems hard to imagine any more recent emancipatory political project from *Black Lives Matter* to *Fridays for Future* and the ideas about social organization that they stand for without relying on the power of each individual to understand and judge

[32] Cf. for instance Blackstone's views on the legal status of women, Blackstone, *Law of England*, Vol. 1, 430.

[33] Georg Wilhelm Friedrich Hegel, "Vorlesungen über die Geschichte der Philosophie I," in *Werke*, Vol. 18, eds. Eva Moldenhauer and Karl Markus Michel (Frankfurt am Main: Suhrkamp, 1986), 441: "*welthistorische Person*."

morally. This egalitarian epistemic stance, politically empowering each human being, should not be abandoned without compelling reason.

I.7 THE SPHERES OF RIGHTS

The *Universal Declaration* outlines moral and political aims that justify and ask for political action and legal institutions. It is important to emphasize that the system of legal human rights protections that the *Universal Declaration* was designed to inspire is by no means limited to international law. On the contrary, the *Universal Declaration* imagines itself as an element of a realm of human rights that are protected effectively on the state level, usually through constitutional law, and complemented internationally through elements of regional and universal public international law. The project embodied in the *Universal Declaration* is a universalism with a judicious plurality not only of moral and political but also of legal tools.

The international human rights law stemming from the *Universal Declaration* is quite explicit about this particular feature of the project. In the preamble, the *Universal Declaration* underlines that the "recognition of the inherent dignity and of the equal and inalienable rights of all members of the human family is the foundation of freedom, justice and peace in the world" and thus its universalistic cause.[34] These rights are supposed to serve as "a common standard of achievement" for nothing less than "all peoples and all nations."[35] The human rights formulated constitute normative standards for individuals and "every organ of society," which includes at least public authorities. These rights are part of individual and political morality. This morality is authoritative and binding. Human rights are to be promoted by educational efforts and – importantly – national *and* international measures to secure their universal and effective recognition and observance. Evidently, such measures include but are not necessarily limited to legal forms of protection. The morality of human rights is the foundation of the legal realm of human rights.

From the very beginning of the post–World War II human rights culture, its founding document thus envisages a complex architecture that interweaves national and international moral, political and legal modes of human rights protection. At the same time, it clarifies that one of the most influential forms of human rights relativism, namely what one may want to call "colonial relativism," has no place in this project: The rights protected are mandatory standards everywhere, including the

34 UDHR, Preamble.

35 The interweaving of national and international law was a common thread of the drafting process. The preamble of Cassin's draft included the formulation "that the enjoyment of such rights and freedoms by all persons must be protected by the commonwealth of nations and secured by international as well as national laws." The Working Group of the Drafting Committee commented that this passage shall "be retained and modified" – as it was, Schabas, *The Universal Declaration*, 788 (E/CN.4/AC.1/W.1).

still-existing colonies. This set the tone for other legal instruments, including regional systems of human rights protection that have universalist aspirations, although by their very legal nature they are capable of realizing these aims only within the scope of their limited jurisdiction. Referring to the *Universal Declaration*, the preamble of the ECHR accordingly states that it "aims at securing the universal and effective recognition and observance of the rights therein declared."[36] It adds that its intention is "to take the first steps for the collective enforcement of certain of the rights stated in the *Universal Declaration*."[37] As mentioned earlier in this Introduction, the colonial powers went to great effort not to extend the *Convention*'s application to colonies through the colonial exemption clause – a stark reminder of the sway of colonial relativism and the political realities behind the universalist language of the ECHR. This is important even though the further development of the *Convention* system has increasingly vindicated the universalist aims formulated in the preamble and not the power politics of some of its founding members.

The *American Convention on Human Rights* includes language that is equally clear in this respect, "recognizing that the essential rights of man are not derived from one's being a national of a certain state, but are based upon attributes of the human personality."[38] The aim is "to consolidate within the framework of democratic institutions, a system of personal liberty and social justice based on respect for the essential rights of man." International protection of these rights is "reinforcing or complementing the protection provided by the domestic law of the American States." Art. 2 of the *American Convention* consequently calls for the legal implementation of these rights, which are conceptualized as universal, in domestic legislation.

This architecture is bolstered by a pillar made of procedural law: All international systems of human rights protection require that domestic remedies have been exhausted as a procedural precondition of the various forms of judicial, quasi-judicial or nonjudicial scrutiny of human rights violations. This precondition has an implication for the architecture of human rights: It presupposes the existence and desirability of a domestic protection of human rights, strengthened but not replaced by international human rights.

The idea of the international human rights architecture thus seems reasonably clear. It is a federated system of human rights protection, so to speak: States and regional units work to protect these rights under the supplementary umbrella of a subsidiary universal protection system. This system has had significant influence on constitutions that were drafted after 1948. A good example of an attempt to meet this challenge – and an unsurprising one, given Germany's past – is that country's Basic

[36] ECHR, Preamble.

[37] ECHR, Preamble.

[38] Organization of American States (OAS), *American Convention on Human Rights, "Pact of San Jose," Costa Rica* (ACHR), UNTS 1144 (123), November 22, 1969, Preamble.

Law, which considers human dignity to be inviolable and to be the foundation of the "inviolable and inalienable human rights as the *basis of every community*, of peace and of justice *in the world*."[39]

The universal aspirations of current law even reach beyond the core area of human rights to ideas such as the rule of law, which are related to or arguably even founded upon but not identical with human rights. The *Universal Declaration*, for instance, refers to the importance of the protection of human rights by the "rule of law."[40] Respect for the rule of law is a precondition for membership in the Council of Europe.[41] The ECHR regards the rule of law as the common heritage of its member states.[42] One of the fundamental European Union (EU) treaties even explicitly identifies the rule of law as a "universal value,"[43] together with freedom, democracy and equality. The inclusion of democracy as a universal value in such a list also comes as no surprise, given that the *Universal Declaration* already regards central elements of democracy as demands of human rights.[44]

This fundamental structure of modern human rights law, a universal normative idea secured by complementary and mutually reinforcing national, regional and international legal instruments, has deep roots in the human rights project that lies at the core both of modern constitutionalism and – arguably – of earlier important thought. One element of this project is the perception that human rights constitute ideas of universal validity. However, given the political reality, for the time being they can only be secured for certain territories and people until the rule of rights can be guaranteed in other communities as well. Thomas Paine, for instance, voiced a not entirely solitary view when he stated in one of the most influential writings in support of the American Revolution: "The cause of America is in a great measure the cause of all mankind."[45] The reason for this is connected with the idea of human rights: "Many circumstances have, and will arise, which are not local, but universal, and through which the principles of all lovers of mankind are affected, and in the event of which their affections are interested."[46] "[D]eclaring war against the natural rights of all mankind" ranks prominently among the things that affect the "principles of all lovers of mankind."[47] Unsurprisingly, Paine later expresses the same attitude in defense of the French constitutional project and in particular of the *Déclaration des Droits de l'Homme et du Citoyen*: "The cause of the French people is that of all

39 Art. 1 para. 2 Grundgesetz [Basic Law for the Federal Republic of Germany (GG)], May 23, 1949 (emphasis added).

40 UDHR, Preamble.

41 Council of Europe, *Statute of the Council of Europe*, ETS 1, May 5, 1949, Art. 3.

42 ECHR, Preamble.

43 European Union, *Treaty on European Union* (Consolidated Version) (TEU), *Treaty of Lisbon*, Official Journal C 326/1, December 13, 2007, Preamble; cf. Art. 2 TEU.

44 Art. 21 UDHR.

45 Paine, *Common Sense*, Introduction.

46 Paine, *Common Sense*, Introduction.

47 Paine, *Common Sense*, Introduction.

Europe, or rather of the whole world."[48] Jefferson held in a similar vein: "[W]e feel that we are acting under obligations not confined to the limits of our own society. It is impossible not to be sensible that we are acting for all mankind: that circumstances denied to others, but indulged to us, have imposed on us the duty of proving what is the degree of freedom and selfgovernment in which a society may venture to leave it's individual members."[49] In one of his most-quoted remarks, Kant stated that humanity has developed in such a way that the violation of human rights "in *one* place of the earth is felt in all," and justifiably so, given the imperatives of practical reason.[50] For Kant, the institutional consequence was to protect these universal rights in republics, confederated in a world community under universal law – the realm of ends of cosmopolitan thought.[51] Schiller and Wollstonecraft were evidently no exception in their view that a universal human cause truly was at stake in the debates about human rights in particular human communities, though the problem of counting all humans as humans was still not solved, as Jefferson's slaves illustrate, for instance.

Thinking that human rights can only be protected by international law with a universal application therefore would miss an important point of the history of human rights. On the contrary, the bottom-up, layered tradition of the protection of human rights embodied in classical thought on rights and authoritatively restated in the *Universal Declaration* is part of the core of the idea of human rights. Human rights certainly are rights of international concern, but that does not mean that they are not of equal domestic importance and should not be protected primarily where they can be protected most efficiently: at home. Consequently, today, the various domestic systems are – as envisaged by the *Universal Declaration* – complemented but in no way superseded or substituted by regional and universal international law in order to create common standards and to prevent the abuse of rights by state governments and other actors.[52]

1.8 THE INQUIRY INTO MIND AND RIGHTS

The preceding remarks have shown the basic assumption, underpinning human rights culture, its history of reflection and struggles for emancipation, is that insight

48 Paine, "The Rights of Man," 103.

49 Thomas Jefferson, "Letter to Joseph Priestly," June 19, 1802, *Founders Online*, National Archives, accessed August 16, 2021, https://founders.archives.gov/documents/Jefferson/01-37-02-0515. As has been much discussed, this stance was accompanied by Jefferson's practice as slaveholder.

50 Immanuel Kant, *Zum Ewigen Frieden*, *Akademie Ausgabe*, Vol. VIII (Berlin and Leipzig: Walter de Gruyter, 1923), 360; translation: Immanuel Kant, *Perpetual Peace*, trans. Mary J. Gregor, in *Practical Philosophy (The Cambridge Edition of the Works of Immanuel Kant)*, ed. Mary J. Gregor (Cambridge: Cambridge University Press, 1996), 330 (emphasis in original).

51 Kant, *Zum Ewigen Frieden*, 349 ff.

52 Klaus Günther, "Geteilte Souveränität, Nation und Rechtsgemeinschaft," *Kritische Justiz*, 3 (2016): 321 ff.

into the idea of human rights with the content just outlined is not the privilege of just a few, but the epistemic domain of all. However, as we have just seen, gaining such an understanding of human rights is a very challenging task.

Consequently, there are many problems that are worthy of the serious attention and the admirable work devoted to them in contemporary human rights theory, which is particularly rich, lively and full of creative thought. Given the anthropological and epistemological foundational ideas of the human rights project and their intimate relation to the equal autonomy of every human being as a moral and reflective agent, the following questions are of particular interest: What is really the role that reason and conscience play in our understanding of human rights? How can these terms be understood – to what elements of human cognition do they refer? Does the assumption that everybody can understand the idea of human rights make any sense? Does the egalitarian epistemic stance not take an overly optimistic view of human beings' capacity for insight? Is it tenable to suppose that the free exercise of human understanding by potentially anyone will lead to the idea of human rights when reflecting about human existence, informed by its history and the realities of social life? Will this be the result of inquiry if guided by nothing other than the gentle but irresistible hands of reasons that convince? Is there not deep disagreement about these matters? Is human thought not structurally skewed – for instance, by biases and heuristics? Are the answers to these questions relevant for the justificatory theory of human rights? In other words: *What is the actual relationship between human thought, its structure and exercise and the idea and justification of human rights?*

As will become clearer over the course of the following reflections, searching for answers to this question does not imply that the many other questions asked in current human rights theory (some of which were mentioned above) are less worth pursuing. On the contrary, they are evidently of great importance, and quite a number of them actually will be addressed in the course of this study. We are simply claiming that this particular question merits serious attention if we truly want to understand what human rights are about and how intricately they are related to the particularities of the human condition. The research objectives of this inquiry thus aim not to replace but to enrich current human rights theory in a circumscribed but meaningful and potentially profoundly important way.

How timely is this topic? The contemporary world is full of violent conflict on a massive scale and is plagued by severe social problems. Furthermore, human rights have been under political attack for years. In principle, this is nothing new, as mentioned earlier in this Introduction. In addition to these familiar adversaries of human rights, however, there are special new threats from within democratic and constitutional systems in which different political forces undermine important fundamental rights. Prime examples include: the measures taken in the so-called War on Terror; the erosion of fundamental norms such as the prohibition of torture; the profound threat to privacy and self-determination posed by the international surveillance systems; the undermining of the international rule of law (e.g. through ongoing practices of extrajudicial killings through drone strikes);[53] and the symptoms of a new religious illiberalism epitomized by the Swiss ban on the minaret. Moreover, liberal democracies have come under pressure not only from strengthened authoritarian regimes, but also from domestic antidemocratic populist movements.

Given this state of affairs, a reflection on human rights certainly needs no excuse. But why mind and rights? Would an inquiry into the role of human rights in these concrete political conflicts not be a more opportune approach?

And are not other perspectives more promising if we want to engage in the theory of fundamental rights – say, rights and culture, rights and the narratives of modernity, the social construction of rights or the analysis of the social assemblage of rights? Is the question of the relationship between mind and rights not less pressing in both practical and theoretical terms?

There are good reasons to assert that this impression is misleading and that, on the contrary, tackling this problem is crucial if we are to gain an understanding of human rights and assure their political survival. Given the upsurge of interest in the relevance of neuroscience and empirical psychology for the understanding of ethics and law,[54] it is not far-fetched but quite evidently necessary to consider in some

[53] On these latter two examples and their wider impact, cf. e.g. David Cole, "Must Counterterrorism Cancel Democracy?" *The New York Review of Books*, no. 1 (January 8, 2015): 26 ff. On targeted killings, cf. UN Human Rights Council, *Report of the Special Rapporteur on Extrajudicial, Summary or Arbitrary Executions, Addendum: Study on Targeted Killings*, A/HRC/14/24, May 28, 2010, Add. 6.

[54] Cf. the broad range of very different approaches by, for instance, Steven Pinker, *The Blank Slate: The Modern Denial of Human Nature* (London: Penguin Books, 2002); Kwame Anthony Appiah, *Experiments in Ethics* (Cambridge: Harvard University Press, 2008); Michael S. Gazzaniga, *The Ethical Brain* (Chicago, IL: University of Chicago Press, 2005); Matthias Mahlmann, *Rationalismus in der praktischen Theorie*, 2nd ed. (Baden-Baden: Nomos Verlag, 2009); John Mikhail, "Universal Moral Grammar: Theory, Evidence and the Future," *Trends in Cognitive Sciences* 11 no. 4 (2007): 143–52; John Mikhail, *Elements of Moral Cognition: Rawls' Linguistic Analogy and the Cognitive Science of Moral and Legal Judgment* (Cambridge: Cambridge University Press, 2011); Jonathan Haidt, *The Righteous Mind: Why Good People Are Divided by Politics and Religion* (New York: Pantheon Books, 2012); Stephen J. Morse and Adina L. Roskies, eds., *A Primer on Criminal Law and Neuroscience: A Contribution of the Law and Neuroscience Project, Supported by the MacArthur Foundation* (Oxford: Oxford University Press, 2013); Joshua Greene, *Moral Tribes: Emotion, Reason and the Gap between Us and Them* (New York: Penguin Press, 2013); Robin Bradley Kar, "The Psychological Foundations of Human Rights," in *The Oxford Handbook of International Human Rights Law*, ed. Dinah Shelton (Oxford: Oxford University Press, 2013), 104–43; Eyal Zamir, *Law, Psychology and Morality: The Role of Loss Aversion* (Oxford: Oxford University Press, 2014); Michael S. Pardo and Dennis Patterson, *Minds, Brains, and Law: The Conceptual Foundations of Law and Neuroscience* (Oxford: Oxford University Press, 2013); Bartosz Brożek, Jaap Hage and Nicole Vincent, eds., *Law and Mind: A Survey of Law and the Cognitive Sciences* (Cambridge: Cambridge University Press, 2021); Owen D. Jones, Jeffrey D. Schall and Francis X. Shen, *Law and Neuroscience* (Alphen aan den Rijn: Wolters Kluwer, 2020); Shaun Nichols, *Rational Rules: Towards a Theory of Moral Learning* (Oxford: Oxford

detail the lessons that the modern theory of the human mind may have for our understanding of the foundations of human rights and – given the constitutive role of human rights for legal systems in general – for the foundations of legal justice.[55] Neuroscience and psychology have a major impact on the contemporary reflection of normative issues. Consequently, it is no longer possible to imagine a plausible theory of human rights without thoroughly considering whether the contemporary analysis of the workings of the human mind is or is not important for an understanding of these rights.

Two kinds of recent human rights revisionism that are paradigmatic examples of a certain perspective on human rights underline this point.

The first is what might be called a genealogical revisionism with deconstructive normative connotations.[56] This challenge formulates the thesis that human rights are of recent, historically contingent and politically doubtful origin. At first glance, it might appear as though this kind of critique is limited to matters of moral and legal history. On a deeper level, however, the legitimacy of human rights is at stake. According to this view, if human rights have a partisan, politically suspect origin, this undermines their legitimacy. The implicit assumption is that the criteria governing the validity of the claim that human rights are justifiable, and perhaps universally so, themselves have a contingent historical origin that renders their justification obsolete. From this point of view, the idea of universally legitimate human rights turns out to be a harmful historical illusion on a grand scale that limits human ethical and political imagination at best and is a tool for human repression at worst.

This kind of critique leaves us with two tasks. The first is to investigate what the historical record teaches us about the origin of human rights and whether its lesson is that the contingent nature of the idea of human rights precludes any further questions about their origin, nature or justification. Second, if this is not the case, we need to develop an alternative theory of the validity of human rights and explain how this account fits with the historical record.

University Press, 2021). For critical views, cf. for instance, Stephen Morse, "Law, Responsibility, and the Sciences of the Brain/Mind," in *The Oxford Handbook of Law, Regulation and Technology*, eds. Roger Brownsword, Eloise Scotford and Karen Yeung (Oxford: Oxford University Press, 2017), 156, warning against exaggerated claims ("brain overclaim syndrome"); Selim Berker, "The Normative Insignificance of Neuroscience," *Philosophy & Public Affairs* 37, no. 4 (2009), 293 ff.; James Davison Hunter and Paul Nedelsky, *Science and the Good: The Tragic Quest for the Foundations of Morality* (New Haven, CT: Yale University Press, 2018), both making the point that descriptive science has no normative implications, the latter fearing a new moral "nihilism." As we will see, when assessing the merits of such criticisms, all depends on the particular theory discussed. Some do respect the is/ought distinction, while some do not, for instance. On the project of "computational ethics," see Edmond Awad et al., "Computational Ethics," *Trends in Cognitive Science* 25 no. 5 (2022): 388–405.

55 Cf. on the many ways in which the search for the "foundations of law" can be understood, Hubert Rottleuthner, *Foundations of Law* (Dordrecht: Springer, 2005).

56 Samuel Moyn, *The Last Utopia: Human Rights in History* (Cambridge, MA: Harvard University Press, 2010).

It is clear that the legitimacy of human rights cannot be justified without the assumption that a proposition of the kind "human right X is (universally) valid" is in fact an act of cognition – an act of insight and not of error. This brings us to the second challenge to the idea of human rights: a neuroscientific, psychological revisionism that employs a very influential model of the human mind – the dual process model of the mind[57] – against the idea of human rights. It argues that this idea is just the product of a particular mechanism of the mind that should not, however, govern our decision-making. The consequence of such theories is far-reaching: Human rights appear as something like a cognitive illusion in the technical sense; that is, a mental phenomenon that is necessarily experienced by human beings given a certain input because of the structure of the human mind, but that in fact delivers erroneous information about the true state of the world.[58] Beliefs about the validity of human rights are as necessarily experienced and as delusory as the impression arising in our minds when we see the Müller-Lyer illusion.

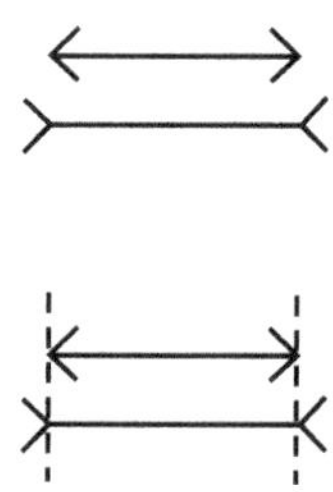

The uppermost of the three parallel lines, each with "arrowheads" and "tails" pointing in different directions, appears to be shorter than the others, although in fact all are of equal length. This is a well-known visual illusion, and even if we are familiar with the effect we still perceive the arrows in this manner. The idea of human rights is the same kind of cognitive illusion, argues the neuroscientific revisionist approach: Human rights are an offshoot of mental mechanisms that deliver certain ideas, whether we want them to or not, and whose erroneous nature can be rectified only by other forms of rational thinking. The impression that human rights are justified stays with us, however, just like the impression of the different lengths of the arrows. Accordingly, we cannot free ourselves entirely from such ideas as human rights, but we can learn to ignore them when it is important to do so.

This position consequently concludes that a proper state-of-the-art scientific understanding of the structure and cognitive conditions of the exercise of human rationality or reason does not yield arguments supporting the legitimacy of the idea of human

[57] Cf. Daniel Kahneman, *Thinking, Fast and Slow* (New York: Farrar, Straus and Giroux, 2011).

[58] Greene, *Moral Tribes*. For a related but not identical argument, see Cass R. Sunstein, "Moral Heuristics," *Behavioural and Brain Sciences* 28, no. 4 (2005): 531 ff.; and the comments by John Mikhail, "Moral Heuristics or Moral Competence? Reflections on Sunstein," *Behavioural and Brain Sciences* 28, no. 4 (2005): 557 ff.

rights, let alone their universality. On the contrary, such theories assert that there are hard scientific grounds for radically and irreverently critiquing such ideas, which have been venerated as admirable human achievements for no reason and properly should be consigned to the dustbin of human thought. If we take seriously and think through the consequences of such a perspective, which regards fundamental principles of morality and the idea of human rights as something like a cognitive illusion, the specter of Descartes' evil demon reappears:[59] The deceiving god Descartes thought to be unimaginable now resides within us as part of our cognitive machinery. Our mind is not ultimately an inner light that leads to insight despite all errors, as Descartes hoped, among many others.[60] Far from it: Right at the heart of human understanding, our vision is clouded by sources of obscurantism, including the idea of the morality of human rights. These claims are embedded in a theoretical background assumption about morality in psychology and neuroscience that contends that there is hard empirical evidence that concern for humanity, evidently crucial for human rights, is not part of the moral makeup of the human mind because the human mind is not structured for such moral ideas.[61] To assess the merits of such claims, we have to engage seriously with the question of the relationship between the theory of mind and human rights and explore what can be learned from such theoretical attacks.

The fundamental question underlying these problems is as follows: Is human knowledge of ethics and normative legal theory possible? How do we identify it if it is? These questions are deeply embedded in a rich and fertile tradition of thought. As we have seen, it is a central Socratic assumption – influential far beyond the so-called history of "Western" practical philosophy – that moral principles and especially justice are objects of true human insight and can be recognized as such.[62] The criteria of genuine insight, as opposed to unwarranted opinion or error, play a crucial role in this reflection.[63] Identifying that which constitutes justice and thus forms such a criterion is therefore a central concern from pre-Socratic[64] thought through to contemporary theories of justice.[65]

Insight is not just there, however. Humans have to achieve it through a mental process of reflection, of thinking, and thus through actively exercising the instrument through which we gain insight: the human mind. A central question of

[59] René Descartes, "Principia Philosophiae," in *Œuvres de Descartes*, Vol. VIII, eds. Charles Adam and Paul Tannery (Paris: Léopold Cerf, 1905), I, XXIX, XXX, 16 f.

[60] Descartes, "Principia Philosophiae," I, XI, XXX, 8 f., 16.

[61] Cf. e.g. Haidt, *Righteous Mind*, 234.

[62] Cf. e.g. Plato, *Gorgias*, 508e–509a. The disavowal of knowledge in this passage after the assertion of knowledge is best understood as "Socratic irony," cf. Gregory Vlastos, *Socrates: Ironist and Moral Philosopher* (Cambridge: Cambridge University Press, 1991), 21 ff., 236 ff.

[63] Cf. Plato, *Euthyphron*, 5d, 6d–6e.

[64] E.g. Simonides' principles, Plato, *Republic*, 331e.

[65] Cf. e.g. John Rawls, *A Theory of Justice* (Cambridge, MA: Harvard University Press, 1971); Amartya Sen, *The Idea of Justice* (London: Penguin Books, 2009); Stefan Gosepath, *Gleiche Gerechtigkeit: Grundlagen eines liberalen Egalitarismus* (Frankfurt am Main: Suhrkamp, 2004).

modern epistemology therefore is whether the structure of the mind is important for what counts as criteria for insight. In other words: Is thought more than just a pure medium of cognition? Does it – by virtue of its properties and structure – determine what appears to humans as truth and not as error? Are the properties and the structure of the mind decisive for the content of thought? If this is so, these mental properties and structures need to be investigated in order to understand the nature and foundation of human cognition, including moral judgment and moral cognition. Reflecting not only on the substance of insight but also on the mind that provides insight is, however, a classical project of modern philosophy. It is – despite different opinions about the structure of the mind – the common attempt of Descartes,[66] Locke[67] and Leibniz[68] to describe the properties of human thought that enable human beings to understand, requiring "art and pains," because "the understanding, like the eye, whilst it makes us see, and perceive all other things, takes no notice of itself."[69] It is the Humean resolve to inquire into the "secret springs and principles, by which the human mind is actuated in its operations,"[70] the Kantian project of a critique of reason, the demand of the "ripened power of judgement of our age, which will no longer be put off with illusionary knowledge, and which demands that reason should take on anew the most difficult of its tasks, namely, that of self-knowledge."[71] To be sure, this project has been subject to

[66] Cf. e.g. Descartes' analysis of the human mind, Descartes, "Principia Philosophiae," I, VIII, 7 ff.

[67] Cf. John Locke, *An Essay Concerning Human Understanding* (Harmondsworth: Penguin Books, 1997), book I, ch. I, § 1.

[68] Gottfried Wilhelm Leibniz, "Nouveaux Essais," in Gottfried Wilhelm Leibniz, *Sämtliche Schriften und Briefe: Philosophische Schriften*, Series VI, Vol. 6, Akademieausgabe (Berlin: Akademie-Verlag, 1990), 48 f., Preface: "*Il s'agit de savoir, si l'ame en elle même est vuide entiérement comme des tablettes, où l'on n'a encore rien écrit (tabula rasa) suivant Aristote et l'auteur de l'essay, et si tout ce qui y est tracé vient uniquement des sens et de l'experience; ou si l'ame contient originairement les principes de plusieurs notions et doctrines que les objets externes reveillent seulement dans les occasions, comme je le crois avec Platon et même avec l'ecole, et avec tous ceux qui prennent dans cette signification le passage de St Paul (Rom. 2, 15.) où il marque que la loy de Dieu est écrite dans les cœurs*" (emphasis in original).

[69] Locke, *Human Understanding*, book I, ch. I, § 1: "The understanding, like the eye, whilst it makes us see, and perceive all other things, takes no notice of itself: and it requires art and pains to set it at a distance, and make it its own object. But whatever be the difficulties, that lie in the way of this inquiry; whatever it be, that keeps us so much in the dark to ourselves; sure I am, that all the light we can let in upon our minds; all the acquaintance we can make with our own understanding, will not only be very pleasant, but bring us great advantage, in directing our thoughts in the search of other things."

[70] David Hume, "An Enquiry Concerning Human Understanding," in *David Hume: Enquiries Concerning Human Understanding and Concerning the Principles of Morals*, ed. P. H. Nidditch, (Oxford: Oxford University Press, 1975), 14.

[71] Immanuel Kant, *Kritik der reinen Vernunft (1st ed. 1781), Akademie Ausgabe, Vol. IV*, (Berlin: Georg Reimer, 1911), 9: a demand "*der gereiften* Urteilskraft des Zeitalters, *welches sich nicht länger durch Scheinwissen hinhalten läßt, und eine Aufforderung an die Vernunft, das beschwerlichste aller ihrer Geschäfte, nämlich das der Selbsterkenntnis aufs neue zu übernehmen,*" (emphasis in original). Translation: Immanuel Kant, *Critique of Pure Reason (The Cambridge Edition of the Works of Immanuel Kant)*, trans. Paul Guyer and Allen W. Wood (Cambridge: Cambridge University Press, 1999), 100 f.

manifold critiques, from Heidegger's doubts about Cartesian metaphysics[72] to Wittgensteinian externalism.[73] But it could still be worthwhile to consider closely "the ways, whereby our understanding comes to attain those notions of things we have"[74] to avoid a philosophical inquiry beginning "at the wrong end."[75]

This approach has its parallel in the modern philosophy of language and its thesis that a theory of language is a necessary element of any theory of human knowledge. One of the philosophy of language's persistent questions is whether the properties of ordinary languages influence the nature of human thought, making it relative to a certain language[76] – bewitching it, perhaps[77] – or, on the contrary, whether they provide reasons that confirm the possibility of universally shared human thought.[78] From this point of view, not only the material criteria for insight but also the medium by which insight may be gained is of central importance, and some even

72 Cf. Martin Heidegger, *Sein und Zeit* (Tübingen: Max Niemeyer Verlag, 1984), 89 ff. on the deficient "*Zugang*" ("access") to the world of Cartesian metaphysics, especially missing its "*Zuhandenheit*" ("readiness-to-hand").

73 Cf. Ludwig Wittgenstein, *Zettel* (Berkeley and Los Angeles: University of California Press, 2007), 606, 608; Hilary Putnam, *Pragmatism: An Open Question* (Oxford and Malden, MA: Blackwell Publishing, 1995), 79: "The mind is not in the head." Concretely on the question of neuroscience and more generally in favor of an externalist account of the mind, cf. Matthew R. Bennett and Peter Michael Stephan Hacker, *The Philosophical Foundations of Neuroscience* (Oxford and Malden, MA: Blackwell Publishing, 2003); Pardo and Patterson, *Minds, Brains, and Law*, 12 ff.: rule-following (with conceptual necessity) is not in the head.

74 Locke, *Human Understanding*, book I, ch. I, § 2.

75 Locke, *Human Understanding*, book I, ch. I, § 7: "For I thought that the first step towards satisfying several inquiries, the mind of man was very apt to run into, was, to take a survey of our own understandings, examine our powers, and see to what things they were adapted. Till that was done, I suspected we began at the wrong end, and in vain sought for satisfaction in a quiet and sure possession of truths, that most concerned us, while we let loose our thoughts into the vast ocean of being, as if all that boundless extent, were the natural and undoubted possession of our understandings, wherein there was nothing exempt from its decision, or that escaped its comprehension."

76 Cf. the classical thesis of Wilhelm von Humboldt, "Über die Verschiedenheiten des menschlichen Sprachbaues," in *Wilhelm von Humboldt, Werke, Vol. III: Schriften zur Sprachphilosophie*, eds. Andreas Filtner and Klaus Giel (Darmstadt: Wissenschaftliche Buchgesellschaft: 2002), 224, that language is an "*eigenthümliche Weltansicht*," language is a kind of worldview. For him, a central task in the study of language is to determine the part that language plays in the creation of beliefs, von Humboldt, "Verschiedenheiten des menschlichen Sprachbaues," 153. For the Sapir/Whorf hypothesis of the determination of thought by language, cf. Benjamin Lee Whorf, *Language, Thought and Reality: Selected Writings of Benjamin Lee Whorf* (Cambridge: Technology Press of Massachusetts Institute of Technology, 1956), 212; on the implausibility of this thesis, see e.g. Steven Pinker, *The Language Instinct: How the Mind Creates Language* (New York: William Morrow and Company, 1994), 59 ff.

77 Ludwig Wittgenstein, "Philosophische Untersuchungen," in Ludwig Wittgenstein, *Werkausgabe Vol. 1: Tractatus logico-philosophicus, Tagebücher 1914–1916, Philosophische Untersuchungen* (Frankfurt am Main: Suhrkamp, 1984), § 109.

78 Cf. e.g. Noam Chomsky, *Language and Thought* (Wakefield and London: Moyer Bell, 1993), 23 f. It is worth noting that von Humboldt underlined the reality of universal understanding, von Humboldt, "Verschiedenheiten des menschlichen Sprachbaues," 158 f.

regard it as crucial for comprehending the reach and limit of human understanding. Here, too, not only the content of that which is regarded (perhaps falsely) as knowledge but also the means of acquiring it are important elements of research.

The critiques claiming to show that human rights are a historical or cognitive illusion are thus helpful because they lead us to questions that any theory of human rights has to deal with. They remind us that we need to think carefully about the historical and cognitive origins of the idea of human rights in order to understand better how, why and with what justification this idea has conquered the world – at least for now.

1.9 WHY IT IS WORTH THE EFFORT

The inquiry into the roots of human rights is no sideshow of current scientific undertakings. Human science is distinguished by many intellectual achievements of impressive sway. It has led to substantial insights into the structure of matter and into the laws that govern the development of the universe. It has deciphered part of the path of the metamorphosis of life from its inorganic origins to today's abundance of forms and peered into the mysteries of how life reproduces itself.

Understanding such matters of scientific inquiry is of considerable human interest. There are sometimes straightforward, practical reasons for this – say, the aim of launching a satellite for telecommunications or of improving medicine. Sometimes, and not infrequently, this importance or even greatness of science stems from other sources than practical interests, however. Approaching some kind of understanding of the structure of the universe, for instance, has no clear instrumental purpose. Nevertheless, cosmology is one of the truly admirable enterprises of the curious human mind. Its importance derives from the occasionally irresistible desire to understand some of the riddles that surround us and the intrinsic value of insight.

Such great intellectual achievements are not reserved to the natural sciences. Other topics are equally important. Comprehending the nature of beauty is no less significant than deciphering the subatomic structure of matter, for instance. It is as honorable to contribute to the understanding of human language as to the understanding of the fate of red giants. Deepening insight in the workings of human societies is as crucial a task as making out what drives the reproduction of life.

The same holds for the study of human rights. Human rights are of evident and even existential practical significance for human beings. Human rights have become part of the moral language human beings speak, and this is true worldwide. They are not just gibberish. Human rights add something very important to the human moral universe. Their message is: Dignity, life, freedom and equality are not crumbs that occasionally fall from the table of the legitimate rulers to be picked at by the undeserving if it so pleases their masters. We are not just granting a favor when we respect the goods of others' human lives. We owe others something.[79] They rightly can demand something from us because they are entitled to it. Rights put people on their own two feet. They secure their agency and status as a subject of human social action.

These moral claims have practical effects. Moral arguments based on rights are influential and sometimes even have the power decisively to determine the course of affairs.

As legal instruments, they are among the most important peaceful means through which human beings can defend their lives, integrity, dignity and liberty and the justice of certain social arrangements. More controversially, they are the means through which human beings can claim certain material goods that are the preconditions for leading a decent human life.

For very long periods of time, states were instruments of power used to secure the privileges of kings, aristocracies and other oligarchical groups, sometimes on a global scale, as the history of colonialism and imperialism illustrates in modern times. They were used for the aggrandizement of dynasties, nations or particular religious creeds. States' power derived from financial and economic control, from ideologies maintaining a belief in the legitimacy of their order and – not least – from the ability to use physical force through their security apparatus and military means to quash dissent.

It is therefore all the more striking that, through a long political process, human societies were able to forge the idea of the necessity and legitimacy of binding these tremendous powers by law, wresting them from the hand of the few and making them tools that served the interests of all in a way that respected the demands of justice. This idea has not become a fully uncontested baseline of our time, as the plethora of flourishing dictators reminds us, but some political orders are seriously committed to it. This is expressed at least in principle in constitutional orders bound by human rights in which political power is generated by democratic means. These orders are not the pinnacle of the political culture possible for human societies. Nevertheless, they are still remarkable achievements if we do not lose our sense of historical proportion and remain aware of the grim nature of humanity's past and of some of the disquieting prospects that may lie ahead.

No person with even brief practical experience of working in legal systems will have the slightest inclination to overestimate the relevance of the law, and in particular of human rights law. But it would be naive to overlook the fact that the basic rights of human beings do have tangible and substantial effects. Powerful institutions enforce human rights, not the least courts. These institutions use state power not to subdue individual freedom but to ensure that human autonomy's

[79] Cf. Griffin, *On Human Rights*, 92: "[G]etting something accepted as a human right transforms one's case. One is transformed from beggar ('you ought to help me') to chooser ('it is my right'). If one can claim by right, one is not dependent upon grace or kindness or charity to others."

dominion is safeguarded against unjustified intrusions and limitations, in particular by the state itself. Today, the protection of human rights has gained an international dimension: The international legal order is oriented towards the realization of human rights in several ways, sometimes achieving substantial results, as in the case of the ECHR or the inter-American system of rights protection – although it should be repeated that the reality is a far cry from anything close to an "international rule" of these rights.

Human rights are thus not just a lofty idea but elements of a very important social practice. Many people think about the meaning of these rights and apply and enforce them. Human rights – both in their moral as well as in their legal dimensions – have thus become building blocks of the social fabric of the world. They are part of the very stuff that current civilization is made of. They form a core aspiration of our epoch that defines its nature and has a clear effect on the lives of many people – at least until human beings abandon it, perhaps to worship anew the false idols of human folly and, even in the intimate realm of their moral hopes, succumb to the fateful lure of power, injustice and domination.

Accordingly, human rights are limited but crucially important concrete expressions of the intimate human longing for justice and a morally decent life. The quest for justice and moral goodness is one of the traits that distinguish the human species. Throughout history, human beings have searched and struggled for a way of life that takes justice and what we owe to each other as seriously as these ideas deserve. These endeavors have occupied, bewildered and at times enchanted human thought. They seem to be one of the undertakings that are key to understanding the core of human existence.

There are many wonders in the natural world, as planets, black holes, red giants, curved space–time, gravitational waves, subatomic particles and the like illustrate. But some of the wonders of this world lie within human beings' inner selves, in their subjectivity, and these are as magnificent in their architecture, as rich in mind-baffling riddles, as fascinating in their surprising properties, as vast in the space they open up for human inquiry as anything in the outside world. One of these remarkable phenomena of the inner human world is the apparent existence of a moral compass, a sense of justice, a principle of humanity, a "conscience," to use the term chosen by the drafters of the *Universal Declaration*. Morality is a constitutive element of human beings' inner world and part of the stuff that defines this rather peculiar species.

Given the very particular role that human rights play in history and contemporary human life and their apparent link to the riddles of morality that are so central to the human life form, they belong among the most important products of human thinking. The desire to understand human rights as such, as elements of pure theoretical inquiry beyond the practical ethical, legal and political interests at stake – the wish to decipher the origin and nature of this element of human thought and practice and to unearth the preconditions of its development in human thinking, history and social development – is consequently a pursuit worthy of very serious effort. Exploring the moral idea of human rights and its manifestations and effects, its history and roots in human beings' inner selves, is no less significant than the attempts of the inquiring human mind to solve the riddles of time and space (or what is left of these traditional forms of human thinking about the world) or to explore the structure of matter deep below the surface. Human rights in ethics and law mirror constitutive features of human moral understanding, and there is no need to defend attempts to determine the exact meaning of what we see in this fragile looking glass.

This remains the case even if we are skeptical about the rise of human rights over the last 200 years or so, as some are; it remains the case even if we deplore the language of rights and see it as depoliticizing intrinsically political struggles, or even as a parochial tool of Western hegemony, which should have no place in a postcolonial world freed from all illegitimate, socially constructed, contingent fetters; and it remains the case even if we see human rights as a chimera sprung from the delusionary workings of our brains – all matters to which we will return. Even in these cases, we should be interested in understanding better the origins and current reality of human rights, firstly because of scientific curiosity and secondly because understanding rights is a precondition for fighting successfully against their rule – if, after reflection, we still find reasons to do so.

1.10 THE LINE OF ARGUMENT

How, then, to approach these far-reaching and important questions? This inquiry will try to get to grips with at least some of the problems involved by proceeding in the following steps: First, given the intense debate about human rights, it has been necessary to show in some detail that embarking on this particular theoretical journey is worth the effort. To this end, the preceding remarks considered the question of why the relationship between the human mind and rights is of significant theoretical interest. Thus, the first question – *Why does an inquiry into mind and rights matter for ethics and law?*[80] – hopefully has been answered sufficiently.

Second, the concept or idea of a human right as a subclass of moral and legal subjective rights (or, to use a different terminology: claim rights) will be outlined and its content clarified. The meaning of the term "human rights" is not obvious. The definitions of this term sometimes vary considerably and are far from uncontroversial, not least in theoretical debates. The questions implied are not just

[80] The term "ethics" is used in a variety of ways. One is to take ethics as a theory that reflects upon morality. Another widespread understanding of the term is to use "ethics" for anything that concerns the good, flourishing life in a roughly eudemonistic sense, e.g. Jürgen Habermas, *Faktizität und Geltung* (Frankfurt am Main: Suhrkamp, 1992), 139 ff.; Ronald Dworkin, *Justice for Hedgehogs* (Cambridge, MA: Harvard University Press, 2011), 13 ff. In the present text, "ethics" is used in the former, not the latter sense.

terminological, however. On the contrary, important issues are at stake. On a very basic level, for example, we can ask whether phenomena such as "rights" are even possible – in the sober light of reflection, is the idea not after all just deplorably obvious "nonsense upon stilts"? If it is not, the question of the structure of rights arises. Another important question concerns the relation between moral and legal human rights. This analysis of the concept or idea of rights is thus indispensable if we are to answer the question: *What precisely are we talking about?*

Human rights as we know them are the products of history. They were not simply present in people's minds in the same way as the perception of a setting sun. Accordingly, there is a rich tradition of studies on the history of human rights, and the field is currently marked by intense debate. It is not possible to discuss human rights credibly from any perspective without situating our argument in what we know about the historical development of this idea that has finally been turned into legal institutions. Therefore, the (fascinating) question *Where do human rights come from?* needs to be addressed as our third step. It will occupy our attention long enough to develop some reasons for a thesis that paves the way for the subsequent line of argument: Human rights have deep roots in the cross-cultural history of ideas and social practices, but not in the sense of a *Universal Declaration* in cuneiform. Rather, there are many clearly related ideas that help us to understand how humans came to form this peculiar concept and illustrate that it is naive to assume that any particular time or culture, including our own, has some kind of epistemic privilege of insight. The history of human rights must include phenomena that *are not human rights* but paved the way to develop this idea. More specifically, history illustrates that important seeds of human rights are moral judgments about individual human beings' justified claims to qualified goods in concrete situations – claims that are addressed to other individuals, who are obliged to act accordingly. When critical reflection leads these judgments to be objectified as to content, generalized across situations and universalized across persons, turned into explicit ethical precepts and finally solidified in legal concepts and institutions, the idea of human rights is born. This process is summarized in a sentence but took centuries to unfold. Furthermore, the present study maintains that reflection on the historical genealogy of human rights necessarily leads beyond human rights history into the deep waters of the theory of human rights, their justification, epistemology and ontology and thus to those kinds of problems that these remarks intend to explore further. Neither history nor historicism offers an escape route from such a theory of human rights.

Fourth, the question *Why are rights justified?* will be considered. The rationale behind this discussion is as follows: There can be no meaningful epistemology of human rights without specifying a normative theory of how they can be justified. This is because the latter formulates the claims whose epistemological merits are assessed by the former. If it emerges that human rights are best justified by qualified interests of agents, the epistemological status of a justification by interest has to be assessed. By contrast, if human rights are successfully grounded on instrumentalist considerations of preference maximization, the epistemological status of instrumentalist arguments is at issue. If loss aversion is the key to understanding the phenomenon of human rights, the epistemic merits of loss aversion have to be scrutinized. If human rights are most convincingly based on arguments from anthropology, political theory and normative principles of solidarity, justice and the intrinsic worth of human beings, as will be argued here, the task is to develop an epistemology of these argumentative pillars of the theory of justification. Only if we identify what the justification of human rights actually entails can we clarify what importance the theory of mind may or may not have for this justification. Admittedly, this step forms a major challenge for our argument because the justification of rights is particularly controversial, and with good reason, given the substantial difficulties to be surmounted. But if we want to proceed, we must meet this challenge as best we can.

These remarks on the analysis of the idea of human rights and what history and the theory of justification teach us about the relation between human understanding and human rights prepare the ground for the fifth and last issue to be addressed: *What, after all, is the importance of the theory of mind for the project of human rights? Can the modern theory of moral understanding vindicate the connection between reason, conscience and rights?* Here, the attack from today's neuroscientific neo-emotivism will be discussed, which is interesting in itself and has the advantage that its critique has considerable heuristic merits. Other important theories of moral psychology will be considered on this basis in order to determine what we can learn from them for a constructive account of the theory of mind and the foundations of human rights.

The next perspective to be explored will be how a theory of human rights could draw from an alternative theory of mind, and more concretely from a mentalist account of ethics and law, to provide such a constructive account. As indicated above, such perspectives on the theory of the moral mind form a necessary element of sufficiently rich explanatory theories of human rights. Without them, a crucial piece of the puzzle that needs to be put together for a theory of satisfactory explanatory power would be missing.

After this argument and on its basis, a central problem that arises in different theoretical settings will be addressed: the role of empirical findings for a normative theory and thus the problem of the trap of a naturalistic fallacy in the study of ethics and law. The present study will argue that while an understanding of the human mind is no substitute for normative theory, normative theory can be bolstered and enriched by a plausible theory of the human mind, not least to defend the idea of human rights against attacks that are motivated by what their proponents regard as the empirical findings of moral psychology. Not only can there be no full understanding of human rights without their theory being embedded in a plausible theory of the makeup of the mind, there can be no full-scale defense of their reign without such a theory either. This study will explain why a defense of human rights strengthened by human moral psychology is entirely in line with a plausible theory of the evolution of human cognition – something that needs to be addressed because evolutionary arguments have become influential in the debate about rights.

The debate about rights is not limited to the rights of humans. The question of animal rights also has attracted much well-deserved attention. We will limit our inquiry, however, to the rights of humans, to avoid overstretching its already rather wide scope, but with the proviso that nothing in this study speaks against a critical theory of rights for nonhuman animals. On the contrary, what is going to be said here may enrich such a theory as well.

I.11 PROBLEMS OF INQUIRY

This research agenda involves particular difficulties. The first is that the questions posed lead to very different fields of inquiry, most importantly the philosophy and legal theory of human rights, the positive law of human rights, the theory of mind, moral psychology and the neuroscience of normative judgment and its evolution. The approach adopted here takes a particular perspective, namely that of practical philosophy and legal theory. As such, it differs from other approaches, has its own particularities and – most importantly – has its own specific limitations.

However, there is no way around such to a certain degree necessarily limited approaches from specific scientific perspectives when addressing a grand topic such as the one at stake here, which forms an object of investigation in other domains of inquiry as well. For example, a moral psychologist necessarily will include theoretical assumptions about the nature of rights in reflections on moral psychology, a moral philosopher assumptions of moral psychology (e.g. that human beings derive all moral concepts *de novo* through education). No one discipline has a monopoly on raising and attempting to answer certain questions. There is no monopoly of insight either: A legal theorist is well advised to listen closely to what a moral philosopher or a cognitive neuroscientist has to say about the topic of human rights. On the other hand, an approach from the point of view of legal theory should be of interest for these other disciplinary perspectives as well. At best, these different perspectives can complement each other and ultimately may help to answer some of the truly big questions at stake.

This mutual interest and benefit are all the more obvious if we remain aware that such disciplinary boundaries are to a certain degree artificial. To be sure, there are differences in the research methods, intellectual cultures and background assumptions in different disciplines. There is common ground, too, however. A psychological fact is no less a fact if it contradicts what lawyers are accustomed to think. An interesting thesis of the theory of law is not irrelevant for philosophy just because it was outlined in an office at a law faculty and not at a desk in a philosophy department in the next building. As far as the topic of human rights is concerned, traditionally many approaches have played a role. This is particularly true for the relation between practical philosophy and moral psychology. It is no coincidence that many important works in the history of ideas wed the two together.

In addition to these problems, another difficulty is that the theoretical questions involved are particularly contested. There is not just one theory of human rights. There are many histories of human rights, too, and, to make things even more complicated, there is profound disagreement about the right method of approaching these questions in the first place. The theory of mind, cognitive science, moral psychology and evolutionary theory are equally divided fields. The basic assumptions of some approaches are taken to be outlandish by others. There is no clear middle ground in these debates. Any question concerning the nature, content and justification of human rights, the history of rights and its lessons, the theory of mind, the insights of neuroscience or the basics of moral psychology or evolution will require us take a stance that appears questionable to some and perhaps even entirely flawed to others. But there is no alternative to proceeding along the outlined course. There can be no history of rights without a concept of rights. There can be no theory of rights, their content and their justification without a concept and some historical understanding of the genealogy of human rights. There can be no theory of the moral and legal mind without understanding what morality and human rights actually mean and how they developed historically. There can be no account of the evolution of moral cognition if there is no theory of what actually makes up moral understanding.

One first aim of these remarks is thus to dispel any hopes that a theory of human rights can be achieved on simpler terms. As we will see, this is not a useless function, as all too often a particular view on any of these issues is too easily accepted as the only defensible approach, sometimes with far-reaching consequences for the plausibility of the argument put forward.

We should be mindful, therefore, of the fact that the particular standpoint from which we approach the question implies limitations, blind spots and disciplinary biases. Furthermore, we should be mindful of the intricate theoretical questions to be answered on the way and their contested nature. Any road taken will lead to path-dependent arguments that may be flawed because of some misconception implied in the background assumptions about the nature of rights, their historical or evolutionary origin, their content and justification and the mechanism of the mind relevant to develop this idea. All of the remarks that follow will be made and should be read with an awareness of this contingency.

The underlying attitude of this inquiry into human rights is thus perhaps best described as a form of *constructively audacious humility*: Substantial theses will be formulated in the hope that they may help us to understand some of the problems at issue, both through occasional insights and through fallacies that may help us to find a better way to proceed by clearly identifying argumentative failures and reflective dead ends. At the same time, there will be no effort made to hide the provisional, fallible and tentative character of any argument formulated here behind pompous language, scientific posturing or robust self-assertion about the things that have supposedly been "shown."

A last difficulty should be mentioned at this point. This difficulty arises in the context of any argument that deals with matters of human morality and profound questions of justice, not least when dealing with human rights. It has two dimensions: First, it is demanding to talk credibly about matters as serious as human rights. Such endeavors can easily sound like moralistic, mawkish hypocrisy, like moral kitsch telling sweet little lies about human goodness and reasonability that are vividly refuted by one glance at the morning papers or one's news feed. They can appear as spinning the metaphysical yarn of the past in a futile effort to salvage a sweet, moving dream when the time for a sobering awaking is already long overdue. Second, important moral issues also can provoke critiques that miss crucial insights because their critics are wedded to the belief that truly unprejudiced human thought cannot leave anything intact that appears grand or noble like human rights, that one truth condition of a theory is that it unveils the profane construction concealed behind a cozening facade. Furthermore, there is a strange intellectual pleasure in defiling that which many seem to cherish highly.

Daring to express irreverent disregard of the false authority of customary thought doubtlessly is a crucial sign of freedom and independence of thought, and this freedom is essential for any serious theoretical endeavor. However, we have to retain an open mind about the possible results of an inquiry into these matters that jettisons false idols. In particular, we need to consider the possibility that an idea like human rights has gained the importance attached to it on very good grounds. We thus have to avoid two pitfalls: moralistic posing on the one hand and gratuitous doubt, which is the born enemy of truly critical thought, on the other.

I.12 THEORY OF HUMAN RIGHTS AND THE ETHICS OF A WAY OF LIFE

The inquiry into these questions is not only of theoretical interest, although this interest alone can already motivate passionate work in this field. These questions are of very concrete political significance, too. This is because there are very serious reasons for concern about the human rights project. We should not take the existence of the level of civilization epitomized by human rights for granted. The history of the last century is sobering. Massive crimes were committed because fantastic ideologies such as National Socialism held their barbarous sway. Camus with good reason called it "*le siècle de la peur*,"[81] a century of fear that formulated the categorical imperative "*ni victimes, ni bourreaux*," to become neither victims,

[81] Albert Camus, "19 Novembre 1946: La siècle de la peur," in *Cahiers Albert Camus Vol. 8: Camus à Combat – éditoriaux et articles d'Albert Camus (1944–1947)*, ed. Jacqueline Lévi-Valensi (Paris: Gallimard, 2002), 608.

nor hangmen.[82] Given this cataclysm and the added experience of the suffering that has followed since around the world, the recent past has certainly taught us that we should not place too much confidence in the decent behavior of human beings. To be sure, such skepticism does not necessarily imply a verdict about reason or an endorsement of theories about its intrinsic dark side[83] or the amoral driving forces of the human will.[84] But it does nourish a very ancient reluctance to underestimate the fragility of civilization. After all, the Athenians did not lack culture but nevertheless sowed destruction in the Peloponnesian Wars, both for others and ultimately for themselves.[85]

Dispelling doubts about the justification of human rights is thus not only a theoretically important but also a politically crucial end. It is necessary to strengthen the (not at all self-evident) motivation to do something to defend human rights' fragile rule where it exists. It is a precondition for helping to increase their sway, which challenges power, injustice and bondage in this world – albeit often without success, given the formidable adversaries of the idea that human beings enjoy certain intrinsic rights. There can be no long-term politically effective defense of human rights without understanding their nature, structure and deeper roots and thus the kind of inquiry to which these remarks intend to contribute.

In the story *Typhoon*, the darkness of the storm that the ship *Nan-Shan* is steaming through is a symbol for the condition human beings find themselves in – the impenetrable riddles of their existence, the immensity of appalling stillness that surrounds them, the threat of being the solitary self-conscious inhabitants of a world without sense and purpose.

The sailors fighting their way through the typhoon, led by the unimaginative but strikingly resilient and morally principled Captain MacWhirr, assert the meaning of human life with their struggle against this menace. Importantly, respect for other persons – in this case, the Chinese coolies, who are herded under deck by the shipowners but who MacWhirr demands be treated with as much decency and fairness as possible even in what appears to be the foundering ship's last minutes – is central to the existential self-preservation of the human beings battling the storm.

82 Camus, "Siècle de la peur," 608.

83 Following e.g. the argument of Max Horkheimer and Theodor W. Adorno, "Die Dialektik der Aufklärung," in *Theodor W. Adorno: Gesammelte Schriften, Vol.* 3, ed. Rolf Tiedemann (Darmstadt: Wissenschaftliche Buchgesellschaft, 1998).

84 Cf. with the consequence of denying the "*Wille zum Leben*," will to life, Arthur Schopenhauer, *Die Welt als Wille und Vorstellung*, Vol. 1 in *Sämtliche Werke*, Vol. 1, ed. Wolfgang von Löhneysen (Frankfurt am Main: Suhrkamp, 1986), § 68; Arthur Schopenhauer, *Die Welt als Wille und Vorstellung*, Vol. 2 in *Sämtliche Werke*, Vol. 2, ed. Wolfgang von Löhneysen (Frankfurt am Main: Suhrkamp, 1986), ch. 48.

85 The perceptive commentator Thucydides takes it as both the premise and the justification of his work that humans will repeat such miseries as the war he describes and may therefore profit from a true account of the past, cf. Thucydides, *History of the Peloponnesian War, Vol. I: Books 1–2*, trans. Charles Forster Smith, Loeb Classical Library 108 (Cambridge, MA: Harvard University Press, 1928), book 1, XXII.

The force of this tale draws our attention to a final point: Human beings have traversed periods of profound darkness, and not only in the recent past. There are probably more dark times ahead, with challenges to the protection of human rights coming both from traditional and new sources that may prove highly significant, as the possible consequences of global warming show with worrisome clarity. Protecting human rights is not only important in order to prevent harm to human beings, however. It is not only a means of fending off the danger of *that* dark night. Rather, this protection forms part of a certain interpretation of the existential condition humans find themselves in as human rights express an attitude towards human life. Simply put, they assert the worth of being human. If humans were dispensable, irrelevant and meritless creatures, there would be no reason to make any effort to respect human persons and protect their capability to lead their lives. It is the very point of human rights that every life is taken to be of equal worth, whether the respective person makes a fortune, excels in physics, leaves behind great sculptures or disappears in the "*immense oubli*," the great forgetting that Camus rightly sees as the fate of people like his hardworking, uneducated and poor parents and family, and which – one might add – will be the final resting place of most of us, regardless of the walk of life from which we come. The language of human rights expresses the persistent consciousness of the meaningfulness of all human life despite the numerous catastrophes of human history, the yaw of intellectual doubt, the many forms of human suffering and the silent vastness of the world in which humanity is seeking its difficult way. Human rights thus reassert the value of naked, simple, unadorned human existence and the spark of greatness that is its core.

Whether a reflection on mind and rights is able to add anything meaningful to these large questions will be scrutinized in the analytical steps outlined above. The path we will follow is beset with particular difficulties. Any step will thus be taken modestly, as indicated above, with the profound conviction that more questions will be raised than answered. The first step is to better clarify what the concept of human rights actually entails.

PART I

The Concept of Human Rights and the Global History of an Idea

1

The Concept of Human Rights

"Sollte eine Entscheidung kommen oder sollte es vorher nötig werden, Sie noch einmal zu verhören, werde ich Sie holen lassen. Sind Sie damit einverstanden?"

"Nein, gar nicht," sagte K., "ich will keine Gnadengeschenke vom Schloß, sondern mein Recht."

Franz Kafka, *Das Schloss*[1]

1.1 PARAMETERS OF ANALYSIS

The concept or idea of a "right" – or, more precisely, a "subjective Right" or "claim right" – is an intricate one.[2] Moreover, as will be illustrated in the historical reflection below, when dealing with terms such as "*ius*," "right," "*Recht*," "*droit*," "*derecho*" and so on, it is important to distinguish – as in other areas of analysis – the words themselves from what they designate. What is referred to by "right" or "subjective right" may also be the meaning of many other terms. It can even be expressed without any such terms, through a circumscription or through the implications of an expression that has very different meanings, too. For instance, the statement "My darling!" tenderly referring to a car parked in front of a house can imply a right (and a complex one at that) called "private property." It can also refer to something quite different if addressed to a human person. In addition, different

[1] "If a decision should arrive or if it should become necessary to interrogate you again first, I shall send for you. Is that all right with you?"
"No, not at all," said K., "I want no favours from the castle, I want my rights."
Franz Kafka, *The Castle*, trans. J. A. Underwood (London: Penguin Books, 2019), 67.

[2] "The notion of a legal right has proved in the history of jurisprudence to be very elusive," not least because of "the interesting though also strange things that jurists and others have said about rights," Herbert Lionel Adolphus Hart, *Essays on Bentham* (Oxford: Oxford University Press, 1982), 162.

normative positions may be all called "rights," though in different senses: The right to free expression does not mean exactly the same thing as a police officer's right to fine a traffic offender.

In view of this fact, we need to outline, however roughly, the content of the concept and idea of human rights and other related terms.[3] This analysis forms the precondition for any discussion of the further questions that need to be addressed in this inquiry – about the history and justification of human rights and what a theory of moral cognition may (or may not) contribute to this important topic. Otherwise, conceptual vagueness will necessarily lead our investigation astray.

Any discussion of these matters needs to take note of legal human rights practice. There is no good reason to snub this practice as tedious, slightly dusty "law stuff" devoid of deeper theoretical interest. After all, the doctrine of human rights has become a rather sophisticated intellectual edifice, built by thousands of industrious legal hands. Examples include intricate concretizations of the scope of different rights, the doctrine of positive obligations, direct or indirect horizontal effects, the principle of the extraterritorial application of human rights, the concept of interference with rights, the doctrine of proportionality and the idea of weighing and balancing rights and interests. Some of these ideas are relevant for a better understanding of the concept of a subjective right, as the discussion in this chapter will illustrate.

This edifice is not simply a descriptive restatement of the content of positive law. Positive law remains silent on many of these issues. And not only that: Core elements of current human rights law are the products of case law and doctrine. Court decisions are not mindless reproductions of what is stated by positive law but demanding examples of often theory-laden normative arguments that incorporate elements of legal doctrine and develop it further. Positive law on human rights is itself often based on these interwoven jurisprudential and doctrinal developments. It is a shortcoming of some discussions in the field that they fail fully to take account of this body of thought.

1.2 MORAL AND LEGAL RIGHTS

A first, much-discussed question that requires an answer for the purpose at hand is whether there are moral rights alongside legal rights.[4] A major issue is the supposed

[3] There is an important methodological question here: What are we investigating exactly? Or, as Hart put it, what are the criteria for the success or failure of such conceptual work, in his view an exercise of "'rational reconstruction' or refinement of concepts in use," Hart, *Essays on Bentham*, 163 f. As will become clear in the following discussion, from our point of view, it is not just the changing factual *use* of words – in the ordinary or specific jurisprudential sense – that is at issue, nor is it a matter of *definition*. The task is rather the analytical understanding of a distinct idea or concept constitutive of human normative thinking and theory building.

[4] Cf. e.g. for a review Hart, *Essays on Bentham*, 82, 162 f.

"criterionlessness"[5] of moral human rights – one cannot identify human rights with sufficient clarity without the determination of their content by positive law. This question was raised in particular at the time of the demise of Natural Law[6] and has continued to occupy legal reflection ever since. Some scholars regard the ontological status of moral rights as dubious because Natural Law seems the only way to conceptualize nonpositive rights. Natural Law, however, they see as wedded to an outdated metaphysics of normative entities. Consequently, in the view of some theorists, without the basis of Natural Law, the idea of rights beyond positive law has no foundations. Moreover, the idea of rights has appeared to some as being redundant as, in their view, every normatively relevant content can be expressed by moral and legal duties.[7]

Some foundational elements of our contemporary human rights architecture clearly take a stand on these questions. The *Universal Declaration* speaks of the "recognition" (not the creation) of human rights, as do influential constitutional texts that assume the existence of human rights that are not created by law.[8] The same holds true for much of the philosophical discussion concerned with human rights as ethical norms independent of legal systems. This stance is very much in line with a long tradition of thought about human rights as fundamental legitimate claims of human beings, a tradition that ultimately gave birth to the idea of protecting human rights by legal means in the first place. The many varieties of Natural Law theory form an important part of this tradition. It is possible, however, to assert the existence of moral rights without endorsing the metaphysics of certain conceptions of Natural Law – say, Thomas Aquinas' idea of Natural Law as a part of an eternal law permeating and determining the structure of the universe (including the content of God's will)[9] or other such ideas.

Rights are nothing less than a fundamental element of human beings' moral world. Any children's birthday party illustrates the importance of normative incidents such as claims, perhaps to an equal share of the sweets distributed by the birthday child's parent or the (occasional, thrilling) permission, privilege or liberty to do just as you please – for example, to eat these sweets whenever you want this afternoon (including: all at once, now!).

Human rights create normative positions on the basis of incidents such as claims. As we will discuss in more detail in this chapter, it is an analytical misunderstanding to think that rights can be reduced to duties of others. Importantly, rights empower the rights-holders: They invest them with control over their own lives because

[5] Hart, *Essays on Bentham*, 82, 90.

[6] Cf. Bentham's dictum that a subjective right must be "the child of law" instead of giving it a "spurious parentage" by laying it "at Nature's door," Bentham, "Nonsense upon Stilts," 400.

[7] Cf. e.g. for discussion Hart, *Essays on Bentham*, 162 f.

[8] Cf. in Germany Art. 1.2 GG (Basic Law).

[9] Cf. Thomas Aquinas, *The Summa Theologica*, trans. Fathers of the English Dominican Province (Notre Dame: Christian Classics, 1981), I–II, Q. 91 a. 2.

rights-holders can justifiably demand something of others.[10] As such, for many people rights have long formed part of the foundations of a considered ethical outlook. Moreover, as we will see in our discussion about the justificatory theory of human rights in Part II, it is not an entirely hopeless task to identify those moral rights that are plausibly taken as moral *human rights* – "criterionlessness" is not the ultimate verdict.[11]

The historical and contemporary positions distinguishing moral and legal rights consequently are entirely on the right track. There are no convincing reasons to deny the existence and importance of moral human rights.

These findings have a very concrete political consequence: They open the door to the principled ethical critique of social practices, structures and institutions that violate human rights in a moral sense. They are also a crucial source for critiquing existing forms of human rights protection in law, identifying their possible shortcomings and developing them further. Moreover, there is good reason to believe that such ethical considerations may play a role in reasonable interpretations of human rights as positive law – many questions raised by positive human rights law are answered convincingly only if guided by the sound principles of a normative theory of human rights.[12]

1.3 THE COMPLEX MAKEUP OF SUBJECTIVE RIGHTS

What is a right? What distinguishes it from an interest in or a wish for something? There is a long, partly neglected tradition of analytical work on the idea and concept of a right, with important contributions by Natural Law theorists like Grotius,[13] deontic logicians like Leibniz[14] or legal theorists like Bentham.[15] Hohfeld's

[10] Hart, *Essays on Bentham*, 183: (Legal) rights turn an individual into a "small-scale sovereign" in the area of conduct covered by the right. This observation does not entail implausible tenets of the will theories of rights, cf. on the critique of will theories Leif Weinar, "The Nature of Rights," *Philosophy & Public Affairs* 33, no. 3 (2005): 223, 238 ff.

[11] Which is not Hart's verdict either. He regards some qualified goods essential to human beings in conjunction with respect for personhood as such a criterion, Hart, *Essays on Bentham*, 95, 103, 189 f.

[12] Cf. Matthias Mahlmann, *Elemente einer ethischen Grundrechtstheorie* (Baden-Baden: Nomos Verlag, 2008).

[13] Hugo Grotius, *De Iure Belli ac Pacis Libri Tres, Ed. Nova, Vol. I, reproduction of the ed. of 1646 by James Brown Scott* (Washington, DC: Carnegie Institution of Washington, 1913), I, I, IV ff.; I, I, XVII, 2; Jean-Jacques Burlamaqui, *Principes du droit naturel* (Geneva: Barrilot & File, 1747), 81: "*Le Droit & l'Obligation sont donc deux termes corrélatifs, comme parlent les Logiciens : l'une de ces idées suppose nécessairement l'autre.*"

[14] Gottfried Wilhelm Leibniz, "Aus der Neuen Methode, Jurisprudenz zu lernen und zu lehren (1667)," in Gottfried Wilhelm Leibniz, *Frühe Schriften zum Naturrecht: Lateinisch-deutsch*, trans. Hubertus Busche (Hamburg: Felix Meiner Verlag, 2003), § 16.

[15] Jeremy Bentham, "An Introduction to the Principles of Morals and Legislation," in *The Collected Works of Jeremy Bentham*, eds. James Henderson Burns and Herbert Lionel Adolphus Hart (Oxford: Oxford University Press, 1996), XVI, 25, n. e; for more details cf. Hart, *Essays on Bentham*, 164 ff.

approach has the great merit of bringing much of what has been discussed in this tradition into a clear conceptual framework. He understands rights not as simple monoliths but as a complex bundle of the normative positions of a bearer or many bearers (or holders) and an addressee or the addressees of a right. These normative positions or incidents include, first, what in standard terminology is interchangeably called a right (in a narrower sense), claim, claim right or subjective right of the rights-holder to an action or forbearance on the one hand and the corresponding duty of the addressee towards the bearer to perform or forbear from the action on the other.[16] If a person has the right to free speech, the bearer has a claim against the addressee not to interfere with the bearer's expression, and the addressee (e.g. the state) has the duty to forbear from interfering. This is a necessary connection. There are no claims without duties, although there are morally good acts that are not normative correlatives of the claims of the patients of the acts – for example, in the case of an action that is supererogatory. Certain duties, however, necessarily imply claims – for instance, the duties of justice imply the claims of the addressees of just acts. This reveals a major analytical deficiency of the idea that rights are a redundant normative category – for many obligations, a normative system of duties is necessarily also a normative system of rights.

Second, the bearers of a large group of rights are permitted but not obliged to use the normative position they hold: They enjoy a privilege to do so or not.[17] The bearers of a right to free speech can express themselves or not, for example. The addressee has no normative claim against the bearers for them to do one or the other – the adressee's position is characterized by a "no-right." A right opens up a normatively protected space within which the bearer can exercise discretion,[18]

16 Wesley Newcomb Hohfeld, *Fundamental Legal Conceptions as Applied in Judicial Reasoning*, eds. David Campbell and Philip Thomas (Abingdon: Routledge, 2001), 12 f.

17 Hohfeld, *Fundamental Legal Conceptions*, 14 ff. On "unilateral" privileges, which, unlike "bilateral" privileges, imply only the freedom to do something and not the freedom not to do something, because of an obligation to act, Hart, *Essays on Bentham*, 166, 173; Weinar, "The Nature of Rights," 223, 225 ff. distinguishes single and paired privileges: the former being an exemption from a general duty, such as a police officer's right to break open a door, the latter providing the bearer with discretion – two "entirely independent" functions. A police officer has the privilege, however, not only to break open the door, but also not to break open the door – for example, if the suspect opens it. Only if the officer is under a duty to break open the door (because the suspect does not open it) is the privilege unilateral, in Hart's terms. Similarly, an arrestee has the privilege not only not to speak, but also to speak, cf. on this example Weinar, "The Nature of Rights," 229.

18 This is the truth of the so-called will theory, cf. Friedrich Carl von Savigny, *System des heutigen Römischen Rechts*, Vol. 1 (Berlin: Veit, 1840), § 4; Bernhard Windscheid, *Lehrbuch des Pandektenrechts*, Vol. 1 (Aalen: Scientia Verlag, 1906), § 37; Hart, *Essays on Bentham*, 80 ff. The assumed opposition to the interest theory, cf. Rudolph von Jhering, *Geist des römischen Rechts auf den verschiedenen Stufen seiner Entwicklung*, Teil III (Leipzig: Breitkopf und Härtel, 1924), 337 ff., is perhaps the product of an incomplete conception of subjective rights: The protection of autonomy (the free exercise of an individual's will) may be one of the interests such rights serve and is not without limits, which was the core of Jhering's concern with the will theory of rights. On the other hand, freedom of choice is of the essence for a right. For a

defined by the nonexistence of a duty with a content precisely opposite to that of the bearer's privilege.[19] If Serena enjoys, for instance, the privilege of expressing her opinion, she is under no duty not to express her opinion. If she enjoys the privilege of not expressing her opinion, she is under no duty to express her opinion. Standard subjective human rights thus are constituted not only by claims, but also by the privilege to do or not to do something. Other kinds of rights, such as guaranteeing the equality of human beings, are, however, constituted only by claims and duties – the claim to equal treatment or nondiscrimination and the correlated duties of the addressee.

Third, rights can contain but are not the same as normative powers to change one's own or others' normative position, such as the power of a police officer to create the duty of the addressee of an order – say, an unfortunate law professor caught cycling up a sidewalk on a one-way street – to stop and explain his deplorable lack of respect for traffic rules before being fined (severely, as he should know better). Such powers are sometimes also understood as rights. The "right" of a police officer to fine a traffic offender refers to a power in this sense. The expression "the right of the police officer" implies more normative incidents, however, namely claims, duties and privileges: The police officer has a claim against the offender to stop and against bystanders that they will not interfere, and the offender and bystanders have a corresponding duty not to do so. The police officer may have the privilege to fine or not to fine the offender – for example, if the respective law allows for some form of discretion in this respect. If so, the police officer is under no duty to fine or not to fine the offender.

Fourth, the normative ability embodied in a power correlates with the liability of the patient of this exercise of the power.[20] It is the opposite of the patient's immunity to such a power, which implies the agent's disability to effect such normative changes.[21]

Bare privileges are conceivable: Their normative force is weak and consists in the possibility of acting or not acting in a certain way without violating the rights of another person.[22] At the same time, hindering the exercise of the bare privilege does not violate a normative position of the bearer of the privilege.[23] To say that the normative force of privileges is weak does not mean that they have no practical relevance. There are, for instance, important legal institutions based on such

critique of certain forms of will theories and interest theories, Weinar, "The Nature of Rights," 238 ff., arguing for a several functions theory, 246 ff., to account for such examples as the right of a judge to sentence a person.

19 Hohfeld, *Fundamental Legal Conceptions*, 14.

20 Hohfeld, *Fundamental Legal Conceptions*, 21 ff.

21 Hohfeld, *Fundamental Legal Conceptions*, 28 ff.

22 Hohfeld, *Fundamental Legal Conceptions*, 16.

23 Hohfeld, *Fundamental Legal Conceptions*, 16; Judith Jarvis Thomson, *The Realm of Rights* (Cambridge, MA: Harvard University Press, 1990), 46 ff.; Robert Alexy, *A Theory of Constitutional Rights* (Oxford: Oxford University Press, 2010), 144 ff.

normative positions: A classic example would be the ability to appropriate things that are no one's property – an ownerless object or a *res nullius*. That this is an important legal idea may sound less than obvious if we think of the used office chair that somebody has put out on the sidewalk with a "for free" sign attached. Anyone has the privilege to appropriate this chair, a normative position that does not imply a duty on anyone's part not to take the chair first.[24] Our perception of the matter may change, however, if we consider other cases. An interesting example stems from the law of the high seas, which ultimately is rooted in the idea of free seas, of *mare liberum*.[25] One consequence of this idea is the guarantee of freedom of fishing and thus of access to a key nutritional resource.[26] There are some limits to this freedom in international law, including those stemming from sustainable fishing policies[27] or the duty not to prevent others from going anywhere on the high seas to fish. However, the freedom of fishing imposes no duty not to fish first where others want to fish too, and thus it implies nothing but the privilege to harvest the fish one is able to find.[28]

Another example of the practical relevance of this normative idea and at the same time of the possibility of its abuse is the doctrine of *terra nullius* that was applied to entire continents and the millions of people living there in the context of colonialism and imperialism to justify grave injustices, including the atrocity called the "Scramble for Africa."

Human rights are not bare privileges. The permission to do or not to do something goes along with and is buttressed by a claim of the bearer against the addressee and a respective duty to do or not to do something, depending on the nature of the right. In addition, a legal right is enforced by the institutions and the sanctions of the law. Human or fundamental rights consequently are understood in the contexts discussed in this volume as a cluster of four normative positions: the claims and privileges of the bearer and the duties and no-rights of the addressee.[29]

Such moral or legal (human) rights can have a power as their content, such as the freedom to contract the power to create contractual obligations – a power that is buttressed by the bearer's privilege to contract or not to contract and the bearer's claims such as the claim not to be prevented from concluding a contract by third parties and the duties of the addressees (e.g. not to interfere with the conclusion of the contract). Another example is the freedom to relinquish ownership (within the

[24] A more detailed analysis would account for the factual elements (e.g. the taking of the chair) and the normative consequences of the actions, including possession and property.

[25] Hugo Grotius, *Mare Liberum: Sive – De iure quod Batavis competit ad Indicana commercia – Dissertatio* (Amsterdam: Elzevir, 1618).

[26] UN General Assembly, *Convention on the Law of the Sea* (UNCLOS), UNTS 1833 (3), December 10, 1982, Art. 87 I e).

[27] Art. 116 ff. UNCLOS.

[28] Other interesting examples are certain normative positions enjoyed in competition law, Hart, *Essays on Bentham*, 166.

[29] For an expression of these relations with the means of deontic logic, cf. e.g. Alexy, *Theorie der Grundrechte*, 171 ff.

limits of other legal norms) traditionally derived from the right to property.[30] This normative position can be accompanied by immunities – for example, not to be obligated by contracts unless the agent has agreed. Such powers can be limited not only as regards a change of the normative positions of others, but also as regards a change of one's own normative position. One may be immune to one's own powers: The right to bodily integrity includes the right that others do not touch us without our consent. We can waive this claim under certain circumstances – for example, enjoying a caress. We cannot waive it in order to enable a third person to cut off our leg to sell it for profit, at least according to standard human rights morality and law. Many human rights imply some such powers and immunities, too.

The powers, immunities and liabilities create the possibility of layered normative systems, a central feature of morality and law – for instance, expressed in the hierarchy of laws, including constitutions that regulate the powers of a parliament to create new law that in turn establishes the power of a public authority to issue an ordinance.[31]

It is an important finding that rights can be analytically broken down into a well-defined, limited set of normative incidents, and universally so. This invites further reflection on the origin of this logical structure of rights.[32]

1.4 THE HOLDERS AND ADDRESSEES OF RIGHTS

The personal scope (that is, the set of bearers or holders) of a right varies according to the right concerned. It can be one single individual who has a specific right – for example, in contractual relations. A class of people, such as the residents or citizens of a country, can enjoy the same rights. In the case of human rights, properly speaking, the bearers of these rights are all human beings, based on no other further characteristic than the humanity of the persons concerned.[33]

30 Weinar, "The Nature of Rights," 231 argues that there are paired powers – the power to waive a right and not to waive a right, for instance. The normative position is more precisely described as a privilege to use the power or not to use the power (a bilateral privilege in Hart's and a paired privilege in Weinar's terminology).

31 Cf. on second- and third-order powers (and so on) Weinar, "The Nature of Rights," 230, n. 8; Kar, "Psychological Foundations," 112: "Consider the constitutional right to contract as an example. This right is easy enough for most people to understand, and so it might be surprising to learn that it in effect gives each member of a state a (fourth order) immunity right to be free from the (third order) power right of the state to limit his or her (second order) power right to contract – which, when exercised, could be used to create new (first order) claim rights against the original holder of the right to contract. Recursive complexities like these are rarely consciously articulated or perceived, but they can operate quite effectively in human unconscious life." Moreover, the right to contract includes claim rights against the state, not only immunity rights.

32 Cf. for substantial thought about this problem Kar, "Psychological Foundations," 109 ff.

33 There is intense discussion about animal rights. Nothing in these remarks has any direct bearing on the question of the normative status animals enjoy and whether they can enjoy rights and, if so, which. This is a question that deserves independent scrutiny. Cf. for a recent case against human superiority Christine Korsgaard, *Fellow Creatures: Our Obligations to the Other Animals* (Oxford: Oxford University Press, 2018), 3 ff., 53 ff.

At this point, some terminological clarification is in order, as the term "human rights" is often used in a wider, generic way that encompasses more than rights in this particular, technical sense of the rights of all human beings – for example, rights to vote that are limited to citizens of a state. This broader usage is found in many contributions to the theory, philosophy and history of human rights. This creates a certain difficulty if we are aiming for terminological precision but at the same time want to avoid terminological pedantry. In the following, the term "human rights" therefore will be used to designate rights in this wider generic sense as long as no greater precision is required. If the need arises, however, the term "human rights" will be used in this narrow, technical sense, too. The text will make clear which meaning is the relevant one in the context in question.

"Fundamental rights" is another term that can help to steer us through the maze of incongruent terminological usage in debates about human rights. However, it, too, first requires clarification. In the following, fundamental rights are understood as encompassing human rights in the narrow sense of the rights of all humans and rights of central importance that are, however, not granted to all persons in legal systems, often for good reason. In these latter cases, the legal situation mirrors the fact that there is no moral right in this respect either. The guarantee of human dignity as a central fundamental right, for instance, is a human right in this technical sense in many legal systems: Everybody under this state's jurisdiction is the bearer of this right, not just the state's citizens. This normative position is entirely justified morally because there are no ethically relevant reasons not to protect everyone's human dignity. The right to vote, by contrast, is universally restricted to citizens or long-term residents of a state or other state-like structures like the EU. There are obvious reasons for this: Voting rights presuppose some kind of long-term relation with a state; tourists not only have no legal right to participate in elections in the countries they visit, they have no moral right either. Nevertheless, the right to vote in such a specific community is of particular importance and thus a fundamental right, though not a (moral or legal) human right in the narrower sense. However, the right to participate in *some* community where one satisfies some minimum requirements (citizenship, long-term residence, etc.) is a human right (in the narrow sense).[34] Insofar as the law contains this right (as customary international law arguably does),[35] it conforms to the demands of ethics in this respect – for example, because this right is interpreted

[34] Cf. Art. 21 UDHR.

[35] On a right to democracy, cf. e.g. Sigrid Boysen, "Remnants of a Constitutional Moment: The Right to Democracy in International Law," in *The Cambridge Handbook of New Human Rights: Recognition, Novelty, Rhetoric*, eds. Andreas von Arnauld, Kerstin von der Decken and Mart Susi (Cambridge: Cambridge University Press, 2020), 465 ff.; Samantha Besson, "The Human Right to Democracy in International Law: Coming to Moral Terms with an Equivocal Legal Practice," in *The Cambridge Handbook of New Human Rights: Recognition, Novelty, Rhetoric*, eds. Andreas von Arnauld, Kerstin von der Decken and Mart Susi (Cambridge: Cambridge University Press, 2020), 481 ff.

as a necessary consequence of the "right to have rights"; that is, the right to be an active part of a human political community.[36] Fundamental rights therefore are synonymous with human rights in the wider, generic sense and will be used interchangeably with that term for the sake of linguistic variation.

A right can address a single individual, a plurality of addressees or everybody. In the former two cases, rights are said to be relative, in the latter to be absolute or *erga omnes* rights[37] – however, the term "absolute" is used in another context as well, albeit in a different sense, namely that of rights without limitations. We need to distinguish between both senses. Property rights are absolute in the first sense but not in the second: The right to property creates claims towards everybody (e.g. not to dispose of an object owned by someone without the owner's consent) but can be limited by laws (e.g. the property in a medieval house can be affected by the heritage protection laws of the country in question).

Legal human rights are directed against public authority on the national, supranational and international levels. Depending on the respective system's level of development, they also have a direct or indirect horizontal effect, thus obligating private persons and legal entities.[38] The same practical effects create positive obligations that are widely accepted around the globe,[39] with some exceptions.[40] Given positive obligations based on fundamental rights, public authorities not only have to refrain from violating human rights but are obligated to take measures actively to protect human rights. Such positive obligations have become important tools of human rights protection, not least of the rights of women, and they continue to

36 Arendt, *Origins of Totalitarianism*, 388.

37 In public international law *erga omnes* rights are directed against all states, cf. Barcelona Traction case: International Court of Justice (ICJ), Barcelona Traction, Light and Power Company, Limited, Judgment (Belgium v Spain), Judgement of February 5, 1970, ICJ Reports 1970, 3 para. 33.

38 For an influential example of the direct horizontal effect of human rights norms, cf. the standing case law of the CJEU, for example on the direct horizontal effect of the EU, *Charter of Fundamental Rights of the European Union* (CFR), C 326/02, October 26, 2012, Art. 21, the equality and non-discrimination clause and a human rights norm in the narrow sense, Court of Justice of the European Union (CJEU), Egenberger (C-414/16), Judgement of April 17, 2018, EU:C:2018:257, para. 76; CJEU, Cresco/Achatzi (C-193/17), Judgement of January 22, 2019, EU:C:2019:43, paras. 76 ff. This case law is modelled along the lines of the standing case law on the direct horizontal effect of the fundamental freedoms of EU law, cf. ibid. para. 77 with further references to the Court's jurisprudence. On this traditional question of fundamental rights doctrine, cf. for example Andrew Clapham, *Human Rights Obligations of Non-state Actors* (Oxford: Oxford University Press, 2006).

39 Cf. the standing case law of the ECtHR since Belgian Linguistic Case, ECtHR, Case "Relating to certain aspects of the laws on the use of languages in education in Belgium" v Belgium (Merits), Judgment of July 23, 1968, Application no. 1474/62; 1677/62; 1691/62; 1769/63; 1994/63; 2126/64, para. 3; Inter-American Court of Human Rights (IACrtHR), Velásquez-Rodríguez v Honduras, Judgement of July 29, 1988, Series C no. 4, paras. 174 ff.

40 Notably the US Supreme Court, cf. e.g. US Supreme Court, DeShaney v Winnebago County Department of Social Services, 489 U.S. 189 (1989).

develop to meet very important challenges. For instance, they have been extended to the protection against the severe adverse effects of climate change.[41]

Moral human rights are directed at private actors. Nigerian peasants, for example, have a moral right that their environment not be destroyed by the actions of powerful individuals or private companies producing oil. Moral rights can obligate public authorities, including the legislature, as well. Though one may not have the legal right to build a minaret in Switzerland as the law stands[42] (although the case is far from clear), there are plausible grounds to believe that there is a moral right of believers to determine the shape of sacred buildings (within the framework of the general rules, such as building safety), and that this moral right is interfered with illegitimately by the constitutional ban on minarets. Public authorities should be mindful of that – for instance, if the legislature is considering proposals for the reform of the law.

1.5 THE BASIC CONTENT OF HUMAN RIGHTS

Human rights are primarily distinguished from other rights by their specific scope of protection. The content of human rights catalogues varies, and often in crucial details. However, there is a cluster of central positions that constitute the basic elements of fundamental rights protection: Dignity, life and bodily integrity are among these objects of protection, as are liberties constitutive of modern constitutional orders, such as freedom of expression, of religion and belief, of assembly and of the press, or more recently established rights like rights to privacy and data protection. Human rights catalogues protect human equality and demand equal treatment through open-ended equality guarantees and prohibitions of discrimination on at least those grounds that traditionally form the reason for discriminatory treatment, including so-called race and ethnic origin, religion and belief, sex and gender, disability, sexual orientation and, more recently, protected grounds like age.[43] Human rights assure solidarity through social rights. In addition, developed codes include other rights derived from the general *telos* of human rights catalogues to serve and protect these core contents, such as political rights and the right to institutions and procedures relevant for the application of rights – for example, to a judicial system, to access to courts and to judicial review, among others. The *Universal Declaration* is a prime example of this.[44]

[41] Bundesverfassungsgericht (German Federal Constitutional Court [BVerfG]), Beschluss des Ersten Senats vom 24. März 2021, Judgement of March 24, 2021, 1 BvR 2656/18.

[42] Cf. Bundesverfassung (Swiss Federal Constitution [BV]), SR 101, April 18, 1999, Art. 72 para. 3.

[43] Cf. e.g. the grounds protected by EU anti-discrimination law, Art. 21 CFR; Council of the European Union, *Council Directive 2000/43/EC*, OJ L 180, 07/19/2000, 22–26, June 29, 2000; Council of the European Union, *Council Directive 2000/78/EC*, OJ L 303, 12/02/2000, 16–22, November 27, 2000.

[44] Cf. e.g. for social rights, Arts. 22–27 UDHR; for political rights, Art. 21 UDHR; for institutional rights, Arts. 10 and 28 UDHR.

The backbone of human rights' legitimacy is the belief that human beings have worth, that they are not just expendable, ephemeral beings of no relevance compared to the values of a higher order of things. Human *dignity* is the term commonly used to denote this particular value status in international human rights law, in many constitutions and in political ethics.[45] Human rights are conceptualized as equal rights of human beings equal in worth: Their aim is to create the normatively safeguarded ability for every individual to lead a human life according to their own preferences in a just system of entitlements under conditions of preserved dignity of all. All of this is conceptualized in the terms of rights, as something that human beings can justly demand from others. This is the burden of consideration for others that human beings have to shoulder.

Rights can be an entirely formal category, without the claim to be legitimate and just. But this is not the case for human rights, which are underpinned by the idea that these rights are deeply justified.

As normative categories, human rights intend to affect agents' reasons for action by specifying what is permitted and obligatory and thus what agents ought to do. An important element of the idea of human rights is thus that they have motivational force and cause individual and collective social action.

1.6 CO-POSSIBILITY AND LIMITATIONS OF RIGHTS

One substantial question of importance in debates about the structure of human rights is whether human rights can conflict, and if so, how to resolve such conflicts. One argument states that rights are co-possible without such conflict,[46] not just because they have been forfeited or waived by one party. That such conflicts of rights do exist seems hard to deny, however. The (moral and legal) right of Jason to live by the commands of his faith may collide with the same (moral and legal) right of a neighbor – for example, when the latter is woken up by loud, religiously edifying music at two o'clock in the morning, played by the former with the aim of proselytizing the wicked unbelievers next door. The same is true for conflicts of rights with public interests, which in many cases are rooted in the rights of people. The owner of a landmark historic building's right to property can collide with the legitimate interest of a community (and arguably the community members' right to cultural heritage that is the reason for this interest) that it not be destroyed, despite the owner's wish to do so to erect something more profitable.[47]

[45] Cf. Matthias Mahlmann, "Human Dignity and Autonomy in Modern Constitutional Orders," in *The Oxford Handbook of Comparative Constitutional Law*, eds. Michel Rosenfeld and András Sajó (Oxford: Oxford University Press, 2012), 370 ff.

[46] Cf. Robert Nozick, *Anarchy, State, and Utopia* (Oxford and Malden, MA: Blackwell Publishing, 2008), 166: "Individual rights are co-possible: each person may exercise his rights as he chooses."

[47] For such considerations in moral philosophy, cf. Griffin, *On Human Rights*, 63 ff., who distinguishes rights/rights, rights/welfare and rights/justice conflicts, the latter concerning, for instance, conflicts of justice-based punishment and the rights of offenders. There are other

The structure of standard human rights law mirrors this state of affairs. The possibility of such collisions forms the basis of a universal feature of modern bills of rights: The formulation of the scope of the right is accompanied by a system of justified limitations of that right, most importantly because of the rights of others and public interests. Human rights catalogues therefore include either rules on such permissible limitations for any single human right[48] or an overarching horizontal clause on limitations.[49] If there are no explicit clauses of limitations, the possibility of implicit limitations is adduced from the purpose of a bill of rights: A workable bill of rights cannot reasonably be interpreted as establishing unlimited rights, apart from a specific exception to which we will return, because such rights are impossible in a community of equal persons.[50]

In fact, a large bulk of highly significant legal debates are concerned with this area of the law. The problem in legal practice is not so much whether there is freedom of religion, for example, but how to solve conflicts between this right and other legitimate public concerns, including, of course, the freedom of religion of other rights-holders. The relevant legal question therefore is not whether there are such collisions, but whether there are perhaps *some* exceptional rights that are not open to limitations. One concrete example is the right not to suffer torture, inhuman or degrading treatment (Art. 3 ECHR), which is – in the interpretation of the European Court of Human Rights (ECtHR) – absolute.[51] Another – at least according to standard interpretations of that norm – is the guarantee of human dignity in the German Basic Law.[52]. The same may hold for Art. 1 *Charter of Fundamental*

imaginable concerns (e.g. protection of animals or the environment) that are not reducible to a nonvacuous concept of welfare. Such considerations answer the worry, contra Rawlsian constructivism, that there is no way to determine an optimal set of co-possible rights because there are "multiple nondominated sets of copossible rights," cf. Onora O'Neill, "Children's Rights and Children's Lives," *Ethics* 98, no. 3 (1988): 445, 455. The answer lies in the principles governing the weighing and balancing of claims in concrete cases and the incremental construction of a concrete system of rights from the results of these exercises. This is the daily work of human rights lawyers (activists, public officials, advocates, judges, etc.).

48 Cf. e.g. Art. 2 para. 2, Art. 8 para. 2, Art. 9 para. 2, Art. 10 para. 2, Art. 11 para. 1 ECHR; Art. 2 para. 1, Art. 2 para. 2 sent. 2, Art. 5 para. 2; Art. 5 para. 3 sent. 2, Art. 8 para. 2, Art. 10 para. 2, Art. 11 para. 2, Art. 12 para. 1 sent. 2, Art. 13 paras. 2–5, Art. 13 para. 7, Art. 14 para. 3 GG.

49 Cf. Art. 29 para. 9 UDHR, Arts. 52–54 CFR, Art. 36 BV.

50 Cf. e.g. on implicit limitations of rights, the standing case law of the German Federal Constitutional Court since BVerfG, Judgement of May 26, 1970, BVerfGE 28, 243 (261).

51 ECrtHR, Gäfgen v Germany, Judgment of June 1, 2010, appl. no. 22978/05, para. 87: "The Court reiterates that Article 3 of the Convention enshrines one of the most fundamental values of democratic societies. Unlike most of the substantive clauses of the Convention, Article 3 makes no provision for exceptions and no derogation from it is permissible under Article 15 §2 even in the event of a public emergency threatening the life of the nation. The Court has confirmed that even in the most difficult circumstances, such as the fight against terrorism and organised crime, the Convention prohibits in absolute terms torture and inhuman or degrading treatment or punishment, irrespective of the conduct of the person concerned."

52 Cf. Ingo von Münch and Philip Kunig, eds., *Grundgesetz-Kommentar, Band 1* (Munich: C. H. Beck, 2021), Art. 1 para. 17.

Rights of the European Union, which reproduces the wording of the dignity guarantee of the Basic Law.

Two (standard) distinctions may help us to understand more about the basic structure of rights: First, *prescriptive norms* such as "You shall not kill" have to be distinguished from evaluative propositions expressing axiological judgments, such as "Liberty is a supreme value" or, more concretely, "Freedom of speech is a central concern for any democratic society." Second, *prima facie norms* have to be distinguished from *norms all things considered*. There is a prima facie right to freely exercise one's religion, but there may be no right, all things considered, to exercise one's religion by playing loud, edifying music at two o'clock in the morning to save one's unrepentant neighbor from eternal damnation.

These differentiations help us to restate the (influential) distinction between *rules* and *principles* that identifies the former with all-or-nothing prescriptions, which are either applicable or not, and the latter with norms that can collide with other such norms, in which case their respective weight has to be considered to determine the principle to be applied.[53]

Rules in this sense are thus – to use the terms outlined above – *prescriptive rules all things considered*. This is the reason why they apply in an all-or-nothing fashion. By contrast, the examples of principles in the rules-and-principles theory very often are stated as *prima facie prescriptive rules*, like "Nobody shall profit from their wrong." A norm such as this is highly abstract and general and its content is thus unspecified, but it is still a prescriptive rule: It prescribes a certain human conduct in abstract and general normative terms.[54]

The disadvantage of the rules-and-principles approach is that it does not account well for the difference between prima facie prescriptive rules and evaluative statements. "You shall not lie" is an example of a prescriptive rule with a prima facie character, as there are cases (all things considered) where one is permitted or even obliged to lie (e.g. to hide the whereabouts of a victim of domestic violence from the perpetrator). There is no reason to refrain from understanding "You shall not lie" as a rule and to prefer to regard it as a principle in the particular sense of the rules-and-principles approach just because it is not a rule all things considered. Rather, it is a prototype for a rule. For the same reason, it seems artificial to take a norm like Art. 3 ECHR, "No one shall be subjected to torture or to inhuman or degrading treatment or punishment," as something other than a prescriptive rule. If that is so, there is no

53 Cf. Ronald Dworkin, *Taking Rights Seriously* (London: Duckworth, 1991), 22 ff.; Alexy, *A Theory of Constitutional Rights*, 44 ff.

54 The logical form of such a prescriptive rule can be expressed, for instance, by $(x)(Ax \rightarrow OBx)$, where (x) means for all x; x ranges over addressees of a rule, "$\rightarrow$" is material implication and reads as "if . . . then," O is the deontic operator for "obligatory" and A and B are descriptive predicates – for example, Ax meaning "x is a human being" and OBx meaning "x ought to help others"; of an evaluative statement about any object of evaluation p using the (evaluative) predicate G "(morally) good" by Gp.

structural difference between these rules and the norm "No one shall profit from their wrong" mentioned above and thus no reason to call it a "principle."

Prescriptive rules regularly have an axiological kernel – for example, that it is unjust to inflict harm and reap advantages from the harm caused as a reward or that torture is unjustifiable. For an analysis of rights, rescuing this axiological content from analytical oblivion can prove useful: Judgments about the value of certain goods – say, free speech – are after all part and parcel of any moral or legal discourse on human rights. Identifying them properly is the precondition for their justification – or critique. And in this respect, the rules-and-principles account suffers from a crucial deficit: Because this approach couches both rules and principles in terms of prescriptive rules – all things considered in the former case, prima facie in the latter – the existence and importance of evaluative statements may be overlooked, to the detriment of analytical precision. The distinction between prescriptive rules (prima facie and all things considered) and evaluative statements therefore offers analytical tools that are preferable to the rules-and-principles approach and will form the basis of the following discussion.[55]

How does the outlined legal practice of human rights fit with these findings? A three-step process forms the core of this practice, though there are many differences in particular legal systems: first, the determination of the scope of a right; second, the ascertainment of an interference; and third, the justification of the interference, the latter today in many jurisdictions including a proportionality analysis, part of which is a weighing and balancing exercise.

This practice is in line with the analytical approach proposed here, which distinguishes between prima facie and all things considered prescriptive rules and axiological propositions: The structure of human rights law – rights with a specific though abstract scope of protection and a regime of justifications – mirrors the step-by-step process of arriving from different prima facie norms at a norm all things considered, which finally enables a court or a state official to determine whether a certain act or omission has violated a right (all things considered) or not.

Value judgments can help to render the scope of rights more concrete: The perception that control over personal data is central to personal autonomy, for instance, can lead to an interpretation of privacy rights that gives them a distinct protective scope – for example, including (under certain circumstances) a right to be forgotten. In addition, such value judgments play an important role in weighing and balancing exercises, generating norms all things considered – for instance, by determining the weight of privacy (including a right to be forgotten) in relation to other rights such as economic freedoms in a concrete case.[56]

[55] It should be noted that in Alexy's restatement of the approach, the distinction of rules and principles ultimately disappears as both enjoy only a prima facie character, cf. Alexy, *A Theory of Fundamental Rights*, 57 ff. The reason for this is that one cannot state all exceptions to a rule, which remains defeasible and is thus not categorically different from a principle.

[56] CJEU, Case C-131/12, Judgement of May 13, 2014, EU:C:2014:317, para. 92 ff.

Moral reflection about rights will take similar reflective steps if considering a moral right to privacy, for instance. It will try to define the content (or scope) of this right, think about possible kinds of interference with it and discuss its limits and thus the question of which interferences may be justified – for example, in the name of the moral right to economic self-determination (if such a moral right is assumed to exist). In such reflections, the distinctions between prescriptive rules and axiological judgments, between prima facie norms and norms all things considered, evidently will play a similar role as in legal arguments.

1.7 RIGHTS AND THE NATURE OF OBLIGATIONS

The nature of obligations has been controversially discussed in the current theory of human rights. This discussion takes its lead from a distinction from the Natural Law tradition that was restated prominently by Kant (who was, however, by no means its author): the distinction between perfect and imperfect obligations. According to Kant, there are perfect and imperfect obligations, both to oneself and to others. Perfect obligations do not allow for considerations of personal inclinations and interests and thus are fully specified, while imperfect obligations allow for such considerations and thus are not fully specified.[57] Another central (and, for the discussion, often decisive) source is J. S. Mill, who explicitly argued that imperfect duties do not create correlative claims.[58] Other interesting accounts with different conclusions attract less attention.[59]

Some theorists argue that, in light of this approach, certain kinds of human rights – namely social rights – make no sense, whereas others argue that it is not the idea of social rights but this approach to obligations that is flawed.[60]

57 Immanuel Kant, *Metaphysik der Sitten, Akademie Ausgabe*, Vol. VI (Berlin: Georg Reimer, 1914), 390 ff.

58 John Stuart Mill, "Utilitarianism," in *The Collected Works of John Stuart Mill, Vol. X – Essays on Ethics, Religion, and Society*, ed. John M. Robson (Toronto: University of Toronto Press and London: Routledge, 1985), 247.

59 Cf. for example for a differentiated discussion of the distinction between perfect and imperfect obligations and rights in a work of considerable importance and much admired by Kant, Moses Mendelssohn, "Jerusalem oder über religiöse Macht und Judentum," in *Moses Mendelssohn, Gesammelte Schriften. Jubiläumsausgabe, Vol. 8: Schriften zum Judentum II*, ed. Alexander Altmann (Stuttgart and Bad Cannstatt: Frommann-Holzboog, 1983), 99–204, 115 ff.

60 Cf. O'Neill, "Children's Rights", 445, 447. O'Neill's argument runs as follows: There are three kinds of obligations: (1) Universal, perfect obligations owed by everybody to everybody else, which specify completely not merely who is bound by the obligation, but to whom the obligation is owed. If such an obligation is fundamental, because they are not derived from any other basic ethical claim, "then the rights that correspond to it are also fundamental rights." (2) Special, perfect obligations, which are perfect obligations owed to specific persons – for instance, by parents to their children. (3) Not universal, imperfect obligations, which are obligations owed to some but are not fully specified – for instance, duties of charity, the "ordinary acts of kindness and consideration," O'Neill, "Children's Rights", 450. Imperfect obligations are a third category between perfect obligations implying rights and supererogatory

To assess the merits of this debate, it is useful to note that this distinction can be interpreted as being in tune with the structural analysis outlined above: In Kant's case, the way to identify perfect obligations (or rights) is to probe any proposition about possibly existing obligations (and rights) with Kant's "testing device,"[61] the categorical imperative in its formal and material sense. The proposition would pass this test if it implied neither a contradiction nor a maxim that a person could not will to apply universally nor treated a person merely as a means to an end. If the respective norm fulfills these conditions, the determined concrete normative position is – in Kantian terms – a perfect obligation directed towards others.[62] For instance, to take a contemporary example, the duty to respect the right to be forgotten is a perfect obligation if it passes this test (perhaps under some qualifying conditions). The same holds for the (perfect) right to be forgotten itself. These concrete normative positions (the right to be forgotten and the duty to respect it) would be definite normative positions and thus rights and duties all things considered in the terminology adopted here.

The same result can be achieved by the step-by-step approach to determining the content of prima facie rights by defining the scope of the right and identifying the interferences and possible justifications for the interferences in concrete cases. This approach has the advantage of clarifying the sometimes-conflicting norms that have to be included in the normative deliberation, in particular the rights of others, and it facilitates the transparent and differentiated discussion of these rights.[63] The normative point of this process and a "testing device" such as the categorical imperative are congruent, however. Both aim to determine a universally justified order of rights.

What about moral obligations to help others and their legal siblings in the form of certain social rights? According to Kant, the duty-bearers enjoys discretion concerning the manner in which to discharge their obligation in this respect, because in this case considerations of their own inclinations are admissible. This does not mean that the interpretation of these obligations by the concrete actors in question need not be reconcilable with the categorical imperative, nor that the duty-bearers could reasonably conclude that there are no such obligations at all.[64] On the contrary, the actors

acts. O'Neill derives positive (social) rights from the institutionalization of imperfect fundamental obligations, ibid. For more critique, see O'Neill, "The Dark Side of Human Rights," 427 ff. (social rights create overly complex regulatory regimes stifling initiative and fostering a culture of self-pity and blame). For a defense of social rights, cf. for instance Griffin, *On Human Rights*, 96 ff.; Charles R. Beitz, *The Idea of Human Rights* (Oxford: Oxford University Press, 2009), 164 ff.

61 Cf. John Rawls, *Lectures on the History of Moral Philosophy* (Cambridge, MA: Harvard University Press, 2000), 162 ff.

62 And thus a "*Pflicht des Rechts*," Kant, *Metaphysik der Sitten*, 390.

63 Cf. on alternative views in fundamental rights doctrine, building exceptions into the elements of the right, Mahlmann, *Grundrechtstheorie*, 366; for a defense of the related doctrine of "specificationism," John F. K. Oberdiek, "Specifying Rights Out of Necessity," *Oxford Journal of Legal Studies* 28, no. 1 (2008): 127 ff.

64 Kant, *Metaphysik der Sitten*, 390.

are morally obliged to do something in this respect. Consequently, it seems to follow that other persons have the claim that the duty-bearers discharges this obligation in some kind of meaningful way, although the addressees of the obligation do not, of course, have a right to supererogatory action.[65] Such claims to others' action can become well-defined and concrete all things considered: If children fall into a pool and you can save them at the expense of wet clothes, you are obliged to save them, and the children have the right that you do exactly that. A claim to the proper exercise of discretion about a certain kind of action, sometimes even narrowed down to an obligation to act in one well-defined way (getting the child out of the water), is an entirely well-defined concept – one that is incorporated, by the way, in much detail into the legal practice of several countries' administrative laws.[66]

What does this mean for the understanding of social rights? Is the traditional distinction between different forms of obligations at work here at odds with the idea of social rights as some maintain? Are such rights merely aspirational "manifesto rights?"[67] Given what just has been said about the nature of obligations towards others and the claims arising from them in Kant's theory and the tradition of which it is part, this is far from obvious. A central issue here is claimability as a precondition for the existence of rights. Claimability implies that there is an identified (or at least identifiable) addressee of a right who is under the duty that the right creates. The existence of an addressee can have a moral and an institutionalized legal meaning. Given that duties are the necessary correlative of claims, there is indeed no right without an addressee in this sense. The specification of such an addressee can vary in terms of concreteness, however. Rights can address specifically identified or generically determined actors. Negative rights are often straightforward cases in this respect: Freedom of speech is a claimable right against a public authority, for instance. Positive rights are more difficult: If Serena collapses on the high street, she has a right to be helped by any bystander or anyone else in a position to help. This takes on practical importance in the debate about the existence of social rights. Here, too, the case can be straightforward,

65 Kant's remarks about this are ambiguous. On the one hand, he emphasizes that imperfect obligations do not create the permission for exceptions to the demands of duty (which seems to imply claims), Kant, *Metaphysik der Sitten*, 390, but he argues that lack of respect violates a claim (*Anspruch*) of others, whereas violations of duties of love (*Liebespflichten*) show a lack of virtue (*Untugend*), Kant, *Metaphysik der Sitten*, 464. That there are no claims to supererogatory acts is uncontroversial.

66 Cf. for instance Verwaltungsverfahrensgesetz (German Law on Administrative Procedure [VwVfG]), May 25, 1976, § 40 and the doctrine of control of administrative discretion, Hartmut Mauer and Christian Waldhoff, *Allgemeines Verwaltungsrecht* (Munich: C. H. Beck, 2020), 139 ff. For Switzerland, Verwaltungsverfahrensgesetz (Swiss Law on Administrative Procedure [VwVG]), SR 172.021, December 20, 1968, Art. 49; Ulrich Häfelin, Georg Müller and Felix Uhlmann, *Allgemeines Verwaltungsrecht*, 8th edition (Zürich: Dike, 2020), 237 ff.

67 Joel Feinberg and Jan Narveson, "The Nature and Value of Rights," *The Journal of Value Inquiry* 4 (1970): 243, 255.

when legal social rights are addressed to a public authority, demanding some kind of identifiable action, although the public authority often enjoys discretion on how to discharge its responsibility.[68] In the political and moral spheres, the addressees of such rights are often generically identified. It makes sense to say that human beings suffering from hunger in the Global South have a moral right to international solidarity, though the addressees of this right are only vaguely defined. A reasonable interpretation of such a right implies a duty of relevant public authorities, both national and international, and of individual citizens – from financial donations to relief organizations to political efforts to improve the economic architecture of the international community.[69] These may be somewhat amorphous rights and duties, but they are still reasonably called such because they demand – entirely in line with Kant's argument – action and identify violations of these rights, such as a total lack of action and concern for the plight of the poor. Such rights thus are not normatively empty or merely vaguely aspirational, as they imply identifiable normative commands and are felt to constitute such commands by many people around the world, sometimes even strongly so.[70]

Even if this were not the case, there is no reason to redefine the concept of rights to accommodate social rights – they are rights if their nature can be properly understood in the terms of the features of rights outlined above (as argued here); otherwise, they are not.

1.8 THE PEREMPTORY NATURE OF RIGHTS

These findings are helpful in a further respect, namely in understanding the sense in which one can speak of rights as trumps, to use a popular

[68] In the debates about the right to water and the nature of states' obligations, it is debated in particular whether the right demands reasonable efforts, maximum use of available recourses and/or guarantee of a minimum core of water access, cf. e.g. South African Constitutional Court, Mazibuko and Others v City of Johannesburg and Others (CCT 39/09) [2009] ZACC 28; 2010 (3) BCLR 239 (CC); 2010 (4) SA 1 (CC) (October 8, 2009), para. 9 ff., finding that a minimum provision (of twenty liters of water per person) met the standard of reasonableness derived from the Constitution of the Republic of South Africa, December 10, 1996, Art. 27 para. 1b; UN Human Rights Council, *Progressive Realization of the Human Rights to Water and Sanitation: Report of the Special Rapporteur on the Human Rights to Safe Drinking Water and Sanitation*, A/HRC/45/10, July 8, 2020.

[69] Cf. on the question whether claimability is an existence condition of a right, Griffin, *On Human Rights*, 110: "The acceptable requirement of claimability is that the duty-bearer be specifiable, not that they exist. It is possible, in certain states of the world, for the duty to fall on specifiable bearers but for no one actually to meet the specification. Even then, there would still be a point in publicly announcing and justifying the description of the duty-bearer, if there might eventually be some."

[70] There is nothing strange about thinking that everybody has a claim to "ordinary acts of kindness and consideration," in particular children, to use O'Neill's example (n. 57), though the addressees have discretion as to how they realize these duties. For a defense of the view that imperfect obligations imply duties, cf. for instance Amartya Sen, "Elements of a Theory of Human Rights," *Philosophy & Public Affairs* 32, no. 4 (2004): 338 ff.

metaphor – that is, as normative positions that decisively exclude other normative considerations.[71]

In light of what has been said earlier in this chapter, rights are trumps in this sense in concrete cases if there is a moral or legal right with a specific content and the weighing and balancing of this right with other rights or normatively relevant considerations and the values implied lead to the conclusion that this right takes precedence over these other normative considerations in the concrete case at hand. This includes arguments concerning rights of others, the common good or social welfare as a possible source of limitations of rights.

The value of a human person and the rights attached to this value form a central concern in this context. After all, one foundational tenet of human rights is a person's value, their intrinsic worth, which means that the individual cannot be disregarded in the context of the justification of particular rights and the concretization of their content in the specific case at hand, not the least in weighing and balancing exercises.[72] As a result, there are certain protected individual goods where numbers do not count.

This can be illustrated by an example that is probably uncontroversial because it concerns the socially irrelevant issue of personal taste: Even if 100,000 people find a tie with a Swiss cow pattern abominable, this gives them no (moral, let alone legal) right to forbid someone else who does like it to wear this tie. There is no right not to be exposed to bad taste, although questions may arise even in this respect – for instance, if the cow were a holy animal in some belief system and a certain religious outlook resents their depiction on fashion items. Other standard examples exemplify the same point on a more serious level: Even saving the lives of five patients does not justify cutting open Peter, who is another healthy patient, to use his organs for this purpose.[73] The ultimate justification of this prohibition to use others as organ banks depends on the justification of the supreme value of individual human beings or, in contemporary human rights language, their dignity, a matter of significant difficulty, which will be discussed in Part II as part of our attempt to provide a plausible justificatory theory of human rights.

It may be necessary to qualify this principle for some extreme emergency situations, and not only from the perspective of consequentialism, but also from the point

[71] Cf. Dworkin, *Taking Rights Seriously*, XI; Griffin, *On Human Rights*, 20. Nozick, *Anarchy, State and Utopia*, 28, argues for rights as "side constraints."

[72] This is a traditional critique of utilitarianism, which is no "respecter of persons," Hart, *Essays on Bentham*, 97 f.; Rawls, *A Theory of Justice*, 3.

[73] Or, to use J. S. Mill's famous formulation: "If all mankind minus one, were of one opinion, and only one person were of the contrary opinion, mankind would be no more justified in silencing that one person, than he, if he had the power, would be justified in silencing mankind," John Stuart Mill, "On Liberty," in *The Collected Works of John Stuart Mill, Vol. XVIII – Essays on Politics and Society Part I*, ed. John M. Robson (Toronto: University of Toronto Press and London: Routledge, 2008), 229, which leads to interesting questions about the complex normative content of Mill's utilitarianism.

of view of (threshold) deontology. Winning the war against Nazi Germany most probably involved acts in which people with no responsibility for the unleashed aggression and crimes of Nazi Germany were killed (say, a resistance fighter in a bombing raid against a German city). This does not mean that there was any morally preferable alternative to the military defeat of Nazi Germany. There is no hidden contradiction here between the normative principles implied in this account, in particular the worth of individual persons. Such emergency situations are situated on a very particular plane and involve the question of how to act when the available path means doing not good, but simply as little harm as possible, given circumstances in which only tragic choices are on offer.

1.9 GROUP RIGHTS

The matter of group rights is another question relevant for an analytical theory of rights. Here, the background consists not only of conceptual questions, but also of intrinsically political issues concerning the decent and just treatment of minorities and other collective entities regarded as embodying cultures or nations.

Do groups have rights in more than a metaphorical sense? It is useful to remember that artificial entities called "legal persons" form a standard tool used by legal systems to organize a normative order. These entities can enjoy rights, a fact that is uncontroversial. There has been a long debate on what these entities are, in particular whether they are real or fictitious. However, they serve a well-defined practical purpose. Such legal persons can be formed of large groups of persons, such as the legal person of a state or the legal person of the international organization called the EU. This tool offers many ways of accommodating the need to include certain groups of people in a wider political order, allowing, for instance, some kind of self-rule that considerably reduces the practical problems posed by group rights.

Groups as such, however, are ultimately not real entities beyond the individuals that form them at any given moment in time. If all lovers of rowing (regrettably) switched their interest to darts, there would be no group of rowing enthusiasts as such left. There are social structures with a certain degree of permanence that are usually thought to stay unchanged even if the members change, such as a rowing club or the Swiss Army. These entities are, however, dependent on the continuing social actions of their members that create and maintain them. If the members of the rowing club decide to dissolve the club, no right of the club is violated – it simply ceases to exist, both as a legal entity and as a *fait social*, to use Durkheim's terminology. The same would hold for the Swiss Army if the Swiss citizens decided they would be better off without it. This is true for any group, including cultures and nations. If their members give up certain cultures – for instance, the militaristic culture of pre-1945 Germany (with good reason in this case) – no right of a group as such is interfered with. What may remain are abstract ideas, like the "essence of rowing" or the "content of pre-1945 German militarism," but no entity that reasonably could be regarded as possessing rights. Rights, therefore, are bound to individuals. Group rights that are more than political rhetoric or slogans are derivative constructs that serve, if they are to be legitimate, the rights of individual persons to autonomous self-determination, in particular through and by a body politic and other forms of meaningful representation, and to the freedom to search for self-fulfillment in joint activities with others.[74] The politics behind the debate about the right to self-determination, which features prominently in international human rights law, illustrate the importance and controversial nature of these analytical findings. One core question is whether the right to self-determination is a tool to realize the rights of individuals or is independent of this purpose.[75] In particular, this point becomes relevant if the rights of individuals collide with (supposed) group rights – for example, the rights of women with group rights enforcing patriarchal group traditions. It strengthens the case of the rights of the individual considerably, because if group rights – properly understood as the rights of a plurality of persons – themselves have the purpose of bolstering individual rights, then the rights of groups as such cannot be turned into political weapons against the rights of individuals. We are simply moving onto the familiar terrain of conflicting rights and the necessity of their reconciliation.

1.10 ETHICS, LEGAL HERMENEUTICS AND JUSTIFICATION

A final remark on the relation of moral rights and legal rights: Kelsen famously attempted to rid the law of nonlegal influences, particularly ethical ones, not least

[74] Joseph Raz, *The Morality of Freedom* (Oxford: Oxford University Press, 1986), 207 ff., argues that a single person cannot have a right to national self-determination, while a specific group of persons can. He, too, argues (along the lines of his interest theory of rights, which we will discuss in detail in Part II) that individual interests motivate this right. These interests are interests of individuals as members of a group concerning public goods – for instance, in a shared culture. Only as the interests of individuals in a group do these interests have sufficient weight to impose duties on others. Cf. for related arguments Will Kymlicka, *Multicultural Citizenship* (Oxford: Oxford University Press, 1995), ch. 3, among many others. For some critical remarks, cf. for instance Griffin, *On Human Rights*, 256 ff. There are many goods that can only be enjoyed in a group because they only emerge as a group activity – for instance, rowing an eight in a boat race. It is obvious that one person does not have the right to row an eight because it depends on others who wish to do so, too. This does not imply, however, that the "eight" as such enjoys rights. Similarly, a single individual has no right to national self-determination, only a plurality of persons forming the respective body politic. The fact that there are goods that are the products of group activities is no argument for the existence of rights of these groups in their own right. Rather, it is an (important) argument for those individual rights that enable human beings to form such groups and engage in activities with others (e.g. to row an eight) and, in the political sphere, of a plurality of persons to decide their own fate themselves in political processes, instead of being dominated by colonial powers, for example. Similar considerations hold for other important concerns, such as the preservation of indigenous cultural heritage, languages, etc.

[75] Cf. Chapter 2.

because ethics are regarded as intrinsically contentious, subjective and thus detrimental to the law's political goal of establishing an authoritative order based – in a democracy – on common, not subjective grounds.[76] This attempt cannot succeed. A realistic legal hermeneutic teaches us that legal rights are not wholly independent of the understanding of moral rights.[77] It will hardly be possible to delineate the scope of many important fundamental rights without recourse to an elementary account of what the particular right in question and fundamental rights in general are about. Open-textured norms such as human rights require interpretation and concretization. Interpretation will necessarily – whether explicitly or implicitly, knowingly or unknowingly – draw upon such more or less reflexive theories of fundamental rights that have an ethical dimension, among others.[78] Whatever one thinks of the jurisprudence of the ECtHR on the absolute prohibition of torture and its interpretation of Art. 3 ECHR in this respect, the argument for or against this understanding will include, whether one wants it to or not, intricate ethical arguments about the absolute or relative value of human life, the existence and scope of human dignity and the competing importance of other values – for example, the rights of third parties in cases where torture is used not for repressive means but to prevent harm to other persons, as in the leading case of the ECtHR on the matter.[79] None of this is stated in the positive law, but it is the result of its interpretation in the light of rich normative background assumptions.

In addition, and crucially, a catalogue of fundamental rights cannot be justified without ethical considerations, as these are the ultimate sources of normative justification. There is no bill of human rights that does not claim the justness of the rights it guarantees. Consequently, there can be no escape from ethics if we want to engage seriously with the law, and with human rights law in particular.

In light of these observations, it does not seem entirely outlandish to assume that a background theory of human rights is very useful for the project of interpreting existing human rights, determining their meaning in greater detail in the face of old and new challenges, developing the current ethics and law of human rights, evaluating their relation to any existing body of social rules, including the

[76] Hans Kelsen, *Reine Rechtslehre* (Vienna: Deuticke, 1960). On the discussions on exclusive and inclusive positivists, cf. Wilfrid J. Waluchow, *Inclusive Legal Positivism* (Oxford: Clarendon Press, 1994); Jules L. Coleman, *The Practice of Principle: In Defence of a Pragmatist Approach to Legal Theory* (Oxford: Oxford University Press, 2001); Joseph Raz, *The Authority of Law: Essays on Law and Morality* (Oxford: Clarendon Press, 1979), 49 f.

[77] Cf. Mahlmann, *Grundrechtstheorie*; Alexy, *A Theory of Constitutional Rights*. Dworkin recently has argued that law should be conceptualized as a subbranch of (political) morality, cf. Dworkin, *Justice for Hedgehogs*, 405.

[78] Cf. Matthias Mahlmann, "The Dictatorship of the Obscure? Values and the Secular Adjudication of Fundamental Rights," in *Constitutional Topography: Values and Constitutions*, eds. András Sajó and Renáta Uitz (The Hague: Eleven International Publishing, 2010), 343 ff.

[79] ECtHR, Gäfgen v Germany, Judgment of June 1, 2010, appl. no. 22978/05.

heterogenous set of norms referred to as 'traditional values',[80] critically assessing the status quo and addressing the important question of whether all rights that are protected as human rights in law are in fact legitimately regarded as human rights.[81] None of this calls the distinction of law and morality into question: Legal reflection and court decisions are not constraint-free intellectual enterprises. Legal doctrine is developed on the basis of a given body of positive law with the aim of influencing or even determining the action of norm-applying authorities, in particular authoritative court decisions. These decisions themselves, more or less openly discursive depending on the legal system, interpret the law of the land on the basis of positive law as it stands and are bound by said positive law. Not every well-justified normative position of human rights theory can therefore be interpreted into the body of human rights law, given its fragmented and limited scope.

These remarks are cursory, of course, and have left out many qualifications of rights, especially those of developed legal systems. But they suffice for the limited purpose at hand.

1.11 WHAT ARE WE TALKING ABOUT?

To sum up: Human rights are a subclass of subjective or claim rights. They are constituted by a set of normative incidents: claims, duties, privileges and no-rights. Claims, and duties, privileges and no-rights are necessarily correlated. Powers can form part of the content of these rights, which may protect the holder through immunities, too. The rights-holders are either all human beings or a subclass of all

80 Cf. on this debate, including the Human Rights Council resolutions on human rights and traditional values, Christopher McCrudden, "Human Rights and Traditional Values," in *Law's Ethical, Global and Theoretical Contexts*, eds. Upendra Baxi, Christopher McCrudden and Abdul Paliwala (Cambridge: Cambridge University Press, 2015), 38–72, drawing attention to the ambiguous nature of what is discussed as 'traditional values' – they can violate human rights or offer new progressive interpretations.

81 Cf. e.g. Griffin, *On Human Rights*, 26: "[H]aving agreement only on a list of human rights, and not on any reasons behind it, has major drawbacks. A greater measure of convergence on the justification of the list might produce more wholehearted promotion of human rights, fewer disagreement over their content, fewer disputes about priorities between them, and more rational and more uniform resolution of their conflicts – all much to be desired." Similarly, Samantha Besson, "Justifications," in *International Human Rights Law*, 3rd edition, eds. Daniel Moeckli, Sangeeta Shah and Sandesh Sivakumaran (Oxford: Oxford University Press, 2018), 23 f. On the view that the problem of indeterminacy shows the ultimately political nature of legal decision-making in the framework of structural biases, see Marti Koskenniemi, *From Apology to Utopia: The Structure of International Legal Argument*, reissue with a new epilogue (Cambridge: Cambridge University Press, 2005), 67, 601. Koskenniemi refers, however, to the importance of inclusion and rights – evidently itself a normative stance with a claim to justification, cf. Marti Koskenniemi, *The Gentle Civilizer of Nations: The Rise and Fall of International Law 1870–1960* (Cambridge: Cambridge University Press, 2001), 516: "International law's energy and hope lies in its ability to articulate existing transformative commitment in the language of rights and duties and thereby to give voice to those who are otherwise routinely excluded."

persons – for instance, the citizens of a state. In the former case, they are human rights in the narrow, proper sense. The term "human rights" understood in a wider sense is used to designate both cases, as is the term "fundamental rights." In the following, it will be clear from the context which class of rights the term "human rights" refers to.

Human rights can be moral or legal. In both cases, they can be addressed to private persons, legal entities and public authorities. Their basic content is related to a limited class of goods, in particular life, bodily integrity, freedom, equality and nondiscrimination, access to the material provisions necessary for human existence and respect for human worth. A useful structural theory of rights distinguishes between prima facie rights and rights all things considered as a subclass of general and abstract prescriptive rules on the one hand and axiological statements ascertaining the value of something (e.g. of freedom) on the other. The current legal structure of human rights law mirrors this distinction. Rights are trumps if – all things considered – they invest a rights-holder with a definite claim to something and impose a corresponding duty on the addressee. The traditional distinction between perfect and imperfect obligations chimes with this analysis and does not provide any argument to deny the existence of social rights: There is no reason stemming from the analysis of the structure of rights – including the claimability of rights – that would speak against understanding social rights as proper rights. In particular, social rights create identifiable meaningful duties of the addressees. Group rights create no structurally different class of human rights as they are best understood as being reducible to the rights of individuals. Moral and legal rights need to be distinguished. The theory of moral rights can, however, enrich the interpretation of human rights and is necessary for their justification. The separation of ethics and law consequently does not mean that the ethical understanding of rights is irrelevant for the legal theory of rights.

2

The Truth of Human Rights

A Mortal Daughter of Time?

It was against my wish that prisoner came to me at night, being a slave, I was afraid.

Yahling Dahbo, Court testimony, Gambia, August 2, 1893

two white men came running torge the women and baby, they stabed the women and the baby and, and threw both of them over the bank in to the water. she said she heard the woman say, O my baby; she said when they [the survivors] gathered the dead, they found all the little ones were killed by being stabed, and many of the women were also killed [by] stabing … They called it the siland creek.

Report on a massacre against the Pomo, California, 1850

Darkness was here yesterday.

Joseph Conrad, *Heart of Darkness*

2.1 APOLOGIZING FOR GENOCIDE

In October 2007, an interesting meeting took place in the town of Omaruru in central Namibia. The heads of six Herero royal houses met members of the German von Trotha family, who had come to Namibia on a rather unusual mission. Their aim was to apologize for what is widely regarded and, since 2021, has been officially accepted by Germany[1] as the first modern genocide in the technical legal sense of a mass killing with the specific intent to exterminate an ethnically or religiously defined group:[2] "We, the von Trotha family, are deeply ashamed of the terrible

[1] Federal Foreign Office, "Foreign Minister Maas on the conclusion of negotiations with Namibia," Press Release, May 28, 2021.

[2] Cf. on the discussion on the law, ethics and politics of the fight against genocide and the role of the genocidal campaign against the Herero and Nama, Ben Kieran, *Blood and Soil: A World History of Genocide and Extermination from Sparta to Darfur* (New Haven, CT: Yale University Press, 2007), 381 ff.; Eric Weitz, *A Century of Genocide* (Princeton, NJ: Princeton

events that took place 100 years ago. Human rights were grossly abused that time," Wolf-Thilo von Trotha said in this honorable attempt to give an honest account of a major crime.[3] Von Trotha is descended from the military commander of the German expedition forces that brutally subdued the 1904 Herero and Nama revolt against German colonial rule, carrying out mass shootings and driving the surviving members of the Herero into the desert with the explicit intent of exterminating them as an entire ethnic group. This campaign spearheaded other means of extermination, including concentration camps and inhumane practices such as medical experimentation, which later were brought to lethal perfection by the Nazis. Some 50,000–80,000 people were killed in this campaign. Notably, a Herero leader called for restraint during the revolt, asking that German women, children and missionaries not be killed, whereas General von Trotha explicitly told his troops to kill every Herero they could find.

Wolf-Thilo von Trotha's statement about his ancestor's deeds appears the obvious thing to say at such an occasion. And in moral terms, it clearly is. Yet it still invites us to engage in a moment of reflection. The German troops had come from the country of Kant well over 100 years after the *Virginia Bill of Rights*, the *Declaration of Independence* and the *Déclaration du Droits de l'Homme et du Citoyen* had made the idea of human rights explicit. Nevertheless, they clearly were thinking within the framework of what has been referred to in the Introduction as *colonial relativism*: Ethical concerns, including rights that applied to Europeans (or Germans), did not also apply to indigenous people in Africa. The Herero had no developed concept of human rights either. They had warred with neighboring peoples for dominance in the region for decades, engaging (like every other group) in other practices that today would be rightly criticized on ethical grounds. There is no reason to romanticize indigenous people or other collectives of human beings, and this goes for the Herero, too. Nevertheless, von Trotha's statement seems to imply that the Herero had, for example, a right to life, irrespective of what the Germans assumed and of how the Herero themselves articulated the normative position they believed themselves in. It presupposes, too, that the Germans were the addressees of these rights and had duties stemming from this normative position. Von Trotha's statement clearly posits that the Herero had these rights and the Germans these obligations, irrespective of the historic period and the framework of thought prevalent at the time. This statement understands human rights as a

University Press, 2003), 12, 46, 240; generally on the law, ethics and politics of genocide, Timothy Snyder, *Bloodlands* (New York: Basic Books, 2010); Samantha Power, "*A Problem from Hell*": *America and the Age of Genocide* (New York: Harper Collins, 2007); Tzvetan Todorov, *Face à l'Extrême* (Paris: Seuil, 1991), 296 with pessimistic conclusions as to the lessons learned; Jonathan Glover, *Humanity: A Moral History of the Twentieth Century* (London: Jonathan Cape, 1999).

3 Cf., "German family's Namibia apology," *BBC News*, accessed November 29, 2021, http://news.bbc.co.uk/2/hi/africa/7033042.stm.

time-independent truth about a specific normative status of human beings – humans as the holders or addressees of rights – even if the rights-holders and addressees themselves have no or only a vague concept of it.

Such a statement, indisputable as it appears on first sight, is not easily reconcilable with certain tenets of contemporary theoretical and historical debates, according to which human rights are culturally relative, historically contingent and dependent upon a certain epistemic framework that itself has no claim to universality but is relative to a specific society at a given time. From this point of view, von Trotha's statement and others like it are anachronistic and epistemologically naive.

This example already shows quite clearly that we need to ask what lessons the historical trajectory of the idea of human rights teaches about their origin and claims to justification. "How did the idea of human rights evolve?" is a central question for any inquiry into human rights.

There are two dimensions to this question: The first concerns the evolution of the principles of human rights, the normative propositions that posit their content and justification; the second concerns the faculty of human beings to conceive of these normative principles, to have epistemic access to them. In both cases, the problem of historical contingency arises. What steps were necessary to develop an explicit concept of human rights in ethics and law? What are the insights that are the preconditions for and what are the obstacles to conceiving of something such as human rights? What does history tell us about the modes of human understanding – prominently including the idea of *reason* – the exercise of which is supposed to lead to the conclusion that human rights are justified normative principles? Most importantly perhaps: How time- and culture-dependent is the *ability* to form the idea of human rights? Bacon famously held that truth is the daughter of time.[4] Does this mean that reason is historically indexed? Is the truth about human rights a daughter of time in this sense, too – more precisely, the daughter of our time, destined to fade away as new historical circumstances arise? Could a humanity legitimately stripped of rights be the truth of tomorrow? Or is there such a thing as an exercise of human understanding that is a child of but not bound entirely to the epistemic framework created by a particular epoch and therefore transcends it? Is this conceivable, or is it a naive illusion of the past, untenable after the many historicizations of human insights?[5] Bacon himself understood the ancient saying about the pedigree of truth as identifying time as a precondition of scientific

4 Francis Bacon, *Novum Organum*, Vol. I, ed. Wolfgang Krohn (Hamburg: Felix Meiner Verlag, 1999), LXXXIV.

5 Theories arguing for the historical relativity of human insights come in many forms. Cf. for some influential examples Herder's theory of cultures (which has a universalist core, however), Johann Gottfried Herder, "Ideen zur Philosophie der Geschichte der Menschheit," in *Johann Gottfried Herder: Werke*, Vol. 6, ed. Martin Bollacher (Frankfurt am Main: Deutscher Klassiker Verlag, 1989), 1784 ff., 336 ff.; Hegel's assumptions about the unfolding of Spirit in history, through a "gallery of pictures" of historically embodied forms of the Spirit, Georg Wilhelm Friedrich Hegel, "Phänomenologie des Geistes," in *Werke*, Vol. 3, eds. Eva Moldenhauer and

progress: Sufficient time spent in scientific work would ultimately yield new forms of genuine understanding.[6] Has the long reflection on the justified claims of human beings provided us with such insights? Or, to put it in more specific terms: Was Wolf-Thilo von Trotha mistaken in his evaluation of what his ancestor had done to the Herero, or was he right to claim that at that time the Herero already had rights and the German troops duties that they violated, even though neither perpetrators nor victims probably had any conscious concept of such a normative status, let alone a status rendered explicit *in human rights terms*? Did Germany acknowledge its guilt for the genocide unnecessarily? Furthermore, did the Herero and the German soldiers possess the cognitive ability to understand the nature of the crime committed? Was it, at least potentially, within the reach of their understanding? Or were the soldiers and their genocidal commanders excused because they simply were unable to get the idea of the human rights of the Herero, given how history and society had shaped their moral thought?

This brings us to further important questions. In particular, what was the Herero's subjective experience of their own situation? Was their ordeal limited to physical suffering in the desert, or did they also consider the actions of the German troops to be unjust, a moral outrage? Did they perhaps feel that they had a *claim* – conceived of in whatever form – not to be starved to death in the desert and that the Germans had a correlating *duty* to let them live? Were traces of the idea of rights (though not of human rights in current terms) thus present in their thought, or would it be an ahistorical anachronism to even consider this possible? Do we have to assume that the Herero were a blank slate in ethical terms because they had not partaken in the cultural development of European civilization, which would have provided them – for instance – with a concept of individuality and certain emotional capacities

Karl Markus Michel (Frankfurt am Main: Suhrkamp, 1986), 590; Kuhn's theory of the role of paradigms in scientific research, Thomas Kuhn, *The Structure of Scientific Revolutions* (Chicago, IL: University of Chicago Press, 1970), and Foucault's "archeology" of knowledge, Michel Foucault, *Les mots et les choses: Une archéologie des sciences humaines* (Paris: Gallimard, 1966), 13: "*Une telle analyse, on le voit, ne relève pas de l'histoire des idées ou des sciences: c'est plutôt une étude qui s'efforce de retrouver à partir de quoi connaissances et théories ont été possible; selon quel espace d'ordre s'est constitué le savoir; sur fond de quel a priori historique et dans l'élément de quelle positivité des idées ont pu apparaître, des sciences se constituer, des expériences se réfléchir dans des philosophies, des rationalités se former, pour, peut-être, se dénouer et s'évanouir bientôt.*" Evidently, every theory is embedded in the scientific insights and cultural background of its given time. If the idea of a *causa finalis* is constitutive of theory building, scientific theories will be formed accordingly. If you do not have access to the mathematical tool of calculus, certain scientific theories are not available to you. The question is only – is this all there is to say about human understanding?

6 Bacon, *Novum Organum*, Vol. I, LXXXIV, 180 writes: "*Authores vero quod attinet, summae pusillanimitatis est authoribus infinita tribuere, authori autem authorum atque adeo omnis authoritatis, Tempori, jus suum denegare. Recte enim Veritas Temporis filia dicitur, non Authoritatis*": "It forms an example of small mindedness, to attribute all desert to the [ancient] authors and thereby to deny the author of all authors, Time, all authority. It is namely true, that Truth is the daughter of Time, not of Authority."

formed not least while reading novels, as some historians have argued?[7] But why did the German expeditionary forces (like other Europeans) behave so much worse than the Herero, despite coming from the country of Goethe and Beethoven?

This case is of additional interest because from a certain perspective it implies an encounter of different ages: The German troops came from one of the scientifically and culturally most advanced countries in Europe (well on its way, however, to barbarous wars and further genocides), while the Herero lived the life of a nomadic tribe. It is a common methodological assumption that we can learn something about the more remote human past from those groups whose current forms of life remain in certain respects similar to some of those of a bygone age even if one avoids the assumption that such groups are simply "contemporary ancestors," without a complex history of their own, providing "direct windows on the past."[8] Thus, Herero ethical thought is of substantial interest from a historical perspective, as it may help us to understand the basis from which the historical trajectory that led to the fully developed idea of human rights began.

Moreover, the Herero example is helpful in illustrating that these questions are of deep moral concern. In the end, the answers determine how the death of the Herero in the desert should be evaluated, particularly as to whether it was already wrong to kill people in such imperial enterprises at *that* time under *those* circumstances within *those* cultural frameworks of perpetrators and victims with *those* cognitive abilities. These questions are decisive, too, in determining whether it will continue to be wrong to commit such atrocities in the epochs to come, because they would violate human rights, regardless of what people in the future, who may be living under new forms of barbarism, may think. This future-oriented dimension of the problem – the question of whether human rights are valid only relative to the contingent belief system of a certain epoch – is not treated with much care in current debates.[9] However, the question of whether the historicization of human rights extends into the future or not is a very serious matter. Torture is prohibited in many constitutions and in *ius cogens*, as a peremptory norm of international law. Could this (legitimately) be different 100 years from now?

Understanding the historical emergence of human rights is a first decisive problem for the cognitive interests governing our inquiry. We need to address this problem if we are to avoid the fundamental fallacy of seeing the contingent products of historical processes as related to structures of the human mind. History may be the

7 Cf. Lynn Hunt, *Inventing Human Rights: A History* (New York: W. W. Norton & Company, 2007), 29 ff., 33: "My argument depends on the notion that reading accounts of torture or epistolary novels had physical effects that translated into brain changes and came back out as new concepts about the organization of social and political life."

8 On the concept and problem of theories about "contemporary ancestors", cf. Graeber and Wengrow, *Dawn*, 15, 103, 121.

9 But cf. the thoughts (at least partly hopeful) that "human rights ideology" will become a matter of the past in Onara O'Neill, "The Dark Side of Human Rights," *International Affairs* 81, no. 2 (2005): 439.

key to understanding human rights, not anything that has to do with the nature of human thinking, as influential contemporary theory maintains. If this is so, the historical inquiry already answers the question of the relation between mind and rights: History is all you need to know. Studies in moral epistemology, psychology and cognitive science that jump directly to assumptions about the natural properties of the human mind and their relation to human rights may thus be missing their target entirely because of the mind's protean quality, the simple truth being that ideas of human rights are as historically relative as the forms of human understanding employed to gain normative insights. Both have taken as many shapes as Homer's "Old Man of the Sea"[10] and will continue to do so in future.

What seems clear is that human rights are not simply a given of all normative human cultures. On the contrary, very many things that make up the idea of human rights and their practice are the products of very complex historical developments. We will return to the question of what we know about the normative evaluations of people such as the Herero when confronted with European savagery, but they certainly did not employ twenty-first-century human rights language to describe what was going on. There are complex early legal codes – such as the *Code of Ur-Nammu* or the *Code of Hammurabi* – that merit closer investigation to see what moral and legal ideas we can unearth in them.[11] But the search for a cuneiform inscription of a Sumerian *Universal Declaration of Human Rights* will – as already indicated – be a vain one.[12] These concrete rights evidently are the product of human beings' long intellectual and practical quest for justice. This is true for the normative principles finally proclaimed and fought for as explicit political and legal demands in the revolutions of eighteenth-century America and France, and it is true for their evolving content. To take a very simple example: Freedom of the press is a bedrock human right, but it assumes that a press (and its contemporary digital equivalents) exist – a precondition that is hardly trivial in historical terms, presupposing not only technological innovations but also cultural developments such as the growth of a politically relevant public sphere.[13]

What is more, the discovery that certain normative ideas or the social institutions that embody them are historically contingent is without doubt a central

[10] Homer, *Odyssey, Vol. I: Books 1–12*, trans. Augustus T. Murray, rev. George E. Dimock, Loeb Classical Library 104 (Cambridge, MA: Harvard University Press, 1919), Book 4, 349–570.

[11] Consider, for instance, the following passage from the prologue to the *Laws of Ur-Nammu* (ca. 2100 BCE) that praises the deeds of the king: "I did not deliver the orphan to the rich. I did not deliver the widow to the mighty. I did not deliver the man with but one shekel to the man with one mina (i.e., 60 shekels). I did not deliver the man with but one sheep to the man with one ox." What concept of justice is implied in this passage? Why are these deeds praiseworthy?

[12] But cf. on the controversial claim that the Charter of Cyrus, inscribed on the Cyrus Cylinder from the mid-sixth century BCE, is the first human rights charter or that the *Code of Hammurabi* contains such rights, Paul Gordon Lauren, *The Evolution of International Human Rights: Visions Seen* (Philadelphia: University of Pennsylvania Press, 2011).

[13] Cf. Jürgen Habermas, *Strukturwandel der Öffentlichkeit: Untersuchungen zu einer Kategorie der bürgerlichen Gesellschaft* (Darmstadt: Luchterhand, 1979).

driving force of human liberation. Many repressive ideas and social arrangements have appeared in the guise of timeless truth or have been presented as derived from indubitable human nature, even though they represented nothing but the prejudice of their times – from the inferiority of persons of a certain skin color to the subjugation of women. Historical analysis is a central precondition for liberating human beings from such chains of the past.

The question to be answered is thus not whether the history of human rights matters for their theory, but whether these rights are *nothing but* a product of history – whether historical analysis is not only a necessary but also a sufficient condition to explain their current reality and influence and perhaps even to justify them, as some maintain.[14]

This necessary inquiry into the history of human rights only appears an easy and straightforward task on the surface, however, and not merely because the historical development of human rights as such is far from comprehensively researched. This is one problem, to be sure. In addition, however, the very object of analysis poses substantial difficulties and is a source of potential misunderstanding. What is this thing whose history we seek to scrutinize? Is it an idea – if so, what kind of idea? Is it a social fact in a sociological sense? Is it a moral concept, a legal institution or both? Are only human rights in the sense of mandatory public international law of interest, or are other legal forms, too, such as constitutional rights? What does legal pluralism tell us about the nature of human rights? What social norms of societies' "living law" should be included? To what entity does the term "moral human right" refer? As the conceptual clarifications of the Introduction and Chapter 1 have shown, there are substantial problems to be solved here. Our results will help prevent us from becoming lost in the maze that these questions form.

Another important concern is: Are there predecessors to human rights in the (itself controversial) contemporary sense that are *not* human rights but that still need to be considered in the history of human rights, and, if so, what criteria mark them as relevant? What is the threshold for including a normative phenomenon in the history of human rights?

As will become clear over the course of the following remarks, all of these questions and their different possible answers have substantial impacts on the kind of human rights history told and therefore require critical reflection. Furthermore, the details of the method of historical investigation are important, too, and they are rife with problems that also demand scrutiny, not least because some of the theories and findings advanced in recent work in this field are profoundly influenced by certain background assumptions on how to study human rights history. Method determines content, and not always fruitfully so. It is thus unfortunate that these issues are not always discussed with sufficient care. Consequently, we need to pay significant attention to these questions first.

[14] For instance with the means of an "affirmative genealogy," Hans Joas, *Die Sakralität der Person: Eine neue Genealogie der Menschenrechte* (Frankfurt am Main: Suhrkamp, 2012).

Our methodological reflection will form the basis for some exemplary discussions of relevant elements of the history of human rights that will pave the way to the central conclusion of this part of the book: History is key to the study of human rights but necessarily leads beyond its own confines to the theory of justification and the structural (not just historical) analysis of the faculties of human understanding that open the epistemic door to the cognition of human rights.

2.2 HOW TO DECIPHER THE HISTORY OF HUMAN RIGHTS?

2.2.1 *History and Human Rights Revisionism*

Clarifying standards for the proper study of human rights history is particularly relevant to current debate. This is because the history of human rights has become a significant battleground in the political, ethical and philosophical war being waged around human rights in general – a war that has shaken the normative edifice established after the World War II to its foundations. In this conflict, the historical origins of human rights are used to question the very legitimacy of these rights and their normative raison d'être.

One central feature of these ongoing debates about the history of human rights is the use of historical analysis with the critical intention of unveiling the dark history of rights. Human rights are taken not to be universal aspirations of humankind, "opening the door to closed societies,"[15] challenging illegitimate authority and empowering the weak, but instead as shrewd plots of partisan politics and politicized religion.[16] This is the challenge posed by the *historical, genealogical human rights*

[15] Lutz Wingert, "Türöffner zu geschlossenen Gesellschaften: Bemerkungen zum Begriff der Menschenrechte," in *Ethik, Politik, Kulturen im Globalisierungsprozess: Eine interdisziplinäre Zusammenführung*, ed. Ralf Elm (Bochum: Projektverlag, 2003), 392 ff. This function as a "door opener" is not only political, but – as Wingert rightly argues – has an epistemic dimension as well: The idea of human rights helps to identify violations of basic normative positions. This is an important claim: Understood in this sense, human rights are a heuristic tool for the discovery of injustice. On the rights revolution and the decline of violence, Steven Pinker, *The Better Angels of Our Nature: A History of Violence and Humanity* (London: Penguin Books, 2012), 456.

[16] Cf. Samuel Moyn, "Personalism, Community, and the Origins of Human Rights," in *Human Rights in the Twentieth Century*, ed. Stefan-Ludwig Hoffmann (Cambridge: Cambridge University Press, 2011), 85 ff., 87; "[H]uman rights need to be closely linked, in their beginnings, to an epoch-making reinvention of conservatism," Moyn, *The Last Utopia*, 47; "After a few years had passed, the meanings the idea of human rights had accreted were so geographically specific and ideologically partisan – and, most often, linked so inseparably to Christian, Cold War identity – as to make the fact that they could return later in some different guise a deep puzzle," Moyn, *The Last Utopia*, 54, 74 ff. See Philip Alston, "Does the Past Matter? On the Origins of Human Rights," *Harvard Law Review* 126 (2013): 2077 on human rights history as a proxy for underlying normative debates. See for a methodological critique of historical findings in legal arguments Anne Orford, *International Law and the Politics of History* (Cambridge: Cambridge University Press, 2021). She convincingly argues that historical studies

revisionism mentioned above. In this view, the contingent origin of human rights is not just an unsurprising historical fact, given that everything has to originate in a particular point in space and time, but the key to a dark heritage showing that they are not a "last utopia." On the contrary, human rights ultimately are delegitimized by their reactionary, religiously and culturally biased origin in Christian doctrine or in neoliberal ideology, despite their various transformations, which, so the argument goes, ultimately are of doubtful effect.[17]

This perspective may appear surprising, because a historical development as such cannot justify or delegitimize a normative institution. After all, the facticity of a historical trajectory provides no normative reason to accept or reject its results. The course of history is one thing, the justification of the products of history quite another, not least in the case of human rights. In addition, the widespread perception is that human rights have ecumenical features – they transcend the boundaries of philosophical confessions and express a common normative perspective for human beings that seems to be founded on something deeper than the false beliefs of a few contingent actors.

Moreover, not many social institutions, in particular those of the law, have sources that are entirely above moral doubt (to put it mildly). If we look at issues directly linked to human rights history, not least constitution making, examples readily present themselves. Nobody who has studied such processes will claim that central norms, including rights catalogues, were the products of pure, benevolent, justice-oriented practical thought. Germany's *Basic Law* is widely hailed as a particularly well-drafted constitutional instrument that has become one of the most influential constitutions in the international context. Many admirable actors had a role in the drafting process. But other motives were at play, too, particularly the desire to make it possible for Germany to reenter the international community after the fall of the Third Reich. Some of those involved may have regarded a democratic, rights-bound, dignity-based form of government as nothing more than the price to pay for this end, a high price perhaps, but – given the total military, political and moral defeat of the German Reich – one to which there was no alternative.

cannot secure legal arguments. Less compelling is her view that an undefined concept of contextual usefulness is the ultimate yardstick for legal arguments, ibid. 316.

[17] Cf. Moyn, *The Last Utopia*, 225 ff. on the intrinsic limits and burdens of the human rights idea. On the case study of human dignity and a critique on similar grounds, with the conclusion that the concept is useless, Samuel Moyn, "The Secret History of Constitutional Dignity," in *Understanding Human Dignity*, ed. Christopher McCrudden (Oxford: Oxford University Press, 2013), 95, 111; cf. for a detailed assessment and different view Christopher McCrudden, "Where Did 'Human Dignity' Come from? Drafting the Preamble to the Irish Constitution," *American Journal of Legal History* 60 (2020): 485–535; Samuel Moyn, "The Continuing Perplexities of Human Rights," *Qui Parle* 22, no. 1 (2013): 107 ff. underlines his skepticism, albeit with some qualifications, given that so far no better alternative exists. On a somewhat more positive note, Samuel Moyn, *Human Rights and the Uses of History* (New York: Verso Books, 2014), 135 ff. On religious bias cf. Samuel Moyn, *Christian Human Rights* (Philadelphia: University of Pennsylvania Press, 2015).

Knowledge of these influences certainly is important. But do they delegitimize the human rights-based democratic order of the *Basic Law*? What about the drafters of the US Constitution? Do the questionable political intentions of some, which partly shaped the Constitution's content, permanently delegitimize the result, irrespective of the further development of the understanding of this remarkable document?

Are not similar conclusions justified in the case of the drafting of other legal instruments important for the history of human rights? Did the role of the racist South African politician Smuts in the drafting process of the preamble of the UN Charter irredeemably contaminate the concepts of human dignity and human rights that were its products? Are not other factors far more important? Were these concepts ultimately wrested from the hands of racist imperialists like Smuts who tried to abuse them?[18] Is this the reason why the South African delegation ultimately opposed (unsuccessfully) the inclusion of a reference to the equality of human dignity and of all human rights in the *Universal Declaration* in an attempt to justify lesser rights for some groups of persons?[19]

The United Nations (UN) with its veto system of the Security Council's permanent members and accommodation of colonial empires was not designed with the single purpose of promoting the egalitarian good of the world community of human beings,[20] nor were the Council of Europe or the ECHR crafted as pure embodiments of the human rights idea, as the latter instrument's colonial exemption clause illustrates.[21] What is more, nation states, international organizations and the law they create continue to be formed by asymmetrical power relations, narrowly defined interests, politics at the expense of (weaker) others and repressive ideologies without there being any prospect of these influences losing any of their force in the years to come. Does this mean that nothing good came out of the national and international

[18] Cf. on Smuts' ideology, Mark Mazower, *No Enchanted Palace: The End of Empire and the Ideological Origins of the United Nations* (Princeton, NJ: Princeton University Press, 2009), 28 ff.; on the inclusion of dignity in the preamble of the UN Charter, Charles R. Beitz, "Human Dignity in the Theory of Human Rights: Nothing but a Phrase?" *Philosophy & Public Affairs* 41, no. 3 (2013): 259, 261 ff. The reference to dignity stems not from Smuts but Virginia Gildersleeve, Beitz, "Human Dignity," 266.

[19] Cf. 95th meeting of the Third Committee, October 6, 1948, and the ensuing debate, in Schabas, *The Universal Declaration*, 2137. The concrete examples used by delegate Charles Theodore Te Water to buttress his general attack on equal human rights were the widely accepted and, in his view, justified unequal rights of men and women.

[20] Mazower, *No Enchanted Palace*, 151 sums up: "Whatever the rhetoric, . . ., this was an international organization designed – much as its predecessor had been – for interstate cooperation and stability in a world of empires and great powers"; Mark Mazower, *Governing the World: The History of an Idea* (London: Penguin Press, 2012), 213: "The Big Three had ended up creating an organization that combined the scientific technocracy of the New Deal with the flexibility and power-political reach of the nineteenth-century European alliance system." Cf. on retrospective narrative constructions about this matter Oliver Diggelmann, "The Creation of the United Nations: Break with the Past or Continuation of Wartime Power Politics?" *Journal for International Peace and Organization* 93 (2020): 371–89.

[21] Cf. Simpson, *Human Rights*, 288 ff., 597 ff.

human rights systems? Most importantly: Does this show that there is no way for critical thought and legal and political work to develop what exists into a meaningful system of human rights protection, a system with an effect that sometimes runs counter to the intentions of some contributors to the making of legal human rights orders and their institutional framework?[22]

The strong arguments not to confuse genealogy and justification notwithstanding, in light of these questions it nevertheless is necessary to ask: Do these critical voices perhaps still have a point? Does the idea of human rights have doubtful roots? Is there a skeleton in the closet we must learn to face? If so – what are the consequences for the justification of human rights? Are human rights indeed delegitimized by their dark origins, which show that they are just a piece of harmful ideology? This would have important consequences for the research object of interest here, because it makes a difference whether we are studying a piece of political ideology or ideas with a justified claim to moral rightness – and the latter claim is what forms the very foundation upon which human rights stand.

2.2.2 *Concepts and Methods of Inquiry*

A first problem for historical inquiry already has been addressed: the concept of human rights, a key element in determining the object whose history is to be investigated. To reiterate our conceptual conclusions: Human rights are most plausibly understood as an intricate web of normative incidents, the ensemble of which determines in important respects the normative positions all human beings enjoy. Through *claims* and related *duties* that obligate everyone at least as moral rights, through *privileges* and through *no-rights*, or, in other words, the *absence of duties* towards others curtailing the exercise of these privileges, human rights establish a normatively protected space for the autonomous existence and action of the individuals whose goods they safeguard.[23] Powers and immunities can form

[22] As many have observed, the development of the UN itself shows how quickly institutions can change – "it turned astonishingly quickly into a key forum for anticolonialism," Mazower, *No Enchanted Palace*, 152. In this forum, in the context of India's famous 1946 initiative against the discrimination of Indians in South Africa, Smuts experienced that he "had defeated himself" by the principles of "human rights and moral anger" he himself had invoked during the drafting of the UN Charter, Mazower, *No Enchanted Palace*, 179. For background, Lorna Lloyd, "'A Most Auspicious Beginning': The 1946 United Nations General Assembly and the Question of the Treatment of Indians in South Africa," *Review of International Studies* 16, no. 2 (1990): 131 ff.

[23] This definition is consistent with but more precise than alternatives used in studies on the history of rights, cf. e.g. Gregory Vlastos, "The Rights of Persons in Plato's Conception of the Foundation of Justice," in *Studies in Greek Philosophy, Vol. 2: Socrates, Plato, and Their Tradition*, ed. Daniel W. Graham (Princeton, NJ: Princeton University Press, 1995), 124, who formulates: "A substitution-instance of the sentence form 'A has the right to X against B' will be true for persons bound by a given moral or legal code if and only if B is required by the norms of that code to engage in X-supporting conduct (action or forbearance) demandable of B by A and/or others acting on A's behalf."

the content of such normative positions. With these normative means, rights secure substantial values such as human dignity, life, integrity, freedom, equality and subsistence in morality and in law for all human beings. They create for all the equally shared opportunity to lead an autonomous human life. The assumption that forms the foundation of their legitimacy is that humans count – that they are not just beings of little worth or even of no concern at all.

The rights through which these normative principles are protected are secured as moral claims and legal norms and institutions that are deeply justified. This claim to deep justification is a central element of the human rights idea: Human rights bind their addressees and thus create legitimate normative burdens for third parties, namely human beings and other normatively accountable entities, most importantly legal subjects, including but not limited to states. The burdens human rights impose are of a particular nature, as they originate in the autonomous critical reflection of the agents themselves as a moral category that is then enforced by law. They create a burden on their addressees but only in a very specific sense, as this burden ultimately is imposed not by others, but by the moral understanding of human beings themselves: It is the offspring of reflective self-rule, not of forced submission to the command of others; the fruit of autonomy, not heteronomy, and thus a burden only in the sense of an obligation to be wholeheartedly embraced.

These findings represent useful tools for historical research. This means that a history of human rights needs to concern itself with three issues in particular: first, the concept of a *right* as foundational normative category; second, the *idea of legitimately protected human liberty, equality, solidarity and worth* as something 'right' in an objective sense; and third, the idea that liberty, equality, solidarity and worth should be spelled out by normative positions of *rights* that apply universally to all humans, and not only by some other political (or normative) means.

This concept of human rights forms an ideal-typical kind of instrument for historical analysis. It is a tool that can aid in the decision as to whether to include a normative phenomenon in the history of human rights or not.[24]

A fully-fledged analytical theory of rights (not just human rights) is the product of twentieth-century thinking and – in one of its constitutive contributions, as we have seen – is motivated by the desire to clarify the ambiguous use of the concept of a subjective right in law, which presupposes that at least some issues were not fully understood beforehand. This does not mean, however, that this kind of analysis has no clearly identifiable predecessors. As noted above, the Natural Law tradition notably captured central aspects of this idea, sometimes with admirable precision, although it failed to make entirely clear what the idea of rights is about – much as we

[24] In light of these clarifications, it is useful to reconsider the heterogeneous normative phenomena in religions and philosophy that Lauren, *Evolution*, 5 ff. lists to decide which of them ought properly to be included in a history of human rights.

today may still appear entangled in misunderstandings from the perspective of future, better analyses of the matter.

Fully explicit *human* rights as moral ideas and – even more so – as legal concepts, practices and institutions are equally recent in nature. Nevertheless, there is much to discover in the more distant past that belongs in a properly complex history of rights in general and human rights in particular. The discussion that follows will illustrate this observation in some detail.

Another relevant point concerns what we might call the difference between the *justification of human rights by the humanity of their bearers* on the one hand and the *inclusion of all beings belonging to the human species in the set of rights-holders* on the other. This distinction is useful as it helps to clarify two separate steps of central importance in the process of the development and realization of these rights. The first step justifies human rights with reference to the normative relevance of something specific about human beings, "human nature" or the "human condition," for instance. The second step determines who qualifies as fully human. Taking the first step does not necessarily mean that the second step also will be taken in a justifiable fashion. Very many human beings were consequently excluded from holding human rights not because there was no concept of human rights as rights of all humans, but because the respective group did not qualify as fully human – women, slaves and religious minorities are classic examples of this. In addition, another relevant issue is frequently neglected when attention focuses first and foremost on classic cases of the unjustified *exclusion* of certain groups of people: There is also the recurring question of whether human rights have now not become *over-inclusive*. After all, some argue, not all human beings legitimately enjoy human rights. Influential voices doubt, for example, that infants, people in a permanent coma and humans with certain disabilities or of a certain age justifiably can be regarded as holders of human rights, as many legal systems posit.[25] The debate about the status of embryos or fetuses is another illustration of the abidingly controversial question of the inclusion or exclusion of potential rights-holders in a human rights regime. These arguments for the exclusion of certain groups of people from protection by human rights do not necessarily doubt that the humanity of humans is a central argument for the justification of human rights. They may even emphasize this point with verve and passion. However, they argue that these groups lack certain properties that are constitutive of full humanity, such as normative agency.[26]

A history of human rights has to account for these complexities. Differentiating between these two steps of justification thus serves as a central tool for producing a fine-grained historical analysis. A thinker, a practice, an institution may be very important for the development of rights based on the humanity of human beings but

[25] Cf. Griffin, *On Human Rights*, 83 ff.

[26] Cf. Griffin, *On Human Rights*, 94 f. If not humanity but some other criterion is taken to be decisive – sentience, for instance – the same problem arises: One has to determine which beings are actually sentient beings.

may have failed dramatically to include all beings that manifestly are fully human. Otherwise we would even have to exclude the classical human rights documents of the eighteenth century from the history of human rights because they disregarded a great many people, and entirely implausibly so. A history of human rights that limits itself to fully inclusive but simultaneously not over-inclusive human rights (assuming that we already know what that means) would be a deficient history of human rights.

The incremental nature of the development of human rights (incremental not implying direction, continuousness or irreversibility) encourages us to ask further questions – for example, about rights that were not justified simply by the bearer's humanity, but because of some other status, such as by being a "free man" of a kingdom, as in the *Magna Carta*. How did such instruments – although evidently not about human rights as understood here – contribute to the history of human rights? Not at all? Or did they pave the way for rights with a more inclusive personal scope by establishing claims for some kinds of people and thereby giving rise to a question with considerable political and historical impact – why only for them and not for others as well? Why not these rights for all? Once again, this question has its modern equivalents. For instance, one major issue of current human rights law is the question of the extraterritorial application of human rights. This issue concerns a state's interference with rights with a cross-border effect. The killing of civilians in the Iraq War by British troops is an important example of this problem from the case law of the ECtHR.[27] Were the soldiers bound by the ECHR, even though they were acting in Iraq and not in Europe? Were the civilians in Iraq as protected as they would have been in Britain? Here, too, the question – why rights for some (the Europeans) but not for others (the Iraqis)? – demands an answer that propels the inclusiveness of human rights forward.

Much current history of human rights is concerned with the (post–World War II) institutionalization of international human rights. This is an important subject. But the history of the institutionalization of international human rights is not the history of human rights. It is just one subchapter in a grander epic. First, in the legal sphere, there is the history of the institutionalization of human rights on the level of national constitutions. As already indicated, at the core of the current international architecture of human rights lies a two-tier system of protection on the national level and of complementary protection on the international level. A history of human rights that fails to pay attention to the primary tier of the system could hardly be assumed to exhaust the subject's history. Second, the history of human rights is not limited to the history of the process of making them a political and – most difficult of all – a legal reality. This history is intriguing and rightly forms the object of profound and

[27] European Court of Human Rights (ECtHR), Al-Skeini and Others v The United Kingdom, Judgement of July 7, 2011, Application No. 55721/07. Cf. for an excellent discussion Angela Müller, *States, Human Rights, and Distant Strangers: The Normative Justification of Extraterritorial Obligations in Human Rights Law* (Abingdon/New York: Routledge, forthcoming 2023).

innovative research. Unsurprisingly, it is influenced by a plethora of factors such as power, ideology, interests both material and nonmaterial, outstanding personalities and their sometimes-remarkable impact, the tides of social passions and beliefs and the like. But the processes through which human rights become a political and legal reality are likewise only one part of the history of human rights. They presuppose an *idea*, one so compelling that people have tried to make its vision politically relevant and even legally binding, first on the national, then on the international level, sometimes at the cost of their lives.

How to trace such a remarkable and powerful idea in history? When and where were the seeds of the empire of rights sown in people's minds? How many times did its harvests wither in the fields of human folly, lust for power and greed? Why did this idea finally develop into a rich crop? Why did it conquer the Earth more fully than virtually any other moral and legal idea in human history? What does this remarkable element of human history tell us about the mind of the creature that developed this idea?

An important step in any inquiry into this matter is not to commit the methodological fallacy of looking for *words* or *terms* such as *rights*, *droits*, *Rechte*, *ius* and so forth, but to search for the meaning of these historical and current terms. We have outlined the central dimensions of the idea of human rights above. A proper history of human and fundamental rights needs to look at all of these dimensions and see whether, how and when they overlap. The moral and legal manifestations of the category of rights therefore form part of this history. The history of freedom as a value is another part, as is the history of the idea that human beings enjoy intrinsic worth and thus dignity, as is the history of equality and solidarity. How did these values become central for human beings' normative aspirations? What suggestions are there that these values were thought of as related to rights? What clues are there that these rights were ascribed to beings with certain well-qualified properties, a thought that finally turned out to be important for the fully developed idea of human rights, namely that all humans enjoy these rights by virtue of their humanity, irrespective of the differences that may exist between them? As highlighted, the latter can only be achieved by processes that include unjustifiably excluded groups of beings, such as women and slaves, among those who are acknowledged to be fully endowed with these properties – for example, with the capacity for autonomous self-determination.

Consequently, when thinking about the history of ideas of human rights, we have to search for both explicit and (the deeper we dig) implicit expressions of these ideas.

These implicit expressions may take the form of normative propositions other than rights, most importantly normative commands. It is rash to assume that an ethical or legal code containing only commands has nothing to say about rights. The command "Congress shall make no law respecting an establishment of religion, or prohibiting the free exercise thereof" is, for instance, self-evidently understood as the legal positivizing of the separation of religion and state (no establishment clause) and a (constitutionally key) subjective right. The question arises for other archetypal commands, too. For example, in the case of the Decalogue, the question is: Do its prescriptions obligate its addressees only in relation to God?[28] Or do they entail a normative claim of those who would suffer from the violation of the commandments, as others have argued?[29] Take, for instance, "You shall not steal." What is the normative position of the potential victims of stealing? Is there none? Or are normative incidents applicable to them? Do they perhaps even have a claim that nothing be stolen from them? There is certainly a very strong argument for the latter. It seems hard to conceptualize that somebody is under a duty not to steal something while at the same time the owner has no correlative claim that this not happen because there is only an obligation to God.

Unsurprisingly, this possibility not only has been observed by historical studies, but also has been debated specifically in the context of the role of subjective rights in Law, prominently, for instance, in Jewish Law.[30] Similar arguments can be advanced for other normative systems formulated in terms of commands.[31] Some examples of this will cross our path over the course of this inquiry.

To imply a right through other normative propositions is but one way to refer to the incidents making up a right, however. We need to broaden our perspective further to become sensitive to implicit expressions of normative ideas, whatever form they may take. This move is crucial not least to avoid another fallacy: the fallacy of intellectual and cultural – more precisely, Western – elitism. Even today, there are people who lack words for human rights but do not lack the central idea, both as regards the normative form and as regards their essential content. An illiterate woman – like the Herero of 1904 – who is mistreated and perhaps raped by military forces may not be able to express the normative claims she thinks she justifiably has in Hohfeldian terms, nor their content with the technical language of Kantian conceptions of dignity, but she may, quite rightly, have the idea, in whatever obscure form, that what is happening to her is not right, that she should be free to be left alone, to not have her body and inner self harmed by such acts, that she, as a human being, can rightly demand not to be treated like this, neither by state forces nor by private parties, and that everybody is obliged to abstain from hurting her in these pernicious ways. It would be a gross and indeed appalling failure of any theory of human rights to not take note of this possibility and account for it.

The same is evidently true of historical perspectives. It is important to ask what human beings thought, felt and experienced during the "Scramble for Africa," when they were attacked, subjugated or enslaved. There are some intriguing sources, including oral history, that give a glimpse of the injustice felt and that should not

[28] This is asserted by Herbert Lionel Adolphus Hart, "Are There Any Natural Rights?" *The Philosophical Review* 64, no. 2 (1955): 175, 182.

[29] Vlastos, "Rights of Persons in Plato's Conception," 128.

[30] Haim Cohn, *Human Rights in the Bible and the Talmud* (Tel Aviv: MOD Books, 1989), 9.

[31] Cf. Lauren, *Evolution*, 11.

be ignored just because they are not formulated in the technical language of an Amnesty International report.

History is fragmented in more than one sense. We reconstruct both history in general and intellectual history on the basis of the shards left by the destructive forces of the past, such as war, ignorance, superstition and accidents. Moreover, many voices in this history of ideas have been silenced. We know what Aristotle and Locke thought about slavery, but not whether the slaves of their time agreed with their stance. The disenfranchisement of women means that half of the human population is excluded almost totally from this history. To conclude from the absence of voices advocating the rights of women at a given time that there is no interesting history of this idea before these rights were explicitly demanded during the eighteenth century may lead to a very selective account of this crucial dimension of the development of human rights.

It is thus not sufficient (though useful) to enter terms into search engines, to search digitized historical texts for occurrences of terms such as *rights*, *Rechte*, *ius*, *droit* and so on if we aspire to write an intellectual history of the idea of fundamental and human rights.[32] We need to look for this idea, or at least for central elements of it, and not only in the canonical texts of high culture, but also in the social practices and not least the struggles of ordinary human beings who over the course of history on many occasions have manifested their belief that they enjoy a particular normative position, a justifiably claimable permission to do or not do something and to have the central goods of their life protected while others were under a duty to act accordingly.

The aesthetic self-representation and self-appropriation of human existence in art is another source of insight. A history of human rights without at least a sense of what has been expressed (e.g. about human dignity in the aesthetic sphere) will miss a crucial aspect of the development of such ideas and some of their intriguing expressions. Odysseus' encounter with the ephemeral shade of his mother in the underworld and what it tells us about the meaning of mortality, the suffering of Euripides' *Women of Troy*, the mourning of the seated, medieval terracotta figures of the Niger delta, Scheherazade's songs against death, Bashō's farewell note[33] or the rebellious defiance of the upright figure with stigmata in front of the firing squad in

[32] As Hunt, *Inventing Human Rights*, 230, n. 5 reports to have done. There is nothing wrong with such research; on the contrary, it may be very illuminating as long as it is not mistaken for a comprehensive search for what a human rights history should be interested in. This is not a new observation. Cf. e.g. Hersch Lauterpacht, *An International Bill of the Rights of Man* (New York: Columbia University Press, 1945), 17 on the history of natural rights: "[I]n order to judge the antiquity of the idea of the natural rights of man we must look to their substance rather than to their designation." On the problem of a "search engine mentality," Alston, "Does the Past Matter," 2049; on the "polycentricity of the human rights enterprise," ibid. 2077.

[33] Bashō writes: "Ailing on my travels/yet my dream wandering/over withered moors," in *The Penguin Book of Japanese Verse*, eds. Geoffrey Bownas and Anthony Thwaite (London: Penguin Books, 2009), 106.

Goya's *El 3 de mayo de 1808 en Madrid* are not entirely irrelevant to the question of whether dignity is a property of the human condition. Giacometti's later sculptures are equally important for this kind of self-reflection, his aesthetic vision decisively shaped by the catastrophes of the first half of the twentieth century.[34] The same holds true – to cite a last example – of Camus' tender description of the world of the illiterate, violent, deprived and desperate poor of colonial Algiers (his family) and their experience of life.[35]

The full meaning of human dignity is not something we learn in philosophical seminars and courses at law faculties about human rights law, important as these are to clarify ethical and legal thought and cultivate certain important moral feelings. Our understanding of human worth is something that grows as part of a lived life and our experience of what this entails. Something similar is true of the growth of the idea of human rights. This idea is no minor thing, and many sources – systematic thought, social struggles, artistic expression – have contributed to it. A history of this idea and its political and legal manifestations needs to remain mindful of this fact.

In recent times, increasing effort has been made to examine critically the biases and limitations of classical elements of legal thought and to do justice to other traditions of practical philosophy outside the so-called Western tradition. This well-justified endeavor adds yet another dimension of complexity to the scope of the history of human rights.

These observations mean that deciding whether or not to include a normative idea or institution in a history of human rights requires us to answer difficult questions. Not all of these answers will be indisputable, and there will be borderline cases. However, broadening the inquiry to ask such questions is a key task of a differentiated history of human rights that hopes to do justice to the richness of its subject.

2.2.3 *Conceptions of History*

There is yet another issue to be addressed: the concept and conception of history that guide historical research, which turn out to be of significant importance for the inquiry into rights and human thought.

This is by no means straightforward. What human history is and how it can be reconstructed form the subject of profound debate. For the purpose of a history of

34 Matthias Mahlmann, "Le Chariot – Bemerkungen zu den Grundlagen des Rechts," *Zeitschrift für Schweizerisches Recht* 131 (2012): 123 ff. Cf. for some more exploration, concretely of Velázquez's *Las Meninas* and the concept of dignity, Christopher McCrudden, "On Portraying Human Dignity," in *Human Dignity in Context*, eds. Dieter Grimm, Alexandra Kemmerer and Christoph Möllers (Baden-Baden: Nomos, 2018), 23–54.

35 Albert Camus, "Le Premier Homme," in Albert Camus, *Œuvres complètes Vol. IV: 1957–1959*, ed. Raymond Gay-Crosier (Paris: Gallimard, 2008); for comments, Matthias Mahlmann, "Menschenwürde in Politik, Ethik und Recht – universelle Fassade, kulturelle Relativität?" in *Rechtsstaatliches Strafrecht: Festschrift für Ulfrid Neumann zum 70. Geburtstag*, ed. Frank Saliger (Heidelberg: C.F. Müller, 2017), 267 ff.

human rights conceptualized in sufficiently differentiated terms, the following remarks may be helpful to illuminate some often-tacit background assumptions of the current historical analysis of human rights.

The first problem is whether history is a gradual, continuous evolution. Within this conception of history, an idea such as human rights is invented at a certain determinable moment in time and then becomes a possible foundation of or influence on further cultural developments, which in turn shape its future content. One important element of this perspective is often (though not necessarily) the assumption that there are no *a priori* foundations of human cultural processes; human existence is a blank slate, determined by its protean nature,[36] the capacity to form any kind of culture, to mold human existence in any form, whatever it may be.[37] Humans are their own continuous creation through and through, so to speak, which implies that the current conception of being human may disappear as it was created at some point in time, like a face drawn in the sand and washed away by the sea.[38]

Anything that now is regarded as foundational for human existence and culture has thus been invented at some point in history. To use an example relevant for the history of human rights: Human beings have no natural sense of individuality. Individuality originated in medieval thought,[39] as some have argued, or in the Renaissance, as others think,[40] but is in any case highly culture specific, not a universal feature of humanity. From this point of view, the Herero dying in the desert possibly had no sense of individuality because they had not benefited from European cultural development.

Some versions of this conception of history may be teleological, but today the emphasis usually will lie on the importance of structure, path-dependent development and contingencies. Conceptions of something unchangeable, something eternal, are, in Walter Benjamin's expression, merely a "ruffle on a dress" of thought, not an idea relevant for conceptions of history.[41]

36 Cf. Rorty, "Human Rights, Rationality and Sentimentality," 115.

37 On the existentialist idea that existence precedes human essence, cf. Jean-Paul Sartre, *L'existentialisme est un humanisme* (Paris: Nagel, 1946).

38 Foucault, *Les mots et les choses*, 398: "*L'homme est une invention dont l'archéologie de notre pensée montre aisément la date récente. Et peut-être la fin prochaine. Si ces dispositions venaient à disparaître comme elles sont apparues, si par quelque événement dont nous pouvons tout au plus pressentir la possibilité, mais dont nous ne connaissons pour l'instant encore ni la forme ni la promesse, elles basculaient, comme le fit au tournant du XVIIIe siècle le sol de la pensée classique, – alors on peut bien parier, que l'homme s'effacerait, comme à la limite de la mer un visage de sable.*"

39 Larry Siedentop, *Inventing the Individual: The Origins of Western Liberalism* (Cambridge, MA: Harvard University Press, 2017).

40 Jacob Burckhardt, *Die Kultur der Renaissance in Italien* (Stuttgart: Alfred Kröner Verlag, 2009).

41 Walter Benjamin, "Das Passagen-Werk," in Walter Benjamin, *Gesammelte Schriften*, Vol. V-1, ed. Rolf Tiedemann (Frankfurt am Main, Suhrkamp, 1982), 578: "*Entschiedne Abkehr vom Begriffe der ‚zeitlosen Wahrheit' ist am Platz. Doch Wahrheit ist nicht – wie der Marxismus es behauptet – nur eine zeitliche Funktion des Erkennens, sondern an einen Zeitkern, welcher im Erkannten und Erkennenden zugleich steckt, gebunden. Das ist so wahr, daß das Ewige*

An alternative view emphasizes the element of discontinuity in history. This model treats skeptically the idea of lines of development that run through centuries, let alone through all of human history. There are no overarching developments connecting different ages and historical cultural formations. The people of the past and their lifeworlds are understood as radically different from others, including our own (whoever "we" may be). To think otherwise means to fall prey to naive anachronisms. The concept of justice found in antiquity, for instance, is thus not something that could inform us today. It is born of its time, and any possibility of understanding it ended with the passing of that epoch. Attempts to connect the lifeworld of the past with current forms of existence lead to distortions of both – of the past because it is reconstructed wrongly using the conceptual means of the present, and of the present because its meaning is established in the light of incongruous concepts of the past. Adherents of this conception of history also mostly understand the infinite malleability of human beings as their defining property.

Yet another approach holds that ideas, institutions, entire forms of life can develop, flourish for a while and then be lost again. From this point of view, it is implausible to assume that good ideas, promising forms of life and useful institutions necessarily become a historical reality and remain so forever having once established themselves. They can simply be suppressed by force, possibly for a long period of time, or subdued by other powers – for example, by the victory of the ignorance, superstition or the partisan interests of powerful groups, individuals or political mass movements. They can also simply be forgotten. But they can be rediscovered as well and reasserted under new historical circumstances. They may have lain dormant, remembered only by a few if not lost in oblivion, not waking to full life until their day finally dawned. Similar ideas, institutions and forms of life can be developed independently at different times and places. Therefore, a time can speak a language that a later time is able to understand quite well, despite there not necessarily being an unbroken link of continuous development between the two.

These competing pictures of history lead to the question of what exactly makes this course of events a *human* history. Is there something species-specific about this history? This question is not particularly far-fetched, for of the many other species that have populated and continue to populate this Earth, no other has undergone any development remotely like the history of human beings. Bonobos or dolphins are admirably complex creatures, with the ability to learn and astonishing acquired skills, some of which are even handed down to new generations (think, for instance, of the hunting techniques of orcas), but none is a historical creature in the way that human beings are. It is safe to guess that bonobos live much the same as they lived a

jedenfalls eher eine Rüsche am Kleid ist als eine Idee." English translation of Benjamin available at Walter Benjamin, *The Arcades Project*, trans. Howard Eiland and Kevin McLaughlin (Cambridge, MA: Harvard University Press, 2002), 463, https://monoskop.org/images/e/e4/Benjamin_Walter_The_Arcades_Project.pdf.

million years ago, whereas human forms of life in comparison have changed quite radically in the 100,000 years that human beings have been shaping their life on Earth. Consequently, there must be something about human beings that is at the core of this very particular history. But what is it? Is this human history best explained by relying solely on the culture-building faculty of human beings? This faculty certainly exists. Nobody doubts that one of the striking qualities of human beings is their creativity, the ability to transcend – unlike other organisms – instinct-driven ways of behavior and to constantly transform their ways of life. That is why any form of biological, genetic determinism and reductionism is so way off the mark. But what is the foundation for this creativity and the specific characteristics of human existence in which this creativity unfolds? Does a richer concept of human nature, in particular a thicker theory of the higher mental faculties of human beings, help to explain some of these characteristics and thus contribute to the understanding of particular properties of human history?

Note that this latter conception is the conception of a radical epistemic egalitarianism. It takes as a heuristic starting point the assumption that human beings share exactly the same creative intellectual and emotional wealth wherever they are born, in whatever cultural circumstances they are brought up and live, whatever skin color, sex, sexual orientation or other surface characteristic they may have and in what particular time they live. From this perspective, a person with the specific culture of a tribe in the Congo Basin in 1900 or the pastoral lifestyle of the Herero enjoys substantially the same set of properties, in particular mental faculties, as Albert Einstein, working on relativity at that time, or an illiterate female bricklayer in today's Delhi. To be sure, there are individual variations – for example, sadly, between Albert Einstein and the author of this text. But these are not differences that transcend the common bond of a shared set of properties that make all humans human, whether they are hunter-gatherers, scientists, bricklayers or confused theoreticians of human rights.

It is important to underline that this is not equally so for anthropological assumptions that take the total malleability of human beings for granted. From this point of view, persons of different times and cultures will not necessarily have the same mental capacities, because certain elements of the human mental world are the product of cultural constructions. People with a certain cultural background (e.g. European) may have certain concepts that others (say, people of the Congo Basin, or the Herero) lack. These questions are particularly relevant for the history of human rights. If one assumes, for example, that human beings have no concept of their individual selves or of separate bodies apart from certain cultural developments,[42] that even "translated into brain changes,"[43] there is basically no point in searching

[42] This seems to be the point of view on the development of cognition adopted by Hunt, *Inventing Human Rights*, 29 ff.

[43] Hunt, *Inventing Human Rights*, 33.

for rights that protect individuality before cultural developments actually define individuality as such. The justification at least of certain rights designed to protect individuality, such as privacy rights, depends upon individuality being a meaningful concept. Accordingly, some histories make the development of individuality a precondition for the conceptualization of the idea of human rights.[44] Even one of the intellectually and morally most impressive accounts of the evils of totalitarianism reveals more than mere traces of this approach. Hannah Arendt condemns unambiguously "the senseless massacre of native tribes" in Africa and other crimes of colonialism and imperialism.[45] The indigenous people of Africa, however, are depicted as beings without culture and without a human world (*Weltlosigkeit*) and thus devoid of full humanity: "They were, as it were, 'natural' human beings who lacked the specifically human character, the specifically human reality, so that when European men massacred them they somehow were not aware that they had committed murder. . . . The great horror which had seized European men at their first confrontation with native life was stimulated by precisely this touch of inhumanity among human beings who apparently were as much a part of nature as wild animals."[46]

If culture is all there is in a human being, and the only truly humanizing culture is a culture similar to that which developed in Europe, a human being without such a culture is nothing at all – this is the dangerous conclusion looming in the background.

If we are open to the possibility that something like a concept of selfhood develops naturally in all human beings, the picture looks quite different, not only for the theory of the justification of human rights, but also for the conceptualization of their history, including the sense of tragedy with which we learn about this history. If there is a case for the individuality of hunter-gatherers in the Congo Basin or of nomadic herdsmen in Namibia, their suffering under Belgian rule or death in the desert at the hands of the German colonial forces gains only more significance. The obvious danger of cultural bias and perhaps even of worth ideologies looms large in the denial of full humanity to people without a specific cultural past, as the history

[44] Cf. Hunt, *Inventing Human Rights*, 27 ff.

[45] Hannah Arendt, *The Origins of Totalitarianism* (London: Penguin Books, 2017), 251.

[46] Arendt, *Origins of Totalitarianism*, 250 ff. The expanded German second edition contains even more explicit passages, among them a longer version of the English passage just quoted, cf. Hannah Arendt, *Elemente und Ursprünge totaler Herrschaft* (Munich: Piper, 2005), 425, where Arendt writes about the Boers: "*In ihnen lebt vermutlich heute noch der erste grauenhafte Schrecken vor den Menschen Afrikas – die tiefe Angst vor einem fast ins Tierhafte, nämlich wirklich ins Rassische degenerierten Volk, das doch trotz seiner absoluten Fremdheit zweifellos eine Spezies des homo sapiens war. Denn was auch immer die Menschheit an Schrecken vor wilden barbarischen Stämmen gekannt hat, das grundsätzliche Entsetzen, das den europäischen Menschen befiel, als er Neger – nicht in einzelnen exponierten Exemplaren – sondern als Bevölkerung eines ganzen Kontinents – kennenlernte, hat nirgends seinesgleichen. Es ist das Grauen vor der Tatsache, daß dies auch noch Menschen sind, und die diesem Grauen unmittelbar folgende Entscheidung, daß solche 'Menschen' keinesfalls unseresgleichen sein durften.*"

that is supposed to constitute humanity or to have produced such concepts as individuality is the history of Europe or the West, thus excluding other cultural trajectories, importantly those of the victims of European cruelty and greed.

Are these conceptions of history fictions or straw men? It does not seem so. There are various examples of historical accounts of human rights or human history in general that imply important features of these different approaches, some of which have already been mentioned and some of which will still cross our path. When engaging with any particular account of human rights, it consequently is useful to ask which background assumptions guide the research in question and how they may color the analysis.

How to decide between these conceptions of history? The question of what history is like cannot be answered on *a priori* grounds. We cannot know how history unfolded before we have studied it – advisably without an *a priori* conception that is immune against falsification.

This open-mindedness should apply likewise to the sketched anthropological assumptions underlying the writing of history. Perhaps human beings of other epochs or from certain contemporary cultures were or are completely different from us (the question of course being – who is "us"?) – with no comparable modes of thought and underlying mental faculties formed by history. Perhaps they had and have no conception of a self, of individuality, of the separateness of one's own body or any other such feature relevant for the idea of human rights. Perhaps, however, quite to the contrary, human beings from other epochs or cultures were or are very much like us in important respects (in this case – irrespective of who is "us"). Possibly humans share certain modes of thought and naturally and inevitably develop a concept of individuality as they develop an upright posture or (it seems) a concept of three-dimensional space as a framework of spatial orientation.

Again, neither of these theories is an *a priori* truth. Both form a hypothesis about human nature that is perhaps right, perhaps wrong. It is particularly important to underline that the assumption of the infinite malleability of human beings implies as many substantial hypotheses about human nature as any other theory. These are assumptions about universal properties of human beings, of all cultures and all times: From this point of view, all human beings share the property of malleability, a protean nature. This is a proposition about a substantial character of the species. The malleability thesis is not anthropologically neutral or "thin" in any kind of relevant sense, as it posits well-defined, rich, natural cognitive properties of human beings, such as a general ability to learn. There is thus no theory or history of human rights without a theory of human nature. The only question is what *kind* of theory of human nature one defends or implies and how well-grounded it is. This point is of some importance and will concern us throughout this study.

It follows that there is nothing outlandish about asking whether a different concept of human nature than the one that the infinite malleability thesis implies may help to formulate interesting research questions for the inquiry into the history of human rights. We might wonder, for instance, whether there are no indications in history that *human beings have always been reasoning, moral, sentient, self-conscious, autonomous and liberty-seeking beings yearning for justice, respect and recognition*. There is some evidence that speaks for seriously considering this hypothesis, such as the testimony of art and not least the social struggles in human history. The search for justice and freedom is not a prerogative of European modernity. In concrete terms, this would mean, for example, that torture hurt as much and was just as humiliating in 2022 as in 1786 or in 500 BCE, that liberty meant something to human beings throughout time (at least after they had experienced it) and that slavery was never a form of life merrily and justifiably accepted by human beings. From this perspective, the mourning of the *Women of Troy* and the real experience it stands for is not incomprehensible noise but resonates in an uncannily familiar manner with the later history of the subjugation of women.

The history of human rights is important for the relation of mind and rights, because, as explained above, we cannot study this topic with historical naivety about the genesis of the ideas and institutions of human rights. But not only that: Conversely, clarifying the relation of mind and rights is in turn highly relevant for the history of human rights itself, because it contributes to strengthening the foundations of the anthropological assumptions that guide this research. Perhaps the theory arguing for the total malleability of human nature is on the wrong track, and consequently the historical account based on this assumption is, too. Historiography and substantial theories of the human mind are of mutual importance for one another: The former casts light upon the historical making of human rights, the latter upon the anthropological foundations of this process.

A final remark about problems of the method of inquiry: The history of human rights is the history of a moral idea and the legal institutions that limit power and privilege and therefore challenge many actors in a given society, including world society. It is thus a history not of benign reflection and good deeds but of often-dirty struggles for social might and material goods that lurk in the background, and sometimes advance into the foreground, too. Furthermore, it is the project of humans and thus of beings who are fallible and often fall prey to error and actions that, even if well-intended, may entangle the actors in guilt and crime.

The history of human rights consequently must be the history of often very mixed achievements, of slow and discontinuous developments, of dead-end roads and noble ideas buried in tragedy. It must be a history of ideas, actions and institutions as imperfect as the beings who drove this project forward through time. The fact that there are many unsavory chapters in the history of human rights thus comes as no surprise. The significant good that this history contains should astonish us more than the bad that marked its path – and we should seek to tell honestly the grand story of both.

2.3 RIGHTS ON THE BARRICADES

2.3.1 *Where to Begin?*

Given these complexities, writing a history of human rights clearly is no easy task. Self-confident assertions about the idea's birth in Stoic thought, in the canonistic reinterpretation of Roman law, in the modern Natural Law tradition, in the Enlightenment, in Christian personalism or even in the policies of Jimmy Carter[47] underestimate the difficulty of the task. This underestimation is even more evident in assertions that the idea of human rights, or normative concepts that reasonably can be taken as related to the history of human rights, are not present in certain periods or cultures. It is far from clear, for instance, that merely because the Herero have not bequeathed to posterity a set of treatises on rights, including normative positions relevant for the idea of human rights, their culture contains nothing of interest to this history – or at least it should be clear if we put aside racist assumptions about the intrinsic inferiority of certain groups of people, in particular due to their cognitive abilities. Given historic events such as the "Scramble for Africa" and what it meant for very many human beings, we should be reluctant to exclude certain cultures from the history of rights from the outset – any intimation of the moral superiority of European or "Western" culture is all too evidently irreconcilable with its (horrific) historic record.

The question of where to start already has no obvious answer. Even if we leave aside implicit (though potentially highly relevant) manifestations of the idea of human rights, ignoring social norms and cultural practices, and instead search only for explicit moral or legal statements of the idea of human rights, we will still find multiple contenders. As explained above, history comes in many shades of gray and thus any such identification of the "beginning" of human rights will (justifiably) remain contentious.

What is clear, however, is that the idea of human rights entered the stage of world history as a major political factor during the American and French Revolutions. This idea had germinated for a long time, becoming increasingly prominent in the political and practical philosophy of the seventeenth and eighteenth centuries and finally turning into a revolutionary force: "The idea moved out of the library on to the barricades."[48]

[47] Cf. S. Moyn, *The Last Utopia*, 217. Moyn, *The Last Utopia*, 6, rightly criticizes human rights historians who approach their subject "the way church historians once approached theirs," without offering a sufficiently complex picture himself, however. See Alston, "Does the Past Matter," 2063 on the problems of "progress narratives" that "leap from one historical moment to another with little if any attempt to demonstrate causality, probe lines of transmission, or explain the political economy involved. They overstate coherence and continuity, marginalize competing understandings, and can be used to delegitimize alternative visions."

[48] Griffin, *On Human Rights*, 1.

The American and French Revolutions were complex historical events in which very different aspirations played important roles. This is also true for the implied politics of human rights. In both revolutionary contexts, however, the idea of human rights had an important part among other, sometimes competing aims, and this makes these events a natural starting point for historical reflection. Subsequently, a wider perspective can be adopted to include other, more remote historical periods.

The history of human rights from the eighteenth-century revolutions to the present is well-charted territory. Nevertheless, it is necessary to highlight some crucial elements of this history in order to make some points that are important for our further inquiry. The discussion will lead to the following conclusion, which will be tested and enlarged upon in Chapter 3: Human rights history since the eighteenth century shows, we will argue, that human rights are a political project based on a particular ethical outlook born from the reflection of historically embedded but autonomously thinking human subjects, a project that is turned into but not limited to positive law and its institutions. To explain human rights history primarily by some often vaguely defined cultural or religious source, as some forms of cultural or religious reductionism do, runs the danger of depoliticizing the profoundly political human rights project, of missing its ethical core and impoverishing significantly the depth and explanatory power of the historical analysis. As we have already seen, in this analysis, human rights as ethical ideas have to be clearly distinguished from their legal and institutional implementation, which can take many forms. The current two-tier system of legal international human rights protection is not the only system in which human rights can play a meaningful role and that needs to be studied to gain a deeper understanding of them.

2.3.2 *From Politics to Law*

The role of human rights at the time of the American and French Revolutions was political, often rhetorical and only legal in a more limited sense. Documents like the *Virginia Bill of Rights* as the first concrete list of such rights and the *Declaration of Independence* gave human rights pride of place. The legal order established by the Constitution of the United States was much more hesitant and took significantly less ambitious steps to follow up these bold statements. In France, the *Déclaration* did not lead to enduring enforceable human rights law either. On the contrary, the French Revolution took the path to *la Terreur* and Napoleonic rule, and the principles of 1789 only bloomed very slowly.

Prominent conceptions of human rights underpinning these developments shared an important feature of the human rights project that has taken shape over the last two centuries, a feature we have already identified: The rights of human beings were to be protected in concrete limited political communities but as part of cosmopolitan normative perspectives. The protection afforded in the context of the nation state from this point of view had a universal aspiration. A kind of stewardship concept was implied: Human rights were to be realized in the available political space, which was the nation state. However, the nation state was acting as a steward of the rights of humanity, which were not limited to any particular political community. Burke identified the problem quite correctly: The *Déclaration* did not secure the rights of Frenchmen; it attempted to secure the rights of human beings in France.[49]

It is hardly surprising that the idea of an international protection of human rights beyond this focus on concrete political communities played no role in this period. To begin with, the idea was violently opposed by various secular and religious powers – including the mightiest that existed. The enemies of human rights had armies, their defenders not necessarily so.

Furthermore, it was not only the forces defending authoritarian regimes and orders based on the perceived unequal worth of human beings, like champions of the *ancien régime*, who opposed human rights. Right from the very inception of these rights, there were movements committed to what they perceived as social progress but on the ground of politics that denied and violated human rights. After all, *la Terreur* followed the *Déclaration de Droits de l'Homme et du Citoyen* after only four years, with long-lasting consequences for the perceived legitimacy of the ideas of the French Revolution.

For a long time, there were other rather substantial impediments to formulating anything remotely resembling a concrete idea of international human rights protection: First of all, at this point in time there was only a vague sense of what humanity actually meant in real terms, given the limited mutual contact and genuine familiarity with the diverse human cultures of that time. Moreover, contact with a given region of the world and knowing something about it does not necessarily lead to the inclusion of that region's inhabitants among humanity, as the colonial practices of the European states vividly illustrate. Finally, it is worth mentioning that there was simply no organizational and institutional space in which such cosmopolitan visions could have been pursued in the revolutionary period.[50] Inevitably, attempts thus concentrated on securing rights for the concrete political entity those involved belonged to; that is, for nation states or other entities, such as the German states or the cantons of the Swiss Confederacy.

Given this state of affairs, other aspirations for a legal world order of human rights were clearly out of reach, if they were developed at all. Establishing rights on the limited national level already required not only revolutionary action, but generations of political struggles that continue to this day. Starting with political action for a

[49] Burke, *Reflections*, 118 ff., though the "rights of man" in comparison to the "rights of Englishmen," a "patrimony derived from their forefathers," for him were chimerical and the root of revolutionary violence.

[50] Cf. Mazower, *Governing the World* for an overview about the development of global governance.

world community of rights would not have been a very promising action plan in 1776 or 1789.

The idea of cosmopolitan perspectives realized in particular political communities, however, found powerful expression, albeit in political practice only as one among other, quite different political aspirations. Moreover, this conception of human rights was often limited in many crucial aspects. The exclusions of women, of slaves and more generally of people of certain imagined races or from particular social classes or religious communities are the most obvious ones. This notwithstanding, this conception of human rights proved to be a central element of the future protection of human rights once these patterns of exclusion were overcome.

2.3.3 *Civil Rights and Human Rights*

Another pertinent issue that came to the fore during this formative constitutionalist period was the relation and sometimes tension between human rights as the rights of all humans and civil rights or the rights of citizens, in the sense that these rights are guaranteed but reserved only to the citizens of a specific community and not extended to all persons resident or temporarily staying in a country. The history of rights in the nineteenth century to a large degree was written in the language of constitutional civil rights, and not only in the USA and Europe. As indicated above, in principle there are legitimate functional reasons for this differentiation that are entirely in harmony with the idea of human rights. In the history of constitutionalism, however, the restriction of rights to citizens was not limited to such functionally legitimate constraints but extended to other and sometimes to all guaranteed rights. This limitation can be understood as a partial realization of universal human rights or can be justified on more narrow grounds – for example, as the traditional rights of members belonging to a particular community or even as a nationalistic conception of rights entitlements.[51]

Despite these limitations and ambiguities, these catalogues of civil rights (understood in this restricted sense as to their personal scope) are relevant for the history of human rights. The content of key rights such as freedom of expression or due process was shaped and developed further within this framework. They are thus examples of how rights that are limited in their personal scope can be relevant for the development of more inclusive human rights. Only one more step needed to be taken – a step of great importance for the history of human rights: the universalization of rights granted to particular individuals, extending the personal scope of these

[51] Cf. the eloquent defense of such a traditionalist account of rights wedded to the specific history of a nation, Burke, *Reflections*, 150: "If civil society be the offspring of convention, that convention must be its law. That convention must limit and modify all the descriptions of constitution which are formed under it. Every sort of legislative judicial, or executory power are its creatures. They can have no being in any other state of things; and how can any man claim, under the conventions of civil society, rights which do not so much as suppose its existence?"

rights to all human beings. Here, too, this one step was a major one, full of preconditions, but one that very much forms part of the history of rights as human rights.

The idea of human rights in the narrow sense, however, continued to play a variety of important roles in nineteenth-century thought. It remained not only the object of legal inquiry and its ambivalent conceptions of human rights' origin and content,[52] but also served as a rallying cry for revolutionary grassroots action struggling to overcome the monarchical order reinstated after the Napoleonic Wars. To take one particularly interesting example, in one of the most famous revolutionary pamphlets in German history, *Der Hessische Landbote* (1834), one of the greatest playwrights in the German language, Georg Büchner, wrote of human rights as the normative anchor of his demands for freedom and equality – demands that drove him into exile in Zurich and landed many of his associates in prison – yet another example of the struggles for human rights from below.[53]

Büchner's courageous actions illustrate that achieving guarantees of these rights after their revolutionary declaration continued to be an arduous political project involving major historical tragedies. One example with particularly far-reaching consequences for world history is Germany, of whose political development Büchner's fate is in many ways a paradigmatic case: The suppression of the democratic revolution in the German states after years of political unrest and its remarkable constitution of 1848, the subsequent rise of German authoritarianism, the admirable constitutional attempt of the Weimar Republic after World War I, its collapse, the rise of Nazism, the catastrophe of World War II and the mass murder taking place in its shadow and the resurrection of German constitutional democracy based on human rights in 1948 in the form of the *Basic Law* in one part of the country, divided until its reunification in 1990, illustrate what kind of historical forces have to be mastered before a constitutional order based on human rights can become a reality. The fascinating history of constitutionalism in the nineteenth and

[52] Cf. for instance Johann Caspar Bluntschli, *Das moderne Völkerrecht der civilisirten Staaten als Rechtsbuch dargestellt*, 2nd edition (Nördlingen: Beck, 1872), 64 on human rights binding states and demanding the abolition of slavery; Pasquale Fiore, *Le droit international codifié et sa sanction juridique* (Paris: Librarie Marescq Ainé, 1890), 14 ff., 164 ff., 164: "*Les droits de l'homme au point de vue international sont ceux que lui confère sa personnalité, au regard de tous les États, de tous ses semblables et de toutes les autres personnes formant la Magna civitas. Ce sont, à proprement parler, les droits de la personnalité humaine, appartenant à chacun, à raison même de son existence, et indépendamment du lien de nationalité qui l'unit à un État déterminé.*" For critical comments, for instance, on elements of racism and antisemitism in Bluntschli's work, Marcel Senn, "Rassistische und antisemitische Elemente im Rechtsdenken von Johann Caspar Bluntschli," *Zeitschrift der Savigny-Stiftung für Rechtsgeschichte* 110 (1993): 376–405; on both, Koskenniemi, *The Gentle Civilisers*, 42 ff.; 54 ff.

[53] Cf. Georg Büchner, "Der Hessische Landbote," in Georg Büchner, *Werke und Briefe*, Münchner Ausgabe, eds. Karl Pörnbacher et al. (Munich: Deutscher Taschenbuch Verlag, 2001), 39 ff., 44, 52, 56, 58. The secret society Büchner founded was called *Gesellschaft für Menschenrechte*, "Society for Human Rights," following a French example.

twentieth centuries unfolding on all continents[54] provides many other examples of how the development of rights proceeded, halted, regressed and had to give way to authoritarian regimes until new developments opened the door to the pursuit of rights once more.

There is a further important point. In addition to their role in the ethics and law of eighteenth-century declarations of rights and of nineteenth-century constitutionalism, human rights also contributed to important ethical and political movements that led to far-reaching change in social, political and legal terms. Important examples are the antislavery movement, including as one of its most dramatic and increasingly less neglected expressions, the 1791 Revolution in Haiti and the campaign against torture that had originated before the great declarations of rights. The women's liberation movement is another crucial example. The rights of women were claimed eloquently during the French Revolution, albeit with limited concrete success.[55] These rights continued to be the object of struggles that concerned not only women's right to vote, but other issues as well, such as property, contract and family law, challenging the many restrictions women faced.[56] One last example is the labor movement, important parts of which had an explicit fundamental rights agenda, despite Marx's skepticism about rights.[57]

These movements developed heterogeneous political views, some of them becoming increasing hostile to the idea of human rights. But even where this was not the case, human rights were not their only concern. Nevertheless, these efforts

[54] An interesting example is South American constitutionalism since its beginnings in the nineteenth century. Here as elsewhere the question of the concrete meaning of fundamental rights was intertwined with different visions of social organization, giving more or less weight to traditional social and religious forces, social and economic oligarchies, individual autonomy or social welfare, cf. for an overview Roberto Gargarella, *Latin American Constitutionalism, 1810–2010: The Engine Room of the Constitution* (Oxford: Oxford University Press, 2013), 6 ff. on conservative, republican and liberal visions of constitutions and rights.

[55] Olympe de Gouges, *Déclaration des droits de la femme et de la citoyenne: Suivi de préface pour les Dames ou le portrait des femmes* (Paris: Mille et une nuits, 2003); Wollstonecraft, *Vindication.*

[56] Harriet Taylor Mill, "Enfranchisement of Women," in *The Complete Works of Harriet Taylor Mill*, eds. Jo Ellen Jacobs and Paula Harms Payne (Bloomington: Indiana University Press, 1998), 72: "What is wanted is equal rights, equal admission to all social privileges; not a position apart, a sort of sentimental priesthood."

[57] Cf. for an example of nineteenth-century social democracy, Gothaer Programm, *Protokoll des Vereinigungs-Kongresses der Sozialdemokraten Deutschlands, abgehalten zu Gotha vom 22. bis 27. Mai 1875*. Leipzig, 1875, 78–9 (equal rights to socially created wealth, freedom of opinion, thought and research, electoral rights, right to form unions) and Karl Marx, "Kritik des Gothaer Programms," in *Marx-Engels-Werke*, Vol. 19, ed. Ludwig Arnold (Berlin: Dietz Verlag, 1987), 13–32. For many decades, the anthem *The Internationale* was sung by members of the labor movement. Its original version by Eugène Pottier, an activist of the Paris Commune, written in 1871 after the subjection of the Paris Commune, contains the verse: "*Le droit du pauvre est un mot creux/C'est assez, languir en tutelle/L'égalité veut d'autres lois/Pas de droits sans devoirs dit-elle/Égaux, pas de devoirs sans droits.*" In the most popular German 1910 version by Emil Luckhart, the chorus explicitly refers to "*Menschenrecht*," the right of humans as a central aspiration of the labor movement.

had some ideas in common: Slaves and workers rebelled against being reduced to beasts of burden, claiming the right to different treatment as humans. Women resisted repressive patriarchal structures and demanded freedoms as beings endowed with as much reason, morality, sentiment and capacity for self-determination as men. The movement for the abolition of torture and more generally for penal reform highlighted the humanity of the tortured persons that seemed to forbid such treatment. The demands of these movements may not have been couched in the words of twenty-first-century human rights terminology, but their more profound normative structure was very much about the legitimate claims of slaves, workers, women or convicts *as humans* and therefore belong in any history of human rights. Mary Wollstonecraft's thoughts about women's rights, recalled above, are just one example, as are W. E. B. Du Bois' demands for human rights as a crucial element of post-slavery emancipation.[58] Accordingly, various provisions of modern human rights law finally embodied these demands.

The protection of human rights in specific political communities, a protection with universalist aspirations despite the limited and exclusionary form in which these rights initially were conceptualized, forms the first key step in the development of the contemporary architecture of human rights. This idea was audacious despite its limitations, as its history shows. The concrete history of legal developments saw substantial human rights realized predominantly in the personally limited form of civil (constitutional) rights. The revival of the full idea of human rights and the project of their international protection beyond the means of the state form the second step of this development. This step led to the highly imperfect and even in its most solid parts constantly threatened order of human rights in which we live today: their primary protection by national means and a supplementary, subsidiary protection through the international systems of rights, both regional and universal. How did this come about?

2.4 THE GROWTH OF THE MULTILAYERED PROTECTION OF HUMAN RIGHTS

2.4.1 *Contours of the Project*

The concrete project of an enlarged protection of human rights through the means of international law emerged more concretely in the twentieth century. From at least the 1920s onwards, the idea of the international protection of human rights became an explicit ethical, political and legal project.

The protection of human rights developed not as a natural outcome of the long-standing humanitarian traditions of the major powers. Traditionally, the political

[58] Cf. for instance the reference to the "manhood rights of the Negro," William Edward Burghard Du Bois, *The Souls of Black Folk* (W. W. Norton: New York, London, 1999), 13, 32, 40 ff., 45, quote at 39, in the framework of universalist perspectives, ibid. 16, 39, 136.

praxis of the world powers of the Global North had nothing to do with human rights: The European powers – despite the constitutional and democratic movements of the nineteenth century – in the time between the American and French Revolutions and the creation of the UN Charter and the *Universal Declaration* in many cases were authoritarian orders with little or no effective protection of fundamental rights, some even in newly established forms such as the fascist dictatorships in Italy and Spain and the Nazi dictatorship in Germany, leading the way to the ultimate negation of human rights. Catastrophic wars were conducted without much consideration for things such as ethical principles. Beyond Europe's boundaries, colonialism continued to inflict great suffering on people around the world, demanding a staggering death toll and including actions that even in the later, narrow, technical legal sense were genocidal, both in colonized Africa – for example, in the case of the Herero – and in other parts of the world, including North America.[59]

These practices were deeply ingrained in the culture and political thinking of the times.[60] It was no coincidence that Joseph Conrad's *Heart of Darkness*, published at the beginning of the twentieth century, became a key aesthetical reflection of the historical forces at play: The real heart of darkness beat in the chest of European culture. Conrad's wandering protagonist Marlow thus notes plausibly that "all of Europe contributed to the making" of the mass murderer Kurtz.[61] Kurtz himself concisely summarizes the maxim guiding his own actions on the margin of his edifying pamphlet about Europe's civilizing mission, revealing the real truth behind the lofty humanitarian rhetoric, drenched with the cynicism, hypocrisy and self-delusion of the colonial empires: "Exterminate all the brutes!"[62]

A sober summary of the situation at the time of the slow inception of the international protection of human rights therefore cannot be a narrative about the triumphant, long-standing ethical tradition of Europe or the Global North, but rather must echo Marlow's self-reflective observation at the beginning of his narrative on the cruising yawl *Nelly*, anchored at the mouth of the Thames: "Darkness was here yesterday."[63]

The idea of taking a step forward, of improving the protection of human rights was thus an element of the *ethical counterculture* to the imperial Global North: the attempt to keep alive some of humanity's more worthy aspirations against powerful and unquestioned political traditions of the time.

As indicated above, the international protection of human rights is very much dependent on some kind of constant and stable organization of the international

[59] Cf. e.g. Benjamin Madley, *An American Genocide: The United States and the California Indian Catastrophe, 1846–1873* (New Haven, CT: Yale University Press, 2016).

[60] Cf. on the sometimes so-called Columbian Epoch and some of its main characteristics, Noam Chomsky, *Year 501: The Conquest Continues* (Boston, MA: South End Press, 1993), 1.

[61] Joseph Conrad, *Heart of Darkness* (London: Penguin Books, 2000), 83.

[62] Conrad, *Heart of Darkness*, 83.

[63] Conrad, *Heart of Darkness*, 19.

community. The first major step was undertaken after World War I. The *Covenant of the League of Nations*,[64] however, did not contain any reference to human rights. The USA and the UK had proposed clauses protecting religious freedom. Japan attempted to include a provision against discrimination on the grounds of race and religion but was unsuccessful because of the opposition of the USA and the UK, who withdrew their proposal after Japan's broader initiative[65] – unsurprisingly, given the racial segregation in the USA and the UK's colonial empire. Proposals for other human rights issues suffered the same fate, including the rights of women.[66]

Human rights played a role in the instruments creating the system of minority protection in the aftermath of World War I. This system contained, first, guarantees of life and liberty to all inhabitants of the respective country or region, without distinction of birth, nationality, language, race or religion. Second, it provided for equality before the law for all nationals and guaranteed their equal civil and political rights, without distinction as to race, language and religion. Third, it protected some cultural assets of minorities – for example, with regard to language or the right to establish social and religious institutions.

This system was limited to certain countries.[67] Proposals to extend the established duties to all League members were repeatedly rejected.[68] However, on September 21, 1922, the League of Nations passed a resolution that voiced the hope that all League Members would abide at least by these standards.

This system was limited in many ways, not least because it established obligations of the states towards other states and not subjective rights of the individual persons under international law. However, the treaties were "still of historical significance as unprecedented limitations on national sovereignty under international law."[69]

[64] League of Nations, *Covenant of the League of Nations*, April 28, 1919.

[65] André Mandelstam, *La Protection Internationale des Droits de l'Homme* (The Hague: Academie de droit international de La Haye, Recueil des cours, 1931), 133 ff.; Jan Herman Burgers, "The Road to San Francisco: The Revival of the Human Rights Idea in the Twentieth Century," *Human Rights Quarterly* 14, no. 4 (1992): 447, 449.

[66] Woodrow Wilson commented that this "was only because the League could not begin by arranging all the affairs of mankind," not because of any disagreement with the cause, cf. David Hunter Miller, *The Drafting of the Covenant*, Vol. 2 (New York: G.P. Putnam's Sons, 1928), 362, referring to such basic demands as universal women's suffrage or the abolition of trafficking with women and children, presented by the International Council of Women and the Suffragist Conference of the Allied Countries and the United States.

[67] Clauses were included in the peace treaties with Austria, Bulgaria, Hungary and Turkey; special treaties were concluded with Czechoslovakia, Greece, Poland, Rumania and Yugoslavia; declarations were made by Albania, Estonia, Finland, Latvia and Lithuania as a condition for their admission to the League of Nations; bilateral treaties were concluded between Poland and Germany and between Lithuania and Germany; cf. Burgers, "Road to San Francisco," 449 f.

[68] Burgers, "Road to San Francisco," 450.

[69] Burgers, "Road to San Francisco," 450. On the political meaning of the minority rights system in comparison to later international policies, in particular population transferal, Mazower, *No Enchanted Palace*, 104 ff.

The substance of the human rights idea was influential in other areas, too. The Constitution of the International Labour Organization (ILO), created at the Paris Peace Conference, is a good example, as it established a framework for the protection of workers inspired by the idea of their human rights.[70]

The efforts of legal scholars from a range of backgrounds to develop the idea of the international protection of human rights form an important chapter in these rights' history. These scholars' concrete reflections and proposals tried to flesh out the possible makeup of such an international order of human rights. The prominent players included the cofounder of the American Institute of International Law and later judge of the International Court of Justice, Alejandro Álvarez of Chile, who as early as 1917 presented a list of individual liberties that ought to be protected for everybody on the territory of any state.[71] Among the other major actors were A. N. Mandelstam, a Russian émigré who moved to Paris after the Bolshevik Revolution, and A. F. Frangulis, a Greek likewise living in Paris because of his opposition to the rule of Venizelos in Greece. Both were involved in the International Diplomatic Academy set up by Frangulis and Álvarez among others, and in this context they played a central role in formulating a 1928 resolution generalizing the rights provided for by the minority system and thus guaranteeing life, liberty and equality before the law and protecting against discrimination on the grounds of race, language and religion.[72] Mandelstam had drafted a text on human rights for the *Institut de Droit International*, which led to the *Declaration of the International Rights of Man* of October 12, 1929, which contained rights of every individual residing in the territory of a state and rights of the nationals of a state. It explicitly stated that the rights guaranteed in national constitutions needed to be extended to everyone and guaranteed by every state.[73] This declaration was endorsed by various associations concerned with human rights and complemented with further and alternative demands.[74] Its aim was to define on the international level a set of rights

70 Cf. Art. 1 in conjunction with the Preamble, International Labour Organization (ILO), *Constitution of the International Labour Organization (ILO)*, April 1, 1919, though not referring explicitly to human rights.

71 As part of a larger project on the future principles of international law, cf. Burgers, "Road to San Francisco," 451.

72 Mandelstam, *La Protection*, 218; Burgers, "Road to San Francisco," 452.

73 As an inspiration, the Fourteenth Amendment to the US Constitution is quoted. Cf. for the text Mandelstam, *La Protection*, 205 f.; George A. Finch, "The International Rights of Man," *The American Journal of International Law* 35, no. 4 (1941): 662 f.; Burgers, "Road to San Francisco," 452. An earlier editorial comment had underlined that it "repudiates the classic doctrine that states alone are subjects of international law," "Draft Convention on Rights and Duties of Neutral States in Naval and Aerial War," *The American Journal of International Law* 33 (1939): 182.

74 Burgers, "Road to San Francisco," 453 f. For an interesting list, drafted by the *Ligue des droits de l'homme* with some influence on the French postwar discussion and *Universal Declaration*, cf. "1936: The Complement to the Declaration of the Rights of Man and of the Citizen by the French League of Human Rights," www.ldh-france.org/1936-COMPLEMENT-DE-LA-LDH-A-LA, *Ligue des droits de l'Homme*, accessed August 13, 2021. It underlines the equality of rights

that states had to guarantee to all human beings residing on their territory and subject to their jurisdiction. This was nothing less than – in a nutshell – the core of the international human rights protection of the post-1945 period.[75]

Comparative studies about human rights protection in the constitutions of various countries[76] formed an important part of these efforts to flesh out the possible content of human rights. These studies were the forerunners of the background research preparatory to the drafting of the *Universal Declaration*. Note that this technique yet again illustrates the percolation of human rights from the national to the international level, which makes it pointless to study the development of the one without the other. This method was put to use on many occasions in the decades to come, as we will see.

These efforts were not entirely theoretical. In 1933, Frangulis, then a delegate of Haiti, introduced a draft resolution to the Assembly of the League of Nations that was identical to the resolution of the Diplomatic Academy of 1928. Its aim was not only to generalize the minority rights protection system, but also to establish a genuine protection of human rights by international law. This initiative was unsuccessful, however. The apparent reasons for its failure are recurrent themes along the path to the international protection of human rights: The guarantee of universal human rights evidently challenged colonial practices as well as racial segregation in the USA. Furthermore, the German Reich was still a member of the League at this point and attempts to appease it continued.[77]

Later endeavors met with equally little success, indicating that the international protection of human rights was not (yet) a matter of sufficient public concern.[78] However, by now the idea had taken on a quite concrete shape and continued to linger in the *ante-chambres* of history until its moment finally came.

and the prohibition of discrimination, Art. 1, contains a right to an amount of work that leaves some time for leisure, similarly to Art. 24 *Universal Declaration of Human Rights*, and derives from human rights an imperative against colonization, Art. 10, referring to the dignity of the human person (*dignité personelle*) as a yardstick for international collaboration. It underlines the familiar point that human rights have to be protected nationally and internationally, Art. 1.

75 Mandelstam's arguments are interesting examples of the blind spots and ambiguities of historical conceptions of the human rights idea. Cf. for instance his view that the colonialism of his time is reconcilable with human rights, Mandelstam, *La Protection*, 170, while at the same time defending the general applicability of human rights in all states, criticizing the idea of backward states ("*civilisation arrière*") and discussing the danger of a new tyranny of great powers that might abuse the idea of human rights for their political purposes, ibid. 197 ff., 215 ff. Cf. for comments Helmut Philipp Aust, "From Diplomat to Academic Activist: André Mandelstam and the History of Human Rights," *The European Journal of International Law* 25 (2015): 1105–21.

76 Cf. the collection by Alphonse Aulard and Boris Mirkine-Guetzévitch, *Les déclarations des droits de l'homme: Textes constitutionnels concernant les droits de l'homme et les garanties des libertés individuelles dans tous les pays* (Paris: Payot, 1929).

77 Burgers, "Road to San Francisco," 458.

78 Burgers, "Road to San Francisco," 459.

In the same year of Frangulis' failed attempt at the League of Nations, the International Union of the Associations for the League of Nations passed a resolution endorsing the idea of the generalization of the protection of human rights, to be enforced, if needed, by humanitarian intervention.[79]

A range of important voices continued to contribute to the idea's promotion. One of the best known of these was H. G. Wells, who, with his writings and other activities, endorsed the idea of an international declaration of rights as a statement of the "broad principles on which our public and social life is based."[80] The final product of these efforts, his treatise *The Rights of Man*, was published in 1940 and gained international traction,[81] succeeding in attracting the attention of President Roosevelt.[82]

2.4.2 *Constructing the Postwar World*

Roosevelt's famous State of the Union address on January 6, 1941, was crucial in bringing human rights back to the center of international politics. In this address, he proclaimed the "supremacy of human rights everywhere," spelled out in the four freedoms – freedom of speech and expression, freedom of worship, freedom from want and freedom from fear – summing up and drawing on several decades of debate on the topic.[83]

The *Atlantic Charter* of the USA and UK of August 14, 1941, referred to the protection of certain rights, including self-government, improved labor standards, economic advancement, social security and freedom from want and fear. These statements were echoed by the *Declaration by United Nations* of January 1, 1942, underlining that "complete victory over their enemies is essential to defend life, liberty, independence and religious freedom, and to preserve human rights and justice in their own lands as well as in other lands."

79 Burgers, "Road to San Francisco," 454.

80 Herbert George Wells, "War Aims: The Rights of Man," *The Times*, October 25, 1939, The Times Digital Archive, link.gale.com/apps/doc/CS100873561/GDCS?u=unizur&sid=bookmark-GDCS&xid=31252630.

81 Herbert George Wells, *The Rights of Man; or, What Are We Fighting For?* (Harmondsworth: Penguin Books, 1940), explicitly evoking the tradition of bills of rights since the *Magna Carta*, ibid. 29. It is useful to compare Wells' bill of rights with the *Universal Declaration* to appreciate the latter's normative qualities. Cf. also Burgers, "Road to San Francisco," 464.

82 Burgers, "Road to San Francisco," 470.

83 Samuel L. Rosenmann, ed., *The Public Papers and Addresses of Franklin D. Roosevelt: Vol. IX: War and Aid to Democracies 1940* (New York: Harper & Brothers, 1950), 672. Roosevelt may have been motivated by the desire to mobilize public opinion in the USA in favor of American involvement in the war by convincing the public of a worthy cause, Burgers, "Road to San Francisco," 469. He knew Wells and was an early member of the Diplomatic Academy. It is thus conceivable that he was acquainted with the resolution of 1928, Burgers, "Road to San Francisco," 470 n. 55. Cf. ibid. on similar formulations used by Frangulis and Roosevelt.

It is, however, not the case that the international protection of human rights from this point onwards became a cornerstone of the concrete political activities of the US Government and the UK that aimed at defining the architecture of the new world order that would emerge after the defeat of the German Reich and the Axis powers.[84] While an international bill of rights played a role in some concrete activities within the US State Department concerning the postwar international order, these did not determine policy in any crucial respects.[85] There was a significant discrepancy between Roosevelt's famous stance and the small print (and sometimes large print) of the USA's foreign policy up to the founding of the UN, including, together with the other Great Powers, opposition to the incorporation of meaningful provisions on human rights in the Dumbarton Oaks proposals on the new world order.[86] Importantly, human rights continued to be violated domestically through the mechanisms of racial segregation, as powerful voices such as W. E. B. Du Bois had underlined for many years.[87] The UK policy was guided by the determination not to apply human rights to the colonies.[88] This set the stage – together with the repressive policies and lethal terror of the Stalinist system – for the problem of double standards in the human rights policies of the major powers, of a "divided world" of human rights protection[89] and the instrumentalization of human rights for political purposes that has haunted the human rights project ever since.

An increasing number of wartime activities by civil society actors were inspired by the idea that one element of the order at stake was human rights. Given the war, these activities to a large extent took place in the USA.[90] Some of the associations involved produced recommendations that closely prefigured the postwar development, including the subsidiarity of international human rights, implying the necessity of human rights protection and enforcement mechanisms on the state level.[91]

[84] Cf. Mark Mazower, "The Strange Triumph of Human Rights 1933 – 1950," *The Historic Journal* 47, no. 2 (2004): 379–398.

[85] Burgers, "Road to San Francisco," 472.

[86] Cf. Lauren, *Evolution*, 160.

[87] Cf. Du Bois, *The Soul of Black Folk*, 13, 32, 39 ff., 45.

[88] Cf. Fabian Klose, *Human Rights in the Shadow of Colonial Violence* (Philadelphia: University of Pennsylvania Press, 2013), 12 on Churchill's will not to apply the Atlantic Charter to the colonies. This was not a secret, as the statement of the African National Congress illustrates, African National Congress, *Africans' Claims in South Africa*, December 16, 1943, Congress Series No. II.

[89] Cf. Klose, *Human Rights*, 5, 16 ff., 39; Mazower, "The Strange Triumph of Human Rights," 397: "So far as the Superpowers were concerned, human rights were strictly for export."

[90] Burgers, "Road to San Francisco," 471 ff.

[91] Cf. e.g. the activities of the American League of Nations Association, which included work on human rights, cf. Quincy Wright, "Human Rights and the World Order," in Commission to Study the Organization of Peace, *Third Report* (1943); Commission to Study the Organization of Peace, *International Safeguard of Human Rights* (1944), 552–75, 574, proposing "that measures be taken to safeguard throughout the world by (1) convening without delay a United Nations Conference on Human Rights to examine the problem, (2) promulgating as a result of this conference an international bill of rights, (3) establishing at the conference a

Major intellectual contributions were published by J. Maritain[92] and H. Lauterpacht[93] among others. R. Lemkin had meanwhile started his campaign for an international instrument against genocide.[94] The ILO passed its *Declaration of Philadelphia* on May 10, 1944, which was annexed to the ILO Constitution in 1946, affirming that "all human beings, irrespective of race, creed or sex, have the right to pursue both their material well-being and their spiritual development in conditions of freedom and dignity, of economic security and equal opportunity," and that "the attainment of the conditions in which this shall be possible must constitute the central aim of national and international policy."

The American Law Institute appointed a committee of twenty-five experts "representing principal cultures of the world" that carried out substantial work on the content of an international bill of rights, including a survey of the protection of human rights in national constitutions and a "statement of essential human rights" comprising liberal and substantial social rights because "Hitler's extermination of

permanent United Nations Commission on Human Rights for the purpose of further developing the standards of human rights and the methods for their protection, (4) seeking the incorporation of major civil rights in national constitutions and promoting effective means of enforcement in each nation, (5) recognizing the right of individuals or groups, under prescribed limitations, to petition the Human Rights Commission, after exhausting local remedies, in order to call attention to violations."

92 Jacques Maritain, *Les Droits de l'Homme et la Loi Naturelle* (New York: Édition de la Maison Française, 1942), 84 ff. The rights he discusses are in line with other rights catalogues of this time and include substantial social rights, in particular for workers, ibid. 93 ff., 114 ff. He criticizes a secular justification of human rights as insufficient, however, ibid. 86 ff., 101 ff. Unlike the French *Déclaration* of 1789, the American rights conception is close to the "*caractère originellement chrétien des droits humains*," he argues, ibid. 102, without making quite clear why.

93 Hersch Lauterpacht gave a lecture in Cambridge in 1943 expounding a differentiated draft of an international bill of rights. Cf. Lauterpacht, *International Bill*, which is of substantial interest for the history of the codification of fundamental rights as one of the "transformative legal works of the twentieth century," Phillippe Sands, "Introduction," in Hersch Lauterpacht, *An International Bill of the Rights of Man* (Oxford: Oxford University Press, 2013), vii. The preamble highlights that the protection of human rights formed a central aim of the war, Lauterpacht, *International Bill*, 69. He underlines the importance of a substantial normative background theory of rights to defend the individual against tyranny and abuse, ibid. 3, 52. This is the core heritage of the tradition of Natural Law and Natural Rights, purged of their reactionary interpretation and "clericalism," ibid. 35 ff., 120. International law is necessary for the protection of human rights, ibid. 27 ff., 50; Hersch Lauterpacht, *International Law and Human Rights* (London: Stevens & Sons, 1950), 79, 313 ff. Lauterpacht's draft, like other such examples, exemplifies the need to criticize and improve any such concretization of rights, cf. for instance the lack of a prohibition of the discrimination of women or his struggle with the question: "How far can the Bill of Rights leave full scope to 'the law of the State' and permit disenfranchisement on account of colour, race, and religion?" His answer was that the egalitarian principles of human rights needed time to overcome the political obstacles blocking the way to their realization.

94 Raphael Lemkin, *Axis Rule in Occupied Europe: Laws of Occupation, Analysis of Government, Proposals for Redress (Foundations of the Laws of War)* (Clark, NJ: Lawbook Exchange Ltd, 2008); Mazower, *No Enchanted Palace*, 124 ff.

peoples has demonstrated to all who can read that a world society with so much power as ours must be organized to serve the dignity and welfare of the individual being or it will destroy itself."[95] It provided key material for the *Universal Declaration*.[96] This is yet another example confirming that these national constitutional rights are not alien to international human rights, but rather are their fertile breeding ground.

All of this notwithstanding, the reluctance to make human rights a real policy issue persisted. The proposals put forward by the USA, the UK, the Soviet Union and China at the conference of Dumbarton Oaks in 1944 referred ultimately only to a new world organization to "promote respect for human rights and fundamental freedoms" in the context of "arrangements for international economic and social cooperation," but not in any more ambitious sense.[97] A US proposal for a mainly rhetorical statement of principle about respecting human rights found no support by the UK and the USSR.[98] China's idea to include a provision on the equality of all races in the Charter (not a minor point for the protection of human rights) was opposed by the USA, the UK and the Soviet Union.[99]

The Charter of the United Nations, signed at the United Nations Conference on International Organization held in San Francisco in 1945, marked a more substantial step forward. This was due not to the policy aims of the great powers, which continued to be in line with the restrictive Dumbarton Oaks proposals, but to the substantial influence of other states and of nongovernmental organizations (NGOs) on the outcome.[100] The Latin American states had decisively influenced the outcome of a conference already held from February 21 to March 8, 1945, in Chapultepec Castle, Mexico. The Chapultepec Conference passed a resolution calling for an international declaration of human rights as well as instruments to implement these rights. It instructed the Inter-American Juridical Committee to prepare such a draft declaration.[101] The Latin American states were active forces for the promotion of human rights at the San Francisco Conference, forming the largest regional group of states, many at that time with democratic political

95 "Statement of Essential Human Rights," drafted by a Committee representing principal cultures of the world, appointed by the American Law Institute, distributed by Americans United for World Organizations 1945, accessed August 13, 2021, www.ali.org/media/filer_public/fc/ea/fcea8b14-8d49-4263-8cd9-e0133751ff64/statement-of-essential-human-rights.pdf.

96 John P. Humphrey, *Human Rights & the United Nations: A Great Adventure* (New York: Transnational Publishers, 1984), 32.

97 United Nations, *The United Nations Dumbarton Oaks Proposals for a General International Organization*, October 9, 1944, ch. IX, Section A 1.

98 Lauren, *Evolution*, 161 f.

99 Lauren, *Evolution*, 161.

100 Lauren, *Evolution*, 165 ff.

101 Lauren, *Evolution*, 168 ff.; Burgers, "Road to San Francisco," 475; Kathryn Sikkink, *Evidence for Hope: Making Human Rights Work in the 21st Century* (Princeton, NJ: Princeton University Press, 2017), 68 f.

systems.[102] Other smaller countries played a significant role, too, including Lebanon and the Philippines.[103]

NGOs also contributed to the process.[104] Forty-two NGOs were invited to join the US delegation as consultants, with a view to securing public support for the new world organization.[105] The US Senate had not ratified the Covenant of the League of Nations, and one of the aims for the UN Charter in the making was to ensure that this did not happen again. The NGOs promoting human rights were politically and culturally heterogeneous and represented voices from various religious perspectives.[106] Their representatives had a decisive influence on the US delegation, which in turn convinced the delegations of the UK, the USSR and China to include references to human rights in the Charter[107] – albeit to an admittedly limited degree. Importantly, human rights became part of the purpose of the UN, which was mandated to establish a commission for human rights under the Economic and Social Council. The Charter was certainly no glorious dawn of the age of human rights, not least because it accommodated the colonial aspirations of Britain, France, Portugal, Spain, the Netherlands, Belgium and the USA. But some seeds were sown that had the potential to grow into something different. In particular, the Charter's provisions provided tools for the next major step in the development of human rights, namely the drafting of the *Universal Declaration*, proclaimed by the UN General Assembly in Paris on December 10, 1948.[108]

It should be noted that the demands for the more forthright language used by the Charter were articulated not least by the Global South.[109] This does not come as a surprise, because one major driving force of the history of human rights was the prohibition of racial discrimination and decolonization, which had a decisive influence on the establishment of the human rights regime as we know it, as will be discussed in more detail below.

[102] Morsink, *Origins*, 130 ff.; Paolo G. Carozza, "From Conquest to Constitution, Retrieving a Latin American Tradition of the Idea of Human Rights," *Human Rights Quarterly* 25, no. 2 (2003): 284; Sikkink, *Evidence*, 70.

[103] Lauren, *Evolution*, 178 ff.

[104] Lauren, *Evolution*, 178 ff.

[105] Lauren, *Evolution*, 179.

[106] The organizations included the Committee on Religious Liberty, created in 1943 by the Federal Council of Churches, the American Jewish Congress and the Synagogue Council of America. Important voices of the human rights movement included Judge Proskauer of the American Jewish Committee, Frederick Nolde of the Joint Committee on Religious Liberty and James Shotwell, cf. Lauren, *Evolution*, 171; Burgers, "Road to San Francisco," 476.

[107] Lauren, *Evolution*, 182; Burgers, "Road to San Francisco," 476; Sikkink, *Evidence*, 70.

[108] The Charter of the United Nations refers to human rights in United Nations, *Charter of the United Nations* (UN Charter), 1 UNTS 1 (XVI), October 24, 1945, preamble, Art. 1, Art. 13, Art. 55, Art. 56, Art. 62, Art. 68, Art. 76 lit. c.

[109] Sikkink, *Evidence*, 72 f.; Klose, *Human Rights*, 36: Fifth Pan-American Congress, October 1945, endorsing the demand for human rights and declaring the readiness to resort to resistance by force.

The question of whether human rights could limit sovereignty (as secured by Art. 2 Sec. 7 UN Charter) cast the universal aspirations of some actors into sharp relief. Art. 2 Sec. 7 UN Charter was widely held as safeguard against any intervention in the internal affairs of states, including those based on the protection of human rights. A fundamental problem lurks here that has continued to trouble the international human rights systems ever since: The protection of human rights was created by those agents – the states – that human rights are designed to protect against. States have therefore a strong incentive to make any international human rights obligation as little burdensome as possible. The tension between international human rights protection and sovereignty was not merely a theoretical issue. For instance, on the initiative of India, the UN General Assembly had already voted in 1946 that the UN had the competence and the duty to investigate the discriminatory treatment of Indians in South Africa.[110]

2.4.3 *Pushing the Agenda from the Periphery of Power*

One major step in the development of the international protection of human rights was the drafting and passing of the *American Declaration of the Rights and Duties of Man*. The Inter-American Juridical Committee worked out a complete draft by December 31, 1947. This draft was amended, in particular with regard to the duties of human beings, and adopted at the Ninth International Conference of American States in Bogotá, Colombia, in April 1948 as the first international general human rights instrument. There were discussions about institutions of enforcement, most importantly an Inter-American Court of Human Rights.[111] The *Declaration*'s content was shaped by different political forces. Social democratic, liberal and Catholic traditions contributed to the set of rights protected, which encompassed classic liberal rights, social and economic rights and – a distinguishing feature – a number of concrete duties.[112] Some voices called for the *Declaration* to be binding and included in the Charter of the Organization of American States, demanding an effective system of enforcement, while other voices opposed this. One reason for this opposition was authoritarian regimes' fear of being bound by human rights.[113] On the other hand, the fear of intervention, which loomed large given Latin America's experiences with US policy, motivated some actors to endorse a declaration of human rights, arguing that it would prevent such intervention as it would

110 Cf. n. 22.

111 Sikkink, *Evidence*, 99.

112 On the background, Carozza, "Conquest to Constitution," 281, arguing for a specific Latin American tradition of human rights, growing out of Las Casas' neo-Thomism, Latin America's nineteenth-century constitutional thinking and the Mexican constitution of 1917, blending individual rights, freedom and social concern in a form of "social liberalism," ibid. 311. Sikkink, *Evidence*, 75.

113 Sikkink, *Evidence*, 76.

protect the rights of persons.[114] Others feared that such a declaration on the contrary would increase the danger of intervention on the grounds (or pretense) of rights protection.[115] These arguments illustrate the complex matrix of reasoning – principles, political expediency and tactics, interests in maintaining or limiting power, different political visions, contextual factors of power relations – that fed into the making of a particular human rights instrument, shaping the actions of those involved in this process, with opposing positions sometimes pursued by different governments of the very same country.[116] The internal divisions underlying these policy changes became vividly clear in Bogotá itself – following the assassination of the politician J. Gaitán, violence broke out, starting one of the civil wars that tormented the country for decades.

The *American Declaration* was of considerable significance for the drafting of the *Universal Declaration*, as were the submissions of Latin American countries to the UN Commission on Human Rights, not the least in the field of social and economic rights, drawn from their particular political tradition.[117] The idea of duties entered into the text of the *Universal Declaration*, Art. 29, only in limited form. We should avoid drawing rash conclusions about the meaning of this, however, such as equating the existence of duties with more community-oriented outlooks and a lack of them with individualism. The question of whether or not to include duties in a rights catalogue is not easy to answer. Duties are the necessary correlative of claims – a rights catalogue thus implies very many duties, both of states and, given a doctrine of positive obligations and a (direct or indirect) horizontal effect, of private actors. Duties can not only serve benign community-oriented purposes, but also curtail legitimate liberty. Thus, one may well be very sympathetic to the importance of community and still opt against a strong language of duties in legal documents.

One controversial topic of international human rights in the making regarded women's rights. These rights were promoted by actors from quite different backgrounds. Influential voices came from the Global South in this field, too, pushing for the inclusion of normative content concerning the equality of women in Art. 8 of the UN Charter on the equal eligibility of men and women to participate in UN organs and in the *Universal Declaration*.[118] They sometimes faced resistance even

[114] Sikkink, *Evidence*, 76.

[115] Sikkink, *Evidence*, 76.

[116] Cf. the politics of Mexico during the drafting process of the *American Declaration*, Sikkink, *Evidence*, 76.

[117] Morsink, *Origins*, 131: "Humphrey took much of the wording and almost all of the ideas for social, economic, and cultural rights of his first draft from the tradition of Latin American socialism by way of the bills submitted by Panama (ALI) and Chile (Inter)."; cf. for a more differentiated interpretation, including traditions of Catholic social teaching, Carozza, "Conquest to Constitution," 303; Sikkink, *Evidence*, 77.

[118] Morsink, *Origins*, 116 ff.; Sikkink, *Evidence*, 79 ff. Katherine M. Marino, *Feminism for the Americas: The Making of an International Human Rights Movement* (Chapel Hill: University of North Carolina Press, 2019), 198 ff.; Torild Skard, "Getting Our History Right: How Were the

from women delegates and their advisors from countries such as the USA, the UK and Canada, including comments that such efforts were "unlady-like."[119] One telling episode that took place during the drafting of the *Universal Declaration* was the initiative to use language clearly including women in the preamble and Art. 1 *Universal Declaration*. The Dominican Republic filed a proposal to make the reference to equal rights of men and women in the preamble explicit.[120] Eleanor Roosevelt did not consider this amendment necessary because "the time had come to take for granted that such expressions as 'everyone', 'all persons' and 'mankind' referred to both men and women."[121] However, the Indian delegate, Lakshimi Menon, together with the female delegate of the Dominican Republic, Minerva Bernardino, argued forcefully for this clarification because the reference to "everyone" or similar expressions may be misconstrued as not creating equal rights for men and women, drawing from constitutional experience such as the interpretation of the Fourteenth Amendment to the US Constitution allowing racial segregation.[122] The initiative was ultimately successful – against the vote of China and the USA – in securing a reference in the preamble of the *Universal Declaration* to the "equal rights of men and women."[123] The issue also arose concerning the language of Art. 1 *Universal Declaration*. Among others, Hansa Mehta from India argued for a language that explicitly includes women in human rights protection to avoid any misunderstanding. This initiative was only partly successful: Art. 1 refers to "all human beings."[124]

One issue of decisive importance for the history of human rights was the question of the inclusion of people living in colonies in human rights protection. Attempts to do so explicitly were forcefully opposed by colonial powers such as Britain and France, albeit with only limited success, given the universalist language of the introductory paragraph and Art. 2 Sec. 2 of the *Universal Declaration*.[125]

Equal Rights of Women and Men Included in the Charter of the United Nations?" *Forum for Developmental Studies* 35, no. 1 (2008): 37 ff.

[119] Marino, *Feminism for the Americas* (comment by Virginia Gildersleeve, who was, however, herself a women rights' activist), 203; Sikkink, *Evidence*, 81; Skard, "Getting Our History Right," 37 ff.

[120] Cf. Schabas, *The Universal Declaration*, 2073 (A/C.3/217).

[121] Cf. Schabas, *The Universal Declaration*, 2895 (A/C.3/SR.165).

[122] Cf. Schabas, *The Universal Declaration*, 2895 f. (A/C.3/SR.165) (Menon); Schabas, *The Universal Declaration*, 2903 (A/C.3/SR.166). Menon was not explicitly mentioning but clearly referring to the "separate but equal" doctrine of the US Supreme Court, Plessy v Ferguson, 163 U.S. 537 (1896).

[123] Schabas, *The Universal Declaration*, 2921 f (A/C.3/SR.167).

[124] Cf. Schabas, *The Universal Declaration*, 1255 (E/CN.4/SR.34). On the debate, Morsink, *Origins*, 118 ff. In the long run, the final formulation ("all human beings") may, in an ironic twist, have turned out to be even more inclusive than the reference to "men and women," at least from current perspectives of critical gender theory. This is an example that the evaluation of certain legal formulations is dependent on a (changing) political context.

[125] Cf. Morsink, *Origins*, 96 ff.; Klose, *Human Rights*, 39; Sikkink, *Evidence*, 79.

Another controversial theme that continues to be significant is the system of enforcement – examples of the debates in the 1920s and 1930s and during the drafting of the *Universal Declaration* have already been mentioned. Various attempts to strengthen the system were made – for example, by Charles Malik and Hansa Mehta.[126] Australia even proposed an International Court of Human Rights with the competence to make judgments binding on states.[127] Successful attempts of Mexico to promote the right to effective remedy, which became Art. 8 *Universal Declaration*, belong in this context, too.[128]

The experience of the "horrors of war and totalitarianism," as the Chilean delegate, Santa Cruz, put it, of the Holocaust and other forms of mass murder were of foundational importance for the drafting of the *Universal Declaration*. The very recent past had shown very clearly what a world without respect for human rights looked like, and the drafters lost no opportunity to draw on what they had seen.[129]

[126] Cf. for example Charles Malik's remarks in Schabas, *The Universal Declaration*, 163 (E/CN.4/SR.2). For Mehta's repeated interventions, e.g. Schabas, *The Universal Declaration*, 162 (E/CN.4/SR.2); Schabas, *The Universal Declaration*, 204, 207 (E/CN.4/SR.15); Schabas, *The Universal Declaration*, 210 (E/CN.4/SR.16). Cf. also the draft Resolution of India, including implementation of human rights obligations by the Security Council, Schabas, *The Universal Declaration*, 175 f. (E/CN.4/11). Malik and Mehta among others in 1947 attempted to allow the Human Rights Commission to study individual petitions submitted to the Human Rights Commission. Such and other proposals met with the resistance of Western states and the Soviet Union, leading to ECOSOC Resolution 75 (V), which prevented the Commission from investigating petitions, cf. Roland Burke, *Decolonization and the Evolution of International Human Rights* (Philadelphia: University of Pennsylvania Press, 2010), 61 ff. Cf. also Lauren, *Evolution*, 217; Sikkink, *Evidence*, 79. The lack of "true and enforceable" obligations was the main reason for Lauterpacht's critique of the *Universal Declaration* and his doubts about its moral authority: "That authority is a function of the degree to which states commit themselves to an effective recognition of these rights guaranteed by a will and an agency other than and superior to their own. The moral influence of ideas flows from the sincerity of those who proclaim them," Lauterpacht, *International Law*, 419.

[127] Schabas, *The Universal Declaration*, 203 (E/CN.4/15); Schabas, *The Universal Declaration*, 2343 (A/C.3/SR.112).

[128] Schabas, *The Universal Declaration*, 2340 (A/C.3/309); Carozza, *Conquest to Constitution*, 287, drawing, for instance, from the Latin American institution of *amparo*; Sikkink, *Evidence*, 78 f.

[129] There were many references to the recent past in the drafting process, cf. e.g. René Cassin: Schabas, *The Universal Declaration*, 801 (E/CN.4/AC.1/SR.8): "He explained that his text alluded to the three fundamental questions of liberty, equality, and fraternity because, during the war, these great fundamental principles of mankind had been forgotten." Vladimir Koretsky: Schabas, *The Universal Declaration*, 854 (E/CN.4/AC.1/SR.13): referring to the "Fascist destruction of feeble-minded people"; Santa Cruz (Chile): Schabas, *The Universal Declaration*, 1667 (E/CN.4/SR.50): referring to the "horrors of war and totalitarianism"; Cassin: Schabas, *The Universal Declaration*, 1670 (E/CN.4/SR.50), referring to the "inherent equality of human beings, a concept which had recently been attacked by Hitler and his ideological disciples." On the untenable thesis, e.g. Moyn, *The Last Utopia*, that the Holocaust was irrelevant for the drafting of the *Universal Declaration*, Johannes Morsink, *The Universal Declaration of Human Rights and the Holocaust: An Endangered Connection* (Washington, DC: Georgetown University Press, 2019).

2.4.4 *From the* Universal Declaration *to the Differentiated International Bill of Human Rights*

2.4.4.1 Human Rights Turned into Constitutional Law

The *Universal Declaration* formed an important source of inspiration for constitutional law after World War II. One example that became particularly influential is Germany's *Basic Law*. Its catalogue of fundamental rights, many of them designed as human rights in the narrow sense of rights of all humans irrespective of nationality, is very much inspired by the *Universal Declaration*. The fundamental rights system of the *Basic Law* influenced other constitutional orders that became influential in their own right. The Constitution of South Africa is a prime example. After 1989, a great number of Central and Eastern European states transformed into constitutional orders protecting fundamental rights. As outlined above, effecting exactly this protection on the level of states was an essential aim of the *Universal Declaration*. The shift towards constitutionalism of the last decades thus forms a crucial element of the history of human rights after 1948. Nothing about this development is irreversible, of course, as recent attacks on constitutional orders based on liberal rights vividly illustrate.

2.4.4.2 Human Rights Turned into International Law

Once the *Universal Declaration of Human Rights* had been passed, a further element on the international human rights agenda was to turn the rights declared into international law and create a system of meaningful implementation. The process of achieving these ends following the adoption of the *Universal Declaration* proved as difficult as might be expected, given this extraordinary legal project's scope and quality. Today, we have covenants of universal application covering a broad range of rights, regional covenants of this kind and specialized conventions dealing with specific issues or groups of persons. There is neither a uniform system of state obligations nor a uniform system of human rights implementation. This situation very much mirrors the convoluted, politically unlikely process of the creation of international human rights law.

A first step was already taken in 1948 with the adoption of the Genocide Convention, one of the archetypical pieces of international human rights law.[130] The Geneva Convention on Refugees is another issue-specific piece of international law serving the protection of a particularly vulnerable group of people.[131]

[130] UN General Assembly, *Convention on the Prevention and Punishment of the Crime of Genocide* (CPPCG), UNTS 78 (277), December 9, 1948. For some comments on the relation of the Genocide convention and the UN minority policy, in particular the idea of population transferal as a solution to minority problems, Mazower, *No Enchanted Palace*, 104 ff.

[131] UN General Assembly, *Convention Relating to the Status of Refugees*, UNTS 189 (137), July 28, 1951.

On the regional level, the 1950 ECHR set out a catalogue of human rights that over the decades has become the core of the arguably most advanced and effective system of the international protection of human rights existing to date. Its creation had to overcome considerable political obstacles, not least in the context of decolonization:[132] "The truth was that a majority in the Council of Europe were, whatever their pretensions in public, unenthusiastic at the prospect of international European human rights protection."[133] Not least because of its effectiveness that has tangible and uncomfortable consequences for states, the ECHR continues to be an object of various forms of critique.[134] The Inter-American system of protection developed more slowly and in many ways under more difficult circumstances, given the number of authoritarian regimes it had to accommodate. By now, however, it has achieved a standard of protection comparable to that of the European system and has contributed many innovations to the understanding of international human rights.

The first international treaty of universal application was the 1965 *Convention on the Elimination of All Forms of Racial Discrimination* (ICERD),[135] which catalyzed the final adoption in 1966 of the two major human rights covenants on civil and political rights (ICCPR)[136] and social, economic and cultural rights (ICESCR),[137] although these only entered into force in 1976. Recent decades have witnessed the development of an increasingly differentiated system of international human rights protection. Its landmark elements include the *Convention on the Elimination of All Discrimination Against Women* (1979),[138] the *Torture Convention* (1984),[139] the

[132] Including the attempt by France and Britain to take the project of the political agenda, cf. Steven L. B. Jensen, *The Making of International Human Rights: The 1960s, Decolonization, and the Reconstruction of Global Values* (Cambridge: Cambridge University Press, 2017), 39. For a slightly different interpretation, Simpson, *Human Rights*, 667. The ECHR was extended by the UK and France to the territories the international relations of which they are responsible for in 1953 and 1974, respectively.

[133] Simpson, *Human Rights*, 667.

[134] One consequence of this critique is Council of Europe, *Protocol No. 15 Amending the Convention on the Protection of Human Rights and Fundamental Freedoms*, ETS 213, June 24, 2013, entering into force August 1, 2021, "affirming that the High Contracting Parties, in accordance with the principle of subsidiarity, have the primary responsibility to secure the rights and freedoms defined in this Convention and the Protocols thereto, and that in doing so they enjoy a margin of appreciation, subject to the supervisory jurisdiction of the European Court of Human Rights established by this Convention." The protocol intends to diminish worries of Member States about an ever-expanding reach of the European Convention system.

[135] UN General Assembly, *International Convention on the Elimination of All Forms of Racial Discrimination* (ICERD), UNTS 660 (195), December 21, 1965.

[136] UN General Assembly, *International Covenant on Civil and Political Rights* (ICCPR), UNTS 999 (171), December 16, 1966.

[137] UN General Assembly, *International Covenant on Economic, Social and Cultural Rights* (ICESCR), UNTS 993 (3), December 16, 1966.

[138] UN General Assembly, *Convention on the Elimination of All Forms of Discrimination Against Women* (CEDAW), UNTS 1249 (13), December 18, 1979.

[139] UN General Assembly, *Convention Against Torture and Other Cruel, Inhuman or Degrading Treatment or Punishment*, UNTS 1465 (85), December 10, 1984.

Convention on the Rights of the Child (1989)[140] and the *Convention on the Rights of Persons with Disabilities* (2006).[141]

A further element of the international human rights system is international humanitarian law based on the *Geneva Conventions* of 1948 and their additional protocols[142] that intend to protect the fundamental rights of persons in armed conflicts. Yet another pillar is international criminal law, born of the Nuremberg and Tokyo Trials. Following the ad hoc tribunals for Yugoslavia and Ruanda, international criminal law took on tangible form in the *Statute of Rome*[143] and the establishment of the International Criminal Court among other institutions. It should be noted that the ideas of humanitarian and international criminal law are deeply rooted in the history of legal thought.

The law of the EU is another important element of international human rights protection on the regional level that comes with its own new and legally challenging qualities. Fundamental rights – beyond the so-called fundamental freedoms of movement, establishment, services and capital, which are at least partly similar to fundamental rights – were first established pretorian style by the case law of the then European Court of Justice (ECJ) (now Court of Justice of the EU; CJEU) as part of EU law.[144] The Charter of Fundamental Rights, which initially was only declaratory in character, was turned into mandatory primary law by the Treaty of Lisbon.[145] It binds the EU and all Member States implementing EU law.[146] Given the expansion of EU law in recent years, its scope of application encompasses significant areas of law. One major issue encountered when the Charter was being drafted was the question of which rights under EU law were to be understood as human rights in the

140 UN General Assembly, *Convention on the Rights of the Child*, UNTS 1577 (3), November 20, 1989.

141 UN General Assembly, *Convention on the Rights of Persons with Disabilities*, A/RES/61/106, December 13, 2006.

142 International Committee of the Red Cross (ICRC), *Geneva Convention for the Amelioration of the Condition of the Wounded and Sick in Armed Forces in the Field (First Geneva Convention)*, UNTS 75 (31), August 12, 1949; ICRC, *Geneva Convention for the Amelioration of the Condition of Wounded, Sick and Shipwrecked Members of Armed Forces at Sea (Second Geneva Convention)*, UNTS 75 (85), August 12, 1949; ICRC, *Geneva Convention Relative to the Treatment of Prisoners of War (Third Geneva Convention)*, UNTS 75 (135), August 12, 1949; ICRC, *Geneva Convention Relative to the Protection of Civilian Persons in Time of War (Fourth Geneva Convention)*, UNTS 75 (287), August 12, 1949. ICRC, *Protocol Additional to the Geneva Conventions of 12 August 1949, and relating to the Protection of Victims of International Armed Conflicts (Protocol I)*, UNTS 1125 (3), June 8, 1977; ICRC, *Protocol Additional to the Geneva Conventions of 12 August 1949, and relating to the Protection of Victims of Non-International Armed Conflicts (Protocol II)*, UNTS 1125 (609), June 8, 1977; ICRC, *Protocol Additional to the Geneva Conventions of 12 August 1949, and relating to the Adoption of an Additional Distinctive Emblem (Protocol III)*, UNTS 2404 (261), December 8, 2005.

143 UN General Assembly, *Rome Statute of the International Criminal Court* (last amended 2010), UNTS 2187 (3), July 17, 1998.

144 Cf. Matthias Mahlmann, "1789 Renewed? Prospects of the Protection of Human Rights in Europe," *Cardozo Journal of International and Comparative Law* 11, no. 3 (2004): 903–38.

145 Art. 6 para. 1 TEU.

146 Art. 51 para. 1 CFR.

narrow sense.[147] Central rights finally were enacted as such human rights, including human dignity,[148] the right to life and physical integrity,[149] the prohibition of torture,[150] freedom of religion,[151] freedom of speech,[152] habeas corpus rights[153] and the prohibition of discrimination.[154] This means that every person can invoke these rights within the scope of application of EU law. The justificatory reason is clear: Persons are entitled to these rights because they are humans, not because they are citizens of a Member State of the EU. For other rights, citizenship of an EU Member State is a precondition – such as the right to vote for the European Parliament.[155] The fact that such a right is not a human right in the narrow sense is uncontroversial, although the question of whether people permanently residing in a country should enjoy this right is. In other cases, the personal scope of the rights was the object of intense debate and criticism – for example, concerning freedom of movement.

The creation of the abovementioned ICERD in 1965 also spearheaded important steps down another thorny road: the road towards the institutionalization of implementation mechanisms. It did so in concrete terms through a "treaty body" entrusted with this task (the Committee on the Elimination of Racial Discrimination; CERD) and competences including an individual petition mechanism, interstate complaints and reporting duties.[156] This became one model of how to implement human rights.

Ideas on how to enforce human rights on an international level, including some kind of international human rights court, had been pursued and proposed early on in the development of international human rights, as we have seen.[157] Such implementation mechanisms represent an important step in making human rights effective limits to state power. Even mandatory human rights norms remain no more than a harmless nuisance if they are not backed with effective mechanisms of implementation. Ideally, these will take the form of an individual complaint mechanism to an independent court with the power authoritatively to determine the meaning of human rights and the concrete content of state obligations, such as the ECtHR or the Inter-American Court of Human Rights, approaching the quality of implementation on the state level. One major challenge is creating trust in the workings of such international institutions so as to overcome resistance against their creation and maintain their legitimacy once established. This problem – which in principle arises for such institutions on the national level as well – is a particular issue on the international level because many states without democratic, human rights-based systems are involved in appointing these

147 Cf. Mahlmann, "1789 Renewed?"
148 Art. 1 CFR.
149 Art. 2 CFR.
150 Art. 4 CFR.
151 Art. 10 CFR.
152 Art. 11 CFR.
153 Art. 6 CFR.
154 Art. 21 CFR.
155 Art. 39 para. 1 CFR.
156 Art. 8 ff. ICERD.
157 Cf. n. 126.

institutions' decision-makers. If we are committed to the idea of an international rule of law, this problem needs to be taken very seriously indeed.

Unsurprisingly, many efforts were made to prevent the development of such effective implementation mechanisms by powerful actors from both the Global North and the Global South.

The implementation mechanisms that were finally established despite this resistance vary considerably. On the national level, they include a fully-fledged constitutional review with courts having the competence to nullify laws as unconstitutional because they breach fundamental rights (including human rights in the narrow sense).[158] Then there is supranational jurisdiction that is binding for Member States, with a direct effect on and supremacy over national law, as in the case of the EU and the CJEU.[159] There is binding international jurisdiction, albeit not with the effect of nullifying laws or the decisions of public authorities,[160] and there are individual petition procedures[161] and other mechanisms, such as periodic reviews of state actions,[162] special rapporteurs,[163] advisory opinions[164] with sometimes opaque (if any) legal effects and work "to promote and protect the effective enjoyment by all of all civil, cultural, economic, political and social rights" in a variety of extrajudicial ways.[165]

2.5 THE PARAMETERS OF CHANGE

2.5.1 *Policy and Politics*

The growth of this heterogeneous and fragmented human rights system was conditioned by the factors shaping world politics after 1948. These included the Cold

[158] Cf. Bundesverfassungsgerichtsgesetz (German Federal Constitutional Court Act [BVerfGG]), March 12, 1951, § 31.

[159] Art. 19 TEU; European Union, *Consolidated Version of the Treaty on the Functioning of the European Union* (TFEU), C 326/49, October 26, 2012, Art. 256 ff., Art. 260 para. 1. Cf. ECJ (European Court of Justice), NV Algemene Transport- en Expeditie Onderneming van Gend & Loos v Netherlands Inland Revenue Administration, Judgement of February 5, 1963, Case 26-62; ECJ, Flaminio Costa v E.N.E.L., Judgement of July 15, 1964, Case 6/64.

[160] Art. 46 para. 1 ECHR.

[161] Cf. for instance Art. 14 ICERD.

[162] Cf. Art. 9 ICERD.

[163] Cf. "Special Procedures," Human Rights Council, accessed August 16, 2021, www.ohchr.org/EN/HRBodies/HRC/Pages/SpecialProcedures.aspx.

[164] Cf. Art. 64 (1) ACHR; Inter-American Court of Human Rights, *Advisory Opinion OC-23/17, The Environment and Human Rights*, November 15, 2017.

[165] Cf. the mandate of the UN High Commissioner of Human Rights, UN General Assembly, *Forty-eighth session: Agenda item 114 (b)*, A/RES/48/141, January 7, 1994, Nr. 4 (a)–(k). It is important to note that individual rights in international law are not limited to human rights, see Anne Peters, *Beyond Human Rights: The Legal Status of the Individual in International Law*, trans. Jonathan Huston (Cambridge: Cambridge University Press, 2016), concluding: "The individual is a full, i.e., a primary, original, *erga omnes* subject in the international community, a potential bearer of new international rights and duties. The catchphrase for describing this new legal status, including the totality of rights under international law, might be the international individual right" (emphasis in original).

War, in which human rights were used as a tactical weapon to weaken the respective opponent in more than one form, albeit interwoven with other power-political considerations.[166] Major powers in both West and East, North and South were reluctant to commit themselves to a system of human rights, fearing scrutiny of some of their policies or of the regimes they supported – from apartheid South Africa to Pinochet's Chile or the Argentinian Junta.[167] Colonial regimes were still a major element of the world order at the time when this project began, and racism still formed part of major actors' institutional structures.[168] Much depended on policy changes in the governments of states and their shifting attitude towards human rights in general and international human rights in particular. Both policies and attitudes often were influenced by domestic considerations, such as the southern US states' fear that an international human rights regime might challenge their system of racial segregation.[169] Such domestic influences are the reason for the resistance in the US Senate to binding human rights treaties that led Eisenhower and Dulles to decide not to ratify the international human rights instruments prepared at the level of the UN after the *Universal Declaration* as part of a foreign policy that did not support the development of international human rights,[170] the UK's 1966 policy shift following the electoral victory of the Labour Party under Wilson in 1964 that accepted broader human rights obligations of states, not least to bring the UK in line with international developments,[171] or the shift of opinion of Western states about the right to self-determination in the Conference on Security and Co-operation in Europe (CSCE) Helsinki Process.[172] The wide-ranging reforms taking place in many societies from the 1960s onwards as part of liberalization and cultural transformation played another important role for domestic and international human rights issues,[173] although some of the competing political projects, including those

[166] An interesting example of such complex considerations is Willy Brandt's letter to President Kennedy of August 16, 1961, proposing to condemn the building of the Berlin Wall at the UN level as a human rights violation. Brandt at that time was mayor of Berlin and later became the first Social-Democratic Chancellor of the Federal Republic of Germany. The USA did not support this initiative. By not highlighting human rights violations in international fora, it was hoping to shield France from international criticism following a colonial massacre at Bizerte during the Algerian War. The Federal German Government followed the US policy requests after a meeting with Vice President Johnson and General Lucius Clay, cf. Jensen, *Making*, 48, citing Johnson's official archived report.

[167] Cf. on the Nixon–Kissinger policies towards Pinochet and its context, Jensen, *Making*, 244 ff.

[168] Cf. the examples of colonial relativism above.

[169] Burke, *Decolonization*, 68.

[170] Jensen, *Making*, 40 f. on the debate about the Bricker amendment; Burke, *Decolonization*, 127.

[171] Burke, *Decolonization*, 79; Jensen, *Making*, 67, 91 and 252 on the second Wilson premiership.

[172] Jensen, *Making*, 205, 226 f.

[173] Cf. Jensen, *Making*, 3: "The European imperial powers, among the most powerful opponents of universality in the first two decades after the Second World War, went through a political process that reformed their views on human rights as they were increasingly liberated from their own empire in the middle decades of the twentieth century. It transformed their approaches to foreign policy and international human rights diplomacy." Ibid. 3, 104 ff. on the process in which the USA "confronted its own long-lasting and foundational tradition of racism" and its effects on US policy on international human rights.

proposing radical, revolutionary transformation, were skeptical about human rights – for example, on the Marxist–Leninist left. The rise of NGOs like Amnesty International as part of wider political movements that they themselves shaped in turn forms part of this context.

2.5.2 *Regime Change and the Creation of New Political Bodies*

Regime change and – given the increasing number of new states – regime creation were further crucial factors.[174] The process of decolonization increasingly led to authoritarian regimes gaining power in the newly independent states. The First UN Human Rights Conference was attended by eighty-three countries, of which about two-thirds were undemocratic.[175] Twenty-six coups took place in Africa in the 1960s alone, followed by Idi Amin's rise to power in Uganda in 1971, the introduction of martial law in the Philippines by President Marcos in 1972 and the putsch in Afghanistan that put an end to some (albeit severely limited) democratic endeavors in that country, including its 1964 constitution.[176] There were many reasons for the rise of authoritarian regimes as part of the decolonization process. In the context of a history of human rights we should remember, however, that this development was majorly influenced by the actions of world powers from the Global North, from the coup against Mosaddegh and support for the Shah's regime in Iran in 1953 by the USA and the UK, to the 1961 coup against Lumumba in Congo that paved the way for Mobutu's dictatorial rule,[177] to the military action by what was then West Pakistan against what is now Bangladesh in 1971.[178] A wave of authoritarianism swept Latin America, too, in the decades after World War II,[179] including US-backed coups – for instance, in Guatemala in 1954, disposing democratically elected President Arbenz.[180] The USA supported dictators throughout the region – Jiménez in Venezuela, Batista in Cuba, Trujillo in the Dominican Republic, Somoza in Nicaragua, Pinochet in Chile[181] and the military governments in Argentina and Brazil after the coup of 1964[182] – as did other Western states. All of this created a massive human rights toll.[183]

[174] In 1955, twenty-nine states took part in the Bandung Conference; in 1968, forty more states joined this group, Burke, *Decolonization*, 94.

[175] Burke, *Decolonization*, 97.

[176] Burke, *Decolonization*, 129.

[177] Belgium officially apologized for its role in the coup in 2002.

[178] Sikkink, *Evidence*, 110.

[179] Cf. the 1948 military coup of Jiménez in Venezuela and the 1952 military coup by Batista in Cuba.

[180] Sikkink, *Evidence*, 98.

[181] Cf. for documentation, "The Chile Documentation Project," The National Security Archive, accessed August 16, 2021, https://nsarchive.gwu.edu/project/chile-documentation-project.

[182] Cf. for instance on Brazil, "Brazil Marks 50th Anniversary of Military Coup," The National Security Archive, accessed August 16, 2021, https://nsarchive2.gwu.edu/NSAEBB/NSAEBB465.

[183] Cf. on the gruesome human rights consequences, e.g. the report of the Brazilian Truth Commission 2014, "Conheça e acesse o relatório final da CNV," accessed August 16, 2021,

In addition, the authoritarian socialist regimes consolidated after World War II. The USSR's record includes the crushing of uprisings in East Berlin in 1951 and in Budapest in 1956 and of the Prague Spring in 1968, as well as the invasion of Afghanistan in 1979 – again with awful consequences for the human rights of very many people.

On the other hand, some regime changes also served the cause of human rights, as illustrated prominently by postapartheid South Africa, post-Pinochet Chile or the end of the Argentinian junta in 1983, which helped to pave the way to the adoption of the *Convention against Torture* in 1984.[184] In addition, the collapse of the socialist state systems after 1989 opened the door to major progress in the development of international human rights, as exemplified by the expansion of the membership of the Council of Europe and concomitant expansion of the protection system of the ECHR. A major driver of this development was represented by the politics of human rights, not only top down in the official channels of the CSCE Helsinki Process, but also courageously bottom up – for instance, in the Charter 77 movement in Czechoslovakia.[185]

2.5.3 *Political Ideologies*

These regime changes went hand in hand with shifting political ideologies that held very different attitudes towards the idea of human rights. Authoritarian regimes employed arguments of cultural relativism to shield their power against critique, from apartheid South Africa to post-Tiananmen China:[186]

> The concepts that relativists champion in terms of respect for Third World cultures has ended up providing a powerful excuse for those who murder, torture and abuse Third World people. … The fundamental similarity between states that assert cultural objections to human rights is not the culture of the people they represent but the authoritarian character of their government. Misuses of cultural difference unites European colonial dictatorships, like the British in Kenya, racial police states like apartheid South Africa, African Marxist autocracies like Ethiopia, Islamic theocracies like Iran, and medieval absolutisms like Saudi Arabia.[187]

http://cnv.memoriasreveladas.gov.br/index.php/outros-destaques/574-conheca-e-acesse-o-relatorio-final-da-cnv.

184 Jensen, *Making*, 267 f.

185 Cf. on the Helsinki Process and the Helsinki Final Act, Jensen, *Making*, 209 ff.

186 On the shift of the parameters of politics from the Asian–African Conference in Bandung, Indonesia, in 1955 and the first UN Human Rights Conference 1968 in Tehran, Burke, *Decolonization*, 13 ff. For a less differentiated account, Glendon, A *World*, 223 f. Burke, *Decolonization*, 128 ff. on the "westernizing" of human rights in the debates about the creation of a UN Human Rights Commissioner.

187 Burke, *Decolonization*, 143 f.

Unsurprisingly, the World Conference on Human Rights held in Vienna in 1993 struck an uneasy compromise between universalist aspirations and emphases on cultural difference, the latter promoted not least by Iran, China and Singapore.[188]

Yet another influence was the Communist vision of social organization in which human rights were interpreted primarily in terms of economic development and well-being – a position that met with criticism, including from prominent Marxist thinkers.[189] This debate was embedded in the larger question of the relation between human rights and development.[190] In some political outlooks, the latter took priority over the former, sometimes as a serious political platform, sometimes as a useful justificatory tool for authoritarian regimes.

Such different political visions were important for the conceptualization of concrete human rights. A good example is the struggle over what religious freedom means, not least in the context of the (ultimately unsuccessful) attempt from 1962 to 1967 to create an international human rights treaty securing freedom of religion and conscience. Here, again, the dividing lines were political, not cultural or religious.[191]

Given these political parameters, the multifaceted powers opposing a meaningful institutionalization of human rights and the – at first glance – rather weak forces mustered in its support, what is surprising is not that the development of the international protection of human rights was a slow and often dirty process and remains highly limited today, but rather that it did not grind to a halt altogether. Civil society played an important role in effecting this change, influencing the institutionalization of human rights in profound ways, not least by bringing human rights concerns home even to those lucky enough not to experience severe human rights abuses themselves. As it turned out, Kant's eighteenth-century perception of

[188] Cf. UN General Assembly, *Vienna Declaration and Programme of Action*, A/CONF.157/23, July 12, 1993, I Nr. 5; Burke, *Decolonization*, 141.

[189] Ernst Bloch, *Naturrecht und menschliche Würde* (Frankfurt am Main: Surhkamp, 1961); cf. the comments of Charles Malik on the different opinions of Third World delegates at Bandung, as quoted by Burke, *Decolonization*, 20: "One of the basic issues on which we were sharply divided … was the question of Human Rights. What are the ultimate fundamental Human Rights? For the Communists these rights are for the most part social and economic rights; but for some of the rest of us the ultimate human rights that should now be guaranteed by the world and by the diverse nations are the personal, legal, political rights to freedom – to freedom of thought, to freedom of expression, and certainly free elections. So, on this issue too, of the concept of human rights, we were sharply divided … Liberation! To the Communists, in the present context of this Conference meant the liberation of the various nations and peoples of Asia and Africa from foreign Western rule. But to some of us – while this certainly belongs to the notion of freedom, freedom was much larger and deeper than liberation from foreign rule. To us freedom meant freedom of mind, freedom of thought, freedom of press, freedom to criticise, to judge for yourself – freedom in short, to be the full human being. And in these respects, the Communists could not possibly agree with some of the rest of us."

[190] Cf. UN General Assembly, *Thirty-second Session*, A/RES/32/130, December 16, 1977.

[191] Cf. Jensen, *Making*, 138 ff. An example for different opinions about this issue among Muslim states is the restrictive stance of Saudi Arabia and its critique by Pakistan.

universal sympathy for and moral solidarity with victims of human rights abuse was quite clear-eyed. This sympathy and solidarity became a political factor increasingly to be counted on. The groundswell of human rights in civil societies in the twentieth and twenty-first centuries is one of the most impressive vindications of the power of the human rights idea – just as the rising tide of contempt for fundamental rights is a warning that the power of its foes is undiminished.

2.6 THE MYTH OF THE WESTERN ORIGINS OF INTERNATIONAL HUMAN RIGHTS

We have already encountered the hypothesis that the international human rights regime is both the outcome and the normative embodiment of the hegemony of the Global North.[192] This is perhaps the most common foundation for the view that human rights are the product of particular, culturally relative outlooks, a view of some importance for our current inquiry because – as mentioned above – it matters whether the inquiry into the foundations of rights is an inquiry into a piece of Western ideology or something more profound than that.

Several elements of the historical development show that this hypothesis is a misperception, besides the influence of actors from the Global South on the drafting of the *Universal Declaration* and on the subsequent development of the human rights system, which was decisive, although some of these actors became entangled in politics that were not true to the idea of human rights at some stage in their careers.[193]

One major set of issues during the first period of international human rights law were the abovementioned colonial exception clauses, promoted by the colonial powers such as the UK, France, Belgium and the Netherlands. These clauses were often defended on the grounds of the colonies' cultural difference and lack of development – the form of colonial relativism encountered above.[194] President

[192] Cf. much-quoted Fareed Zakaria, "Culture Is Destiny. A Conversation with Lee Kuan Yew," *Foreign Affairs* 73, no. 2 (1994): 109; Makau Mutua, *Human Rights: A Political and Cultural Critique* (Philadelphia: University of Pennsylvania Press, 2002).

[193] One example is Carlos Romulo of the Philippines, an important voice in international human rights politics, who championed universality and liberal rights and criticized authoritarian politics in the Third World, but nevertheless at the end of his career served the Marcos government, cf. Burke, *Decolonization*, 93. Another is Minerva Bernardino, Dominican Republic, given her involvement with Trujillo's regime, Burke, *Decolonization*, 115.

[194] Cf. Burke's summary of the debate of October 26, 1950, on such clauses in the draft human rights covenants, Burke, *Decolonization*, 40: "Speaker from Belgium, France, and Great Britain explained that the 'backward' indigenous inhabitants were not ready for 'Western' human rights. Even René Cassin, famous co-architect of the *Universal Declaration*, defended the clause, advising that it was unwise to hold 'different people to uniform obligations'," a stance Cassin later abandoned, Burke, *Decolonization*, 105. In November 1950, the colonial clause was removed from the draft covenant due to an initiative of the Philippines and Syria, Burke, *Decolonization*, 41.

Nixon's observation that "some of the people of Africa have been out of the trees only for about fifty years"[195] was a late echo of these views.

The anticolonial forces mobilized universalist principles of the equal rights of all human beings against these clauses, ultimately with success.[196] One major precondition of any meaningful human rights system, namely the nonselectivity and universalism of human rights, owes its existence to a large extent to the Global South's struggle for recognition.[197] Cultural relativism at this stage was a shield deployed against the aspirations of the colonies, not a sword challenging Western hegemony.[198] Following the publication of *Atlantic Charter*, the colonial powers already had to face the problem that many people in the colonies demanded that the values of freedom, democracy and rights defended in World War II be applied to them, too. After all, they were expected to provide crucial material support for the war effort and even to risk their lives in great numbers. The attempt to maintain the colonial system embodied a blatant self-contradiction. Moreover, massive human rights violations by colonial powers, including atrocious colonial military operations like the French campaigns in Madagascar, Southeast Asia and Algeria or the British counterinsurgency violence in Malaya, Cyprus and Kenya, which for a long time were "a taboo in public debate"[199] in many countries, showed the true colors of the colonial regimes.[200] Human rights thus became an "anticolonial inspiration."[201] Other liberation movements relied on human rights, too. One good example is the human rights catalogue that the African National Congress drafted after the publication of the *Atlantic Charter*, calling all to unite in "this mass liberation movement and struggle, expressed in this Bill of Citizenship Rights until freedom, right and justice are won for all races and colours."[202]

One concrete long-term legal effect of this was the broadening of the scope of international humanitarian law to include anticolonial and internal armed conflicts.[203] Another was the colonial powers' resistance to the development of a robust

[195] Burke, *Decolonization*, 146.

[196] On the attempts to include a separate article on the colonies in the Universal Declaration, Fn 125 above.

[197] Jensen comments on the implied "process of civilization": "[I]t would be timely to acknowledge the ways that the Global South civilized the West," Jensen, *Making*, 279, 218, 232.

[198] Cf. Burke, *Decolonization*, 114: "Cultural relativism did not appear with the influx of African, and to a lesser degree, Asian states into the UN in the late 1950s and early 1960s. On the contrary, in the early 1950s, it was driven by imperial powers and strongly opposed by the few Third World delegates then present in the UN. The first struggle for universality was the exact opposite of what academic proponents of cultural relativism hold as orthodoxy."

[199] Klose, *Human Rights*, 2.

[200] Cf. the detailed account by Klose, *Human Rights*, 56 ff.

[201] Klose, *Human Rights*, 17 ff.

[202] African National Congress, *Africans' Claims in South Africa*, December 16, 1943, Congress Series No. II.

[203] Protocol Additional to the Geneva Conventions of August 12, 1949, and relating to the Protection of Victims of International Armed Conflicts (Protocol I), June 8, 1977: Protocol Additional to the Geneva Conventions of August 12, 1949, and relating to the Protection of

international human rights regime. Only once the colonial powers were forced to give up control over their colonies and the ethical corruption that the colonial regime entailed no longer played a role did this obstacle to a meaningful rule of human rights fall away.[204]

The debate on the *Convention on the Political Rights of Women*,[205] the UN's first attempt to improve women's rights, is a further good example of the role of relativism. Arguments about cultural difference played a major role here, and an attempt even was made to reintroduce colonial exception clauses into the covenant. These arguments were ultimately defeated by defenders of women's rights, including Begum Ra'ana Liaqat Ali Khan from Pakistan,[206] who later in life stood up for women's rights against the dictator Zia-ul-Haq, who himself used the argument of cultural relativism in his attempts to curtail these rights in Pakistan. The struggle against cultural customs continued to be an important issue in the efforts to protect women's rights, not least in the context of arguments for modernization and development.[207] These efforts culminated in the *Convention on the Elimination of All Discrimination of Women* (CEDAW) of 1967, central provisions of which cannot be justified without recourse to universal, not culture-dependent rights of women.[208]

The arguments supporting the establishment of the apartheid regime on the grounds of cultural relativism – citing the Bantu laws, for example – provide another example of the ideological functions cultural relativism may serve.[209]

It should be noted that this form of relativism differs in decisive aspects from varieties of cultural relativism current today. Importantly, it was based on an ideology of some cultures' lack of development, paternalism and racism, whereas contemporary forms of cultural relativism predominantly are inspired by the equality of different cultures and the equal worth of all human beings. However, the history

Victims of Non-International Armed Conflicts (Protocol II), June 8, 1977, cf. Klose, *Human Rights*, 238.

204 Klose, *Human Rights*, 228 ff.

205 UN General Assembly, *Convention on the Political Rights of Women*, A/RES/640(VII), December 20, 1952.

206 Burke, *Decolonization*, 121 ff.

207 Cf. e.g. General Assembly resolution concerning the status of women in private law: UN General Assembly, *Status of Women in Private Law: Customs, Ancient Laws and Practices Affecting the Human Dignity of Women*, A/RES/843(IX), December 17, 1954; UN General Assembly, *Convention on Consent to Marriage, Minimum Age for Marriage and Registration of Marriages*, opened for signature and ratification by General Assembly resolution 1763 A (XVII) of November 7, 1962, entry into force: December 9, 1964; Burke, *Decolonization*, 125 ff.

208 Cf. Art. 2 (f) CEDAW, obliging state parties "[t]o take all appropriate measures, including legislation, to modify or abolish existing laws, regulations, customs and practices which constitute discrimination against women" and Art. 5 (a) CEDAW, mandating state parties to take all appropriate measures "[t]o modify the social and cultural patterns of conduct of men and women, with a view to achieving the elimination of prejudices and customary and all other practices which are based on the idea of the inferiority or the superiority of either of the sexes or on stereotyped roles for men and women."

209 Burke, *Decolonization*, 122.

of human rights teaches us to consider closely whether not only the former variant, but the latter, too, can serve as a tool to secure the dominion of illegitimate power. We will return to this problem and the question of whether an egalitarian relativism can be held without refuting itself by self-contradiction below.

The politically motivated selectivity of human rights standards was another issue, well exemplified by the many discussions about whether Soviet rule over Eastern Europe constituted colonialism or not[210] and the lack of criticism by some political actors of Soviet power politics in Eastern Europe, including in Hungary in 1956 and in Czechoslovakia in 1968.[211] Rulers used human rights arguments hypocritically for all kinds of political purposes, without applying these arguments to their own regimes.[212]

In subsequent human rights politics, actors from the Global South continued to play a decisive role[213] – from initiatives on early human rights instruments to the initiation of covenants like the ICERD that catalyzed further development,[214] through to influencing important steps towards meaningful monitoring systems, focusing first on apartheid and gaining successively universal application,[215] although such initiatives always faced opposition from the Global South, too – unsurprisingly so, given the kind of regimes involved.[216] One interesting example is Jamaica, which for some years became a global leader in human rights initiatives.[217] The universality of human rights as rights to be claimed by all human beings remained the key idea underpinning these politics.[218] Powers from the Global North often opposed these initiatives, sometimes successfully, sometimes not.[219]

210 Burke, *Decolonization*, 27 ff.

211 Burke, *Decolonization*, 46 f. The problem of (politically motivated) selectivity of UN action on human rights has a long history, cf. Jensen, *Making*, 259 ff.

212 Cf. the criticism by South Vietnam of the Democratic Republic of Vietnam and "dictatorial communism," Burke, *Decolonization*, 29.

213 Cf. Jensen, *Making*, 51 ff., 67, 102 ff., 139 ff. On the background, Burke, *Decolonization*, 6 ff., including a lack of interest of Western powers in human rights development, the perception that human rights were an issue where states from the Global South had more political leeway than in other fields because the issues had no significant consequences for their security or that of the Western democracies, less pressure from the West or Soviets on the issues or the quality and initiative of individual delegates.

214 Jensen, *Making*, 102.

215 Burke, *Decolonization*, 70 ff. Jensen, *Making*, 125.

216 Cf. the opposition against the draft enforcement article of the ICERD by the delegate of Baath Party-led Iraq, Burke, *Decolonization*, 74, or the arguments of African authoritarian regimes (e.g. of the Mobuto regime in Congo) against such mechanisms in the ICPPR, moving the provision finally to an optional protocol, Burke, *Decolonization*, 77 f.

217 Jensen, *Making*, 69 ff.: Jamaica was a main broker of progress in UN human rights diplomacy from 1962 to 1968. Examples include its role in promoting the ICERD and the International Year of Human Rights in 1968. Importantly, this was not a single-issue policy but embedded in wider political visions, ibid. 85.

218 Cf. Final Communiqué of the Asian–African Conference, Bandung, April 24, 1955, Burke, *Decolonization*, 19 ff.

219 Cf. n. 125 or the June 1949 initiative to study allegations of human rights abuses, Burke, *Decolonization*, 8.

One important issue in the development of human rights as international law is their relation to the idea of self-determination, which features prominently in the international covenants as a central right.[220] This seems defensible in light of human rights doctrine. Individual self-determination and liberty, necessarily including political rights, cannot be reconciled with a colonial rule that entirely denies or severely limits these rights. Furthermore, colonial rule was often brutal and repressive and led to a plethora of human rights violations. The denial of racial equality is incompatible with the basic human rights of equality and dignity.

Understood in this light, there is no contradiction between individual human rights and the right to self-determination. In fact, the latter serves the purpose of the former. The American revolutionaries' demand for self-determination was based on this kind of thinking: Independence served the cause of inalienable rights. The constitutional systems of democratic states around the world accordingly are built on the idea of national self-determination under a democratic government bound by human rights.

As a consequence, the anticolonial movement seems naturally wedded to the idea of human rights not only because of the experience of colonial human rights violations, but also because of the aspiration of political autonomy.[221] But this is just one way in which the right to self-determination was understood – a democratic interpretation based on human rights. The right to self-determination was also put to other political uses in the process of decolonization, where it was basically decoupled from individual rights and turned into a collective right used to justify encroachment upon individual human rights in the domestic system. In these political ideologies, collective independence trumped human rights. In addition, self-determination functioned as a shield against foreign critique and intervention. This stance could and indeed did serve authoritarian regimes. It is important to note the background of this position, however, which was many

[220] Art. 1 ICCPR; Art. 1. ICESCR. Cf. on the development Burke, *Decolonization*, 35 ff. Adom Getachew, *Worldmaking after Empire: The Rise and Fall of Self-Determination* (Princeton, NJ: Princeton University Press, 2019), 71 ff.; Klose, *Human Rights*, 40 f..

[221] Cf. for example the UN General Assembly, *Declaration on the Granting of Independence to Colonial Countries and Peoples*, A/RES/1514(XV), December 14, 1960, 1: "The subjection of peoples to alien subjugation, domination and exploitation constitutes a denial of fundamental human rights"; UN General Assembly, *The Situation with Regard to the Implementation of the Declaration on the Granting of Independence to Colonial Countries and People*, A/RES/1654(XVI), November 27, 1961, with different nuances, UN General Assembly, *Declaration on Principles of International Law concerning Friendly Relations and Co-operation among States in Accordance with the Charter of the United Nations*, A/RES/2625 (XXV), October 24, 1970 (Declaration on Friendly Relations); Burke, *Decolonization*, 43. On Bandung, Burke, *Decolonization*, 14: "On the Bandung agenda, support for rights was balanced, albeit precariously, with the intense desire for national liberation." UN General Assembly, *The Right of Peoples and Nations to Self-Determination*, A/RES/637, December 16, 1952, had asserted that "self-determination is a prerequisite to the full enjoyment of all fundamental human rights."

Third World states' experience of foreign intervention, often under the pretext of protecting rights and freedom. The right to self-determination is an important normative asset to protect a political community against the many forms of domination and power politics. Justifying such an intervention in the name of human rights consequently is not a step to be taken lightly (if at all). The right to self-determination soon became an internal issue for newly independent states facing their own secessionist movements.[222]

The question of the relation between decolonization and human rights is thus answered not only by the obstacles that the political forces of decolonization were up against, but also by the kind of postcolonial order that was established. For the anticolonial movements, the crucial matter to determine was the nature of the postcolonial regime: "Is political freedom achieved when the national banner rises over the seat of government, the foreign ruler goes, and power passes into the hands of our own leaders? Is the struggle for national independence the struggle to substitute a local oligarchy for the foreign oligarchy?"[223]

The fact that self-determination resulted in regimes disrespectful of human rights has led some to question whether there is in fact any connection between decolonization and human rights.[224] History teaches a different lesson, however: The ambiguous role of the right to self-determination in the history of international human rights underlines the need for a very nuanced and differentiated approach to the complex role of decolonization in this process. Decolonization was neither simply a human rights movement nor unrelated to human rights.[225] Sometimes human rights were the foundations of its politics, sometimes they were of no concern.[226]

These ambiguities illustrate the Jamaican diplomat Richardson's famous observation about "the moment of truth" of global human rights aspirations. At the First UN Conference on Human Rights in Tehran, Richardson, who contributed

[222] "The limits of the right to self-determination were brutally illustrated in 1968 by the Biafran conflict and the atrocities of the Nigerian Federal Government. Once European colonialism had departed, the right to self-determination ceased to exist," Burke, *Decolonization*, 57.

[223] Carlos Peña Rómulo, *The Meaning of Bandung* (Chapel Hill: University of North Carolina Press, 1956), 67.

[224] Cf. Simpson, *Human Rights*, 300, because its "primary aim was not to reduce the power of the state over the individual." Simpson grants, however, that colonialism violated basic human rights, including equality and dignity, ibid.; Moyn, *The Last Utopia*, 111; Burke, *Decolonization*, 3; Getachew, *Worldmaking*, 33 for some discussion.

[225] Burke, *Decolonization*, 6: "The politics of anticolonialism both advanced and obstructed the progress of international human rights."

[226] Burke, *Decolonization*, 12: "A historical exploration problematizes the easy oversimplifications that are so often made about the role of the Asian, African, and Arab states. Decolonization's impact on the human rights enterprise cannot be captured in a single historical moment, or defined solely by the claims of its most prolific ideologues. The Third World of the 1950s spoke with just as much legitimacy as that of the 1970s and what it said then was much less amenable to the defenders of authoritarianism."

significantly to the development of human rights, spoke of the moment "when we came face to face with the nature of the beast – when we saw what it means to be promoting the cause of human rights by working through governments" – often, one might want to add, authoritarian or dictatorial governments.[227]

The ambiguous role of the Global South in the development of international human rights is further underlined by the fact that the principled support of human rights from (state) actors from the Global South diminished in lockstep with the increase in the authoritarian regimes that in many countries tragically were the successors of colonial rule.[228]

The vagaries of international politics led to some progress in the development of human rights despite this evolving political landscape, however, with the ironic result that those regimes that had to fear much from the system of human rights supervision contributed significantly to its creation and to the possibility of future scrutiny of their regimes in several important regards (e.g. the development of the right to individual petition to the Commission on Human Rights).[229] This once again illustrates why it is wrong to overly quickly equate the political intentions of agents with the actual political outcomes of their actions – the mismatch between intentions and results is a basic element of political processes, often with tragic results, but sometimes also with beneficial consequences.

[227] Burke, *Decolonization*, 94. Eagerton Robertson was a driving force behind the organization of this conference. The hosts, the Shah Reza Pahlewi and his regime, backed by the USA, well exemplify how important it is to be clear about which political regime one is talking of when referring to the Global South. On the conference, Burke, *Decolonization*, 92 ff., 109: "The events of Tehran were emblematic of fundamental changes that had emerged in political systems that characterized much of the Third World, with a tendency toward diminution of democracy and individual rights. Sandwiched between the oppression of the colonial era and the oppression of postcolonial dictatorships, the early and mid-1950s were unique for their relatively widespread support for human rights. As the decade wore on, many of Bandung's democracies had collapsed into authoritarianism. Indonesia, Egypt, Burma, Iraq, Pakistan, the Philippines, Sudan, and Ghana were all more authoritarian in 1968 than they had been in 1955. The spirit of Tehran was radically different from the legendary 'spirit of Bandung'."

[228] Cf. for instance Jensen, *Making*, 167 ff.

[229] As Burke, *Decolonization*, 91 sums up the development leading to the right to individual petition to the Commission on Human Rights in the 1960s in comparison to the 1950s: "The most stunning paradox in the history of the human rights program was that a UN dominated by dictatorships should prove more successful in expanding human rights monitoring than one occupied by a majority of democracies. Only in an environment of Afro-Asian solidarity, where repressive states could be confident of the immunity granted by bloc voting, was such an impressive reform of the Commission's powers possible. Perversely, the most impressive achievements of the Afro-Asian bloc in the international sphere occurred when human rights were approaching their nadir in many of the countries across Asia and Africa. The diplomats of the undemocratic Third World had inadvertently succeeded in accomplishing what their democratic predecessors had begun. Hence the extraordinary irony of the 1960s, where an alliance of African and Asian dictatorships facilitated the construction of a human rights system that contained unprecedented potential for the future investigation of their own regimes."

2.7 LESSONS TO BE DRAWN

2.7.1 *A First Lesson: The Rediscovery of the Political Roots of Human Rights*

The process of the slow becoming of human rights as powerful ethical principles fleshed out and made into the increasingly densely woven law of the land, from the aspirational declarations of the eighteenth century and their roots in the history of ideas to the drafting of the *Universal Declaration* and – on this basis – to the developed contemporary system of the protection of human rights, was the unsurprising stuff of which historical developments are made. It involved multiple agents with often-competing aims as well as deep controversies, some even leading to violent struggle. Agents' options were conditioned by social structures, such as pre-World War II nationalism, an established, violently defended colonial system, the facts and political parameters created by World War II, including the power relations of the Cold War, heterogeneous social and political movements, the complex economic parameters of political action in a world with very different economic systems, changing profoundly over time and in the impact they had, decolonization and European integration. Support for human rights in the process spanned a very wide political spectrum, in both religious and secular terms. This is manifest in the making of national constitutions and is also evident for international human rights.

The complex matrix of reasoning of the agents shaping the current human rights system – principles, political expediency and tactics, interests in maintaining or limiting power, different political visions, contextual factors of power relations, for instance – highlights that arguments about the determination of human rights by culture (e.g. the Global North) or religion (e.g. Catholic personalism) miss the point and divert attention from the deeper political and ethical issues at stake.

The historical record displays the major conclusion to be drawn quite clearly: It is as erroneous – be the thrust of the argument apologetic or critical – to make an imaginary essentialized homogeneous Global South the true source of human rights as it is to understand human rights as the product of an imaginary essentialized homogeneous Global North. Human rights are a political project derived from an ethical outlook centered on the respect for individual human beings. The political orientation of the relevant actors is decisive for the development of human rights, not whether they came from the Global North or the Global South. This is illustrated vividly by the ups and downs of the process establishing the current imperfect human rights architecture, both in the Global North and in the Global South. Overlooking this means to depoliticize the struggle for human rights – a fatal flaw of any analysis of such a deeply political project. Arguments that make the legitimacy of human rights' content dependent upon the particular background of the protagonists or institutions that played a role in shaping them have the unfortunate effect of obfuscating the central conclusions to be drawn from the history of human rights. The question then no longer is what the normative principles and the politics of human rights protagonists and of their foes are, but what their cultural background is.

Eleanor Roosevelt's stance on the explicit extension of rights to "men and women," however, was certainly not simply that of a representative of the Global North, nor had she a hidden patriarchal agenda. The activities of persons such as Lakshimi Menon or Hansa Mehta likewise indicate the limited explanatory power of reductionist accounts that link human rights to a particular religious outlook or cultural background – Menon and Mehta were very important for the drafting of the *Universal Declaration* but were not agents of the Global North, nor of "Christian human rights." Nor were they early spearheads of the "neoliberalism" that some believe to be at the core of the rise of human rights, as we will see in greater detail later in this inquiry. Colonial powers like the UK or France opposed the application of human rights in their colonies not because of their respective Christian (though confessionally different) religious culture, but because of their colonial interests.[230] What is important about Pinochet is not that he was from Chile, but his vision of dictatorship. What is important about Álvarez is not his Chilean background, but the force of his arguments for the international protection of human rights.

The central normative issue is whether there is *the intention to protect individuals against state power and other threats to central goods of their human existence as a matter of right or not*, whatever the background of the actors or institutions involved may be. The question is whether the individual counts and to what degree they do so compared to other aims that motivate political action – from the protection of received power and privilege to the achievement of a classless society where all antagonisms cease to exist. Human rights are the language neither of the Global North nor of the Global South.[231] They are the language of all who concluded from their principles and experience that human beings matter, that their opportunity to pursue their own idea of personal well-being cannot be traded for other goods and that – in light of centuries of political practice – societies need to establish legally protected rights to secure the possibility for humans to flourish. There were forces that promoted and forces that acted against this idea in both the Global North and the Global South. During the time when the International Bill of Human Rights was made, countries of the Global North were engaged in colonial and postcolonial wars, from Algeria to Vietnam. Democratic movements were crushed, as in the Prague Spring. Dictatorship, often supported by the power centers of the Global North, ruled for decades in the Global South, from Chile to Uganda, from Argentina to the Philippines. Human rights found both champions and vicious foes

[230] Cf. Morsink, *Origins*, 96 ff.; Klose, *Human Rights*, 234 f. on the results of his detailed study of the colonial wars in Kenya and Algeria: "European democracies like France and Great Britain were not the stronghold and defender of liberal values but the source for the negation of basic universal rights," including arbitrary detention, torture and forced resettlement; Sikkink, *Evidence*, 79.

[231] Sikkink, *Evidence*, 71 argues for human rights as the language of the Global South.

in working-class movements, in different religious communities and in diverse political currents.

Furthermore, we simply cannot draw conclusions about an individual's or political group's attitude towards human rights from their general political outlook, aside from extreme cases such as fascism. It is possible to be a working-class activist who deeply (and honestly) believes in the equality of human beings and still be prepared to forfeit the rights of persons for the greater good of a classless society (part of the tragedy of some major socialist and communist movements). It is possible to believe in the duty of charity on religious grounds and still be prepared to sacrifice individuals on the altar of the higher purposes of organized religion. It is possible to be a champion of freedom but nevertheless support the suppression of strikes because of the towering importance of economic profits. It is possible to fight colonial oppression and still show little regard for human rights because of the perceived needs of the struggle against the colonizer or because of the perceived necessities of development. All of these justifications may be nothing but cynical ideology masking other interests – but they need not be.

One of the key lessons of the twentieth century and its twisted political course is that the idea of human rights cuts across simply drawn religious and cultural divides and political party lines – this is both part of its frailty and part of its strength. The analysis of these historical processes becomes shamefully diminished in depth if these intricacies are glossed over with the rough brush of simplistic monocausal explanations.

The analysis of the origin of human rights therefore requires much more precise historical and political analysis, looking at the kind of regimes that acted and their political agendas and goals, always differentiating between governments and those governed. The views on human rights embraced by those imprisoning or killing their opposition and repressing dissent are after all not necessarily the same as the views of those who are the object of these measures. This analysis admittedly is much more demanding than thinking in the rough grids of North/South divides and the like. However, there is no alternative for a serious history of human rights.

2.7.2 *A Second Lesson: The Rediscovery of Autonomous Critical Thought*

In the light of these findings, it is important to clarify what exactly is meant by "origin of human rights." One understanding seems to be that "origin" refers to an identifiable agent with a particular background (say, Field Marshal Smuts, or the philosopher Jacques Maritain). Some properties of this agent's respective background are then taken to determine their views and intentions, which in turn somehow determine the nature of human rights – Smuts' racism the content of the idea of human dignity, or Maritain's Catholicism the true meaning of the *Universal Declaration*, for instance. This thought can be framed in broader terms, including the wider cultural context in which these individuals were working. It can encompass institutions and the organs of states (e.g. "the government of the USA") and peter out in very thinly defined ideas such as "the Global North," "European," "Indian," "the (semi-)

periphery," without determining what "European" means exactly and what element of the concept of human rights depends on the "Europeanness" of a specific actor in any sufficiently precise manner. Which element of "Indianness" made Hansa Mehta pursue gender-neutral language in the *Universal Declaration*, and which element of "Americanness" led Eleanor Roosevelt to oppose it? Why does this matter for our understanding of human rights norms?

Origins can mean other things as well, such as a social structure, the capitalist economy or a system of ideas like "Western thought." Here, again, the problems arise of what these mean exactly and what the supposed causal connection to a concrete human rights position is. Why is Hansa Mehta's opinion about gender-neutral language capitalist or an expression of "Western thought" (as some take all human rights to be), even though it goes against what Eleanor Roosevelt, who came from a Western capitalist country, admonished her to do?

This kind of analysis seems to imply that individuals' independent and critical ethical or legal reflections and insights do not play an interesting role in the process of developing the human rights idea. The origin of human rights must lie somewhere else, it is assumed. The free exercise of human thought, leading more often than not to error and illusions, but in principle capable of grasping something that stands the test of critical reflection, plays no decisive role in such accounts. But is this plausible? Did these agents not think? How exactly was their background relevant for their reflections? How important was it? Could they just not help thinking in a European, Indian or South American way? Are human beings mere puppets on the strings of their culture?

This stance also seems to imply that there cannot be some common human framework of experience and understanding. It leads to the highly dubitable consequence of diminishing the importance of human beings' capacity for autonomous, authentic thought independent of the properties of their respective backgrounds, most importantly the place and cultural context in which they happen to live.

Social history, the struggles for progress and in particular the history of human rights tell a different story, as we have seen. There are of course many social and cultural influences on human beings. The place and time of a given human life matters profoundly for that person's outlook. But time and place are capacious concepts in the intellectual and emotional lives of human beings – one can communicate with voices from very different times and places and profit, grow with and learn from them. Moreover, human beings as subjects of autonomous thinking ultimately are able to transcend given social and cultural contexts – this is part of the epistemic dignity of individuals, and the ultimate cause of the constant transformation of human cultures.[232]

[232] It is consequently ill-advised to question the authenticity of actors during these debates, asking whether delegates from the Global South were sufficiently "global-southern" to authentically represent this region – for instance, because of their education in Europe.

2.8 POLITICS, ETHICS AND A PRELIMINARY CONCLUSION

These two lessons are no mere side issues for the cognitive interests of this inquiry. On the contrary, they refocus our attention on a crucial problem. If everything hinges upon the *ethical and political reasons* for establishing a system of legal protection of human rights on the constitutional and international level and on the *reasons* for the work creating the political structures for this endeavor in institutional frameworks and civil society, and if these reasons are not simply the function of geographical settings and cultural or religious background factors, then the central questions are: *What are the grounds for this struggle for human rights? If human rights are about the ethical calibration of political purposes and legal institutions, what are the ethical determinants of political and legal thought in the defense of human rights? And can these ethical principles be justified?* What about the justification of the many detailed questions that flesh out what human rights really mean – from their personal scope to their possible legitimate limitations? *What does the understanding of the human mind add to the answers to these questions?*

If, by contrast, the result of our inquiry had been different, if it had shown that human rights are an expression of the colonial ideology of the Global North, the inquiry would have a very different object – the study of the psychology of ideology, perhaps.

The central lesson of the genealogy of human rights is that this genealogy is not enough to understand the ascent and current reality of human rights. The argument about the actual manifold origins of the current human rights system is – as already mentioned – both true and important. But even if this were not so, the case of the legitimacy of human rights would not have been settled. Even if human rights had been of purely European (or Indian or African) origin, we would still face the question of how convincing this idea of human rights is, after all (wherever it stems from). Are there reasons that are relevant to all human beings or not? Are all humans able to comprehend these reasons? In order to understand human rights and their role in history, it seems, we have to turn to the grounds of their justification and the cognitive preconditions of their formulation.

The explicit formulation of human rights did not spring from nowhere. The declarations of the eighteenth century had deep roots in history. The question to address now is whether the results formulated concerning the more recent history of human rights resonate well with what the earlier history of human rights – or, more precisely, the history of those normative ideas that ultimately led to explicit human rights in ethics and law – teaches us. Does this history confirm these findings, or does it present them in an entirely different light? The following chapter will shed some light on this question.

3

Down the Deeper Wells of Time

Oh unhappy women! O the criminal deeds of the gods! What is to happen? To what tribunal can we appeal when we are being done to death by the injustice of our masters?

Euripides, *Ion*

They were very well formed, with handsome bodies and good faces. ... They do not carry arms nor are they acquainted with them, because I showed them swords and they took them by the edge and through ignorance cut themselves. They have no iron. Their javelins are shafts without iron and some of them have at the end a fish tooth and others of other things. All of them are alike are of good-sized stature and carry themselves well. ... They should be good and intelligent servants .... They brought balls of spun cotton and parrots and javelins and other little things that it would be tiresome to write down, and they gave everything for anything that was given to them. I was attentive and labored to find out if there was any gold; and I saw that some of them wore a little piece hung in a hole that they have in their noses. ... And these people are very gentle .... [W]henever Your Highnesses may command, all of them can be taken to Castile or held captive in this same island; because with fifty men all of them could be held in subjection and can be made to do whatever one might wish.

The Diario of Christopher Columbus's First Voyage to America 1492–1493, 11 – 14 October 1492, Abstracted by Fray Bartolomé de las Casas

Manifiesto es que ... la libertad sea la cosa más preciosa y suprema en todos los bienes deste mundo temporales, y tan amada y amiga de todas las criaturas.[1]

Bartolomé de Las Casas

How dare you talk to us of duty when we stand waist deep in the toxin of our past?

Toni Morrison, *The Nobel Lecture in Literature*

[1] "It is obvious that ... liberty is the highest and most precious of all worldly goods and is beloved of all creatures."

3.1 BACK TO THE ROOTS OR TRAPPED IN ANACHRONISM?

The history of human rights since the eighteenth century teaches us that these rights are based on ideas that seem to transcend the parochial boundaries of culture, religion, imaginary race, class or any other such characteristics. They appear to speak forcefully to human understanding, albeit not irresistibly so.

One question raised by the development of the last 250 years concerns the deeper roots of these ideas about human rights in history. Are there any, and if so, of which kind? The answer to this question adds a further piece to the puzzle of the origins of human rights in the ethical and legal life of the human species. Furthermore, it helps us to clarify the exact nature of the object of our inquiry by investigating whether human rights, seen from this wider perspective, are a Western idea of the Enlightenment or the Natural Law tradition, a piece of twentieth-century ideology, a justified normative concept accessible to all (the foundational assumption of the human rights movement) or something else altogether. This question opens up a vast territory, many aspects of which are not particularly well charted, although outstanding scholarship has explored some of them. The following remarks cannot aspire to fill all of these gaps. They also cannot engage with the full complex social, political, economic, religious and cultural context of the historical examples of thought about rights we will discuss. Moreover and importantly, they imply no assumptions about a linear, continuous historical process, coherent ideas about rights over millennia or simple causal connections between the thoughts about rights of different epochs, but serve limited expository purposes: They pursue merely the modest aim of highlighting some important findings for the specific cognitive interests of our inquiry.

3.2 A STANDARD THESIS

A standard thesis encountered in discussions about the history of human rights holds that neither antiquity nor cultures not considered "Western" had any concept of *rights*, let alone human rights. Rather, the term *right* referred only to a property of a state of affairs, "namely that the state of affairs is right or just or fair."[2]

According to this view, the modern sense of a subjective right emerged in the European Middle Ages in the work of canonists. Only since the twelfth and

[2] Griffin, *On Human Rights*, 9. Cf. on this thesis Hart, *Essays on Bentham*, 163; on the discussion but doubting the thesis, acknowledging the existence of subjective rights in Roman Law Brian Tierney, *The Idea of Natural Rights* (Michigan: Wm. B. Eerdmans Publishing Co., 1997), 13 ff.,16 f., 34, 42, including the observation that authors pursuing this historical thesis, like Villey who defended a neo-Aristotelian, neo-Thomist objective Natural Law theory buttressing a conservative social ethics, are motivated by disagreement with an ethics and legal philosophy that gives rights a central place, as this approach is supposedly "Utopian, arbitrary and sterile," Tierney, *Idea of Natural Rights*, 21. Richard Tuck, *Natural Rights Theories* (Cambridge: Cambridge University Press, 2002), 1 ff.

thirteenth centuries has the term *ius* come to cover not only what is fair, but also the meaning of the modern sense of a right – an "entitlement that a person possesses to control or claim something."[3] This set in motion the process that finally led to the idea of human rights. In this process, the idea of *natural rights* played a key role. Rights instruments and documents before the eighteenth century, such as the *Edict of Milan* (313) by Emperor Constantine on freedom of religion, the *Magna Carta* (1215), the *Virginia Charter* (1606), the *Petition of Right* (1628), the *Habeas Corpus Act* (1679) and the *Bill of Rights* (1688/1689) are not seen to properly belong to the history of human rights, however. This is because they did not protect rights of humans by virtue of their humanity, but the rights of specific groups of people – for instance, the entitlements of the feudal lords of England secured by the *Magna Carta* or the ancient rights of Englishmen secured by the *Bill of Rights*.[4] Consequently, it would be an error to list such rights as predecessors of human rights.

This thesis implies that not only ancient cultures, but also non-European cultures were unfamiliar with the idea of rights. Before the efforts of the glossators, who brought something new into the world, human beings around the world lived in a world without rights, this thesis seems to suggest.

What to think of this thesis, especially if one gives up certain simplistic "evolutionary prejudices"[5] about the development of law from primitive beginnings to complex modern (European) codes? Important documents such as the abovementioned *Edict of Milan* (313) date to before the supposed invention of the concept of "rights" in medieval thinking. The fact that much medieval thought on law and justice is based on ancient sources, in philosophy as much as in law, is another reason that should deepen our interest in the contributions of earlier epochs.

But not only that. As already mentioned above, events like the "Scramble for Africa" led to a confrontation between different epochs of human cultural development. The modern, technologically and scientifically advanced culture of Europe encountered the cultures of Africa and other continents, which in many respects were often more like some of those many and diverse human ways of living of an earlier age. Some indigenous cultures may thus serve as one indirect clue to the moral conceptual framework of earlier human societies, which were acephalous and based on oral traditions, like the few human groups who still live under comparable conditions today.[6]

3 Griffin, *On Human Rights*, 30.

4 Griffin, *On Human Rights*, 12.

5 Cf. for an instructive case study on such unhelpful prejudices José Louis Alonso, "Fault, Strict Liability, and Risk in the Law of the Papyri," in *Culpa: Facets of Liability in Ancient Legal Theory and Practice*, ed. Jakub Urbanik (Warsaw: The Raphael Taubenschlag Foundation, 2012), 19, 74.

6 For an example of such an approach from the study of Hereros, cf. Andrew B. Smith, "The Origins of Pastoralism in Namibia," in *People, Cattle and Land: Transformations of a Pastoral Society in Southwestern Africa*, eds. Michael Bollig and Jan-Bart Gewald (Cologne: Rüdiger Köppe Verlag, 2000), 72.

Given the history of racism, it is important to note two things about this methodological approach: First, it does not imply any hierarchy between these cultures, simplistic notions about cultural advancement aside that are already refuted by the comportment of Europeans during colonization. Second, such developmental differences obviously do not say anything about the rights of the individuals living in these cultures, which are independent of this development. Just because somebody has not acquired the skills to build computers, it does not follow that they have less worth as a person. Your right to life does not depend on your digital competences.

These indigenous cultures will form our first object of study, based on the assumption that what we know about the moral ideas of indigenous African people during the colonial period, for instance, will tell us something about our remoter past. The point of this inquiry is not to show that people like the Herero already had a differentiated bill of human rights, including the doctrinal tools of a proportionality or strict scrutiny test. Nor is it to assume that they were "contemporary ancestors."[7] The point of studying the moral universe of indigenous people is a much more subtle but still crucially important one. This study may tell us something about the moral intuitions and concepts with which these human beings reacted to the practices of slavery, exploitation, mass killings and – as in the case of the Herero – genocide even in narrow technical legal terms, all of which today are regarded as paradigmatic cases of human rights violations. These intuitions were not moral judgments in explicit human rights terms. But they may tell us something important about the seeds of human moral thought that slowly grew into the concept of human rights.[8] This inquiry has a moral dimension, too: By reasserting their inner moral world, it contributes to restoring the full humanity and individuality of the victims of these crimes.[9]

3.3 NOT A MORAL BLANK SLATE: THE PERSPECTIVE OF INDIGENOUS PEOPLE

Indigenous people seem to be something of a blind spot for many current human rights histories. This is not surprising if the leading research paradigm is that human

7 Cf. Chapter 2 n. 8.

8 Tierney, *Idea of Natural Rights*, 13 comments: "The concept of individual subjective rights has become central to our political discourse, but we still have no adequate account of the origin and early development of the idea. The lack of such work leaves open one of the central questions of modern debate – whether the idea of human rights is something universal, common to all societies, or whether it is a distinctive creation of Western culture, which emerged at some specific, identifiable point in European history." This is a good example of identifying an important question but framing it imprecisely. The question is not whether there are human rights in every society, because obviously there are not. The question is rather: In a specific historical and social context, are there specific normative phenomena – including incidents such as claims and duties or intuitions about normatively demandable freedom and equality – that are possible building blocks of the ultimately formed explicit human rights idea?

9 Which helps to address a problem of genocide studies: "Victims left behind mourners. Killers left behind numbers," threating to extinguish both humanity and individuality, Snyder, *Bloodlands*, 407.

rights are the product of European culture, whether stemming from the revival of Roman law in the Middle Ages,[10] novel reading in the eighteenth century[11] or other such culture-specific developments.

There is a traditional strand of research that investigates the law of early human acephalous societies and includes famous early and controversial work in legal anthropology on so-called primitive societies[12] – which are in fact not primitive at all. This research already shows in often-fascinating detail that these societies have intricate normative codes and concepts.

A prominent example of contemporary research – much praised and controversially discussed – that underlines the importance of not neglecting indigenous cultures when writing the history of normative concepts was produced by David Graeber and David Wengrow. They argue that there is much new archaeological and anthropological evidence from early cultures, including those from the Upper Paleolithic, to suggest that there was a great variety of political forms – egalitarian, proto-democratic, participatory, cooperative and peaceful, but also hierarchical, authoritarian and full of violence and cruelty.[13] Indigenous cultures were not living in some kind of dream-like mode of existence that never changed, but rather they took conscious choices about what we today call the political organization of their societies – sometimes increasing equality, care for others and participation, sometimes erecting authoritarian systems, among many other forms of social order.[14] Graeber and Wengrow try to show that some expressions of indigenous thought even influenced the Enlightenment's political philosophy of freedom and equality, which was stimulated by the indigenous critique of European civilization.[15] Moreover, the desire for liberty is well-documented in many ancient societies.[16]

Contrary to some popular conceptions that hunter-gatherers lived in small, competing groups, the respective cultures often spanned geographically huge spaces, in which individuals moved widely, creating groups that were not based on biological kinship relations in any discernable sense but rather on common cultural bonds:[17] "[T]he common stereotype that 'primitive' peoples saw anyone outside their particular local group only as enemies appears to be entirely groundless."[18] Hunter-gatherers already created city-like communities producing impressive

[10] Tuck, *Natural Rights Theories*, 13: "It is among the men who rediscovered the Digest and created the medieval science of Roman law in the twelfth century that we must look to find the first modern rights theory, one built round the notion of a passive right."

[11] Hunt, *Inventing Human Rights*, 35 ff.

[12] This is a classic thesis, cf. Edward Adamson Hoebel, *The Law of Primitive Man: A Study in Comparative Legal Dynamics* (Cambridge, MA: Harvard University Press, 1954).

[13] Graeber and Wengrow, *Dawn*, 85 ff., 119, 197, 203.

[14] Graeber and Wengrow, *Dawn*, 86, 107, 112, 115, 349, 354, 482.

[15] Graeber and Wengrow, *Dawn*, 17 ff., 29 ff.

[16] Graeber and Wengrow, *Dawn*, 41 ff., 452, 473, 492, 523.

[17] Graeber and Wengrow, *Dawn*, 122, 279 ff.

[18] Graeber and Wengrow, *Dawn*, 547 n. 4.

artifacts and architecture.[19] In particular, hierarchical state-like structures were not the necessary outcome of the slow introduction of agriculture – large-scale communities based on forms of communal participation developed in different forms as well.[20] This variety of social organization was based on complex normative concepts, including subjective rights, from the right to perform certain sacred actions to differentiated rights to the use of (communal) property.[21] Thus, not only the myth of the "noble savage" but also the myth of the "stupid savage" has to be abandoned.[22] As soon as modern humans had developed, they started – endowed with common biological and cognitive abilities constituting the "psychic unity of mankind" – "doing human things,"[23] which encompassed, one may add, normative "human things." History has to stop "infantilizing Non-Westerners" and restore "our ancestors to their whole humanity."[24]

If we return to the example of the subjugation of Africa, particularly in the nineteenth century, we find a considerable body of work that documents indigenous African people's reactions to these events. Such studies on indigenous people around the world present evident methodological problems, not least that some of this evidence has been produced and handed down through the colonial machinery, such as governmental reports, court proceedings, diaries of missionaries and so forth. Analyses thus have to factor in the fact that such sources may be heavily influenced by colonial perspectives and particular interests.[25]

Having said this, there are still many impressive testimonies about the suffering of colonized people at this time and – crucially for our inquiry – about their sense of the normative wrongness of what had happened to them.

The Herero rebellion is a case in point. The Herero were a nomadic people. Their pastoral way of life changed over time, and many aspects of its precolonial development remain unclear.[26] In the second half of the nineteenth century,

19 Cf. for instance Graeber and Wengrow, *Dawn*, 89 ff. on Göbekli Tepe.

20 Cf. for instance Graeber and Wengrow, *Dawn*, 211 ff. on Çatalhöyük; 297 ff.; 329 ff.

21 Graeber and Wengrow, *Dawn*, 150, 157 ff., 179, 181, 250, 502.

22 Graeber and Wengrow, *Dawn*, 71 ff. Cf. for a recent example of sophisticated knowledge Tim Ryan Maloney et al., "Surgical Amputation of a Limb 31,000 Years Ago in Borneo," *Nature* 609 (2022): 547 ff.

23 Graeber and Wengrow, *Dawn*, 80, 83 ff., 95, 118, 96: "Anthropologists who spend years talking to indigenous people in their own languages, and watching them argue with one another, tend to be aware that even those who make their living hunting elephants or gathering lotus buds are just as sceptical, imaginative, thoughtful and capable of critical analysis as those who make their living operating tractors, managing restaurants or chairing university departments."

24 Graeber and Wengrow, *Dawn*, 31, 24.

25 Cf. Madley, *American Genocide*, 10 ff.

26 Cf. Dag Henrichsen, "Ozongambe, Omavita, and Ozondjembo – The Process of (Re-) Pastoralization amongst Herero in Pre-colonial 19th century Central Namibia," in *People, Cattle and Land: Transformations of a Pastoral Society in Southwestern Africa*, eds. Michael Bollig and Jan-Bart Gewald (Cologne: Rüdiger Köppe Verlag, 2000), 149 ff., 152: "pastoral/pastroforaging social formation." For an overview, Michael Bollig and Jan-Bart Gewald, "People, Cattle, Land – Transformations of Pastoral Society," in *People, Cattle and Land:*

influences of various kinds, including those of the Christian missionaries, made themselves felt. The Herero had sophisticated sets of rules that organized and structured their communal life. These included rules for the use of land, the ownership of cattle, defining the territorial claims of certain groups, ceremonial matters, spiritual practices, family life and so forth. It is impossible to describe this way of life and the normative concepts and thoughts that underpin it without a terminology including concepts such as claims (to cattle, to land use, to territory) and duties (not to take away the cattle of somebody else, to accept the land use or territory of others) – let alone to practice it without access to normative categories like *claims* and *duties*. It thus seems implausible to assert that such normative phenomena were alien to the Herero.

The Herero's fight against their German aggressors underlines these findings, and in matters that relate directly to human rights. Trying to reconstruct the normative world of people such as the Herero and their perception of the events at that time obviously is not an easy task. Various sources and studies document the reasons for the rebellion – basically, it constituted self-defense against invaders who took away the Herero's land, property and possibility of gaining their livelihood, threatening their way of life. The Germans failed to uphold prior arrangements by contract. The Herero's complaints about these matters are based on normative ideas, not least the claims they thought they had to their land, cattle and way of life.

One such source, the report of the German General Staff about the military campaign against the Herero, provides an interesting glimpse into what was going on. This report cannot be suspected of idealizing the enemy, although the caveat about the effects of colonial perspectives holds here, too. The report outlines the reasons for the rebellion and in this context highlights the Herero's will to resist the appropriation of their land, cattle and labor by the colonizing power. In addition, it underlines two other factors: first, the warlike characteristics of the Herero; and second, their desire for freedom and independence. The report states that the Herero possess a "sense of freedom and independence" (*Freiheits- und Unabhängigkeitssinn*) rarely found among African peoples.[27] They united with former adversaries to fight the "intruder" who threatened their "independence"

Transformations of a Pastoral Society in Southwestern Africa, eds. Michael Bollig and Jan-Bart Gewald (Cologne: Rüdiger Köppe Verlag, 2000), 3 ff. On the evidence for earlier periods Andrew B. Smith, "The Origins of Pastoralism in Namibia," in *People, Cattle and Land: Transformations of a Pastoral Society in Southwestern Africa*, eds. Michael Bollig and Jan-Bart Gewald (Cologne: Rüdiger Köppe Verlag, 2000), 55 ff.; Thomas Frank, "Archeological Evidence from the Early Pastoral Period," in *People, Cattle and Land. Transformations of a Pastoral Society in Southwestern Africa*, eds. Michael Bollig and Jan-Bart Gewald (Cologne: Rüdiger Köppe Verlag, 2000), 77 ff. For later developments Jan-Bart Gewald, "Colonization, Genocide and Resurgence: The Herero of Namibia 1890–1933," in *People, Cattle and Land: Transformations of a Pastoral Society in Southwestern Africa*, eds. Michael Bollig and Jan-Bart Gewald (Cologne: Rüdiger Köppe Verlag, 2000), 187 ff.

[27] Kriegsgerichtliche Abteilung I des Grossen Generalstabs, *Die Kämpfe der deutschen Truppen in Südwestafrika, Vol. 1: Der Feldzug gegen die Hereros* (Berlin: Mittler und Sohn, 1906), 2.

(*Unabhängigkeit*) and "freedom" (*Freiheit*). Their resistance showed "how strong [their] sense of freedom and independence" was. They were not "weaklings" (*Schwächlinge*) who could be won over by "being bought" (*Kauf*) or negotiation, but instead were determined not to be subdued without offering fierce resistance.[28] The main reason for the rebellion, the report concludes, thus ultimately is this "warlike and freedom-loving nature" of the Herero.[29]

So freedom clearly mattered to the Herero, and enough to fight one of the world's major military powers. Furthermore, it does not seem plausible that the freedom they fought for was only the *factual ability* to act in certain ways without obstacle – the freedom of the hare to escape the fox, as it were – and not the defense of a *normative position*, the normative *claim* to freedom accompanied by the correlated *duty* of the German invaders to respect this freedom. The sources show that the Herero framed their fight in normative terms, referring to the injustice of their treatment by the Germans, including the unjust lack of sanctions for perpetrators of crimes. This implies that they believed that they could *claim* to be treated differently and that the Germans had a *duty* to do so. The Herero defended *claims* to land, cattle and the integrity of holy sites, and there is no reason to believe that this was not true for their freedom as well.

Such conclusions underline how important it is to break with the often-racist idea of "savages." A "savage" is someone who lacks basic cognitive abilities, including moral orientation, and is prey to beast-like impulses. The truth is that the European invaders encountered not savages, but human beings with complex moral concepts and rules, embodied in proto-legal or legal norms (depending on the concept of law used). This only deepens the horror of what happened to the Herero: The human beings starved to death in the Namibian desert must have felt not only the physical pain of their treatment, but also the moral outrage of their death.

This brief account encourages us to consider more closely what the history of slavery and the mass killings or even genocide of indigenous peoples can teach us about the deeper sources of human rights. Two more examples from different backgrounds indicate the kinds of question that arise if one reflects on the meaning of the testimonies of the indigenous victims.

Our first example concerns Yahling Dahbo, a former slave. Dahbo gave an account of the conditions of her life as a slave at a trial concerning her emancipation after British rule was established in The Gambia in 1889. Britain took some (albeit limited) measures to end slavery in the Crown Colony, although the practice persisted until 1930. Dahbo stated: "It was against my wish that Prisoner came to me at night, being a slave I was afraid. . . . I was at Prisoner's as a slave. Nobody has put the word slave into my mouth. Prisoner himself used to tell us that we were his slaves. That is all the reason I have for saying I am a slave. It is not because I [was

[28] Generalstab, *Feldzug gegen die Hereros*, 3 f.
[29] Generalstab, *Feldzug gegen die Hereros*, 3 f.

beaten] that I say that I am a slave. All the world beats. Not because I make rice farms. If you are in the hands of a person, if you are free born you will know."[30]

At the same trial, another woman, Dado Bass, testified about her life with the slaveholder: "I know I am a slave because they never tie free people or put them in irons. Prisoner used to tie me and put me in irons. He used to tie my hands with a rope. He used to put me in irons."[31]

A third women, Maladdo Mangah, had this to report: "It was not my will or pleasure to go with the prisoner. I could not help myself. I am a slave. . . . I have a child. She is in the hands of Mr. Edwin [the slaveholder]. Fatou James took the child at Bathurst saying she was a slave. It was not with my consent. I cried."

What are we to conclude from this dry protocol of the answers given by these women to the questions of the court? Does Yahling Dahbo's testimony simply report the brute fact of harm, or is there a normative dimension to her suffering? Did she evaluate the rape she endured in some kind of normative framework? Did she think (in whatever terms) that she could justifiably demand that this not happen and that the slaveholder was bound not to rape her, even though the customs of a slave society were on his side? What are the reasons why this is naturally assumed for European women of this time but not for her? Conversely, what are the reasons to think that the experience and evaluation of both African and European women share crucial common elements? Does rape only constitute a normatively evaluated harm after a cultural development comparable to that of Europe?

What about Dahbo's longing for freedom? Did it have a normative dimension, or was it just a non-normative wish, like "I wish I could fly?"

How did Dado Bass feel, and what did she think when the slaveowner placed a rope around her hands and put her in irons? What about Maladdo Mangah? What does it mean that it was not her "will or pleasure to go" with the slave holder? What does it mean that she thought her consent should have mattered when she was forcibly separated from her child? Did she think she had a claim to be asked about the separation? What was going on inside her when she cried? Was her pain accompanied by some kind of moral outrage?

Our second example is taken from the report of a chief of the Native American Pomo. Based on the oral accounts of eyewitnesses of an 1850 massacre during the genocide against Native Americans in California, he stated:

> [O]ne old lady a (indian) told about what she saw while hiding under abank, in under aover hanging tuleys [bulrushes]. . . . alittle ways from she, said layed awoman shoot through the shoulder. she held her little baby in her arms. two

[30] Alice Bellagamba, "'Being a slave, I was afraid. . .': Excerpt from a Case of Slave-Dealing in the Colony of the Gambia," in *African Voices on Slavery and the Slave Trade*, eds. Alice Bellagamba, Sandre E. Green and Martin A. Klein (Cambridge: Cambridge University Press, 2013), 343 ff., 351 ff.

[31] Bellagamba, "Being a slave," 355.

> white men came running torge the women and baby, they stabed the women and the baby and, and threw both of them over the bank in to the water. she said she heard the woman say, O my baby; she when they [the survivors] gathered the dead, they found all the little ones were killed by being stabed, and many of the women were also killed [by] stabbing ... They called it the siland creek (Ba-Don-Bi-Da-Meh).[32]

What do we assume about the perceptions of this dying mother in the last moments of her life? What was the exact nature of her attitude towards the death of her child? What did the people of her community think? What would we assume if the mother were Swiss? Is the inner emotional and moral world of an indigenous woman flat and impoverished, whereas the inner world of a Swiss woman is differentiated and rich? Why the one, why the other?

Many such questions present themselves if one engages more intensely with this kind of research. However, the above remarks should suffice to show plausibly that some basic elements relevant for the history of the idea of human rights can be found in sources other than the canonical texts of the European history of thought and European or "Western" cultural practices and historical records. These basic elements include powerful intuitions about the value of freedom and strong moral beliefs about one's claims to goods of fundamental importance for human life and correlated duties of others.

These findings are important for the question of who has epistemic access to the idea of human rights. Further analysis will show that many steps and transformations were required to bridge the gap between such elementary intuitions and beliefs and the explicit concept of human rights as understood today. These intuitions and beliefs are, however, part of the ethical raw material for developing the idea of human rights, and as such they are not beyond the reach of any human being.

A further conclusion suggests itself, if we take the methodological step mentioned above and interpret such results as providing some clues about the lifeworlds of cultures in the more distant past, albeit not mistaking them for a "direct window on the past," as clarified above. In light of these findings, we should take seriously the possibility that the human beings of these times were no moral blank slates, but rather lived in a differentiated normative lifeworld, as did the Herero, other indigenous peoples or indeed any other human group (including ourselves) – a lifeworld that historians of human rights have taken too little interest in thus far.

Consequently, the normative dimensions of events such as the Herero rebellion, the slave women's perception of their lot and the precise nature of the experience of the dying Pomo mother cradling her stabbed child properly belong in a history of human rights. Indigenous people are no strangers to this history, and their experience matters.

[32] William R. Benson, quote: Madley, *American Genocide*, 130.

These remarks do not imply that indigenous people only had rights because they entertained subjective moral beliefs about their justified claims. There is no doubt that human beings have rights even if they are not conscious of them. A four-year-old child has a right to life, even though they have no understanding of this idea. The subjective belief that one is a rights-holder is not an existence condition of the rights of humans. The point of these observations is only to identify the traces of this idea in the moral experience of human beings in order to understand its deeper roots in the human life form.

The next step of our inquiry will investigate whether such findings are challenged or bolstered by what we know about the relevant normative ideas in antiquity. Here, too, the aim is not to discover full concepts of human rights in ancient texts or practices. Rather, the goal continues to be to go back to the roots of the idea of human rights to identify the elementary moral notions that make it possible to form the idea of human rights.

3.4 THE MANY FORMS OF NORMATIVE THOUGHT IN ANCIENT TIMES

3.4.1 *The Imagery of Epics*

When talking of antiquity, our interest goes beyond just European or even only Greek and Roman antiquity. Such a narrow focus would unduly neglect important recorded sources of other regions and cultures (e.g. from India or China). Nor should we conclude from the fact that we do not have many recorded sources of certain times and cultures (e.g. the oral cultures of Africa) that these cultures have produced nothing of interest. They almost certainly did.

Despite these limitations and the fragmentary nature of the historical record, surviving sources offer many interesting points of departure for research on the wider history of subjective rights and their connection with liberty, equality and ideas of human worth as a subchapter of the history of human rights. Serious, open-minded study of cultures that formerly and wrongly were called "primitive" may provide some interesting hints about the use of rights in early human forms of life, as we have just seen. In addition, the oldest known legal codes of the third and second millennia BCE from Sumer and Babylon seem to express or imply a concept of a right – a finding that is hard to reconcile with the thesis that the concept is a much more recent invention of European legal thought.[33] The question of whether the

[33] Consider, for instance, from the *Laws of Ur-Nammu* (ca. 2100 BCE): "§ 30 If a man violates the rights of another and cultivates the field of another man, and he sues (to secure the right to harvest the crop, claiming that) he (the owner) neglected (the field) – that man shall forfeit his expenses." Martha Tobi Roth, *Law Collections from Mesopotamia and Asia Minor* (Atlanta, GA: Scholars Press, 1997), 20, or from the *Laws of Hammurabi* (ca. 1750 BCE): "§ 244: If a man rents an ox or a donkey and a lion kills it in the open country, it is the owner's loss. § 245 If a man rents an ox and causes its death either by negligence or by physical abuse, he shall replace

same holds for the Vedas, the oldest of which also stem from the second millennium BCE, is an important matter. It is equally fruitful to investigate whether rules such as the Ten Commandments entail something about rights. This is no trivial question, for the formulation of the normative content of a given moral or legal code as a command is not sufficient to rule out the possibility that this code implies such rights, as we have seen above.

For open-minded research that at the same time is critically aware of the danger of anachronism, in light of our methodological findings about the historiography of human rights, it may turn out to be a fruitful research strategy not to turn immediately to legal texts, as is often done, but to include wider cultural manifestations of normative ideas in our analysis to gain a more inclusive picture of the normative thinking of a given culture and epoch, which is never limited to the sphere of law.

One very interesting issue in this context is the imagery of epics. A good example of the depth of the questions these works of art raise is Homer's *Odyssey*, a text whose outstanding importance for the cultural development of humankind is beyond doubt. One central part of the epic concerns the suitors' abuse of Odysseus' property. They "continue to slay his thronging sheep and his spiral-horned shambling cattle," as Athena observes,[34] and they harass Penelope because "all prayed, each that he might lie in bed with her."[35] This is described as a moral outrage, justifying the anger of Odysseus and his son, Telemachos. The suitors are wrong to use Odysseus' goods because the cattle, wine and other amenities they feast on are the property of the absent Odysseus and of Telemachos. There is no doubt that the suitors are violating a rule by indulging in this behavior. It seems equally obvious that Odysseus and his heir, Telemachos, had a claim that their cattle not be slaughtered and their goods not squandered, and that the suitors were under a correlative duty not to do so. In addition, Odysseus and his son enjoyed the liberty to either dispose of their goods (e.g. by organizing a feast) or not do so, and the suitors could not demand the one or the other – they had, to use Hohfeldian terminology, a no-right that Odysseus and Telemachos do so, in the same way that Odysseus and Telemachos enjoyed a privilege to throw a party. This normative position is acknowledged by one of the suitors: "Never may that man come who by violence and against your will shall wrest your possessions from you, while men yet live in Ithaca."[36]

the ox with an ox of comparable value for the owner of the ox." Roth, *Law Collections from Mesopotamia and Asia Minor*, 127. These norms from the *Laws of Hammurabi* clearly imply the notion of legal responsibility, cf. Alonso, "Fault," 74 f. and thus very substantial notions about human action and agency. But not only that: The interesting question also arises of whether the owner of the borrowed ox has a *claim* to compensation.

34 Homer, *Odyssey*, *Vol. I*: *Books 1–12*, trans. Augustus T. Murray, rev. George E. Dimock, Loeb Classical Library 104 (Cambridge, MA: Harvard University Press, 1919), Book 1, 91–2: οἵ τέ οἱ αἰεὶ μῆλ' ἁδινὰ σφάζουσι καὶ εἰλίποδας ἕλικας βοῦς.

35 Homer, *Odyssey*, *Vol. I*: Book 1, 366: πάντες δ'ἠρήσαντο παραὶ λεχέεσσι κλιθῆναι.

36 Homer, *Odyssey*, *Vol. I*: Book 1, 403–4: μὴ γὰρ ὅ γ' ἔλθοι ἀνὴρ ὅς τίς σ' ἀέκοντα βίηφιν κτήματ' ἀπορραίσει, Ἰθάκης ἔτι ναιετοώσης.

Odysseus' terrible revenge on the suitors when he finally returns is not presented as a wanton act of cruelty but justified with reference to the abuse of the goods of his house and the attempt to force Penelope into marriage while he is still alive, thus being the violation of rights he is entitled to protect, some of them concerning Penelope evidently of a patriarchal nature. Not surprisingly, then, the attempt of the suitors to appease him consists in offering to pay him compensation for the damage inflicted, which implies that he had a claim that they forbear from what they have done.[37]

Such observations are an invitation to track down the concept of a right in more detail – for example, in private law in the pluralistic normative orders of antiquity, which were of great complexity comparable in more than one respect to contemporary legal systems.[38] Some such rules even have clear significance for issues that haunt human rights law today, though evidently not in the form of current rights conceptions. A good example is represented by the legal rights of women – very limited in Athens, but quite strong in Egypt in the Hellenistic period, for instance.[39]

No attempt, however, can be made to do any justice even to these and other very ancient sources that are of evident importance if one takes this wider, non-Eurocentric perspective on the genealogy of rights. Nor is this necessary for the subject matter at hand. Instead, the discussion will turn to an example that is particularly relevant for the history of human rights: the first politically, ethically and legally entrenched democratic order on record in ancient Athens. The reason for this choice is that democracy is not just any system of government but the attempt to create an institutional framework that does justice to the autonomy, equality and dignity of human beings and thus to those values that today are understood to be at the core of human rights. There is an intense debate about the exact relation between democracy and human rights.[40] That human rights are central for any theory of democracy is, however, beyond doubt. It seems therefore worthwhile to investigate what traces of these ideas can be found in the rudimentary forms of democracy of antiquity.

The discussion of this and other related matters, its necessary selectivity notwithstanding, will add further arguments to bolster the point that the idea of rights is far

[37] Homer, *Odyssey, Vol. II: Books 13–24*, trans. Augustus T. Murray, rev. George E. Dimock, Loeb Classical Library 105 (Cambridge, MA: Harvard University Press, 1919), Book 22, 55–9.

[38] Cf. for a very fundamental example from peregrine law, Alonso, "Fault," 19, 74, on fault and strict liability in the Papyri.

[39] Cf. the analysis of the legal institute of *katochè* in Egypt, illustrating the strong legal position of women in ancient Egypt, who were able to act without a legal guardian and could include clauses in marriage contracts that prevented their husbands from disposing of the husband's own property without the consent of his wife – a legal position evidently including complex subjective rights, José Louis Alonso, "Interpretatio graeca: Rechtspluralismus und Umdeutungsvorgänge in den Papyri," Inaugural Lecture, February 25, 2019, University of Zurich, manuscript on file with author, 8 f.

[40] Habermas, *Faktizität und Geltung*, 109 ff. argues, for instance, for the "co-originality" of public sovereignty and human rights.

from a recent invention, as already suggested in the discussion of the normative lifeworlds of indigenous societies. Moreover, innovative thoughts about equality, freedom and human worth are not the prerogative of modernity, even in an explicitly cosmopolitan perspective.

There are many other examples from other spheres of the law of antiquity where rights play a role – for example, if a concrete person was awarded quasi-citizenship rights as a specific honor, including the right to enter a city, to reside there or to be professionally active.[41] These examples further illustrate that rights were part of the normative currency of the age.

3.4.2 *Democracy and Rights*

Many regarded democracy in ancient Greece as the political expression of equality and the principles of justice spelled out by equality. Accordingly, *Isonomia*, equal law, most probably even preceded *Demokratia* as a proper name for a democratic form of government.[42]

The egalitarian character of the democratic form of government established in Athens was limited in obvious and significant ways, not least through the exclusion of women and slaves. Furthermore, democratic policy made no attempt to create social equality. Despite these grave shortcomings, from a historical perspective the idea of equalitarian self-rule as the core meaning of *Isonomia* was still a striking achievement, in particular for the disadvantaged classes: "It promised the poorest citizens an equal right in the law-making, law-administration, law-enforcing power of the state. It expressed the spirit of a constitution, hitherto undreamed of in civilized society, which declared that the poor man's share in law and political office was equal to that of the noble and the rich."[43]

This order was established in several steps that gradually increased equality and transformed the Solonian order, which had limited magistracies to the members of the wealthier classes but already admitted every citizen to the courts before which officials could be held accountable under the law: "The demand for political equality, first voiced by only the poorest sections of the demos, became the first article of the democratic creed and was progressively implemented in waves of far-reaching reforms which swept away one by one all constitutional guarantees of political privilege for the upper classes."[44]

[41] Cf. the differentiated set of rights granted to Polos of Aegine, 306 BCE, Haritini Kotsiduou, *TIMH KAI ΔΟΞΑ: Ehrungen für hellenistische Herrscher im griechischen Mutterland und in Kleinasien unter besonderer Berücksichtigung der archäologischen Denkmäler* (Berlin: Akademie Verlag, 2000), 256 f. (including rights as a citizen, right to enter and leave the port during peace and war, access to the public assembly, for him and his descendants).

[42] Gregory Vlastos, "Isonomia," *The American Journal of Philology* 74, no. 4 (1953): 337 ff.

[43] Vlastos, "Isonomia," 355 f.

[44] Vlastos, "Isonomia," 353. This included the Cleisthenean Constitution of 508 BCE and further reforms that followed it; the reforms of Ephialtes, 462 BCE; the eligibility of Zeugitai for

The democratic constitution of Athens enabling "the rule of the majority" included as its key elements the selection of magistrates by lot, the auditing of public officials, thus holding them accountable, and the referral of all resolutions to the authority of the public, as Herodotus put on record in one of the oldest reflections on the topic of democracy.[45] A further key element was the citizens' ability to initiate motions and legislation in the assembly (*ekklesia*).[46] The entitlements to political participation and to access to office doubtlessly can be called rights. They encompassed the claims to be included in the group from which a person was selected by lot, to attend the assembly with a vote that counted and to initiate a decision of the assembly, as well as corresponding duties of others to act accordingly: Officials in fact were obligated to include persons with such entitlements among those that could be drawn by lot, to count the votes of such persons as ones codetermining the final outcome of an assembly decision and to deal appropriately with initiatives of entitled citizens.[47]

Ancient Greek had no proper term for what is now called a subjective right or claim. The meaning of this term was expressed in various paraphrases[48] or implied in particular human practices, as not only Odysseus' and Telemachos' actions illustrate. The importance of the idea in practical terms is illustrated perhaps most dramatically by its decisive role in the fundamental normative architecture of the democratic political order outlined above. This is another reminder that we should not allow ourselves to be led astray by the linguistic particularities of a given language and draw wrong conclusions about the ideas important to a particular culture. Just because a certain human community expresses itself differently than another does not mean that certain ideas are alien to this culture.

Political rights were an explicit and decisive issue in the political struggles about the democratic constitution – for example, in the context of active or passive electoral rights, access to office and decision-making. These issues were not arcane

appointment by lot to archonship, 457 BCE; financial remuneration for jury services, councilors and, finally, for attending the assembly, ca. 450 BCE and after 403 BCE.

45 Cf. the outline of democracy in the discussion about the different forms of government, Herodotus, *The Landmark Herodotus: The Histories*, trans. Andrea L. Purvis, ed. Robert B. Strassler (New York: Anchor Books, 2009), Book III, 3.80.6.

46 Cf. Jochen Bleicken, *Die athenische Demokratie* (Stuttgart: UTB, 1995), 196 ff. This right was supplemented by the inclusion of the council (*boule*).

47 The democratic state was widely regarded as "a common pool of rights and privileges equally shared by all its citizens," Vlastos, "Isonomia," 348 with further references n. 38.

48 Cf. Vlastos, "Rights of Persons in Plato's Conception," 124 on the irrelevance of the linguistic fact for a theory of rights that to express the idea of a right various ancient Greek terms were employed. To express the same notion "one would resort to a variety of makeshifts: (1) 'what is due to one' (*ta opheilomena*), as in the definition of justice ascribed to the poet, Simonides, in R. 331e, 'rendering to everyone his due'; (2) 'the just' (*ta dikaia*), as in Demosthenes 15 (*Rhodians*), 29, 'in commonwealths the laws have made participation in private rights (*idiōn dikaiōn*) common and equal for the weak and the strong'; and (3) 'one's own' in the phrase 'to have one's own' (*ta hautou echein*), as in the definition of *justice* in Aristotle's *Rhetoric* (1366b9), 'the virtue because of which each has his own and in conformity with the law.'"

elitist debates but the daily bread of politics. Consider the classic speech of Athenagoras, the democratic leader of Syracuse during the early stages of Athens' doomed Sicilian campaign during the Peloponnesian War, who in his address to the popular assembly on the eve of war asked the young oligarchs the following rhetorical question: "Do you dislike having the same rights like all others? But how it is just for people who are the same not to have the same?"[49] The core of democracy, he argues, is that everyone has the same rights and duties.[50] The explicit linking of equal rights and justice in Athenagoras' speech echoes widely held democratic beliefs: "There is nothing more hostile to a city than a tyrant. In the first place, there are no common laws in such a city, and one man, keeping the law in his own hands, holds sway. This is unjust. When the laws are written, both the powerless and the rich have equal access to justice, ... and the little man, if he has right on his side, defeats the big man."[51] These views draw attention to the relation between justice, equality and rights, as well as to the empowering function of rights, and thus to questions crucial for our inquiry.

Isonomia, equal law in this sense, and *Isokratia*, equal share in government, were essential to what later was termed the democratic idea. A further foundational feature was *Isegoria*, free speech, to which we will turn after exploring the meaning of equality.

3.4.3 *Equality*

In Greek antiquity, the discussion about equality was interwoven not only with topics such as democracy and the political rights of citizens. Social inequality, relations with – in the Greek case – barbarians (that is, all non-Greek-speaking people) and, of course, slavery were also of great importance. These are all issues that remain intimately linked to or even form core areas of human rights debates today. A short glance at these issues thus may prove fruitful.

Despite the egalitarian political structure of the Athenian democracy among the limited group of people that counted as equals, democratic politics did not aim at material redistribution within the Athenian society. There were utopian

49 Thucydides, *History of the Peloponnesian War, Vol. III: Books 5–6*, trans. Charles Forster Smith, Loeb Classical Library 110 (Cambridge, MA: Harvard University Press, 1998), Book 6, 6.38.5. The original reads: ἀλλὰ δὴ μὴ μετὰ τῶν πολλῶν ἰσονομεῖσθαι; καὶ πῶς δίκαιον τοὺς αὐτοὺς μὴ τῶν αὐτῶν ἀξιοῦσθαι; *Isonomisthai* is here rendered as equal in rights. The translations vary, but it is clear that the passage concerns political rights, cf. William Keith Chambers Guthrie, *The Sophists* (Cambridge: Cambridge University Press, 2005), 148.

50 Thucydides, *History of the Peloponnesian War*, Vol. III: Book 6, 6.39.1.

51 Euripides, "Suppliant Women," in Euripides, *Suppliant Women, Electra, Heracles*, ed. and trans. David Kovacs, Loeb Classical Library 9 (Cambridge, MA: Harvard University Press, 1998), 429–34: οὐδὲν τυράννου δυσμενέστερον πόλει, ὅτου τὸ μὲν πρώτιστον οὐκ εἰσὶν νόμοι κοινοί, κρατεῖ δ'εἷς τὸν νόμον κεκτημένος αὐτὸς παρ'αὑτῷ· καὶ τόδ'οὐκέτ' ἔστ' ἴσον. γεγραμμένων δὲ τῶν νόμων ὅ τ' ἀσθενὴς ὁ πλούσιός τε τὴν δίκην ἴσην ἔχει, ... νικᾷ δ' ὁ μείων τὸν μέγαν δίκαι' ἔχων.

schemes that failed to become reality and instead ended up the object of comedic ridicule.[52] The social reality of democracy was based on the "astonishing fact that the man who, as citizen, shares the kingly dignity, the sovereign power of the demos, may yet as a private individual labour under the indignity of utter destitution."[53]

The equality discussed thus far was the political equality of Athenian (male) citizens – as it was still 2,500 years later at the dawn of the human rights revolutions. But at least some of the limits of equality were the object of debate. The sophist Antiphon, for instance, famously argued against distinctions based upon birth and importantly ethnic origin, very clearly stating a universalist, cosmopolitan idea of the equality of all human beings:

> The sons of noble fathers we respect and look up to, but those from humble homes we neither respect nor look up to. In this we behave to one another like barbarians, since by nature we are all made to be alike in all respects, both barbarians and Greeks. This can be seen from the needs which all men have. [They can all be provided in the same way by all men, and in all this] none of us is marked off as either barbarian or Greek; for we all breathe the air with our mouth and nostrils and [eat with our hands].[54]

This passage rejects distinctions based upon social class, race and ethnic origin. It does so on the grounds of an anthropological theory that asserts the basic equal properties of all human beings. Antiphon explicitly includes the non-Greeks, the barbarians, which we should note means *all* non-Greeks. The argument of all humans' shared existential conditions is a powerful one and of great significance for the history of ideas. It has been appealed to by human beings in greatest need throughout history – as mirrored both in Shylock's plea for recognition in Shakespeare's literary reflection of human life[55] and in Primo Levi's self-assertion

[52] Aristophanes, "Assemblywomen," in Aristophanes, *Frogs, Assemblywomen, Wealth*, ed. and trans. Jeffrey Henderson, Loeb Classical Library 180 (Cambridge, MA: Harvard University Press, 2002).

[53] Vlastos, "Isonomia," 355. He rightly adds: "No impartial estimate of the democratic state can close its eyes to the consequences of this contradiction in terms of moral degradation, political corruption, and ceaseless class conflict to which Plato with merciless logic directs our attention," ibid.

[54] Hermann Diels and Walter Kranz, *Die Fragmente der Vorsokratiker*, Vol. 2 (Zürich: Weidmann, 2005), B 44: <τοὺς ἐκ καλῶν πατέρων ἐπ <αιδούμεθά τε κ<αὶ σεβόμεθα, τοὺς δὲ <ἐκ μὴ καλοῦ οἴκ<ου ὄντας οὔτε ἐπ<αιδούμεθα οὔτε σεβόμ<εθα. ἐν τούτω<ι δὲ πρὸς ἀλλήλους βεβαρβαρώ<μεθα, ἐπεὶ φύσει πάντα πάντ<ες ὁμοίως πεφύκ<αμεν καὶ βάρβαροι καὶ Ἕλλην<ες εἶναι. σκοπεῖν δὲ παρέχει τὰ τῶν φύσει <ὄντων ἀναγκαίων πᾶσιν ἀν<θρώποις· π<ορίσαι τε κατ<ὰ ταὐτὰ δυνα<τὰ πᾶσι, καὶ ἐν <πᾶσι τούτοις οὔτε β<άρβαρος ἀφώρισ<ται [δ] ἡμῶν ο<ὐδεὶς οὔτε Ἕλλην <·> ἀναπνέομεν τε γὰρ εἰς τὸν ἀέρ<α> ἅπαντες κατὰ τὸ στόμ<α κ> αἰ κατ<ὰ τὰς ῥῖνας κ<αὶ ἐσθίομε>ν χ<ερσὶν ἅ<παντες . . . >. Translation Guthrie, *Sophists*, 153.

[55] William Shakespeare, *The Merchant of Venice*, The Arden Shakespeare, ed. John Drakakis (London: Bloomsbury, 2010), 284, Act I, Scene 1: "I am a Jew. Hath not a Jew eyes? Hath not a Jew hands, organs, dimensions, senses, affections, passions?"

against the deathly and very real grip of racist ideology in Auschwitz.[56] It also lends itself quite clearly to a critique of patriarchal power structures. One needs, however, to recognize that the argument for the equal respect of all persons based on the equal properties of all human beings applies to women, too – unfortunately no small step in cultural and political terms, as history has proved.

In Antiphon's view, the equality of human beings has a normative consequence. We owe everybody equal *respect*, as otherwise we are behaving like "barbarians" (in this context, "barbarian" is used to refer to uneducated people who lack proper understanding rather than "non-Greeks").[57] At this point an interesting question arises: What is the normative correlative to respect owed to others? What are the normative positions of those to whom respect is owed in relation to the agent who owes respect? The fragment remains silent on this issue. It does not say that people without a "noble father" have a *right* to respect. One could therefore argue that there is no such right, that there is simply a blank space, that there is an entirely one-sided relation that consists of nothing but, first, a person's respect for others and, second, the obligation to show this respect to others but no correlative claim of these others. We already encountered this problem during the discussion of command-based ethical and legal codes: Such normative voids are hard to conceptualize. Another interpretation seems less far-fetched, namely that the others who are equals to be respected have a correlative *claim* to this kind of respect. If one reads the many pieces of democratic argument such as Athenagoras' speech, this seems to be an evident implication: Equals have a claim to equal rights because they deserve equal respect.

Antiphon's thought illustrates the depth of the reflection on equality and its normative consequences during Greek antiquity. Antiphon was, however, one voice in an obviously rich and controversial debate about human equality. His views align with some theorists[58] and clash with others, most notably (at least in certain respects) with the theories of Plato[59] and Aristotle,[60] which in different and complex ways defended the view that there are different classes of human beings. These anti-egalitarian arguments have political consequences, including the perceived legitimacy of slavery – the next issue to be considered. They also resonated through the centuries. Aristotelian arguments for inequality were, for instance, directly applied to justify the conquest of America, as we will see.

[56] Primo Levi, *Is This a Man?* (London: Abacus, 1987).

[57] Cf. Guthrie, *Sophists*, 153 on these difficulties.

[58] Cf. for instance the discussion by Aristotle, *Politics*, trans. Harris Rackham, Loeb Classical Library 264 (Cambridge, MA: Harvard University Press, 1932), 1277b.

[59] Cf. Plato, *Republic, Volume I: Books 1–5*, eds. and trans. Christopher Emlyn-Jones and William Preddy, Loeb Classical Library 237 (Cambridge, MA: Harvard University Press, 2013), 469b–c: only enslavement of barbarians permitted, but cf. also the picture of the wise Egyptians in Plato, "Timaeus," in Plato, *Timaeus, Critias, Cleitophon, Menexenus, Epistles*, trans. Robert Gregg Bury, Loeb Classical Library 234 (Cambridge, MA: Harvard University Press, 1929), 21e.

[60] Aristotle, *Politics*, 1254a.

3.4.4 *Slavery and the Search for Freedom, Equality and Equal Worth*

Slavery concerns questions of human equality, freedom and worth in equal measure. Consequently, it is a crucible of the pivotal normative principles that stand at the core of the human rights debate. It thus comes as no surprise that recent history has focused strongly upon the abolitionist movement, interpreting it – rightly – as a manifestation and moving aspect of human rights culture. It consequently is hard to talk about slavery and not think about its role in the history of the idea of human rights.

For very long stretches of time, slavery was a simple and self-evident social given. Slavery took very different forms – the life of a slave in a copper mine in Attica was scarcely comparable to that of a slave running a business for an Athenian citizen. There were even complaints that slaves in Athens had too much freedom of speech[61] and more rights to free expression than the citizens of other states.[62]

However this may be, there is little evidence that slavery was experienced as pleasant, and many documents attest to the suffering of slaves and the value of freedom. Euripides wrote: "[O] son . . . just one thing I urge upon you: never consent to live and go into slavery when you can choose to die as befits a free man."[63] The losses imposed by slavery included not only particular freedoms, such as freedom of speech,[64] but also self-determination more generally. Euripides' *Trojan Women*, for instance, is one great, heart-wrenching indictment of the "yoke of slavery."[65] The play is of particular interest because it concerns the fate of women. Women were not free in Athenian society, and even less free than in other ancient societies. Despite this, slavery is depicted as something even worse than the usual subjugation of women, testifying to the perceived importance of freedom for any human life.

Moreover, slavery was questioned in principled terms in antiquity. One good example is furnished by the observation of a loyal slave in Euripides' *Ion*: "Only one

[61] Aristophanes, "Frogs," in Aristophanes, *Frogs, Assemblywomen, Wealth*, ed. and trans. Jeffrey Henderson, Loeb Classical Library 180 (Cambridge, MA: Harvard University Press, 2002), 949.

[62] Demosthenes, "The Third Philippic," in Demosthenes, *Orations 1–17 and 20, Olynthiacs, Philippics, Minor Public Orations*, trans. James Herbert Vince, Loeb Classical Library 238 (Cambridge, MA: Harvard University Press, 1930), 226; Guthrie, *Sophists*, 156.

[63] Euripides, "Archelaus," fr. 245: ὦ παῖ, προβαλλ[ἓν δέ σοι μόνον προφωνῶ· μὴ ᾿πὶ δουλείαν ποτὲ ζῶν ἑκὼν ἔλθῃς παρόν σοι κατθανεῖν ἐλευθέρως. In Euripides, *Fragments, Euripides Vol. VII*, eds. and trans. Christopher Collard and Martin Cropp, Loeb Classical Library 504 (Cambridge, MA: Harvard University Press, 2008).

[64] Euripides, "Phoenician Women," in Euripides, *Helen, Phoenician Women, Orestes, Euripides Vol. V*, ed. and trans. David Kovacs, Loeb Classical Library 11 (Cambridge, MA: Harvard University Press, 2002), 388–93; Euripides, "Ion," in *Trojan Women, Iphigenia among the Taurians, Ion, Euripides Vol. IV*, trans. David Kovacs, Loeb Classical Library 10 (Cambridge, MA: Harvard University Press, 1999), 670–75; cf. below.

[65] Euripides, "Trojan Women," in *Trojan Women, Iphigenia among the Taurians, Ion, Euripides Vol. IV*, trans. David Kovacs, Loeb Classical Library 10 (Cambridge, MA: Harvard University Press, 1999), 600: ζυγὰ . . . δούλια.

thing brings shame to slaves, the name. In all else a slave who is valiant is not at all inferior to free men."[66] The equality of slaves and free human beings and thus the accidental nature of slavery find forceful expression in such passages.[67] As rightly has been concluded, "it would be perverse not to recognize an outright denial of natural divisions within the human race whereby one can be born to serve and another to rule, with the corollary that slavery is wrong in itself. A slave as such is of no less worth than a free man."[68]

Such statements about the equality of slaves and nonslaves were discussed widely some decades later, including by Aristotle. From this egalitarian perspective, slavery is unjust, for it is based on force, as Aristotle reports – even though he himself did not accept this conclusion, given his nonegalitarian anthropology.[69]

Here, too, we can inquire into the normative position enjoyed by human beings perceived as unjustly forced into slavery. Did they enjoy no such position? How plausible is this? Is it not less far-fetched to assume that those people unjustly enslaved by brute force had an implied moral right to be freed? As the discussion thus far has already amply illustrated, the category of a right enjoyed wide currency in the normative thinking and practice of antiquity, and it is certainly no anachronism to assume that this category was of importance in the context of slavery, too.

This debate about slavery implies a stance about the worth of freedom for human beings. There are very clear statements about what enslavement meant for the persons concerned, as the examples discussed powerfully illustrate. It did not take the dawn of modern individualism to feel the pain of bondage. It is not as if there were no strong arguments against slavery in antiquity. The problem was rather that they did not prevail. The situation was therefore no different from other epochs in

66 Euripides, "Ion," 854–56: ἓν γάρ τι τοῖς δούλοισιν αἰσχύνην φέρει, τοὔνομα· τὰ δ᾽ ἄλλα πάντα τῶν ἐλευθέρων οὐδὲν κακίων δοῦλος, ὅστις ἐσθλὸς ᾖ. The context does not contradict this statement: The slave advises Creusa to seek just self-protection and revenge without being depicted as somebody whose words cannot be taken seriously. Cf. as well Euripides, "Phrixus A or B," in Euripides, *Fragments: Oedipus-Chrysippus, Other Fragments, Euripides Vol. VIII*, eds. And trans. Christopher Collard and Martin Cropp, Loeb Classical Library 506 (Cambridge, MA: Harvard University Press, 2008), fr. 831: "For many slaves their name is a thing of shame, but their mind is freer than those who are not slaves"; Euripides, "Helen," in Euripides, *Helen, Phoenician Women, Orestes, Euripides Vol. V*, ed. and trans. David Kovacs, Loeb Classical Library 11 (Cambridge, MA: Harvard University Press, 2002), 728–33.

67 Another example is a passage from Alcidamas' Messenian speech: "God has set all men free; nature has made no man a slave," which Aristotle discusses in the context of his argument for a natural, not just legal justice, Aristotle, *The "Art" of Rhetoric, Aristotle Vol. XXII*, trans. John Henry Freese, Loeb Classical Library 193 (Cambridge, MA: Harvard University, 1926), 1373b, the Alcidamas quote supplied by the scholiast, Aristotle, *Rhetoric*, 140 f.: ἐλευθέρους ἀφῆκε πάντας θεός· οὐδένα δοῦλον ἡ φύσις πεποίηκεν.

68 Guthrie, *Sophists*, 159; cf. also Bernhard Williams' observation that slavery was regarded as an unjust evil, albeit one without a practical alternative, Bernhard Williams, *Shame and Necessity*, 2nd edition (Berkeley: University of California Press, 2008), 105 ff.

69 Aristotle, *Politics*, 1253b 20.

the struggle against slavery: One needs not only good arguments, but also the political and cultural leverage to make them count.

3.4.5 *Liberty and Tyranny*

Freedom also played an important role in other contexts. One central example is freedom of speech. *Isegoria* or *parrisia*, free speech, was robustly protected in the Athenian democracy. It was regarded as one of the hallmarks of the democratic order. At various points limitations were imposed, but these were often lifted again and did not do away with the practice in any case. On all accounts, freedom of speech was a fundamental right that citizens enjoyed. The political importance of this freedom is mirrored in the wider culture of the time. Take the following exchange between Jocasta and her son by Oedipus, Polynices, after the latter's clandestine return to Thebes from exile:

JOCASTA: What is it like to be deprived of your country? Is it a great calamity?
POLYNICES: The greatest: the reality far surpasses the description.
JOCASTA: What is its nature? What is hard for exiles?
POLYNICES: One thing is the most important: no free speech.
JOCASTA: A slave's lot this, not saying what you think.
POLYNICES: You must endure the follies of your ruler.[70]

Ion voices much the same sentiment in Euripides' eponymous drama. He does not know who his mother is but hopes that she is Athenian "so that I may have free speech as my maternal inheritance! For if a foreigner, even though nominally a citizen, comes into that pure-bred city, his tongue is enslaved and he has no freedom of speech."[71]

These passages are of interest in more than one respect. They make the supreme worth of freedom of speech vividly and directly tangible. They do so using the term *parrisia*, which refers to normatively protected liberty, not just to a factual ability to do something. Both passages understand freedom of speech as a right guaranteed by a particular community, in the case of Ion protected only for natives of the Athenian (mythical) polis. Ion does not know his origins. He only hopes he is Athenian. He nevertheless expresses quite clearly that in his view it would be legitimate for him to enjoy freedom of speech, whatever his origins. There is no indication that he considers it justified for the tongues of foreigners (such as he might be himself) to

[70] Euripides, "Phoenician Women," 388–93: ΙΟΚΑΣΤΗ: τί τὸ στέρεσθαι πατρίδος; ἦ κακὸν μέγα; ΠΟΛΥΝΕΙΚΗΣ: μέγιστον· ἔργῳ δ' ἐστὶ μεῖζον ἢ λόγῳ. ΙΟΚΑΣΤΗ: τίς ὁ τρόπος αὐτοῦ; τί φυγάσιν τὸ δυσχερές; ΠΟΛΥΝΕΙΚΗΣ: ἓν μὲν μέγιστον· οὐκ ἔχει παρρησίαν. ΙΟΚΑΣΤΗ: δούλου τόδ'εἶπας, μὴ λέγειν ἅ τις φρονεῖ. ΠΟΛΥΝΕΙΚΗΣ: τὰς τῶν κρατούντων ἀμαθίας φέρειν χρεών.

[71] Euripides, "Ion," 671–75: ἐκ τῶν Ἀθηνῶν μ' ἡ τεκοῦσ' εἴη γυνή, ὥς μοι γένηται μητρόθεν παρρησία. Καθαρὰν γὰρ ἤν τις ἐς πόλιν πέσῃ ξένος, κἂν τοῖς λόγοισιν ἀστὸς ᾖ, τό γε στόμα δοῦλον πέπαται κοὐκ ἔχει παρρησίαν.

be enslaved. It simply is a political and legal reality that this right is not protected if one is not a citizen of the city. His claim to freedom of speech is thus based on other grounds than belonging to a certain polis – most probably on the fact that he is a human person.

Jocasta's reaction to Polynices' assessment is interesting, too: The right to free speech was not guaranteed for women in Athens, nor was it guaranteed in the mythical Thebes where the dialogue is set. But this does not mean that she, as a woman, does not fully understand Polynices' point. Rather, it seems that she resents "a slave's lot" as much as her son. This was a view not only formulated by Euripides but heard and understood, if not endorsed, by his audience in the elevated social and cultural context of Athenian tragedy.

The right to free speech is singled out as a key element of democracy that contrasts democratic social orders with tyranny. Importantly, this is because it gives a person the freedom not only to speak, but also *not* to speak: "Freedom consists in this: 'Who has a good proposal and wants to set it before the city?' He who wants enjoys fame, while he who does not holds his peace. What is fairer for a city than this?"[72] The right thus explicitly has the content of a privilege to express oneself or refrain from doing it, with others having a no-right to the one or the other course of action.

In these ancient works, we thus find important questions relevant to the history of human rights: first, questions concerning the value of freedom of speech; second, the reasons for legitimately claiming it as a right; third, the difference between rights that are actually legally and politically guaranteed and the legitimate claims that people have that their rights be thus protected; and fourth, the reasons for the limited inclusion of certain groups of people among the bearers of such rights and the justification of these reasons. All of these works illustrate that the debate concerns rights in the proper sense, not some other kind of normative or non-normative position. Above all, they manifest a deep sense of the importance and human interest of these questions.

Another significant issue when considering the role of freedom in antiquity is why tyranny was regarded as a problem in Athenian democracy. The fact that it was seen as a major problem is illustrated by the great efforts made to avoid such rule, dubious as the means adopted against the abuse of power may have been – considering, for instance, the practice of ostracism. The answer can only be: because political liberty, freedom from power unrestrained by democratic decision-making, was regarded as an important good.[73] No defense of democracy or critique of tyranny is possible without valuing political freedom, though the structure of suppression of women and slaves shows the limits of this concern for liberty and equality.

[72] Euripides, "Suppliant Women," 438–41: τοὐλεύθερον δ' ἐκεῖνο· Τίς θέλει πόλει χρηστόν τι βούλευμ' ἐς μέσον φέρειν ἔχων; καὶ ταῦθ' ὁ χρῄζων λαμπρός ἐσθ', ὁ δ' οὐ θέλων σιγᾷ. τί τούτων ἔστ' ἰσαίτερον πόλει;

[73] Cf. the vivid warnings in Herodotus, *Histories*, Book III, 80, 3.

The desire for freedom is also one reason for the political importance of the equality of citizens and the rule of law. The rule of law is a tool guaranteeing the equality of citizens. At the same time, the equal political power of citizens in a democracy maintains the rule of law because it prevents the use of arbitrary power by individual tyrannical rulers.[74] The rule of law thus protects equality, equality the rule of law.[75] The equality of citizens under the rule of law has a central aim, however: to secure the citizens' freedom. The protection against arbitrary power by the rule of law and equal political rights thus underline the importance of freedom and political autonomy.

3.4.6 *Rape, Injustice and Human Self-Determination*

One recurrent theme of Greek mythology is the rape of women by both men and gods. This should be of interest to us, for rape brings together the issues of patriarchy, self-determination, bodily integrity, equality and violence – all of which are intricately connected with human rights and human rights law. "A curse on that night and its fate" is what the women of Troy have to say about being "brought to the bed of a Greek."[76] Such passages leave us in no doubt whatsoever that the horrific and degrading meaning of rape was already perceived very clearly in antiquity – in fact, it was thematized on the grand stage of the theater with chilling intensity.

What do such representations of suffering tell us about the normative framing of rape? The fate of Creusa in Euripides' *Ion* is a further interesting example that is relevant when answering this question. Creusa, an Athenian princess, is raped by Apollo. She gives birth to Ion, whom she abandons in despair[77] and with whom she is reunited only after years of deep sorrow. Not only is the pain of the act of rape itself deplored,[78] but the god also is accused of violating normative principles and crucially – inflicting a wrong upon *her*.[79] What does this imply for the normative position in which Creusa finds herself? Could these passages possibly be understood

[74] An important part of the radical shift in Plato's theory consists in the rehabilitation of the rule of law to prevent arbitrary power and of some of the democratic rights to protect human freedom in a constitution combining elements of monarchy and democracy, cf. Plato, Nomoi,, 693b ff., 714a ff.

[75] Herodotus, *Histories*, Book III, 80, 3. Vlastos, "Isonomia," 356 ff. For a warning analysis of how democratic mass rule under the influence of demagogues can destroy the rule of law, Aristotle, *Politics*, 1292a.

[76] Euripides, "Trojan Women," 204: ἔρροι νὺξ αὕτα καὶ δαίμων. Ibid. 203: λέκτροις πλαθεῖσ' Ἑλλάνων.

[77] Cf. the heart-wrenching line in Euripides, "Ion," 961: If you had seen the child stretching forth its hands to me! (εἰ παῖδά γ' εἶδες χεῖρας ἐκτείνοντά μοι).

[78] Euripides, "Ion," 342, 368.

[79] Euripides, "Ion," 972: ἀδικήσαντα. Cf. also ibid. 288, 367, 425–8, the remarkable reflection of Ion 429–51, Creusa's accusation of Apollo 859–922, 939, 941.

as implying that she had no claim that violence not be done to her and the god no corresponding obligation towards her, even though she passionately accuses him of doing her an injustice? There is nothing in the play that justifies Apollo's behavior. It does not seem plausible that Creusa and other characters in the play can accuse the god of inflicting the gravest injustice upon her and at the same time hold that she had no claim that he not violate her. She comments on the plight of women: "O unhappy women! O the criminal deeds of the gods! What is to happen? To what tribunal can we appeal when we are being done to death by the injustice of our masters?"[80] This observation is clear enough: The reason for her despair is not that she feels she and other women have no claim to be spared the indignity of rape, but that there is no institution able to enforce this legitimate claim given the perpetrators' overwhelming power. Is this merely a problem of the very distant past, unheard of in more recent attempts to protect the rights of human beings? If that is doubtful, then Creusa's remarks and the real suffering for which they stand deserve to be remembered.

3.4.7 *Justice and Rights*

Justice was a central concept for both ethics and law in the thought of this period. Its meaning and consequences were a core concern not only for Socrates, Plato and Aristotle – the remarks of Athenagoras indicate its particular political traction in public debate.

It has been underlined – and quite plausibly so – that central theories of justice in antiquity contain an implicit statement of rights. This implicit statement can be traced not by hunting for specific words that occur in the texts, but by undertaking an in-depth, substantive analysis of these theories, challenging as such an analysis may be.[81]

One common point of reference in these debates was Simonides' formula that justice consists in giving everybody that which they are owed.[82] Socrates saw this formula as relevant to but not exhaustive of justice. He clarified that it cannot mean that one does good to one's friends and inflicts harm upon one's foes. Justice, in his view, means not harming anybody.[83]

80 Euripides, "Ion," 252–4: ὦ τλήμονες γυναῖκες· ὦ τολμήματα θεῶν. τί δῆτα; ποῖ δίκην ἀνοίσομεν, εἰ τῶν κρατούντων ἀδικίαις ὀλούμεθα;

81 Vlastos, "Rights of Persons in Plato's Conception," 104 ff.; and the semantic analysis of Gregory Vlastos, "The Theory of Social Justice in the Polis in Plato's Republic," in *Studies in Greek Philosophy, Vol. 2: Socrates, Plato, and Their Tradition*, ed. Daniel W. Graham (Princeton, NJ: Princeton University Press, 1996), 70 ff.

82 Plato, *Republic*, 331d: *ta opheilomena*, "that what is owed to somebody."

83 Plato, *Republic*, 335e. Plato's Socrates is here understood as voicing genuine Socratic ideas – as widely assumed for the Socrates of Book I of the *Republic*.

This principle forms the starting point of Plato's argument in *The Republic* for a very particular understanding of justice.[84] The idea also is endorsed and qualified by Aristotle, among many other relevant voices: "Justice is a virtue which assigns to each man his due [τὰ αὑτῶν] in conformity with the law; injustice claims what belongs to others, in opposition to the law."[85]

Some interpretations see this formula as empty, understanding it to presuppose an additional standard for what is due to a concrete person – a lot, little, nothing? – without specifying what this standard might be. At first glance, this is true. However, all of the theories mentioned clearly understand the formula as a principle of the equality of persons, and this connection with equality, together with background assumptions about the natural interests of human beings, fills the formula with substance. Socrates' understanding is paradigmatic in this respect: The prohibition of harm, applied equally to everyone, whether friend or foe, already constitutes a substantial, nontrivial moral principle and derives from the formula of what is owed to others – it is everyone's due not to be harmed given that it is a fundamental interest of equal human beings not to suffer.

Importantly, the formula implies that rights are a normative correlative of just distribution. This does not mean only that justice demands the equal protection of given rights. This would leave open the question of what the normative reasons are for assuming that persons have these rights in the first place. Its additional, important point is that people have a right to a share of a just distribution of goods (their due). A just distribution is an equal distribution to which one has a right. If it is just to distribute a pie equally, Peter cutting the pie does not have free discretion to allocate the pieces as he will – the recipients have a right to an equal slice of the pie and the distributor a duty to distribute it accordingly.

This principle was reformulated by Ulpian and became one of the classic definitions of justice in the Western legal tradition through its incorporation into the *Corpus Iuris Civilis* and the reception of Roman law from the Middle Ages onwards. It appears in two versions, one with an explicit reference to rights (*iustitia est constans et perpetua voluntas ius suum cuique tribuere*; justice is the constant and unremitting will to render to everyone their own right), the other without (*suum*

[84] Plato's conception was at odds with the public conception of justice of his time (as far as we can reconstruct it), especially because he connects the harmony of the soul with justice and argues for radical inequality of political rights and his functional understanding of rights, cf. Gregory Vlastos, "Justice and Happiness in the Republic," in Gregory Vlastos, *Platonic Studies* (Princeton, NJ: Princeton University Press, 1981), 117; Vlastos, "Rights of Persons in Plato's Conception," 117: "A more extreme inequality in the tenure of political power has never been conjured up by the Greek imagination"; ibid. 122: The idea that only functional rights exist puts him at odds with the morality of his own society: "For Plato's public the question concerning the rights of persons whose urgency remained paramount over that of all other public issues concerned the just allocation of political rights which, for the Greeks, meant the right of direct participation in functions of government and therewith a share in the control of the state."

[85] Aristotle, *Rhetoric*, 1366b 7–8: ἔστι δὲ δικαιοσύνη μὲν ἀρετὴ δι' ἣν τὰ αὑτῶν ἕκαστοι ἔχουσι, καὶ ὡς ὁ νόμος, ἀδικία δὲ δι'ἣν τὰ ἀλλότρια, οὐχ ὡς ὁ νόμος.

cuique tribuere; to render to everyone their due).[86] The two versions need to be interpreted as synonymous, underlining the fact that the formulation "justice assigns to each person their due" implies a right, as it can be used interchangeably with a formulation that refers explicitly to rights.[87]

Another reading of this formula is possible, too. Here, the formula can be understood in an objective sense – for instance, as assigning the sanction for a crime that is just and in this sense due to the offender. What is meant, therefore, depends on the context.[88]

In the Greek debate, the principle encompassed not just one subset of rights, such as property rights,[89] but in fact included any entitlements, including far-reaching political claims.[90] Socrates' understanding of the issue once again is helpful in this respect: It refers to not inflicting any harm, not just harm to property.

Even the theory of justice that seems to break most radically with the concepts of justice common at that time, Plato's ideas in *The Republic* (later significantly modified in *The Laws*), needs to be understood as saying something about rights.[91] His shorthand formula for his concept of justice as "to do one's own" not only determines the duties of the members of the polis, but also indirectly defines what is due to them.[92] The members of the polis have a right to exactly those things that are necessary for doing what is "their own."[93] Therefore, the guardians, even women, have the right to rule if they have the required intellectual ability.[94] Otherwise, they could not fulfill their function, which is to govern the polis. Conversely, the guardians have no claim to any material privileges – the latter would just prevent

86 Corpus Iuris Civilis, Dig. 1.1.10.

87 Vlastos, "Social Justice in the Polis," 72 f. n 19: Ulpian relies on "one's own" to have fully as general and abstract a signification as "one's own *right*" (emphasis in original).

88 As a consequence, it is a fallacy to take only the objective sense of the formula as its true sense, as Michel Villey, "Suum Jus Cuique Tribuens," in *Studi in onore di Pietro de Francisi*, Vol. 2 (Milan: Giuffrè, 1956), 361–71 argued – for example, that it was the *ius* of heresy to suffer the death penalty, ibid. 364; for discussion cf. Tierney, *Idea of Natural Rights*, 16.

89 Cf. for this view Hart, "Are There Any Natural Rights?" 176.

90 Vlastos, "Justice and Happiness in the Republic," 120 n. 27: "As the Aristotelian definition shows, the scope of ta autou and ta allotria in such contexts is broad enough to cover everything to which persons would be morally or legally entitled." He illustrates this with Demosthenes, "Second Olynthiac," in Demosthenes, *Orations 1–17 and 20, Olynthiacs, Philippics, Minor Public Orations*, trans. James Herbert Vince, Loeb Classical Library 238 (Cambridge, MA: Harvard University Press, 1930), 26, where the reference is to rights to political sovereignty.

91 "Plato undertakes to do something never previously attempted in the history of the West: to determine on purely rational grounds all of the rights which all of the members of a particular society ought to have," Vlastos, "Rights of Persons in Plato's Conception," 105.

92 Plato, *Republic*, 433a ff., 433e f. formulates that justice consists in doing and having one's own.

93 This is the core of Plato's functionalist account of rights, cf. Vlastos, "Rights of Persons in Plato's Conception," 110: "All members of the polis have equal right to those and only those benefits which are required for the optimal performance of their function in the polis."

94 This includes explicitly the vision and achievement of the highest good, cf. Plato, *Republic*, 540c.

them from doing "their own," namely to rule the polis based on true justice.[95] These rights are not human rights, because they are rights dependent on membership in a polis and (importantly) dependent on the fulfillment of a social function.[96] For Plato, being human in itself is no reason to have rights. This is a key reason for the hierarchical, antiegalitarian structure of his imagined ideal polis, and one of the main reasons it is so unconvincing.[97]

For the purpose at hand, these examples suffice to elucidate that ancient discussions about rights were intimately related to question of justice – and not only in the political sphere, but also in the fascinating debates about the idea of justice that continue to shape important aspects of the search for the right order even today. The concept of rights was simply presupposed in all of these debates. As in the case of indigenous culture, without this concept, neither a description nor an analysis of ancient thinking and practice is possible.

3.4.8 *The Worth of Human Beings*

The abovementioned debate about slavery already implied an important question: What are the essential features that characterize a being as morally relevant, with a claim to respect, freedom and equal rights? Who shares these features? All human beings? Just a subclass of humans? What are the normative consequences of such properties?

The worth of human beings and their special status in the order of the world – the themes that inspired the discourse about human dignity in its many, not only modern variations – were the subject of explicit reflection. One famous (and very beautiful) example can be found in the verses in Sophocles' *Antigone* in which he praises on the one hand human beings' ability to build (to use a later term) a second nature through culture, prevailing over their many foes in the physical world. On the other hand, however, humans are described as tragic beings, always prone to harming others and themselves if they lose their way by acting contrary to the laws of justice, which are the laws of the gods. The Greek epithet *ta deina*, used to capture the core of human existence, refers to a being that is not only great and wonderful, but also uncanny and full of destructive forces – as Antigone's tragedy vividly

[95] Cf. Plato, *Republic*, 419a ff.

[96] The inclusion of Plato's theory of the *Republic* in the predecessors of human rights, cf. Paul Gordon Lauren, "The Foundations of Justice and Human Rights in Early Legal Texts and Thought," in *The Oxford Handbook of International Human Rights Law*, ed. Dinah Shelton (Oxford: Oxford University Press, 2013), 173, is, despite the role of women (and some other remarks) in his theory, ultimately unconvincing.

[97] Cf. Karl Popper, *The Open Society and Its Enemies, Vol. 1: The Spell of Plato* (London and New York: Routledge, 2009), 91 ff.; Vlastos, "Social Justice in the Polis," 91, 101 correctly observes: Plato has no concept of human dignity and thus of humans as ends-in-themselves; Vlastos, "Rights of Persons in Plato's Conception," 105, 120 ff.

illustrates.[98] Those wanting to write a history of the idea of what today is called human dignity would be well advised not to ignore such thoughts.

Encouraged by these examples, we can start to search for other traces of the idea of human worth. For example, Socrates' understanding of justice as (at least) implying that one should not harm anybody seems to make little sense if there is not something about other human beings that demands that much respect for their well-being. Socrates' respect for human autonomy, displayed in his attitude towards his partners in dialogue, appears to support this interpretation. He wants to incite them to think independently and is not trying to betray, manipulate or dominate them. In particular, he trusts in his interlocutors' moral autonomy, in their ability to truly understand what is just and to act accordingly.[99] His irony is a statement of respect for others' power of judgment, their ability to discern the serious meaning of thoughts dressed in the light colors of irony. This attitude towards others entails an acknowledgment of their worth as thinking and self-determined subjects, an acknowledgment that unsurprisingly has resonated as both an encouragement and an inspiration through the ages.

3.4.9 *The Human Polis*

The Stoics and their reflections on the content and nature of Natural Law provide another important body of thought that is of interest in our search for the deeper sources of the idea of human rights.[100] The thinkers counted as part of this tradition held many differing opinions. Some voices underlined the particular value of human beings because of certain properties they enjoyed – an argument that even today remains a central, albeit controversial source of the ascription of the predicate of dignity to humans. Furthermore, some Stoics developed a distinctly cosmopolitan vision: All human beings are members of one polis and therefore live under one kind of Natural Law. Stoic Natural Law criticized slavery as a violation of human equality, although some Stoics also defended slavery from this point of view. Here, we once again can ask: If some Stoics understood slavery as a violation of a cosmopolitan Natural Law of equality, then what was the slaves' normative position? Did they enjoy an entitlement to be freed? There is no doctrine of rights in Stoic philosophy, but it is certainly at least as plausible that claims were implied in the normative propositions of this philosophy as in the other examples discussed.

Cicero is an heir to the Stoic tradition in many ways, albeit with a strong dose of theoretical eclecticism. One important idea of his was to use *dignitas*, dignity, not

98 Sophocles, "Antigone," in Sophocles, *Antigone, The Women of Trachis, Philoctetes, Oedipus at Colonus*, ed. and trans. Hugh Llyod-Jones, Loeb Classical Library 21 (Cambridge, MA: Harvard University Press, 1994), 332 ff.: "πολλὰ τὰ δεινὰ. . ."

99 Cf. on the implied moral autonomy of his partners in dialogue, cf. Vlastos, *Socrates*, 44.

100 Cf. for more details Matthias Mahlmann, *Rechtsphilosophie und Rechtstheorie*, 7th edition (Baden-Baden: Nomos, 2023), 60 ff.

only to refer to the relative social position of human beings, but also to designate their worth as human beings as such – although he certainly did not draw the same practical conclusions as we do today with 2,500 more years of experience and reflection.[101]

3.4.10 *Actions and Rights in Roman Law*

Roman law developed a particularly sophisticated legal system that remains influential to this day. One seasoned topic of discussion is the existence of subjective rights in this action-based legal system. Because of this constitutive feature of Roman law, some scholars deny that it had any concept of subjective rights. The actions, the lawsuits, the *actio in rem* concerning objects and the *actio in personam* concerning mainly the law of obligations, however, do not support this conclusion. After all, a claim or subjective right, which is enforced by the lawsuit, forms the necessary basis of legal action. Moreover, the category of subjective rights played an important role in Roman law, including property rights, the rights making up the *patria potestas* over one's children or rights concerning one's wife (*manus*), the right to inheritance, the rights of tutors and curators and the patronage of the liberator over the slaves the liberator has freed. It seems difficult to interpret the given body of Roman law plausibly without reference to the category of subjective rights.[102] In addition, important instruments such as the *actio iniuriarum* made it possible for persons to sue others over violations of personal injuries, implying that respect for one's person was indeed a right.

Furthermore, famous passages of Roman law echo parts of the older traditions of Natural Law. These include the assumption of the equality of human beings and their freedom under Natural Law.[103] When setting out the foundational assumptions of Roman law, Ulpian underlines that originally all persons were just called human beings. According to Ulpian, slavery is an artificial creation. The distinction between free persons, slaves and liberated persons was only introduced later.[104] Freedom is defined as the ability to do what one wants to unless one is prevented from doing so by force or law.[105] The legal status of a free person entails not just the *factual ability* to do as one pleases unless prevented by force or law. It is a normative status, *iusta*

[101] Cf. on dignity as relative to social position Cicero, On invention, II, 166; Cicero, *De re publica*, I, 43. On dignity as the specific value of human beings as human beings, cf. for instance Cicero, *De officiis*, 1, 11 ff., 105 or his formulation that human beings are an image of god – "*cum deo similitude*," Cicero, *De legibus*, I, 25. For comments, Mahlmann, *Elemente*, 109 f.

[102] Cf. Max Kaser and Rolf Knütel, *Römisches Privatrecht*, 20th edition (Munich: C. H. Beck, 2014), § 4.

[103] Ulpian, Dig. 1.1.4.

[104] Ulpian, Dig. 1.1.4.

[105] Inst. 1.3.1: "*Et libertas quidem est, ex qua etiam liberi vocantur, naturalis facultas eius quod cuique facere libet, nisi si quid aut vi aut iure prohibetur.*"

libertas,[106] which implies subjective rights. These include the claim that others do not circumscribe the liberty of a free person and treat him as slaveholders are allowed to treat their slaves. That means, more concretely, for instance, that a free person enjoys not only the legal ability (the power in Hohfeldian terms), but also the entitlement to acquire property for himself, not just for the slaveholder and under the restrictive conditions set out by the law on slavery, among many other concrete claims based on the legal status of a free person.[107] This legal status was not lost when a person was forced into slavery without legal grounds, implying that legal claims arising from the status of a free person continued to exist.[108]

The doctrines on original equality and freedom as part of Natural Law did not act as a shield against the legal entrenchment of institutions such as slavery. On the contrary, these institutions were put into practice in often gruesome and appalling legal detail. As the reference to the original equality and freedom of human beings shows, the architects of this system were well aware of other positions. They were conscious, too, that slavery meant misery for the person concerned. Accordingly, the legal possibility to be freed by *manumissio* was highlighted as a benefit (*beneficium*),[109] whereas slavery was a *calamitas*, a misfortune, as the *Digests* note, for instance, in passing – a misfortune great enough that it should not be legally imposed on children when their mother had conceived while she was still free but had borne the child when she already was enslaved.[110] It is consequently an oversimplification to state that criticism of institutions such as slavery on the grounds of human liberty were unknown in Roman law. Other considerations, unconcerned with the misfortune imposed on many human beings, simply prevailed, as they did in the many centuries of slavery to follow. Moreover, we should not overlook the elements of human freedom and equality protected in this normative system. Not only the conceptual tools of Roman law were important for subsequent developments, but also these elements. They were used, sometimes centuries later, as argumentative resources to reclaim liberty – for instance, when the idea of human beings' freedom under Natural Law was invoked to counter another misfortune imposed on others: the conquest of America.[111] This illustrates the methodological point made above: The history of the development of human rights is a history of expanding the scope of the content and the class of beneficiaries of certain rights, which were at first selectively guaranteed – a scope, moreover, that sometimes contracted again over the course of history. The intricacies of Roman law are relevant for this history – not because this law already formulated human rights

[106] Cf. Inst. 1.5.3 on the development of the differentiated rights associated over time with the status of a freed person.
[107] On the *potestas* of the slaveowner, Inst. 1.8. Dig. 1.6.1.1.
[108] Inst. 1.4.1.
[109] Inst. 1.5.
[110] Cf. Inst. 1.4.
[111] Cf. on the use of Dig. 1.1.4. in Las Casas' argumentation against slavery below.

proper, as some argue,[112] but because it illustrates the many forms that systems operating with individual rights and with content related to human rights (like freedom) can adopt. These systems form the raw material from which the idea of human rights ultimately was molded. They show what steps need to be taken to make this idea explicit and what obstacles stand in its way. Even in the system of Roman law, a reference to the universal freedom of human beings was inscribed, an idea that was irrelevant in practical terms but whose time would come. The fact that this reference to a Natural Law of freedom existed offers not only a hopeful, but also a sobering lesson, however: An explicit idea of universal freedom is no guarantee that a culture and its legal systems will not disregard its commands.

A final remark: As already discussed above, one of the most influential definitions of justice by no less a figure than Ulpian echoes the older Greek discussion linking justice and rights. This alone is sufficient evidence to show that claims or subjective rights were part of Roman law – unsurprisingly so, given that this law was one of the technically most sophisticated pieces of legal thinking ever developed.

3.4.11 *Varieties of Rights*

Even a brief discussion of these selected ancient sources already shows how lively, controversial and profound the debate about the equality, freedom and worth of human beings was, a debate with grand stakes for political rights, institutions such as slavery and the lives of women. This debate included thoughts about the universality of ideas such as equality, forging arguments that in principle remain current today about the existential equality of human beings and its normative consequences, arguments that in contemporary frameworks are discussed in universalist terms. They naturally included – implicitly or explicitly, and expressed using different linguistic means, as the Greek example in particular shows – the complex category of subjective rights in many variants.

These debates about competing ideas prevent us from regarding the complex world of Greek and Roman antiquity as a monolithic whole, stating, for instance, that this period had no concept of equality, freedom or rights. This is a crucial finding for the purpose of our study. Another point is worth mentioning: One cannot argue that Antiphon's defense of the equality of all human beings and Aristotle's critique of this idea had simple cultural causes, as very different thoughts were put forward eloquently in the same culture. These controversies *within the same cultural framework* were a matter of competing ideas and arguments and were not due to simple and superficial properties of their exponents' backgrounds.

To be sure, rights in the examples discussed were not part of human rights catalogues. Some theories were quite contrary to a plausible set of human rights

[112] Tony Honoré, *Ulpian: Pioneer of Human Rights* (Oxford: Oxford University Press, 2002).

in many respects – prime examples include Plato's division of humanity,[113] Aristotle's defense of slavery and slavery's legal regulation in Roman law. The examples nevertheless illustrate that these ancient sources contain aspects that are relevant and quite interesting for the convoluted history of the concept of subjective rights.

Acknowledging this does not mean glossing over the less attractive features of slave societies without rights for women, in the case of the Athenian democracy pursuing an exploitative, aggressive foreign policy ultimately to its own detriment. Nor does it mean that the admirable features of these cultures led to current human rights systems in a continuous line of development. Rather, these thoughts exemplify what later epochs, including our own, have underlined: There are many voices in history, including powerful ones that incite human beings to injustice, cruelty, subjugation and often self-destruction. However, there are other voices, too, which make a case for the equality, freedom and worth of all human beings, sometimes even couched in the language of rights. We should listen to these voices if we want to do justice to the greatness and tragedy of the history of the deeper sources of the human rights idea.

3.5 RIGHTS SINCE ANTIQUITY

3.5.1 *Rights at the Dawn of a New (European) Era*

One important document from the twilight of antiquity is the document commonly called the *Edict of Milan* (313), following Galerius' *Edict of Toleration*, issued in 311.[114] The *Edict* is part of Christianity's slow rise from a proscribed faith to the state religion of the Roman Empire.[115] It grants religious freedom not only to Christians, but also to members of other religions, ordering the restitution of the property people have lost through religious persecution. It establishes a right (*potestas*, *facultas*) to the free exercise of religion in broad and clear terms, including some

[113] As already mentioned, the core problem of Plato's theory of justice is that the citizens of the polis are ultimately not regarded as an end-in-themselves, Vlastos, "Social Justice in the Polis," 91.

[114] Cf. for the debate about the nature of the document, in particular whether it formed an edict and its context, Noel Lenski, "The Significance of the Edict of Milan," in *Constantine: Religious Faith and Imperial Policy*, ed. Edward Siecienski (London and New York: Routledge, 2017), 27–56.

[115] Lenski, "Edict of Milan," 33 sums up: "As this scheme indicates, the period between 306 and 313 represented a water-shed in the history of the legitimization of the Christian faith. As often happens in periods of social change, this process did not occur all at once but was slow and confusing. … The Edict of Milan represents the culmination of this process and stands apart from other related legal pronouncements of the era in its combination of the three principles of the restoration of public rights, the restitution of churches, and the return of other confiscated real estate to Christians. The concatenation of these three principles in a single legal text is attested for the first time ever in the Edict of Milan."

justificatory arguments about the need to protect this right for the sake of peace.[116] The *Edict* represents yet another example from late antiquity illustrating the important role played by the idea of rights at that time – rights as a naturally used normative resource for political action. With freedom of religion, the *Edict* concerns an issue that is fundamental for the history of human rights. It grants this right to all persons under the rule of the Emperor and does not limit it to persons with certain characteristics. The *Edict* also indicates the distance to be crossed from a right such as this, granted by an Emperor not fully living up to its promise, to later ideas about freedom of religion, including the natural rights tradition and finally the idea of human rights as inalienable rights of human beings that are not granted by an Emperor, but rather deny his claim to power.

It should be noted, however, that the *Edict* does not tell the whole story of ideas of rights at that time, such as the thoughts that the Christians had about their normative position. The *Edict* certainly did not grant to Christians and other believers something they had never heard of – a right to religious freedom – but rather mirrored their demands or at least their aspirations, issues that were of fundamental importance for them. While not formulated in the language of modern human rights, the *Edict* thus is a highly significant testimony of the prevalence of the issue of a right to freedom of religion at that time as well as to the wishes of human beings of different creeds concerning their normative status. As such, the *Edict* is very much part of the history of human rights.[117]

[116] Cf. Lenski, "Edict of Milan," 46 for a comparison of the language of the versions rendered by Lactantius and Eusebius, respectively. Cf. for example: "*Quae sollicitudini tuae plenissime significanda esse credidimus, quo scires nos liberam atque absolutam colendae religionis suae facultatem isdem Christianis dedisse. Quod cum isdem a nobis indultum esse pervideas, intellegit dicatio tua etiam aliis religionis suae vel observantiae potestatem similiter apertam et liberam pro quiete temporis nostri <esse> concessam, ut in colendo quod quisque delegerit, habeat liberam facultatem. <Quod a nobis factum est. Ut neque cuiquam> honori neque cuiquam religioni <detrac tum> aliquid a nobis <videatur>.*" *Edictum Mediolanense*, Lactantius, Mort. Pers. (Fritzsche, Lactantius, Opera, II, Leipzig, 1844), 288–9; "We thought it fit to commend these things most fully to your care that you may know that we have given to those Christians free and unrestricted opportunity of religious worship. When you see that this has been granted to them by us, your Worship will know that we have also conceded to other religions the right of open and free observance of their worship for the sake of the peace of our times, that each one may have the free opportunity to worship as he pleases; this regulation is made that we may not seem to detract aught from any dignity or any religion." Text and translation: https://droitromain.univ-grenoble-alpes.fr/Constitutiones/ed_tolerati.htm (accessed September 1, 2021). Importantly, the *Edict* is not motivated by *indulgentia*, "unmerited forbearance granted by an emperor to a religion that remained for him fundamentally repugnant," as explicitly Galerius' edict of 311, but by the idea of religious liberty, perhaps inspired by Lactantius himself, cf. Lenski, "Edict of Milan," 46 ff.

[117] Lenski, "Edict of Milan," 50: "Even if Constantine – as, indeed, all other rulers down to the present – never truly enacted these principles in full, their open and reasoned expression in this document remains remarkable. In this sense, the Edict of Milan was perhaps the first official document in the Western tradition to enact the principle of religious liberty into law."

This illustrates the methodological point made above about the many sources of ideas of rights. It is thus a fallacy to take certain political or legal documents as the only key to determining the state of a given idea's historical development. The fact that the Emperor granted a right does not mean that his subjects did not entertain other, more capacious concepts of legitimate claims. The fact that women had few rights in many ancient societies does not mean that women had no ideas that transcended this state of affairs – as powerfully expressed in the most important artworks of that time, as we have seen. We need to remember this point when turning to other important instruments of the development of the law.

3.5.2 *Natural Rights and Medieval Rebellion*

Medieval and scholastic thought worked with a well-developed notion of subjective rights. Twelfth-century authors referred to a faculty or power (*facultas*, *potestas*), using a traditional terminology to describe a normative position that, according to the analytical account above, can count as a right, though often with remaining analytical ambiguities. The rediscovery of Roman law acted as a catalyst for the development of legal thinking, spearheaded by canon law since the *Decretum Gratiani* (1140). It profoundly influenced the terminology and conceptions of rights.[118]

The *Magna Carta* (1215) belongs to this time. It grants certain rights to the nobility and freemen of England, and thus to a limited group of people. It was inspired by the English barons' desire to defend their existing rights against encroachment by King John. One of its most famous articles – 39, later 29 – concerns the right not to have one's rights interfered with without the Crown abiding by some medieval standards of the due process of law. There are, however, other interesting provisions, too – for example, concerning freedom of movement.

It is often argued that the *Magna Carta* does not belong in the history of human rights proper because of its limited personal scope and aim to reinforce the traditional rights of the nobility. On the other hand, it had an enormous impact on the development not only of English, but also of American constitutional law, as it was interpreted (not least under Coke's influence) as an instrument to protect freedom. The personal scope expanded given the increasing number of freemen. Accordingly, the *Magna Carta* is a good example of the incremental steps in which rights developed, leading from securing a right within a certain area of protection for a limited group of privileged people to the slow inclusion of wider circles of persons into the personal scope of protection – often against the resistance of the privileged minority.[119]

[118] Cf. for detailed studies, Tierney, *Idea of Natural Rights*; Tuck, *Natural Rights Theories*.

[119] Cf. James Clarke Holt, *Magna Carta*, 3rd edition (Cambridge: Cambridge University Press, 2015), 36: "For Coke, Magna Carta was an affirmation of fundamental law and the liberty of the subject. For the modern historian it is a statement of liberties rather than an assertion of liberty; a privilege which was devised mainly in the interests of the aristocracy, and which was

The idea of explicitly stated "natural rights" gained importance in this period. These rights concerned different issues, from Godfrey of Fontaines' idea of a right in mounting a case against papal power in the 1280s to Ockham's inalienable right to property.[120] Moreover, there are good arguments for holding that Thomas Aquinas included rights in his Natural Law theory. One example is his argument that persons in need can take the property necessary for their subsistence lawfully if they are in concrete danger because this property is owed to them by the owners. Under these circumstances, the property becomes the lawful property of the needy. It does not seem very plausible to deny that, according to this argument for basic human solidarity, persons in need have substantial claims to the support of others.[121]

The struggles for the restoration and protection of rights were not limited to the nobility and philosophical reflection. Fundamentally important rights were demanded from below in popular revolts. The famous proverb "When Adam delved and Eve span, who was then a Gentleman?" was used (and perhaps formulated) during the Peasants' Revolt of 1381 in a sermon of the preacher John Ball.[122] It reasserts the fundamental equality of human beings and clearly implies the claim to be treated accordingly. Another important and tragic example stems from the German Peasant Wars of 1525, one of the major popular uprisings in European history in which Luther ultimately sided with the feudal lords against the peasants whose movement in the end was crushed by force.[123] A central document of the

applicable at its widest to the 'free man' – to a class which formed a small proportion of the population of thirteenth-century England." This, however, was just the starting point of the further development, in particular concerning cap. 29, ibid. 39 f.: "Between 1331 and 1368, in six acts, Parliament passed statutory interpretations of this clause which went far beyond any of the detailed intention and sense of the original Charter. First, it interpreted the phrase 'lawful judgement of peers' to include trial by peers and therefore trial by jury, a process which existed only in embryo in 1215. Secondly, the 'law of the land' was defined in terms of yet another potent and durable phrase – 'due process of law', which meant procedure by original writ or by indicting jury. It was construed to exclude procedure before the Council or by special commission and to limit intrusions into the sphere of action of the common-law courts; it was even applied against trial for trespass in the Exchequer. Thirdly, the words 'no free man' were so altered that the Charter's formal terms became socially inclusive. In the earlier statutes of Edward III of 1331 and 1352 they became simply 'no man', but in 1354 in the statute which refers for the first time to 'due process of law', 'no free man' became 'no man of whatever estate or condition he may be'. ... The seventeenth-century interpretation which Coke typified produced some additions to the fourteenth century glosses, but they were in the main minor extensions to, or clarifications of, an already widely extended range of interpretations." This included the application of cap. 29 to villeins, interpretation of liberties as "liberty" and the argument that *Magna Carta* established grounds for the writ of Habeas Corpus, ibid. 41 f. On the influence of *Magna Carta* on the Levellers and American Law, ibid. 45.

120 Tierney, *Idea of Natural Rights*, 13 ff.

121 Cf. Thomas Aquinas, *Summa Theologica*, II-II, q. 66, 7. This is an indication that the neo-Thomists who criticize the idea of subjective rights are less Thomist than is sometimes assumed.

122 Cf. Susan Marks, A *False Tree of Liberty: Human Rights in Radical Thought* (Oxford: Oxford University Press, 2019), 46 ff.

123 Cf. Peter Blickle, *Die Revolution von 1525*, 4th edition (Munich: Oldenbourg, 2004).

uprising lists twelve articles with the peasants' demands. They concerned the abolishment or easing of the burdens imposed on the peasants by their lords and asserted the right to freedom of all human beings who are created equal. Therefore, they also insisted on the abolishment of serfdom. Such demands echoed older views, including those found in such important restatements of customary medieval law as the *Sachsenspiegel* (1215–1235), which influenced the law of the German states for 700 years. Its author, Eike von Repgow, argued for the initial equality and freedom of human beings: "All people were free when our ancestors came here to this land. My mind cannot comprehend that one person could belong to another." He regarded serfdom (the legal meaning of which the rules reported in the *Sachsenspiegel* flesh out in great detail), in contrast, as unjust violence: "The genuine truth, however, is that bondage resulted from coercion, imprisonment, and unlawful exercise of force, which has become unjust custom since ancient times, and now people take it to be right and good custom."[124]

These examples show the important role that rights and ideas of freedom and equality, explicitly derived from the existential conditions of human beings and conceptualized in religious terms, played in the struggles for social justice and liberation of ordinary people of that period – a role they continued to play in the centuries to come.[125]

3.5.3 *Natural Rights and the Conquest of America*

Spanish late scholastic thought contributed a further famous chapter to the history of natural rights. This school of thinking serves as another example for the purpose of our historical overview, and for two reasons: first, the depth of its arguments; and second, the political issue that stands in the background and sometimes in the foreground of reflection, namely the European subjugation and exploitation of South and Central America and the human suffering and loss these caused.

The founder of the School of Salamanca, Francisco de Vitoria, developed a differentiated theory of natural rights, particularly in his comments on Aquinas.[126] These rights form part of Natural Law. According to Vitoria, this law can be understood by all human beings, including non-Christians, and thus also can be

[124] Cf. Eike von Repgow, *Der Sachsenspiegel*, trans. Paul Kaller (Munich: Beck, 2002), Book III, 42 § 2, 4, 6; Eike von Repgow, *The Saxon Mirror*, trans. Maria Dobozy (Philadelphia: University of Pennsylvania Press, 1999), Book III, 125 f.; Blickle, *Revolution*, 105 ff.; David von Mayenburg, *Gemeiner Mann und Gemeines Recht. Die Zwölf Artikel und das Recht des ländlichen Raums im Zeitalter des Bauernkriegs* (Frankfurt am Main: Vittorio Klostermann, 2018), 240.

[125] Cf. for some more examples and comments Bloch, *Naturrecht*; Marks, *A False Tree*.

[126] Francisco de Vitoria, "On Law: Lectures on St. Thomas Aquinas," in Francisco de Vitoria, *Political Writings*, eds. Anthony Pagden and Jeremy Lawrence (Cambridge: Cambridge University Press, 1991), 155 ff.

comprehended by the inhabitants of the Americas, as they, too, enjoy the natural light, the common human faculty of understanding.

Vitoria provided a definition of a subjective right in line with earlier formulations: "A right is the power or faculty that somebody enjoys by law, which means a faculty, provided for me by law, concerning anything that I need."[127] Vitoria's theory of property is particularly relevant for such subjective rights. It is based on the idea that every human being has a claim to the goods of this Earth. Vitoria conceptualized the concrete order of property as the product of a common agreement establishing human law. This meant, among other things, that the indigenous Americans had a title (*dominium*) to their land – that it was not *terra nullius*, not a territory that belonged to nobody and was therefore up for conquest. It is clear that he is concerned with a normative claim, as he distinguishes this normative position from the factual ability to take somebody's goods.[128] The scope of the rights he discusses overlaps in crucial respects with current human rights positions, including the rights to life, bodily integrity, freedom and property, though traditional limitations apply – for instance, as to the freedom of women. In addition, he assumes a right to freedom of movement and to commerce between peoples based on their natural society and communication. There are also political rights, not least the right to determine the form of government.

A particular conception of the normative status of human beings forms the basis of this argument. They are subjects who are entitled to determine themselves, are free and exist for their own sake.[129] His discussion of the four reasons why the indigenous Americans could not have rights illustrates this clearly: This could be so because they are sinners, infidels, lunatics or insane.[130] None of these arguments proves valid: Sinners still can enjoy *dominium* because they are created in God's image and exist for their own sake. Infidels can have rights, as can lunatics and insane persons. In any case, indigenous Americans are no lunatics but self-determining human beings.

Vitoria assessed Spain's claims in America on this basis, dismissing influential voices that defended the Spanish conquest. Vitoria considers seven arguments that in his view are not sufficient to justify denying indigenous Americans *dominium*:[131]

[127] Francisco de Vitoria, *De Iustitia, Über die Gerechtigkeit, Teil 2*, ed. Joachim Stüben (Stuttgart and Bad Cannstatt: Frommann-Holzboog, 2017), quaestio LXII, articulus I, 8: "*Ius est potestas vel facultas conveniens alicui secundum leges, id est facultas data, v.g. mihi a lege ad quamcumque rem opus sit.*"

[128] Francisco De Vitoria, "De Indis," in *Vorlesungen (Relectiones) Vol. II: Völkerrecht, Politik, Kirche*, eds. Ulrich Horst, Heinz-Gerhard Justenhoven and Joachim Stüben (Stuttgart: Kohlhammer, 1997), 401; English translation in Francisco Vitoria, *Vitoria: Political Writings*, eds. Anthony Pagden and Jeremy Lawrence (Cambridge: Cambridge University Press, 1991), 248.

[129] Vitoria, "De Indis," 403; Vitoria, *Political Writings*, 249.

[130] Vitoria, "De Indis," 387 ff.; Vitoria, *Political Writings*, 240 ff.

[131] Vitoria, "De Indis," 407 ff.; Vitoria, *Political Writings*, 251 ff.

Neither the emperor nor the pope have power over the whole world sufficient to abrogate the rights of indigenous Americans. The discovery of America justifies the denial of rights of indigenous Americans as little as the discovery of Europe by indigenous Americans would have justified abrogating the rights of Europeans. Indigenous Americans had not been given sufficient reason to believe in Christianity, so proselytizing does not provide justification either. Sins do not justify the derogation of rights because it is unthinkable to be entitled to conquer all countries where there are sinners, as there are quite a few. The indigenous Americans have not elected the Spanish kings, nor was America a gift of God to Spain.

Vitoria based a possible justification for Spain's claims on the right to movement and commerce, including to war to defend this right. Spaniards enjoyed the right to spread Christianity peacefully and protect converters. These rights could be defended by force if denied. The indigenous Americans could elect Spanish kings voluntarily. Spaniards could lend support to other indigenous Americans in war. Another argument, likewise of interest for the history of human rights, was that indigenous American societies violated Natural Law by sacrificing humans and even practicing cannibalism. This violation justified intervention to stop this practice. In Vitoria's view, there were no slaves by nature, though he kept open the possibility that the Spanish dominion could be justified by indigenous Americans' need to be ruled because of being close to be incapacitated – but only if this rule aimed at their benefit and they indeed did not have the ability to rule themselves, which he was not asserting as proven.[132]

This leaves Vitoria in an ambivalent position towards the conquest of America. His thought contains strong critical potential, and his theory made it much more difficult to justify the atrocities perpetrated by the Spanish, not least on the ground of natural rights. He explicitly voiced strong doubts that the conquest could be justified, considering all of these reasons. On the other hand, rights and rights violations were used to justify the use of force against others. The Spanish conquest certainly had nothing to do with protecting the rights of indigenous Americans, and in political practice it was not based on restrictive arguments like Vitoria's. Vitoria's argumentation nevertheless represents an early example of the danger of potential misapplications of these notions, strengthening (albeit unwillingly) the ideological foundations of projects such as the conquest of America.

A now-famous voice that also forms part of the context of Spanish late scholastic thought is Bartolomé de Las Casas. His critique of the Spanish conquest of America starts from points that lie right at the heart of the idea of human rights.

The first of these points is the ascertainment of the equality of human beings as reasonable beings with the capacity for autonomous self-determination and consequently with equal worth:

[132] Vitoria, "De Indis," 457 ff.; Vitoria, *Political Writings*, 277 ff.

> All peoples of the world are made up of human beings, and there is only one definition of all human beings and of each one of them, which is that they are rational creatures; they all have their own reason and will and freedom of decision, because they are created in the image and likeness of God. All human beings have five outer and four inner senses and are driven by the same purposes; they all possess the natural or seedlike principles through which to understand, study, and discern the sciences and things that they do not know, and this goes not only for those with virtuous tendencies, but also can be found in those who are bad because of their depraved customs; all delight in the good and take pleasure in what is enjoyable and amusing, and all reject and abhor evil and are displeased by what is unpleasant and harmful to them.[133]

The second is the capacity for free self-determination and the central value of freedom for human beings:

> It is obvious that liberty is the highest and most precious of all worldly goods and is beloved of all creatures, both sentient and non-sentient, and most of all of rational creatures. . . . If human beings do not agree to an interference with their aforementioned liberty of their own free, uncoerced will, then everything is based only upon duress and violence, is unjust and perverted, and is null and void according to natural law, for this turns the state of freedom into that of servitude, which is the greatest detriment apart from death.[134]

Liberty is understood as a natural right of all humans: "Freedom is an inborn right that humans possess necessarily and in themselves from the beginning. Therefore it is a matter of Natural Law."[135] It is hard to find any qualitative distinction between

[133] Bartolomé de Las Casas, *Obras Completas Vol. 7: Apologética Historia Sumaria II* (Madrid: Alianza Editorial, 1988), Cap. 48, 536: "*todas las naciones del mundo son hombres y de todos los hombres y de cada uno dellos es una no más la definición, y ésta es que son racionales; todos tienen su entendimiento y su voluntad y su libre albedrió como sean formados a la imagen y semejenza de Dios. Todos los hombres tienen sus cinco sentidos exteriores y sus cuatro interiores y se mueven por los mismos objectos dellos; todos tienen los principios naturales o simientes para entender y para aprender y saber las sciencias y cosas que no saben, y esto no sólo es los bien inclinados, pero también se halla en los que por depravadas constumbres son malos; todos se huelgan con el bien y sienten placer con lo sabroso y alegre, y todos desechan y aborrecen el mal y se alteran con lo desabrido y que les hace daño*" (translation M. Hiley).

[134] Bartolomé de Las Casas, *Obras Completas Vol. 10: Tratados de 1552, Impresos por Las Casas en Sevilla* (Madrid: Alianza Editorial, 1992), Octavo Remedio, Razón Nona, 327 f.: "*Manifiesto es que . . . la libertad sea la cosa más preciosa y suprema en todos los bienes deste mundo temporales, y tan amada y amiga de todas las criaturas sensibles e insensibles, y mucho más de las racionales. . . . E, si no sale de su espontánea e libre y no forzada voluntad de los mismos hombres libres aceptar y consentir cualquiera perjuicio a la dicha su libertad, todo es fuerza e violento, injusto y perverso, y, según el derecho natural, de ningún valor y entidad, porque es mutación de estado de libertad a servidumbre, que, después de la muerte, no hay otro mayor perjuicio*" (translation M. Hiley).

[135] Bartolomé de Las Casas, *Obras Completas Vol. 12: De regia potestate, Questio Theologalis* (Madrid: Alianza Editorial, 1992), Notabile I, § I, 1; 34, 36: "*Nam libertas est ius insitum hominibus de necessitate et per se ab exordio rationalis naturae, et sic de iure naturali,*" with reference to Dig. 1.1.4 and Decretum Gratiani, D.1., c.7.

this right and what is understood as a moral human right today. There is a further interesting point: Las Casas argues for liberty with reference to the idea – found in Thomas Aquinas among others – that human beings exist "per se" and thus not as a mere tool for others' ends. To use other, more modern words, humans are ends-in-themselves.[136] There consequently are no slaves by nature.[137] Las Casas for some time accepted the widely held idea that slavery was justified in war, and even proposed using such slaves from Africa for work in South America – a position he later famously renounced as a great error.

This liberty is the root of people's political self-determination, including their choice of government.[138] This extends to all human beings, including the indigenous Americans, a position that – in Las Casas' later thought – denied the legitimacy of Spanish imperial rule on the grounds of Natural Law, which implies subjective rights to self-determination:

> All non-believers, whichever religious sect they belong to and whatever sins they may have committed, according to natural and divine law as well as according to so-called *ius gentium* entirely justifiably possess the power over the things they have acquired without harming anybody. And by the same right they possess their principalities and kingdoms, their estates, dignities of office, their jurisdiction and powers to rule.[139]

Las Casas interpreted the 1493 Bull *Inter Caetera* of Pope Alexander VI, which permitted the Spanish conquest and missionizing of America, in a correspondingly narrow manner as legitimizing (if any) only a supervisory role of the existing Spanish rule for the purpose of religious teaching by gentle means, such as good example – "peaceable, loving and indulgent, charitable and enticingly, through gentleness, humility, and good examples."[140]

[136] Las Casas, *regia potestate*, Notabile I, § I, 1; 34: "*Quia in natura pari Deus non facit unum alterius servum, sed per omnibus concessit arbitrium. Cuius ratio est secundum Thomam …, quia natura 'rationalis, quantum est de se, non ordinatur ut ad finem ad alium, ut homo ad hominem'.*"

[137] Las Casas, *regia potestate*, Notabile I, § I, 1; 34, 36.

[138] "*La razón es porque la elección de los reyes e de quien hobiere de regir los hombres y pueblos libres, pertenece a los mismos que han de ser regidos, de ley natural y derecho de las gentes, sometiéndose ellos mismos al elegido por su proprio consentimiento, que es acto de la voluntad, que en ninguna manera puede ser … forzada, comoquiera que los hombres todos al principio nasciesen y fuesen libres.*" Bartolomé de Las Casas, *Obras Completas Vol. 10: Tratados de 1552, Impresos por Las Casas en Sevilla* (Madrid: Alianza Editorial, 1992), Tratado comprobatorio del imperio soberano, 447.

[139] Bartolomé de Las Casas, *Obras Completas Vol. 11.2, Doce Dudas* (Madrid: Alianza Editorial, 1992), Respuesta, Cap I, Principio 1, 35: "*Todos los infieles, de qualquiera secta o religión que sean, o por qualesquiera peccados que tengan quanto al derecho natural y divino y al que llaman derecho de las gentes, justamente tienen y poseen señorio sobre sus cosas que sin perjuycio de otro adquirieron. Y también con la misma justicia posseen sus principados, reynos, estados, dignidades, jurisdicciones y señorios.*"

[140] Bartolomé de Las Casas, *Obras Completas Vol. 10: Tratados de 1552, Impresos por Las Casas en Sevilla* (Madrid: Alianza Editorial, 1992), Treinta proposiciónes muy jurídicas, Prop. XXII, 210:

The concept of subjective rights likewise played an important role in Francisco Suarez's approach to Natural Law. Natural Law defines a scope of permitted action that gives rise to subjective rights to do or not to do those things permitted – for instance, to marry or to preserve one's freedom, to use Suarez's examples.[141] Freedom is of central importance: Human beings are free by nature and subject only to their creator.[142] As in Vitoria and Las Casas, there are no natural slaves. Suarez argues, however, that humans can subject themselves to slavery and – echoing a principle of his time – that legitimate slavery can be established by enslaving prisoners of war in a just war.[143]

Within this framework, political authority is legitimized with reference to the preservation of freedom. It originates in the will of all who unite in a political community: "According to nature, the perfect civil community is free and not subjected to any person outside of it; it enjoys total power over itself, which would be democratic if not changed."[144] The people have a natural right (*naturalis potestas*) to defend themselves against tyranny.[145]

Suarez's Natural Law theory included the whole of humanity, which he thought of as possessing a "certain unity" (*aliqua unitatis*), not only as a species, but also in political and moral respects, as indicated by the natural obligation of mutual love and compassion, "which extends to all, including the foreigner of whatever nation."[146] In addition, the mutual dependency of communities demands cooperation and mutual help, which form the basis for the idea of international law.[147]

3.5.4 *Natural Rights and the Worldly Law of Reason*

A further important exponent of the Natural Law tradition is Grotius, whose work for centuries formed the textbook not only of the legal but also of the ethical thought of

"*pacifica y amorosa y dulce, caritativa y allectivamente, por mansedumbre y humildad y buenos ejemplos*" (translation M. Hiley).

[141] Francisco Suárez, *De Legibus ac deo legislatore, Liber II*, eds. and trans. Oliver Bach, Norbert Brieskorn and Gideon Stiening (Stuttgart and Bad Cannstatt: Frommann-Holzboog, 2016), ch. 18 n. 2.

[142] Francisco Suárez, *De Legibus ac deo legislatore, Liber III, Teil* 1, eds. and trans. Oliver Bach, Norbert Brieskorn and Gideon Stiening (Stuttgart and Bad Cannstatt: Frommann-Holzboog, 2014), ch. 1 n. 1: "*homo natura sua liber est et nulli subiectus nisi creatori tantum.*"

[143] Suárez, *Legibus*, III, ch. 2 n. 9.

[144] Francisco Suárez, *Defensio fidei catholica et apostolica, Pars Prima* (Naples: Ex Typis Fibrenianis, 1872), 186: "*Sic ergo perfecta communitas civilis vere naturae libera est, et nulli homini extra se subicitur, tota vero ipsa habet in se potestatem, quae si non mutaretur, democratica esset.*"

[145] Suárez, *Defensio*, 190.

[146] Suárez, *Legibus* II, ch. 19 n. 9: "*Ratio … est quia humanum genus, quantumvis in varios populos et regna divisum, semper habet aliquam unitatem, non solum specificam, sed etiam quasi politicam et moralem, quam indicat naturale praeceptum mutui amoris et misericordiae quod ad omnes extenditur, etiam extraneos et cuiuscumque nationis.*"

[147] Suárez, *Legibus*, II, ch. 19 n. 9.

influential parts of the European societies.[148] He is therefore our next example of complex thought about the rights of human beings.

Grotius is widely regarded as restating the Scholastic idea of Natural Law rooted in patristic thought and the Stoa,[149] and transforming it into the conception found in the modern Natural Law tradition.[150] According to Grotius, human beings are able to understand Natural Law because of their natural reason – they are legislators guided by insight. The principles he derives reflect the social nature of human beings. These principles, like those of his predecessors, contain a highly differentiated notion of natural rights, including a sophisticated concept of rights that in many ways is on par with later analysis.[151] These rights are not fundamentally restricted to certain groups but apply to all human beings,[152] even though Grotius' theory was not short of elements able to buttress the imperial ideology of the European states.[153] These rights of all human beings include the right to self-preservation,[154] to the pursuit of well-being[155] and, as a precondition for this, to life, bodily integrity and freedom.[156] These rights establish duties of others to refrain from violating them. Grotius also discussed the right to receive what is one's due and thus the traditional relation between justice and rights.[157] Grotius outlined a theory of the extraterritorial enforcement of the rights of humans under qualified circumstances,[158] underlining the universalist dimensions of his theory.

Natural rights do not exclude the possibility of unrestricted, absolute power, however.[159] Human beings can relinquish their freedom[160] – a position important

148 Robert Warden Lee, "Hugo Grotius," *Proceedings of the British Academy* 16 (1930): 267: *De jure belli ac pacis* "supplied the nations, particularly the protestant nations, of Europe with what they wanted – a rational theory of international relations emancipated from theology and the authority of churches. It was well adapted to be the textbook of the New Europe (a congeries of independent powers) to which the Peace of Westphalia had set its seal."

149 On the scholastic and antique roots cf. e.g. Terence Irwin, *The Development of Ethics: A Historical and Critical Study, Vol. II: From Suarez to Rousseau* (Oxford: Oxford University Press, 2008), 99.

150 Cf. e.g. Christian Thomasius, *Fundamenta juris naturae et gentium* (Halle: Salfeld, 1718), 4, § 1 on Natural Law theory: "*Uti enim Grotius hanc utilissimam disciplinam pulvere scholastico commaculatam & corruptam, ac tantum non exanimatam primus iterum suscitavit ac purgare incepit*"; or Knut Haakonsson, "Hugo Grotius and the History of Political Thought," *Political Theory* 13, no. 2 (1985): 239–65, 239.

151 Cf. Grotius' notion of rights, Grotius, *Iure Belli ac Pacis*, I, IV, V, XVII.

152 Grotius, *Iure Belli ac Pacis*, I, IV ff.

153 Cf. his opinions in Hugo Grotius, *De jure praedae commentarius* (The Hague: Martinus Nijhoff, 1868). On the context of Dutch colonialism Richard Tuck, *The Rights of War and Peace* (Oxford: Clarendon Press, 1999), 79 ff.

154 Grotius, *Iure Belli ac Pacis*, I, II, III.

155 Grotius, *Iure Belli ac Pacis*, I, II, I, 6.

156 Grotius, *Iure Belli ac Pacis*, I, II, I.

157 Grotius, *Iure Belli ac Pacis*, Prol., para. 44.

158 Grotius, *Iure Belli ac Pacis*, II, XX, XL. He underlines that any such action by means of war can only be justified by the gravest sort of crimes (*atrocissima & manifestissima*), ibid. II, XX, XLIII, 3.

159 Grotius, *Iure Belli ac Pacis*, I, III, VIII.

160 Grotius, *Iure Belli ac Pacis*, I, III, VIII.

for Grotius' idea of justified slavery, one example of those elements of his thought that were put to use to justify European imperialism.

3.5.5 *Transitions of Natural Law*

Samuel Pufendorf's theory of Natural Law strongly influenced the debates in the late seventeenth and eighteenth centuries that ultimately led to the explicit formulation of human rights, imperfect as this formulation remained. Important elements of Pufendorf's thought are his account of God's will as the source of Natural Law's obligatory power, his theory of international relations and his theory of sovereignty. The substantive content of Natural Law is spelled out by duties and the rights of persons. Like other thinkers in the Natural Law tradition, Pufendorf drew on a differentiated analytical notion of subjective rights. Natural Law's main aim, which determines its content, is to preserve the peaceful sociality of all humans.[161] Some of the duties of Natural Law are directed towards all human beings, men and women.[162] These absolute duties towards others include the prohibition of injury and the accessory obligation of reparation[163] and mutual respect between human beings.[164] For Pufendorf, too, there is no natural slavery.[165] He argues not only for the prohibition of injury of others, but also for an (imperfect) obligation to benefit others.[166] Where distribution is concerned, only an equal distribution honors the equal dignity of human beings.[167] Such obligations are connected to rights claims – as illuminated by the example of human beings' justified claims for equal respect based on the concept of human dignity: Human beings have a right to this respect.[168]

3.5.6 *Rights in the Best of All Possible Worlds*

Yet another interesting example is G. W. F. Leibniz, whose ideas on Natural Law for the most part remained unpublished during his lifetime, and for whom Grotius served as point of departure in his own complex thought on Natural Law, including subjective rights. Like Grotius, his thoughts include a sophisticated analysis of the structure of rights. In addition, he outlines some substantive content of human rights. Leibniz distinguishes three levels of Natural Law: *ius strictum*, *aequitas* and *pietas*. *Ius strictum* – importantly for our topic – encompasses the protection of life,

[161] Samuel Pufendorf, *De Jure Naturae et Gentium* (Lund: Junghans, 1672), II, 3.1.
[162] Pufendorf, *Jure Naturae et Gentium*, II, 3.24.
[163] Pufendorf, *Jure Naturae et Gentium*, III, 1.
[164] Pufendorf, *Jure Naturae et Gentium*, III, 2.1.
[165] Pufendorf, *Jure Naturae et Gentium*, III, 2.8.9.
[166] Pufendorf, *Jure Naturae et Gentium*, III, 3.1.
[167] Samuel Pufendorf, *De Officio Hominis et civis juxta legem naturalem* (Lund: Junghans, 1673), VII, § 4.
[168] Pufendorf, *De Officio Hominis*, VII, § 1.

physical and mental integrity, liberty and property. These are clearly conceptualized as normative positions with the quality of rights.[169] These rights are not created by legal communities; rather, liberty has profound metaphysical roots. It is the inalienable right of rational souls.[170] *Ius strictum* is based on the equality of persons[171] and, with reference to Aristotelian categories, on corrective justice.[172] Its principle is not to harm anybody (*neminem laedere*).[173]

The next level is *aequitas*, which concerns the proportional balance of normative claims. In this sphere, it is not the equality of human beings that is central, but rather their inequality, which stems from specific unequally distributed abilities and talents. On the basis of these inequalities, applying Aristotelian principles of distributive justice, the goods of society are to be distributed in a way that serves the common good.[174] This distribution is effected by law and through the action of authorities applying the maxim of this sphere, *suum cuique tribuere*,[175] a maxim implying rights, as discussed above. The political order is one of just inequality because of these differences between human beings. Importantly for our topic, just inequality includes the political rights of human beings. Leibniz argues that the "equality of human rights" (*l'egalité du droit des hommes*) would be self-evident if human beings' capability to rule was equal. Given that this capability differs, those who are the most capable are the ones who legitimately govern.[176] Though

[169] Vgl. Gottfried Wilhelm Leibniz, "Aus der Neuen Methode, Jurisprudenz zu lernen und zu lehren," in Gottfried Wilhelm Leibniz, *Frühe Schriften zum Naturrecht*, trans. Hubertus Busche (Hamburg: Felix Meiner Verlag, 2003), 79.

[170] Gottfried Wilhelm Leibniz, "Sur la nature de la bonté et de la justice," in *Das Recht kann nicht ungerecht sein...: Beiträge zu Leibniz' Philosophie der Gerechtigkeit*, ed. Wenchao Li (Stuttgart: Franz Steiner Verlag, 2015), 177. An interesting question concerns the meaning of Leibniz's monadology for the conception of individual rights, cf. Gottfried Wilhelm Leibniz, "Monadologie," in *Monadologie und andere metaphysische Schriften*, trans. Ulrich Johannes Schneider (Hamburg: Felix Meiner Verlag, 2003).

[171] Gottfried Wilhelm Leibniz, "Vorrede zum Codex Juris Gentium Diplomaticus," in *Die philosophischen Schriften von G. W. F. Leibniz*, ed. C. I. Gerhardt (Berlin: Weidmann, 1887), 388.

[172] Vgl. Leibniz, "Neue Methode," 81.

[173] Leibniz, "Neue Methode," 81; Gottfried Wilhelm Leibniz, "Entwürfe zu den Elementen des Naturrechts," in Gottfried Wilhelm Leibniz, *Frühe Schriften zum Naturrecht*, trans. Hubertus Busche (Hamburg: Felix Meiner Verlag, 2003), 137.

[174] Gottfried Wilhelm Leibniz, "Sur la notion commune de la justice," in *Das Recht kann nicht ungerecht sein...: Beiträge zu Leibniz' Philosophie der Gerechtigkeit*, ed. Wenchao Li (Stuttgart: Franz Steiner Verlag, 2015), 168, 173.

[175] Leibniz, "Neue Methode," 81.

[176] Cf. Leibniz's comments on Locke's *Second Treatise*, Gottfried Wilhelm Leibniz, "Letter to Thomas Burnett of Kemney, 2 February 1700," in *Sämtliche Schriften und Briefe*, Series I, Vol. 18, Akademieausgabe (Berlin: Akademie-Verlag, 2005), 380: "*Il y a pourtant quelques endroits peutestre qui demandoient une plus ample discussion, comme entre autres ce qu'on dit de l'Estat de la Nature, et de l'egalité du droit des hommes. Cette egalité seroit certaine si tous les hommes avoient les mêmes avantages[,] mais cela n'estant point[,] il semble qu'Aristote a eu plus de raison icy que Mons. Hobbes. Si plusieurs hommes se trouvoient dans un même vaisseau en pleine mer, il ne seroit point conforme à la raison ny à la nature, que ceux qui n'entendent rien à*

often highly critical of monarchs and the aristocracy, he thinks that a "rule of reason" is more likely to be achieved in the hierarchical order of the monarchies of his day.

The principle of the highest sphere of Natural Law, *pietas*, which demands that human beings live decently,[177] is justice as the love of those who have gained wisdom.[178] This demands a principled concern for the well-being of others.[179] Leibniz thinks that the ultimate motivation of agents for action is to realize their own interests. These interests, however, include the desire to see others becoming happy.[180] The happiness of others is an intrinsic good. This stance has concrete consequences. Leibniz formulates very substantial demands of human solidarity: There is a duty not only to abstain from harming other people, but also to make their well-being possible, if no substantial disadvantages are incurred by the agent,[181] which raises the familiar question: What claims are implied?

Leibniz pursued a cosmopolitan perspective: The City of God is a moral universe formed by all rational souls under the same principles of justice that guide God's thought, decisions and actions.[182]

3.5.7 *Closing the Circle: The Explicit Doctrine of Human Rights*

The idea of human rights was finally formulated explicitly in the eighteenth century. For moral philosophers, thinkers and political theorists of the Enlightenment, human rights were a central, foundational and explicit element of their thought

la marine pretendissent d'estre pilotes, de sorte que suivant la raison naturelle le gouvernement appartient aux plus sages. Mais l'imperfection de la nature humaine fait, qu'on ne veut point écouter raison, ce qui a forcé les plus sages d'employer la force et l'adresse pour établir quelque ordre tolerable, en quoy la providence même s'est m'êlée. Mais quand un ordre est etabli, il ne faut point le renverser sans une necessité extreme, et sans estre asseuré d'y réussir pro salute publica d'une maniere qui ne cause pas des plus grands maux"; Gottfried Wilhelm Leibniz, "Letter to Thomas Burnett of Kemney, July 18, 1701," in *Sämtliche Schriften und Briefe*, Series I, Vol. 20, Akademieausgabe (Berlin: Akademie-Verlag, 2006), 284.

177 Leibniz, "Neue Methode," 83.

178 Gottfried Wilhelm Leibniz, "Vorrede zum Codex Juris Gentium Diplomaticus," in *Die philosophischen Schriften von G. W. F. Leibniz*, ed. C. I. Gerhardt (Berlin: Weidmann, 1887), 386; Leibniz, "Elemente," 241.

179 Leibniz, "Neue Methode," 83; Gottfried Wilhelm Leibniz, "Universale Gerechtigkeit als klug verteilte Liebe zu allen," in Gottfried Wilhelm Leibniz, *Frühe Schriften zum Naturrecht*, trans. Hubertus Busche (Hamburg: Felix Meiner Verlag, 2003), 215 ff.

180 Leibniz, "Elemente," 225, 237. However, there are also passages in which the reference to one's own interests disappears, cf. Leibniz, "Sur la notion commune," 172.

181 Leibniz, "Elemente," 101, 153; Leibniz, "Sur la notion commune," 166 f.

182 Leibniz, "Monadologie," paras. 85–6; Gottfried Wilhelm Leibniz, "Initium institutionum juris perpetui," in *Rechtsphilosophisches aus Leibnizens ungedruckten Schriften*, ed. Georg Mollat (Leipzig: J. H. Robolsky, 1885), 1: "*Itaque justum est, quod publice interest, et salus publica suprema lex est. Publicum autem non paucorum, non certae gentis, sed omnium intelligitur, qui sunt in civitate Dei et, ut sic dicam, republica universi.*"

both before and after the political declaration of these rights.[183] Approaches such as Locke's social contract theory and his defense of the natural rights to life, liberty and property already directly influenced the formulation of the *Declaration of Independence* in 1776. Moreover, Locke's triad of rights is based on another important idea we have repeatedly encountered, namely that human beings exist for their own sake, a position Locke ultimately framed in religious terms. These natural rights "belong to men as men and not as members of society."[184]

Natural Law theorists such as Barbeyrac,[185] Burlamaqui,[186] Wolff and de Vattel outlined in theoretical depth and with a political thrust different accounts of the idea of the natural, inalienable rights of individuals, in some cases making them the foundations of their conceptions of the rights of states and nations.[187] Wolff develops a specific concept of innate rights (*iura connata*) within the framework of a perfectionist theory of Natural Law. These rights are derived from Natural Law obligations based on the nature and essence of human beings, are inalienable[188] and encompass not only freedom, equality and the means of subsistence, but also other means of attaining the perfection of their human physical and mental faculties as the core command of Natural Law.[189] Human beings have all of the rights necessary

[183] Cf. Vincenzo Ferrone, *The Enlightenment and the Rights of Man* (Liverpool: Liverpool University Press, 2019), 9: "A decisive battle for the history of the rights of man in the Western world was being fought everywhere: from the most prestigious universities to the Berlin and Munich gazettes; at court as well as in the theatre."

[184] John Locke, *Two Treatises of Government*, ed. Peter Laslett (Cambridge: Cambridge University Press, 1988), The Second Treatise, ch. 2, para. 14.

[185] Jean Barbeyrac, "Preface," in Gerard Noodt, *Du pouvoir des souverains et de la liberté de conscience*, 2nd edition (Amsterdam: Pierre Humbert, 1714), XXXI: "*Nous qui somme Hommes, avons-nous besoin qu'on nous apprenne quels sont les droits naturels des Hommes, & jus-qu'où chacun veut ou peut y renoncer? Le Peuple est-il fait pour le Prince, ou le Prince pour le Peuple?*"

[186] Cf. Burlamaqui, *Principes du droit naturel*, 80 on the "*fondement général des Droits de l'homme.*"

[187] Cf. Emer de Vattel, *Le droit des gens ou Principes de la loi naturelle appliqués à la conduite et aux affaires des nations et des souverains*, Tome 1 (London: s.n., 1758). Preliminaires, § 5, 6. According to Natural Law, individuals are free and independent, § 4. Cf. on the equality of human beings and their rights and duties and the equality of nations big and small, § 18. On the right to resistance to protect basic rights against tyrants, § 51. There are many examples illustrating how far such conceptions still were from a plausible account of human rights. For instance, de Vattel also includes the right to abduct women in a demographic crisis (but not to force them into partnership or to rape them) among the rights that human beings can claim (on the exceptional ground of necessity) to preserve their group, Livre II, § 122; Christian Wolff, *The Law of Nations Treated According to the Scientific Method*, trans. Joseph H. Drake, rev. Thomas Ahnert (Carmel, IN: Liberty Fund, 2017), § 16, 17.

[188] Christian Wolff, *Institutiones Naturae et Gentium* (Halae Magdeburgicae, 1750), § 74: "*Jus* quoque *connatum homini ita inhaeret, ut ipsi auferri non possit*" (emphasis in original).

[189] Wolff, *Institutiones*, §§ 103, 107, 114 ff. Frank Grunert, "The 'Iura Connata' in the Natural Law of Christian Wolff," in *Philosophy, Rights and Natural Law, Essays in Honour of Knud Haadkonssen*, eds. Ian Hunter and Richard Whatmore (Edinburgh: Edinburgh University Press, 2019), 200 comments: "If we consider this list, . . ., there is no doubt that it looks very like an early catalogue of human rights, especially when we consider the construction of its philosophical basis."

to promote their happiness.[190] These innate, inalienable and explicit rights of human beings are embedded in a theory of the state, public welfare and security, which are themselves based on Natural Law and form values that can override individual rights in the civil state (*status civilis*), though not beyond the purpose of the state to enable human perfection.[191] As members of a human society organized in a state, natural rights continue to exist and serve as critical yardsticks for civil law but are substantially limited and not properly enforceable by the rights-holders against the sovereign.[192] The subjects maintain the right to resist abuses of power, derived from their innate rights, however.[193] Vattel took Wolff as a reference point for his reflections on Natural Law, which in turn influenced core ideas of the American Revolution, including the *Declaration of Independence* and its conception of unalienable rights.[194]

From a Jewish perspective, Mendelssohn, for instance, defended human rights within the conceptual framework of the natural rights tradition, including a most impressive account of freedom of religion, "the most valuable treasure of human bliss" – to be expected, perhaps, from a courageous member of suffering minority.[195]

Mendelssohn's correspondent Kant, to take this most influential last example of the practical philosophy of the epoch, formulated his doctrine of freedom as a human right. This is a complex and intricate right, because the freedom of the individual must be compatible with the freedom of all under a universal law of liberty. Kant's conception of human rights is based on the idea of human dignity in the concrete sense of respect for human beings as ends-in-themselves, which is the source of their equality.[196]

Human rights permeated art as much as they did theory. Internationally acclaimed plays of the epoch illustrate this, such as Schiller's *Don Carlos* or his *Wilhelm Tell*, in which the rights of human beings constitute crucial and explicit elements of great tragedy.[197] Human rights are a centerpiece of Schiller's theory of

190 Wolff, *Institutiones*, § 118.

191 Wolff, *The Law of Nations*, § 14.

192 On the debate as to whether the innate rights are relinquished in the civil state, cf. Grunert, "Iura Connata," 196 ff., 201, opting for a differentiated solution: "iura connata: more than lost rights and less than human rights."

193 Wolff, *Institutiones*, § 1079.

194 Cf. William Ossipow and Dominik Gerber, "The Reception of Vattel's Law of Nations in the American Colonies: From James Otis and John Adams to the Declaration of Independence," *American Journal of Legal History* 57, no. 4 (2017): 521–55. As e.g. Wolff's treatment of the issue shows, the reference to the "pursuit of happiness" derives not only from de Vattel's work – and may simply form an obvious point.

195 Mendelssohn, "Jerusalem," 1: "*das wertvollste Kleinod menschlicher Glückseligkeit.*"

196 Kant, *Metaphysik der Sitten*, 224.

197 Cf. Matthias Mahlmann, "On the Foundations of a Democratic Culture of Freedom: Law and the Normative Resources of Art," in *The Quest for Core Values in the Application of Legal Norms: Essays in Honor of Mordechai Kremnitzer*, eds. Khalid Ghanayim and Yuval Shany (Berlin: Springer, 2021), 15–35.

political aesthetics, too, as we have seen. For the purpose of this illustrative historical sketch, there is consequently no need to elaborate further on these thoughts – the historical record is uncontroversial.

These theories were often limited in many ways, excluding large groups of persons, as we have repeatedly underlined, and sometimes were clearly contradictory, not least because the radicalism of some normative insights had not permeated the whole theory. One good example of this is Kant's idea that human beings are to be respected as the ultimate ends of human decision-making, as ends-in-themselves, a maxim that gained significant influence in contemporary ethics and law in the context of discussions about human dignity.[198] Kant's powerful critique of political practices on these grounds did not prevent him from denying suffrage to women and servants or justifying the rights of men over women, however – positions obviously irreconcilable with the idea that they are ends-in-themselves as human beings.[199] Such positions are thus best and most effectively criticized by the normative principles that Kant himself made explicit. Moreover, theoreticians' ideas did not necessarily determine their behavior – as Locke's involvement in the slave trade demonstrates. However, the idea of human rights had now been formulated in modern terms, entered the stage of world history and at last become a revolutionary force.

3.6 THE MANY ROOTS OF HUMAN RIGHTS

This review in outline of the concept of rights is far from exhaustive, particularly bearing in mind that not only the history of ideas, but also the history of ordinary human lives and struggles is important. There are many other periods and events that lend themselves to a fresh look from the perspective of human rights – from slave revolts in antiquity, the liberties granted under the Moghul rulers in India[200] or the rights claims of religious dissenters[201] to the claim by one of the leading protagonists involved in the drafting of the *Universal Declaration*, P. C. Chang, that Confucianism at its core is about human rights,[202] a statement comparable to the

[198] Cf. Mahlmann, "Human Dignity and Autonomy," 379 ff.

[199] Kant, *Metaphysik der Sitten*, 279, 313 ff. Other examples are some remarks on religious and ethnic minorities. However, he sharply criticized the European subjection of the world, cf. for instance Kant, *Metaphysik der Sitten*, 266.

[200] Cf. on the example of the emperor Akbar, Sen, "Elements of a Theory of Human Rights," 352 f.; Sen, *Idea of Justice*, 36 ff.

[201] Cf. Roger Williams, "The Bloudy Tenent of Persecution," in: *The Complete Writings of Roger Williams*, Vol. 3, ed. Samuel L. Caldwell (Paris, AK: The Baptist Standard Bearer, 2005) or the famous study by Georg Jellinek, *Die Erklärung der Menschen- und Bürgerrechte* (Berlin: Duncker & Humblot, 1895), 31 ff.

[202] Cf. on P. C. Chang's interpretation of Confucianism and human rights, Hans Ingwar Roth, *P. C. Chang and the Universal Declaration of Human Rights* (Philadelphia: University of Pennsylvania Press, 2018), 3 ff., 207 ff.

view of a spiritual leader of current Buddhism.[203] For the purpose of our inquiry into the history of human rights, however, avoiding ahistorical naivete in the theory of human rights is sufficient. In particular, our review sought answers to the following questions: What (if anything) does the history of human rights teach us about the relationship between human rights and human moral cognition? Is history all you need to know to understand the roots of human rights in the human life form? Answering these questions proved a difficult task, as the history of human rights is a minefield of controversies – so much so that even the method of inquiry itself required clarification.

Despite these difficulties and the limitations of the review, this endeavor produced some important results, which we will recapitulate in the following.

3.6.1 *The Importance of Methods of Inquiry*

The above discussion has shown that any historical account of human rights needs to pay close attention to: first, the need to search for implied ideas instead of for words or terms; second, the importance of a keen awareness of the many forms of human expression beyond theoretical thought, including art and the oral history of indigenous communities and their often highly significant content; third, the need to respect the profound ethical implications of human practices beyond elite circles, not least of human struggles; and fourth, the need to abandon Eurocentric or otherwise parochial perspectives. The example of the "freedom-loving" Herero or the questions generated by attention to the experience of enslaved women indicated the interesting results such an approach is able to generate. When we follow these methodological admonitions, we see that the traces of the idea of human rights are manifold – indeed, they are so copious that no existing history of human rights has done them justice so far, despite the sterling work carried out in this field.

3.6.2 *Varieties of Rights and the Significance of Distinctions*

Our historical review has shown that the idea of subjective rights played a central role in cultures and contexts as diverse as pastoral, indigenous societies, Greek antiquity, Roman law and Roman imperial politics, Scholastic thought, Natural Law and the law of reason, up to the Enlightenment, when human rights were explicitly (albeit imperfectly) stated more or less in their current form and became a revolutionary force. These rights did not deal merely with minor issues but addressed decisive human concerns such as autonomy and self-determination, political participation and decision-making, bodily integrity, freedom of speech and political equality. Some discussions involved major social and political

[203] Dalai Lama (XIV), *Human Rights and Universal Responsibility, Non-Governmental Organizations, United Nations World Conference on Human Rights*, June 15, 1993, Vienna.

controversies of their time, such as the fight for *isonomia*, equal political rights (even though these were guaranteed highly selectively) in the democratic era of ancient Athens, as well as the legal advice given to arguably the most powerful monarchs of their time about the rights of indigenous Americans during the conquest of America when the lives of many human beings were at stake (and not saved), to take just a few rather dramatic examples.

Unsurprisingly, these debates were not couched in modern human rights language. However, this does not mean that they are irrelevant for the history of human rights, as this history is – as emphasized above – not about *words* or *terms*, but about a normative *idea*. In light of the historical record, it seems obvious that the examples discussed above were in fact dealing with normative phenomena related to (but not identical with) the idea that currently is called "human rights." The examples are highly selective, particularly if one considers the methodological steps proposed above for the study of human rights to be reasonable. The baseline of these steps is, after all, that a history of human rights needs to be much more inclusive than traditionally assumed, not only going beyond Eurocentric perspectives, but also including other sources than canonical texts. There have been some hints that such a broader perspective would only strengthen the points made so far, as the discussions about indigenous cultures and the rich normative tools of antiquity show.

Our review of historical thought on rights included very different examples – varying in form, in their metaphysical and religious background, in their concrete conclusions as to central topics and in their anthropological assumptions, theories of society and understanding of human history. Euripides' poetic reflection about rights (quite evidently) differs in many important ways from Leibniz's metaphysical perfectionism. These distinctions should not be glossed over in some kind of romantic tale about the triumphant march of human rights, implying that they were already conceived in full in the very early stages of human reflection. They were not, and this almost trivial point has been repeatedly underlined.

Frequently, these reflections had no political influence – they were political hopes, aspirations, often mere desperate dreams that did little to better the conditions of human beings. They included many instances of minority positions, even singular views of outsiders, entirely marginalized in their social environment. Euripides did not simply adopt the consensual positions of his era, as Aristophanes' derision shows. The theories of the Spanish Scholastics remain impressive despite their flaws and inconsistencies, but the reality in America was decided by the sword and the greed for gold and land. Las Casas was a total anomaly, not only in his own time, but also in subsequent centuries that happily embraced the racist ideology of conquest. Unsurprisingly, the Inquisition banned some of his works after his death. Sometimes major powers were moved to protect certain rights for certain moments in the historical trajectory, but only for a limited time, as evident in the Roman Emperor's protection of freedom of religion in the *Edict of Milan*, which ultimately yielded to religious intolerance.

The rights discussed were often limited to certain groups of persons, whether because of the aristocratic stratification of society, as in the case of the *Magna Carta*, or because the set of legitimate bearers was thought to be limited on other grounds – excluding women, for instance. Another challenge proved to be that the concept of "human beings" or "humanity" expanded as human cultures on different continents encountered one another. These developments posed the question of inclusion (and exclusion) anew.

A further important observation is that the starting point of reflections about rights is one thing, the concrete conclusions drawn from these reflections quite another. One may agree that human beings have a right to freedom but disagree substantially about what this actually means in specific cases. Yet another question is whether any of the insights drawn determine concrete action, as opposed to other motives such as individual interests. One position in Natural Law theory, reaffirmed throughout the centuries, was that there are no natural slaves. This did not prevent some of the theorists from justifying slavery on other grounds (e.g. as legitimate captives in war) or from becoming commercially involved in the slave trade themselves, like Locke, who most probably was motivated by financial interest and not by deep philosophical principles to do so.

Moreover, events of the historical proportions of the conquest of America gave rise to profound and honest critique based on the rights of indigenous Americans on the one hand, but on the other hand led to arguments that could be abused to justify imperialist policies by the back door – for example, the rights to free movement and commerce to justify some of the violence committed by the Spanish *conquistadores*. Other historical examples show that the use of rights-based arguments for political purposes that seek to empty these rights of their meaning is far from a recent invention.

Today, human rights are widely regarded as connected with democracy. Many of the theories discussed, however, were developed in the context of monarchical orders. Some theories challenged these orders – albeit sometimes half-heartedly – on the basis of rights, but not necessarily so. Leibniz's theory offers an interesting account of the role that subjective rights can play in a conservative concept of politics that legitimizes monarchy. Leibniz was an adherent of Europe's stratified order that ultimately was to be overcome by the developments sparked off by the eighteenth-century democratic revolutions. This does not mean that his conception of rights was meaningless: Asserting the inalienable "freedom of rational souls" considerably limits the actions of others, including political powers, as illustrated by Leibniz's measured but significant critique of slavery.

The constraints of religion are likewise important. In the examples discussed, Christianity obviously is particularly significant, although, for instance, the Herero's cult of their ancestors raises interesting questions as to their social fabric, too. The limits of the cosmopolitanism of Natural Law theories form a recurrent theme of this review. The ambivalent effects of the Christian background of some accounts and the consequences of these effects for persons of other faiths are important issues here. While a cosmopolitan theory based on a particular religious perspective certainly is not sufficiently inclusive from the point of view of a critical human rights theory, it nevertheless is of interest for a history of human rights. This is because such theories based on a particular religious outlook assert the normative relevance of some common properties of all human beings, creating a moral community that is not limited to specific societies – a doctrine that proved to have wide-ranging consequences once religious and other biases were transcended.

Religious beliefs were important in other respects, too. Even a radical critic like Las Casas, for example, felt compelled to accommodate the papal bull legitimizing the subjugation and exploitation of America in his (nevertheless critical) doctrine. Thinking beyond the Christian systems of institutions was beyond even his reach, faithful believer that he was.

Notwithstanding these many limitations, inconsistencies, cultural and religious biases, incorporated injustices, racist distortions and apologetic abuses among other problems, we should not overly quickly dismiss these theories and ideas as irrelevant for the history of human rights simply because they come from a different time and a different cultural, social and religious context. This would not do justice to the important contributions to the idea of human rights that can be detected in this history despite all of their flaws. Human rights history is not an all-or-nothing issue – many normative phenomena below the threshold of human rights as stated in modern constitutions or international law are highly significant if one wants to understand the deeper roots of the human rights idea. There is, after all, a line that runs through these debates. This line is made up of: first, the *concept of a right as a specific set of correlated normative incidents*, often explicitly identified in a sophisticated analysis such as that developed over the centuries in Natural Law; and second, the *particular content of such rights*, securing existential concerns such as life, bodily integrity, liberty and equality as fundamental entitlements of human beings.

As to the first point: Given the amount of evidence reviewed, it is clear that the normative category of a subjective right is no recent invention. The historical record shows that this category played an important role as a building block of normative systems in very different historical and cultural settings. There is ample evidence showing that this category does in fact (contrary to some historical reconstructions) form part of early normative orders, including those of antiquity about which we have reliable information and of indigenous societies that may give us some hints about the normative elements of even earlier forms of life. The cultural narcissism of some studies claiming that the European or Western tradition has a monopoly on the idea of rights needs to be overcome once and for all.

As to the second point: Demands for respect for life, bodily integrity, liberty and equality are likewise not prerogatives of Europeans since the eighteenth century, as the Herero example or the rich normative reflection of the poets and thinkers of Greek antiquity vividly illustrate. Brushing aside the many centuries of reflection about rights related to existential concerns of human beings would not do justice to those remarkable thoughts of the past.

A failure to take this history seriously into consideration when discussing contemporary human rights would not do justice to the many victims of this history, either. Their voices are heard faintly at best in many historical accounts. We know what Columbus thought when he discovered human beings he was able to easily exploit. We do not know what his victims thought of his arrival, even though this knowledge would be crucial for understanding this fateful historical event. The least one can do, given this situation, is to pay very close attention to those testimonies we have.

3.6.3 *Rights and Models of History*

These broader perspectives of the slow emergence of human rights sit well with our previous findings about the development of human rights following their explicit statement in the eighteenth century as revolutionary principles of political reorganization. There is no simple, continuous, linear, progressive trajectory from the idea's inception to universal acceptance – neither before nor after the idea of human rights flew its flag visibly on the philosophical and political barricades of the eighteenth century.

There is no teleology, no comforting "this had to happen" to be detected in this process. And certainly there is no "all's well that ends well" fanfare appropriate today – not only because we do not know whether this history will indeed end well, but also because of what was (and continues to be) done to so many victims along the way, the unjustified, wanton, avoidable suffering that cannot be redeemed by a bright human rights future, the metaphysical kitsch of teleological theories of history aside.

These results show that the remarks made above (in Chapter 2) about the different theories of history were useful: The history of human rights is neither one of simple linear progress, nor one of disconnected events without an overarching meaning. Rather, it is a history of recurrent attempts made in various diverse cultural and social contexts to secure the most important goods of human beings with the normative tool of rights, sometimes informed by predecessors, sometimes not, sometimes with long-lasting constructive influence, sometimes entirely forgotten, sometimes resounding through history, sometimes nothing more than the desperate whisper of the victims of injustice.

These complex findings underline another point highlighted in the discussion about the models of history guiding research on human rights: It is crucial to be self-critical about one's implied anthropological assumptions. A naive adoption of the blank-slate theory, for instance, might lead historical research to overlook the intricate normative world (including a richly textured inner world) of indigenous human beings, wrongly taking them and their cultures to be "primitive." More interesting problems may be hidden here than is widely assumed.

3.6.4 *A Key Finding: The Long Way from Moral Intuitions to Explicit Rights*

Our historical review leads us to an analytical point about the genesis of the human rights idea as an explicit ethical, political and ultimately legal concept. This point is of crucial importance for our argument. As we have just underlined, human rights do not come in an all-or-nothing fashion. There are many possible intermediary stages between the (hypothetical) possibility that there is neither the normative category of "rights" nor ideas about claims to bodily integrity, liberty, equality or respect in a given cultural context on the one hand, and fully developed beliefs that human beings enjoy the now-canonical human rights of codes such as the *Universal Declaration* as moral or even enforceable legal rights on the other.

If one tries to reconstruct the steps necessary to develop an idea of human rights in light of these findings, the following picture emerges: The most basic first step on the long road to the formulation of an explicit, critically reflected idea of human rights appears to be a moral intuition with a specific, claim-related content which is not arbitrary and in this sense principled, although not necessarily based on explicit ethical principles. This is an important observation which will be analyzed below in Chapter 8. Second, according to this moral judgment, a person – for instance, Creusa – first perceives herself as having a claim that is of qualified concern to her life, and second perceives somebody else as being under a duty to act in certain ways demanded by this claim. Third, according to this moral evaluation, it is often the case that she can decide herself whether or not to do something that is within the material scope of the perceived claim, the other party having no right that she do the one or the other. In other cases, she simply enjoys an entitlement – for instance, that her bodily integrity is respected.

One example is Creusa's intuition, first, that she should remain unmolested by Apollo; second, that he is under a duty to restrain himself; and third, that she has the privilege to decide herself about whether or not to have an intimate encounter with him. It is crucial that there is such a claim, not just an interest or a wish – this is the decisive step into the realm of normativity and rights.

Intuitions about such claims, duties and privileges can concern many different things, including trivial matters. For the history of human rights, only very particular contents of claims, duties or privileges are relevant. In Creusa's case, for example, her bodily integrity and personal self-determination certainly qualify in this respect. If claims cross this threshold, they are potentially relevant for the history of human rights.

As this claim and the correlative duty are normative incidents, some normative principles must be involved that give rise to the complex normative position a right defines for its holder and addressee. Justice was of central importance for the justification of rights in more than just one epoch – Athenagoras' speech in defense of equal political rights in Syracuse in the face of the Athenian attack is just one example.

Such justice-based claims to important personal goods by individual persons in particular circumstances do not already constitute human rights, however. Several more steps need to be taken to transform these individual moral judgments about legitimate individual claims towards specific other persons into human rights. These steps are quite demanding in more than one sense.

The first step is the *generalization* of the *abstractly determined ethical content* of specific claims. The material scope of human rights is not just about the claim of W to X against Y under the specific circumstances Z – Creusa's claim not to be raped by Apollo in the holy cave – but to respect (in this example) the bodily integrity and autonomy of women under any circumstances. Another step (historically perhaps the most difficult one) is *universalization* – the inclusion of all human beings in a right's personal scope. This step rests upon two major presuppositions: first, that the same rights-conferring reasons apply to all human beings – for instance, because they all share some rights-conferring properties; and second, that (roughly) the same goods are of particular importance for all human beings. Both presuppositions evidently require substantiation, seeing as they remain controversial even today.

As we have seen, such moral claims can remain implicit, as in Creusa's case. The idea of human rights, having defined their content in abstract terms, generalizing and universalizing them, now renders them *explicit*, another step with far-reaching consequences. It presupposes various conditions that are neither individual nor culturally and historically trivial. First of all, it requires a reflective stance towards moral intuitions, taking one's own individual moral judgments as the possible object of critical scrutiny, improvement and change. Impartial moral reasoning, adopting the point of view of an "impartial spectator," is the aim.[204] Ethical reflection needs to abstract from the personal interests and wishes of a particular agent and determine in explicit terms what claims anybody may have under normative principles such as justice. We can call this the *objectification* of human rights content.

Finally, human rights, derived from the generalized, universalized and objectified abstract core content of moral intuitions made explicit, can be conceptualized and institutionalized as *law*. The historically most important form of this conceptualization and institutionalization is, as we have seen, the protection of human rights in the legal systems of concrete political communities, a foundational idea of modern rights-based constitutionalism. In the twentieth century, humanity even made the audacious attempt to do something that never had been tried before: to erect a system of the legal complementary protection of human rights by international law on a global scale, including mechanisms of enforcement that are meant to be (and sometimes are) effective.

We do not maintain that these steps follow a consecutive historical order, nor that they describe stages in the development of individuals, let alone of humanity as a whole. There is no parallelism of ontogeny and phylogeny. Rather, these steps are

[204] Adam Smith, *The Theory of Moral Sentiments* (New York: Prometheus Books, 2000), 19 ff.

theoretical constructs, a kind of ideal-typical description of the preconditions of the genesis of the human rights idea. The historical record, however, elucidates that in reality such intermediary steps were taken in many different forms – on a road that not only was long, but also needed to be paved while it was already being traveled, without clear directions on which way to go.

3.6.5 *How to Miss the Point of Human Rights: Some Lessons from the Past*

The historical record teaches another lesson. It illustrates the central *obstacles* that may prevent the development of the idea of human rights. These obstacles arise at every level of this idea's evolution.

As we have seen, rights are often limited to certain groups of people or as to the specific content they protect. The *Magna Carta* implied that only parts of the population of the Kingdom of England were entitled to certain important goods – for example, not to be arrested without legal grounds. The same goes for the *Virginia Charter* (1615) or the *Bill of Rights* (1688/1689). Widening the personal scope to include more groups of persons through a process of personal universalization requires the overcoming of religious, social, cultural and ethnic boundaries, as well as the age-old dividing line of gender. The preceding remarks have made the huge historical steps involved sufficiently clear. There are other challenges as well, likewise of no small scope. One example is the need to reformulate the concept of humanity because of encounters with other cultures, expanding it to the entire globe. That these encounters would result in an inclusive concept of humanity was far from obvious, given that they were accompanied by the rise of extremely powerful ideologies very alien to the idea of human rights, as the uncanny attraction of racism and its political manifestations exemplify.

These processes are accompanied by the struggle to further define the material scope of the rights protected – a separate and equally difficult task, full of further obstacles. There are theories of rights that are meaningful even though certain rights that reasonably seem to fall under human rights are not included – for instance, equal political rights do not form part of the set of rights defended by Leibniz. This illustrates the importance of the question of which rights exactly are to be protected as human rights. If good reasons are found to secure a particular right, the next (no less complex) question arises: What precisely is the scope of the rights guaranteed – what does habeas corpus, for instance, mean exactly? This is a question that haunts lawyers, courts[205] and ethicists to the present day.

[205] Cf. for instance the question of whether the procedures for review of the detainees' status provided by the Detainee Treatment Act of 2005 (DTA), 119 Stat. 2739, are an adequate and effective substitute for habeas corpus, which the US Supreme Court denied in a landmark case, Boumediene v Bush, 553 U.S. 723 (2008).

In this respect, the guarantees of certain rights catalogues limited to certain persons have often spearheaded the development of the material content of human rights. The right to be arrested only under some form of rule of law under the *Magna Carta* was not a human right. But within the framework of *the Magna Carta*'s limited personal scope, the content of a right was developed that later was vindicated for all human beings,[206] illustrating that "the historic value of any single pronouncement affirming the rights of man as against authority is not dependent upon the degree of its completeness."[207] Even in the opinion of its most ardent supporters, freedom of religion for a long time excluded atheists[208] – until they finally were included in its personal scope and enjoyed the protection of a right initially designed for religious believers.

This process is of great importance. The exclusion of certain marginalized groups can be the precondition to establishing a certain claim as a right. The peasants of England could not claim habeas corpus under the rule of law in 1215 – the noblemen could. Many believed that atheists could not claim freedom of religion while believers could, because otherwise the moral structure of society would be subverted. These personally selective rights form a first crack in the wall of the unlimited power and privilege of certain persons or social institutions. Moreover, the exclusion of often large swathes of the population gives rise to questions with subversive power: What is the reason for this exclusion? Why do they enjoy this right and not us? The impossibility of providing good, principled answers to these questions turned out to be the seed of those revolutions that built the modern world of rights. *The privileges for a few spearhead the rights for all* – this has been a central theme of the history of human rights to the present day.

Another key obstacle to the development of human rights is their challenge to the distribution of power in social orders. Any expansion of the content of rights reduces somebody's power and privilege – the power to determine what is said in a community, which criticism is allowed, what the ruler can do to their subjects

206 Cf. Holt, *Magna Carta*, 46: "The history of Magna Carta is the history not only of a document but also of an argument. The history of the document is a history of repeated re-interpretation. But the history of the argument is a history of a continuous element of political thinking. In this light there is no inherent reason why an assertion of law originally conceived in aristocratic interests should not be applied on a wider scale. If we can seek truth in Aristotle, we can seek it also in Magna Carta. The class and political interests involved in each stage of the Charter's history are one aspect of it; the principles it asserted, implied or assumed another. Approached as political theory it sought to establish the rights of subjects against authority and maintained the principle that authority was subject to law. If the matter is left in broad terms of sovereign authority on the one hand and the suject's right on the other, this was the legal issue at stake in the fight against John, against Charles I and in the resistance of the American colonists to George III."

207 Cf. Lauterpacht, *The International Bill of the Rights of Man*, 58, commenting on the meaning of the *Magna Carta* for the development of human rights. Cf. on the expansion of the meaning and scope of application of central provisions, n. 119.

208 Cf. John Locke, *A Letter Concerning Toleration*, ed. James Tully (Indianapolis, IN: Hackett, 1983), 51; Mendelssohn, "Jerusalem," 130 f.

and ultimately even whether these rulers may lose their positions because the ruled claim the right to rule themselves. These rights reshape the social fabric, directly or indirectly challenging social and economic power. This does not require sophisticated social rights or doctrinal instruments such as direct or indirect horizontal effects of rights between private parties. If one grants freedom of speech, freedom of association and freedom of assembly, one empowers unions to start renegotiating the distribution of wealth in a society, for instance, and women to unite to challenge patriarchy. If people are entitled to education irrespective of their skin color, the outcome quickly undermines ideas of racial superiority. If women cannot be treated disadvantageously because of their gender in labor law, this subverts discriminatory structures of domination in the workplace.

A further impediment is that, as indicated above, human rights as an explicit idea presuppose something like detached reflection, transcending merely personal perspectives and interests. They demand a readiness to be bound by the conclusions drawn from reflecting upon normative questions and to act accordingly – exacting demands for creatures such as human beings. The fact that the results of this thinking took a very long time to be formulated clearly, elevated to political demands and institutionalized in the law, finally even on the global level, is another unsurprising feature of the development of human rights. Human beings live in lifeworlds full of prejudice, narrow-mindedness, ignorance, resentment, egoism and aggression. The pursuit of domination, power and material advantage is a significant historical factor. In history, social structures that maintain power and privilege define entire epochs. Developing an idea like human rights in this framework evidently is an arduous task – not least because many competing theories deny that human rights really serve justified ends well, a matter we will discuss in Chapter 4.

The history of human rights is thus not just a smooth ride to paradise. It is worth remembering the many incremental steps, the dead-end roads taken, the errors and the striking thoughts formulated on the way. Furthermore, debates on human rights are far from over: Questions concerning the personal and material scope of human rights arise to the present day, as illustrated by current theories about the legitimate bearers and content of human rights that, in the opinion of some, do not include certain groups of human beings such as infants,[209] or do not in fact encompass certain content, such as the right to democratic self-government,[210] which in the eyes of others is central to the idea of human rights.[211]

3.6.6 *Not from Nowhere*

These findings are very useful in determining what exactly we are talking about when addressing the topic of human rights. They illustrate that the idea of human rights was not formulated explicitly in all cultures since the beginning of time but is

[209] Griffin, *On Human Rights*, 95.
[210] Griffin, *On Human Rights*, 242 ff.
[211] Habermas, *Faktizität und Geltung*, 156.

no creation *ex nihilo* of ingenious eighteenth-century thinking either, let alone a ephemeral partisan concept of the second half of the twentieth century, stemming from, say, Amnesty International (admirable as they are),[212] the Carter administration[213] or Catholic personalism.[214] Rather, the building blocks of this idea have been long in the making. Casting these ideas as a recent invention of modern, perhaps even twentieth-century normative ingenuity misses important dimensions of the history of human rights and does not do justice to the great contributions of the past of more than one cultural tradition.

The development of the idea of human rights is embedded in the wider history of thought about justice, goodness and the right political order. From a very early stage onwards, these debates concerned not only what is objectively right, as some have maintained, but also the justified claims that human beings have. The history of the search for equality, liberty, solidarity and human worth speaks against simplistic accounts – for example, that antiquity (which antiquity?) had no concept of a subjective right or of human equality and dignity. The historical record is highly fragmented, not only because of the destructive forces of history, but also because very many human beings were prevented from contributing to its records, which already should caution us against drawing one-dimensional conclusions. Moreover, even the sources we have show a differentiated picture – there were voices for equality and voices against, and even statements such as this have to be carefully nuanced for each individual case. Plato and Aristotle were no champions of democratic egalitarianism. But shelving their complex thought as irrelevant for the history of the idea of human equality would be ill-advised, too, given their contribution to the theory of justice and its relation to rights, as we have seen.

All of these debates were couched in a great variety of intellectual contexts – Plato's theory of ideas, Aristotle's concept of forms, the metaphysics of religiously framed Natural Law, the rational deductions *more geometrico*, the perfectionist Natural Law of Leibniz and the *a priori* principles of practical reason in Kant's thought, for example.

The history of human rights thus is full of complications and of "continuity *and* discontinuity."[215] But, as we have seen, many traces of the idea of human rights can be discovered in history, in the thought and art of many cultures, as well as in the backyards

[212] Cf. Moyn, *The Last Utopia*, 3 ff.: "The drama of human rights, then, is that they emerged in the 1970s seemingly from nowhere."

[213] Cf. Moyn, *The Last Utopia*, 217: "During the Carter administration, to which it clearly owed its newfound public role, the human rights movement generally treated government as an ally."

[214] Moyn, "Personalism," 85 ff.

[215] Cf. Christopher McCrudden, "Human Rights Histories," *Oxford Journal of Legal Studies* 35, no. 1 (2015): 181 (emphasis in original), Moyn, "Continuing Perplexities of Human Rights," 96 ff. admits this. He defends his view with the remark that he is interested in conceptual history, not the history of an idea, ibid. 98. This is not what his historical account is about: It traces not just the use of terms (if that is what is meant by conceptual history as opposed to a history of ideas), but what he takes as the emergence of an apolitical, moralist and impoverished utopia. On problems of some kinds of conceptual history Orford, *International Law*, 299 ff.

of history, where dwell those who are forgotten and downtrodden but still show, in acts of rebellion and daily uprightness, what rights, albeit denied, are truly theirs.

This winding course of human rights history is to be expected, because human history itself is a long journey towards human self-understanding, a meandering, often-tragic course with early advances and epochs of regress, slowly fathoming humans' most important concerns and vulnerabilities, finally forming a concept of humanity itself that is not biased and fragmented by ideologies of exclusion based on sex, skin color, cultural origin and the like as the basis of ethical thought.

The roots of human rights in history thus are deep. They are not the monopoly of just one culture, one system of thought, one religion or one political agenda. The idea of human rights draws on the best traditions of human thought, on the defense of human equality, liberty, solidarity and human worth. For this idea to see the light of day, human thinking needed to shed the fetters of prejudice, resentment and concern for comfortable privilege and to breathe life into the hope for equal respect for all. Human rights do not make up the totality of justice, but they are an important element of what a just order may be.

To be sure, human rights have been and indeed currently are abused for political purposes. This seems to be the fate of any great human idea. But the idea itself is not necessarily delegitimized by its abuse by its political foes. Human rights as embodied in law are equally not just the innocent offspring of beautiful moral minds. They are the product of many political forces, including ones that were sometimes far from any serious attachment to the idea of human rights. Again, this comes as no surprise in light of the way human institutions are formed in history. But human rights are not necessarily contaminated by these origins if they are otherwise justified. If we overlook this, we fail to provide "a historically convincing account of the normative power of the human rights idea,"[216] and thus we neglect a crucial element of human rights history.

Seen in historical perspective, *human rights are the late child of ethical concerns at the core of the human life form*. This finding considerably raises the bar for any theory seeking to address the relation between human rights and the human mind. The task is not to say something meaningful about a political whim of a generation or an ideological artifact of the post-1945 intellectual culture of the West. If it is to succeed, this account needs to contribute to the understanding of nothing less than a central, enduring element of human beings' deepest moral and legal aspirations, an element that often fails tragically, at irredeemable human cost.

3.7 THE CHARISMA OF HUMAN RIGHTS: WHERE FROM?

The interesting lessons of the history of ideas thus raise questions that differ significantly from those discussed by current historical human rights revisionism. These questions already suggested themselves during our reflection on the lessons of

[216] McCrudden, "Human Rights Histories," 203.

the more recent history of human rights and can be put like this: Why did the moral intuitions related to the core building blocks of the explicit human rights idea and the principles underlying it emerge in quite different historical and cultural contexts? Why is the human rights idea prospering today, not least at a grassroots level, despite its many political (and academic) foes? Why was it not just one idea among others, but a notion that exerted a fascination like few before it? Why did it capture the moral, political and legal imagination of human beings around the globe and from all walks of life, prompting committed political and even revolutionary action that still rightly is heralded as a proud chapter in the self-liberation of human beings? Why does this tradition continue in the attempts of very many people, who often are far removed from academic discourses, to secure justified claims of human beings against suppression and contempt? Why does it appear as one example in human history that nourishes the hope that this species may be capable of something better than folly, superfluous harm and mishap? What are the deeper reasons for this fact?

The history of the idea of human rights is not a history of cultural developments without human subjects. On the contrary, in crucial respects it is the history of inquiring, fallible human beings who developed certain ideas, enlarged their scope, ironed out inconsistencies, established new connections to other beliefs that appeared insightful, made explicit what before was only tacitly implied and through these labors of thought and passion for understanding forged the concepts that finally became reliable foundations upon which to build something new through political action. It is the history of great insights that are lost and rediscovered, transformed and finally grow into an almost self-evident part of a human way of living. These insights can seem secure for some time until doubt sets in again and the destructive forces of failing to comprehend, of ignoring or, to use Benjamin's phrase, of "Penelope's work of forgetting"[217] what already has been understood take their toll – forces that can make people turn their back upon what earlier generations won at very high cost, occasionally even with a bored shrug of their shoulders and a contemptuous grin.

As we have seen, this picture also appears to aptly describe the more recent developments after the explicit proclamation of human rights on the world stage in the age of revolutionary constitutionalism. Our historical review showed that the human rights idea has its true source in a particular position, in an ethically calibrated political and ultimately legal substantial stance about whether human beings enjoy fundamental rights, what these rights are and how they relate to other concerns of human beings and the social communities in which they live. This stance convinced very many people around the globe, including governmental actors. It enjoyed great influence for some periods of time, but also was eclipsed,

[217] "*Penelopewerk des Vergessens*," Walter Benjamin, "Zum Bilde Prousts," in Walter Benjamin, *Gesammelte Schriften*, Vol. II-1, eds. Rolf Tiedemann and Hermann Schweppenhäuser (Frankfurt am Main: Suhrkamp, 1992), 351.

as we have seen. This was the case not only for obvious political reasons, such as the rise of new forms of authoritarianism after the end of colonialism, but also because of other factors as well, as exemplified by recent theoretical human rights skepticism.

What is the source of the attraction, the "charisma" of human rights, to adopt a term used by Max Weber in the context of his (skeptical) discussion of the rise of human rights?[218] What led human beings to politically declare rights to liberty, equality, solidarity and respect for equal human worth the basic conditions for any legitimate human political order? Why did they turn these rights into law, finally embarking on the ambitious project of extending the realm legally secured by these rights to all human beings, protecting them preferably by the means of national legal orders, but with international law and international institutions as residual safeguards?

In the end, human rights are nothing less than a powerful *yes* to human existence, a *yes* to the worth of every person being more important than other concerns, a *yes* to the respect for human beings as the minimum condition for a decent human life. Why did the idea of human rights convince sufficient numbers of people? It appeals to the best in human beings, to their sense of justice, to their concern for the well-being of others, to their respect for their moral status and the shared humanity of all. Usually such appeals die away unheard. Why was it, then, successful to a remarkable degree, despite all of its evident shortcomings? Why did the seasoned projects of domination, of secured privilege for some and contempt for others, fail to win the day (at least for now)? Given the course of human history, there is ample reason to be astonished about this course of affairs, as this history allows no illusions about the necessarily victorious force of justice and goodness and its relative strength in comparison to other baser pastimes of humanity. The fact that something as noble as the idea of human rights could be formed, survive and even prosper might thus be cause for considerable bewilderment.

One possible reason for the success of human rights is the "peculiarly compulsionless compulsion of the better argument," to borrow a famous phrase.[219] From this perspective, the partial victories of the human rights idea and its underlying principles first in the realm of thought and then as political projects and legal institutions are, despite all epistemic differences, due to some of the same factors that led to the acceptance of the theory of gravity or the Darwinian theory of evolution and their successors in scientific theory building. Of course, arguments in physics or the theory of evolution convince on different grounds than arguments in ethics or legal thought. However, there is a common denominator in one respect. In all of these cases, the reason for the "charisma" of these ideas is that they are well

[218] Max Weber, *Wirtschaft und Gesellschaft – Herrschaft*, in *Max Weber Gesamtausgabe*, Vol. I/22-4, eds. Hanke Edith and Kroll Thomas (Tübingen: Mohr Siebeck, 2005), 678 f.

[219] Jürgen Habermas, *Theorie des kommunikativen Handelns*, Vol. 1 (Frankfurt am Main: Suhrkamp, 1981), 47: "*eigentümlich zwanglose Zwang des besseren Arguments.*"

justified and because of this have the power to convince, sometimes slowly, sometimes by leaps and bounds.

To be sure, good reasons hardly have been a strong force in history. But we should not underestimate their subversive power either. After all, the attraction of some arguments has slowly altered our views about the structure of the universe and matter, or about our origins in natural history. These were hardly small intellectual labors. Consequently, there is nothing strange in assuming that the same can happen in the process of chiseling out the politically effective and legally enforceable ideas from the bedrock material of some basic moral intuitions of what justice and moral decency command.

The precondition for this perspective is the assumption not only of good justificatory *reasons* for the legitimacy of human rights, but also of the existence of a *capacity of moral understanding that in principle is shared by all human beings*. It is exercising this capacity that leads to insights about rights when human beings reflect impartially on their existential situation within a community of others like themselves and on what the human condition might normatively demand.

To explore such perspectives and to assert, first, that there are good arguments for human rights; second, that all human beings enjoy the ability to understand their point; and third, that the conviction of the justifiedness of human rights has been and continues to be a relevant, sometimes even decisive historical and political factor determining human political action leads in no way to a surprising or strange conclusion. It is rather the fundamental assumption underpinning many lines of thought in human history, not only of obvious cases such as Natural Law theory and the theory of moral understanding of the Enlightenment. It is the hidden working hypothesis of contemporary human rights culture, of literally millions of people, despite the importance of various relativisms for academic and some political debate. The foundational assumption of the human rights movement after all is that human rights make sense for everyone. The whole project starts from the idea that all human beings are endowed with "reason and conscience" and thus are capable of understanding that there are human rights for themselves and others, irrespective of culture, upbringing, gender, skin color and the like. The human rights project represents optimism about the possibility of common human insight. Despite its many obstacles – not least powerful ideologies, incited hatred and the cultivation of moral parochialism in some intellectual quarters – this project considers it possible that humans can come to understand that such rights are justified and that they are worth the effort, passion and sacrifice required to make them living things.

Thus, the true answer to the challenge of historical human rights skepticism is not to prove the universal historical presence of human rights in human history. This proof is neither possible nor necessary. The true answer to the historical and, as an intended consequence, normative relativizing of human rights is to reassert the strength of the reasons, first, for the validity of human rights and, second, for assuming the reality of a fundamental and universal faculty of human beings for moral cognition that provides everyone with epistemic access to the idea of human rights. To avoid any misunderstanding: The existence of a capacity of practical cognition is not the criterion for the truth of the propositions perceived as true. The fact that empirically human beings judge something to be true or justified is no reason to assume that it is in fact true or justified. This capacity only creates the cognitive possibility of *understanding* what is justified on whatever grounds there are for this justification, as we will see in the following chapters.

According to this fundamental assumption of modern human rights culture, this human faculty of moral insight is not just the privilege of some philosopher-kings, of some special people, of a particular culture, class or religion. It is not the privilege of white people or of men, nor is it the privilege of just one time. As we have seen, the history of the idea and practice of human rights is the history of constantly renewed approaches to this great idea in very different forms and in very different historical, social, cultural and religious contexts, approaches that often are implicit and always are fragmentary, tentative and imperfect. Our own time is no more than another chapter in this history. We can be sure that other times will discern and perhaps wonder about the limits of our present understanding and practice of fundamental rights, as there is no reason to assume that we – unlike all who came before us – are able to grasp fully something that is so difficult to develop and even harder to fill with real life.

The history of human rights consequently puts two questions on the table. First, are human rights justifiable, and if so, how? Second, how are we to understand the thesis of universal epistemic access to the idea of human rights? In other words: What are the conditions for the epistemological plausibility of such a theory of justification? What kind of theory of practical cognition and of the kind of objects that cognition in this field is concerned with does the justification of human rights presuppose?

Historical or even historicist accounts of human rights thus offer no escape from the theory of the justification of human rights and their psychological, epistemological and ontological aspects. On the contrary, a review of the history of human rights and, in this context, of the merits of historical human rights revisionism leads to the question of the relationship between human thought and the idea of human rights. More precisely, it raises the questions of whether these good arguments for human rights do indeed exist and of whether the idea of a universal faculty of moral insight – of practical reason or a sense of justice, if you will – that is shared by all human beings and provides justified insight into these matters makes any sense for contemporary thought.[220]

[220] That this is not obvious is illustrated by Habermas' remark that subjective reason is "*zerbrochen*," shattered into pieces, Habermas, *Faktizität und Geltung*, 17, applicable to the practical reason of subjects, too.

The precondition for answering these questions is a theory of the justification of human rights beyond the particular political or religious strategies that hoped to use the idea of human rights for their purposes. Only once the problem of justification has been clarified can we ask whether a certain structure of the human mind has any importance for the project of justification, not least to delegitimize it, as is claimed by various quite influential theories of the human moral mind to be discussed below. This question needs to be taken very seriously, as it challenges the idea of a potentially shared human understanding of human rights more radically than other forms of human rights critique, such as the various forms of relativist perspectivism discussed today.[221]

These results of the history of human rights constitute a crucial benchmark for assessing the merits of any psychological or neuroscientific theory of human rights. This theory has to be able to account for the *cognitive preconditions of the possibility of the historical trajectory and its immense complexity*. Given the historical analysis and what it tells us about the making of the human rights idea, thus far it seems implausible that human rights intuitions are either a simple given of human cognition, despite what influential contemporary theories maintain, or that human beings are merely moral blank slates.

This brings us to a very important finding. In order to develop something like a theory of moral cognition relevant for human rights, we consequently need to take a different route. The most promising points of departure are *the fundamental intuitions about claims to goods (e.g. the ability to speak one's mind, so cherished by Polynices and Jocasta), correlated with duties and often accompanied by privileges, based on justice and moral obligations towards others that seem to be the root for what has become the explicit idea of human rights, now institutionalized as law.*

These findings prove the need to reconstruct some elements of human rights history for the cognitive interests of our inquiry. The discussion has shown that a historical account such as this is not a mere digression for a theory of human rights that is willing to confront the challenges of psychology, neuroscience and the theory of mind. On the contrary, history is crucial if we are properly to determine the object of research and the key theoretical questions that such a theory needs to answer.

A fundamental lesson thus is that *studying the genealogy of human rights is a necessary condition but in itself is not sufficient to understand the ascent and current reality of human rights*. The argument for the cross-cultural origins of contemporary human rights discussed above is important. But even if matters were different, the case of human rights would not be settled. Even if this idea were of purely European (or Indian or African) origin, the question would still remain: How convincing is this

[221] On perspectivism cf. Nietzsche, *Jenseits von Gut und Böse*, 12. Historical revisionism is not necessarily wedded to perspectivism: It could claim that human beings do share a fundamental perspective on the world through time that did not, however, produce a concept of human rights until the 1970s.

idea of human rights after all? Are there reasons relevant for all human beings or are there not? Are all human beings able to understand these reasons, as all human beings are able (in principle) to grasp the arguments for the theory of gravity, even though not many of them are born in Woolsthorpe-by-Colsterworth in Lincolnshire, like Newton? In order to understand human rights and their role in history, it seems that we have to turn to the grounds of their justification and the sources of moral cognition in the still largely unfathomed human mind.

PART II

Justification

4

Far from Obvious

The Quest for the Justification of Human Rights

Die Leute glauben, unser Tun und Schaffen sei eitel Wahl, aus dem Vorrat der neuen Ideen griffen wir eine heraus, für die wir sprechen und wirken, streiten und leiden wollten, wie etwa sonst ein Philolog sich seinen Klassiker auswählte, mit dessen Kommentierung er sich sein ganzes Leben hindurch beschäftigte – nein, wir ergreifen keine Idee, sondern die Idee ergreift uns.[1]

Heinrich Heine, *Vorrede zum ersten Band des Salons*

Die Gesammt-Entartung des Menschen, hinab bis zu dem, was heute den socialistischen Tölpeln und Flachköpfen als ihr "Mensch der Zukunft" erscheint, – als ihr Ideal! – diese Entartung und Verkleinerung des Menschen zum vollkommenen Heerdenthiere (oder, wie sie sagen, zum Menschen der "freien Gesellschaft"), diese Verthierung des Menschen zum Zwergthiere der gleichen Rechte und Ansprüche ist möglich, es ist kein Zweifel! Wer diese Möglichkeit einmal bis zu Ende gedacht hat, kennt einen Ekel mehr, als die übrigen Menschen, – und vielleicht auch eine neue Aufgabe! ...[2]

Friedrich Nietzsche, *Jenseits von Gut und Böse*

We must remember that Fascism and racism will emerge from this war not only with the bitterness of defeat but also with sweet memories of the ease with which it is possible to commit mass murder.

Vasily Grossman, *The Hell of Treblinka*

1 "People believe that our doings and workings are nought but choice, that from the hoard of new ideas we selected one for which we desired to speak and work, argue and suffer, much as a philologist selected the classics whose commentary was to occupy him for the rest of his life – no, we do not grasp an idea, rather the idea grasps us" (translation M. Hiley).

2 Friedrich Nietzsche, *Beyond Good and Evil*, trans. Reginald John Hollingdale (London: Penguin Books, 2003), 127 f.: "The *collective degeneration of man* down to that which the socialist dolts and blockheads today see as their 'man of the future' – as their ideal! – this degeneration and diminution of man to the perfect herd animal (or, as they say, to the man of the 'free society'), this animalization of man to the pygmy animal of equal rights and equal pretensions is *possible*, there is no doubt about that! He who has once thought this possibility through to the end knows one more kind of disgust than other men do – and perhaps also a new *task*!" (emphasis in original).

4.1 HOW TO JUSTIFY HUMAN RIGHTS

4.1.1 *An Idle Question?*

The justification of human rights is no straightforward matter. This justification involves various problems that stem from different sources: Some issues are related to the specificities of human rights, some originate in fundamental questions of ethics and metaethics that are relevant for human rights but not limited to their justification, some stem from issues of human epistemology that cut across a range of fields and some even touch upon the question of the limits of human understanding.

To complicate matters yet further, there is some debate as to whether human rights require any justification at all. Maritain's account of the by now proverbial summary of a postwar exchange of opinions on the foundation of human rights – "we agree about the rights but on condition that no one asks us why" – already has been recalled above. This summary could be interpreted as stating something even stronger than mere factual disagreement about the justification of human rights, accompanied rather luckily by a consensus about the list of rights to be protected; it could be interpreted as stating that agreement about their content is *conditioned upon* a lack of engagement with deeper background theories. One of the last decades' most influential theories of political liberalism could be understood as claiming something to this effect: An "overlapping consensus" is all that is needed, and this can be achieved on the basis of different background theories within the framework of reasonable disagreement.[3] Engaging with these background theories is unnecessary and may even impede such an overlapping consensus. Agnosticism about the deeper justification of human rights may turn out to be the high road to consensus about their content, which is all that matters, one could think.

When seeking to address these problems, it is useful to distinguish between *justificatory theories*, which will form the focus of attention in the following, and *explanatory theories*, some of which will be discussed in Part III below.

Justificatory theories provide normative reasons for the legitimacy of human rights, explanatory theories tell us about the causes of the existence of human rights. Many such causes can be imagined – social, historical, political, economic, anthropological, evolutionary and cognitive. There is theoretical work on the foundations of rights that combines explanations of human rights with statements about their legitimacy or illegitimacy – for example, in the genealogical revisionism discussed above as well as in other approaches that aim to defend the idea of human rights.[4] However, none of the possible causes for the emergence of human rights as such has

[3] Cf. J. Rawls' idea of an "overlapping consensus," not dependent on underlying "comprehensive doctrines," Rawls, *Political Liberalism*, 144.

[4] Joas, *Sakralität der Person*.

any bearing on the justification of human rights, as this justification ultimately is based not upon any causal account of the origin of human rights, but on the normative grounds of their legitimacy – a topic related to the intense debates about the is/ought distinction and thus full of intricacies to which we will return.

There are various justificatory theories of human rights, some with deontological or with consequentialist leanings, others from the quarters of virtue ethics or other philosophical background theories – from Marxism and Critical Theory to post-modern phenomenology. These theories naturally are very different and raise many difficult issues, both as to concrete arguments about human rights and as to theoretical background assumptions. These questions need not be necessarily linked – from a variety of theoretical points of view, conceptions of human rights can be entertained that may be open to criticism, but not because of their underlying theoretical orientation. For example, one can criticize the view that human rights should be understood solely as rights of international law and not also as rights of national constitutional law – a position that may be held from quite different theoretical points of view. Such critical analysis is possible without any need to engage with the theoretical background of this thesis. Other questions are different in kind and only can be answered if one tackles these underlying theories at least to some degree.

Accordingly, the following remarks will discuss not all but some of the currently most influential and (which is not always the same thing) the constructively most promising theoretical approaches to the justification of human rights. We will avoid theoretical overkill if a question can be answered without reference to wider theoretical frameworks, but we will not shy away from difficult philosophical questions if necessary.

The findings of our historical review form a useful starting point for this discussion. Studying the historical development of the human rights idea has given us substantial reason to believe that basic, not arbitrary intuitions about claims to fundamental human goods need to be transformed substantially before they can become ethical, political and legal principles akin to the idea of human rights. This transformation requires both a generalization of issues abstracted from the particulars of a specific case to form the material scope and a universalization of the status of being a rights-holder to establish the personal scope of these rights as moral principles. Their content needs to be determined impartially and thus objectified. Human rights have to be made the explicit objects of critical, reflective deliberation. Finally, they needed to be turned from moral ideas into political demands and finally into justiciable legal norms and working legal institutions.

Given these findings, the question is: *How are we to justify such generalized, universal, objectified, impartial moral claims abstracted from specific cases that have been made explicit and turned into a transformative political agenda and ultimately powerful institutions of the law?*

At least three fundamental problems can be distinguished that a theory of human rights seeking to answer this question has to deal with.

4.1.2 A *Critical Theory of Human Goods*

Human rights are, first, rights to something; they have a scope, an area of protection and a particular content. This protected something is of value, worth or importance to human beings – otherwise protecting it would not make any sense. The right to life, for instance, protects the good of human life, the right to freedom of speech protects the good of unfettered human expression and so on. The things protected by rights are taken (rightly or wrongly) to be important, precious, even of existential concern to human beings. Rights thus protect what this inquiry has called human *goods*. The term "goods" in the sense employed here encompasses anything that is of value for human beings, without any particular theoretical implications.

This starting point may seem straightforward enough, but there is a problem lurking in the background. There are important theories justifying human rights that appear to refrain from relying on such substantial theories of goods. This is hardly surprising – after all, it is widely assumed in various quarters of modern theory, not least in economics, that it is impossible to come up with any such theory because there can be no such account (or even an "objective list") of such goods. The first line of argument against this stems from the idea of human beings' historical and social malleability. There is obvious truth to this thesis: Human ways of living have changed radically through history and differ profoundly depending upon social circumstance. The honor of winning a knight's tournament is currently not an important good for many people. There is a normative point as well, namely that any concrete image of what is central to being human, to human existence and to human good wrongly essentializes human beings and ossifies a certain parochial vision of human existence – say, of white male heterosexuals from elite groups of the Global North – and that this has profound illiberal consequences. These wrong conceptions of human life may serve to repress the full unfolding of new ways to pursue happiness and innovative experiments of living. From the point of view of influential theories, the prohibition of images of God thus has normative significance for the secular sphere, too, where not the image of a supreme being but the image of humans is of concern. The secular prohibition against forming a fixed image of human beings serves the demand not to reduce them to something they are not.[5]

[5] Cf. Adorno, *Negative Dialektik*, 293 f.; the standing case law of the Swiss Federal Court includes an explicit reference to the "indeterminable essence" ("*nicht fassbare Eigentliche*") of human beings in its definition of human dignity, Bundesgericht (Federal Supreme Court [BGer]), Judgement of March 22, 2001, BGE 127 I 6 E. 5b, 14 to avoid any essentialist definition of human nature.

The second line of argument against a theory of substantial human goods originates in the respect for human autonomy and diversity: How is a theory of goods possible if humans have very diverse ideas of such goods and by the basic principle of human autonomy are entitled to pursue their particular path to happiness? How can such a theory be constructed, given that this diversity seems to lead inevitably to the assumption that individual conceptions of the good are diverse and incommensurable?

Given these two assumptions of, first, a constantly changing, self-reinventing humanity and, second, the importance of autonomy, how can a theory of substantial human goods be formulated that is more than mere historical contingency and personal idiosyncrasy?

This clearly is a crucial question. What might encourage the inquiry is the recognition that such theories themselves presuppose a substantial theory of the good in their argument – the good of the liberty to invent and autonomously determine oneself. This illustrates the fact that the issue is not whether one needs a theory of human goods for a theory of human rights, but rather what the content of this theory of human goods is.

Undoubtedly, human rights protect not just any good, but a highly selective subset of all imaginable objects that are valuable to human beings in one sense or another. This is true both for moral and for legal human rights. There is neither a moral nor a legal human right to have freshly baked strawberry cake delivered to one's office every afternoon because one (understandably) likes it so much and it fosters one's work in the theory of law considerably, nor a moral or legal human right to see the right side (one's own team, of course, incomparable as it surely is) always win the soccer World Cup, accompanied by a corresponding duty of the other (quite useless) teams to let it happen. Consequently, some kind of threshold criterion needs to be identified in order to determine whether a human concern is of such weight that it is a possible candidate for protection by human rights.[6]

The rights protected by law are subject to further qualifications and may be narrower than moral rights because the specific properties of legal rights need to be accounted for – for instance, institutionalized justiciability and enforceability.

Any theory of human rights therefore needs, first, a *critical theory of human goods* to account for the reasons for including particular goods in the catalogue of human rights in morality and law and not others. More precisely, such a theory must identify the reasons that qualify something as a potential good for protection in the first place as well as the reasons its weight is sufficient to be protected by the special means of human rights.

The details of the scope of human rights are highly contentious. They are shaped and refined daily through the work of thousands of lawyers, court decisions,

6 Threshold criteria represent a classic theme of human rights theory, cf. James W. Nickel, *Making Sense of Human Rights*, 2nd edition (Malden, MA: Blackwell, 2007), 53 ff.

legislative acts and legal, political and philosophical deliberations about old and new normative challenges. However, their core elements include respect for human beings' particular, supreme and inalienable worth, their physical and mental integrity, freedom, equal treatment and – more controversially perhaps – the means for their physical subsistence and, more ambitiously, the minimum material conditions of a dignified life. A theory of human goods needs to consider closely why these goods are protected (in many cases uncontroversially), whether this protection is justifiable and which other goods could possibly qualify as worthy of protection.

4.1.3 *A Political Theory of Human Rights*

Human goods, including those that qualify as possible objects of protection as human rights, can be secured by more than one means, not only rights. Sometimes, rights are not even an option to achieve a given end, because the enjoyment of many goods very important to human beings obviously cannot be fostered by the specific normative tool of rights. For example, it is very important to be loved, but love cannot be secured by rights. The obligation of the addressee of the right and the correlative claim of the rights-holder presupposes the possibility of voluntary control of the obligatory act: *ultra posse nemo obligatur*. Therefore, nobody can have a duty to do something that is not a matter of their choice – as falling in love is not, if one is among the many unfortunate (or perhaps fortunate) individuals who do not possess Puck's magic flower.

For the justification of rights, this means that we need a convincing account of the *possibility* and, if the possibility exists, the *reasons* to secure certain important goods of human beings by the particular means of rights. This is obvious for freely created, positive legal rights, which by their very nature imply a conscious choice on the part of the lawmakers. For moral rights the problem takes a slightly different turn, at least if one believes (as many do) that they are not freely created as positive legal rights but are somehow the object of cognition by thought bound by reasons and arguments, and that they are valid even if people do not think they exist – just as Jewish people's right to life certainly existed even though many people around them in the Third Reich thought otherwise. But in the case of moral rights, too, one needs to answer the question of whether a supposed right serves morally justified ends or, on the contrary, defies such ends.

In many cases, the fact that rights do serve justified aims is not obvious. For example, one can be of the opinion that important democratic institutions should not be subjected to vilifying critique that is not based on facts. The integrity and stability of such institutions is an important good for human life – quite clearly so. But this does not mean that citizens should have a moral or legal right that others do not utter this kind of baseless, vilifying critique – at least, this is a thought upon which much of current free speech doctrine is based. One reason for this is the argument (given its canonical form by Mill) that reasonable decisions in a democracy in the long term are best served by the free exchange of ideas[7] and not by their suppression, even if they "shock, offend and disturb," as the ECtHR has put it.[8] Another argument stems from the normative weight of free speech, which speaks – at least in many cases – against any control of the content of human expression because of its importance for human life.

This example shows that human rights imply prudential considerations, as in the first-mentioned argument for free speech based upon the instrumental value of the free exchange of ideas, and normative arguments – for instance, arising from the question of how to balance the normative value of individual freedom of expression and the normative value of democracy. The latter aspect already points to a problem to be discussed below: the problem of the normative principles implied in the justification of human rights.

These questions are far from trivial. In addition, on a more fundamental level, important theories forcefully deny that human rights contribute to the achievement of human goods. This is obvious for authoritarian theories of various ilk, vividly illustrated, for instance, by the critique of the ideas of the *Déclaration des Droits de l'Homme et du Citoyen*. This line of argument can be found in other contexts as well, however. Theories with a considerable impact on world history, such as Marxism, argued (at least in some classical forms) that freedom is an important good, even the ultimate aim of a unalienated society, but at the same time offered a radical critique of rights that still resonates today: Rights are held to be tools not for the liberation but for the repression of the working class in capitalist societies. Radical proceduralist democratic theory argues that the best way to secure human liberty is unfettered democracy, not a realm of rights. Deconstruction theories interpret rights as at best ambiguous tools to foster justice (among other reasons because of the abstract generality of rights), while at worst as forms of unjustified violence, if only in the sublimated residual form of performative force.

Given all this, the point of rights needs to be made. For legal rights, furthermore, the particularities of the legal form, such as justiciability and enforceability, need to be taken into consideration. This is even more obvious if one is familiar with the realities of legal rights in practice: Much hinges on the argument that a particular public good is actually fostered by specific legal rights, which is by no means always clear, even if one endorses the underlying moral right. Certain social rights are classic examples of this kind of difficulty. There is a very good case for a moral right to work. It is, however, an entirely different question whether the underlying aim – income and meaningful work – would be fostered if courts were entitled to allocate jobs on the basis of a fully-fledged subjective right of guaranteed employment. More complex mechanisms are therefore often sought to operationalize social rights as

7 Mill, "On Liberty," 228 ff.

8 ECtHR, Handyside v The United Kingdom, Judgement of November 4, 1976, appl. no. 5493/72, para. 49.

legal rights – for example, government action that fosters employment, institutions that secure sufficient benefits in case of unemployment and the availability of measures to assist reintegration into the workforce through vocational training and the like. Even if one is convinced that, despite all obstacles, courts should have the competence to decide on employment, this conclusion certainly requires more argument than the thesis that courts legitimately decide on problems of free speech.

As a consequence, one needs – and this is the second fundamental problem of a theory of human rights – a theory of the proper conditions for the realization of human goods in human societies and, in particular, a theory of the role of moral and legal rights in achieving this end. This theory of the possibility and desirability of the realization of human goods by means of rights will imply answers to intrinsically political questions and thus constitutes a *political theory of the role of rights in a well-ordered society*.

4.1.4 A *Theory of Fundamental Normative Principles*

The third problem is the problem of the normative principles constitutive for the justification of rights. There are two dimensions to this problem. The first dimension concerns the *normative structure of rights*. Rights are normative *relations* between persons and, more precisely, between a plurality of intricately connected persons and other rights-holders such as legal persons. Rights create a highly subtle web of such normative relations between agents – claims and privileges of the rights-holder towards the addressee, correlated duties and no-rights of the latter towards the former, powers and immunities, disabilities and liabilities, as explained above. The question that any theory of human rights has to answer is: What is the normative source of these intricate normative relations? How and why do they come into being? How, for example, are principles of justice related to rights? The answer to these questions is relevant for both moral and legal rights. In order to make sense of moral rights, one needs to be able to clarify the ground on which they come into existence. Otherwise, they may be regarded as metaphysical illusions, mere fictions without significance, nonsense upon stilts, as skeptics argue.

For legal rights, the answer may seem easier because they constitute positive law. The normative relations between rights-holder and duty-bearer(s) exist because the law posits them, one could say. The law, however, does not create the notions constituting a subjective right *de novo* and regularly either fails to define them or does so only in a highly limited, sometimes openly tautological manner.[9] Instead, it presupposes the meaning of the term *right*, which is the very reason why the current analytical theory of rights developed: The practice of the law was insufficiently clear on what it understood as a *right* in different contexts. It is thus necessary to clarify the

[9] For an example from a famous code: The German Civil Code (BGB) defines claims in Art. 194 (1) as: "The right to demand that another person does or refrains from an act (claim)."

meaning of terms such as *claim* or *obligation*, *privilege* or *no-right*, and to establish whether this meaning is similar or the same as in in the moral domain. This is not a banal question. Terms like "obligation" are, after all, crucial concepts, the meaning of which "haunts legal reflection."[10] This analysis helps to solve the next problem, namely to determine whether these normative relations and concepts are mere legal artifacts or the legal equivalent of underlying fundamental moral notions turned into law. Ascertaining whether the positive law mirrors some deeper principles of a plausible theory of rights that clarifies in particular the relation between the fundamental normative categories constitutive of rights and normative principles like justice would be an insight of great interest.

The second dimension – unlike the first question, which relates to the normative structure of rights as a formal category independent of their content – is at the forefront of many debates. It concerns the *material content of those normative principles that justify the ascription of rights to human beings*. Human rights imply the idea of a justified distribution and allocation of central goods such as respect, status, freedom and resources. Which normative principles give rise to the particular kind of rights that persons possess and that justify the allocation of goods realized by rights? Can they be identified? If so – what are they? In particular, what is the role that basic principles of morality such as justice and altruism play in this respect? What about human dignity? Are these moral principles a key to the question of the origin of human rights? Or are other principles at play? Agency, perhaps? There seems to be something special about moral principles, as other principles do not lead to rights. For instance, the principle that everybody should strive to fulfill their wishes in order to be happy does not give rise to the right to see one's wishes fulfilled. The principle that everybody should treat equals equally does create the right to such a treatment. Why?

As we will see, an explicit theory of normative principles as the foundation of human rights is of considerable importance. There are influential theories that do not address this problem, instead assuming that the identification of something as a legitimate, important concern for individuals suffices to give rise to rights (given that certain further conditions are satisfied, which are – and this is crucial – not related to normative principles). This is not the case, however. The fact that any concern of individuals creates claims towards others and related duties on their side – and that these individuals may enjoy privileges and are shielded from the demands of others because these others have no claim that they do or forbear something and thus only have no-rights – is something that can be explained only on the basis of normative principles. These principles are the reasons that oblige others in normative terms to act in certain well-defined ways that respect the interests of others and enable their actions. The fact that one person's interest in

10 Herbert Lionel Adolphus Hart, *The Concept of Law* (Oxford: Oxford University Press, 2012), 87.

free expression, for instance, is of such normative relevance for another person that the first person enjoys a right such as freedom of speech with the normative incidents implied can be explained only on the basis of normative principles that turn the concerns of others into the material of their rights and our obligations. It should be noted that not every normative principle gives rise to a right, however. Supererogatory acts are good examples of this. This is because such an act, which benefits others beyond the call of duty, while highly laudable in moral terms, is not required. The patient of this act has no claim to it. This example already indicates that rights do not exhaust the domain of morality. The task is therefore to identify not only justified normative principles, but also the members of that subset of justified normative principles that give rise to rights. Consequently, third, there is no full theory of human rights without a *normative theory of the foundational principles of rights*.

Thus, in sum, the first question is: What is a promising basis for determining the selective, highly qualified goods protected by human rights? The second is: Is there a convincing account of the political point of human rights? The third is: What are the normative foundations of human rights?

As a first step, we will turn now to core elements of current debates about the *justification* of human rights. This review should help us to ascertain whether these questions really direct reflection to the core of the matter, miss important points or already have been answered convincingly. For the sake of accessibility, we will distinguish *affirmative* human rights theories from *revisionist* human rights theories, the former making a case for, the latter against human rights. The former will be discussed first, and subsequently the Chapter 5 will turn to the possible sources of critique of these affirmative claims in the framework of political theories of human rights, thus addressing the question: Are human rights the proper tools of human liberation or, to the contrary, elements of humanity's persistent repression?

In order to maintain an overview of the somewhat heterogeneous debate on human rights, it may be equally useful to group the affirmative theories according to certain theory clusters: Human rights are theorized with a focus on their *functions*, in particular for social differentiation, the efficient allocation of goods, the accommodation of bounded rationality and the maximizing of aggregate happiness. They are legitimized by *procedures*, such as by consensus or contract, if only in counterfactual thought experiments. Another approach is to refer to *substantive elements of human existence* as sources of legitimacy – autonomy, needs, interests and capabilities are examples of these. A *political conception* turns to the practice of human rights to clarify their point, whereas a *eudemonistic* perspective derives their importance from their role for a life lived well. These clusters serve expository purposes and do not possess deep theoretical meaning. As a whole, they promise to cover if not all, then at least a sufficiently wide range of topics that a critical theory of human rights needs to address.

4.2 THE FUNCTIONS OF HUMAN RIGHTS

4.2.1 *Human Rights as Tools for Social Integration*

One way to look at the justification of human rights is to deny that they protect goods for the sake of individuals. Influential theories assert that human rights can only be understood as means to serve certain *functions of society*. The fact that they serve the interest of individuals is a mere by-product. The attraction of this view stems from the fact that it sidesteps questions about normative foundations and furthermore explains in functional terms why these quarrels about normative foundations occupy people in the first place. Marxist theory of law is a paradigmatic case, seeing human rights as a functional tool to preserve and perpetuate power both in concrete social terms and in the realm of epistemic regimes. More recent examples include post-structuralist theories of human rights. As these theories predominantly are critical of human rights, they will be discussed as part of our review of the critique of human rights.

Affirmative social functionalist theories argue instead that human rights are best understood on the basis of their function in successful social integration.[11] The most recent and arguably currently most influential theory of this kind stems from systems theory, which conceptualizes society as an autopoietic social system. It is regarded as autopoietic because the elements of this system reproduce themselves through the means of the system itself. In the case of the law, for instance, there are legal norms that regulate the creation of new law or court decisions that determine the content of law. In a systems-theoretical analysis, law creates law and thus is autopoietic.[12] The basic elements making up social systems – the atoms, so to speak, of society in general and of its subsystems like the law – are taken to be "communications," not in the sense of meaningful human utterances, but as social incidents that convey meaning.[13] The evolution of systems is driven forward by increased social differentiation – that which augments social differentiation is incorporated into the social system over the course of its historical evolution. This is the reason why things such as the rule of law or constitutional states evolved: They are functional tools that allow for social differentiation.[14] Human rights, too, are held to have a particular function in such systems: They keep "the future open" for the self-reproduction of the autopoietic social system.[15] They have this desirable effect, it is argued, because

[11] Cf. on social integration driven by the interdependence of persons from the perspective of legal sociology, Émile Durkheim, *De la division du travail social* (Paris: PUF, 2007); Eugen Ehrlich, *Grundlegung der Soziologie des Rechts* (Berlin: Duncker & Humblot, 1989), 65.

[12] Niklas Luhmann, *Das Recht der Gesellschaft* (Frankfurt am Main: Suhrkamp, 1995), 41.

[13] Niklas Luhmann, *Soziale Systeme* (Frankfurt am Main: Suhrkamp, 1987), 346.

[14] Luhmann, *Recht der Gesellschaft*, 239 ff.

[15] Cf. e.g. Niklas Luhmann, *Die Gesellschaft der Gesellschaft Vol. 1 and 2* (Frankfurt am Main: Suhrkamp, 1998), 1094 ff.

they give individuals space to act and thus to change the social system, which allows it to evolve.

This function of human rights is regarded as a powerful analysis of the reasons for the emergence of human rights. Human rights are interpreted as modern complex societies' functional answer to the need for differentiated organization, and not as the renaissance of Natural Law or other forms of human societies' normative orientation. Making individuals the normative center of legal systems means to engage in old-fashioned metaphysics of the person. In systems theory, individuals instead are regarded as "*Funktionsträger*," as the "function bearers" of society.[16] The social system allocates a function to the individual, namely to initiate social development, and provides the crucial tools required to fulfill this function, which are fundamental rights. Individual rights are protected not for the sake of the individual but for the functional sake of society – to enable its differentiated development. The classical idea of the relation between rights and society – that rights are secured because of the justified normative claims of the individual – is turned upside down or, as systems theorists would claim, is turned from its metaphysical head onto its social-functionalist feet.

The traditional view that anchors human rights in the goods of the individual is not only incorrect according to this perspective, however. In systems theory, this traditional view is regarded as a necessary product of social mechanisms and thus as the object of functionalist explanations *itself*. It is part of the "self-descriptions" created by social systems in the form of their members' beliefs about the justification of the elements of the social world in which they live.[17] These beliefs include, for example, the idea that human rights are justified by substantial, rationally defensible, valid reasons. According to systems theory, however, the belief that human rights are justified is false. From the point of view of social theory, there are no valid justifications, only social constructions that erroneously are regarded as reasons for the justification of human rights. In fact, these apparent reasons are nothing but contingent beliefs that depend on the given evolution of the social system. As it is useful for the system's functioning that people entertain these beliefs – for instance, the belief that human beings enjoy human rights because of their human dignity – the system reproduces these beliefs. Human rights theorists and activists unwillingly and unwittingly are serving the functional needs of differentiated social systems. Accordingly, this theory is comparable to Marxist theories of a false consciousness that the class structure of society necessarily produces and that serves the functional purpose of preserving this society but has no claim to justification.

We need to address this argument, for if it is true, the aim of formulating something like a normatively relevant theory of human rights would fail to grasp the functional point of human rights. Moreover, the theory itself might be nothing

[16] Niklas Luhmann, *Grundrechte als Institution* (Berlin: Duncker & Humblot, 2009), 50.

[17] Luhmann, *Gesellschaft der Gesellschaft*, 886 ff.

more than the offspring of social mechanisms that normative human rights theory has failed to understand.

Social-functionalist theories are open to various forms of critique – from the idea that the atoms of social theory are "communications" (and not, as, for instance, Weber thought, the meaningful social action of individuals) to the idea that social systems such as the law are autopoietic. Is the law not rather the purposeful creation of human beings, applied by identifiable agents, institutionalized as social fact by the coordinated meaningful social action of persons, such as creating law, accepting certain norms by a legislature, applied by another institution called courts, as valid, binding and enforceable law?[18]

For the purpose of the theory of human rights, the following points are central, however: Systems theory claims to be purely explanatory. Because of its radical constructivism, it argues that there is no valid justification of normative propositions; every normative stance is taken to be historically and socially contingent. What remains are functional explanations of social institutions and accompanying justificatory beliefs. At first view, systems theory thus does not formulate any claims about legitimacy. However, the development of the preconditions for social differentiation is regarded as an essential tool of complex social organization. Societies with this level of differentiated organization can thus claim something like functional legitimacy: Living in a more differentiated society clearly is preferable to life in a less differentiated society, according to systems theory. This functional superiority then – against its own theoretical stance – tends to turn into a normative claim of the legitimacy of functionally differentiated societies organized around human rights – which brings us back to our question of the normative legitimacy of these rights.

Moreover, systems-theoretical approaches misunderstand the true function of human rights in wedding them to social functions of the kinds described. Human rights are about protecting central individual goods, irrespective of whether this serves a function for the differentiation of society or not. Free speech can be used for purposes that are quite dysfunctional in social terms but is rightly protected in principle even in such cases. This is because human rights are instruments to protect persons, not instruments to protect functions of society abstracted from the concerns of individuals. Regarding human rights as tools that instrumentalize individuals for social purposes is a profound misunderstanding of the function of human rights in modern societies. Their central function is the very opposite: to protect individuals against the intrusion of public authorities and other actors into their lives and ultimately to shield human beings against being used for purposes that denigrate their autonomous subjectivity.

[18] Cf. Mahlmann, *Rechtsphilosophie und Rechtstheorie*, 301 ff.; Matthias Mahlmann, "Katastrophen der Rechtsgeschichte und die autopoietische Evolution des Rechts," *Zeitschrift für Rechtssoziologie* 21, no. 1 (2000): 247 ff.

There is a further fundamental problem for any social-functionalist theory of human rights. The aims of society are not simply a given. Societies are not natural kinds with fixed purposes. The word "society" is a term used for a variety of reasons. Usually, it designates associations of human beings who are connected in some kind of qualified manner – for instance, by the shared institutions of a state. Societies in the latter sense have one central kind of purpose – the purposes their members define. Rights formulate yardsticks, limiting conditions for these chosen aims of a society – whatever the aims are, they must not violate human rights in the first place. Erecting such limits to its own decision-making can in itself be a defining part of the wider aims of society – the protection of human rights signals human beings' decision to take their humanity seriously. This is – at least in principle – the point of the project of creating public authorities bound by national, regional and international human rights. Human rights in this sense *constrain and determine the purposes of society*; accordingly, they are not just functional tools for achieving some given non-normative aim of social organization, such as the high-level differentiation of social interaction. Rather, they define the legitimate aims of society itself.

Because of this misconception, functionalist theories fail to address, let alone specify the normative principles underlying the allocation of rights and determining the social purposes these rights serve, which include the normative calibration of what societies are there for. The question of the criteria for the proper identification of the goods protected remains unanswered likewise because these are the goods of individuals, not of society as such. Whether there is an epistemologically convincing justificatory theory of human rights or not is something that the following discussion will reveal.

4.2.2 *Engineering Social Efficiency?*

Arguments for human rights from the perspective of the *economic analysis of law* point out that certain forms of human rights increase efficiency,[19] based on a conception of human beings as utility maximizers who make rational choices.[20] Efficiency is defined as an allocation of resources in which value is maximized,

[19] Cf. for an example of such reasoning from the analysis of constitutional rights Richard A. Posner, *Economic Analysis of Law* (New York: Wolters Kluwer, 2014), 978: "A search (or seizure) is reasonable if the cost of the search in privacy impaired (B) is less than the probability (P) that without the search the target of the search cannot be convicted or otherwise rendered harmless . . ., multiplied by the social loss (L) if he eludes punishment." For an analysis of torture, ibid. 984, arguing that under normal circumstances torture is regularly too costly but is efficient in the case of prevention of terrorist attacks: "The cost-benefit analysis of coercive interrogation would be dramatically altered if for example the interrogation concerned a terrorist plot and the person interrogated – a peripheral figure in the plot but a possessor of vital information – faced no criminal punishment but merely deportation as an illegal alien, continued surveillance, or a warning."

[20] Posner, *Economic Analysis*, 4 ff.

value being measured by the willingness to pay. Willingness to pay is dependent on ability to pay, which creates an (unsolved) problem for this approach: The assessment of a thing's value depends on the given resources of the agent.[21] Not factoring an agent's financial background out of the willingness to pay has the effect that potentially any good is more valuable for rich persons than for poor persons – because of the rich persons' financial resources, they may be willing to pay more for everything.[22]

Efficiency-based rights accounts have shortcomings comparable to those of functionalist theory: They fail to capture appropriately the central point of human rights, which is to provide normative principles beyond efficiency, understood in the terms of standard economic efficiency criteria.[23] Rights formulate limiting conditions for any efficiency regime and therefore presuppose a justification that transcends the limits of an efficiency-based cost–benefit analysis.[24] Making the value of a thing dependent on the contingent financial resources of an agent is already a very implausible analytical starting point for a theory of efficiency, utility, value and the law. Moreover, the worth of liberty or other goods protected by human rights is not what a person is willing to pay for them anyway. Their value is certainly not lower for the poor than for the financially affluent. It is a category error to try to assess the worth of a good such as liberty in monetary terms. Moral evaluation depends on moral principles – in Kant's pithy words, "for that an object of justice is small does not prevent the injustice done to it from being great."[25]

A more promising approach stems from *behavioral economics*. Its main advance in comparison to classical law and economics is the attempt to base theories upon empirical research in human psychology, particularly in decision-making. Psychological research of this kind points to structures of bounded rationality: Under certain conditions, human decision-making is determined by other reasons than merely rational ones. Studies within prospect theory on psychological mechanisms such as heuristics, framing patterns and biases like risk aversion form the common starting points of such research.[26]

[21] Posner, *Economic Analysis*, 11 ff.

[22] On the conclusions of this starting point, which are unethical from his point of view, too, cf. Posner, *Economic Analysis*, 11 ff.

[23] For an example of a discussion of the limits of criteria like Pareto optimality and Kaldor–Hicks efficiency, Posner, *Economic Analysis*, 13.

[24] To take the example mentioned previously: The point of limiting governmental searches and seizures is the protection of human freedom and autonomy. This idea can justify much stricter limits than conceived in Posner's formula quoted above (see n. 19). This is even more evident for the crucial example of torture, where the dignity of a person justifies an absolute prohibition of such practices. A cost–benefit analysis of the kind imagined by Posner, *Economic Analysis*, creates a gateway for practices that cannot be reconciled with human rights.

[25] Kant, *Zum Ewigen Frieden*, 384; translation in Kant, *Perpetual Peace*.

[26] An interesting example is the reconstruction of the debate about civil and political rights on the one hand and social and economic rights on the other from the perspective of framing them as losses or gains, cf. Zamir, *Law, Psychology and Morality*, 143 ff.

Behavioral law and economics are no substitute for justified normative principles: Skewed decisions due to heuristics, framing effects or biases are important elements of a realistic theory of human decision-making. The findings on bounded rationality, however, lead to the question of what principles should guide human decision-making instead, not least which normative principles should be decisive in overcoming its shortcomings.[27]

Sophisticated theories on behavioral law and economics factor a deontological threshold into the cost–benefit analysis, which aims at achieving harmony with common moral intuitions.[28] This move underlines the importance of normative principles. It invites us to consider closely the nature of common moral intuitions and their role in normative theory. In particular, it raises the question of why common moral intuitions should be decisive in *normative* terms.[29] As these theories formulate some of the currently most influential empirical hypotheses about the human mind, they will be discussed in more detail in the analysis of current theories of cognition that forms Part III of this study.

4.2.3 *Human Rights and Maximizing of Happiness*

There is a rule-utilitarian defense of human rights – despite Bentham's proverbial critique of these norms. This argument holds that having human rights in the long run secures the greatest happiness of the greatest number and thus satisfies the basic utilitarian principle for justifying individual and social norms. This is the case, it is argued, because everybody will profit from the goods protected by rights as social rules, even though, in particular cases, the principle of utility could demand that the goods of the individual are sacrificed for the greatest happiness of the greatest number.

One good example for this kind of argument is the enslavement of a minority, because a classic counterargument to utilitarianism is that it offers no theoretical defenses against the justification of the enslavement of a group of persons if the happiness of the slaveholders outweighs the misery of the enslaved. Utilitarians answer that this is not so, because it is not clear that the misery of slaves is not so profound that the benefits for the slaveholders become irrelevant. Even if under very particular circumstances – for example, some kind of privileged form of household slavery where the slaves are treated well – this were not the case, as a rule the prohibition of slavery

[27] The debate about libertarian paternalism and its limits is exactly about this question, cf. Richard H. Thaler and Cass R. Sunstein, *Nudge* (London: Penguin Books, 2008). For a critique, Jeremy Waldron, "It's All for Your Own Good," *The New York Review of Books* 61, no. 15 (2014); Christopher McCrudden and Jeff King, "The Dark Side of Nudging: The Ethics, Political Economy, and Law of Libertarian Paternalism," in *Choice Architecture in Democracies: Exploring the Legitimacy of Nudging*, eds. Alexandra Kemmerer et al. (Oxford and Baden-Baden: Hart and Nomos, 2015).

[28] On threshold deontology Eyal Zamir and Barak Medina, *Law, Economics and Morality* (Oxford: Oxford University Press, 2010), 41 ff.

[29] Cf. Zamir and Medina, *Law, Economics and Morality*, 65.

would still be justified: Overall, given the many forms of slavery and the experience of the cruelty it engenders in at least sufficiently many cases, it is reasonable to assume that the institution of slavery causes more suffering than well-being and thus as a rule is not justified according to the principles of utility.

Utilitarian support of this kind for the justification of human rights is certainly welcome. It is not a reliable defense, however. The central reason for this is that the point of ethics and justified law is not to maximize goods abstracted from individuals. Individuals cannot be factored out of a normative argument and be substituted by aggregate social goods. Rather, they are at the heart of it.[30] Thus, even if enslavement did promote the greatest happiness of the greatest number, it could not be justified.

There is another important point. What is good and admirable about utilitarian doctrine is its sense for the equality of human beings. Its central pillar is, after all, that the happiness (determined quantitatively[31] or qualitatively,[32] depending on the utilitarian outlook) of all humans should count equally. This is an important and, in many ways, a progressive doctrine. However, it presupposes the normative principle of the equality of human beings and thus normative content beyond the principle of utility itself.[33] The same is true for the radical selflessness that utilitarianism implies and that demands that individuals relinquish any good if it serves the greatest happiness of the greatest number. This presupposes a selfless, other-regarding moral motivation and not just the pursuit of pleasure and the avoidance of pain. As such, it shows that we cannot escape the question of the normative ideas that lie at the heart of the discussion of human rights and that therefore have to be confronted head on.

4.3 JUSTIFICATION BY AGREEMENT

4.3.1 *Discourse and Consensus*

A further influential approach stems from *discourse theory*. To many, this theory recommends itself because it seems to rely only on very thin theoretical

[30] Cf. on this standard criticism from the "separateness of persons" for instance Herbert Lionel Adolphus Hart, "Between Utility and Rights," *Columbia Law Review* 79, no. 5 (1979): 828 f.

[31] Bentham, *Principles of Morals and Legislation*, I, 1.

[32] Mill, "Utilitarianism," 211.

[33] Bentham, *Principles of Morals and Legislation*, I, 13, note d; Mill underlines the importance of the principle of equality for utilitarianism emphatically: "The entire history of social improvement has been a series of transitions, by which one custom or institution after another, from being a supposed primary necessity of social existence, has passed into the rank of a universally stigmatized injustice and tyranny. So it has been with the distinctions of slaves and freemen, nobles and serfs, patricians and plebeians; and so it will be, and in part already is, with the aristocracies of colour, race, and sex," Mill, "Utilitarianism," 259. On the problem that this apparent egalitarian starting point "may license the grossest form of inequality in the actual treatment of individuals, if that is required in order to maximise aggregate or average welfare," Hart, "Utility and Rights," 830.

preconditions. It consequently appears well adapted to a “post-metaphysical” age that is skeptical about substantial normative theory.[34] It starts from the assertion that neither a teleology of history, nor human nature, nor traditions are able to furnish the foundations of ethics and legal systems.[35] Instead, subjective practical reasons need to be replaced by *communicative reason*.[36] The core principle for the justification of any ethical principle, including human rights, is the *discourse principle*. According to this principle, those norms that all participants in rational discourses are able to agree upon are justified.[37] A discourse is rational when its outcome is determined solely by arguments and not skewed by the power of some participants. This deliberative process respects human beings’ foundational right to justification:[38] People are bound to principles that are not imposed upon them but rather prove to be justified once everybody’s interests are taken into account. It is only adhering to such principles that enables the self-endorsement of everybody’s subjectivity without domination by others.[39] Ultimately, the culture of reason-based argument is rooted in specific historically grown lifeworlds (*Lebenswelten*).

Discourse theory correctly highlights the importance of individual autonomy that is the non-negotiable yardstick of legitimate normative content.[40] This notwithstanding, it faces a substantial theoretical problem: A discourse that includes everybody’s concerns in the sense outlined above is a normatively charged enterprise. It presupposes equality, freedom and respect for other human beings. These normative principles are partly implied in any form of communication that is based on arguments between equals, as discourse theorists correctly maintain.[41] However, this discursive practice is not the source of these normative principles. Morality is not the child of the structure of communication. Rather, equality, freedom and respect for human beings are the preconditions for the obligation to enter into such forms of communication with everybody in the first place. Doing so is not self-evident. Many people throughout history and in the present have not had and do not have a voice because they are not respected as free and equal subjects worthy of respect. The normative principles demanding equal respect for free individuals cannot then be

34 Cf. on the genealogy of post-metaphysical thinking, Jürgen Habermas, *Auch eine Geschichte der Philosophie, Vol. I: Die okzidentale Konstellation von Glauben und Wissen* (Berlin: Suhrkamp, 2019), 21.

35 Habermas, *Faktizität und Geltung*, 17

36 Habermas, *Faktizität und Geltung*, 17.

37 Habermas, *Faktizität und Geltung*, 138: “*Gültig sind genau die Handlungsnormen, denen alle möglicherweise Betroffenen als Teilnehmer an rationalen Diskursen zustimmen können.*”

38 Cf. Rainer Forst, *Das Recht auf Rechtfertigung* (Frankfurt am Main: Suhrkamp, 2007).

39 Cf. Klaus Günther, “Anerkennung, Verantwortung, Gerechtigkeit,” in *Sozialphilosophie und Kritik*, eds. Rainer Forst et al. (Frankfurt am Main: Suhrkamp, 2009), 269, 286 f.

40 The fact that the individual is not replaceable does not mean that the results of moral thought are private, cf. Lutz Wingert, *Gemeinsinn und Moral* (Frankfurt am Main: Suhrkamp, 1993), 290 f.

41 On a “minimal ethics” implied in communication, cf. Jürgen Habermas, *Erläuterungen zur Diskursethik* (Frankfurt am Main: Suhrkamp, 1991), 194.

the products of the application of the discourse principle, because these principles are the normative preconditions for the legitimacy of the discourse principle itself. The discourse principle is not normatively foundational but dependent on the acceptance of other, truly justifying norms of equality, liberty and respect for others. Thus, it is thin, but too thin.

Moreover, the norms demanding the kind of respect for human beings embodied by human rights reach beyond normatively structuring patterns of communication. Human life is not a discourse. A human life has many dimensions beyond communicating with others, and human rights take account of this fact. The right to bodily integrity, for instance, protects a pain-free existence, which is a value not only because it enables the rights-holders to enter into political deliberation. Freedom of faith protects belief for the sake of individuals, whether they want to share this belief with anybody or not. One cannot rely only on the supposed normative implications of communication to justify such rights, because these rights protect spheres of human life beyond such communication. Nor can one simply rely on a supportive lifeworld: Respect for other humans and their rights is the ultimate normative precondition for the historical and political *creation* of discursive and deliberative practices and lifeworlds. Such a lifeworld can only come into existence and persist over time if people feel obliged to respect others as free and equal individuals. Discursive and deliberative practices and lifeworlds thus cannot be the ultimate normative foundations of human rights – they depend on the cultural ethical appeal of these very rights.

Discourse theory professes ultimately to leave open the question of the normative principles that would be justified by a rational discourse. But precisely this is the central question to be answered for the topic at stake here: Are there any reasons why agents who are respectful of good reasons should regard human rights as justified, and if so, what are these reasons? The fact that discourse theory engages in this enterprise irrespective of its professed normative abstinence only underlines the importance of this point.[42]

4.3.2 *Justification by Contract*

Another self-proclaimed *thin* normative theory is *contractualism*, which draws on the long tradition of social contract theories that majorly influenced normative thinking on modern constitutionalism and fundamental rights. In the history of thought, social contract theory has been a powerful tool for rationalizing, individualizing, secularizing and universalizing norms crucial to a body politic. The baseline

42 The theory of human rights within discourse theory sets out to derive a "system of rights" from the discourse principle: The defense of a standard catalogue of human rights is charged with normative assumptions about the worth, equality and liberty of human beings. Cf. Habermas, *Faktizität und Geltung*, 151 ff.

is that norms, including those constitutive of the state, are justified by the consent of the parties to a contract. In contemporary approaches (as in most older social contract theories), this contract is not real but a thought experiment. It serves to test the legitimacy of norms by checking whether it reasonably could be assumed that these norms could be the result of agreement between free and equal individuals. The conditions under which such an agreement is reached can be very specific in order to highlight the importance of impartiality, as is the case, for instance, in Rawls' theory.[43]

This approach faces a problem related to that of discourse theory: Social contract theories presuppose the freedom, equality and right to respect of all human beings. Otherwise, there would be no reason to include them in the imagined contract. The very point of a contract is to honor human beings' liberty, equality and equal worth by making their agreement the precondition of their obligations. As the norms underlying liberty, equality and respect for human worth form the foundations of the social contract, they ultimately cannot be its products. Contractualism leaves the question of the contract's normative foundations open: Why is it legitimate that human beings are bound only by obligations that can be imagined as accepted by free persons of equal worth?[44] Where do the noncontractualist preconditions of contractualism stem from?

The problem of normative principles independent of and foundational for contractualist justification is the reason for an influential critique of contractualism that focuses on the formality of contractual principles, as this formality misses the decisiveness of material normative principles. The reason for the justification of normative principles is not that people would agree that certain principles are legitimate (under whatever specified conditions honoring their freedom and equality) but, contrariwise, that people could be imagined to agree upon the legitimacy of certain principles because these norms are justified by good substantial reasons. As J. J. Thomson stated pointedly:

> For my own part, I cannot bring myself to believe that what *makes* it wrong to torture babies to death for fun (for example) is that doing this "would be disallowed by any system of rules for the general regulation of behavior which no one could

[43] The central tool of his argument is the "veil of ignorance," cf. Rawls, *Theory of Justice*.

[44] This may be true but is not evidently so. Hegel, for example, was repulsed by the idea that a contract could be imagined as founding something sublime like a state, cf. Georg Wilhelm Friedrich Hegel, "Grundlinien der Philosophie des Rechts," in *Werke Vol. 7*, eds. Eva Moldenhauer and Karl Markus Michel (Frankfurt am Main: Suhrkamp, 1986), § 273. The same problem also arises for other contractualist theories – for instance, the second-person standpoint and its implied contractualism, cf. Stephen Darwall, *The Second-Person Standpoint: Morality, Respect, and Accountability* (Cambridge, MA: Harvard University Press, 2009). Darwall argues that any claim to moral authority is subject to a test of reasonable acceptance or rejection from the second-person standpoint of any second-personally competent being. This test presupposes the normative equality of these agents and their legitimate claims to equal treatment, concern and respect.

> reasonably reject as a basis for informed, unforced general agreement". My impression is that explanation goes in the opposite direction – that it is the patent wrongfulness of the conduct that explains why there would be general agreement to disallow it.[45]

The contractualists' answer is that the contractualist formula is about "what it is for an act to be wrong. What *makes* an act wrong are the properties that would make any principle that allows it one that it would be reasonable to reject (in this case, the needless suffering of the baby)."[46] This answer, however, is not enough to save the contractualist paradigm. The answer itself underlines that material normative standards are crucial (those that would make any principle that allows, for instance, the torturing of babies, one that it would be reasonable to reject), not a formal, content-free, thin contractualist principle. Moreover, the hypothetical agreement that it is reasonable to reject a rule allowing certain actions is not "what it *is* for an act to be wrong." "What it *is* for an act to be wrong" is the fact that it constitutes a violation of one of those moral principles that are justified. What it *is* for torturing babies to be wrong is the fact that torturing babies violates basic principles of human ethics. The agreement about this – whether hypothetical or real – is the consequence of the cognition of this state of affairs. This agreement does not, however, constitute the nature of wrongness.

One of the strengths of Rawls' theory is that it acknowledges the limits of contractualism. According to Rawls, the original position in which the agreement is concluded is a *device of representation*.[47] This stance is important for contractualism in general. Through a formidable metaphor, it illustrates profound ethical intuitions that are crucial for the justification of modern constitutionalism and fundamental rights. It does not, however, substitute these normative principles by the foundational idea of a social contract. Instead, it derives this idea from these principles and therefore remains dependent on their justification.

4.4 HUMAN RIGHTS AND HUMAN EXISTENCE

4.4.1 *The Rights of Autonomous Agents*

Human rights are rightly associated with the protection of and the respect for autonomy as a central element of human existence. Accordingly, influential theoretical approaches that are both sophisticated and highly demanding in philosophical terms rely on *agency* as the foundation for the justification of human rights. There are basically two kinds of agency theories. One is based upon what one might

[45] Thomson, *Realm of Rights*, 30 n. 19 (emphasis in original).

[46] Thomas M. Scanlon, *What We Owe to Each Other* (Cambridge, MA: Harvard University Press, 2000), 391 n. 21 (emphasis in original).

[47] Rawls, *Political Liberalism*, 24.

want to call the *logic of action*. This theory relies on a variant of a transcendental argument by identifying the protection of human rights as the precondition for the possibility of agency.[48] The other variant refrains from statements about the logic of action and centers its argument on the normative consequences of what is called *normative agency*, the value of autonomously defining and pursuing one's own course in life. We will look at these two theories in some detail in turn, as this will allow us to distill certain important systematic insights.

4.4.1.1 Human Rights and the Logic of Action

Two questions form the starting point of the argument for human rights from the logic of action perspective: "First, what logical or rational justification is there for attributing to self-interested individuals a concern for their own having rights or making rights-claims? Second, what logical or rational justification is there for a self-interested individual's moving, or having to move, from an acceptance that she herself has rights to the much broader moral judgment that every individual has rights, so that there are human rights and correlative duties?"[49] The answer is found by a "dialectically necessary method"[50] deriving normative principles from human action, which is the foundation of a rational argument for morality and human rights.[51] This foundation has a particular quality as nobody can escape the context of action, not even by committing suicide (which is itself an action).[52] The key features of action are voluntariness or freedom and purposiveness or intentionality. As agents act to actually fulfill their purposes, purposiveness is extended to the general conditions for succeeding in this endeavor and thus to well-being.[53] Therefore, it is concluded, "freedom and well-being are the proximate necessary conditions and generic features of action and of generally successful action."[54]

Human rights are justified on this basis. It is argued that, first, "every agent must logically accept that he or she has rights to freedom and well-being" and, second, "that the agent logically must also accept that all other agents also have these rights equally with his or her own, so that in this way the existence of universal moral rights, and thus of human rights, must be accepted within the whole context of action or practice."[55]

48 Alan Gewirth, *The Community of Rights* (Chicago, IL: University of Chicago Press, 1996), 13 ff.
49 Gewirth, *Community*, 8.
50 Gewirth, *Community*, 16.
51 Gewirth, *Community*, 13.
52 Gewirth, *Community*, 13.
53 Gewirth, *Community*, 13. Gewirth distinguishes different levels of well-being that become increasingly rich: basic well-being (life, physical integrity, mental equilibrium), nonsubtractive well-being (not being lied to, not being stolen from) and additive well-being (education, self-esteem, opportunities for acquiring wealth and income).
54 Gewirth, *Community*, 14.
55 Gewirth, *Community*, 17.

To show that self-interested agents must (with logical necessity) attribute rights to themselves, eight steps are outlined that set out the argument very clearly.

The first step consists of the agents each setting an aim: "I do X for end or purpose *E*." Second, *E* is identified as a good. Third, the agents must accept that their freedom and well-being are necessary goods, because they are the proximate necessary conditions of action and of acting successfully in general, and thus of attaining any purpose. Given this, the agents must, fourth, conclude that they must have freedom and well-being. The fifth step is of particular importance: The agents, it is argued, logically must accept not only that they must have freedom and well-being, but that they have *rights* to freedom and well-being. The alternative would be self-contradictory: It would amount to, sixth, rejecting the proposition that others ought at least to refrain from removing or interfering with the agents' freedom and well-being. It would imply, seventh, that others are permitted to remove or interfere with the agents' freedom and well-being. This in turn would mean, eighth, accepting that they may not have freedom and well-being, a proposition contradicting the conclusion of step four that the agents must have freedom and well-being as the proximate necessary conditions of action and of acting successfully in general.[56]

The logical principle of universalizability[57] builds the bridge from these findings to the justification of moral rights for all: If any agents hold that they have rights by virtue of them being a prospective agent, they must grant this right to all.[58] This is an application of the central moral principle of this theory, the *principle of generic consistency:* "[A]ct in accord with the generic rights of your recipients as well as of yourself."[59]

From this foundation, particular rights are deduced, most prominently positive rights to welfare. These thoughts also set the stage for the important argument that rights and community are not opposed but that, on the contrary, rights establish a community – a community of rights.[60]

4.4.1.2 Human Rights and Normative Agency

A different approach puts *normative agency* center stage.[61] Normative agency as a qualified form of agency[62] is understood as a rights-generating reason that at the same time offers a well-defining and content-limiting existence condition of moral human rights. This is taken to be crucial, as the "term 'human rights' is nearly

[56] Gewirth, *Community*, 17 f.

[57] Stated as "if some predicate P belongs to some subject S because S has a certain quality Q (where the 'because' is that of sufficient condition), then P logically must belong to all other subjects S_1 to S_n that also have Q," Gewirth, *Community*, 18.

[58] Griffin, *On Human Rights*, 18.

[59] Griffin, *On Human Rights*, 19.

[60] Griffin, *On Human Rights*, 1 ff., 71 ff.

[61] Griffin, *On Human Rights*, 2.

[62] Griffin, *On Human Rights*, 45.

criterionless," it is argued.[63] There is a certain consensus about the term's extension but not about its intension, at least not in a sufficiently thick sense, because "the fragment of intension we have – namely, a claim that we have on others simply in virtue of our being human – holds of moral claims in general, and not all moral claims are rights-generated. For example, the claim that one has on others that they not gratuitously cause one pain is not."[64] That task is thus "to remedy the indeterminateness – to do what the Enlightenment failed to do."[65]

Normative agency is the proper starting point to achieve these ends, the argument goes. Normative agency and what it entails spell out the meaning of the term "human dignity,"[66] which is not human beings' most important moral status, however.[67] Normative agency is of intrinsic value: "If normative agency is valuable, it is intrinsically valuable. One can only try to make it sufficiently clear what normative agency is and expect others to see that it is valuable."[68] Such a teleological *personhood theory* is based on an "expansive naturalism" that justifies human rights because they are preconditions for human agency.[69]

Normative agency consists in the possibility to form a conception of a worthwhile life and to pursue one's life accordingly. Normative agency in this wider sense, it is argued, encompasses three elements: autonomy, liberty and minimum provision, which enable normative agency.[70] Autonomy concerns self-decision, "a capacity to recognize good-making features of human life, both prudential and moral, which can lead to the appropriate motivation and action."[71] Liberty refers to the possibility to follow one's choices.[72] With minimum provision, the important aspect of the

[63] Griffin, *On Human Rights*, 14.
[64] Griffin, *On Human Rights*, 17.
[65] Griffin, *On Human Rights*, 18.
[66] Griffin, *On Human Rights*, 3, 44: "What we attach value to, what we regard as giving dignity to human life, is our capacity to choose and to pursue our conception of a worthwhile life."
[67] Griffin, *On Human Rights*, 94.
[68] Griffin, *On Human Rights*, 152.
[69] Griffin, *On Human Rights*, 32 ff.
[70] Griffin, *On Human Rights*, 32 f.: "[W]e value our status as human beings especially highly, often more highly than even our happiness. This status centres on our being agents – deliberating, assessing, choosing, and acting to make what we see as a good life for ourselves. Human rights can then be seen as protection of our human standing or, as I shall put it, our personhood. And one can break down the notion of personhood into clearer components by breaking down the notion of agency. To be an agent, in the fullest sense of which we are capable, one must (first) choose one's own path through life – that is, not to be dominated or controlled by someone or something else (call it 'autonomy'). And (second) one's choice must be real; one must have at least a certain minimum education and information. And having chosen, one must be able to act; that is, one must have at least the minimum provision of resources and capabilities that it takes (call all of this 'minimum provision'). And none of this is any good if someone then blocks one; so (third) others must also not forcibly stop one from pursuing what one sees as a worthwhile life (call this 'liberty'). Because we attach such high value to our individual personhood, we see its domain of exercise as privileged and protected."
[71] Griffin, *On Human Rights*, 156.
[72] Griffin, *On Human Rights*, 149 ff.

material preconditions of real agency enters the picture – a plausible and classic thought of the justification of social and economic rights. From this basis, other human rights can be derived, the ensemble of which forms the well-founded bill of moral human rights.[73]

According to its proponents, this approach allows the crucial critical function of human rights theory – namely to sharpen the vague contours of the term "human rights" – to be fulfilled. The human rights project is said to have led to an implausible proliferation of rights.[74] Given this development, one central driving force behind the normative agency account is the need for critical yardsticks to determine what is rightly called a human right and what is not. The agency account is thus deliberately restrictive. Human rights are not "anything that promotes human good or flourishing, but merely what is needed for human status."[75] The personhood account "is deflationary in three related ways. It supplies a ground for rejecting certain actual declarations of rights. It tends to narrow the content of individual human rights. And it reduces the importance of human rights."[76] This restrictive approach encompasses the personal scope of human rights as well. Contrary to current human rights practice, not all human beings, only "functioning human agent[s]"[77] qualify for protection by human rights,[78] excluding infants,[79] those with severe mental disabilities or people in an irreversible coma.[80] This does not mean that there are no moral obligations towards these persons. They just do not have human rights, it is argued.[81] If the threshold condition is met, however, anybody above it counts as an agent without differentiation.[82] According to this argument, the diminishing capacity for agency in the elderly can curtail their human rights – for example, to health care (e.g. when medical resources are scarce).[83] On the other

[73] Griffin, *On Human Rights*, 33 provides a list: "[T]he generative capacities of the notion of personhood are quite great."

[74] "Unacceptable cases" are supposed to include the right to peace, the right to inherit, the right to protection of honor and reputation and the right to residence, Griffin, *On Human Rights*, 194 ff.

[75] Griffin, *On Human Rights*, 34.

[76] Griffin, *On Human Rights*, 95.

[77] Griffin, *On Human Rights*, 35.

[78] Griffin, *On Human Rights*, 34 f., 83 ff. The underlying theory of personal identity makes capacity for self-consciousness the crucial criterion, preventing a "temporally backward proliferation" of personal identity. On the debate on the factors of personal identity, with other results, Mahlmann, *Grundrechtstheorie*, 298 ff.

[79] Griffin, *On Human Rights*, 87, because infants do not have full consciousness yet.

[80] Griffin, *On Human Rights*, 92: "My belief is that we have a better chance of improving the discourse of human rights if we stipulate that only normative agents bear human rights – *no exceptions*: no infants, not the seriously mentally disabled, not those in a permanent vegetative state, and so on" (emphasis in original).

[81] Griffin, *On Human Rights*, 90 ff., 95: "To deny an infant the chance to reach and exercise and enjoy maturity is a far more horrendous wrong than most infringements of human rights."

[82] Griffin, *On Human Rights*, 44 f.

[83] Griffin, *On Human Rights*, 101.

hand, agency can provide reasons to accept new and hitherto contested rights – for example, to same-sex marriage,[84] or what are called positive rights; that is, rights to the provision of goods,[85] including welfare rights.[86]

Practicalities are a second existence condition of human rights: Human rights must be suitable for real human individuals and social life. Therefore, practicalities encompass "features of human nature and of the nature of human societies."[87] Knowledge constraints and a realistic account of human motivation play important roles in delineating the content of human rights.[88]

It is stressed that the human rights thus justified do not encompass the whole domain of morality, which is identified with equal respect.[89] Other and equally important normative principles exist that are not identical to, related to or reducible to human rights.

The existence conditions of legal human rights are said to be different from moral rights. Nevertheless, the importance of a theory of moral human rights for the conception of the law is (quite plausibly) understood to be significant. Court decisions are no substitute for such a theory – on the contrary, they require this theory to solve some of the crucial puzzles of how to understand human rights law.[90]

The normative agency account hopes to renew the argument, rightly taken to be a key element of the human rights tradition, "that these rights are grounded in natural facts about human beings."[91] The account is universalist: The existence conditions of human rights are taken to be valid for any human community.[92] Changes in social and cultural circumstance are no counterargument because universality can be defended for higher-level rights that are, in turn, the foundation of derived rights relative to a certain time, like freedom of the press.[93] The challenge of relativism can thus be met.[94]

These thought-provoking proposals resonate well with the uncontroversial connection of human rights and the respect for human autonomy. Let us consider, then, how promising these approaches are in making the case for human rights.

84 Griffin, *On Human Rights*, 163.
85 Griffin, *On Human Rights*, 97 ff. He is critical of some, e.g. right to health, ibid. 99 ff.
86 Griffin, *On Human Rights*, 176 ff., 181: "The value concerned is being a normative agent, a self-creator, made in God's image." Therefore, the proximate necessary conditions for normative agency must be secured, ibid. 183.
87 Griffin, *On Human Rights*, 38.
88 Griffin, *On Human Rights*, 98 ff. on the effects on positive rights, which are rights to the provision of certain goods.
89 Griffin, *On Human Rights*, 39.
90 Griffin, *On Human Rights*, 205.
91 Griffin, *On Human Rights*, 36, 93.
92 Griffin, *On Human Rights*, 48 ff.
93 Griffin, *On Human Rights*, 50.
94 Griffin, *On Human Rights*, 38 f.

4.4.1.3 The Concept of Agency

The first step in assessing the reach of these theories is to clarify the different aspects of the concept of agency. One possible understanding of agency is that it refers to a particular property of human beings, the capacity of human subjects to initiate chains of events, undetermined and free, as uncaused causes, if you will. If so, this kind of capacity (if it exists) seems to be inalienable, and human beings cannot lose it (apart from certain extreme situations to be discussed shortly) as it is part and parcel of their existence. This is the understanding of agency in the sense relevant for the question of free will.

Only in rare cases is this capacity for autonomous decision-making as such endangered, restricted, made irrelevant or even extinguished. These cases are far from banal. The most obvious example is killing a person – there can be no agency if the agent is not alive. Another important example of such cases is torture. Among the many evils of this practice is the tortured human being's loss of the ability to form an autonomous decision. To be sure, in a certain sense, a person who is being tortured can still decide about their course of action – for example, to remain silent. In practical terms, however, leaving ideas of superhuman willpower aside, this possibility is only theoretical – for every human being has a breaking point, everybody has their Room 101, where their autonomy is wrested from them by the pain and degradation inflicted. Other instances of this kind include brainwashing, drug-induced behavior, forced "reeducation" and the like.

The second understanding of agency is the possibility of acting in line with autonomous decisions. Agency can be rendered meaningless if there is no scope to act in a way that corresponds to the agent's intentions, even if the possibility of making a decision as such remains unimpaired.[95]

4.4.1.4 Agency and the Problem of Justificatory Underdetermination

It is far from clear whether all particular liberties and other important classes of human rights are in fact necessary preconditions for agency in the senses discussed by agency theories, which seem mostly related to agency as the possibility to act in line with autonomous decisions. Can one only be an agent in the sense of being the subject of action by acting according to one's will if one enjoys freedom of expression, of religion, of assembly or the freedom to choose a profession? There are all kinds of repressive regimes that violate very many classic human rights but do not call agency as such into question, only certain uses of agency. For instance, the use of agency to criticize the government may be proscribed while other fields

95 There is a gray area between these two kinds of impairments of agency: The total lack of possibilities to act upon one's choices may have a very considerable influence on the decision-making itself.

remain untouched – say, the agency as to one's narrowly circumscribed (but still very important) private life. History is full of such regimes. This does not mean that human beings only became full agents after human rights were established. Consequently, the logic of action as such does not carry very far in justifying particular rights. By deducing a full set of rights from agency, the theory over the course of the argument in fact implicitly enriches the preconditions of agency to such a degree that it is not just the *logic of action* that carries the argument through but something else, namely the normative relevance of the *minimum conditions of a meaningful life*. This is an important point but no longer is based solely upon the logical necessities of being an agent.

The normative agency conception fares much better in this respect. But even in an illiberal society without much freedom, meaningful normative agency remains imaginable, as explained above.[96] In addition, human rights are more capacious than this argument implies – the freedom guaranteed by human rights, at least in some crucial cases, is not limited to the *minimum* of what is necessary to assure agency but to the *maximum* that is compatible with the same equal freedom for all human beings and some other constraining public interests – in the case of free speech, for instance, as much as in the case of freedom of religion.

Equality guarantees, a further building block of human rights thinking, raise some questions for an agency approach, too. Why is equal treatment as such a human right enlisted in every bill of human rights? Interestingly, equality guarantees are somewhat neglected in reconstructions of the legitimacy of rights in agency accounts. Filling in this gap in the spirit of agency theories, one may want to argue that equal treatment is important for agency in the normative sense if discrimination is such that it curtails or takes away certain freedoms. If you are unable to rent an apartment because of your skin color, your liberty is substantially limited because you cannot choose your preferred dwelling place. Such arguments are important, but not the whole story about equality guarantees. Another important reason for the protection of equality as a human right derives from considerations of justice,[97] yet another from the respect due to a person. Discrimination on the ground of race is forbidden (and thus equal treatment secured) at least partly to make sure that

[96] Griffin, *On Human Rights*, 46 f. accepts the objection that repressive regimes do not negate any form of agency but maintains that such regimes prevent individuals from a central element of normative agency: "By 'agency' we must mean not just having certain capacities (autonomous thought, executive action) but also exercising them," ibid. 47.

[97] Griffin argues that only issues of procedural justice are part of human rights, not other forms of retributive and distributive justice, Griffin, *On Human Rights*, 40 ff. This fails to convince for, as Griffin himself notes, human rights have distributive effects, ibid. 41, which, however limited they may be, must be legitimized with reasons of distributive justice. In addition, some forms of "fairness" like equality of men and women are regarded as being internal to human rights because of the equal agency of men and women, ibid. 41. All of this explicitly points to principles of justice as a central legitimizing reason for human rights.

everybody is treated with such respect as is due to them.[98] It thus is not just agency that is at stake but these other normative considerations as well.[99]

A further example for a lacuna in the theory is the widespread view that human rights provide yardsticks for just punishment, contrary to what agency theorists assume.[100] Personality rights including human dignity play an important practical role in this respect, and plausibly so. A system of sanctions that instrumentalizes human beings for the purpose of deterrence certainly creates a human rights issue. High-profile court cases underline the importance of this approach.[101]

Agency theories thus seem to have the problem of *underdetermining the precise content of human rights*. This problem is relevant both for the logic of action variant and for the more capacious normative agency approach, though the latter is less affected by it because it has the resources to legitimate at least some important substantial rights.

This leads to another critique of agency theories, which is the flipside of the argument just mentioned: They fail to include important goods other than agency that are protected by human rights. A good example is the right to life. Agency theories derive this right, as they do any other, from the importance of agency.[102] However, life is protected not just as a precondition of action or to enable normative agency. It is protected as the precondition of the many things – including agency, of course – that make up a meaningful human life, from the possibility of enjoying a gentle spring breeze to the many other fruits to be reaped in the fertile gardens of human thought and sentiment. Not all of these goods of life are secured for the sake of agency: Falling in love (the sheer event, not the actions stemming from it) is not an exercise in autonomy. On the contrary, it is entirely beyond autonomous decision-making, which is the source of its bliss and sometimes of its tragedy.

98 Griffin argues for protection from discrimination because being a "member of a hated minority" impairs agency – for example, by inhibiting such a person from speaking out, Griffin, *On Human Rights*, 42. In addition, he (rightly) takes it as a "monstrous injustice, a flagrant violation of equal respect," 42. This, however, points to the importance of justice and respect for the foundations of human rights, as argued here.

99 As a consequence, Griffin's account sits uneasily with current human rights practice beyond the examples mentioned. He argues that racism and sexism are human rights issues, while ageism is not. A huge bulk of current antidiscrimination law, generating much case law, today is concerned precisely with the latter and is widely regarded as a human rights issue, cf. e.g. for the EU context Council of the European Union, *Council Directive 2000/78/EC*, OJ L 303, 12/02/2000, November 27, 2000, its transposition into Member State law and the case law on the matter by the CJEU and national courts.

100 Griffin, *On Human Rights*, 43.

101 Cf. for instance ECtHR, Vinter and Others v The United Kingdom, Judgment of July 9, 2013, appl. nos. 66069/09, 130/10 and 3896/10, [2016] III ECHR 317.

102 Griffin, *On Human Rights*, 100: "On the personhood account, we have a right to life, because life is a necessary condition of normative agency." There are arguments that make the account harder to grasp, because the value of life, it is said, is derived from the value of the person concerned for others and from the intrinsic value of life. The most consistent interpretation is that all of these are ultimately based on the value of normative agency.

Nevertheless, it is something that many would regard as the prime gift (in a very deep and literal sense) of human life. Life consists of a myriad of other such good things that make it the precious thing it is. Life in this sense is of intrinsic value as such, not only in an instrumental sense as the precondition of action or normative agency.

The same seems to be true for the goods protected by other rights. Part of the point of freedom of expression is to satisfy an existential need: the desire to talk, to express thoughts and the many other aspects of one's inner human life. One important dimension of freedom of religion is the possibility to live according to something that many people would regard as beyond personal choice – their particular faith and what it means for them. A normative agency theory may argue that these kinds of expression are covered by the capacious concept of agency, but this underestimates what is at stake, namely expression or belief as manifesting a form of exercising human potential that is valuable for humans as such and not only as the manifestation of a choice or the pursuit of an autonomously formed conception of a good life.

Even torture is an evil not only because it means a threat to or even the abrogation of agency in the sense discussed above. Part of the evil is the pain inflicted, whatever other goods are impaired as well.[103] The same holds for the protection of bodily integrity. To be sure, it is true that a violation of this right has consequences for agency, but avoiding the impairment of bodily integrity is a good in itself. A last example: Social rights, including to basic subsistence, are important preconditions of agency. In underlining this, agency theories have made a very important contribution. But not being hungry is a good in itself, too, irrespective of the further benefits of secured agency.

4.4.1.5 Why Protect Agency?

Another issue concerns the value of agency itself. Agency forms the fulcrum of the argument for human rights. Why is agency of such importance? Agency theories imply that enjoying agency is a central human good. This may not be obvious, at least for the logic of action variant. From the logic of action perspective, the agency-based argument for human rights appears to imply nothing about human goods. From this point of view, rights are a precondition for the possibility of action. As humans have to act, the precondition for the possibility to do so needs to be

[103] Griffin, *On Human Rights*, 52 accepts this but argues that not just any pain qualifies as giving rise to human rights – in his example, the pain inflicted by a callous husband does not. However, this only proves the need for arguments that concrete manifestations of human goods (e.g. a pain-free existence) are candidates for protection by human rights, not that some of these (an existence free of torture) are not protected by human rights for the reason of shielding human beings from the pain of torture. Whether Griffin's claim is correct that a theory cannot sufficiently specify the goods legitimately protected will be discussed in the further argument of this book.

protected. This appears to be a straightforward and watertight argument. But is it valid? What if acting were nothing but a pain and burden for human beings? What if a life of wordless meditation, refraining from action as far as possible, were preferable to the *vita activa*? What if there is no good answer to the question of why *not to be*? After all, it is not only noble young men facing a rotten world of baseness and betrayal who take this question seriously. One may grant that human rights are the precondition of agency but nevertheless ask: What is the point of agency?[104]

How, then, does the agency theory justify the fact that the existence of agents needs to be protected? This seems the most fundamental concern of human rights – to assert the intrinsic, inalienable, supreme value of human beings and spell out its normative consequences for human life and institutions. There are two possible answers to this. The first relies on some kind of argument that agency is of value as such irrespective of what human beings may think of it, independently of whether they enjoy it as a gift or curse it as a burden. Perhaps there is such an argument. Agency theories, however, seem not to be wedded to any such argument despite considering agency an intrinsic value.[105]

Consequently, agency theory needs to base its justification of this right – and this is the second option – on the value of life *for* an (average) human agent, which brings us back to the most fundamental good: the good of human life.[106] Agency theory (correctly) presupposes the value of human life as lived by agents, which is not, however, an *a priori* truth but an evaluative stance that needs to be accounted for. In particular, there is a need to explain that not only some agents are protected (say men or whites or North Americans) but all human beings equally, because the value of life is equal for all. Agency theory thus is wedded to some egalitarian theory of human worth that argues for this equal value of human life. This indicates that the principle of equal respect is of great importance for a theory of human rights and that such a theory cannot do without it.[107]

Furthermore, agency theories refer to the interests that people have and the qualified nature of some of these interests that justifies "ring-fenc[ing] them with

[104] Gewirth considers the possibility of suicide. It is true that suicide is an action, too. However, this finding has no bearing on the question at issue, which is, if you will, Camus' question of the philosophical reasons against suicide, cf. Albert Camus, "Le Mythe de Sisyphe," in *Œuvres complètes Vol. I: 1931–1944*, ed. Jaqueline Lévi-Valensi (Paris: Gallimard, 2006).

[105] Cf. Griffin, *On Human Rights*, 152 or 200: "The dignity is then to be seen as deriving from the value we attach to our normative agency." This assertion is embedded in a teleological not deontological argument, ibid. 36, 57 ff., 73: "It is teleological somewhat in the way that Aristotle's ethics is: the only values used in the derivation of moral principles are the ends of life."

[106] Griffin's argument in Griffin, *On Human Rights*, 71 ff. that the prohibition of killing is a conservative "policy" because it is too unclear what the benefits of abandoning it may be is not particularly convincing.

[107] Griffin's argument in Griffin, *On Human Rights*, 39 that equal respect is too abstract a concept to form the foundation for the derivation of human rights is thus only right in that this principle is only a part of a full justificatory account of human rights.

the notion of human rights."[108] This shows that agency does not do away with the need for a substantial account of interests or (more generally) human goods. This is all the more so if we bear in mind that human life, as indicated above, is valuable not just because it is a precondition for agency (though this is important, too), but because of the many other human goods it enables us to enjoy.

4.4.1.6 Is There a Bridge from Agency to Rights?

These findings lead us to the next problem. Agency theories – as we just have seen – presuppose that agency is so important that it should be protected by rights. This is certainly correct, but there is a gap in the reasoning, even if – for the sake of the argument – one assumes that the case for the importance of agency is fully made. It is an example of a structural problem for any justificatory theory of human rights and consequently merits close attention.

This problem concerns the concrete normative implications drawn from agency. Where does the *right* to agency (with its particular complex normative meaning) stem from? Why is the importance of something for agent A not just a reason for, say, the agent's urgent wish to have this important thing protected, but rather an existence condition for a very specific normative position of the rights-bearer A and the addressee(s) of the rights – a *claim obliging* the addressee(s) of this right? It is plausible that individuals value their agency. But why should potential addressee(s) be concerned about these individuals' agency? Why should they bother about the agency of *others*? Why should the importance of agency for a meaningful human life create a specific web of normative incidents – including a claim of the rights-holder and obligations on the part of the addressee(s)? A transformative step is taken from the self-interested perspective of an individual to the normative position called a *right*, a step that requires explanation. Why do the needs or interests of others obligate agents to respect the preconditions of agency of these others? Universalization is of no help in this respect. Universalization presupposes that others count morally – the very question at issue here.

The importance of this problem can be illustrated by the eight steps outlined in the logic of action argument. The issue arises when taking the step from the conclusion that agents *must have* freedom and well-being in order to pursue their goals to the assertion that they have *rights* to freedom or well-being. A right is a

[108] Griffin, *On Human Rights*, 36. Because of this importance of interests that can be balanced against other interests and goods, Griffin understands his theory as teleological (in a broader sense than "'consequentialist' or 'utilitarian'") and not deontological, ibid. The important role of interests is underlined in his "metaphysics" of human rights, ibid. 115: "One way to see something as worth wanting is to see it under the heading of some general human interest." Or ibid. 116: "To see anything as making life better, we must see it as an instance of something generally intelligible as valuable and, furthermore, as valuable for any normal human being." Ibid.: He sets up a list such as accomplishment, enjoyment, etc. In his view, this amounts to "a kind of need account: what is needed to function as a normative agent."

normative notion that implies duties on the part of the addressee. If only self-interest and no normative principles are relevant, the fact that agents must have freedom and well-being in order to attain their goals does not imply (with logical necessity) that they have a right to freedom and well-being. To begin with, another normative position of the agents is entirely possible: They could have a privilege, namely that attaining their freedom and well-being would not violate the rights of others, although they have no right that others do not interfere with them achieving their purpose.

In assuming that agents are motivated only by self-interest and not some moral principle, the logic of action argument aligns better, however, with a different view of the world, a world of adversarial, competing self-interest. It could even be a deeply antagonistic, survival-of-the-fittest world, where the agents understand that in order to be able to act, they have to fight for their freedom and well-being and can only realize their agency if they are victorious in this fight. It is a world not of rights, but of power. In such a world, the agents most probably would wish that other agents did not interfere with their attempt to achieve their purposes. Nevertheless, if only self-interest matters, this wish does not translate into a right just because it concerns important goods of the agents. For such a right, the agents need to recourse to a normative principle that *entitles* them to realize their agency and other goods of human existence and *obliges* other agents to refrain from obstructing their pursuit of these goods.

This does not imply that others are *permitted* to interfere with a person's freedom and well-being in this world, only that they *can do* it. Permission is a normative notion as much as a right. It cannot be derived from the self-interest of the agents either. In this amoral world of self-interest, the situation is simply that others can (and probably will) in fact interfere with a person's freedom and well-being, not that they are permitted to do so. If they are stronger, they will succeed; if not, the person will prevail.

There is thus no contradiction if agents hold that they must have freedom and well-being and, at the same time, that others may in fact prevent the agents from enjoying these goods – if, as is assumed, normative principles do not play a role. What the agents *must* have specifies the factual preconditions of their acting but does not imply anything about their rights and about what others ought to do. The agents would contradict themselves if they held – at the same time – that they must have freedom and well-being and do not need freedom and well-being in order to act. They do not contradict themselves if they hold that they must have freedom and well-being but (unfortunately in this tough world) have no right to obtain either and that they consequently will not get what they need in order to act.

The fact that there is no connection between something necessary for human action and a right to this something can be illustrated by a practical example, too: There are cases where it is justified not to provide agents with something that they must have in order to be agents, even something that is of existential importance for them. For example, no person has a right to the lifesaving organ of another person, even if taking the organ from this latter person would not endanger that person's life. This is because of normative principles that delineate the scope and limits of rights.

It is no counterargument to maintain that the action-based argument is formulated from a first-person perspective.[109] The argument starting from action concerns not just any kinds of possible, erroneous beliefs of agents, but logically necessary and thus justified beliefs. Given what has been said above, one cannot conclude from the fact that something is important to an agent (as a precondition for action) that they have a right to this something. This is true irrespective of the point of view.

This analysis highlights the importance for a theory of human rights of something already underlined above: the intrinsic value of human persons. While it is a grave inhumanity to deny others the possibility of becoming or continuing to be agents through slavery or even extermination, it is not a logical error to do so if one does not accept the key moral principle of the equal intrinsic value of human persons and certain basic principles of justice. If the perpetrator of such crimes denies the victims of his deeds either any or sufficient worth and assumes that whatever worth they have is outweighed by other considerations – such as the interests of a master race – he is not committing a logical fallacy. Victims may even agree (at least this is a theoretical possibility) that, given their properties, there is no point in protecting their agency because these properties make them (in their own eyes) worthless creatures. Only if any of the agents as individual persons are of intrinsic worth is there an argument for protecting the possibility to act as a *right*, and only if principles of justice count is there an argument for *equal* rights.

This raises difficult normative questions. The humanity of persons commands respect. Respect in this sense is a normative concept and differs from non-normative appreciation or admiration – for example, for a free kick into the corner of the goal from thirty meters away. As a consequence, one *ought* to respect persons, and one *ought* to treat them accordingly. But where do these normative demands stem from? The idea that there is something about human beings that commands this kind of respect is not self-evident and requires solid arguments, as illustrated by the many examples of contempt for human beings and the power of the forces that motivate inhumanity. The step from the precondition of *being an agent* to the *right to act as an agent* is therefore surely entirely justified, but only under much richer premises than the theories of agency identify.

4.4.1.7 The Objective Reason Argument

There is one important argument still to be considered, which we can call the *objective reason argument* or the argument from the perspective of (logical)

[109] Gewirth, *Community*, 21.

universalization. This argument holds that we have to accept duties towards others as correlatives of their rights because the same reason that justifies the predication of value to us justifies the predication of value to others. The same normative conclusions – rights for us and others – thus follow, given that this objective reason is applicable to all.[110] Griffin provides a concise formulation of this argument:

> It is tempting to treat the reason-generating consideration that moves me when my autonomy is at stake as different from the one that moves me when yours is at stake. The obvious difference between these two cases is that in the one it is *my* autonomy, and in the other it is *yours*. But the most plausible understanding of the engine of these two judgements is *autonomy: because a person's quality of life is importantly at stake*. The *my* and *your* are not part of the reason-generating consideration. The clause *because a person's quality of life is importantly at stake* lacks reference to me or to you, but it lacks nothing of what we understand the reason to be. To try to deny "autonomy" its status as a reason for action unless it is attached to "my" would mean giving up our grasp on how "autonomy" works as a reason for action.[111]

A related argument holds that one only respects the objective value of one's own humanity if one respects the humanity of all – because the reasons for this respect are the same, a line of reasoning that is called "Kant's argument" and that we will discuss below.[112]

In a certain sense, this is a good, important and valid argument. There is no discernible reason why some consideration X applicable to human being A should invest A with some kind of normative status, including rights, but the same consideration X should not invest human being B with the same normative status. It is thus contradictory to treat A (even if A is oneself) differently from B (some other person) if consideration X is the reason for this treatment.

There is still a fundamental problem here, however. As discussed, the implications of the logic of action or of the consideration "a person's quality of life is importantly at stake" are not sufficient conditions for generating rights. Agency theories simply have not made the point that agency is a consideration applicable to A that gives rise to rights of A and there is thus no reason to accept that other agents to whom the same consideration applies also enjoy such rights. An argument insufficient to ground rights for an agent A is insufficient to ground the rights of other agents as well.

[110] Gewirth, *Community*, 19; Griffin, *On Human Rights*, 135.

[111] Griffin, *On Human Rights*, 135 (emphasis in original). Similarly, ibid. 58: "The ground for my liberty is a ground for your equal liberty; the ground cannot justify my being more at liberty than you are. That identifies a formal constraint on the content of the right; each person's liberty must be compatible with the same liberty for all." In Griffin's view, this kind of argument seems to account for the transition from prudence to morality, from value judgments like "this is cruel" to prohibitions of torture, ibid. 126.

[112] Dworkin, *Justice for Hedgehogs*.

One further issue is a matter of substantial debate. As we have seen, the framework of agency theories provides insufficient reasons for the justification of human rights. If that were different, however, the following problem would arise. It is inconsistent to think that there are reasons for oneself having rights but not to accept that others – for the same reasons – also have rights. The nonacceptance of rights of others is, however, not only a logical error. It also is a violation of moral principles as one *ought* to treat others equally for moral reasons, not the least justice, not just because of the demands of consistent reasoning. This is a matter of analyzing the phenomenon properly.

In addition, there is a dimension at issue that leads to a problem haunting a substantial part of moral philosophy: the problem of moral motivation. An insight as such has no motivational force. One can agree that people have such things as rights, shrug one's shoulders and go about one's business without being affected by this insight, just as one does not need to be particularly affected by the insight that 1 + 1 = 2. The fact that an insight into the existence of rights has a different status – that to assert, "Yes, A has a human right to X" implies "Because of this right of A, I have an obligation to Z," an obligation with a motivational effect – is a consequence of the normative nature of the right at issue, not a consequence of the demands of consistent thinking.

The gap in the argument from agency to human rights can only be bridged by normative principles, namely the respect for human beings, for egalitarian principles of justice and for basic obligations of human solidarity, as will be explained in more detail below.[113]

4.4.1.8 The Important Point of Agency Theories

In sum, agency theory encounters at least the following problems: First, the reference to agency fails to sufficiently determine the content of human rights, as the differentiated set of human rights transcends what is necessary to secure agency. Second, human rights protect goods other than agency for their own sake. Third, agency theories rely on a theory of human goods, which crucially includes the good of the life of a human agent, which they do not spell out. Fourth, agency theories imply but do not identify the normative principles that turn the existence conditions of agency and other goods important for human rights into the content of claims towards others and their correlated duties.

The critique of agency theories thus confirms the importance both of a theory of human goods and of normative principles for the justification of human rights. These findings may prove helpful with regard to a question of great practical importance, namely the question of who the bearers of human rights are. Agency

[113] Griffin, *On Human Rights*, 160 underlines that a constraint on liberty is the equal liberty of all. This is true but rests ultimately on the principles of justice at issue here.

theories sometimes determine this group quite narrowly, excluding human beings such as infants,[114] who are protected uncontroversially in human rights law. If one is willing to relinquish the persuasion that agency alone is the key to understanding the foundations of human rights, the door may open to form an inclusive concept of human rights that is more convincingly justified and is a better match for the state of current human rights law.

The importance of normative principles does not mean that human rights and morality are coextensive. They are not. There are indeed "most heavyweight moral obligations"[115] that are not part of human rights. However, this does not mean that these moral principles are not foundational for human rights theory. The fact that justice and human solidarity and human rights are not coextensive does not imply that justice and solidarity are not central for the foundations of human rights. This seems crucial to understanding the whole project of human rights. Human rights are a part of the language of justice and human solidarity, and this is what the further argument of this book will try to spell out.

Agency theories thus do not answer all questions that need to be answered concerning the justification of human rights. However, they do underline a central element of the edifice of human rights that needs accounting for: the importance of autonomy.

4.4.2 *Needs and Interests as the Engine of Rights*

4.4.2.1 The Argument Based on Needs and Interests

Need and interest theories share some common ground: Both hold that some needs or interests of human beings are so important that they give rise to human rights.[116]

Need theories argue that certain basic human needs are the reason for the existence of rights, at least for the fundamental ones. The need to live without bodily harm thus justifies the protection of bodily integrity by rights, for example. The need not to starve justifies certain social rights. Other rights are derived from these fundamental rights by further considerations that depend on the right in question. Due process rights, for example, can be derived from rights to bodily integrity or the protection of liberty, because due process rights are necessary preconditions if these fundamental rights are to have substantial content.

114 Cf. Griffin, *On Human Rights*, 83 ff., assuming that children's rights are acquired in "stages," ibid. 95.

115 Griffin, *On Human Rights*, 43.

116 On need theories, cf. e.g. David Miller, "Grounding Human Rights," *Critical Review of International Social and Political Philosophy* 15, no. 4 (2012): 407 ff., 422. On interest theories, cf. Raz, *Morality of Freedom*, 166. For a critique of need theories and in defense of interest theories, John Tasioulas, "On the Foundations of Human Rights," in *Philosophical Foundations of Human Rights*, eds. Rowan Cruft, S. Matthew Liao and Massimo Renzo (Oxford: Oxford University Press, 2015), 63 ff.

Current influential need theories face criticism on various grounds. One important critique argues that need theories are implausibly restrictive because not all rights are linked to true human needs.[117]

Interest theories provide an alternative. Joseph Raz's influential version offers what is called a definition of rights, but in fact includes a theory of the justification of rights through interests:

> Definition: "X has a right" if and only if X can have rights, and, other things being equal, an aspect of X's well-being (his interest) is a sufficient reason for holding some other person(s) to be under a duty. Capacity for possessing rights: An individual is capable of having rights if and only if either his well-being is of ultimate value or he is an "artificial person" (e.g. a corporation).[118]

From this perspective, interests are of sufficient importance to generate rights if a certain threshold criterion has been met. However, Raz's theory is not clear on the argument's crucial step, as it does not spell out how interests are transformed into normative incidents, into claims and corresponding duties, privileges and no-rights. It limits itself to asserting that some interests are of such a nature that they give rise to rights and duties: "Only where one's interest is a reason for another to behave in a way which protects or promotes it, and only when this reason has the peremptory character of a duty, and, finally, only when the duty is for conduct which makes a significant difference for the promotion or protection of that interest does the interest give rise to a right."[119]

The respect for persons, which plays a prominent role in the justification of human rights, also is derived from interests: "[A] person has an interest in being respected as a person. That shows that rights grounded in respect are based on interests."[120] There is, however, another step in the argument that grounds it on something other than naked interest, namely the value of the well-being of persons: "It is, as was indicated before, the duty to give due weight to the interests of persons. And it is grounded on the intrinsic desirability of the well-being of persons."[121] The proposition about the "intrinsic desirability" itself seems not to be derived from interests, but from an evaluative judgment about the value of the well-being of persons.

John Tasioulas' approach formulates a much more differentiated argument that is particularly helpful for understanding promising ways to justify human rights. Importantly, it is pluralistic in the sense that not only interests, but also other considerations play a justificatory role. In particular, the crucial role of human dignity for the justification of human rights is highlighted, which marks a major difference from other interest-based approaches.

[117] Tasioulas, "Foundations," 66.
[118] Raz, *Morality of Freedom*, 166.
[119] Raz, *Morality of Freedom*, 183.
[120] Raz, *Morality of Freedom*, 188.
[121] Raz, *Morality of Freedom*, 190.

The derivation of rights from interests takes the following shape:

(i) For all human beings within a given historical context, and simply in virtue of their humanity, having X (the object of the putative right) serves one or more of their basic interests, for example, interests in health, physical security, autonomy, understanding, friendship, achievement, play, etc.
(ii) The interest in having X is, in the case of each human being and simply in virtue of their humanity, pro tanto of sufficient importance to justify the imposition of duties on others, for example, to variously protect, respect or advance the interest in X.
(iii) The duties generated at (ii) are feasible claims on others given the constraints created by general and relatively entrenched facts of human nature and social life in the specified historical context. Therefore:
(iv) All human beings with the specified historical context have a right to X.[122]

These steps are spelled out in helpful detail: The universal interests are objective, standardized, pluralistic, open-ended and holistic. They are objective in the sense that they exist independently of the attitude of the subjects of these interests. They are standardized because they abstract from individual cases and are derived from standard cases of ordinary human beings' interests. There is an open-ended plurality of interests, meaning that there is no single overarching value underpinning all human interests and that the interests may change and evolve over time. Their holistic character leads to an interpenetration of different interests – the prudential value of freedom for agents, for example, is said to be dependent on moral values: "[M]ultiplying trivial or morally depraved options does not enhance their freedom."[123] Freedom may have an important impact on other values, too: A partnership based on autonomous decisions is more valuable than one that is based on the decisions of others, as in the case of arranged marriages. However, freedom is not an element for every prudential value.[124]

This theory includes the idea of human dignity in its account of the foundations of human rights:

> The interests on which the pluralist account draws are always the interests of individual human beings, and understanding their normative significance requires that we grasp the intrinsically valuable status equally possessed by all human beings, one grounded in the fact that they are humans. What emerges is a form of the interest-based theory which regards the interests in question as generative of human rights in crucial part because they are the interests of human beings who possess equal moral status: human dignity and universal human interests are equally fundamental grounds of human rights, characteristically bound together in their operation.[125]

[122] Tasioulas, "Foundations," 50 f. (emphasis in original).
[123] Tasioulas, "Foundations," 52.
[124] Tasioulas, "Foundations," 53.
[125] Tasioulas, "Foundations," 53 f.

The reference to dignity adds an important dimension to Tasioulas' approach: In particular, it answers the question of why interests of persons cannot be aggregated to form a collective notion of interest that then is taken as the true yardstick for individual and social norms: "If human beings matter in themselves, as sources of ultimate moral concern, each potentially with their own life to lead, then it is a travesty simply to 'detach' their interests from them with a view to maximizing the overall fulfilment of interests across persons. The individuals with these interests count in themselves and not because the satisfaction or frustration of their interests is ultimately assimilated to some overarching aggregative concern."[126]

Tasioulas argues that this provides a key to the puzzle of why rights are hostile to trade-offs: Every individual counts, and their interests must be taken into due account.[127] The dignity of human persons is based on a set of particular properties of human beings, properties that are not limited to humans' rational nature.[128]

According to Tasioulas, the following criteria must be met for a qualified interest to give rise to a right: the possibility of fulfilling the duty imposed by the right, the limitation to duties that do not confound the point of the right and, importantly, the compossibility of this right with others' rights of the same content and a burdensomeness test. If the overall duties imposed by human rights are too burdensome for the addressees of the rights, these rights are not justified.[129] Moreover, he argues, human rights are intrinsically connected to principles of justice.[130]

4.4.2.2 The Reach of Need and Interest Theories

4.4.2.2.1 NEEDS OR INTERESTS – OR SOMETHING ELSE? Need and interest theories make an important constructive point by underlining that there can be no theory of human rights without reference to and sufficiently detailed specification of the goods these rights protect – an account that explains why these specified needs or interests count and not others.

There is much intense debate between need and interest theorists. When reviewing these discussions and controversies, many of the arguments seem to be directed not at need or interest theories as such, just at certain *versions* of these theories. In addition, seen from a slight distance, there appears to be a considerable overlap between these theories. In particular, the real question at stake hinges not so much on the problem of whether needs or interests are the better starting point for theory, but on which particular human goods count as relevant for the justification of

[126] Tasioulas, "Foundations," 55.
[127] Tasioulas, "Foundations," 55.
[128] Tasioulas, "Foundations," 54.
[129] Tasioulas, "Foundations," 56 ff.
[130] John Tasioulas, "Justice, Equality, and Rights," in *The Oxford Handbook of the History of Ethics*, ed. Roger Crisp (Oxford: Oxford University Press, 2013).

human rights. The main difference between the variants of the theories as they are formulated in contemporary discussions is that the term *interests* is taken to be more capacious than *needs*. For example, it is argued that freedom of religion cannot be derived from basic human needs, or at least that the protection of manifestations of belief that usually are included in the scope of this right cannot be.[131] Is this indeed so? Can we be sure that at the base of the concern for the manifestation of one's belief there really is not some kind of deep-seated human need not only to entertain religious beliefs, but also to live according to their commands? We can even go a step further and ask: Are there any independent interests that are not connected to human needs in one way or another?

It appears that the problem with some need theories is not the idea that needs are important for human rights but the concrete interpretation of what human needs are.

Interest theorists rightly criticize certain need theories for overly restricting the goods included in the set of goods worthy of protection by human rights.[132] However, given what already has been said, there is no reason to assume that all need theories must be so restrictive. Furthermore, there is no reason not to include both needs and interests in a wider theory of human goods worthy of protection by human rights. This has the advantage that one does not have to answer the question of where precisely needs end and interests begin – if this is indeed possible at all. Consequently, this will form part of the approach developed over the course of the further argument, while taking on board the insights that the debate about needs and interests is offering. From this point of view, it is not crucial whether one calls the deep longing of human beings to manifest their religious beliefs a need or an interest (although much speaks in favor of seeing it as a fundamental need) as long as one agrees (as one should) that this longing is a human good worthy of protection by the special instrument of human rights.

4.4.2.2.2 NEEDS, INTERESTS AND HUMAN DIGNITY As we have seen, an important schism runs through the interest theory camp: One influential version of the interest theory bases respect for other people on interests by pointing to people's interest in being respected. This argument is not sufficient, however. What needs to be explained is why one *ought* to respect others (and respect their interest in being respected). This cannot be achieved by pointing to the interest of the agent herself in being respected because a normative element is missing from the argument. This almost becomes explicit when Raz refers to the "intrinsic desirability" of the well-being of persons, which is an evaluative judgment.[133] Even if the theory referred to

[131] Tasioulas, "Foundations," 21.

[132] Others criticize interest theories as being too expansive, cf. Griffin's critique of Raz, Griffin, *On Human Rights*, 54 ff. In addition, he argues, rights are not only exclusionary reasons.

[133] Cf. on the normative status of human beings and human rights, Joseph Raz, "Human Rights in the Emerging World Order," in *Philosophical Foundations of Human Rights*, eds. Rowan

non-normative reasons for the interest in well-being (its intrinsic desirability in a non-normative sense), the question still remains of how the normative dimension of respect for others is derived. How is the intrinsic desirability of being respected as an aspect of well-being turned into one's right (and the right of others) to be respected?

Tasioulas' version of interest theories that includes human dignity therefore constitutes a major improvement, offering substantial insights into the justification of human rights. It correctly highlights the importance of the equal, supreme normative status of human beings that is the reason for respecting the interests of others. This paves the way to understanding the question of possible limitations of human rights or of trade-offs. The theory provides space for weighing and balancing rights with other rights and legitimate public concerns. Such weighing and balancing exercises are, however, limited by the rights of persons to be protected as ends-in-themselves. Weighing and balancing is no license to abrogate the intrinsic value of persons and instrumentalize them. This has entered into doctrinal findings – for example, that there is an essence of fundamental rights that needs to be protected and that there are nonderogable rights or absolute rights that cannot be limited. A prime, widely accepted example of the latter is the prohibition of torture, a *ius cogens* norm.[134]

At this point, however, the theory of justification has to take one more step, a step already encountered in our discussion of agency theories. This step consists of introducing normative principles into the argument to transform interests that as such are of no moral concern to others into something that is the object of claims and correlated duties.

This step is indispensable because both need and interest theories face a common problem we have encountered before. How do certain needs or interests give rise to normative claims and privileges on the part of the rights-holder and obligations and no-rights on the part of the addressee of rights? This is far from obvious. All kinds of needs and interests have no normative consequences at all. Why is it different in the case of some needs and interests? There is a gap in the argument between the descriptive proposition that humans have certain (important, existential) needs or interests and the normative proposition that they legitimately have the right to have these needs and interests secured:

> [R]educing human rights to universal interests is a category error. Interests belong to the domain of prudence or well-being, which concerns what makes a life better for the person living it, whereas human rights are moral standards that impose duties on others, where the violation of the duty entails *wronging* someone in

Cruft, S. Matthew Liao and Massimo Renzo (Oxford: Oxford University Press, 2015), 217–31, 225: "[O]ne crucial contribution of individual rights to the emerging world order is underpinning its commitment to the value of human life."

134 Cf. ECtHR, Gäfgen v Germany, Judgement of June 1, 2010, appl. No. 22978/05, which states that the prohibition of torture allows for no exceptions whatsoever.

> particular – the right-holder. Our interests, by contrast, can be impaired in all sorts of ways without any *moral* wrongdoing being in the offing, let alone a directed wrongdoing of this specific kind.[135]

To refer once again to a standard example: A person for sure has a need and interest of the highest order not to die. This does not mean, however, that this person has a right to any kind of medical treatment, even if treatment is available that could save this person's life. No person has the right that another person relinquish involuntarily a kidney, even if this would save the life of the first person and the donor would still be able to continue their life.

This remains the case even if we qualify the theory with a (very helpful) threshold criterion, according to which one precondition for the justification of a human right is that the interest protected is possible to satisfy and the consequences of the right are not too burdensome for others.[136] However, the introduction of this criterion still leaves open the question of why these qualified interests entail normative consequences. The problem of the category error remains unsolved.

Among the threshold criteria, the importance of the compossibility of the content of rights is (correctly) underlined. This points in the same direction, revealing the importance of the principles of justice that are the ultimate reason for the justification of this demand: Justice demands the compossibility of the content of the right of one person with the rights of others because otherwise the agents would be treated unequally without any justified reason.

The constitutive role of dignity allows for similar conclusions: Human dignity is a central building block of the theory of human rights, as the pluralist interest theory rightly and importantly highlights. Dignity correctly is not derived merely from interests to be respected. It is a fundamental value status of persons. Moreover, it is the origin of a normative principle, namely the principle that one ought to respect a person who enjoys this value. Human dignity is an axiological judgment with prescriptive effect. Again, the importance of normative principles becomes manifest over the course of the argument.

Such normative principles are the reason why nobody is obliged to donate their organs to save the lives of others (laudable as this would be): Such a duty would violate normative principles, in particular the principle of equal respect for personhood that prohibits the instrumentalization of persons, even for the benefit of others.

In view of these findings, the best way to bridge the gap that still remains between needs and interests even if one considers sophisticated and convincing threshold criteria is to take one more step. This step consists of including among the justificatory reasons for human rights not only human dignity as a status, but also

[135] As John Tasioulas correctly observes in "Human Dignity and the Foundations of Human Rights," in *Understanding Human Dignity*, ed. Christopher McCrudden (Oxford: Oxford University Press, 2013), 296 (emphasis in original).

[136] Tasioulas, "Human Dignity," 297 ff.

normative principles as further coeval grounds of human rights: Humans enjoy fundamental rights because of normative principles of justice, equal respect and human solidarity that prescribe the conditions under which the needs and interests of persons to enjoy certain goods are normatively relevant and may generate claims, privileges and obligations of the rights-holders and the addressees.[137]

4.4.3 *The Capability Approach*

4.4.3.1 Determining Desirable Functionings

The capability approach has become a paradigm in various areas of research, from economics, where it originated, to philosophy. Its core concern is how to properly measure the advantages of persons in a society. As such, it concerns a central element of normative theory and is relevant to both distributive justice and human rights. Capabilities, it is argued by leading proponents like Amartya Sen and Martha Nussbaum, give the best answer to the question of how a person's overall advantage is properly assessed.[138] They are "the relevant space within which to make comparisons of quality of life across societies."[139] A person's well-being consists of qualified "functionings," of being able to act in certain manners ("doings") and of certain states of being ("beings"). Capabilities are neither the functionings themselves nor the formal opportunity to do or be something. Rather, a capability is a "real opportunity to achieve valuable functionings."[140] It is a comprehensive opportunity: One central element of capabilities is choice,[141] because it is not only the opportunity to achieve something that is valuable; the possibility to choose already is valuable in itself (and crucially so).[142] Given different circumstances, needs and interests, trade-offs between capabilities are necessary.[143]

The focus on capabilities presents an alternative not only to welfare approaches, which foreground happiness, pleasure or utility as the basic units for assessing a human being's advantage, but also to other influential theories in which primary goods[144] or resources[145] fulfill this function. Happiness, pleasure and utility are not

[137] Therefore, Tasioulas is right to underline the intrinsic connection between justice and human rights, Tasioulas, "Justice, Equality, and Rights."

[138] Sen, *Idea of Justice*, 231. M. Nussbaum and A. Sen disagree about some aspects of the theory, cf. e.g. Martha C. Nussbaum, *Women and Human Development* (Cambridge: Cambridge University Press, 2001), 70 f. In the following, these disagreements will be discussed only if they are relevant for the course of the argument.

[139] Nussbaum, *Women and Human Development*, 63.

[140] Sen, *Idea of Justice*, 371.

[141] Nussbaum, *Women and Human Development*, 88; Sen, *Idea of Justice*, 232.

[142] Nussbaum, *Women and Human Development*, 88; Sen, *Idea of Justice*, 228 ff., 235 ff., 370 ff.

[143] Nussbaum, *Women and Human Development*, 81; Sen, *Idea of Justice*, 233; Sen, "Elements of a Theory of Human Rights," 315 ff.

[144] Rawls, *Theory of Justice*, 78.

[145] Ronald Dworkin, *Sovereign Virtue* (Cambridge, MA: Harvard University Press, 2002), 65 ff.

the only things that are valuable, capability theorists argue.[146] What is valuable may even determine what brings human beings satisfaction and increases their utility[147] – a traditional argument already considered. From this perspective, freedom is of particular importance beyond welfare.[148] Capability theorists agree with the argument already encountered that aggregating across distinct lives and distinct goods, as in a utilitarian approach, overlooks the importance of the individual and the different values that certain goods hold for different persons. The aggregation of utility thus gives only a distorted image of persons' advantages.[149]

Primary goods and resources are only means to achieve valuable ends, not these ends themselves.[150] By contrast, capabilities offer the opportunity to directly assess freedom, rather than counting the means to achieve it. The capability approach thus provides a broader informational basis than its alternatives.[151] Capabilities are assessed on an individual level, because capabilities of groups are reducible to capabilities of individuals.[152] Capabilities are not "interests," because choices may concern actions that are not in the interest of the agent.[153] Sen underlines that capabilities are not the only concern for a normative theory. There are other considerations as well, such as fairness or other demands of distributive justice.[154]

The background of the capability theory is informed by a certain idea of human existence and the worth of persons flourishing according to their own choices. In Nussbaum's version of the approach, it is interpreted as a "freestanding" Aristotelian argument, not "deduced from natural teleology or any non-moral source"[155] about "the human being as a dignified free being who shapes his or her life in cooperation and reciprocity with others."[156] For Nussbaum, the core of dignity is to regard human beings as ends-in-themselves: "We want an approach that is respectful of each person's struggle for flourishing, that treats each person as an end and as a source of agency and worth in her own right."[157] The peron's individual well-being therefore is not to be traded off for the well-being of others,[158] depriving the person

146 Sen, *Idea of Justice*, 274. In addition, happiness – unlike capabilities – does not create obligations. On the latter point, ibid. 270 f.

147 Sen, *Idea of Justice*, 276.

148 Sen, *Idea of Justice*, 282, 286 ff.

149 Nussbaum, *Women and Human Development*, 62, following Rawls, *Theory of Justice*, 156 ff.

150 Sen, *Idea of Justice*, 233, 253 ff. In addition, focusing on resources can result in a skewed picture because of further factors, importantly conversion opportunities; that is, the real ability to convert resources in quality of life (e.g. because of gender discrimination), ibid. 255 ff.

151 Sen, *Idea of Justice*, 236.

152 Sen, *Idea of Justice*, 246.

153 Sen, *Idea of Justice*, 377 ff.

154 Sen, *Idea of Justice*, 295 ff.

155 Nussbaum, *Women and Human Development*, 76.

156 Nussbaum, *Women and Human Development*, 72.

157 Nussbaum, *Women and Human Development*, 69.

158 Nussbaum, *Women and Human Development*, 56 f., 72 f., 74.

of autonomous decision-making: "For it is all about respect for the dignity of persons as choosers."[159]

Nussbaum's account identifies the ethically and politically relevant capabilities according to their importance in any human life.[160] There is an overlapping consensus about many such capabilities.[161] In this respect, not only their instrumental value is relevant, but also their intrinsic worth for human flourishing. Depriving human beings of a basic level of capabilities constitutes a violation of political justice.[162]

How does the argument build the bridge between capabilities as real opportunities for certain functionings and human rights? Human rights are "an especially urgent and morally justified claim that a person has, simply by virtue of being a human adult, and independently of membership in a particular nation, or class, or sex, or ethnic or religious or sexual group."[163] Capabilities are the key to identifying and justifying those claims that in this sense are especially urgent and morally justified: "The importance of freedoms provides a foundational reason not only for affirming our own rights and liberties, but also for taking an interest in the freedoms and rights of others – going well beyond the pleasures and desire-fulfilment on which utilitarians concentrate."[164]

Threshold criteria identify those capabilities of such a nature that they qualify to be protected by human rights. The key is their importance and the possibility for others to bring about their realization: "For a freedom to be included as part of a human right, it clearly must be important enough to provide reasons for others to pay serious attention to it. There must be some 'threshold conditions' of relevance, including the importance of the freedom and the possibility of influencing its realization, for it to plausibly figure within the spectrum of human rights."[165]

The human rights thus justified include at least central liberties, equality and claims to material goods that assure that the agent has sufficient resources to pursue a fulfilling life. In Nussbaum's view (unlike Sen's), it is possible to formulate something like an "objective list" of desirable human capabilities.[166] The theory of capabilities argues for a social structure that enables agents to achieve their goals and does not place obstacles in their way. Human rights may

[159] Nussbaum, *Women and Human Development*, 61 f.
[160] Nussbaum, *Women and Human Development*, 74.
[161] Nussbaum, *Women and Human Development*, 76.
[162] Nussbaum, *Women and Human Development*, 71.
[163] Martha C. Nussbaum, "Capabilities and Human Rights," *Fordham Law Review* 66, no. 2 (1997): 273 ff., 292.
[164] Sen, *Idea of Justice*, 367.
[165] Sen, *Idea of Justice*, 367. It should be noted that, for Sen, freedom is a capacious concept, including, for example, the freedom not to be tortured, ibid.
[166] Sen argues with the open space of public reason, Sen, "Elements of a Theory of Human Rights," 315, 333 n. 31.

contribute to assuring this. The discussion of capabilities and rights primarily concerns human rights as moral rights. However, these moral rights sometimes need to be turned into legal rights.[167]

Sen's account underlines the difficulty of justifying *duties to act*, not just *reasons to act*, for the benefit of others – a distinction already highlighted above. In Sen's view, one particular fundamental other-regarding duty is key: "The basic general obligation here must be to consider seriously what one can reasonably do to help the realization of another person's freedom, taking note of its importance and influenceability, and of one's own circumstances and likely effectiveness."[168] There is a duty to concern oneself with the well-being of others, particularly if an agent has the capability to reduce injustice. Power entails responsibility.[169] This duty is not based on considerations of reciprocity:

> Unlike the contractarian argument, the case for duty or obligation of effective power to make a difference does not arise, in that line of reasoning, from the mutuality of joint benefits through cooperation, or from the commitment made in some social contract. It is based, rather, on the argument that if someone has the power to make a difference that he or she can see will reduce injustice in the world, then there is a strong and reasoned argument for doing just that (without having to dress all this up in terms of some imagined prudential advantage in a hypothetical exercise of cooperation).[170]

This duty does not offer quick and simple solutions for practical questions but demands that the concern for others be included in the process of decision-making about what it is right to do: "There is a universal ethical demand here, but not one that automatically identifies contingency-free, ready made actions."[171]

Nussbaum emphasizes the egalitarian thrust of her argument.[172] Human beings have a capability to relate to others and should exercise it if they do not want to lead an impoverished life.[173] The "worth and dignity of basic human powers" forms the basis for "thinking of them as claims to a chance for functioning, claims that give rise to correlated social and political duties."[174] She underlines the importance of "human rights language": It serves as a reminder of legitimate and urgent claims of human beings, is rhetorically more direct than other ways of speaking, highlights autonomy and indicates a common ground in debates.[175]

[167] Sen, *Idea of Justice*, 361 ff.
[168] Sen, *Idea of Justice*, 372 f.
[169] Sen derives this idea from Buddhist thought, Sen, *Idea of Justice*, 205.
[170] Sen, *Idea of Justice*, 270 f.
[171] Sen, *Idea of Justice*, 373.
[172] Nussbaum, *Women and Human Development*, 86.
[173] Nussbaum, *Women and Human Development*, 92.
[174] Nussbaum, *Women and Human Development*, 84.
[175] Nussbaum, *Women and Human Development*, 100 f.

As mentioned above, capabilities are not the only concern of ethics. There are other topics that are taken to be relevant for human rights, too, such as fairness, although the consequences of such principles are not spelled out in any detail.[176]

In Sen's theory, the justification of his ethical theory rests on a particular concept of reason. Reason means viability in impartial reasoning, which allows for objectivity.[177] Sen denies that there is any reason to reduce rationality to the pursuit of self-interest and to exclude, for example, the commitment to alleviating the suffering of others.[178] The demand that people be seen as equals, which is a cornerstone of human rights theory, relates to "the normative demand for impartiality and the related claim of objectivity."[179] This reasoning is central to the rational vindication of human rights.[180]

4.4.3.2 Capabilities as Key?

The concern behind the concept of capabilities relates to a classic debate about the problems of equality of opportunity. One persistent theme in reflections on justice and equality concerns the shortcomings and sometimes even moral cynicism of conceptions of formal equality.[181] In the theory of justice and in the legal field of equality and nondiscrimination law, one major thrust consequently is to overcome the deficits of identifying equality with mere formal opportunities. Women have equal opportunities in formal terms to achieve highly qualified positions, for example, but this does not mean that they actually reach these positions. The formal opportunity of a person with a foreign-sounding name to rent a flat does not mean that the person will not be denied access to housing because of this name. Having formal opportunities thus constitutes only the first step towards equality. Such opportunities must be made substantial and real, empowering agents to reach those aims that are the conditions for a meaningful life. By now, a sophisticated set of legal instruments and extensive case law dealing with this matter have developed.

The concept of capability has the broader purpose of enlarging the informational basis for assessing what advantages for human beings consist of beyond concepts such as utility, preferences, pleasure and resources. In this context, the capability approach convincingly insists that opportunities are central elements of human goods and should be understood in a way that makes them more than just hollow promises society does not keep. In many respects, its detailed analysis has fleshed out

[176] Sen, "Elements of a Theory of Human Rights," 336 f.; Sen, *Idea of Justice*, 370 f.

[177] Sen, *Idea of Justice*, 180 ff., 293, 359, 365 f., 385.

[178] Sen, *Idea of Justice*, 180 ff.

[179] Sen, *Idea of Justice*, 293 f.

[180] Sen, *Idea of Justice*, 359, 365 f.

[181] Cf. the almost proverbial observation of a character in Anatole France's *Le lys rouge* (Paris: Calmann-Lévy, 1894) that the majestic equality of law prohibits the rich and the poor equally from sleeping under bridges, begging on the roads and stealing bread.

what opportunities that are not just formal and comprehensive mean in real terms. The capability approach therefore marks an important contribution to a theory of human goods. This should be borne in mind in the following.

Human rights are (explicitly or implicitly) understood as preconditions for the opportunity of persons to lead a flourishing life. Capabilities indexed to such a way of life are more capacious than the preconditions of agency, for instance. This allows the capability approach to provide reasons for the importance of a wide variety of rights. The arguments mustered against the agency approach in this respect consequently do not hold for the capability approach. More difficult to justify from this perspective are the demands of equality. Even an unequal freedom to live according to the demands of one's faith still may be sufficient to live a meaningful life, albeit perhaps not to the utmost extent. This raises the question of the origins of the demands of equality – a problem we already encountered when discussing the agency approaches. It is therefore right to underline – as Sen does – that there is more to a normative theory of human rights than a foundational recourse to capabilities.

A certain liberty such as freedom of expression protects a particular human good – for instance, the need to express oneself without censure. The capability approach presupposes these kinds of needs and other sources of human goods – a capability is a capability for something, and the question is where these valuable somethings stem from. The answer to this question refers to a certain valuable form of existence, the existence of free, dignified human beings who lead a truly human life. It is argued that certain capabilities are important in any form of human life an agent may want to choose and that there is something like an overlapping consensus on what these capabilities are. These are further helpful observations on the way to a comprehensive theory of human goods, and they chime well with traditional arguments in the history of human rights – say, Las Casas' defense of the value of freedom not only for Spaniards, but also for indigenous Americans. A question that remains to be answered, however, is what criteria determine which human capabilities are sufficiently important to generate rights and ultimately form such a consensus. This is particularly relevant for human rights because they are highly restrictive with respect to the goods they protect. This selectiveness needs to be justified.

A capability approach thus is no alternative to a theory of the sources of human goods. Rather, it depends on such a theory. Even if a capability approach were to interpret the capabilities protected in a formal fashion, not only (rightly) underlining the importance of choice, but also leaving it entirely up to the agents to autonomously determine what the content of a flourishing life might be, a statement about human goods is implied, as we already have seen. The protection of autonomy presupposes at least that human life is worth living and that freedom and autonomy as preconditions for making choices constitute elements of any meaningful life. Otherwise, there would be no reason at all for their protection. Here, too, the question of the reasons for this valuation of autonomy arises. This confirms a key insight of the discussion so far: A human rights theory implies a substantial theory of human goods.

One challenge that the capability approach faces as much as any other human rights theory stems from the fact that rights consist of claims towards others and create obligations. They impose normative burdens to be shouldered by all that often translate into real, material burdens on the addressees and are the price to be paid for respect for human rights. As we have seen, these claims and obligations cannot be derived solely from the importance of a good for agents – for example, the importance of the real opportunity to speak their mind. One can acknowledge readily the significance of such a good for oneself and others and still ask: "Why do I have any duties concerning things that are (admittedly) important for others?" Normative principles are thus required that can serve as the foundations of such other-directed claims and obligations.

The capability theory makes some very important theoretical moves that help to provide a deeper understanding of the issue. Particularly crucial in this respect is a more capacious and thus plausible concept of rationality and reason, which includes certain other-regarding principles that are not derived from self-interested, utility-based calculations. In addition, principles of obligatory respect for equality and equal treatment play an important role. Finally, the principle of human dignity and the worth of individuals as ends are highlighted, notions that play a central role in the wider discourse on human rights in both ethics and law and that indeed seem to be key to understanding the importance of the individual in the idea of human rights.

Nevertheless, based on these results further questions arise. In Sen's account, the other-regarding duties result from the power to change the situation of another person for the better.[182] This seems to presuppose some duty to be beneficent to others rather than explain the foundations and content of this duty. A power entails responsibilities only if others exposed to this power count in normative terms. As such, it does not entail any duties not to harm others or to promote their well-being. Grounds for these duties independent of the factual ability to influence the lives of others are required. The same holds for an argument based upon the importance of a good for others (or oneself): The importance of a good as such has no normative implications.

In Nussbaum's account, these other-regarding duties seem to be equated with the capability to relate to others. This capability, however, important as it is, is something other than the normative duty to care for others. The ability to relate to others is not the same as the duty to care for their well-being. The powers of human beings, Nussbaum argues, give rise to claims to be able to exercise them. How can the transition of the fact of given human powers into normative claims be explained without committing the category error identified above?

[182] As indicated, Sen relates this idea to Buddhist thought, Sen, *Idea of Justice*, 205.

Similar problems arise for the principles of justice invoked. The thrust is clearly egalitarian. But what exactly does the argument look like? How is equality as a normative principle to be understood? How does it provide foundations for human rights? Furthermore, what is the relation between human beings, viewed as ends because of their dignity, and the wider normative conclusions drawn about claims on others in the form of human rights? Is the dignity of "choosers" all there is at stake?

In this context, it should be underlined that human rights are not just about a "language of rights" in the sense of a rhetorical device or a way of speaking. The theoretical problem they pose is that of a particular, deontic status of human beings. This status has an identifiable content. The central problem of the justification of human rights is to account for the reasons to assume that human beings do in fact enjoy this particular status with its concomitant claims of the rights-holder and duties of the bearer of the rights. This deontic status is what the language of rights refers to – and correctly so, if this idea is successfully justified.

This leaves us with a task. The structure and content of the normative principles that render the importance of enjoying a rich set of capabilities normatively relevant need to be spelled out in more detail than the capability approach provides, as does the way that these normative principles translate into arguments for the justification of human rights. Only if these principles are exposed in the full daylight of critical reflection can answers be provided to the questions of their justification and their relation to human moral psychology and their epistemological status, a central concern of this inquiry. In this respect, it is interesting to investigate whether equality as a normative concern is wedded to impartiality and objectivity in reasoning, and if so, in which sense, or whether the normative principle of equality has different sources.[183] The origin of rights in normative principles, the coming into being of this intricate web of normative incidents that empowers the rights-holder through claims and privileges and entangles the addressee in obligations and no-rights under some apparently nonarbitrary conditions thus still needs to be fully accounted for, despite the many insights provided by the capability approach.

One last point: Sometimes capabilities appear as synonymous with effective human rights, contrasted to moral rights to something.[184] It is, however, important to distinguish the function of fully realized capabilities as yardsticks for human rights rendered effective (in particular in the legal domain) from the prior question of how to account for the normative content of human rights that is to be made effective. How to make the right to education effective for girls in the Global South is a highly

[183] We have already encountered this question, cf. the discussion of the objective reason argument above.

[184] Nussbaum, *Women and Human Development*, 98, understanding human rights as combined capabilities; that is, the internal capability of the agent to act and external conditions that enable the exercise of the function, ibid. 84 f., contrasting rights in this sense to moral human rights.

important question, but it differs from the problem of why it is justified to think that such a right exists in the first place.

4.5 POLITICAL CONCEPTION

4.5.1 *Human Rights and the Veil of Ignorance in the International Sphere*

A prominent approach in human rights theory developed by Charles Beitz outlines a political conception of human rights. The starting point for this approach is Rawls' transferal of his own contractualist theory of justice, already discussed in part above, to the international sphere. In this framework, human rights are understood as those rights that form a shared normative framework for liberal democracies and other "decent peoples," in particular hierarchical, nondemocratic societies, the latter characterized by a conception of justice linked to an idea of the common good and a consultative, albeit nondemocratic process of political decision-making. This shared normative framework is based on public reasons, because there is a "duty of civility requiring that they offer other peoples public reasons appropriate to the Society of Peoples for their actions."[185] Both kinds of societies form the set of "well-ordered peoples."[186] These peoples need to be seen alongside "out-law states" without respect for human rights, "burdened societies," which are poor, and "benevolent absolutisms."[187] Human rights in the international sphere are the products of deliberation behind a "veil of ignorance," Rawls' famous tool for neutralizing bias and interest. This deliberation is performed not by individuals, however, as when determining the basic principles of justice, but by peoples, which are the moral subjects of international law.[188] The veil deprives the peoples of knowledge about the size of their territory, their number of inhabitants, their strength and the like, information that may skew their judgment about the appropriate international order.[189]

Human rights are defined by being of international concern. One central indicator for this concern is the fact that these rights may justify an international intervention by other actors in the affairs of a state, in particular an outlaw state.[190] This approach to human rights thus is a functional account: The content of human rights is dependent on the function human rights serve, which is to determine the grounds for intervention. The list of rights derived from this starting point is considerably shorter than standard human rights catalogues – for example, it does not encompass a cornerstone of the international protection of human rights such as

[185] John Rawls, *The Law of Peoples* (Cambridge, MA: Harvard University Press, 1999), 59.
[186] Rawls, *Law of Peoples*, 63.
[187] Rawls, *Law of Peoples*, 63.
[188] Rawls, *Law of Peoples*, 23 ff.
[189] Rawls, *Law of Peoples*, 34 ff., 68 ff.
[190] Rawls, *Law of Peoples*, 81.

the equal protection of freedom of religion, among other liberties.[191] The reason is that "decent hierarchical peoples" do not accept such rights and cannot be coerced into doing so.[192]

4.5.2 *The Political Conception Reframed*

On this basis, Beitz outlines further arguments for a political conception of human rights, which in some important aspects breaks new ground and provides fresh insights into the problems of the nature and justification of human rights. This approach does not argue on the basis of some kind of abstract foundational normative principle: "We do better to approach human rights practically, not as the application of an independent philosophical idea to the international realm, but as a political doctrine construed to play a certain role in global political life."[193]

Consequently, this approach turns its attention to a political practice in which human rights count as reasons for a specific restricted set of actions – human rights are "transnational action-justifying norms."[194] The content of human rights, Beitz argues, is best derived by understanding the meaning of this practice. The task consists of determining the concept of human rights that best fits the nature of this practice. The approach "tries to grasp the concept of human rights by understanding the role this concept plays within the practice. Human rights claims are supposed to be reason-giving for various kinds of political action which are open to a range of agents. We understand the concept of a human right by asking for what kinds of actions, in which kinds of circumstances, human rights claims may be understood to give reasons."[195]

The international practice of human rights is only emergent.[196] Its outline needs to be derived from an informal construction of its content.[197] Thus, admittedly, the properties of the practice of human rights are in many ways amorphous, but they are still sufficiently established for this approach to succeed.[198]

[191] Rawls, *Law of Peoples*, 65, 78 ff.

[192] Rawls, *Law of Peoples*, 68: "The Law of Peoples does not say, for example that human beings are moral persons and have equal worth in the eyes of God; or that they have certain moral and intellectual powers that entitle them to these rights. To argue in these ways would involve religious or philosophical doctrines that many decent hierarchical peoples might reject as liberal or democratic, or as in some way distinctive of Western political tradition and prejudicial to other cultures."

[193] Beitz, *Idea of Human Rights*, 48, 68. Allen Buchanan, *The Heart of Human Rights* (Oxford: Oxford University Press, 2013), 3, also bases his account of human rights on the practice of international (legal) human rights.

[194] Beitz, *Idea of Human Rights*, 42.

[195] Beitz, *Idea of Human Rights*, 9.

[196] Beitz, *Idea of Human Rights*, 43.

[197] Beitz, *Idea of Human Rights*, 107.

[198] Beitz, *Idea of Human Rights*, 10.

The political conception of human rights allows their practice to be criticized from a normative point of view.[199] It argues, however, that one has "to distinguish between the problem of describing human rights [and] the problem of determining what they may justifiably require and identifying the reasons we might have for acting on them."[200] The approach intends as a crucial step to identify what agents commit themselves to if they participate in the practice of human rights.

The reasons for this approach are, first, that there undeniably is a substantial social practice connected with human rights.[201] Second, there is a "prima facie reason to regard the practice of human rights as valuable. On the face of it, its norms seek to protect important human interests against threats of state-sponsored neglect or oppression which we know from experience are real and can be devastating when realized."[202]

Human rights are distinguished from other norms by being of global concern: "The central idea of international human rights is that states are responsible for satisfying certain conditions in their treatment of their own people and that failures or prospective failures to do so may justify some form of remedial or preventive action by the world community or those acting as its agents."[203]

Importantly, human rights practice is not only a *legal* practice. On the contrary, it is argued, important dimensions of the international practice of human rights are political, not legal. Consequently, this account diverges from the legal paradigm.[204]

Beitz develops a two-level model[205] that underlines the priority of the (legal and political) protection of human rights by states.[206] The international protection of human rights adds a second level with its own particular features. Emphasizing that human rights are of international concern does not mean equating the practical expression of this concern with military intervention. On the contrary, military intervention represents an exceptional case of political action motivated by this international concern.[207] The international community has at its disposal a variety of other legal and political means that are far more important in practical terms to enforce (or try to enforce) human rights.[208]

The political approach not only provides a piece of descriptive human rights sociology, but also aims to identify criteria to justify or criticize certain human rights

199 Beitz, *Idea of Human Rights*, 10, 78.
200 Beitz, *Idea of Human Rights*, 11.
201 Beitz, *Idea of Human Rights*, 11.
202 Beitz, *Idea of Human Rights*, 11.
203 Beitz, *Idea of Human Rights*, 13, quoting United States Court of Appeals, Filártiga v. Peña-Irala, Judgement of June 30, 1980, 630 F.2d 876 (1980), 881: "[I]n this modern age a state's treatment of its own citizens is a matter of international concern."
204 Beitz, *Idea of Human Rights*, 40.
205 Beitz, *Idea of Human Rights*, 108, 114, 160.
206 Beitz, *Idea of Human Rights*, 31 f., 108 f., 119 f., 122.
207 Beitz, *Idea of Human Rights*, 116.
208 Beitz, *Idea of Human Rights*, 33 ff.: Mechanisms include accountability, inducement, assistance, domestic contestation and engagement, compulsion and external adaption.

contents.[209] It tries to contribute to answering all of the questions identified above.[210] Its basis is a kind of interest theory of the justification of human rights: Human rights claims are justified, it is argued, if there is a qualified interest, if the state has effective means at its disposal to foster this interest and if the failure of a state to protect the interest would be a legitimate object of international concern.[211]

Such a justificatory account of human rights claims includes empirical generalizations about causes for grievances and effective policy means and thus about social behavior and the working of social institutions.[212] Interestingly, "an empirical truth about human nature" also plays a central role: Following Rawls, Beitz argues that the ability of every human being to form a conception of the good constitutes such an empirical truth.[213]

According to Beitz, this kind of account shows that human rights are not the whole but only a part of social justice.[214] The practical conception of human rights has a justificatory function that makes it possible to critically assess human rights claims – for example, as to welfare rights,[215] rights to political participation[216] or women's rights.[217] This account is not called into question by the plurality of moral outlooks in different societies: The toleration of such divergent perspectives is (ultimately) conditional upon the respect for individual interests,[218] the most fundamental of which – like physical integrity – are by no means parochial Western concerns.[219]

[209] Beitz, *Idea of Human Rights*, 137.

[210] Beitz argues that the primary question is not why human rights are "sources for reasons for action for us," but how human rights "operate in the normative discourse of global political life," Beitz, *Idea of Human Rights*, 105. The emphasis on the critical function of human rights and the justificatory theory outlined illustrate the normative thrust of the argument.

[211] Beitz, *Idea of Human Rights*, 137: "We might therefore imagine a schema for justifying claims about the content of human rights doctrine with three parts. An argument for any such claim should make good three contentions.

1. That the interest that would be protected by the right is sufficiently important when reasonably regarded from the perspective of those protected that it would be reasonable to consider its protection to be a political priority.
2. That it would be advantageous to protect the underlying interest by means of legal or policy instruments available to the state.
3. That in the central range of cases in which a state might fail to provide the protection, the failure would be a suitable object of international concern."

[212] Beitz, *Idea of Human Rights*, 129: "Historically, the argument for a global practice with the functional features of human rights turns on an empirical thesis about the pathologies of a global political structure that concentrates power at dispersed locations not subject to higher-order control"; ibid. 139.

[213] Beitz, *Idea of Human Rights*, 146.

[214] Beitz, *Idea of Human Rights*, 142, 143.

[215] Beitz, *Idea of Human Rights*, 161 ff.

[216] Beitz, *Idea of Human Rights*, 174 ff.

[217] Beitz, *Idea of Human Rights*, 186 ff.

[218] Beitz, *Idea of Human Rights*, 144 ff.

[219] Beitz, *Idea of Human Rights*, 203.

4.5.3 *A Fresh Start?*

The political conception of human rights hopes to offer a "fresh start" for human rights theory that is better than other accounts. But does it succeed in its aim to make the normative meaning of current human rights practice fruitfully explicit?[220] And is this the key to the many riddles of human rights?

One problem that may be worth considering is the descriptive adequacy of the political conception's account of human rights practice. As indicated above, important rights guarantees are found in constitutions and other national legal instruments. In addition, regional, international or (in a technical sense) supranational layers of human rights guarantees are added to this primary element of human rights protection. Finally, there are universal international law systems of human rights protection. The international system of human rights is consciously designed to be complementary to the initial municipal level of their protection, which is of crucial importance in practical terms.

Consequently, it is important that – unlike in Rawls' own account – Beitz's conception highlights the primacy of the domestic protection of human rights.[221] Despite this, however, there is no substantial engagement with regional or national systems of the protection of human rights and with what they may teach us about the concept of human rights. Human rights are certainly of international concern, but not only that. Considerations of reasons for international agents to take action highlight only part of the practice of human rights and only part of their function in political orders, and in fact not the most important ones.[222]

This focus runs the risk of obscuring important differentiations. The domestic protection of human rights and the complementary regional and international systems (ideally) share a common goal but follow their own rules in certain respects. For instance, one crucial (practical) debate concerns the deference of the international interpretation of human rights to national human rights practice – the doctrine of a "margin of appreciation" of states in the ECHR system illustrates this question's content and key importance. Arguments are required to define the scope of such a "margin of appreciation" and – importantly – its limitations. This aspect of the practice of human rights may have important consequences for understanding

[220] Beitz refers to some of R. B. Brandom's thoughts on implicit normative commitments and the need to make them explicit, Beitz, *Idea of Human Rights*, 9 n. 14, as developed fully in Robert B. Brandom, *Making It Explicit* (Cambridge, MA: Harvard University Press, 1994).

[221] Beitz, *Idea of Human Rights*, 23, 31 f., 108 f., 119 f., 122, 143.

[222] Cf. for a related critique Griffin, *On Human Rights*, 24: The Rawlsian account of the function of human rights reduces them to establishing rules of war between nations and conditions for one nation being allowed to intervene in another. It overlooks the intranational role – for instance, to justify rebellion, to establish a case for peaceful reform, to curb an autocratic ruler or to criticize a majority's treatment of racial or ethnic minorities. Beitz rightly highlights the many forms of reactions to human rights violations, including on the domestic level, but he draws no clear conclusions from this observation for his general theoretical enterprise.

the idea of human rights – for example, as to its universality and the manner in which it relates to the many ways of interpreting the concrete meaning of human rights. This example shows that just looking at human rights in international law does not tell us enough about the true practice of human rights.

Another element of the practice of human rights – from an international perspective – is its robust inclusion of private individuals and legal persons as addressees of human rights, although this takes place to varying degrees and in controversial ways. It thus is important for conceptions of human rights to account for the idea of such horizontal effects.

The most important point, however, is the following. The practice of human rights is understood as the key to determining what kind of actions in which kind of circumstances are justifiably demanded by human rights claims. The practice appears to be a settled given. The first question one can ask is: Why should one take the practice *as it is* as a starting point? A practice may be flawed, being based on error and ideology, for instance. There needs to be a way of addressing the challenge that the current human rights practice may make no sense at all, that it may be ill-conceived from its very beginning. The argument thus starts from the assumption that a practice makes sufficient sense from a normative point of view. It is not naked facticity that is the reason for forming a conception of human rights on the basis of a certain practice, but rather the (assumed) legitimacy of this practice.

A second question relates to and confirms this point: What *kind* of practice is actually taken as relevant? The current practice of human rights has very many, often conflicting aspects – even more so if one seriously considers its past and keeps the distinction between morality and law in mind. Human rights often do play the role they are supposed to play as normative demands with which human beings try to do justice to their human dignity. However, they very often also are no more than ideological talk used for political purposes, not least to camouflage narrow interests. They can serve as pawns in geostrategic conflicts, as during the Cold War, when human rights were deployed as useful tools against authoritarian enemies but considered of little relevance if an equally authoritarian regime was seen as an ally.

Identifying what counts as a practice of human rights properly speaking thus already is a normatively loaded enterprise. This identification is not independent of a philosophical, theoretical normative standpoint – it implies it. More concretely, it hinges on some kind of assessment of the importance of the goods protected, of the proper politics of rights and (at least) of some normative principles. It is therefore crucial to spell out the theory of goods (as agency, need, interest and capability theories rightly do), the political assumptions and the normative principles involved, as these are the sources of the idea that the particular practice is in fact legitimate and worth considering, as we will see in more detail below.

Let us take the example of humanitarian interventions that seek to protect human rights. There are certainly some elements here of an emergent practice, though its status under international law is far from clear. Why should this practice be able to determine the content of the concept of human rights? Perhaps the practice is in fact nothing but disguised imperialism and thus leads to a less than convincing conception of human rights. The question of whether or not human rights are of sufficient weight to be of international concern and may even justify intervention requires some kind of standards for assessing their importance. It is unclear how the weight of human rights can be assessed without (among other things) a principled account of the importance of the protected goods for human beings and of the human goods that may be at stake as a consequence of such an intervention. The political conception of human rights offers no alternative to a theory of goods – on the contrary, it presupposes such a theory. The same is true for the political evaluation of rights and for the normative principles involved. Would a practice of human rights distorted to the detriment and disadvantage of less powerful countries, as some claim the practice of humanitarian intervention is, not be an illegitimate violation of normative principles – for example, of international justice and equal respect for human beings, irrespective of the country in which they live? It is worth remembering that for many years the practice of human rights relied on the exclusion of a vast number of human beings from the protection of human rights – the colonial exception clause of the ECHR has been mentioned various times in this respect. The political and normative presuppositions of arguments challenging such exclusionary practices thus need to be identified and spelled out.

All of this points to a central conclusion: *Only from a normative point of view* can a human rights theory achieve its twofold aim, namely to refute skeptics who think that the whole practice makes no sense and to calibrate the concrete content of human rights. It is not a given practice that is the key to the concept of human rights; rather, a justificatory theory of human rights is the key to identifying (and building) a legitimate practice of human rights.

That this is indeed the case seems to be confirmed by the fact that the political conception of human rights explicitly states that the practice it considers serves prima facie legitimate normative aims.[223] The reason for this can only be that the existing emergent practice gives due weight to the dignity, freedom and equality of human beings. Clearly, those elements of the international practice of human rights that are identified as the relevant parts of the overall social practice of human rights are chosen because they live up to the promise of protecting these core values. By contrast, the ideological use and the political abuse of human rights and the hypocrisy and window dressing practiced in their name are taken to be irrelevant for the central task of determining what the relevant practice really is because they violate the normative vision of human rights.

In addition, the political approach even outlines a theory of legitimacy, or, in more concrete terms, a modified interest theory of the justification of human

[223] Beitz, *Idea of Human Rights*, 11.

rights.[224] It underlines the critical power of the political conception of human rights,[225] which is, after all, not just a descriptive sociology of certain facts of international political life.[226] One example, and a telling one at that, is the Helsinki Process.[227] This process and the transformative influence it had (in the circumscribed way this can be said in complex historical cases) upon Europe came about because a certain conception of human rights was made politically relevant – a conception that is not just a rhetorical facade but takes individual liberty, in particular political liberty, seriously. This example shows that the practice of human rights is a contested territory, shaped and continuously reshaped by the struggle over the meaning of human rights and the normative principles that should guide their understanding. Human rights practice is not a simple given that can be relied on to build a theory of human rights.

The same conclusion can be drawn from the discussion of the limits to the acceptable differentiation of normative terms or the demands of international tolerance. The argument that the concerns of individuals are central and may trump those of communities rests on a normative thesis, namely the importance of individual autonomy, an idea that guides the entire theoretical enterprise.

The political conception of human rights therefore relies on an argument without a completely explicit premise: Its conception of human rights is not just derived from a given identified practice and its content determined on other than normative grounds. A prior normative stance is itself the foundation upon which the identification and evaluation of the practice as justified prima facie unfolds.[228] The possibility of determining the content of a legitimate set of human rights depends on this normative stance.[229] Everything thus hinges on this normative theory. The

[224] Beitz, *Idea of Human Rights*, 137 ff.

[225] Beitz, *Idea of Human Rights*, 105. He argues in the context of what he calls agreement theories, ibid. 78: "Human rights are supposed to be critical standards: they are supposed to provide a basis for criticizing existing institutions and conventional beliefs and justifying efforts to change or revise them. Confining the content of human rights doctrine to norms that either are or could be agreed to among the world's moral cultures threatens to deprive human rights of their critical edge." One can ask why this is not also true for the identification of human rights with a particular practice if there are no normative reasons justifying this practice's normative authority.

[226] Beitz, *Idea of Human Rights*, 104.

[227] Beitz, *Idea of Human Rights*, 82.

[228] The theory of goods and the normative principles cannot be derived from some other higher-order practice, because this would beg the question of the legitimacy of this higher-order practice.

[229] The possibility of deducing substantial content from the functional role of human rights as outlined by a political conception of human rights is limited, cf. Griffin, *On Human Rights*, 144: "The serious weakness in Rawls' functional explanation of human rights is that it leaves the content of his shortened list – the content both of the list itself and of each individual right – unworkably obscure." Buchanan, *The Heart of Human Rights*, 12, 107 ff. argues that international human rights should not be identified with moral rights, but he argues at the same time for the need for a "genuinely moral justification" of these rights – which seems to confirm the importance of normative principles for a theory of human rights.

attempt to leave the problems of justificatory philosophical theories behind leads right back to the very theories that the political conception of human rights had hoped to transcend.

This notwithstanding, the political theory provides many insights. One key point for the current argument is the fact that it highlights the "beneficiary-centeredness" of some of the discourse on human rights: Such a perspective does not provide sufficient reasons to normatively account for the duties implied by human rights.[230] These theories focus on what is at stake for the rights-holder and go into far less detail on why the implied burden for the addressee (whoever that may be) is supposed to be justified. This burden can be substantial. The social price paid for the protection of human rights often is considerable; society may even incur great risks in their protection. Liberal rights entail the possibility of abusing of these liberties, with potentially severe consequences: "So there is the further question why an agent who is in a position to respect and protect the right should do so?"[231] This is the case for all levels of human rights protection. Why should human beings accept the rights of strangers who happen to share the same citizenship but perhaps nothing else? Why should they feel obliged towards people in faraway countries? Why does the suffering and well-being of individuals other than oneself matter in a particular manner that gives rise not only to pity or compassion, but also to rights and the duties they imply?

The reasons discussed for imposing such burdens are not entirely satisfactory, not least because attention is focused upon the international protection of human rights.[232] However, the formulation of the problem underlines a key finding of our discussion of justificatory theories of human rights so far: The burdens imposed by rights and the normative position the addressees of these rights find themselves in point to the relevance of normative principles. What else could be a promising candidate as the source of these sometimes-exacting duties?

4.6 HUMAN RIGHTS AND THE ART OF LIVING WELL

A theory pioneered by Ronald Dworkin understands rights as trumps in structural terms, analyzing them in terms of rules and principles (as discussed in Chapter 1 on the concept of rights). Substantially, Dworkin argues, human rights are a central pillar of lives lived well so that they become "tiny diamonds in the cosmic sands."[233]

[230] Beitz, *Idea of Human Rights*, 65.

[231] Beitz, *Idea of Human Rights*, 70.

[232] These reasons include the ability of a political agent to act significantly, the permissibility of the action, the nature and importance of the threat, the burdensomeness of the actions, the harm implied and the nature of the historical relationship, Beitz, *Idea of Human Rights*, 137, 140. If one includes the national, supranational and regional protection and natural and legal persons as potential (direct or indirect) addressees, additional questions about the legitimacy of such burdens arise.

[233] Dworkin, *Justice for Hedgehogs*, 423.

The foundational principle of human rights is human dignity. This obviously tallies with explicit statements of modern human rights law, though this is only a subchapter of his thought. For Dworkin, dignity in concrete terms means self-respect and authenticity.[234] From this, explicitly following Kantian lines, he derives the guiding principle for ethics, political philosophy and (as part of the latter) law: "Kant's principle," as he calls it, holds "that a proper form of self-respect – the self-respect demanded by that first principle of dignity – entails a parallel respect for the lives of all human beings. If you are to respect yourself, you must treat their lives, too, as having an objective importance."[235] One only respects oneself if one respects the humanity of all. The moral standard derived from dignity therefore is equal concern for all and respect for personal responsibility – a standard that, unlike the concrete shape it takes in different systems of positive law, is universal.[236] The canonical human rights can be derived from this principle. In light of this standard, norms that prohibit acts exhibiting a belief in the superiority of certain groups, the protection of basic liberties and the impermissibility of torture and punishing people for the benefit of others rightly are regarded as human rights.[237] The exact details form the object of debate – for example, about the meaning of controversial concepts like dignity that are neither criterial (i.e. for which no set criteria of use applies) nor natural kind concepts but interpretative; that is, in need of interpretation to determine their content.[238]

Like the other theories discussed, this argument strikes an important note by emphasizing the connection between dignity and rights. In central aspects, it is an objective reason argument of the kind already encountered and therefore poses a related question: Why is dignity a source of the special normative status of having *rights*? Why does it create duties? Is dignity the only foundational principle in this respect, or are other normative standards important, too? Framing the theory in the terms of a eudemonistic concept of a life lived well does not solve this problem. Living well does not just mean to feel pleasure but to live according to a normatively loaded vision of life – which leads back to the content and justification of the normative principles defining this vision of life. The problems that seem to haunt the theory of human rights raise their heads once again.

[234] Dworkin, *Justice for Hedgehogs*, 203 f.: "The first principle is a principle of self-respect. Each person must take his own life seriously: he must accept that it is a matter of importance that his life be a successful performance rather than a wasted opportunity. The second is a principle of authenticity. Each person has a special, personal responsibility for identifying what counts as a success in his own life; he has a personal responsibility to create that life through a coherent narrative or style that he himself endorses. Together the two principles offer a conception of human dignity: dignity requires self-respect and authenticity."

[235] Dworkin, *Justice for Hedgehogs*, 255.

[236] Dworkin, *Justice for Hedgehogs*, 338.

[237] Dworkin, *Justice for Hedgehogs*, 336 ff.

[238] Dworkin, *Justice for Hedgehogs*, 157 ff.

4.7 SUMMARY: AFFIRMATIVE THEORIES OF HUMAN RIGHTS

This discussion of some exemplary justificatory theories has not provided a full map of the theoretical landscape but has allowed for some constructive insights important for our inquiry. The discussion of social functionalist theories of human rights underlined that human rights prioritize the goods of individuals, not the functional imperatives of societies. Contrariwise, these functional imperatives themselves are dependent on the normative yardsticks of social organization, including human rights. The classic economic analysis of law faces a related problem: Rights are limiting conditions for any efficiency regime and therefore presuppose a justification independent of the efficient allocation of resources in society. Behavioral economics provides important insights into the psychology of decision-making to which we will return. The idea of bounded rationality, however, demands an answer to the question of what fully rational decision-making would mean and which normative principle should guide its exercise.

Rule-utilitarian defenses of human rights face at least two problems: First, it is not socially aggregated goods that are relevant for normative theory but individuals, who thus cannot be ignored when building a normative theory. Second, the power and many beneficial consequences of utilitarianism derive from its respect for the equality of human beings. This normative principle of equality is not itself derived from the principle of utility, however, but is its foundation.

Discourse theory relies on normatively loaded presuppositions that are the precondition, not the product of moral deliberation. Contractualism points to its own normative foundations that transcend a contractual compact. Theories discussing agency, needs, interests or capabilities as the foundation of human rights have illustrated the importance of the following point: It is a category error to draw normative conclusions such as the existence of rights from the importance of a human concern. Normative principles need to explicate why such concerns of individuals become the object of rights and the normative burdens of duties of the addressees. Moreover, they provide important insights for a plausible theory of human goods relevant to the theory of human rights.

The political conception of human rights reminds us of the weight of human rights: They are not just parochial concerns but central commitments of the entire human community. The political theory thus renders human rights theory a very important service: It reminds us of the stakes of justification. The practice of human rights is not a simple given but contested territory that takes its shape according to the normative theory of the human rights defended. Accordingly, it cannot become the ultimate foundation of the idea of human rights.

The derivation of human rights from a conception of a life lived well that is centered on human dignity, understood as authenticity and autonomy, underlines the importance of dignity for the theory of human rights, as the pluralist interest theory and the capability approach do as well. Among other questions, this derivation raises the issue of how to bridge the gap in the argument between the perceived worth of one's own life and ensuing rights and duties of oneself and others. A normatively loaded vision of a life lived well does not offer an escape route from these questions.

These findings only scratch the surface of the sophisticated thoughts underlying these approaches. Much can be learned from these theories, and no one working in this field should feel confident to be able to produce anything remotely as thoughtful. This notwithstanding, none of these theories seem to answer the question of the justification of rights in an entirely satisfactory manner. Therefore, it may be useful to take a step back and once again consider how we can make some progress in this respect. This review seems to suggest that the problems initially identified are of real relevance. So far, there appears to be no way around a theory of human goods, a political theory of human rights and a theory of their normative foundations. Let us explore, then, how far we can travel along this path.

5

A Castle of Sand?

Man darf nicht vergessen, daß am Anfang dieses Krieges, der nicht 1939, sondern 1933 begann, die Abschaffung der Menschenrechte stand. "Die Menschenrechte sind abgeschafft", verkündete damals Dr. Goebbels im Berliner Sportpalast, und zehntausend blöde arme Teufel brüllten ihren kläglich-widersinnigen Beifall. Es war eine geschichtliche Proklamation, die prinzipielle Grundlage für alles, was Nazi-Deutschland heute den Völkern, einschließlich des eignen Volkes, zufügt ....[1]

Thomas Mann, *BBC radio address*, January 1942

Ob die anderen Völker in Wohlstand leben oder ob sie verrecken vor Hunger, das interessiert mich nur soweit, als wir sie als Sklaven für unsere Kultur brauchen, anders interessiert mich das nicht. Ob bei dem Bau eines Panzergrabens 10.000 russische Weiber an Entkräftung umfallen oder nicht, interessiert mich nur insoweit, als der Panzergraben für Deutschland fertig wird. ... Das ist das, was ich dieser SS einimpfen möchte und – wie ich glaube – eingeimpft habe, als eines der heiligsten Gesetze der Zukunft: Unsere Sorge, unsere Pflicht, ist unser Volk und unser Blut; Dafür haben wir zu sorgen und zu denken, zu arbeiten und zu kämpfen, und für nichts anderes. Alles andere kann uns gleichgültig sein.[2]

Heinrich Himmler, *Posener Rede*, 4 October 1943

[1] "One must not forget that the abolishment of human rights marked the beginning of the war, which started not 1939 but 1933. 'Human rights are abolished,' proclaimed Dr. Goebbels in the Berlin Sportpalast, and ten thousand poor stupid devils roared their deplorably absurd approval. It was a historical proclamation, the fundamental basis for all that Nazi Germany is now doing to the peoples, including its own people" (translation M. Hiley).

[2] "Whether the other *Völker* are prosperous or starving to death only interests me to the extent that we require them as slaves for our culture, it does not interest me in any other way. Whether 10,000 Russian women keel over from exhaustion or not when building an antitank ditch interests me only insofar as the antitank ditch is completed for Germany. ... This is what I want to inculcate and – I believe – have inculcated in this SS, as one of the most sacred laws of the future: our concern, our duty is our *Volk* and our blood. That is what we must care, think, work, and fight for, and nothing else. Nothing else need matter to us" (translation M. Hiley).

By every civilized and peaceful method we must strive for the rights which the world accords to men ….

W. E. B. Du Bois, *The Soul of Black Folk*

5.1 THE SOURCES OF HUMAN GOODS

5.1.1 *No Foothold for Rights?*

Our discussion of affirmative theories of human rights has clarified many of the aspects that a theory of the justification of human rights needs to address. Our review has shown that, in one way or another, the theory of human rights needs to determine the sources of the goods to be protected by human rights, outline the political theory of human rights and identify the normative principles that generate human rights. Our initial assessment to this effect in the last chapter proved to be correct. Accordingly, we will address these topics – goods protected, political theory, normative principles – each in turn. The question to be dealt with first is: Which goods are justifiably protected by the normative instrument of human rights?

The goods that rights protect are defined by the material scope of rights. This seems clear enough at first view: The right to free speech protects the freedom to express oneself as one pleases, freedom of religion the ability to pursue one's own spiritual path in both thought and deed. However, it is important to note that such abstract definitions of the scope of rights leave many questions unanswered. The practice of fundamental rights law illustrates this vividly: The prima facie scope of these rights already is often unclear, failing to determine, for example, whether hate speech is part of the content protected by free speech rights or not. The different legal traditions are divided regarding this issue, as the different approaches in Europe and the USA show. In addition, the meaning of rights and thus the definition of the goods protected are not set in stone; they are shaped and refined daily in the sphere of law by the work of thousands of lawyers, by court decisions, by legislative acts and by public deliberation about new normative challenges.

In this context, it should be noted that if we seek to understand the full meaning of a right in a given legal framework, it is not enough just to look at the scope of this right as guaranteed in the respective catalogue of rights. The *system of limitations* is important as well. For instance, in German constitutional law there is no right derived from freedom of faith (which is a human right in the technical sense) not to be exposed to religious symbols of others – an important matter where the constitutionality of wearing, for example, a hijab as a teacher in state schools is concerned.[3] Only in this concrete sense is freedom of religion protected all things considered.

[3] Cf. BVerfG, Judgement of January 27, 2015, BVerfGE 138, 296.

To take another example illustrating why limitations matter greatly for the scope of rights: In some systems, there is a residual right protecting any kind of exercise of human freedom, which in German constitutional law includes riding one's horse in a forest, to use this famous case from German law.[4] However, this does not mean that any kind of use of freedom is protected – quite to the contrary, as interferences with this right are easily justified by reasonable considerations of common goods or rights of others. Riding on prohibited paths is not a trump of German equestrians.

Including a right in a human rights catalogue thus is just one step along the road determining this right's scope of protection in concrete cases. A further crucial step is the system of limitations. In order to determine the proper content of such a system of limitations, it is necessary to consider the weight of other rights and other concerns. These considerations themselves need to be informed by criteria determining the importance of the rights and common concerns at issue for human life and society. The theory of goods is therefore relevant when determining the proper limitations of human rights, too.

The same kind of issues can arise in moral reflection if we turn our attention to concrete questions of human rights protection.

Leaving these necessary qualifications aside for a moment, it is easy to identify some core elements of what human rights protect. In particular, we said, these include the inalienable worth of human beings (called their dignity), their physical and mental integrity, a set of specific liberties, equal treatment and – controversially – the means for their physical subsistence and, more ambitiously, the material preconditions for a dignified life secured by social rights.

Is this a good start to a list of goods worthy of protection for *all* human beings, irrespective of gender, cultural and social background, skin color and ethnic origin, age, religion or belief, sexual orientation or any other of the myriad differences between human beings? Is it a useful first step towards a more detailed account of what is justifiably protected by human rights? How can we cross the apparent gap between these abstract goods and the concrete questions to be answered in law and applied ethics? What are the deeper reasons for including these goods in the human rights catalogues of greatest practical relevance (with the exception of social rights, which are more selectively found in positive law)? How culturally and historically relative are these concerns? How malleable are human beings in this respect? Can the reasons for including certain goods in human rights catalogues help to solve the problems posed by recent approaches seeking to expand the reach of human rights? What about privacy in the digital age, for instance? To take a concrete example: The right to be forgotten – does this make sense?[5]

[4] Cf. BVerfG, Judgement of June 6, 1989, BVerfGE 80, 137.

[5] Cf. CJEU, Google Spain SL, Google Inc. v Agencia Española de Protección de Datos, Judgement of May 13, 2014, C-131/12, and from national constitutional law BVerfGE, Judgement of November 6, 2019, BVerfGE 152, 152 ff.

One promising way to determine how a human good becomes a suitable object of protection by human rights is to look first at clear cases. Why is there little controversy about certain liberties – for instance, as suitable objects of protection? One interesting fact about the drafting of the *Universal Declaration* is that a whole range of rights were pretty much beyond doubt. The ultimate abstentions did not stem from opposition to the whole rights catalogue. They were motivated instead by the nonacceptance of certain rights, not least freedom of religion, not of human rights as such.

The freedom of the person from unjustified detention, for example, is a classical human right – in the words of Art. 9 *Universal Declaration*, the right not to "be subjected to arbitrary arrest, detention or exile." This right is an archetypal element of the development of rights and its foundational documents such as the *Magna Carta*. The human good protected is personal liberty, the freedom not to have to stay in a certain confined place due to incarceration or being banned from a certain territory if there is no sufficient reason for this. In addition, this right protects related goods of which an agent is deprived if in custody or exile. It protects a central precondition of the many uses of liberty and the free development of the individual. The question to be answered in more concrete terms is, then: How are we to justify the selection of certain goods as suitable for protection by human rights without succumbing to cultural bias and parochial perspectives?

The central rationale of human rights is to protect those goods that are of particular, even existential importance for all human beings. This implies that a good such as not being subjected to arbitrary arrest does not protect mere personal preferences that vary from person to person. This is not a theoretically innocent move but is based on very substantial assumptions: Human rights presuppose that there are certain objects that are valuable to *all* human beings. Consequently, the goods that are candidates for protection by human rights somehow need to be plausibly related to what is intrinsically human and transcend merely adventitious needs dependent on individual idiosyncrasies. In this first sense, they are objective.[6] Such goods also are objective in the second sense that they are regarded as worthy of protection even if an individual disagrees: Freedom from arbitrary arrest is justifiably also protected for those who deny its value – for example, the advocates of an authoritarian police state. These assumptions only make sense if the further precondition that these goods must be of approximately equal value for all human beings is met: Freedom from arbitrary arrest must mean roughly the same for person *A* as for person *B*. Importantly, there is a diachronic element, too: Human rights attempt to capture more than the fads of a particular group at a certain transient moment in time. They aspire to be relevant for long stretches of time, if not in detail, then at least in their main normative tenets: Freedom from arbitrary arrest was of considerable worth in 1215 not only for the nobility, and it remains

[6] Griffin, *On Human Rights*, 88 f.: Needs must be characteristic of human life generally.

valuable today. This is also true for human rights' most fundamental principles: The guarantee of human dignity in human rights ethics and law has no expiration date. This stance clearly does not mean to imply that there is no cultural change.[7] The underlying assumption is rather that whatever change takes place unfolds legitimately only under the condition that the goods protected by human rights are preserved. Whatever the cultural evolution of certain groups or humanity in general brings, not being arbitrarily detained, for instance, will be a condition of its normative legitimacy.

In sum, the theory of human goods presupposes *idealization*, in the technical sense of abstraction from difference, not in the sense of making something better than it actually is, nor in the sense of denying difference and particularity. This move is necessary in many scientific fields – a predication about the functioning of human kidneys abstracts from the differences between individual human kidneys without denying that these differences exist. For the purpose at hand – say, some nephrological thesis – these differences are simply not relevant. For the purpose of human rights, the fact that freedom from arbitrary detention is of substantial value for both person X and person Y is relevant, not other facts that distinguish X and Y. There are various such goods. In real life, they are interrelated in many ways, and their enjoyment is full of trade-offs.[8]

Accordingly, it is not an accidental, historically contingent convergence of preferences of human beings at a particular time that is at issue, but the idea that there is something in the human condition that persists over time, something in the existential makeup or – to use the most traditional, albeit rather controversial term – the *nature* of human beings that makes these goods valuable to all of them.

This presupposition that certain goods are valuable to all human beings because of their particular *human condition, existential makeup* or *nature* points to a difficult step that a theory of the justification of human rights has to take: It appears that no theory of these human goods protected by human rights is possible without a *substantive anthropology*. Human rights protect the goods not of any being but of

[7] There is a discussion about Stone Age human rights. Is not a point of view that understands human rights as not entirely relative wedded to such an idea? The answer to this question can be derived from what has been said so far: Evidently, there was no explicit formulation of human rights in year 27,000 BCE. It is quite another matter whether there were not moral intuitions that formed part of the building blocks identified so far of the later human rights idea and its predecessors in the history of thought. Cultural and technological innovation forms a second layer of historical development. As already highlighted, you need a press to start thinking about a right to freedom of the press. Furthermore, there is nothing outlandish about something being justified when it has not been made explicit that it is justified. In 27,000 BCE, people presumably had no idea that the Earth was round. Nor did they presumably think that in a right-angled triangle the square of the hypotenuse is equal to the sum of the squares of the other two sides. This does not mean that it is not justified to hold that the Earth had this shape or that Pythagoras' theorem was correct at that time and that human beings, in principle, could know it.

[8] Cf. in a similar vein Tasioulas, "Foundations," 52.

human beings, irrespective of personal differences. Therefore, we need to determine what makes a human being *human*.

How can there be a justification of the importance of liberty and self-determination for human rights, for instance, without the assumption that human beings are made in such a way that liberty and self-determination are of great worth to them, and that arbitrary detention, for instance, holds little attraction for them?

Is this kind of substantive anthropology possible at all, however? If not, the project of human rights rests on shaky foundations. Unfortunately for the case for human rights, very influential lines of thought cast doubt on precisely this possibility. Human beings' ability to leave the bounds of nature behind and to create a second world of culture is a central theme in the history of ideas, and rightly so. According to influential theories, some of which we already have recalled, this ability includes their own nature: Human nature is not stable and fixed but is constantly changed and recreated throughout history. As Marx formulated paradigmatically in his theses on Feuerbach, human nature is the ensemble of all social relations.[9] Nietzsche considered human beings to be "*nicht festgestellte Tiere*," animals without a fixed nature.[10] Formerly openly fascist anthropologists such as Gehlen, who remained influential after 1945, held that humans are deficient beings (*Mängelwesen*) that need to be formed by powerful institutions.[11] Rorty talked about humans as "protean beings."[12] At a certain stage in his thinking, Foucault held that humans' self-conceptions are nothing but faces drawn in the sand by social forces, sketches that will be obliterated by future social change.[13]

From this perspective, a supposedly fixed "human condition" is thus in fact dependent on the social and not least economic structures that create the characteristics of the humans of a given age in their own image, the capitalist society the *egoistic bourgeois*, the panoptical society of domination the socially adapted *subject of modern society*, a subject that has internalized the epistemic structures of its own subjugation or in colonialism the ideologies of the *colon*.

Some of these theories have contributed greatly to our understanding of the historical and social contingency of elements of human lifeworlds that are indeed far from natural. Whatever one may think of the capitalist economy – or, more precisely, of its many very different conceptions from Manchester capitalism to the social market economy – it is certainly the product of history and political choices. The ways of living developed within this framework, be they a life guided by

9 Karl Marx, "Thesen über Feuerbach," in *Marx-Engels-Werke*, Vol. 3 (Berlin: Dietz Verlag, 1975), 6th thesis.

10 Friedrich Nietzsche, *Jenseits von Gut und Böse*, aphorism 62.

11 Arnold Gehlen, *Der Mensch, seine Natur und seine Stellung in der Welt* (Berlin: Junker und Dünnhaupt, 1940), 59, 64, 453 ff, 709 ff. Gehlen deleted the explicit reference to Nazi ideology in later editions of the book.

12 Rorty, "Human Rights," 115.

13 Foucault, *Les mots et les choses*, 398.

something like the "spirit of capitalism" described by Weber or forms of consumerism, are equally contingent. The critique of racism has been fostered considerably by the denial of any racial differences in human nature. The critique of the false naturalization of historically contingent forms of life is thus hugely important.

It is quite another matter, however, to assume that there is no such thing as an identifiable existential makeup of human beings – a human nature, if you will. It is important to note that doubts about a shared set of human characteristics concern not the physical makeup or even all mental properties but only particular psychological properties of human beings and the consequences of these properties in human thought, emotion and action. Nobody holds that the intricate functions of the human body – say, upright posture – are the product of the ensemble of human social relations. Upright posture (a cognitively demanding faculty) is not interpreted as a product of capitalism, for example. Nor does anyone hold that the specific makeup of visual cognition – say, the ability to interpret certain visual experiences as permanent solid bodies located in three-dimensional space – is historically contingent. The fact that there is a human nature in these physical and cognitive areas is thus uncontroversial. The question is, rather, whether and in which sense this human nature extends to such sublime desires as the longing for freedom and respect.

No demonstrably true insights exist in this area. The question of what human beings are ultimately like is too complex for this. The best one can do is review the plausibility of the arguments that speak for and against the assumptions implied by human rights about certain shared human properties, such as the desire for self-determination, and their importance for the design of rights.

Before one can even start to consider this line of thought, one has to take seriously the possibility that something like a human nature extending to the cognitive domain actually exists. As we just have seen, there are many areas of cognition where this kind of human nature is not seriously doubted, such as visual cognition. Some discussions of human nature appear to overlook this. In addition, it is a standard thesis of hardheaded, empirical, evidence-based paleoanthropology that a specific cognitive endowment of human beings exists – as in any other hominid species. This does not imply that anything of relevance to the search for the foundations of human rights forms part of this endowment. It simply means that human beings are not blank slates. These findings will be discussed in Part III of this study.

Even if these theories are not sufficient to make the case for the substantive anthropology underlying the human rights project, they do show that there is nothing *a priori* wrong about such a theory. It is simply a matter of the evidence that can be adduced for certain assumptions (e.g. that human beings are made up in such a way that self-determination is of value to them) in contrast to other assumptions (e.g. that authoritarian orders suit human beings' depraved nature best).

Evidence *against* the idea of a natural human inclination to liberty can be seen in the many authoritarian systems that persisted over long periods of time. Orders of freedom are the historical exception, not the rule. Influential voices have consequently concluded that human beings are actually not made for freedom at all – that, quite to the contrary, being ruled by superiors fulfills their deepest needs.[14] Accordingly, such ideas infuse the ideologies of very many repressive orders of past and present, from the Christian Inquisition to communist party oligarchies and other forms of dictatorship, or, another option, they are used to support the thesis that subjection means profound suffering for the subjected today but did not in the past because those past cultures were different.

There are some strong arguments that cast such conclusions into doubt, however. The history of human rights already lends less support to them than some thinkers tend to assume. As our historical review showed, the perception of what rights human beings enjoy and who is actually entitled to these rights has developed and changed significantly. The repeatedly discussed problem of the slow and gradual inclusion of all human beings in the personal scope of rights is a vivid example. But there is an interesting strand of continuity as well, in particular as to life, physical integrity, vulnerability to degradation, liberty and equality. As far as the kind of rights and their material scope are concerned, the formulation of some core rights has remained remarkably constant over long stretches of time, in spite of the major social transformations taking place. The *Virginia Bill of Rights* basically speaks a normative language that as far as core rights are concerned is clearly related to the language of the *European Charter of Fundamental Rights*, a recent example of a full human rights catalogue. Why the *Magna Carta* secured certain rights for the freemen of England is no riddle, nor are the concerns of the *Edict of Milan*. As our little journey deeper into history and farther afield, including indigenous peoples, showed, it is not at all clear that the concerns embodied in these documents do not resonate with the feelings and ideas of human beings of other times and places, too, although these people were in no way close to expressing them in the form of explicit human rights as we know them. After all, what, for instance, Yahling Dahbo experienced when the slaveholder came to her at night does not seem wholly mysterious.

A range of reasons speak for the protection of freedom. The theory of liberal rights importantly underlines the instrumental value of freedom. Freedom of expression is regarded as the catalyst of truth and better political decisions, for instance. The free exchange of ideas helps to identify better arguments and preferable political action. Human rights have more than just this instrumental value, however. Liberty is of intrinsic value as well. Human rights norms and institutions go to great lengths to secure the enjoyment of liberty. This only makes sense under the assumption that liberty holds particular importance as a political good.

One striking feature of human history that lends support to this assumption is the persistent struggle for self-determination. It is simply not true that history shows that

[14] For a version of this thought, cf. Nietzsche, *Jenseits von Gut und Böse*, aphorisms 188, 199 on the need of humans for obedience.

human beings have no deep desire for freedom. On the contrary, the longing for freedom has been one of history's crucial moving forces. Unsurprisingly, in our historical review we encountered many examples taken from theory, political life and art that reflected this longing, from the mourning of the women of Troy forced into slavery and sexual exploitation to the fight of the "freedom-loving" Herero, to quote the term used by the German general staff. Where are the credible counter-examples showing with equal force that human beings prefer to be enslaved, raped or subdued?

To be sure, as Wilhelm von Humboldt observed, after a long tradition of subjugation human beings sometimes first have to learn to feel their chains before they can try to shake them off.[15] "Habits of submission make men as well as women servile-minded. ... Custom hardens human beings to any kind of degradation, by deadening the part of their nature which would resist it," commented Harriet Taylor Mill, discussing the argument that women were, in fact, not seeking for liberty.[16] But once such obstacles have been overcome, the promise of freedom has proven to be quite irresistible. The liberation of women in the last centuries, as far as it has been achieved, and the fight to abolish slavery bear witness to this, as do the many other attempts of human beings throughout history to gain that freedom. How different are future human beings imagined to be? Can any argument be discerned to suggest that, given some future historical development, the subjugation of women and their sexual exploitation or enslavement will with good reason come to be regarded as properly mirroring the human condition of women and those groups of people selected for slavery? Are such thoughts not rather revenants of the totalitarian dream that it is possible to create natural slaves through indoctrination and force, a dream whose consequences it hopefully is needless to recall?

Nor should these huge social struggles lead one to forget the importance of freedom and self-determination in the personal sphere. Not many people enjoy being deprived of making their own choices in their private lives. Children already fight to assert their own will (any parent having faced the task of dressing children for bad weather knows the intensity of this struggle, seeing that denim jackets are so much cooler than raincoats).

All in all, such observations seem to lend substantial support to the idea that the "freedom-loving" Herero were perhaps more representative of the deep desires of other human beings than is sometimes assumed.

When human rights imply that freedom is an important good for human beings, they consequently draw on anthropological assumptions that are more plausible than the competing thesis that human beings are made up in such a way that

[15] Wilhelm von Humbodt, "Ideen zu einem Versuch, die Gränzen der Wirksamkeit des Staates zu bestimmen," in *Wilhelm von Humboldt, Werke, Vol. I: Schriften zur Anthropologie und Geschichte*, eds. Andreas Filtner and Klaus Giel (Darmstadt: Wissenschaftliche Buchgesellschaft, 2002), 218.

[16] Taylor Mill, "Enfranchisement of Women," 70.

self-determination has no meaning for them. Nevertheless, this is not a self-evident truth, as repeatedly underlined. Human beings could be very different. There are many organisms with a different makeup for which certain things are not valuable. For ants, for example, the problem of self-determination does not arise, admirable creatures though they are. For human beings, however, this problem does arise. Bees do not have a problem with monarchies, human beings do. Human rights thus necessarily imply *a substantive empirical falsifiable assumption about the kind of creature human beings are*. They posit a certain degree of sameness in the makeup of human beings as well. Human beings undoubtedly put the freedom to determine themselves to use in an infinite variety of ways. As far as the value of the ability for self-determination is concerned, however, human beings are made of roughly the same stuff. Underlining this is particularly important given the long history of anthropologies of inequality – for example, of racist or misogynist ilk.

A further task of our inquiry into the sources of human goods is to determine the grounds for the necessary selectivity of the goods protected. Formulating assumptions such as the importance of self-determination about human beings' ways of life does not, after all, entail any denial of their many other sides. There is a very plausible case that part of what makes up human beings is their inclination to greed, to aggression, to cruelty, to enjoy and strive for domination. A theory of human goods must therefore evaluate those objects for which human beings strive in order to determine those that justifiably deserve protection. What are the criteria that determine selection among such different inclinations? Are some elements of human nature supposedly more "natural" than others? How could this be?

These questions need an answer, and not only for inclinations such as aggression and the like. It may be granted, for instance, that freedom is a basic human good because of human beings' particular makeup. But why is it legitimate to satisfy this particular desire? Why is it not advisable to extirpate this longing for freedom as hubris and wicked lust? These questions relate to problems that have been discussed ever since antiquity. Is something valuable because it is desired, or is it desired because it is valuable?[17] If the former – why not satisfy the desire for domination? If the latter, we next face the issue: What are the criteria determining whether something is valuable (apart from being desired), and where do they stem from? What does this mean for the place that various desires have in a theory of human goods – from innocent pastimes like the urge to count the blades of grass in different lawns[18] or to make the collection of matchbox pictures the center of one's life[19] to

[17] Plato, Republic, 505c; Aristotle, "Metaphysics," in Aristotle, *Metaphysics, X–XIV, Oeconomica, Magna Moralia*, ed. George Patrick Goold, Loeb Classical Library 287 (Cambridge, MA: Harvard University Press, 1990), 1072a 29.

[18] Cf. Rawls, *Theory of Justice*, 432, introduced in the context of the "Aristotelian principle" that human beings desire things for their own sake; Griffin, *On Human Rights*, 112, proposing a life-enhancing function as a criterion for evaluation.

[19] Dworkin, *Justice for Hedgehogs*, 257.

sadism? In addition, one needs to clarify what value judgments are in the first place. Are they expressions of subjective desires (which would take us back to square one) or acts of cognition? If acts of cognition – cognition of what?

Two kinds of criteria are relevant for selecting some of the things human beings strive for as human goods plausibly protected by rights.[20] First are *normative standards*, the third issue of a human rights theory identified above, to which we will turn in Section 5.6. The fact that such principles exist and censor some human desires seems obvious: The desire to inflict cruelty on others, for instance, cannot be protected because it unjustifiably harms others. Moral judgments of this kind are clearly more than the expressions of idiosyncratic tastes and desires as they are able to censor and direct choices about the pursuit of such tastes and desires. As there ultimately is no convincing reason to assume that they refer to some objective, mind-independent order of value either, they seem to be of a third, *sui generis* kind. Part III of this study will investigate why that is so and what this could plausibly mean.

Second, there is the old question of *eudaimonia* or what makes a life worth living. Arguments worthy of serious consideration suggest that the life of powerful dictators, despite applauding acolytes, bowing satraps and free rein for their desires and wishes, is less attractive than it might seem. The apparent normative constraints on the permissible fulfillment of desires may thus turn out to be one of the things that actually constitutes quality of life because of the importance of moral integrity, and this has to be factored into a convincing theory of human goods. After all, the goods ultimately protected by human rights are not just individual freedom, for example, but a *just* system of freedom for all.

Moreover, it is useful to look at goods in themselves, such as freedom, for instance, in comparison to the lures of submission, under the condition that no needs or interests of others are diminished. One reason to prefer freedom even from a purely individual standpoint is its sheer attractiveness as a way of life. Preferring subjugation to liberty is like preferring a damp, dark, soiled dungeon to a clear, crisp day with bright sunlight and fresh air. A second reason is liberty's intrinsic value as something that can be reconciled with the dignity of autonomous human beings, something that the fascination with self-subjugation or even self-annihilation is not, even though the strange force of the latter was able to captivate the destructive mass movements of the twentieth century.

[20] A theory of rational desires, that is, of desires upheld after reflection, as in Richard Brandt, *A Theory of the Good and the Right* (Oxford: Clarendon Press, 1979), 10, is not sufficient to answer this question, as the example of the persistent sadist shows. As Griffin, *On Human Rights*, 112 ff. rightly argues: The standard must get stronger, reach a level of appropriateness, of getting something right, ibid. He argues, with reference to Wittgenstein and Davidson, that the form of life constituted by language provides guidance: "Certain values are part of the necessary conditions for our language, which sets for us the bounds of intelligibility," ibid. 113. Part III of this study will investigate what other kinds of parameters of thought might exist.

Such judgments about the eudemonistic value of certain actions and ways of life are more than mere expressions of personal tastes and desires. They ascribe value to certain forms of life and form critical yardsticks by attempting to capture something relevant to any human pursuit of happiness.[21] Neither in their case nor in the case of moral judgments is there any good reason to assume that they refer to some objective, mind-independent order of value.[22] This does not mean that they cannot be debated. Aesthetic judgments plausibly do not refer to an objective order of beauty either. This does not mean, however, that Caravaggio's *Adoration of the Shepherds* of 1609 cannot be argued to be aesthetically superior to the drawing of an elephant produced by a struggling theoretician of human rights to the amusement of his daughter, who at the age of five was already more artistically able than he.

Critical reflection thus does not lack guidance when weighing the respective merits of gratifying some rather than others of the many passions and desires springing in the labyrinthine depths of the human self.

5.1.2 *The Anthropology of Human Rights and the Thresholds of Inclusion*

Human rights ultimately are not about abstract notions such as freedom, but about concrete liberties. Including freedom of speech or religion in a catalogue of human rights means that one assumes that these particular liberties are of key importance for human life. This is not an *a priori* truth but requires arguments in its support. The long and painful history of the attempts to secure human rights manifests this clearly. After all, great minds argued powerfully against these very rights – Augustine, for instance, against freedom of faith, following his change of opinion in this respect. But such reasons do exist – for example, that the possibility to express oneself or to hold and live by certain religious beliefs is important for human beings to flourish. The rich theory and doctrine on such rights spell these arguments out, and often compellingly so.

[21] This conclusion is drawn by various theories of human rights, without, however, always distinguishing between normative and other eudemonistic reasons, cf. Griffin, *On Human Rights*, 115: "To see anything as making life better, we must see it as an instance of something generally intelligible as valuable and, furthermore, as valuable for any normal human being. Deliberation about human interests ends up, I think, with a list of values. I am less concerned with precisely what is on the list than I am with the conclusion that deliberation ends with a general profile of values, a chart of the various high points that human life can rise to."

[22] There are many approaches to this question, in an Aristotelian, Humean or Kantian mode, for instance. For a recent answer, a variant of a "perception model," see Griffin, *On Human Rights*, 119 f.: "So I think that we may conclude that judgements about human interests can be correct or incorrect. They report deliverances of a sensitivity to certain things going on in the world, namely, interests being met or not met. These interests are part of *human* nature, and not just human nature as seen by society. These judgements seem to be correct or incorrect, not, say, in the way that conclusions in mathematics can be, but rather true or false in the way that statements of natural fact can be" (emphasis in original).

The same seems to be true for other tenets of human rights, including the experience of the intrinsic value of life, the desire for respect as equals, the importance of equal treatment for human beings or – particularly controversially – the material preconditions of their lives such as food, water, shelter and so forth.

In light of the conclusion reached above that some kind of tentative substantive anthropology is possible, these goods protected by human rights are reasonably regarded as of equal objective value in the double sense outlined earlier: They are plausibly understood as goods of all human beings, independently of the opinion of possible dissenters. For the same reason, they are regarded not only as valuable, but as *equally* valuable for all human beings. There is nothing suspiciously paternalistic about this kind of claim to objectivity: Every moral principle and legal rule faces some kind of dissent – the prohibition of theft, for example, on a daily basis – without an overly paternalistic attitude of the community towards the autonomy of thieves casting the legitimacy of this norm into doubt. The legitimacy of norms would only be called into question if there were good reasons for this critique.

Moreover, identifying such goods is not an easy task if one is aware of the danger (already highlighted above) of parochial perspectives, of a repressive essentializing of human beings and of skewed, perhaps even racist or misogynist anthropological assumptions. In this regard, any thesis is fallible and in need of repeated critical scrutiny in which dissenters can make their case. This scrutiny is a crucial source of moral and legal progress. As human rights at their core are about respect for individuals, self-determination and freedom, not least of expression, their very point demands the freedom of every human being to engage in a better, more inclusive, less prejudiced understanding of what the proper goods of protection are. No one has an epistemic or political prerogative to authoritatively determine the content of the pivotal human goods worthy of protection by human rights, let alone any entitlement to imperialistically enforce certain visions. What counts are the reasons adduced, and there is nothing paternalistic about compelling reasons. In procedural terms, in the world of political decision-making and law-giving, this has to be spelled out in democratic, participatory and deliberative forms of determining the content of human rights – demands that the practice of human rights on a national, supranational and international level often fails to meet.

Theories of goods justifiably protected by human rights need to identify a threshold criterion to determine which of the human goods that constitute possible objects of protection are important enough to qualify as the possible content of human rights. This criterion needs not to be so narrow as to make human rights meaningless in too many areas of human life, nor so expansive as to cause an inflationary use of these rights.[23] There is no criterion that does not leave some kind of gray area in which debate is possible. Such a criterion implies the ascertainment

[23] Cf. Chapter 4. The question is how to determine this criterion. Cf. also Griffin, *On Human Rights*, 88 ff.: Human rights should not include anything needed to avoid ailment or

of the weight of such a good. This weight needs to be determined by considering the role this good plays in the context of a human life, embedded in certain cultural and social circumstances. This already underlines the importance of the second central tenet of the justification of human rights to be discussed: the political theory of human rights. Such judgments involve demanding considerations that evidently are highly controversial. Debating these questions is an important part of the slow development of human rights. However, neither the difficulty of such assessments nor the danger of very subjective approaches to these issues has prevented a consensus from developing about the significance of some rights. The fact that freedom of speech, belief and conscience are important liberties is hardly in doubt. The reason for this is that these liberties create the scope for human activities that both as history and as daily practices play a crucial role in a flourishing life.

The importance of such a threshold condition does not mean that human rights need to be limited to some kind of *minimalist conception* of their reach. Conceptions of human rights can be generous. They can (and should) protect the *maximum of a good* if this is compatible with the rights of others, as we already have seen. If the exercise of a freedom can be reconciled with binding normative principles, there is a prima facie right to the exercise of this freedom. After all, a foundational principle of an ethics of freedom is that whatever is not forbidden is allowed. This principle is even acknowledged as a principle of international law.[24] In this context, the distinction between the *type* of good protected and the different *tokens* of the good is important. Expressing one's opinion about the question of whether or not the goal scored by X was offside or not is not an existential concern (at least once one has had a chance to cool down following the end of the game). Nevertheless, this expression would be protected by many legal systems guaranteeing free speech, and rightly so. A government biased in favor of some soccer team (owned by the president, perhaps) would thus violate free speech if it prevented spectators from drawing the public's attention to unjustified goals.

This notwithstanding, a proper differentiation of the importance of various kinds of claims is required if we are not to call every morally defensible claim a human right. The *type* of good protected (freedom of expression) must be of qualified concern, though not every *token* of this good is of great importance (voicing opinions about offside goals).

Yet another element of the threshold criterion for human rights is relevant historical experience that human beings are in substantial danger of being deprived of these goods by others, not least political institutions such as states. Freedom of religion and freedom of speech are archetypal human rights because it happens to

malfunction. Otherwise, human rights would be in danger to become implausibly lavish. Avoiding harm is overly capacious, too.

[24] ICJ, The Case of the S. S. Lotus, Judgement of September 7, 1927, P.C.I.J. (ser. A) (No. 10 Sept. 7).

be the case that human beings have a strong inclination to impose what they believe on others and to silence their particular voices. The prohibition of slavery is a *ius cogens* norm of international human rights because human beings have found it surprisingly easy to think that others of their kind are made or justifiably used (unlike themselves) to serve.

5.1.3 *Needs, Interests and Capabilities*

This account of the sources of goods protected by human rights helps to clarify some of the problems we identified when discussing theories of needs, interests and capabilities.

As underlined in our discussion of need and interest theories, it is misleading to identify certain versions of such theories with all possible approaches that take needs and interests seriously. The above analysis has shown that human needs are important to specify the content of human rights. Bodily integrity is a human need. The protection of liberty in its various forms by human rights is based on the human need to have scope for actions that are determined by one's own decisions, thoughts, feelings and identity. Whether one prefers to call these sources of strong longings needs or interests is more a question of terminology than of substantive content. Specific rights can be derived from such needs. It may be odd to say that there is a *need* for freedom of the press. That depends, of course, on the understanding of needs in this context. In any case, there is certainly an *interest* in free journalism. It is hard to understand this interest if one does not assume that human beings have a strong desire – a need, if you will – to understand and determine themselves politically on the grounds of insights, and that this political self-understanding and self-determination constitute ends that freedom of the press intends to serve. The ultimate justification of needs and interests thus rests on assumptions of this kind about the particular human condition and the ensuing preconditions for a flourishing life.

The capability approach is very important for ensuring that rights do not remain abstract and do not shoot wide of human beings' real lives under concrete social circumstances. An abstract right to education means little if a society is structured in such a way that girls have no real opportunity to avail themselves of this right – for example, because they are taught to aspire to other ends than education, such as serving the male members of their family.[25]

The identification of the relevant capabilities presupposes that there are criteria for selecting the goods to be brought to life by the idea of capabilities. Such selection criteria ultimately must rely on some kind of substantial theory about the human condition and the deeper needs and interests derived from it.

25 Sen, *Idea of Justice*, 257.

5.1.4 *Contours of a Form of Life*

In a sense, therefore, epoch-making catalogues of human rights like the *Universal Declaration* embody a (defeasible) hypothesis about what constitutes central human goods derived from empirically grounded anthropological assumptions – a hypothesis that is not based on divine revelation, a metaphysical order of perfection, tradition or the teleology of history but on a sober, fallible assessment of basic human historical experience. This assessment is spelled out in the terms of concrete ethical and legal norms. In a full theory of human goods protected by human rights, one consequently needs to engage in detail with such provisions and what they protect exactly, given the system of limitations. Moreover, the next topic of this inquiry, a political theory of rights, has to be factored into such an account. That this is a demanding task is illustrated by the very substantial work carried out in philosophy and legal doctrine, not to forget case law, to determine the content and purpose of specific norms. One needs only to think about the vast amount of work on freedom of speech or freedom of religion and conscience to get a sense of this debate's level of sophistication.

The full theory that is slowly emerging through this work, detailing what the proper objects of protection by human rights may be, is not a simple technical matter. Quite the contrary. The goods that human rights protect are a mirror image of what makes human beings human. They are the reflection in the mirror of ethics and law of the contours of a form of life drawn by the fine pen of historical expressions of the species' most delicate characteristics, contours that define its particular *human* mode of being.

The image emerging, sometimes not clearly visible in the crude looking glass of ethical principles and legal rules, is of a being with subtle longings for respect, moral integrity and freedom, a being full of play that is creative and an inexhaustible wellspring of fresh thoughts and sentiments, seeking a deep understanding of its experience of itself and the world it inhabits, its efforts proving that it is capable of both far-reaching insight and profound error. The mirrored outlines hint at a being looking for meaning in its life, a meaning that is not easily ascertained in an ever-perplexing world, if it is discernible at all; a being looking for and unleashing beauty; a being that is communicative, needing and seeking intimate partnership and community; a being that cares for others, directed by moral principles of justice and other-regarding concern, with a vulnerable body and inner self and constantly forced to secure its precarious survival in a world not made for and unconcerned with its existence, bliss and suffering.

The need to protect every human being against their own kind (and sometimes the distress they bring about themselves) by the means of rights adds further important facets to this picture: This being is also violent, greedy and thirsty for power and domination, superficial and vulgar, selfish, callous and cruel, self-righteous and full of contempt for others. "Man delights not me," Prince Hamlet says, and in doing so has not only melancholic bile but some good arguments on his side.

The fact that human beings are so mixed in kind that the protection of human rights seems reasonable is a contingent fact of their existence. Human beings could be different. There is no hidden or open teleology at play. It is perfectly possible to imagine beings that, for instance, possess consciousness or other higher mental faculties, like human beings, but feel no desire to express their thoughts and feelings, as they are happy to converse with themselves. To protect the freedom of expression of such beings would make no particular sense. Alternatively, human beings could be infinitely malleable, as totalitarian systems imagine them to be. A life of serfdom would then be as appropriate for such a creature as a life with fundamental liberties – after a little bit of reeducation, perhaps, to overcome old habits. But there is no reason to think that human beings are like this, as we already have seen and will find confirmed by some of the findings to follow below.

This directs our attention to an insight of some importance, which we will flesh out in greater detail now: Human rights are bound to and dependent on the human mode of existence and the human lifeworld. *Human rights mark a space of decency defined by human critical thought committed to obligatory moral principles when reflecting on the nature of the human condition and what is valuable in a human life.* They are thus a fragile thing, transient, guaranteed by nothing but a delicate web of justificatory reasons and their precarious command over human thought and passions.

5.2 BETTER OFF WITHOUT RIGHTS?

5.2.1 *The Limited Reach of Rights*

The preceding remarks have provided an outline for the first existence condition of human rights: sufficiently weighty goods as objects of protection, though not every use of such rights needs to be of particularly qualified importance. Not all such sufficiently weighty goods worthy of protection are proper objects of human rights, however. One very evident further existence condition of human rights is that the respective good can in fact be secured by the means of rights. As already mentioned, the principle *ultra posse nemo obligatur* sets an obvious limit. A right to be loved consequently serves as a metaphor for an important human concern, not as the statement of an existing entitlement in the literal sense. This metaphor is not without import – it underlines the significance of being loved and, importantly, the fact that there is no one unworthy of this noblest of affections one can entertain towards another person.

There are other examples. There can be no human right to be happy, because it is beyond the capabilities of other persons and indeed agents themselves to make somebody (including themselves) happy. Happiness is too elusive a gift to become a claim on others; although, once again, metaphorically it makes perfect sense to speak of a human being's right to be happy – meaning, for instance, that happy their life should be. For related reasons, there is no right to sex either, to take an example from the current debate about incels, their misogynistic thoughts and violent acts.[26]

Problems like these can be resolved in a pretty straightforward way. More difficult is the question of whether human rights are the proper means for realizing certain human goods that at least in principle could be the objects of rights. This question arises because many influential voices in the fields of political and legal theory deny that human rights contribute to the realization of human goods, or they maintain that they even prevent the achievement of this end. These arguments are of evident moral and legal relevance. If the case has been made that human rights are useless or even harmful, there is no conceivable argument that still would speak for their justification in ethics and law. Tools to foster human goods that turn out to be useless or harmful are not normatively justified.

Any theory of human rights consequently includes a *theoretical stance on the historical, social and political conditions of the realization of human goods*. Freedom of speech guaranteed as a right, for instance, presupposes the idea that the free exchange of ideas and views does in fact enhance the flourishing of individuals and a community. Dictatorial authoritarianism, on the contrary, presupposes that only narrowly circumscribed expression – say as regards the addressees or the topics permitted (or both) – benefits a community and ultimately the individuals (if its doctrine is not just some cynical ideological device of subjugation). Freedom of faith presupposes that it is not in people's true interest that all religions but the "One True Faith" have to be suppressed. Again, this is not a trivial assumption. Centuries of violent persecution of believers of other faiths and the intellectual defense of this persecution attest how difficult it is to grant this freedom. After all, from the point of view of certain religious creeds, letting those who follow other faiths have their way means that the infidels will go to hell and on the way are allowed to perform all kinds of forbidden, wicked, even blasphemous acts.

The more profoundly one engages with the justification of concrete details of the scope of rights, the more important this aspect of a theory of human rights becomes, because the more arguments are needed to show that a particular framing or interpretation of human rights does in fact serve the ends that human rights are there to foster. One may agree that free speech is important for a rationally governed society – but what about the prohibition of hate speech? Does it really promote social civility, or does it gratuitously curtail an important liberty? If the former – in which form? Does the exclusion of Holocaust denial from the protection by free speech guarantees increase respect for human beings of whatever group, or does it stifle historical debate? Is the answer the same in Germany as in Switzerland? Consequently, the next question to which we will turn is: What could a convincing political theory of human rights look like?

[26] Amia Srinivasan, *The Right to Sex* (London: Bloomsbury, 2021), 73 ff.

5.2.2 *Politics beyond Normativity?*

Our review of justificatory theories of human rights already showed that *functionalist theories* do not provide a good account of human rights as they miss their point, which is to provide a normatively grounded yardstick for the legitimate aims a society can pursue. Human rights are not functional tools to achieve a social purpose determined without recourse to normative principles. Rather, human rights themselves determine the justified purposes of social action. They define what is or is not functional for the operation of society because they play a key role in setting the aims that social organization is to serve. In light of the human rights idea, societies are not there just to reproduce themselves in whatever form; instead, societies are to be organized in a way that respects the worth, liberty and equality of human beings.

Other political theory options are not convincing either. Human rights cannot be reconstructed as a form of *political aestheticism*, for instance.[27] Orders of human rights aim at more than just some kind of aesthetically attractive form of life. They are not an element of political *dandyism*[28] but express a specific, sufficiently well-defined normative standpoint. Human rights therefore also are not a form of *existential decisionism*, which views all normative standards as rooted in a fundamental decision by individuals or collectives to pursue a certain way of life. No prior normative reasons guide such decisions. In this view, normative orders are thus a kind of political *creatio ex nihilo*, a creation from nothing that defines the future political being of a community, including the normative parameters that bind it.[29] Contrary to this perspective, human rights are wedded to the claim that their validity is based not on mere contingent political commitments created by foundational political decisions without normative grounds, but rather on compelling normative reasons. Norm-independent existential political decisions are not the ultimate source of human rights; rather, human rights are decisive normative reasons that must guide all such fundamental political decisions, in particular those of a *pouvoir constituant*. This is exactly the political role they played in the process of constitution-making around the world and in the development of the international architecture of human rights: They were reasons that guided the kind of political order that was designed – from the drafting of the *Universal Declaration* to the South African Constitution after the end of the apartheid regime.

Functionalism, political aestheticism and political existentialism thus are not helpful approaches to the idea of human rights. One needs to look elsewhere for

[27] Cf. Nietzsche's assessment of the aesthetic value of the doomed moral culture of equality, fading away like a beautiful note, Nietzsche, *Jenseits von Gut und Böse*, aphorism 255.

[28] Cf. Albert Camus, "L'homme révolté," in Albert Camus, *Œuvres complètes Vol. III: 1949–1956*, ed. Raymond Gay-Crosier (Paris: Gallimard, 2008), 101 ff.

[29] Carl Schmitt, *Verfassungslehre* (Berlin: Duncker & Humblot, 1928), 75 f.; Carl Schmitt, *Die Diktatur* (Berlin: Duncker & Humblot, 1928), 42.

theoretical guidance. The first step in doing so is to examine a whole battery of theoretical approaches that deny that human rights serve the good of humanity.

5.3 THE CRITIQUE OF RIGHTS

5.3.1 *The Benefits of Authoritarianism*

Human rights diffuse power. They create a protected space for the activity of human beings and set limits to what public power is allowed to do. One important counterargument to at least some such rights claims that an illiberal, hierarchical order is ultimately to people's benefit. This argument has been articulated throughout the ages in various forms and has exerted significant political influence.

One example is Plato's critique of democratic rights, a group of rights that certainly belongs in the history of human rights, as we have seen. Plato's argument was not an attempt to shield the privileges of certain classes, including his own. Rather, it derived from the belief that the authoritarian order he envisaged, which had a functional conception of justice as its lodestar, allocating rights and duties in society according to the best service a person could provide for the community, promoted the best of the polis – and not only of the collective, but of all its members, too.[30]

A further proponent of this idea from a different epoch is Leibniz. He argued, as we have seen, that people have inalienable rights to life, the protection of personal integrity and liberty. However, he thought that natural law spoke against equal political rights. For Leibniz, the criterion of distribution under Aristotelian principles of justice was the capability to rule. He made the factual assumption that monarchs and aristocrats are better suited to ruling than other people. In addition, he argued that popular assemblies are as prone to engage in arbitrary rule as single rulers. Consequently, it seemed most likely to him that the rule of reason would be achieved by the traditional political ruling class of the *ancien régime*.[31] Hegel's metaphysics of constitutional monarchies is yet another example of a vision of political organization that includes authoritarian elements and skepticism about rights.[32]

The idea of benign authoritarian rule has held practical significance in more recent politics, too (e.g. in state socialist systems with a party-led bureaucracy) and continues to be a relevant category today – for example, underpinning the political systems of Singapore or China.

[30] Cf. Plato, Republic, 465e ff. on the happiness of the guardians.

[31] Cf. Leibniz's comments on Locke's *Second Treatise*, Leibniz, "Letter to Thomas Burnett of Kemney, 2 February 1700," 380; Leibniz, "Letter to Thomas Burnett of Kemney, July 18, 1701," 284.

[32] Cf. for instance G. W. F. Hegel's critique of democratic popular sovereignty, Hegel, *Grundlinien der Philosophie des Rechts*, § 279 and his design of a legitimate constitutional monarchy, §§ 260 ff.

Various issues arise here. One is the plausibility of the assessment of the beneficial effects of authoritarian rule. There is ample historical evidence to show that democracies in which a significant portion of the population have political rights may take decisions that are not conducive to the common good – for example, to engage in the Peloponnesian War. It seems hard to argue, however, that there is any substantial historical evidence that the lack of rights leads to the well-being of human beings to a comparatively larger degree than in systems where such rights are recognized. In this context, a crucial question to ask is what "well-being" actually means and whether the respect for the rights of an individual possibly forms part of it. Here, again, the classical argument is important that a life within the framework of respected rights – both of the agent and of others – is an essential element of true human flourishing. Theories that argue for the benefits of social organization without rights thus remain unconvincing: They miss the very point of rights and their significance for a human life worth living.

5.3.2 *Human Rights: Ineffective Ethical and Legal Balderdash?*

Human rights have been institutionalized on a national, regional and – to a certain limited degree – international level. This naturally has given rise to the question of whether they do in fact contribute to achieving the ends they are supposed to serve.

In recent years, various commentators have claimed that human rights lack this effectiveness: They either are of no use in reaching the aims for which they are made, in particular reducing violence and repression and fostering liberty, or are even detrimental to this task.[33] Others have disputed these findings, not least on methodological grounds.[34] The latter point is of some importance, because it underlines the fact that it is exceedingly difficult to say anything about the effectiveness of human rights that is valid by the usual standards of the social sciences. Besides other specific methodological problems, human rights cover a potentially vast area of social life. Human rights catalogues vary considerably. In addition, human rights, as has been emphasized, cannot be reduced to international human rights. Therefore, any analysis of the effects of human rights would also need to include the effects of national constitutional rights protection. The mechanisms

[33] Cf. for example Jack Landman Goldsmith and Eric Andrew Posner, *The Limits of International Law* (Oxford: Oxford University Press, 2005); Eric Andrew Posner, *The Twilight of Human Rights Law* (Oxford: Oxford University Press, 2014); Emilie M. Hafner-Burton and Kiyoteru Tsutsui, "Justice Lost! The Failure of International Human Rights Law to Matter Where Needed Most," *Journal of Peace Research* 44 (2007): 407 ff., arguing that "human rights laws are most effective in stable or consolidating democracies or in states with strong civil society activism," but they fail to make a difference in repressive regimes, ibid. 407.

[34] Beth Simmons, *Mobilizing for Human Rights: International Law in Domestic Politics* (Cambridge: Cambridge University Press, 2009), highlighting in particular the constraining role of international treaties; Sikkink, *Evidence*, 139 ff.

used to implement human rights are equally heterogeneous, ranging from a fully developed constitutional review to a very weak supervisory mechanism, as in many areas of international human rights law. The same right can have quite different regulatory effects in different social areas – freedom of religion may robustly protect a majority religion against encroachment by the state but be less effective at protecting a minority religion.

A further exemplary problem needs to be mentioned: Because of the complexity of the issues with which human rights are concerned, there are many independent (intervening) variables that influence the effects of any legal regulation. The radical change almost worldwide of the understanding of the meaning of rights to privacy, personal autonomy, equality and human dignity for the permissible regulation of same-sex intimate relations, for example, has occurred while the legal texts of the relevant norms remained unchanged for the most part. This cannot be explained without reference to the development of the background social morality, its political ramifications and the attitudinal changes of decision-makers, including judges. Saying that these norms were ineffective before this change is as reductionist as claiming that they now are the only engine of social change. The truth is that a multifaceted interaction of many factors – legal, social, ethical, political – in the end leads to such progress. This complexity renders self-confident arguments about the effects of human rights highly dubious.

Given this wide range of application, the heterogeneous multiplicity of implementation mechanisms, the different spheres of protection and other relevant independent variables to be considered when determining the causation of given social phenomena regulated by human rights, it may be possible to say something meaningful about the effects of a certain right of a particular legal system as to a certain issue – for example, the effects of freedom of religion as a human right guaranteed by the *German Basic Law* on the regulation of vestiary symbols in public services and its application by state authorities concerning the wearing of Islamic headscarves in schools in Germany – but not about the effects of human rights in general across issues, societies and regulatory regimes.[35]

Furthermore, given this rather obvious problem, one needs to ask whether the argument of the ineffectiveness of human rights is in fact a tactic pursuing the political aim to delegitimize human rights, an argument that stems not from a genuine concern for effective human rights protection but from a political agenda hostile to their rule.

[35] This skepticism about the reach of existing studies encompasses some studies that assert the positive effects of human rights, which contain important findings but are often not particularly fine-grained. The dependent variables determined by human rights as the independent variable are sometimes very general and may even tend to become something like the general well-being of the members of society. Cf. as an example the complex example of undernourishment and the many factors that may influence it, Sikkink, *Evidence*, 147 ff.

An abundance of examples illustrates the failure of the various systems of the protection of human rights. It is very important to stay painfully aware of this in order to avoid an overly romantic view of human rights. However, it is wrong to ascribe these failures solely to the human rights systems in their different variants, concepts, conceptions and institutions. This would miss the very point of human rights, which is to confront power. This power is not that of some friendly agent waiting to be convinced by the idea of human rights and swayed by a critical state report it could safely ignore, but power that has no respect for the values protected by human rights and thus for the task performed by these norms. Human rights confront authoritarianism, dictatorship, suppression, violence, torture and murder, sometimes of the worst kind. It is no surprise at all that human rights often are rendered ineffective by the might of the forces working against them, which have included the most powerful political agents in history.

Both the constitutional and, increasingly, some of the regional and international systems of human rights protection show that human rights can be highly effective. They have changed many people's lives for the better, although they certainly have not established a paradise of complete and utter justice.[36]

In any case, the argument based on ineffectiveness has limited force. If it were plausible, the consequence would be to try to increase the effectivity of human rights, not to abolish the project altogether.

All of this mainly concerns human rights as legal rights. The assertion that human rights as moral principles are entirely ineffective seems equally hard to defend, given the far-reaching beneficial effects this idea continues to have as a critical check on ideologies of unrestrained power.

5.3.3 *Human Rights as Means of Economic Disempowerment*

Marxist theory, both traditional and contemporary, provides a classical critique of human rights. Its main claim is that fundamental rights are part of the superstructure of capitalist economies and societies. Property rights and the freedom to contract are understood as paradigmatic rights illustrating the truth of this thesis: Private property and the ability to enter freely into a contract are preconditions for the capitalist mode of production. However, these rights do not set human beings free but through the cunning of the capitalist economy enslave them to this mode of production. The thinkers of the Enlightenment proclaimed rights that they thought embodied the realm of reason, when in fact they were unable to transcend the

[36] One would be hard pressed to name any study that denies the positive effects of, say, the bills of rights of US, German or Swiss constitutional law or doubts the substantial positive effects of the ECHR system. Criticism is mostly directed at international, universal human rights law, which is not, as repeatedly underlined, the whole of human rights law, nor was it ever meant to be its main pillar. Interestingly, Posner, *Twilight*, 139 does not count the ECtHR as an international institution protecting human rights.

limited perspectives of their century, its mode of production and their own class consciousness.[37]

There are reasons for this argument, and they are found not only in nineteenth-century forms of capitalism. Rights to private property can be used to defend by legal means a particular economic power structure – the one established by the existing unequal distribution of wealth, for instance. Marxists have not been the only ones to make this point. To this day, it remains important to reflect critically upon the question of whether or not a particular human rights order serves its purpose of fostering the goods of all members of society or not. It is wrong, however, to assume that all human rights necessarily protect an unequal distribution of power and property. Many human rights cannot be reduced to such a function. To begin with, human dignity as the idea of regarding human beings as ends-in-themselves is one of the normative starting points for criticizing structures of exploitation – a point that Marx himself and other prominent Marxists did not to miss.[38] Liberal rights, freedom of opinion, freedom of the press and other forms of communication and of assembly are (among other reasons for their importance) the preconditions for any political transformation in a society, including any economic reform. Equality guarantees are a tool to maintain or establish a decent level of equity in a society and fend off discrimination. Social rights are far from able to alleviate all social injustice and suffering in the world but can play an important role in taking some steps in that direction. For example, a human right to minimum living conditions

[37] Friedrich Engels, "Die Entwicklung des Sozialismus von der Utopie zur Wissenschaft," in *Marx-Engels-Werke*, Vol. 19, ed. Ludwig Arnold (Berlin: Dietz Verlag, 1987), 189–201: "The great men, who in France prepared the public mind for the oncoming revolution, stood forth themselves as extreme revolutionists. They recognized no external authority of whatever sort. Religion, theories of nature, society, political institutions, all were submitted to ruthless criticism. Everything was summoned before the judgment-seat of reason, there to justify or, contrariwise, give up its existence. Reason was set up as the only standard. Those were the days when, as Hegel put it, the world was placed upon its head; first, in the sense that man's head, and the maxims evolved from thought, claimed to be the foundation for all actions and social adjustments; secondly, in the further sense that the reality which stood in contradiction to those maxims was, in fact, turned upside down. All former social and State institutions, all notions that had come down from ancient days, were pitched into the lumber-room as being against reason. The world, it was claimed, had thitherto allowed itself to be led entirely by prejudices; all the past deserved only pity and contempt. Only then did the light of day, the reign of reason break forth. Thenceforth, superstition, injustice, privilege and oppression were to be superseded by eternal truth, eternal justice, and the nature-born equality and inalienable rights of man. Today we know that that reign of reason was nothing else than the idealized reign of the capitalist class; that that eternal justice found its realization in capitalist law; that that equality reduced itself to the capitalist's phrase: 'equality before the statute'; that one of the essential rights of man proclaimed was – capitalist property; and that the reign of reason, the social contract of Rousseau, did and could only come into existence as a capitalistic, democratic republic. Like all their predecessors, the great thinkers of the eighteenth century were unable to leap the barriers with which their own age hemmed them in." Translation: Friedrich Engels, *Socialism: Utopian and Scientific*, trans. Edward Aveling (London: Swan Sonnenschein & Co., 1892).

[38] Cf. Bloch, *Naturrecht und menschliche Würde*.

secured by a social state is an important asset, and in some legal orders is even anchored in such a core right as human dignity.

Human beings live not on bread alone. Their free self-determination in the many dimensions of human life is a good, too, as is the freedom to live according to one's faith or secular convictions in a community where nobody has to fear for life and limb and in which human beings find the respect they deserve. Some of the best Marxist thought on human rights has (ultimately) underlined the importance of this dimension of social reform.[39]

Reductionist economic theories thus fail to convince. This also is true for a modern variant, which – though not necessarily within the framework of Marxist theory – posits a hypothetical connection between human rights and the rise of neoliberalism.[40] This connection does not exist if neoliberalism is taken to refer to economic policies that disregard the interests of the poor, foster inequality, limit the freedom of the greater part of society through economic hardship and serve the material interest of a few within an instrumentalized, laissez-faire, free-market ideology. Human rights do not establish a just economic order as such, but they are a precondition for the political possibility of achieving this end and already enshrine certain principles that create a framework for decent economic policy, as just underlined. None of this is linked to neoliberalism. Unsurprisingly, various regimes of the Global South applied what are widely regarded as neoliberal policies while at the same time showing no respect for human rights.[41]

5.3.4 *Human Rights as the Handmaidens of Power and the Prospects of Postcolonial Worldmaking*

Another theory weds human rights to political power in the sense of a whole set of structures of domination, including epistemic patterns of subjugation in the "*vaste dispositif*" of a "*societé panoptique*," in which the "*episteme*" contributes to the subject's internalization of the power relations that enslave them, to use Foucault's terms.[42] In postmodern thought, this can be connected to deep-seated structures of force, including the performative force of language: From this perspective, the meaning of expressions is fixed by subtle or visible forms of force.[43] Certain ideas

[39] Bloch, *Naturrecht und menschliche Würde*, arguing for extending the concern of Marxist thinking to securing human beings the respect that they deserve.

[40] Cf. for the argument that the supposed blindness of human rights to issues of material equality prevents them from abetting neoliberalism, Samuel Moyn, *Not Enough: Human Rights in an Unequal World* (Cambridge, MA: Harvard University Press, 2018), 173 ff., 218.

[41] Sikkink, *Evidence*, 38 ff. Moyn, *Not Enough*, 173 ff. does not deny this but fails to fully acknowledge the role of human rights in enabling egalitarian policies and preventing abuses – including, importantly, by progressive movements, as discussed below.

[42] Michel Foucault, *Surveiller et punir* (Paris: Gallimard, 1975), 349 ff.

[43] Derrida, "Force of Law," 3–67; cf. for comments Matthias Mahlmann, "Law and Force: 20th Century Radical Legal Philosophy, Post-Modernism and the Foundations of Law," *Res Publica* 9, no. 1 (2003): 19–37.

conquer human beings' thought through the same mechanism of subtle and not-so-subtle compulsion, not by better arguments – which is hardly surprising, because from this deconstructivist perspective there is no such thing as a "better" argument. Human rights are sometimes even associated with great evils: In their generality and universality, it is argued, they disregard the individuality and otherness of every human being and thus come dangerously close to totalitarian ideologies of contempt for human beings.[44]

In some (but importantly not all) postcolonial theories, human rights are linked in particular to continuing structures of colonial domination. It is claimed that human rights perpetuate these structures both politically and epistemologically because they universalize colonial perspectives and overlook other "epistemologies of the South."[45]

There is an important point here: As in the case of the economic instrumentalization of human rights, any theory of human rights needs to stay mindful of the degree to which it may lend itself to abuse by power. It is also true that the limited, fragile and imperfect order of international human rights exists alongside economic, political, legal and military structures of the domination of powers of the Global North over many states of the Global South. The hypothesis of an intrinsic connection between rights and power is quite another thing, however. Human rights are central tools for criticizing authoritarian orders or power in democratic societies. Political freedoms and the protection of life and bodily integrity are assets for political movements that challenge illegitimate political power. For instance, to the political opposition or dissidents it matters greatly whether they have the means to defend themselves against torture, arbitrary arrest, censorship and other seasoned means of repression or not.

It thus is no accident that the underestimation of the importance of these rights by certain analyses of the period following World War II, not least from the radical left, some of which even postulate the dawn of authoritarianism in constitutional states, is widely perceived as a political shortcoming. As Foucault rightly observed in this context, there is the risk of exaggerating the critique and failing to properly distinguish different forms of state power. The failure to make such differentiations was

[44] Derrida, "Force of Law," 59 ff.

[45] Cf. for instance Tony Evans, *The Politics of Human Rights: A Global Perspective* (London: Pluto Press, 2005); Makau Mutua, *Human Rights: A Political and Cultural Critique* (Philadelphia: University of Pennsylvania Press, 2002); David Kennedy, *The Dark Side of Virtue: Reassessing International Humanitarianism* (Princeton, NJ: Princeton University Press, 2004); Boaventura de Sousa Santos, *Epistemologies of the South: Justice Against Epistemicide* (Boulder, CO: Paradigm Publishers, 2014); Nelson Maldonado Torres, "On the Coloniality of Human Rights," in *The Pluriverse of Human Rights: The Diversity of Struggles for Dignity*, eds. Boaventura de Sousa Santos and Bruno Sena Martins (New York: Routledge, 2021): "[T]he very Western modernity that has generated the hegemonic discourse of the 'Rights of Man' is also the global episteme that generated the view of colonial ontological differences among human beings."

one of the root causes leading to the tragedy of 1970s left-wing terrorism in Western democracies. In addition, Foucault (like many others) rediscovered the importance of rights, even wedding the idea of critique to such rights in the tradition of "natural law," as he states explicitly in his later work.[46]

As our historical review suggested, universal human rights were in no way a project of the ruling groups of European history. They were used as tools to liberate radically suppressed, even enslaved people. Major developments in the institutionalization of human rights were due to the committed work of persons from the Global South. For significant stretches of time, human rights were the instruments used to wrest power from colonial elites and attack systems such as South African apartheid, and thus they were part and parcel of the political project of the democratic and liberty-preserving movements of decolonization and their contribution to a kind of worldmaking beyond the color line that aimed to free human beings from global structures of domination.[47] In addition, the movement towards delegitimizing these rights was advanced powerfully by authoritarian regimes that intended to free themselves from the burden these rights imposed on them.

It is unclear how this historical trajectory can be reconciled with the thesis that modes of thought of the kind hypothesized in "epistemologies of the South" would arrive at entirely different normative principles than those embodied in human rights. Why would this be plausible, when the idea of human rights owes so much to the creative thinking and political determination of people from the Global South? And what would it even mean in concrete terms to design rights according to the "epistemologies of the South"? That taking the life of a dissident by state force is legitimate according to these epistemologies? That censorship is entirely justified due to the epistemic makeup of people from the Global South? That homosexual people are to be treated disadvantageously in comparison to heterosexuals, perhaps even stoned to death, as has been justified recently with reference to local traditions?[48] That racist discrimination, torture and rape are okay? As such conclusions are entirely out of the question, the question at issue here remains what exactly the better alternative to human rights might be. Sometimes, reference is made to a stronger emphasis on community values in, for example, African conceptions of human rights to render the difference from "Western" human rights more concrete. This does not question the idea of human rights as such, however. It asks the entirely legitimate question of how individual claims, the rights of others and communal

[46] Michel Foucault, *Qu'est-ce que la critique? Suivi de La culture de soi* (Paris: Librairie Philosophique Vrin, 2015), 38.

[47] Du Bois, *The Souls of Black Folk*, 5, 17, 33: "[T]he problem of the 20th century is the problem of the color-line." For a reconstruction of some of these aspirations in the process of decolonization, which included references to human rights, from George Padmore to Nkrumah and Eric Williams, cf. Getachew, *Worldmaking after Empire*, 70, 94, 126. On her analysis of the place of human rights in a postcolonial cosmopolitanism, ibid. 33 f., cf. the discussion below.

[48] Embassy of Brunei Darussalam, *Letter to European Parliament*, REF: KBBB 33/2019, April 23, 2019.

interests can be reconciled. This is a classical question *within human rights doctrine* solved by the system of justification of interferences in human rights, in particular by proportionality analyses and the weighing and balancing of competing interests. Incidentally, this includes the doctrine of property, which can be constructed in a way that leaves ample scope for the consideration of community interests.[49] Seen in this light, the matter then turns from supposedly profoundly different ways of understanding justice to questions of the convincing and of course continuously controversial concrete construction of human rights not least as positive law, with all of the political and ethical implications such constructions necessarily entail. It comes as no surprise, then, that documents such as the *African Charter of Human Rights* or the bill of rights of the Constitution of South Africa contain original content that nevertheless rests comfortably within the framework of the universal human rights project.

Other proposals for alternative norms that differ from human rights in any meaningful sense either remain exceedingly vague[50] or implicitly restate the importance of those rights they profess to transcend.[51] There is simply no body of norms in sight that would offer a preferable alternative to the differentiated body of human rights in ethics and law.

Controversies about such questions are not decided simply by the superior power of one side of the debate, as in some epistemological theory. Power can intimidate opponents, bend their thinking to its yoke and make them its

[49] Cf. for some remarks on the legal philosophy and doctrine of property, Matthias Mahlmann, "Autonomie, Gleichheit und Eigentum," *Zeitschrift für Schweizerisches Recht* 140, no. 4 (2021): 377 ff.

[50] Mark Goodale, *Anthropology and the Law: A Critical Introduction* (New York: New York University Press, 2017), quoting Eduardo Kohn, asks, for instance: "So what does a 'living-future logic of a thinking forest' point to for the future of law?" relating this to the "*cosmovisiones*" of epistemologies of the South.

[51] A good example is the claim (e.g. the one mentioned above, Torres, "Coloniality", n. 45) that the Western world that produced the idea also erected a false hierarchical ontological order of human beings. This claim evidently demands and defends human equality – a core idea of the human rights project. So either this critique is colonial itself or the human rights project is already pursuing what this criticism normatively implies. Moreover, it is more than deplorable that such accounts entirely neglect the struggles from below involved in human rights history, trying to overcome human inequality, and overlook the inegalitarianism existing in the South. Another example is Mutua's argument that ultimately endorses human rights. He does not criticize human rights as such but a certain conception of human rights, which in his view neglects in particular the importance of community and people's rights, Mutua, *Human Rights*, 71 ff. This is an important topic of debate, but not one that puts the idea of human rights as such into question – as Mutua's reliance on this idea underlines. Evans, *The Politics of Human Rights*, 142, criticizes human rights policies in the framework of a political analysis of neoliberal globalization, but also demands "a political agenda that expresses a genuine concern for human rights and human dignity." One may also wonder what the normative core of the demand to treat refugees "humanely" actually is and whether it boils down to something else than the human rights of refugees (rhetoric aside), cf. Kennedy, *The Dark Side*, 352.

hypocritical servants or simply silence them. But it is a category error to mistake *being convinced by arguments* for *being compelled to accept a position by force.* One cannot be convinced by force, a seasoned argument of great importance in the struggle against religious intolerance. "One can enter a church without wanting to, one can walk towards the altar without wanting to, one can accept the sacrament without wanting to, but believe you cannot but willingly," Augustine observed aptly, although later in his life he pursued policies at odds with this insight.[52] The same holds true for becoming convinced of a proposition. Convincing presupposes argument and free assent, not force. This is the analytical shortcoming of theories that dissolve reason-giving into the force to subdue others, in however subtle a form. This theory of the constitutive role of violence in the formation of normative convictions can have very dangerous political consequences, a fact that presumably is obvious. It is not good news for human communities if it is seriously maintained that central political, legal and ethical questions cannot be solved or at least promoted by arguments and reasons but only by force. The fact that the Nazis could send a person who resisted their regime to the guillotine did not make their positions right, and it is crucially important to stay aware of this fact.

There is thus no compelling case for the claim that human rights are necessarily instruments of domination, both in practical politics and in the "*epistemes*" of society, the systems of human beings' political, ethical and legal beliefs. There is no reason to think that the promotion of human rights necessarily unwillingly serves the interest of the powerful, whether colonial or not, although human rights may be abused for this purpose. The critique of accounts of human rights as camouflaged instruments of power leads to a clearer perception of the emancipating force of human rights based on reasons accessible to all.

5.3.5 *Feminist Critiques and Restatements of Human Rights*

There is not just one form of feminism. On the contrary, feminist discussions are as controversial and even acrimonious as other areas of theory-building. Traditionally, a distinction is made between different waves of feminist reflections about ethics and law: A first wave claimed the equal rights of different genders, a second emphasized difference, including the unity of normative standards applicable[53] to different

[52] "*Intrare quisquam ecclesiam potest nolens, accedere ad altare potest nolens, accipere Sacramentum potest nolens: credere non potest nisi volens,*" Augustinus, "In Joannis Evangelium," in *Patrologia cursus completus, series latina, tomus XXXV* (Paris: Jacques-Paul Migne, 1845), 1379, 1607.

[53] Cf. for instance the debate about ethics of justice and ethics of care, after Carol Gilligan's critique of Lawrence Kohlberg's theory of ontogenetic moral development, Carol Gilligan, *In a Different Voice: Psychological Theory and Women's Development* (Cambridge, MA: Harvard University Press, 1982).

genders, and a third questioned the sense of binary gender categories in general.[54] In recent years, further perspectives have broadened the picture, importantly, for instance, concerning intersectionality, including, among other factors, skin color ("race," to use English-language terminology) and religion.[55]

In some of these debates, skepticism about human rights has been voiced, in particular concerning whether the idea of human rights is dependent on a concept of humanity that in fact mirrors male perspectives and thus forms an unsuitable tool to foster the liberation of women.[56]

The understanding of human rights as an ethical, political and legal concept has profited significantly from these debates, which have informed and driven forward the protection of equal treatment and freedom from discrimination in law, among others. It is a misunderstanding to assume that human rights cannot accommodate the respect for human difference, including nonbinary gender difference. On the contrary, there is an increasingly sophisticated set of legal tools to fight discrimination and foster the respect for the equality of human beings.[57] Accordingly, as mentioned in the historical review, women's issues were important early elements of the international struggle for human rights – just as they were on the national level. The core areas of protection, such as freedom and self-determination, are significant for all human beings, whatever their gender might be – as Polish, American and Argentinian women's struggle for reproductive autonomy in recent years has shown yet again.

These findings already indicate the main lesson drawn from the history and practice of human rights, a lesson emphasized by many feminist scholars and activists: Nothing in the idea of human rights is hostile to the justified aim to include gender perspectives in ethics and law. This is true both of the normative foundations of human rights, as will be discussed below, and of the concrete normative content of these rights. The task therefore is to purge human rights of

54 Cf. respectively Wollstonecraft, *Vindication*, Introduction: "[T]he first object of laudable ambition is to obtain a character as a human being, regardless of the distinction of sex"; Susan Moller Okin, *Women in Western Political Thought* (Princeton, NJ: Princeton University Press, 1979); Judith Butler, *Undoing Gender* (New York: Routledge, 2004); Judith Butler, *Gender Trouble* (New York: Routledge, 1990). Referring to waves should not be understood, however, as implying that later waves superseded earlier ones. Nussbaum, for instance, emphasizes universalistic, egalitarian perspectives, cf. Martha Nussbaum, *Women and Human Development: The Capability Approach* (Cambridge: Cambridge University Press, 2000), 34 ff., including "central human functional capabilities," 78 ff.

55 Kimberlé Crenshaw, "Demarginalizing the Intersection of Race and Sex: A Black Feminist Critique of Antidiscrimination Doctrine, Feminist Theory and Antiracist Politics," *The University of Chicago Legal Forum* (Vol. 1989): 139–67.

56 Catharine MacKinnon, *Toward a Feminist Theory of the State* (Cambridge, MA: Harvard University Press, 1989), 238: "In the liberal state, the rule of law – neutral, abstract, elevated, pervasive – both institutionalizes the power of men over women and institutionalizes power in its male form."

57 Cf. for an overview of international human rights law Daniel Moeckli, "Equality and Non-discrimination," in *International Human Rights Law*, 3rd edition, eds. Daniel Moeckli, Sangeeta Shah and Sandesh Sivakumaran (Oxford: Oxford University Press, 2018), 148–64.

the many surviving remnants of patriarchal traditions and ideology, not to politically and theoretically subvert the concept of human rights itself.[58]

5.3.6 *Human Rights Curtailing Democracy and Sovereignty*

Fundamental rights have an antimajoritarian edge. There are occasions when a human right will trump even a democratically taken decision. Various laws that criminalized consensual homosexual intimate relations, for instance, were created democratically and nevertheless were struck down by courts entrusted with protecting fundamental rights. There are many examples of such forms of judicial review in international law as well – for instance, in the system of the ECHR.[59]

It is argued that this limitation of democracy is either illegitimate or at least bad policy. Unfettered political self-determination should take priority over human rights and their enforcement by courts or other institutions, it is claimed. In this context, the power of courts, both domestic[60] and international,[61] to strike down legislation is an issue. What is the source of this power?

There is more than one way to solve this problem. One important point is to formulate a properly differentiated account of the relation between democracy and human rights. Human rights are not an irrelevant by-product of democracy; rather, they are essential for its architecture and functioning. There can be no democracy without the protection of fundamental rights. This is true not only for political rights, including electoral rights, which are the precondition of any democratic decision-making. It also is true for liberties like freedom of speech, freedom of the press and freedom of assembly. Democracies need decisions that are the product of sometimes important interpretations of human existence and of what human life and human community are about. Freedoms of religion, of conscience, of science and art create the possibility of a lifeworld where such opinions can be formed,

[58] Cf. as examples from the debate the passionate defense not only of fundamental rights, but also of fundamental rights *protected by judicial review*, Susanne Baer, "Who Cares? A Defence of Judicial Review," *Journal of the British Academy* 8 (2020): 75–104. On the unconditional reciprocal recognition of others embodied in human rights, Elisabeth Holzleithner, "Feministische Menschenrechtskritik," *Zeitschrift für Menschenrechte* 1 (2016): 110–20, 118. Beate Rudolf, "Menschenrechte und Geschlecht – eine Diskursgeschichte," in *Menschenrechte und Geschlecht*, ed. Ulrike Lembke (Baden-Baden: Nomos, 2014), 24–50. For an immanent and universal theory of human rights, Brooke A. Ackerly, *Universal Human Rights in a World of Difference* (Cambridge: Cambridge University Press, 2008). Cf. on the debate Diana Tietjens Meyers, "Feminist Philosophy of Human Rights," in *The Oxford Handbook of Feminist Philosophy*, eds. Kim Q. Hall and Ásta (Oxford: Oxford University Press, 2021), 462–83.

[59] The judgments of the ECtHR do not nullify laws but create obligations of state parties to abide by the decisions of the court, Art. 46 para. 1 ECHR, which often leads to changes of laws.

[60] Cf. for instance Dworkin, *Justice for Hedgehogs*, 395 ff.

[61] Armin von Bogdandy and Ingo Venzke, *In Whose Name? A Public Law Theory of International Adjudication* (Oxford: Oxford University Press, 2014).

interrogated, revived and reformulated and therefore constitute an equally vital element of democracy. The procedures of democracy need to be protected, which implies elements of the rule of law that have a bearing on questions of human rights, including the right to a judicial review of decisions made by public authorities. Moreover, if democrats have to fear for life and limb because of their political activities, the democracy at issue is very limited indeed. The right to life is therefore equally important for democracy, as is the prohibition of torture and other guarantees – for example, habeas corpus.

Rights may thus limit democratic decision-making in certain instances, but their rule serves to protect democracy in the long run. This is essential, because democracy is not just about one majority decision at a given moment of time but is a system of political self-government in which it is possible to exercise political autonomy continuously over a long period of time.

Ideally, courts are created with democratic credentials themselves, whether direct or indirect. The point of courts is that the democratic political process establishes an institution that is functionally independent of concrete majorities and can thus serve as a check on the decision-making of shifting majorities in certain well-qualified respects. Courts with such a function form part of the idea of constitutional entrenchment – the democratic creation of antimajoritarian checks on the decisions of everyday democratic life. Organizing such a system with a claim to legitimacy and securing its credible operation, not least on the international plane, involves many difficulties. However, the claim that no such sufficiently legitimate system can be imagined seems hard to maintain, given the existing practice of institutions that serve these functions quite successfully.

Another point should be considered. Democratic self-determination and sovereignty do not mean arbitrary power unfettered by normative principles. They mean the exercise of political autonomy within the bounds and limits of legitimate norms. This is how they have been conceptualized for a very long time in various domains of thought, and convincingly so: There is no right to determine oneself by enslaving a minority, for instance. Political self-determination has to respect the normative limits drawn by justified normative principles, in particular by the legitimate rights of individuals as equal, autonomous persons.[62]

[62] Schmitt famously states that sovereign is who determines the course of affairs in the state of exception, Carl Schmitt, *Politische Theologie* (Berlin: Duncker & Humblot, 1934), 11: "Souverän ist, wer über den Ausnahmezustand entscheidet"; Carl Schmitt, *Diktatur*, 18 [194], influencing many current debates, cf. for instance Giorgio Agamben, *Homo Sacer: Sovereign Power and Bare Life*, trans. Daniel Heller-Roazen (Stanford: Stanford University Press, 1998). This theory dissolves the normative concept of sovereignty into brute power, unconvincingly, cf. for instance Hans Kelsen, *Das Problem der Souveränität und die Theorie des Völkerrechts* (Tübingen: Scientia Verlag, 1928), 6 ff.; similarly, Beitz, *Idea of Human Rights*, 22, for whom sovereignty is a creation of international law: "In this perspective, the significance of the declaration at the time of its adoption was not so much to pose a challenge to the principle of domestic jurisdiction as to advance a larger project of redescribing it."

Human rights are therefore deeply interwoven with the normative architecture of democracy and the legitimate exercise of sovereignty. There is no argument against human rights from the perspective of democracy and political self-determination, only one that strengthens their cause.

5.3.7 *The Wrong Politics of Human Rights*

Another strand of human rights criticism argues that human rights are bad politics. While human rights are not denied to be a legitimate concern, critics maintain that a focus on human rights has detrimental political effects. It is argued that human rights politics are powerless against inequality,[63] crowd out other concerns, fail to acknowledge the costs of human rights or pursue a narrow concept of human emancipation. Human rights are understood as individualistic, atomistic and insufficiently oriented towards community.

These criticisms are arguably true for certain versions of human rights politics, although it is not as easy to name serious human rights actors both within and beyond the legal sphere that promote human rights as a *passpartout* to all political problems, are unconcerned about the problematic aspects of (legal) human rights or celebrate the egoistic individual free of all community concerns.

In any case, there is certainly no reason why human rights should not be reconcilable with or even profoundly supportive of other political aims. For instance, human rights have done a great deal for human equality – from racial desegregation to the liberation of women. As already indicated, they created a space within which to develop and implement new political visions by protecting those liberties and other goods that are the precondition for any transformative political thought, including the survival of the thinker. A legitimate conception of human rights includes the concerns of other human beings in its architecture, as we will see in a moment. Furthermore, our historical review showed that, from the very beginning, the rights of human beings were closely associated with questions of social justice, which are, thus, not only a concern of recent debate. Today, human rights contribute to the task of promoting social justice in very concrete ways, not least through social rights that work and are effective in more than one legal system.

To be sure, there are wrong politics of human rights. But there is no reason why the struggle for human rights must be bad politics.

5.3.8 *The* Aporia *of Human Rights*

Hannah Arendt famously advanced a critique of human rights that hinges on the thesis that there is an *aporia* of human rights. Human rights are proclaimed to be rights of crucial importance and are thought of as the rights that human beings enjoy

[63] Moyn, *Not Enough*, 173 ff.; Sikkink, *Evidence*, 35, 236.

solely by virtue of their humanity. As ethical ideas and legal institutions, however, they are unable to protect human beings when it matters most. In times of acute crisis and danger, nobody has the slightest respect for the naked humanity of human beings. This became all too apparent when the Nazis launched their full-scale attack on human dignity: The supposedly sacred idea of human rights had no practical traction and remained an empty promise, an object of bitter ridicule in light of the hopes connected with it and the suffering with which these hopes were repaid.[64] The core lesson of this experience is to understand the importance of the "right to have rights," Arendt argues. This means that human beings need to be entitled to belong to the group of morally relevant beings. This status is achieved by being part of a political community,[65] which is the place where human beings achieve their humanity in active life, led in a common sphere created by the exchange of ideas and other ways of human interaction that constitute humans' humanity.[66]

Arendt doubtlessly makes an important point here. The experience of the Third Reich shows vividly that human rights as an ethical and political idea will not necessarily be able to prevail against powerful political foes. On the contrary, any appeal to these standards can be shrugged off with disdain as no more than foolish babble as long as the regime's battalions are advancing victoriously and its police apparatus is functioning well. As our historical review showed, the first steps towards a kind of legal protection by human rights proved no obstacle to the conquering German armies in World War II and the machinery of Nazi terror. This experience is very important. It shows the possibility of merciless, unremitting, outspoken, proudly posturing contempt for central elements of those ideas for which human rights stand – a contempt *with a mass basis in society*. The awareness of this possibility acts as an excellent antidote to the illusion that there is anything natural and self-evident about even the smallest partial victory in the struggle for human rights.

In addition, Arendt's critique of human rights inspired by these observations, which is perhaps more serious and important than any other, directs the analysis of human rights to a crucial point that is relevant for their justification. It underlines the significance of the protection of human rights at the state level. Without such safeguards, there can be no meaningful protection of human rights. As highlighted in the historical review, the drafters of the *Universal Declaration* recognized this fact and included it in the architecture of international human rights that they envisaged. The protection of human rights at the state level has been a baseline of their legal implementation ever since then.

Two elements of the evolved human rights system are important to bear in mind when evaluating Arendt's critique, however. The first is that national systems can incorporate and seriously protect human rights in the narrow sense – that is, the rights

64 Arendt, *Origins of Totalitarianism*, 349 ff.
65 Arendt, *Origins of Totalitarianism*, 388.
66 Hannah Arendt, *The Human Condition* (Chicago, IL: University of Chicago Press, 1958).

of all human beings under the jurisdiction of the respective state, independent of their nationality or residence status. It is not just humanity that can protect human rights, as Arendt formulated. The ranks of the protectors of human rights have been swelled by the legal orders of particular states. This is a crucial development. It shows that a considerable number of states have learned to have more respect for human beings' naked humanity than past political actors, and that they have even institutionalized this attitude. As explained above, this is also the case for supranational legal regimes, as the *European Charter of Fundamental Rights* illustrates. Regional systems of public international law also have expanded the reach of rights, in particular within the framework of the extraterritorial application of human rights.[67]

Moreover, Arendt's critique contains certain ambiguities, perhaps even self-contradictions, because it acknowledges the possibility that societies can evolve to such a degree that humanity as a whole, not only individual states, becomes able to guarantee human rights.[68] This questions the necessary link between the inclusion in concrete communities and the right to have rights that forms the core of Arendt's critical argument.

This leads to the second significant point: The international system of protection has changed since Arendt's critique was formulated. While the current system has its weaknesses, it is certainly better than nothing. States adapt their behavior to human rights standards, some kind of redress for past violations is offered and individuals are saved from human rights violations by this system. In addition, legal means are not the only or even the predominant way of enforcing human rights. Political instruments count a great deal, too.

These two developments – the protection of human rights as the rights of all humans, not just of the members of the respective communities, and the denser protection of human rights on the international level – manifest an evolution of the human rights system that was scarcely on the horizon when Arendt formulated the critique of the *aporia* of human rights. These two developments provide practical proof that belonging to a national community is not a necessary precondition for enjoying human rights. Human beings have taken a step beyond this limitation, or, more precisely, they have picked up some threads of the rich heritage of meaningful universalism in past thought and practice and hold them in their hands – though they may let them fall at any time. Arendt's critique therefore had a kind of traction in the past it now no longer possesses.

This notwithstanding, the thesis of the aporetic structure of human rights leaves us with an important question: What is the justification of the right to have rights? Or is there none, because this right begs the question of what the justification of the right to have the right to have rights (and so forth) is? Are we trapped in an infinite regress? The task is therefore to show plausibly that there is a point in the

[67] Cf. for an overview the Introduction and Chapter 2.
[68] Arendt, *Origins of Totalitarianism*, 390.

justification of human rights where, to use a famous metaphor, the spade is turned[69] because it is impossible to dig deeper. One idea is that the core of the right to have rights is human dignity – the ultimate worth of every individual human being, which, under the condition of valid, universally obligatory rights-generating normative principles, entitles every individual human being to enjoy a protected space for the pursuit of happiness, secured by rights. Whether human dignity and such normative principles (yet to be specified in more detail) solve the problem of the justification of the right to have rights is one of the questions to be addressed in the following. For now, let us simply record that political theory's various attacks on the idea of human rights are not very convincing. This further encourages us to ask what the point is of identifying a selected set of rights as ethical and legal concerns of particular weight and of buttressing these rights through powerful legal institutions.

5.4 THE POLITICAL CASE FOR HUMAN RIGHTS

5.4.1 *The Political Theory of Entrenchment*

A useful approach to answering this question of why one should identify a particular set of rights and take them as particularly weighty ethical and legal concerns is to reflect on the *usefulness of legal entrenchment*. It is no accident that the political idea of human rights is wedded to the political theory and practice of constitutionalism and its basic idea, which is to isolate certain foundational norms from the general political process that these norms frame.[70] This means defending a two-tier system of political organization: Human rights create a framework for the everyday labors of politics, including antagonistic political pursuits concerning the many issues controversial in society. They can even to a certain degree accommodate those political forces that aim to leave a political system based on human rights behind. There are certainly legitimate limits to this accommodation. No majority has the right to enslave a minority, and no majority can enjoy the right to deprive others of their right to pursue their vision of the right and the good in the future, nor has any majority the right to deprive others of their rights to life and liberty. But within these limits, much is possible: In many systems, freedom of speech rightly includes the freedom to think aloud about the merits of abandoning this very freedom.

This kind of second-order entrenchment serves a very important function: It creates the scope for an open political process, which is necessary because political perfection is not ready at hand, political insight is not easy to achieve and human political pursuits – despite the very best intentions and careful self-reflective

[69] Wittgenstein, "Philosophische Untersuchungen," 217.

[70] András Sajó and Renáta Uitz, *The Constitution of Freedom: An Introduction to Legal Constitutionalism* (Oxford: Oxford University Press, 2017), 41 ff.

thinking – continue to be fallible. No philosopher king, no avant-garde of social progress is in possession of absolute political truth. Politics is a search involving trial and error, with no obvious end in sight – and if one shares these assumptions, the entrenchment of secondary norms like human rights makes a great deal of sense. A good and entirely justified dose of epistemic and moral self-distance, a lack of self-righteousness and skepticism about human beings' political wisdom is built into the political project of human rights: This project does not guarantee the end state of human bliss but protects conditions that preserve a framework for humanity's search for a decent political order. In this sense, human rights are a politically mature expression of patience with human fallibility – they provide the scope to pursue very different paths and experiments of living and to learn from failure along the way.

There is a further important point: Human rights aim to preserve the possibility of a flourishing human life independently of whether a final, highest aim of social organization is reached. An imperfect life is still a life worth living – this is one of the insights buttressing the legitimacy of human rights. The value of a life as such suffices to justify their system of protection. These rights consequently are not at the disposal of a policy that justifies current interferences in human rights with the supreme future good that these interferences will bring about. Interferences have to be justifiable here and now. This does not exclude the possibility of considering the interests of future generations – for example, in the context of environmental policies. However, the rights of the people alive now cannot simply be discounted. There is no prerogative of a utopian future; every generation and its particular quest for a life well lived is equally worthy of respect.

Human rights therefore act as a check on certain eschatological political schemes that are prepared to sacrifice human beings in the present on the altar of future bliss. The history of nineteenth- and twentieth-century socialist and communist thought is determined by such ideas in theory, art and political practice. Some noble deeds of self-sacrifice and some of the greatest tragedies of the twentieth century were the consequences. Human rights' insistence on the equal importance of every human being is thus far from a political banality. The question of whether or not one follows this path has turned out to be one of the decisive normative questions of recent history and defining not only for the identity of the post-totalitarian left – a topic to which we will return.

As said above, human rights create a framework for an open political process. However, this framework is to be respected by everybody and is thus based on a claim of substantial legitimacy. This implies that the idea of human rights rests on epistemologically more solid grounds than other political questions. The assumption is that there are better reasons to assume that freedom of speech is justified, for instance, than opinions about particular controversial political questions – say, that the highest percentage of income tax should be 44 percent and not 47 percent. This is quite a plausible stance. There are compelling reasons for freedom of speech, whereas the maximum tax rate is loaded to a much greater extent with difficult problems of political expedience. The content of human rights thus embodies a substantial theory of conditions for justified political aims.

The political idea of entrenchment is relevant not only for *legal* human rights. It is also an important element of a reflective *ethics* that seeks to identify a specific set of rights of other people, rights that carry *pro tanto* specific weight in comparison to other considerations. Religious tolerance as a moral virtue presupposes a sense of the moral entitlement of others to have their religious beliefs respected, not only by law, but also in everyday life. To discriminate against persons because of their religion is therefore not a morally appropriate thing to do.

Such a morality of rights is helpful in political ethics, too. It determines the constraints of one's own political or economic aspirations, which may take different forms but must not violate the human rights of others. This is also true for those cases involving a morally justified bias towards people with whom one enjoys specific relations. There is doubtlessly a morally legitimate special concern for one's children or other persons with whom one enjoys a personal bond. We legitimately do many things for our own children that we do not do for other children. Acknowledging this does not mean committing to a new form of tribalism, because there are limits to such permissible special concerns.[71] Human rights define some of these limits. The legitimate concern that one's own children receive a good education does not justify contributing to social structures that provide for this need at the expense of other children, for instance. Human rights define an ethical baseline in the framework of which other concerns take their appropriate place. Making them explicit ethical principles helps to draw their boundaries properly.

Entrenchment implies a stance on the idea of human *progress*: Whatever the future may look like, human rights underline that respect for human liberty, equality and worth is the condition for any progress. Consequently, progress does not consist – as in some teleologies of history – in humanity being reborn over and over on ever-higher levels of development, but in better ways of living that continue to respect human beings' basic rights.[72]

[71] As Dworkin, *Justice for Hedgehogs*, 324 observes: "Many people do believe, as I do not, that their racial, ethnic, religious, and linguistic connections bestow associational rights and obligations. Perhaps some of these convictions have a genetic foundation; if so they will prove particularly hard to ignore and perhaps pointless to disparage. But the idea of these special rights and obligations has been and remains a powerful source of evil. Throw a dart at a spinning globe, and the odds are good that it will land where tribes of race, religion, or language are killing each other and destroying their communities in the name of some supposed group right or destiny. These hatreds may be as enduring as they are destructive, and we should have no illusions that they will disappear or even ebb from human affairs."

[72] This can be reconciled with a sober concept of history. Arendt, for instance, notes in the expanded German version of *Origins of Totalitarianism* – Arendt, *Elemente und Ursprünge totaler Herrschaft*, 325 n. 36 – that the concept of progress of the Enlightenment, contrary to teleological ideas of limitless progress, included the idea that humanity had ultimately reached maturity and thus an end point of a certain kind of development, and would move onward with freedom and autonomy, not be carried away by the currents of history.

5.4.2 *Scope to Act and the Political Subjects of History*

Human rights empower human beings as the agents of political development and social change. Does this make political sense? After all, one important question of political theory and the philosophy of history is who the subjects of this history actually are. This question only seemingly has an easy answer. Much intellectual effort has gone into showing that it is not human beings who drive human history forward (as it might appear), but forces beyond human control. It is not only religious perspectives that embrace this view. Hegel, for example, famously argued that it is the cunning of reason, the "*List der Vernunft*" that moves history – and in ways contrary to human beings' intentions.[73] Consequently, attempts to create a political order based on normative principles determined by free, autonomous human reflection are futile. Marxism was influenced by the idea of history being driven forward by economic forces, the dialectic of the forces of production and relations of production. Some evolutionary social theories invest the functional needs of social systems with the power to determine the course of human social history.[74] Others (unlike Adam Smith himself) see only the invisible hand of markets at play.

Human rights made explicit and established as powerful institutions of the law imply another story, however. The creation of such ethical systems and institutions manifests the conviction that human beings can influence history in a very profound way. These systems and institutions embody the human attempt to define the normative limits in which the future – whatever it might bring, with all of the surprises both good and bad that it surely holds in store – can unfold. The architecture of human rights intends to prevent certain courses that have plagued human beings in the past. Human rights are made to facilitate a human life that is enriched by a certain degree of normative integrity because individuals pursue their various aims within the morally legitimate limits of human rights. Within these carefully crafted constraints, however, humans are free to act. Human rights are a testimony to human beings' claim to being the autonomous authors of their own political fate.

There is much to be said about the importance of social structures and the many direct and indirect ways in which they influence human beings' political aspirations, political consciousness, motivations and, ultimately, action. Subjective voluntarism is not a convincing theory of political agency. However, acknowledging this does not mean that it is advisable to deny the importance of individuals' political agency. The claim that superindividual forces beyond human control drive the course of history forward has not proven to be a very successful theoretical stance. It was not merely an impersonal social structure that caused masses of human beings to inflict war

[73] Georg Wilhelm Friedrich Hegel, *Vorlesungen über die Philosophie der Geschichte*, in *Werke*, Vol. 12, eds. Eva Moldenhauer and Karl Markus Michel (Frankfurt am Main: Suhrkamp, 1970), Vorrede, 49.

[74] Luhmann, *Gesellschaft der Gesellschaft*.

upon other people and commit crimes during Nazism, but individuals who ultimately were responsible for these deeds. Human rights consequently draw a plausible lesson from the past.

The ethics and law of human rights presuppose that there is no reason for humans, as autonomous agents, to abdicate normative reflection in favor of other forces when determining the proper setup of institutions of social organization. There is no reason to assume the priority of the superhuman wisdom of the markets, for example, which transcends the capacities of human thought. Instead, normative principles form the legitimate framework of social organization. These normative principles are accessible to human understanding. Human beings not only are the authors of the normative framework of humans' social lives, but their ethical thought can also determine this framework's content convincingly. The idea of human rights acknowledges human ethical understanding as a guiding source of political organization.

The empowerment of human beings by human rights poses an important question to the politics of rights: How are we to prepare human beings for freedom? How are we to prevent the abuse of freedom for aims that have nothing to do with human rights? This question strongly exercised important thinkers after the experience of the French Revolution and in particular of *la Terreur*.[75] It continues to be a crucial question for the transition to democracy and the maintenance of democratic structures alike. The answer provided by systems of human rights is to secure rights and try to prevent abuse within this framework of guarantees. There is a case for cultivating the ability to appreciate freedom, including, for example, by such subtle means as art.[76] The rise of illiberal democracy attests the need for this, and dramatically so in recent years. There is, however, no legitimate "maturity test" for individuals or societies that could form a precondition for the enjoyment of rights. The entrenchment of freedom and other rights guarantees that lies at the base of the project of human rights thus involves a significant dose of trust in human beings' capability to exercise their rights conscientiously, with tangible institutional consequences that entail real political risks.

Trusting that human beings are able to use freedom responsibly bets on the sufficient maturity of human beings. Historical experience warns us not to be too sure about the outcome of this bet. It is thus important, as we will see shortly, that human rights not only create scope for action, but also incorporate safeguards against destructive political actions, something that is of decisive importance for the political theory of human rights.

5.4.3 *Human Rights as a Condition of Community*

Human rights are not based on a *collectivist theory of social organization*: Their aim is to protect individuals, not superindividual values of whatever form. However, they are

75 Cf. for instance Humboldt's remarks, Humboldt, "Ideen zu einem Versuch," 218.
76 Schiller, *Ästhetische Erziehung*; Schiller, *Aesthetic Education*.

not motivated by an *atomistic, asocial individualism* either, although there have been plenty of attempts to make fundamental rights serve the interests of a powerful few. The importance of individuals as a limiting condition of political pursuits does not mean that human rights cannot be reconciled with solidarity and duties towards others, as we already have seen. Human rights are concerned with individuals, but individuals who are part of a community. Rights imply duties of others, they impose normative burdens in a variety of forms on everybody: Every individual not only is a bearer of rights, but also has duties derived directly or indirectly from the rights of others. If some persons have a right to freedom of expression, others have a no-right that these persons refrain from expressing themselves in a certain way, even if they strongly (and with good reason) disagree with the content of this expression. This includes their normative inability to make public authorities intervene in others' exercise of free speech – for instance, by action by courts. Respecting an order of rights is a strong statement of human solidarity, because it comes at a price for everybody.

In the law, further technical devices make this concern a legal reality. For instance, the doctrine of legitimate limitations of rights manifests the importance of the community-oriented aspect of human rights. Many codifications explicitly mention the rights of others in their systems of justified limitations alongside other community concerns. Influential courts have strongly emphasized the social nature of human beings.[77] The system of limitations is, after all, an attempt to balance the rights of individuals with the rights of others and community interests. Moreover, human rights catalogues include guarantees of equality and increasingly also incorporate some social rights that embody a minimum of legally guaranteed social solidarity with the needs and interests of others, mirroring moral principles with the same content. There is also a good argument for human rights as promoting the lasting integration of political communities: People's enjoyment of a significant set of shared, equitably distributed rights can create a social bond beyond the many divisions that remain. It is thus a profound misunderstanding to see human rights as opposing a deep concern for the importance of human community, including, on the international level, the community of all human beings.

5.4.4 *Human Rights as Legal Rights*

Human rights as legal rights place particular demands on justification. One is the degree of certainty that law aspires to embody. Human rights, however, are abstract

[77] An interesting and influential case is the case law on human dignity in German constitutional law. In this context, the Federal Constitutional Court has underlined explicitly that the dignity-based freedom of the individual is not the freedom of an "isolated" and "autocratic" individual, but of an individual embedded and bound by human community, BVerfGE, Judgement of June 21, 1977, BVerfGE 45, 187 (227): "*Freiheit versteht das Grundgesetz nicht als diejenige eines isolierten und selbstherrlichen, sondern als die eines gemeinschaftsbezogenen und gemeinschaftsgebundenen Individuums*"; standing case law, cf. BVerfGE, Judgement of January 17, 2017, BVerfGE 144, 20 (para. 540).

and general. As a consequence, there is a need to specify them. Ensuring that this process is methodologically controlled so that it amounts to more than mere arbitrary decision-making by courts is a challenging problem. Nevertheless, through the incremental development of case law and doctrine, working human rights systems prove that this issue can be solved in practice.

A further problem is justiciability. This is an important constraint for legal human rights. The fact that something is a legitimate moral concern is not enough to make it a legal human right. It must be possible to formulate the concern in a way that makes it justiciable. Normative rhapsodizing devoid of legal effect does not foster the cause of human rights. There are intense technical debates about this question within human rights law. Given the vast number of concrete judicial applications of human rights law in courts around the world, it would be absurd to deny that this problem can be solved. To be sure, there are difficult cases, of which social rights represent a key example that we have highlighted several times in our discussion. These rights are very controversial for various reasons, not least because of their potentially redistributive impact on the wealth of society. However, such concerns about the legitimizing principles of social rights – important as they are – do not exhaust the debate. One also needs to be able to formulate social rights in a way that renders them justiciable. But even in this difficult case there is sufficient jurisprudence to show that social rights, too, can be properly integrated into justiciable law.

A further issue we have already touched upon is the role of courts in a theory of political institutions. In democracies, preventing courts from taking over legislative functions is of particular concern. The practice of human rights proves that this problem can be solved as well, not least by judicial self-restraint. These institutional questions are relevant for problems of specific groups of rights, too. As indicated above, one can be entirely convinced that there is a case, say, for a moral right to work and that a political society is under a duty to provide such work but legally question that courts should be the institutions allocating employment in a society.

The legal dimension of human rights therefore merits particular attention in a political theory of human rights. Nevertheless, it seems indisputable that the legal protection of human rights has proven a useful tool for fostering important goods of human beings. As we have seen, theories that doubt this have proven unconvincing.

5.5 RIGHTS AFTER AUSCHWITZ

Political theories do not exist in a historical vacuum. The weight of arguments depends in part on what history teaches us about their relevance. This is particularly true in our time. The many horrors of the last century are not sufficiently remote to have passed into comfortable oblivion. They are not episodes devoid of any deeper relation to our current lives, like castle dungeons that can be visited on a Sunday afternoon, sending a pleasurable shiver down one's spine at the thought of the cruel deeds once committed there but soon forgotten over a beer in the museum bar – as if our present-day lives had exorcised the menacing ghosts – savage, narrow-minded and grotesque, greedy and devoid of remorse or pity – that plagued the unfortunate past. The twentieth century was on all accounts a watershed in human history. The catastrophes of that century – World War II, the Holocaust, the Gulag, the extermination campaign against the Armenians, the atrocities committed against the human beings submitted to colonial domination, including such defining events as the millions of deaths in the Congo under Belgian rule and the mass murder of the Herero by German troops, the massacres under Pol Pot in Cambodia or the genocide in Rwanda among other gruesome events – taught some dire lessons that are of decisive importance for the political theory of human rights.

The thoughts, feelings and actions of all those who have gone before, whether they have left a personal mark in the annals of the past or not, their suffering, humiliation and fleeting bliss are the characters in which history spells out what it really means to be human. History provides the key to what humanity is truly about – understood not as a group of beings but as the epitome of the characteristics with which the human species travels through time. Not only the achievements of art and science, not only the *Peplos Kore* and Newton's optics, the *Creation of Adam* on the ceiling of the Sistine Chapel and Euler's proofs say something about the existential makeup of humankind. Nor are the care and justice of everyday life, the dignity with which humans shoulder the many tasks of their existence as mortal beings the only things to take into account. The fact that an atrocity like the Holocaust was possible, that human beings performed the many tasks required to make mass murder happen, often with the deep conviction – *This is right!* – is another building block of any credible conception of what humanity means. This atrocity thus indicates a deep cultural, ethical and political crisis that enveloped humanity a mere few decades ago. Given the many crimes that have followed since then, there are good reasons to think that this crisis still defines important elements of our lives.

The events of the past cannot be undone. No future degree of decency can reconcile the moral balance sheet of the human species. The colonial massacres, the enslavement of people weak enough to be subdued, the concentration camps and gas chambers will remain on the records defining what it is to be human. The image of ourselves, painted by the trajectory of history, extending not in space but in time, contains elements we cannot digest. There is no way to come to terms with the fact that human beings were torn from their homes, herded into cattle wagons and killed in a production line of death for no other reason than a vile, obscenely shallow and entirely fantastic ideology. So little do thought and reason count, such absurd and dirty fairy tales can become human beings' intimate creed, so feeble is the force of the most basic and obvious demands of justice and human solidarity, so contemptuously can human beings deal with human life. The edifice of human institutions, the pious teachings of religion, the grand systems of ethics born in the better hearts and minds of humanity? Not worth a cent when it counted most.

These experiences have put paid to important hopes. The human species without doubt has the capacity to do good and to act justly. But it will continue to be threatened by these other impulses, which enmesh humans in profound guilt and inflict cruelty and death upon their victims in many shapes. Any view that does not include these experiences in its picture of humanity and give them decisive weight is no more than a dangerous illusion.

Human beings have proved able to explain the motions of heavenly bodies in a universe vast beyond imagination and to decipher some of the codes of matter. But they have neither been nor become the sovereign masters of their social life. The workings of their societies, the economic structures they create, the systems of social interaction they build, the power relations by which their fates are decided, the web of human life woven by the back-and-forth of ceaseless action all seem to elude their full understanding, and thus humans often remain at the receiving end of events that they even sometimes mythologize as destiny. Given the state in which the world finds itself in the twenty-first century, humanity still appears unable to establish social structures at a global level that allow for a decent life for all of its members, prevent the worst atrocities from happening and ensure the survival of the species – tasks one might be inclined to think would not be beyond creatures such as ourselves.

The reality of the horrors of the past and the continued instability and imperfection of social relations suggest that the future of human societies is precarious. It is possible that long-cherished hopes will be brought closer to realization; it is possible that our worst nightmares will come true, including the self-annihilation of the human species.

In this situation, both full of promise and rife with threats, the most important lesson of the twentieth century is that certain normative principles must be protected without compromise. Whatever policy one may wish to pursue, certain norms must not be violated – this is the categorical imperative that the events of the last century have formulated. No aim is lofty enough to justify the abandonment of these norms, which protect some of the most foundational principles of human decency.

This lesson is taught not least by the tragedy of socialism. The ethical core of the best elements of this movement is the search for human equality and the protection of human dignity. However, the politics of key attempts to realize an economic and political order based on these principles made a terrible charade of these ideals: Authoritarian oligarchic party bureaucracies, let alone terror systems such as Stalinism, marked a cruel betrayal of these normative ideas.

The lesson that many thinkers draw from this tragedy deserves to be considered more emphatically than often is the case in debates about the political point of human rights. There are many reckonings with this tragedy, some of them by people who supported concrete socialist politics for some time or throughout their lives, others by critics of these visions – from Arthur Koestler[78] and Ernst Bloch,[79] on to George Orwell[80] and Hannah Arendt,[81] from Bertrand Russell[82] and Albert Camus[83] to Noam Chomsky,[84] from Max Frisch[85] to Uwe Johnson.[86] One recurrent theme is the realization that the political aims pursued do not justify all means and in particular that no human community based on the freedom, equality and dignity of human beings can be built by politics that disrespect these very principles in the process of constructing this community. Individuals must count, not just abstract principles, which can quickly turn into hollow phrases, as the "untouchable" Veluta realizes in A. Roy's tale about the "god of small things" when fleeing caste hatred and vainly seeking help from his fellow communist Comrade Pelay, the refusal spelling his death sentence: "*Individuals' interest is subordinate to the organization's interest. Violating Party Discipline means violating Party Unity*. The voice went on. Sentences disaggregated into phrases. Words. *Progress of the Revolution. Annihilation of the Class Enemy. Comprador capitalist. Spring-thunder.* And there it was again. Another religion turned against itself. Another edifice constructed by the human mind, decimated by human nature."[87]

These insights seem straightforward enough but are clearly in need of defense. Their political foes come in various guises, and not only from the political right. Leftist movements of the 1960s and 1970s did not universally accept that human rights are inviolable. Tactical attitudes towards human rights were widespread, sometimes in the framework of decolonization or revolutionary aspirations. The leftist terror of the 1970s in Europe is just one example of the consequences that such ideas can have. The collapse of the state socialist systems, the moral and political reckoning that followed when the reality of these systems (which now no longer could be shrouded in comforting ideologies) could be inspected in full daylight confirmed beyond doubt the importance of the principle that no social and political good can come of the violation of human rights, whatever aims are pursued.

This lesson is also crucial for current and new attempts at social reconstruction and worldmaking. New egalitarian projects that rightly rebel against injustice in particular societies and in global economic and political structures, searching for a postcolonial cosmopolitanism able to overcome structures of domination and the

78 Arthur Koestler, *Darkness at Noon* (London: Vintage Classics, 2020).
79 Bloch, *Naturrecht und menschliche Würde*.
80 George Orwell, *Homage to Catalonia* (London: Vintage Classics, 2021); George Orwell, *Animal Farm* (London: Vintage Classics, 2021); George Orwell, *Nineteen Eighty-Four* (London: Vintage Classics, 2021).
81 Arendt, *Origins of Totalitarianism*.
82 Bertrand Russell, *The Practice and Theory of Bolshevism* (London: Allen and Unwin, 1962).
83 Camus, "L'homme révolté."
84 Noam Chomsky, *America and the New Mandarins* (New York: Vintage Books, 1969), 72 ff.
85 Max Frisch, *Tagebuch 1946–1949* (Frankfurt am Main: Suhrkamp, 1985).
86 Uwe Johnson, *Jahrestage 1–4* (Berlin: Suhrkamp, 2013).
87 Arundhati Roy, *The God of Small Things* (London: Flamingo, 1997), 287 (emphasis in original).

global "color line," will fail to achieve any meaningful and justified ends if they overlook the importance of human rights. Any form of human progress needs human rights to maintain the public space necessary for thinking and acting. Without rights to political participation, the freedom to communicate about ideas, the rights to associate with others in political groups, NGOs or trade unions, without guarantees for the liberty to be whatever a person chooses to be, from sexual identity to religious belief, without protection against being unlawfully prosecuted, incarcerated, tortured or killed, no political movement will succeed.

There is another point: Disregarding human rights would mean discounting the normative reasons – the human autonomy, equality and dignity at the heart of the human rights idea – that motivate the search for nondomination in the first place. Moreover, this discounting does not even promise success in the long run, as the history of postcolonial dictatorships and their contribution to imperial worldmaking, strengthening global structures of domination over the Global South, has shown – from the oil-producing authoritarian regimes in the Middle East and their role in the current political economy of energy resources to the South American military dictatorships. Ultimately, any emancipatory political project will betray its promises of freedom, equality and dignity if it loses its consciousness of what one does not do to human beings.[88]

As Albert Camus put it when reflecting on the many forms of nihilism that swept European culture in the nineteenth and twentieth centuries, it is not enough for the *l'homme revolté*, the rebellious human being, to say *no*. It is crucial to say *yes* to something, too – to a substantial idea of what human beings are like irrespective of history and social development, and to a set of normative principles that are sufficiently secure to lead the way and crucially are not negotiable.[89] For Camus, as for many others, human rights needed to form the building blocks of this answer to the challenge of nihilism and contempt for human life that dragged human beings into the many catastrophes of recent history.

The consequence of these thoughts for a theory of the justification of human rights seems clear enough: Nothing can redeem the pains and degradation of the victims of the past. However, underestimating the political importance of human rights fails to draw the minimum necessary conclusion from their

88 When considering arguments that the human rights movement has neglected the struggle for substantive equality, cf. for instance Moyn, *Not Enough*, one should therefore also remain aware of what the neglect of human rights has meant for egalitarian movements. It would be a sad irony if contemporary egalitarianism were to reenact key destructive political fallacies of the egalitarianism of the past. Similar considerations hold for visions of postcolonial worldmaking. It is certainly true, as Getachew, *Worldmaking after Empire*, 33 f. argues, that sovereignty is not just a way to shield a regime against critique of its own human rights abuses, but an institution helping to protect political communities against domination, both colonial and of other kinds, cf. Chapter 2. However, this does not mean that it is justified to pursue paths of political self-determination that discount human rights for the sake of collective self-determination.

89 Camus, "L'homme révolté."

suffering, namely to honor those rights the contempt for which was the root of these victims' dire fate.

5.6 NORMATIVE PRINCIPLES

5.6.1 *Justice and Solidarity as the Wellsprings of Rights*

The discussion thus far has led to two conclusions: First, a justificatory theory of human rights depends on reasons why the goods protected are worthy of such protection. The argument was that a plausible theory of the human condition or human nature (not a theoretically suspicious concept if understood properly and purged of speculative metaphysics or repressive ideology) is needed to justify the selection of protected goods embodied in human rights bills and ethical theories.

Second, there are plausible reasons to believe that a convincing political case can be made for human rights as key instruments to secure these goods both as ethical principles and as legal institutions, despite a great number of critiques, both old and new.

Our review of the theories of justification and of the political theory of rights, including the critique of rights, has underlined the importance of normative principles for the justification of rights – hardly a surprising result, albeit sometimes less clearly stated in current debates than one might expect, as we have seen. But what exactly are these normative principles? How do they give rise to rights?

In the history and theory of human rights, one central concept is *equality*. Human rights are concerned with human equality, and part of the foundational principles of the human rights project is the equality of rights. Furthermore, human rights are an expression of *benevolent concern* for other human beings, for their liberty, for the proper treatment that they deserve. It therefore stands to reason that plausible candidates for the normative principles important for the justification of human rights include, first, principles of egalitarian justice and, second, principles of human care and solidarity. Let us look at these two sets of principles first before we turn our attention to another key normative concept for human rights: the idea of human dignity.

Principles of justice are the reason why human rights are conceptualized as equal rights. They also provide the reason why certain goods – be it interests or needs – possess normative relevance. This reason is the *necessary connection between justice and rights*:[90] Interests or needs as such are normatively neutral, as we have seen. The fact that I have an interest, perhaps even a need (given my deep-seated competitive passion) to win a rowing regatta does not mean that I have the right to win a rowing

[90] This is a standard observation, cf. Mill, "Utilitarianism," 247 f.; John Tasioulas, "Justice, Equality, and Rights," in *The Oxford Handbook of the History of Ethics*, ed. Roger Crisp (Oxford: Oxford University Press, 2013).

regatta. If a distribution is just, however, one has a right to this distribution. This seems to be a necessary connection. It is impossible to assert that the distribution D of good X is just, but that the patients of the distributive action have no moral right to their share D of the good X distributed. If sweets are distributed during a children's party, the kids have a moral right to their fair share – and will claim it with considerable moral passion (and noise). This relation between justice and rights is relevant for human rights as well: Human rights imply the idea of a just distribution and allocation of central goods such as respect, status and freedom. Because it is just that human beings are put in a position where they are equally capable of enjoying a certain share of goods as other humans are (e.g. to express themselves freely in way K under circumstances Y), they have a right to that good.

Principles of justice thus are key to transforming certain human goods into the content of rights: The justness of the distribution of goods gives rise to the existence of rights. If the goods meet the threshold condition of importance and have a qualified personal scope, they may be human rights.

What are these principles? This question leads to further vast problems and copious intense debates. Moreover, the concept of justice seems to have various dimensions – standard distinctions include distributive, corrective, retributive and procedural justice and justice in exchange. If we look at basic uncontroversial cases regarded as just or unjust (such as distributing a birthday cake, basic standards of just grading, etc.), however, we are able to make sufficient progress for our purposes in determining what this idea is all about. It is useful in this context to distinguish between normative principles, criteria of justice and spheres of justice, to use Walzer's terms.[91] The first set normative standards – importantly, for instance, the universally accepted principle "treat equals equally." The second determine the normatively relevant reference points of just or unjust intentions, actions and states of affairs – for instance, the criteria for allocating goods in a certain way or for evaluating an already-existing allocation of goods. The third circumscribe certain areas of just or unjust intentions, actions or states of affairs that may follow a specific rationale for allocating goods.

The concrete meaning of the principle of equality has formed the basis of discussions on justice to a large degree ever since antiquity and is universally associated with justice in today's theory and empirical work, too. Accordingly, the most important questions in the theory of justice are not whether justice is connected to equality, but, first, what equality as a prescriptive concept means exactly (formal equality, substantive equality, something else?), second, between which objects this relation has to obtain to satisfy the principles of justice and, third, what the normative consequences of judgments about justice (or injustice) actually are.[92]

[91] Michael Walzer, *Spheres of Justice* (New York: Basic Books, 1983).

[92] A good example of a contemporary debate about these issues is the discussion about Rawls' principles of justice, Rawls, *Theory of Justice*, 60. Some argue that in particular the prudential

If one analyzes standard cases of distributive justice (a dimension of justice particularly relevant for the justification of human rights), the justness of the distribution of goods appears to have the following yardsticks. A just distribution demands proportional equality between the value of the specific criterion of distribution reasonably related to a particular sphere of distribution on the one hand and the amount of the good distributed on the other. Determining which criterion of distribution should count is a persistent problem.[93] This difficulty does not mean that there are not good reasons to prefer one criterion over the other: The criterion for the distribution of grades reasonably related to the sphere of university education is performance, for instance. Giving grades according to the perceived beauty of the student is, in contrast, a rather bad idea because it does not serve the function of grading, such as feedback and information about intellectual achievements. A just grading of an exam is consequently one that awards a good grade to a good performance, because this preserves the proportional equality between the value of the criterion of distribution (a good performance) reasonably related to the sphere of distribution (grading) and the good allocated (a good grade).

Another yardstick is that justice demands an interpersonal comparison and the preservation of the equality of the distribution between persons. The standard of treatment applied has to be equal for all equal patients of an intention or action. For example, if grading is made dependent on performance for some students and not for others, this grading is unjust. If there is no criterion for distinctions between patients of actions, then, as a default rule, a numerically equal distribution among equals is just to preserve the equality of persons. If there is no particular reason to distribute a birthday cake differently, an equal distribution is a just distribution. This principle is not entirely banal, as it is central for the allocation of scarce goods in a society for cases in which a criterion of distribution underdetermines the distribution both of these goods and of the chances to acquire these goods. As far as corrective justice is concerned, the restituting act has to equal the object restituted.[94] Finally, any

modification of egalitarian principles by the difference principle is unconvincing and that justice thus demands stricter egalitarianism than conceived of by Rawls, Gerald Allan Cohen, *Rescuing Justice and Equality* (Cambridge, MA: Harvard University Press, 2008). Others argue that Rawls' egalitarianism goes too far – the principles of justice worth defending are not "end-result or end-state principles" of the distribution of social goods, but historical principles, Nozick, *Anarchy, State, and Utopia*, 153 ff. Sen, *Idea of Justice*, in turn doubts the wisdom of "transcendental institutionalism" observed in Rawls' theory. Michael J. Sandel, *Justice: What's the Right Thing to Do?* (New York: Farrar, Straus and Giroux, 2009), 268 argues for a "connection between distributive justice and the common good." Despite these (serious and important) questions, the debate continues to be one about the meaning of equality.

93 Cf. e.g. Sen's example of three children and a flute in Sen, *Idea of Justice*, 12 f.: Should a flute belong to the maker, the one who can play it best or the one that needs it the most for their well-being? The idea of proportional equality has been a centerpiece of the theory of justice since antiquity, cf. for a classic statement Aristotle, *Nicomachean Ethics*, trans. Harris Rackham, Loeb Classical Library 73 (Cambridge, MA: Harvard University Press), 1129a ff.

94 Cf. Mahlmann, *Rechtsphilosophie und Rechtstheorie*, 423 ff.

treatment or state of affairs (e.g. the distribution of capabilities to lead a meningful life in a society) has to be reconcilable with human beings' basic equality of worth, the ultimate substantive yardstick of justice in human affairs. On this basis, one can start to rationally reconstruct other dimensions of justice, such as substantive or procedural justice, and try to tackle concrete political problems.[95]

In the case of goods that are the objects of protection by human rights, the criterion for distribution reasonably related to the sphere of distribution is the humanity of the rights-holder. As all humans enjoy full humanity in the normatively relevant sense, a just distribution of goods protected by human rights requires that every human being enjoy an equal set of goods protected by human rights, not some classes of human beings (say, women or people with a certain skin color) less and others (say, men and white people) more. Human beings consequently have rights to this kind of distribution of goods. The principles of equality are also important for the justified limitations of rights, which need to ensure that the sometimes-scarce good of liberty is distributed equally so that the liberties of one are reconcilable with the equal liberties of others.

In the theory of rights, there is another dimension to justice: Rights not only secure goods, they are *goods themselves*. To have a right to an asset is itself of great worth. Consequently, the distribution of rights *itself* is a matter of justice. This helps to explain why human beings have a *right to have rights*: Because of their shared humanity (or so it seems thus far), it is a matter of justice that they enjoy *rights* to an equal system of rights to goods crucial to their life as human beings, not only the goods as such.

The necessity to preserve interpersonal equality is another reason why only an equal allocation of rights among different but normatively equal persons forms a just system of rights. Principles of justice demand the equal treatment of persons by the

[95] It is important to underline that this reconstruction of principles of justice does not reduce equality to consistency. It raises, thus, not the concerns discussed e.g. in Sandra Fredman, *Discrimination Law*, 2nd ed. (Oxford: Oxford University Press 2011), p. 8 ff. The criterion for equal treatment determines the respects in which persons are to be treated alike or differently, depending on the value of the criterion. Two persons with equally high incomes are to be taxed equally highly, whereas a high-income earner and a low-income earner are justifiedly taxed unequally (to treat them equally depending on their financial capabilities). Given that the relation of equality has to obtain between the value of the criterion of distribution and the treatment, one does not always need a different person as comparator. A good grade is just for a good exam performance even if only one student participated in the exam. Moreover, in cases of interpersonal comparisons there is the possibility of hypothetical comparators, now widely accepted in equality law. Thus, the account of justice outlined helps to develop an idea of substantive justice that aims to break the cycle of disadvantage of certain groups, to respect the dignity of everyone, to cherish diversity and to secure the equal participation of everyone in society. Cf. on these aims ibid. p. 25 ff. The significance for satisfying the demands of principles of justice to maintain proportional equality between the criteria of distribution and the kind of distribution of goods is one reason why equality is not a redundant concept, as some argue. A second reason is the importance of interpersonal, comparative equality for the just allocation of scarce goods. A third reason is that equal treatment shows respect for the equal worth of human beings. Cf. for an overview Jeremy Waldron, *One Another's Equal: The Basis of Human Equality* (Cambridge, MA: Harvard University Press, 2017), 41 ff. with similar conclusions.

equal distribution of goods and the rights that secure them because of the equal normative status of human beings. This equal system of rights protects everyone's equal opportunity (or capability) to use their potential as a human person. The thesis that already suggested itself in the critical review of theories of justification therefore seems to be on the right track: *Justice is a wellspring of rights.*

The other relevant principle is *care or solidarity*. There are obligations to care for others; this is a core principle of morality and ethics. These obligations are not boundless, but still are meaningful. For example, there is a duty not to let somebody die who can be helped without compromising overwhelmingly important interests of the agent.[96] Some legal systems even buttress such duties with criminal sanctions.[97] Other duties may be more controversial: Leibniz argued that not only Samaritan duties to prevent harm to others exist, but also duties to promote the well-being of others if that is possible at no or a small cost to the agent.[98] Kant thought that the only duty of virtue is to foster the beatitude of others.[99] If one goes yet a step further and holds that loving one's neighbor as oneself captures an important ethical principle, duties to concern oneself with the well-being of others become even more exacting. Be this as it may, for the purpose of these remarks it suffices to say that there is a strong case at least for some basic duties of human solidarity.

The flipside of the coin of the duty to care for others is the prohibition to harm them – the least one can do for the well-being of others is not to harm them. Unlike positive duties of solidarity, this prohibition of harm is rather uncontroversial.

These moral obligations of agents give rise to the rights of others.[100] This is important. There is not only an obligation to help others under certain circumstances, but also a right of those in need that this be done as long as the threshold of supererogatory acts of the agent is not crossed. If Ayodele collapses on the road, bystanders have a duty to call an ambulance, and she has a right that they do (at least) this. The same holds for the prohibition of harm – it creates not only duties, but also entitlements.

Rights protect human goods that are often of existential importance; they can even be matters of life and death. Human beings therefore have a duty of solidarity to help others to enjoy these goods – for instance, the possibility of leading a free and secure life, a duty that gives rise to rights to these goods.

Furthermore, human rights are crucial instruments for protecting the enjoyment of central human goods and – as just highlighted – goods *themselves*. Human solidarity is therefore a further reason for humans' *right to have rights*. Moreover, contributing to

96 This is sometimes discussed as the rescue principle. There is nothing new about this idea, cf. for instance Thomas Aquinas' arguments for strong duties of care for others in need (and the implied claims of the persons in need), discussed in Chapter 2.

97 Cf. Strafgesetzbuch (German Penal Code [StGB]), January 1, 1872, § 323c; Strafgesetzbuch (Swiss Penal Code [StGB]), SR 311.0, December 21, 1937, Art. 128.

98 Cf. Chapter 2.

99 Kant, *Metaphysik der Sitten*, 385.

100 On these problems, including but not limited to the relation of imperfect obligations and claims, see Chapter 1.

the efficiency of the (legal and extralegal) instruments of protection of these goods is a command of human care and solidarity. One consequence of this is the obligation to strengthen mechanisms of rights protection – for instance, by sustaining a legal order that protects such rights by one's taxes, by lending political support to international institutions for the protection of human rights or by participating in an NGO committed to improving the political culture of human rights. These duties are supplemented by the duties stemming from the prohibition to harm anybody – by depriving others of central goods or the rights that protect them.

Accordingly, the next important finding is that not only principles of justice, but also *duties to care for others are a wellspring of rights.*

5.6.2 *Dignity and Rights*

The theory of human goods needs to identify those goods that are plausibly of such qualified value for human beings that they are justifiably protected by human rights. Some reasons for the identification of some such goods have been outlined above. However, the goods identified in this way are only morally significant if the being for which they constitute goods is itself morally significant. One question thus remains that any theory of human rights needs to answer: Why are human beings of normative concern?

This question can be formulated more precisely when one pays due attention to three presuppositions in the argument so far. These are – simply put – first, that individual human beings count *at all*; second, that they count *equally*; and third, that they count *decisively* for any evaluation of a course of action. To address the first point, if human beings were of no *moral significance*, if they did not possess a certain value status, the project of human rights quite evidently would be pointless. The protection of life, liberty, equality, subsistence and well-being is based on the idea that the being for which these things are goods of importance matters. If human beings were creatures of no worth that better would not exist, an unfortunate, corrupted product of natural history that ought to be driven from the face of the Earth, the protection of their life, freedom or other goods would make no particular sense. The protection of life, liberty, equality and well-being is only important because the being whose goods these things are is itself morally significant.[101]

Second, it is important that each individual is of *equal worth*. This is the precondition for protecting life and liberty equally. It is not, as it might appear, a consequence, but rather a precondition of equality guarantees: They presuppose the equal worth of the human beings they are designed to protect. If racism were right

[101] Tasioulas, "Human Dignity," 307 comes to a similar conclusion from the point of view of an interest theory of human rights. Jeremy Waldron, "Is Human Dignity the Foundation of Human Rights?" *NYU School of Law, Public Law & Legal Theory Research Paper Series*, Working Paper No. 12-73 (2013), has correctly pointed out that dignity designates not only a cluster of normative positions, but also an underlying idea.

and certain so-called races were worth more than others, prohibitions of discrimination on the ground of ascribed race would not make any sense.

Third, it is pivotal that human rights not only imply that human beings have worth and that this worth is equal, but also determine the *weight of this worth* in comparison to other considerations. After all, one of the central questions in social history is whether other values ever outweigh the significance of individual human lives, and if so, under which circumstances. It has perhaps been something like the antihumanistic default assumption throughout history that individual human lives are of only relatively small importance, if any at all. Human life and liberty were held to be of little concern in comparison to the desire to build pyramids, to the power of dynasties and ruling groups, to the amassment of riches, to the grandeur of nations, to the future happiness of social classes or to the final, blissful, redemptive victory of religious creeds. Accordingly, many have perished without much ado on the construction sites of the cultural wonders of the world, in wars fought in the interests of dynastic power, in the pursuit of wealth and national glory, in class wars and in the religious suppression of heretical thought. Today, some of these ideas have lost their importance, while others have not: For the managers of the Bhopal factory, the lives of the poor living close to the factory premises were evidently only of limited concern, to take this classical example from economic history. National security is yet another example that continues to be significant. In this context, the idea that individuals have little importance in comparison to greater goods like the security of a nation is defended and put into practice – although there are, to be sure, effective security policies that follow a course respectful of human rights. The war in Ukraine with its many consequences from civilian deaths to starvation in poor countries teaches the same lesson.

What, then, supports the idea that all human beings enjoy a particular inalienable value status?

The central idea underpinning the attribution of equal worth to individuals and determining the qualified weight of this value status in relation to other goods is the notion that human beings enjoy human *dignity*. This is at least the language of contemporary human rights in which human dignity is taken as foundational for human rights – both in fundamental documents and treaties of human rights law and in much theoretical reflection.[102]

[102] Cf. for a reconstruction of the history of the concept and discussion of the current debate Mahlmann, *Grundrechtstheorie*, 97 ff.; Matthias Mahlmann, "The Basic Law at 60 – Human Dignity and the Culture of Republicanism," *German Law Journal* 11, no. 1 (2010): 9–31; Mahlmann, "Human Dignity and Autonomy," 370 ff.; Matthias Mahlmann, "The Good Sense of Dignity: Six Antidotes to Dignity Fatigue in Ethics and Law," in *Understanding Human Dignity*, ed. Cristopher McCrudden (Oxford: Oxford University Press, 2013), 593 ff.; Matthias Mahlmann, "Die Garantie der Menschenwürde in der Schweizerischen Bundesverfassung," *Aktuelle Juristische Praxis* 22, no. 9 (2013): 1307–20; Mahlmann, "Menschenwürde in Politik, Ethik und Recht," 267–81; Matthias Mahlmann, "Dignity and the Philosophy of the Republic," in *The Oxford Handbook of Republicanism* (forthcoming).

There is something in human beings – that is the core of this idea – that bestows particular worth upon them. All humans enjoy it, and the value of their life is thus equal. In addition, the worth inherent in human beings is supremely important. Human dignity means that individuals are of intrinsic, supreme, inalienable value, ends-in-themselves, and everybody equally so. According to this idea, human beings are the justified highest-order ends of human intentions and actions.

Human dignity is thus the expression of a radical egalitarian humanism, of human beings' uncompromising respect both for others and for themselves, not because of ephemeral achievements and contingent merits, but because of the nature of the core of their existence, the humanity they share. Such an interpretation of the value status of each individual cannot be reconciled with ethical principles in which the aggregate welfare trumps individual rights.[103] Furthermore, the idea of human dignity is the most radical critique of those ideas that relativize the importance of human life because of the greatness of dynasties, nations, classes or religions, because of the seductive pull of the pursuit of wealth or because of the heterogeneous interests behind what are often quite misleadingly called "reasons of state."

As we have seen, Arendt's famous assessment of the role of human rights as a force against the abuses of Nazism and Stalinism insisted on the importance of the *right to have rights*. Arendt identified this with the right to belong to a political community that protects the rights of its members, skeptical that humanity itself could fulfill this role.

On the function of integrating people into society and establishing solidarity, Regina Kiener, "Grundrechte in der Bundesverfassung," in *Verfassungsrecht der Schweiz/Droit constitutionell Suisse*, eds. Oliver Diggelmann, Maya Hertig Randall and Benjamin Schindler (Zürich: Schulthess, 2020), 1217 f. Cf. also for instance Christopher McCrudden, "Human Dignity and the Judicial Interpretation of Human Rights," *European Journal of International Law* 19, no. 4 (2008): 655–724; Aharon Barak, *Human Dignity: The Constitutional Value and the Constitutional Right* (Cambridge: Cambridge University Press, 2015); George Kateb, *Human Dignity* (Cambridge, MA: Harvard University Press, 2011); Michael Rosen, *Dignity* (Cambridge, MA: Harvard University Press, 2012); Jeremy Waldron, *Dignity, Ranks, and Rights* (Oxford: Oxford University Press, 2012); Catherine Dupré, *The Age of Dignity: Human Rights and Constitutionalism in Europe* (Oxford: Hart, 2015); Joas, *Sakralität der Person*; Peter Bieri, *Human Dignity: A Way of Living* (Cambridge: Polity Press, 2016). This basic stance encompass thinkers with a somewhat skeptical attitude towards the normative concept of dignity, cf. for instance Griffin, *On Human Rights*, 21: "If the weight we attach to rights is not to be arbitrary, we must have a sufficiently rich understanding of the value that rights represent – for *human* rights that would most likely require a sufficiently rich understanding of the dignity, or worth, of the human person, whatever the proper understanding of that now widely used phrase is. A satisfactory account of *human* rights, therefore must contain some adumbration of that exceedingly vague term 'human dignity', again not in all of its varied uses but in its role as a ground for human rights" (emphasis in original).

[103] This is the normative basis of the standard critique of utilitarianism that it disregards the necessary respect for persons, cf. Chapter 4. The point thus has deep roots in the history of ideas. Griffin, *On Human rights*, 22: "Nozick introduces an element of ethical substance: rights represent the moral significance of the separateness of persons." Such comments underestimate the importance of the long tradition based not least on the idea of dignity that defended the worth of the individual.

It has been argued above that a more promising approach might be to understand justice and human solidarity as the roots of such a right to have rights. Moreover, the right to have rights presupposes that a person is morally significant enough to become a holder of fundamental rights. Human dignity seems to be at the core of this idea. Under principles of justice and benevolent moral concern for others, human beings' worth, their intrinsic value as ends-in-themselves demand that they have rights securing the main pillars that make possible their pursuit of happiness and demand that these rights are those of *equals*. Belonging to a political community continues to be important for the efficient enforcement of rights. However, the right to belong to such a community is itself derived from the value status of human beings, and not, vice versa, this value status being from membership in a political community.

There is no right to have the right to have rights. There is no right to have human dignity to entitle someone to have equal human rights (likewise, Arendt does not argue that there is a right to the right to be a member of a human community that protects human rights in her original statement of the problem). Human dignity is the value status humans enjoy that, together with principles of justice and human concern, provides the *ultimate* foundation of human rights. This is where the spade turns, to return to this metaphor.

One may admit that this argument about dignity as a foundational principle of human rights has some merits. One may agree, too, that it would be beneficial for everybody to have reason to think it correct to ascribe dignity to all human beings, adding dryly that having human dignity as their foundation is all the worse for human rights, because human dignity itself has no justification. The castle of human rights, constructed to shield the essence of humanity, is built of normative sand and is quickly brought tumbling to the ground by a few swift strokes of doubt.

There is a vast debate both about the possible justification for ascribing dignity to all humans and about the concrete meaning of this concept, including the influential opinion that there is no such justification and that dignity is simply a piece of deplorable vacuous rhetoric at best and a harmful (and stupid) political ideology at worst, both in ethics and in law.[104]

Admittedly, it would make theoretical and political life much easier if one did not have to answer demanding questions about the meaning and justification of dignity. It would simplify human life even more if there were no need to take the idea seriously when taking actions that affect other human beings. If the dignity of others were irrelevant, one could just deal with them as one pleases, restricted by much less exacting standards.

[104] Cf. for instance Steven Pinker, "The Stupidity of Dignity," *New Republic*, May 28, 2008, 28; there has been a vast amount of dignity criticism ever since Schopenhauer's much-quoted (and less often seriously assessed) attack on Kant's idea of dignity, Arthur Schopenhauer, *Preisschrift über das Fundament der Moral* (Hamburg: Felix Meiner Verlag, 1979), 64.

But is this really so? The following thoughts indicate that this skeptical view is overly simple. A path that we will now explore further speaks for the plausibility of contemporary human rights' foundational assumption of the dignity of human beings and its consequence, namely the assertion of the respect owed to them.

The first argument to consider draws on the fact that human beings experience their life as intrinsically valuable, as an end-in-itself (pathological cases aside). This is why self-preservation is such a strong impulse. Life in this context cannot be reduced to continuous physical reproduction. It encompasses the totality of a human existence in its manifold dimensions. Life in this sense is not only a good, but the life of every human being is an *equal* good. There is nothing about one person's subjective experience that makes it qualitatively more worthy to be lived than the subjective experience of any other person. Love, friendship, happiness, despair are made of the same stuff in all human beings. Nor is anything objectively better about one life of a human being than about another as far as the basic value of human existence is concerned, although one can obviously do very different things of unequal value with the equally valuable gift of life. Nothing in the life of one person as such elevates it above the value of the life of another.

If that is so, if there is no reason to differentiate the value of life of different persons, then justice demands the equal protection of each human life as an end-in-itself. The universalization of the just, equal concern for the equal value of each life justifies the right to the protection of the intrinsic value of everyone's human existence.

In addition, humans enjoy particular properties that seem to give reason to think that the ascription of dignity is justified. Human beings have unpleasant characteristics, including being the only known organism with genocidal inclinations – no small flaw. The serious accounts of human dignity are therefore those underlining the fact that whatever worth human beings may possess, they continue to be highly ambivalent creatures, living just one step away from often self-inflicted, gratuitous, profound suffering, tragic errors and appalling crimes.

But this is not all that can be said about them. We already beheld some contours of the human life form in the mirror of the ethical and legal norms ascertaining its most important rights. If we take a closer look, some of the following observations may attract our attention: Humans are distinguished by their desire to look behind the facades of appearance and comprehend those parts of the structure of the world that are accessible to their understanding. This is of substantial importance for their position in the world. They cease to be *objects* of forces beyond comprehension and by epistemic means establish themselves as *subjects* within the world. They become capable of mastering some of the forces of nature and using them for their human purposes. For the many aspects of nature beyond such use, the understanding of at least some of their properties still prevents human beings from becoming mere passive things in the chain of events that make up the stuff of the world.

Human creativity is another constitutive factor of human beings' status as subjects. Humans put this creativity to use in very particular ways. In aesthetical representations whose beauty pleases and sometimes even enraptures, human beings critically reflect upon their own form of life and develop accounts of how things could be otherwise. They are themselves the authors of some of their deepest pleasures and of the prudentially and morally preferable imaginary worlds they continue to construct with the fine brush strokes of art. This faculty to produce works of beauty is very important for the concept of human dignity: In aesthetic creation, human beings bring a world according to their own image into being by which and in which their subjectivity can manifest itself in the form of and with the freedom of meaningful and at the same time deeply pleasurable artistic play.

Human existence is characterized by an emotionally rich, conscious, autonomous selfhood with a vulnerable longing for respect: Human beings inhabit a world of sentiment and are conscious of it, which both deepens their joy and can make suffering unbearable. They live with the consciousness of their mortality, which poses the challenge of earnestly striving for one's goals in life while knowing that ultimately one will have to let go of everything one has managed to achieve and holds dear. Thinking and acting despite the transience of one's existence (and the transience of the human species as such) adds to the reasons for the respect that humans rightly desire to enjoy.

The capacity for autonomous conscious self-determination offers humans the striking privilege of being the authors of their one life. They are not the mere plaything of drives that determine the actions they take but are able to choose and themselves decisively shape the course of their existence. They are a product of nature, but one with a demiurgic power to mold anew what human existence means within the limits set by their human nature. At the same time, their acts greatly influence the lives of others. Their autonomy is the source of the responsibility for what they do to themselves and to others – a responsibility to which humans have to be able to stand up, sometimes with dire consequences, including guilt, remorse and punishment. When deciding the course of action they intend to take, humans have the ability to transcend some of their most important interests, motivated by the force of moral obligations to secure what is due to others and to respect their rights, sometimes leading strong souls even to risk and sacrifice their lives.

Human beings are reflective, creative, autonomous, feeling, self-conscious, mortal subjects under moral laws. They unfold their potential and realize their capabilities in human communities and through their many bonds with others. These existential characteristics enable a particular form of life, extended over time, encompassing growth, maturity and decay, and plausibly can be taken as some of the crucial reasons for justifiably ascribing dignity to human beings in all phases of their life and for defending their delicate yet proud sense of their own worth and their unremitting desire for respect.

It is important to note that there are no justificatory resources beyond such reasons. One cannot transcend arguments of this kind and the axiological principles underlying the justified predication of dignity with some kind of striking meta-argument. One can only hope to elicit agreement with these reasons based on the same act of cognition by which one was persuaded oneself – and continue to listen to why these reasons may fail to convince. There is nothing epistemologically spurious about this. An argument about the question of why the Earth is not flat is no different: One provides arguments (we can travel around it, the notion that arriving back where one started is just a dream is not convincing, etc.) and hopes that they convince by a similar act of cognition that persuaded oneself about the truth of this proposition. Critics of the reasons given for human dignity – arguing, for example, that it is nothing but a deplorable example of speciesism to take existential characteristics such as autonomy or feeling, self-conscious subjectivity under moral laws to be relevant reasons for the ascription of dignity – draw on exactly the same epistemic resources: They provide counterarguments that in their view are convincing but have nothing over and above these reasons to make their case.

Understood in this way, dignity has concrete surplus content as compared to other human rights. The core of the matter is the idea – in whatever way one wants to express it – that human beings are ends-in-themselves and thus have to be protected as such, as the autonomous subjects of their life. This implies prohibitions of instrumentalization, objectification and reification and gives rise to correlated rights. It also implies a basic level of respect for every human being beyond these prohibitions. Respect as a normative concept is not just a contemplative appreciation of the qualities of human life, looking at human life as one would at a millipede's astonishing number of legs. Rather, respect has normative consequences, including the duty to refrain from actions irreconcilable with it and encompassing the right to be treated accordingly.

These are hard, applicable and – in the law – justiciable normative principles. They have both implicitly and explicitly guided courts around the world in cases concerning the death penalty, torture, discrimination, social rights, procedural rights and democratic participation.[105] They formulate an uncomfortable need to make individuals matter as they deserve in various normative contexts. They play a decisive role in the weighing and balancing exercises that now are at the heart of the application of human rights law by providing yardsticks for the normative calibration of the value judgments involved.

These remarks provide some important answers to standard objections against dignity. They show that human dignity is not a redundant concept. It is not empty or vague beyond hermeneutical redemption, although of course in practice its application may be dubious and lack precision. One also may want to add that it is not exclusionary. On the contrary, any plausible account of dignity is inclusionary – that is, it includes every human being, and most certainly infants, persons with disabilities, mentally ill and unconscious people. Anything else would amount to drawing distinctions between members of the human species as to who is "human enough"

[105] Cf. Mahlmann, "Dignity and Autonomy," 370 ff.

to count as human, without there being any plausible yardsticks for such distinctions. Besides, it would risk denying the richness of the human experience of some of these persons and the potential for a full human life of some others.[106]

Basing human rights on the respect for the dignity of human beings does not lead to the implausible consequence that human rights fill the whole moral domain, as has been argued.[107] There are very many matters of moral relevance that have nothing to do with human dignity.

To give generously to people in need beyond what might be regarded as obligatory is a morally laudable deed. Not doing so, however, does not constitute a violation of the recipients' dignity. Moreover, there are without doubt many possible violations of human rights that are not violations of human dignity – in fact, this is actually the standard case in human rights law. Making a demonstration dependent on prior authorization, excluding the possibility of assembling spontaneously, is arguably a violation of the right to freedom of assembly, an important fundamental right. However, requiring such a prior permit hardly already constitutes a violation of human dignity. It is simply a disproportionate limitation of a liberty. Therefore, one important element of any credible concept of human dignity is that it must prevent an inflationary use of this idea, which loses its meaning if it is understood as covering any violation of moral or legal norms.

Human dignity in this well-circumscribed sense is neither an ideologically nor a religiously partisan concept. To be sure, it is certainly used in this way. But in this it simply shares the fate of every important normative idea. There is no important normative concept that has not been abused by political forces. In the history of liberty, equality and democracy, examples of this abound. Highly authoritarian systems have been called democracies without this constituting a reason to abandon the normative idea of democracy. This is one of the decisive reasons why one needs to be precise about what dignity means and what its justifications are.

Human rights resting on human dignity are thus built not on imaginary foundations, but on the justified cognition of what ethical reflection about common humanity demands. Human dignity is not a tool for subjugating human ethical, legal, social and political imagination to a reactionary, metaphysical or otherwise obscure concept. On the contrary, it is the skeptical self-assertion of humanity, and it is not to be toyed with given how fragile and stained humanity's claim to decency is.

The principles of justice, human care and solidarity together with the idea of human dignity take the theory of human rights a long way towards its aim of specifying the normative principles that form necessary elements of any justification

[106] In this context, the diachronic identity of human persons is of substantial normative relevance, cf. Mahlmann, *Elemente*, 300 ff. Waldron, *One Another's Equals*, 173 has rightly underlined that dignity is predicated of human beings "conceived not as momentary time slices but as persons extended over time."

[107] Cf. Griffin, *On Human Rights*, 201.

of human rights. Human rights spell out what justice, solidarity and respect for human dignity mean in the hard currency of rights.

5.7 MAKING HUMAN RIGHTS CONCRETE

Human rights as explicit ethical principles and legal norms are regularly formulated in abstract terms. One important task therefore is to render human rights more concrete. This goes not only for the law, but also for meaningful ethical accounts of human rights.

Real-life human rights protection poses many highly intricate problems. One key issue is the question of what morally legitimate burdens can be imposed on others both prima facie and all things considered. In order to assess this, different normative considerations need to be placed in relation to one another. For instance, the constraints of justice mean that there is no right to everything. There is neither a right to the self-abandonment of others nor even a right to their utmost efforts to benefit somebody else, because of the rights of these others to lead their own equally important lives. More complicated are questions in specific cases where a lot hinges on the specific circumstance at stake.

In legal practice, the scope of a right determines the prima facie protection of a certain good. A proportionality analysis is a key practical tool in finding a solution all things considered. This includes reviewing whether a measure that is interfering with a right pursues a legitimate aim, is suitable to achieve this aim, is the least burdensome of all equally effective means and whether the burden imposed on the bearer of the right is not disproportionate as regards the gains of the measure. Proportionality in this sense is ultimately a device of justice: The burdens and secured goods are to be allocated among the rights-holders in a way that remains fair.[108] Other considerations include the possibilities and limits of securing particular human goods by rights – a problem already discussed above. There is no reason why the ethical concretization of rights should not follow a comparable path.[109]

Looking at concrete cases underlines the importance of a caveat concerning the limits of our findings so far: Whether or not banning burqas in public can be reconciled with freedom of religion, for example, can only be answered after substantial reflection about the *telos* of this right, the kind of freedom protected, some serious thought about what a society can demand of a person, whether "*vivre*

[108] It is thus a misunderstanding to equate proportionality with an expansive interpretation of human rights, John Tasioulas, "Saving Human Rights from Human Rights Law," *Vanderbilt Journal of Transnational Law* 52, no. 5 (2019): 1167, 1186. Proportionality is a tool to limit legitimate inference with human rights, not a tool to expand their scope. Cf. for thoughts on the moral point of proportionality and its relation to law George Letsas, "Proportionality as Fittingness: The Moral Dimension of Proportionality," *Current Legal Problems* 71, no. 1 (2018): 53–86.

[109] This includes proportionality. It is a traditional concern of ethics to criticize disproportionate punishment, for instance.

ensemble" is in fact a sufficient reason to force a person not to wear a burqa (as the ECtHR has argued), the impact of such a ban on the women concerned, whether it liberates them from oppression or drives them deeper into the dungeon of isolation and so on.[110] The theory of goods, the political theory of rights and the normative principles considered do not answer all of these questions. They are thus only a part of the full unfolding of human rights, not least in the hard doctrinal work of the law.

Something similar is important for the question of how to derive guidance from what has been said about the new frontiers of human rights – say, the development of privacy rights in the digital age. The results of this inquiry define benchmarks for any solution but do not give all of the answers needed – for example, as to whether a right to be forgotten should be included in the scope of protection of privacy or not.

5.8 SOME MORE RESULTS

What are the results of our inquiry so far? What do they mean for the questions pursued?

First, the concept of rights gained some contours, showing that rights are best understood as an intricate web of normative relations woven by claims and duties, privileges and no-rights, powers and immunities, both in ethics and in law. Human rights deal with a limited set of qualified human concerns protected for all human beings by virtue of their humanity, including the respect for humans' intrinsic worth, life, liberties, equality and some of the material means required for a fully human life.

Second, the long and rich history of the making of the idea of human rights was sketched in rough outline. One lesson drawn was that human rights are plausibly understood as reflective, abstract, objectified generalizations and universalizations of concrete rights claims of individual actors, often stemming from perceived violations of rights under particular circumstances, based on not arbitrary but principled intuitions about justice and moral obligations, rendered explicit after a critical reflection of their possible personal scope and content and finally selectively turned into law in various forms. Their acceptance and slow political and legal realization in incremental, incomplete steps devoid of any teleology, involving both progress and regression at a very high human cost, depended on the political and ultimately ethical choices, convictions and decisions of human subjects embedded in the culture and social structures of their time, which created the preconditions, scope and constraints for insights and possible social action. Human rights faced many foes from different political and ideological corners, depending on historical circumstance. Our historical inquiry revealed the importance of a political and ethical analysis that specifies the heterogeneous actors and interests driving human rights

[110] Cf. ECtHR, SAS v France, Judgement of July 1, 2014, appl. no. 43835/11.

history and refrains from simplistic theses about monolithic cultures and their causal impact on the development of human rights. The history outlined is not about the presence of the full, explicit concept of human rights in all times and places. Rather, it is the history of normative phenomena that *were not human rights* but paved the way to their ultimate formulation. It is the history of islets of decency in the wide seas of injustice, islets that slowly grew into the idea of human rights.

Third, it became clear that the justification of human rights is a large and difficult topic. Some highly demanding theories were reviewed, and much has been learned from these impressive efforts. The questions to be answered about the justified goods protected by human rights, their place in a political theory and their normative foundations are far from trivial. However, some arguments about the sources of these goods, their political rationality and their normative basis have been formulated that seem to stand the test of critical reflection.

So far, this inquiry has traveled on well-known ground, albeit not on paths commonly trodden. But while the findings outlined are necessary elements of a theory of human rights, they are not sufficient to complete our theoretical task. One reason for this is that we now have a new kid on the block. In recent years, moral psychology, behavioral economics, cognitive science and neuroscience have turned their attention to the question of ethics and in particular to human rights, with sometimes far-reaching revisionist theses, holding that the arguments about the justification of human rights that have been mustered here are in fact no more than an intellectual hoax, the post-hoc rationalization of the illusions produced by human beings' psychological machinery. However, such revisionist theories are only one approach to the problem of the cognitive foundations of human rights, and one that does not exhaust the theoretical options available.

This psychological interest is not surprising: After all, human rights are an element of ethics, and ethics is traditionally associated with moral psychology. In addition, this inquiry started from the observation that human rights are a product of human thinking, and that human rights theory suffers from a potentially highly relevant blind spot if it does not concern itself with the theory of the human mind that, after all, generates this thought.

Our inquiry covered some distance to arrive at these findings. This journey has not been a digression. On the contrary, these efforts were necessary in order to formulate the first of the central results of this study: *Our findings about the concept of human rights, the goods they legitimately protect, their history and justification define the plausibility conditions of any meaningful theory of human rights, including the theories developed by psychology, behavioral economics, evolutionary theory and neuroscience.*

The results of our inquiry show that such theories need to address complex issues – that there is much that enters into an understanding of human rights. This includes problems of the origins of beliefs about human rights and in this sense of the epistemological dimensions of theories about these rights. Given the rich and intricate findings produced, one thing seems rather obvious: The epistemology of human rights is the epistemology of many things. *Conceptual questions* need to be addressed. *Factual propositions* of human anthropology enter into the justification of rights, as do multifaceted theses about the *working of human societies* into the assessment of the political theories of human rights. Lessons need to be drawn from history, which presupposes *historical analysis* and understanding. Finally, a *normative theory* needs to be outlined that includes loaded ideas such as justice, solidarity and human dignity.

This is a crucial point. It shows that no psychological or neuroscientific theory can afford any naivete about the complexity of the explanatory task at hand. There is no way to make this clear other than to outline in sufficient detail the many difficulties to which the theory of human rights has to face up, as has been attempted in the preceding chapters. The results of the inquiry formulate important parts of the research agenda in this field. At the same time, these findings from the beginning limit, or so it seems, the role that a psychological or neuroscientific theory can play for the theory of human rights, including its epistemological dimensions. It is a nonstarter to assume that such a theory can explain all of the substantial and epistemological issues raised, ranging from human anthropology to the effects of rights in society to the normative content of human dignity. This does not mean that there are no important insights to be gained or that one does not need to keep an open mind about where the inquiry may lead, only that one should not expect (or promise) too much. The inquiry about the relation between human rights and the mental structure of human beings is an intriguing and important piece of the puzzle of understanding human rights and perhaps human moral orientation more generally. It is, however, only *one* piece of the puzzle alongside other, equally important ones.

Given the cognitive interests of this inquiry into mind and rights, the question is now: What is the origin of the normative principles in human thinking that are pivotal for the idea of human rights? Why have human beings pursued these ideas for such a very long time with such deep conviction? Why do they form such commanding elements of normative systems of belief in the contemporary world across cultural and religious divides? What do psychology, cognitive science and neuroscience add to our understanding of these matters, given that some theories claim to possess the key to answering these questions? What consequences do the answers to these questions have for the epistemological and ontological status of the principles crucial to the justification of human rights? Are they properly regarded as foundational principles in any meaningful sense? Are they justified true beliefs or deeply held but ultimately contingent ideas? Or are they nothing but moral illusions, on par with illusions in other cognitive domains? Do the answers to these questions (if there are any) matter for a normative theory of human rights and thus ultimately for their justification, perhaps even undermining their legitimacy? Or are they entirely irrelevant in this regard? These are the next problems we will consider, problems that are as exciting to address as they are difficult to solve.

PART III

Rights and Moral Cognition

6

Which Kind of Mind, Which Kind of Morals, Which Kind of Rights?

Was ist der Mensch? konnt' ich beginnen; wie kommt es, daß so etwas in der Welt ist, das, wie ein Chaos, gärt, oder modert, wie ein fauler Baum, und nie zu einer Reife gedeiht? Wie duldet diesen Heerling die Natur bei ihren süßen Trauben?[1]

Friedrich Hölderlin, *Hyperion* oder der Eremit in Griechenland

6.1 ETHICS AND THE THEORY OF THE HUMAN MIND

The content of justice and the good forms one prime focus of human reflection about practical matters. Another question that has occupied practical philosophy ever since its beginnings concerns the mental means by which human beings achieve moral cognition. The answers to this question are manifold, mirroring the changing conceptions of what human beings are like. One constant of this debate is the notion that human beings possess a particular faculty through which they are able to gain insight into true normative propositions. One famous example of this is Socrates' daimonion, his inner voice that guided him, taking his decisions about what it was right and wrong to do.[2] The Stoics reflected on a human faculty of moral understanding – an idea that influenced the natural law tradition they so profoundly inspired in other regards, too.[3] In Christianity, Paul's idea of a law written in the human heart already was very influential in Patristic thought: Moral precepts

[1] "'What is man?' I could begin; 'how can it be that such a thing is in the world that ferments like a chaos or moulders like a rotting tree, and never grows to ripeness. How can nature suffer this sour grape amid her sweet clusters?" Friedrich Hölderlin, *Hyperion, or the Hermit in Greece*, trans. H. Gaskill (Cambridge: Open Book Publishers, 2019), 38.

[2] Plato, *Apologia*, 31c; Vlastos, *Socrates*, 280 ff.

[3] Cf. Chryssipus, "Chrysippi fragmenta moralia," in *Stoicum Veterum Fragmenta*, Vol. III, ed. Hans von Arnim (Munich & Leipzig: K. G. Saur Verlag, 2004), 314, 323; Max Pohlenz, *Die Stoa* (Göttingen: Vandenhoeck & Ruprecht, 1992), 133.

seemed somehow ingrained in human nature.[4] In later natural law theory, the question persisted. Thomas Aquinas, for instance, believed that synderesis was the means of understanding natural law.[5] Others assumed a natural light or a *recta ratione*.[6] In modern times, the thesis of innate ideas gained prominence, not only concerning the foundations of mathematics, scientific insight and logic, but also with regard to practical questions. Descartes did not say much about ethics or natural law, though there are some interesting remarks.[7] Leibniz, however, developed quite a differentiated theory of moral judgment in which innate moral ideas played an important part.[8]

One influential idea advanced by the Scottish Enlightenment was that human beings have a moral sense that allows them to perceive the moral status of things.[9] Hume argued that morality is part of humans' mode of thinking because of "some internal sense or feeling which nature made universal in the whole species."[10] Kant argued with practical reason. In his view, the moral law is a "fact of reason," a given property of human understanding.[11] Other psychological assumptions supplement this view: For Kant, one central idea is "respect for the law," the ultimate reason why moral precepts matter.[12] According to this doctrine, the human psyche is structured in such a way that the cognition of the moral law gives rise to respect for this law. This respect for the moral law is the reason why morality matters in practical terms and influences both human motivation and ultimately – if other inclinations do not gain the upper hand – human action.[13]

The same cognitive interest motivated authors such as Locke who considered determining the nuts and bolts of the machinery of human thought a central task, even though they were critical of psychological theories that assumed the existence of innate ideas.

In contemporary thought, moral psychology continues to play a role in influential theories of morality. Habermas, for instance, took Piaget's and Kohlberg's theory of

4 Rom. 2, 15.

5 Aquinas, *Summa Theologica*, I–II, q. 94.

6 Grotius, *De Iure Belli ac Pacis*, I, X.

7 René Descartes, "Les Passions de l'Ame," in *Œuvres de Descartes*, Vol. XI, eds. Charles Adam and Paul Tannery (Paris: Léopold Cerf, 1909), 445 ff.

8 Leibniz, "Nouveaux Essais," 91 ff. Matthias Mahlmann, "Die geistige Wurzel der Gerechtigkeit – Rationalismus und Epistemologie in Leibniz' praktischer Philosophie," in *Rechts- und Staatsphilosophie bei G. W. Leibniz*, eds. Tilmann Altwicker, Francis Cheneval and Matthias Mahlmann (Tübingen: Mohr Siebeck, 2020), 89 ff.

9 Cf. for instance Francis Hutcheson, *An Inquiry into the Original of Our Ideas of Beauty and Virtue* (New York: Garland Pub., 1971), XVIII, 134, 270.

10 David Hume, "An Enquiry Concerning the Principles of Morals," in *David Hume: Enquiries Concerning Human Understanding and Concerning the Principles of Morals*, ed. Peter Harold Nidditch (Oxford: Oxford University Press, 1975), 173.

11 Immanuel Kant, *Kritik der praktischen Vernunft*, *Akademieausgabe*, Vol. V (Berlin: Georg Reimer, 1913), 31.

12 Kant, *Kritik der praktischen Vernunft*, 71 ff.

13 Kant, *Metaphysik der Sitten*, 399.

moral development as the basis for his understanding of the ontogenesis of moral thought.[14] A further example is Rawls, who considered the idea of a parallel between Chomsky's concept of universal grammar and the sense of justice, although he did not develop this systematically after encountering substantial critique.[15]

This rich tradition of thought about the characteristics and the functionings of the mind and moral understanding comes as no surprise. The question of how human beings acquire moral knowledge and which cognitive mechanisms are used to put this knowledge into practice suggests itself too evidently to have been missed in the past.

Throughout much of this tradition, moral psychology was understood as equally important for the understanding and creation of law as for morality. The faculty of understanding that enabled human beings to cognize natural law or the law of reason was seen either as dealing with norms regarded as directly valid law or as constituting the foundation for the determination of the legitimate content of the law. The inclusion of moral psychology in theoretical reflections about the law thus also comes as no surprise. The discussion that follows consequently represents yet another small piece of reflection on a topic embedded in a rich history of creative thought. Despite its brevity, it hopefully will shed light on some problems of human moral understanding that hitherto have not been fully illuminated.

Some theories assume that human beings have a general learning ability that both allows them and at the same time makes it necessary to learn everything anew, including moral concepts. Some of these theories understand humans as protean beings who are infinitely malleable and whose mental makeup is determined by their social surroundings, as we have seen. It should be noted again that all such theories, despite their constructivist bent, formulate a substantial, empirical psychological hypothesis including assumptions about human nature, assumptions that are true or not, depending on evidence. Their thesis is that the human mind is structured in such a way that it can and indeed must learn everything anew. In this sense, consequently, even radically culturalist or constructivist theories are naturalistic or nativist because they presuppose an empirical thesis about the cognitive foundations of the development of morality in human beings. There is no escape from psychology and theories of the structure of human cognition.

The view that there are species-specific properties of the human mind other than general learning abilities that constitute the preconditions of the development of morality has gained considerable influence, although perspectives often differ radically about what this means in detail and whether this is good news for an egalitarian ethics of human justice and solidarity and for the political and

[14] Jürgen Habermas, *Moralbewusstsein und Kommunikatives Handeln* (Frankfurt am Main: Suhrkamp, 1983), 127 ff.

[15] Rawls, *Theory of Justice*, 46 ff.; Mikhail, *Elements*.

cultural project of human rights in particular, or whether it rather calls these projects into question.

It is easy to discern the reason for the view that such species-specific properties of human beings exist. Everybody agrees that human beings acquire a vast number of norms as they grow up, through their upbringing, education and socialization. These norms are products of their culture. At the same time, it is not really plausible that the complex cognitive capacities forming the foundation of morality are not species-specific: The cultural influences are obvious, "[b]ut the household pets growing up in the same cultural and religious contexts do not thereby become moral beings."[16] Therefore, it seems quite reasonable to assert that "there is absolutely no question that human children are biologically prepared for the process as well."[17]

The inquiry into the cognitive preconditions of morality is important, regardless of whether we believe that any findings in this area have *normative* consequences in addition to *explaining* some of the cognitive mechanisms involved in moral understanding, or whether we believe that this would mean committing a naturalistic fallacy or neglecting the is/ought dichotomy.[18] There are various reasons for this importance. First, the question of whether facts of moral psychology have normative consequences or not must be informed by what these facts actually are, and so we need to inquire into these facts. Second, the comprehension of moral cognition and its relation to the law is itself a valuable, even indispensable scientific goal if one wants to gain a profound understanding of the nature of morality and law. We clarified this in the Introduction of the present study. Third, the empirical theories of moral cognition very often do have a direct or indirect normative edge, because they influence the way human beings think about the mechanism that directs their volitions and actions. Just because there are good reasons to take the is/ought dichotomy seriously (as will be argued here) does not mean that everybody in fact agrees with or, even if they avowedly agree, adheres to this stance. Misconceived theories may have significant practical impact. What has been called "evoconservatism" – the justification of reactionary political visions by means of evolutionary theory – is just one such example we will discuss below.[19] Finally, we have to answer the question of the relation between what seems right in normative theory and the facts about human moral cognition. To put it in concrete terms: Do human rights demand the impossible of human beings, as some influential voices argue? Thus, as things stand, the critical assessment of theories of human morality and the law by psychology and neuroscience is of great significance. A lack of interest in the

[16] Michael Tomasello, *A Natural History of Human Morality* (Cambridge, MA: Harvard University Press, 2016).

[17] Tomasello, *Natural History of Human Morality*, 134.

[18] Cf. Selim Berker, "The Normative Insignificance of Neuroscience," 293 ff.

[19] Allen Buchanan and Russell Powell, *The Evolution of Moral Progress* (New York: Oxford University Press, 2018).

cognitive preconditions of human moral understanding is not something moral and legal theorists can afford.

As indicated above, these questions are not of minor concern. As Hannah Arendt correctly observed, a core problem brought to the fore by the horrors of the Holocaust is the question of whether human beings have a faculty of moral understanding that enables them to distinguish between right and wrong, even if this means setting themselves in radical opposition to their environment.[20] The assumption that everybody was able to know that Auschwitz was a crime, irrespective of the drums of Nazi propaganda, presupposes at least two things: firstly, that there *are* standards of right and wrong; and secondly, that people have the *ability to understand* them. The first question already occupied us in our discussion of the justification of human rights, with encouraging results. The second must be informed by what we know about human moral cognition, not least because some theories maintain that moral cognition does not facilitate but rather obstructs doing the morally right thing.

6.2 THE EPISTEMOLOGY OF MORAL COGNITION

There are at least two acts of cognition relevant to this inquiry. First, there are concrete assertions of rights along the line of "X has a right to Y." These can take the form of assertions in concrete circumstances relating to specific people, such as Creusa's complaint about the violation of her rights by Apollo. They can also take the form of more abstract and general assertions – for example, about the rights of women to sexual self-determination.

Second, there are acts of cognition that concern the justification of such rights assertions. The cognition of the justification of a right is achieved by a series of mental acts, by a set of cognitive judgments. The final judgment has the propositional content "right X is justified" – for example, expressions such as "freedom of speech is worth defending." This proposition in fact relies on a number of complex reasons. It implies, as explained above, assumptions about the usefulness of a right such as free speech in human communities (for the expression of humans' personality, the pursuit of truth, the protection of democracy and the like) and – although these are not always made explicit – anthropological claims about the importance of freedom for human beings. In the case of legal rights, further complications arise from their nature as positive law – for instance, as to their justiciability.

One further element of this bundle of predications is of special concern for normative theory: the predication of the *moral* justification of a right. Complex systems of moral legal rights, many details of which are historically contingent, cannot be derived directly from basic moral intuitions. As we have seen, substantial steps are necessary to move from concrete moral judgments to the formulation of

[20] Hannah Arendt, *Eichmann in Jerusalem: A Report on the Banality of Evil* (New York: Penguin Group, 2006), 294 f.

explicit moral human rights. Basic intuitions of justice or impermissible harm are one thing, the formulation and full justification of a norm in the form of an explicit moral human right, let alone in the technical form of a legal fundamental right and its regime of limitations, quite another.

This notwithstanding, making the moral case for human rights forms a necessary element of any justification of human rights.[21] There are many considerations that speak for human rights, but these rights cannot be legitimate if they are not justified from a moral point of view. Nobody would have taken the UN General Assembly seriously if it had stated that adopting the *Universal Declaration* made good sense even though it was quite an unjust catalogue of rights. A human rights catalogue that does not claim to lay down a just and morally appropriate set of norms is not a proper human rights catalogue.

Legal human rights sometimes appear in very abstract form. More often than not, however, the respective norms are stated in more differentiated terms, including a regime of justified interferences. This is of crucial importance, because this regime of justified interferences determines the true content of the right, as we have seen. The final judgment "right X is justified" in this case thus encompasses intricate arguments not only about the prima facie scope of a right, but also about other values that justify restrictions of this right and the degree to which this is possible. In this context, principles of proportionality have become a core element of modern human rights catalogues,[22] sometimes buttressed by the protection of the essence of a right.[23] The determination of a human right's concrete content thus involves the recursive application of normative principles to limit the prima facie scope of the right and determine the meaning of the clauses of limitations, not least by weighing and balancing different rights. As explained above, similar considerations apply for moral rights.

The predication of the normative justification of a right in this sense by a moral judgment (as one element of a bundle of highly complex justificatory arguments about human rights) must be a principled mental act. Caprice cannot provide justification. Rather, the application of normative principles to the case evaluated – the human right under consideration – gives rise to the judgment that this right is morally justified (or not). But what are these principles? And how are these principles, used to justify norms such as human rights, justified themselves? These two major questions of practical philosophy lead us straight to the heart of

[21] For a derivation of a wide range of human rights from basic moral judgments, albeit not from principles of justice and altruism as proposed above and discussed in detail below, John Mikhail, "Moral Grammar and Human Rights: Some Reflections on Cognitive Science and Enlightenment Rationalism," in *Understanding Social Action, Promoting Human Rights*, eds. Ryan Goodman, Derek Jinks and Andrew Woods (Oxford: Oxford University Press, 2012), 196 ff.

[22] Cf. Art. 36 Constitution of the Republic of South Africa, December 18, 1996; Art. 36 para. 3 BV.

[23] Cf. Art. 36 para. 4 BV.

the normative component of the theory of human rights. Accordingly, over the course of the history of ideas, many principles have been formulated that seek to pin down at least some core elements of morality, from Socrates' belief that it is better to suffer injustice than to do injustice to Kant's categorical imperative and beyond. Given what has been said above about the justification of rights, it seems plausible that principles of equality and thus of justice, duties of human care and respect for the worth of human beings play a crucial role in this respect.

It seems likely that these principles also guide moral judgments about concrete claims, the first category of cognitive acts mentioned above, and not only the normative justification of these intuitions following their transformation into an explicit concept of human rights. Such concrete claims are regularly based on intuitions about justice and the moral obligations of others in concrete circumstances that give rise to specific rights and duties. For example, Creusa's rebellion against her abuse implies that what Apollo has done to her is unjust. These kinds of claims, too, originate in the justificatory principles of justice, benevolence and respect.

The problems of the content and justification of the normative principles guiding moral judgment in the context of concrete claims and the justification of rights lead to the core question of interest here. *Is the content of these justificatory principles perhaps dependent on the structure of human thought?* Are these principles possibly even in one way or another determined by the properties of the human mind? Is the nature and structure of human thought a factor that defines the results of reflection – in the moral domain for moral judgments? This is, as indicated above, the Cartesian, Lockean, Humean and Kantian question about the preconditions of the possibility of human moral cognition. Are there such *Verstandesbegriffe*, such "concepts of understanding" in the moral domain, to use a Kantian term? If so – what is their effect? Are the particular nature and structure of human thought crucial to objective, foundational moral insight? Or are they indispensable elements of moral cognition that, however, do not reveal "morality in itself" (to modify another Kantian idea), do not reveal the true, objective morality? Is there thus a parallel to theoretical cognition, in the same way that human thought, in Kant's view, never grasps the nature of the "*Ding an sich*," the thing in itself?[24] Or – a third possibility – do such structures of the mind exist and decisively influence human moral thought but create nothing but cognitive illusions, the moral equivalent to the Müller-Lyer visual illusion mentioned in the Introduction?

These questions lead us to another important challenge to human rights to be considered in this study. A particular line of cognitive psychology and neuroscience has formulated exactly the latter thesis. It holds that the nature and structure of the human mind is indeed decisive for human moral reasoning, but that the moral

[24] Immanuel Kant, *Kritik der reinen Vernunft (2. Ed. 1787)*, Akademie Ausgabe, Vol. III (Berlin: Georg Reimer, 1911), 16 f., 202 ff., 207.

judgment thus determined yields not insight, but error. Accordingly, the idea of human rights is part of this erroneous reasoning, and thus is not qualified to decidedly influence human affairs. This challenge will be considered over the next sections of this chapter, before we turn our attention to the fertile research in behavioral law and economics and then to a related challenge from evolutionary psychology in Chapter 7. Finally, we will consider other potentially very fertile approaches to the relation between mind and rights in the last chapter of this book.

6.3 THE NEUROSCIENTIFIC ATTACK ON HUMAN RIGHTS: HUMAN RIGHTS AND THE MENTAL GIZMO THESIS

The thesis to be examined here accepts as its general framework the dual-process model of the mind. This model holds that there are two kinds of mental processes: "thinking fast" and "thinking slow," to use the popularized terms.[25] Thinking fast means using heuristics, framing operations or biases to solve everyday problems. These mechanisms are hardwired into the human brain. Humans cannot but use them and do so intuitively and unconsciously.[26] Thinking slow means using reflective rationality that abides by standards of logic.[27] Thinking fast works well for many aspects of everyday life but is skewed in important regards. Human decision-making is thus not fully rational. It is possible to become aware of the factors that skew human rationality, such as heuristics, framing effects and biases, and overcome their influence through slow thinking. However, this may not necessarily happen, because the control system of slow thinking may fail in its task.[28] This dual-process model of the mind has become highly influential beyond psychology, inspiring research in many other fields, not least behavioral law and economics. Its pioneers have also explored the place of moral reasoning within this model.[29] The mental gizmo thesis, however, aims to provide more substantial guidance. Most importantly for our inquiry, human rights are prominent topic of the discussion.

The mental gizmo thesis runs as follows: Moral cognition is part of the dual-process mind.[30] Deontological judgments are part of fast thinking. There is a mental "gizmo" that yields such judgments involuntarily, unconsciously, as a product of the

[25] Kahneman, *Thinking, Fast and Slow.*

[26] Kahneman, *Thinking, Fast and Slow*, 19 ff.

[27] Kahneman, *Thinking, Fast and Slow*, 19 ff.

[28] Kahneman, *Thinking, Fast and Slow*, 39 ff. This idea is the origin of nudging, the idea that one can systematically exploit these factors for the benefit of others in the framework of a "libertarian paternalism."

[29] Cf. for a summary of the research Daniel Kahneman and Cass R. Sunstein, "Cognitive Psychology of Moral Intuitions," in *Neurobiology of Human Values*, eds. Jean-Pierre Changeux, Antonio Damasio, Wolf Singer and Yves Christen (Berlin: Springer, 2005), 91 ff., arguing that indignation is key to explaining the outrage heuristic, the centrality of harm, the role of reference states, moral framing and the act–omission distinction.

[30] Greene, *Moral Tribes*, 15, 105 ff.

fast, automatic and emotional operations of the human mind. These deontological judgments are like heuristics or biases: They are useful in certain respects but should be disregarded as general guides for moral judgments because they systematically skew human moral rationality.[31] The mental gizmo thus causes "moral illusions"[32] (in the same way that the Müller-Lyer illusion causes visual illusions), and one prime example of a product of its operations is Kant's principle of humanity that one should never use other human beings merely as means and not as ends.[33] This in itself is already important for the topic of human rights, because this principle is widely regarded as an important element of the concretization of guarantees of human dignity in various national, international and supranational legal systems.[34] Human dignity, in turn, is a constitutive part of the whole architecture of human rights. If human dignity is a moral illusion, then this architecture starts to totter. However, the mental gizmo thesis goes even further than this. Human rights as such are themselves seen as products of the mental gizmo, useful as rhetorical devices and exploitable for good causes but without any claim to rationality as such and often quite harmful in their effects.[35] Instead, for truly rational moral thinking one needs to resort to utilitarianism. Utilitarianism constitutes slow thinking, which is what should govern human moral reasoning in the last instance.[36]

What is the evidence for the mental gizmo thesis? Some of many variants of the familiar trolley problem form the starting point of the analysis.[37] In the so-called bystander case, a bystander can turn a switch so that a runaway trolley is redirected with the consequence that it kills not five persons on one track but one person on another track. In the variant called the "footbridge case," a person is thrown down onto a track from a bridge to stop a runaway trolley, thus saving the five people working on the track. Proponents of the mental gizmo thesis argue that a proper analysis of cases where deontological judgments seem to be at play, because the observers judge it not to be permissible to sacrifice the life of one person to save five (footbridge case), shows that this judgment is in fact determined by hardwired emotional reactions.[38] This analysis is supported by neuroimaging studies. These

[31] Greene, *Moral Tribes*, 132 ff.

[32] Greene, *Moral Tribes*, 252.

[33] Greene, *Moral Tribes*, 105 ff., 115.

[34] Cf. Mahlmann, *Human Dignity and Autonomy*, 370 ff.

[35] Greene, *Moral Tribes*, 302 ff.

[36] Greene, *Moral Tribes*, 290 ff.: Utilitarianism is called "deep pragmatism." Greene sums this thesis up: "The Central Tension principle: Characteristically deontological judgements are preferentially supported by automatic emotional responses, while characteristically consequentialist judgements are preferentially supported by conscious reasoning and allied processes of cognitive control," Joshua Greene, "Beyond Point-and-Shoot Morality: Why Cognitive (Neuro)Science Matters for Ethics," *Ethics* 124, no. 4 (2014), 699. For an endorsement cf. e.g. Peter Singer, "Ethics and Intuitions," *The Journal of Ethics* 9, no. 3/4 (2005), 331 ff.

[37] Greene, *Moral Tribes*, 105 ff.

[38] Greene, *Moral Tribes*, 119 ff. Greene, "Why Cognitive (Neuro)Science Matters for Ethics," 698 states that mechanisms of fast thinking do not need to be "hard wired." In his discussion,

studies, it is argued, show that when deciding on these cases, the ventromedial prefrontal cortex (VMPFC) is active, an area of the brain associated with the production of emotion.[39] The VMPFC is active because these cases involve the agent directly; they are "personal" and thus trigger emotional reactions.[40]

In other cases that are "impersonal," where the judgment reached is different and participants consider it permissible that one person dies and five persons are saved (bystander case),[41] the dorsolateral prefrontal cortex (DLPFC), the center of cognitive control in the brain, is active, showing that this utilitarian judgment is a rational, not an emotional one.[42] Further evidence is provided, it is argued, by studies showing that if the VMPFC is damaged, utilitarian judgments are made by the participants in both the bystander and footbridge cases.[43]

From this perspective, deontological arguments are nothing but the post-hoc rationalization of hardwired emotional reactions.[44] This is not only the "secret joke of Kant's soul,"[45] but, one might add, the secret joke of the souls of a great many thinkers on moral issues from antiquity to the present. Thus, say, Plato's dialogues, the *Critique of Practical Reason* and *A Theory of Justice* are all exercises in self-delusion on the part of their authors. Plato's defense of a nonconsequentialist concept of justice, the formulation of the categorical imperative in its formal and material versions and John Rawls' nonutilitarian principles of justice are ultimately expressions of the secret workings of the emotional mental gizmo, rationalized post hoc and writ large.[46] Human rights are part of these post-hoc rationalizations: "'Rights' are nothing short of brilliant. They allow us to rationalize our gut feelings without doing any additional work."[47] The many people concerned with human rights, such as lawyers, judges, activists, politicians and – most importantly – the people claiming human rights,

the mental gizmo appears, however, throughout to be "hard wired," a given of human nature, shared by Kant, Rawls and us.

39 Greene, *Moral Tribes*, 121 ff., Joshua Greene et al., "An fMRI Investigation of Emotional Engagement in Moral Judgement," *Science* 293, no. 5537 (2001).

40 Greene, *Moral Tribes*, 121 ff.

41 In the bystander case, the bystander can turn a switch so that a runaway trolley is redirected with the consequence that it does not kill five persons on one track but one person on another track.

42 Greene, *Moral Tribes*, 120.

43 Greene, *Moral Tribes*, 124 ff. For more studies taken as support for this thesis, Greene, "Why Cognitive (Neuro)Science Matters for Ethics," 700 ff.

44 Greene, *Moral Tribes*, 298 ff., 300: "The moral equivalent of confabulation is *rationalization*. The confabulator perceives himself doing something and makes up a rational sounding story about what he's doing and why. The moral rationalizer *feels* a certain way about a moral issue and then makes up a rational-sounding justification for that feeling" (emphasis in original).

45 Greene, *Moral Tribes*, 301, quoting Nietzsche: "In other words, Kant has the same automatic settings as his surrounding tribespeople. But Kant, unlike them, felt the need to provide esoteric justifications for their 'popular' prejudices."

46 On Rawls, *Theory of Justice* as being another product of rationalization of the working of the mental gizmo, Greene, *Moral Tribes*, 333.

47 Greene, *Moral Tribes*, 301 ff., 302.

fighting for these rights to be respected, hoping, sometimes desperately, for their protection, are all under the spell of a "moral illusion." Given the importance of human rights in practice, this "moral illusion" has massive consequences that dwarf any practical effects that other elements of a skewed rationality, such as framing effects, may possibly have. These consequences are quite harmful: "Rationalization is the great enemy of moral progress, and thus of deep pragmatism."[48]

The mental gizmo thesis is part of a wider trend in contemporary neuroscience that can be called neuroscientific emotivism. This trend uses the means of cognitive psychology to defend traditional emotivism's idea that human morality is no more than the expression of certain emotions of appraisal and disgust. It represents a very radical critique of human rights: Its punchline is not to deny the cognitive reality and impact of deontological judgments and the idea of human rights, but radically to reinterpret their status and meaning. In this view, deontological judgments and human rights are not manifestations of practical reason, but on the contrary are some of the causes of human moral irrationality. This irrationality has such far-reaching detrimental consequences that it needs to be overcome for the sake of the survival of the species. Only utilitarianism, only slow thinking, it is maintained, is able to solve the great problems of humanity and transcend the parochial moralities of the human tribes created by the mental gizmo,[49] "to free philosophers from the ups and downs of their automatic settings,"[50] and to free all the rest of us, of course, who also often suffer from the "moral illusion" of human rights.

How to answer this interesting challenge, which presumably will be paradigmatic for quite a few discussions to come?

6.4 THE MENTAL GIZMO THESIS RECONSIDERED

One fundamental problem is that the analysis of the trolley problems (and its predecessors, such as those formulated by the German criminal lawyer Hans Welzel) underlying the mental gizmo thesis is deficient.[51] The cases that are taken to prove the workings of emotional gut reactions (instances of the footbridge case) in

[48] Greene, *Moral Tribes*, 301.

[49] Greene, *Moral Tribes*, 289 ff.

[50] Greene, "Why Cognitive (Neuro)Science Matters for Ethics," 720.

[51] The usual reference for the origin of this problem is Philippa Foot, "The Problem of Abortion and the Doctrine of the Double Effect," *Oxford Review* 5 (1967); Judith Jarvis Thomson, "The Trolley Problem," *Yale Law Journal* 94 (1985); Judith Jarvis Thomson, "Killing, Letting Die, and the Trolley Problem," *The Monist* 59, no. 2 (1976). In fact, core elements of the problem were already formulated previously, cf. Hans Welzel, "Zum Notstandsproblem," *Zeitschrift für die gesamte Strafrechtswissenschaft* 63 (1951), 47, 51 (with trains, not trams as in Foot). It is interesting that almost no reference to this earlier paper is found in current international debates, although Welzel was a well-known criminal lawyer and the article has been a standard in German-language criminal law discussions ever since its publication. It would be interesting to know whether Foot was familiar with it. Welzel discusses the concrete case of Nazi doctors' culpability for the mass murder committed as part of the so-called euthanasia program.

fact show something quite different, namely the relevance of the means/side effect distinction in explaining the empirical patterns of moral evaluation observed and, more precisely, the prohibition of the instrumentalization of human beings.[52] A proper analysis of the trolley problems therefore in fact vindicates the relevance of Kant's famous formula of the principle of humanity and thus the relevance of a crucial element of the idea of human rights. In addition, it is far too rash to conclude that a utilitarian reasoning is at play in the other cases where choosing the death of one person is taken to be permissible if the alternative is the death of five (or more victims, as in Welzel's initial train case). Thinking that it is permissible to choose the lesser of two unavoidable evils, though perhaps feeling at the same time that this is a tragic choice, is one thing, endorsing utilitarianism in the sense that it is always permissible simply to count lives quite another. The analysis of the trolley problems needs to be much more sophisticated and transcend such simple dichotomies.[53]

[52] The most advanced analysis of the trolley problem is provided by Mikhail, *Elements*, including the introduction of formal modes of representation of structures of the human actions evaluated, such as act trees, cf. Mikhail, *Elements*, 118 ff. Greene discusses Mikhail in some detail, cf. Greene, *Moral Tribes*, 230 ff. As Mikhail correctly argues, the core of the footbridge scenario is the use of the patient as a means. More precisely, in Mikhail's analysis, a battery (not the death) is a means to stop the trolley, not just the foreseen side effect of an action taken to save five, Mikhail, *Elements*, 123 ff. One can question whether the means to stop the trolley is just a battery or the death of the person, and this may be a significant difference. The means–ends distinction is, however, of crucial importance in any case. An explanation relying on the alternative account of the personal character of the action (pushing the patient over the bridge) is unconvincing, given scenarios that remove this personal element, cf. Mikhail, *Elements*, 109 (drop man) and passim; Mikhail, "Moral Grammar and Human Rights," 183. Empirical evidence quoted by Greene, *Moral Tribes*, 215 ff. is inconclusive, given empirical evidence that on the contrary buttresses the relevance of the means/side effect distinction, Mikhail, *Elements*, 319 ff. and other studies with quite different results, cf. n. 63. The "loop case" does not call these findings into question. On this case adduced by Greene, *Moral Tribes*, 220 ff. as a counterexample, Mikhail, *Elements*, 336 ff., 359. In the latter case, the issue of what counts as the origin of data (i.e. the problem of the criteria for the selection of judgments taken as evidence) is of crucial importance, because some scenarios can be so complicated that their moral point becomes obscure; see the remarks on "considered judgments" below. The "modular myopia hypothesis" that Greene, *Moral Tribes*, 224 ff. formulates as an explanation and according to which the emotional (deontological) cognitive subsystem is blind to harmful side effects is therefore not convincing. Kahnemann and Sunstein, "Cognitive Psychology of Moral Intuitions," 102, are consequently mistaken in evading the question of whether there are principled interpretations of the trolley problems. This question is decisive for understanding how moral cognition operates.

[53] Cf. for an attempt to move forward in this respect Mikhail, *Elements*; on alternative explanations for the reactions to trolley problems, cf. Guy Kahane and Nicholas Shackel, "Methodological Issues in the Neuroscience of Moral Judgment," *Mind & Language* 25, no. 5 (2010); Guy Kahane, "Sidetracked by Trolleys: Why Sacrificial Moral Dilemmas Tell Us Little (or Nothing) about Utilitarian Judgment," *Social Neuroscience* 10, no. 5 (2015): 555 f.; Guy Kahane et al., "Beyond Sacrificial Harm: A Two-Dimensional Model of Utilitarian Psychology," *Psychological Review* 125, no. 2 (2018): 132 ff. As Zamir, *Law, Psychology, and Morality*, 188, has pointed out, given sufficiently large "net good outcomes," subjects may reason as if they were consequentialists. One important question in this context is whether there is a significant moral difference between cases where harm is inflicted on others and are

Another problem of the mental gizmo thesis is that it is self-refuting. The reasons for this are as follows. Utilitarianism in all its classical and contemporary rule- or action-based variants is guided by the principle of utility: Any rule or action that creates the greatest happiness of the greatest number is normatively justified.[54] The foundation of this principle is the idea that each person's happiness counts equally because the persons who are happy count equally. This egalitarian thrust of utilitarianism explains its persistent attraction and forms the core of what is truly admirable in this line of thought.[55]

This maxim rests on two pillars: the equality of persons and the prescriptive principle that equal persons ought to be treated equally. Only given these two propositions does it follow that everyone's happiness shall count equally, as presupposed by the principle of utility. Consequently, the obligation to respect the equality of equal persons by counting their happiness equally in the utilitarian calculus is not the consequence, but the precondition of utilitarianism. The obligation to respect the equality of persons is not and indeed cannot be derived from the application of the principle of utility: Being its foundation, the obligation to treat equals equally cannot be the consequence of that latter principle. Rather, the obligation to respect the equality of persons is a principle that forms the nonconsequentialist normative precondition of consequentialism. There is thus a deontological residue at the core of utilitarianism, because the principle of the obligatory equal treatment of equals (the reason for being obliged to value everybody's happiness equally, as presupposed by the principle of utility) is the foundation of any utilitarian argument.[56]

widely regarded as (morally and legally) justified and cases such as the bystander case in the trolley problem. The perception that the latter case involves tragic choices implies that there is such a difference. Shaun Nichols and Ron Mallon, "Moral Dilemmas and Moral Rules," *Cognition* 100, no. 3 (2006) distinguish between broken (apparently explicit) rules and permissibility all-things-considered. This distinction raises interesting and important issues. However, the issue discussed here as an incident of tragic choices arises precisely in the case where an action is regarded as permissible all-things-considered and consequently has to be accounted for.

54 Cf. Bentham, *Introduction to the Principles of Morals and Legislation*, I, n. 1.

55 Cf. Bentham, *Introduction to the Principles of Morals and Legislation*, I, 13 n. d; Mill, "Utilitarianism," V, 200 and 198, on the principle of equality: "It is involved in the very meaning of Utility, or the Greatest Happiness Principle. That principle is a mere form of words without rational signification, unless one person's happiness, supposed equal in degree (with proper allowance made for kind), is counted exactly as much as another's." Cf. Chapter 4.

56 There is the argument that utilitarianism is not about the equality of persons but only about the equality of happiness, cf. for instance Hart, *Essays on Bentham*, 98. In this case, too, a prescriptive rule is implied, however – the rule that you ought to treat equal matters of fact (e.g. happiness) equally by including any equal amount of happiness on an equal footing in the utility calculus. Moreover, to value any degree of happiness equally seems to imply the equality of the persons experiencing it. The happiness of a king is therefore not worth more than the happiness of a beggar. Greene realizes that the foundation of utilitarianism is such a principle of equality, Greene, *Moral Tribes*, 163, 170: "The second utilitarian ingredient is impartiality,

This analysis of utilitarianism leads us to the central catch of the mental gizmo thesis. The catch is this: Either it is true that utilitarianism is slow thinking (as utilitarianism presupposes deontological principles of equality, it follows in that case that such deontological principles are slow thinking, too, because these deontological principles of equality are the normative core of what is regarded as slow thinking) or it is true that such deontological principles are fast thinking (as utilitarianism presupposes these deontological principles of equality, which is fast thinking, utilitarianism must constitute fast thinking, too). In either case, the mental gizmo thesis is refuted by internal contradictions.[57]

the universal essence of morality, that's distilled in the Golden Rule. Having added this second ingredient, we can summarize utilitarianism thus: Happiness is what matters, and everyone's happiness counts the same."

[57] Greene does not provide any justification of the foundational principle of utilitarianism that he identifies (impartiality, the Golden Rule, cf. Greene, *Moral Tribes*, 163, 170) and draws no consequences from it, even though this evidently calls his analysis in question. What is "impartiality" or the "Golden Rule"? Slow thinking? Why is it not just another one of those ethical principles that he derides as dangerous rationalizations of gut reactions? What is the difference in this respect between "impartiality" or the "Golden Rule" and, say, the categorical imperative or Rawls' principles of justice? This question needs to be asked not least because the point of the categorical imperative or Rawls' principles of justice is precisely to reach "impartiality" by universalization or by deliberation behind a "veil of ignorance." The "Golden Rule" is certainly related to one of the key ideas of the categorical imperative, namely the idea of universalization. Greene's argumentation is thus circular: Principles such as the categorical imperative are criticized as dangerous rationalizations of emotional gut reactions on the basis of principles such as the Golden Rule that are in fact similar to the very principles criticized.

Greene, "Why Cognitive (Neuro)Science Matters for Ethics," 717, claims that his argumentation "favors consequentialist approaches to moral problem solving, ones aimed solely at promoting good consequences, rather than deontological approaches aimed at figuring out who has which rights and duties, where these are regarded as constraints on the promotion of good consequences." The critique developed here can be stated in the terms of constraining rights and duties, too: The principle of equal treatment ("impartiality") at the foundation of utilitarianism implies that all human beings have a *right* that their happiness should count equally and that others have a *duty* to count their happiness equally. Only given these normative constraints is the application of the principle of utility legitimate for utilitarianism. The doctrine of rights and duties is thus criticized using a doctrine that itself relies on very important rights and duties. Again, the circle is complete. Greene even states that utilitarianism presumably rests on an "affectively based evaluative premise," Greene, "Why Cognitive (Neuro)Science Matters for Ethics," 724. That this "affectively based evaluative premise" is supposed to be a high-level intuition does not change the fact that – by relying on such an *affectively* based premise to replace emotional gut reactions – the theory has become quite visibly inconsistent. It is a useful exercise to reconsider on the basis of this observation the meaning for Greene's argument concerning the studies (interesting as they are) listed in Greene, "Why Cognitive (Neuro)Science Matters for Ethics," 701 ff. Another example of these kinds of contradictions is the following statement, referring to emotional and cognitive neural structures: "It seems that healthy humans engage both responses and that there is a higher-order evaluation process that depends on the ventromedial prefrontal cortex, a structure that across domains attaches emotional weight to decision variables. In other words, the brain seems to make both types of judgement (deontological and consequentialist) and thus makes a higher-order judgement about which lower-order judgement to trust, which may be viewed as a kind of wisdom (reflecting virtue or good character)," Joshua Greene et al., "Embedding Ethical

When thinking about these kinds of claims advanced by certain psychological theories, we should bear one thing in mind: While neuroimaging studies have provided many fascinating results in recent years, as yet there are limits to these insights. These limits are not only the product of the constraints imposed and problems implied in the methods of neuroimaging, such as the level of the spatial and temporal resolution of the methods applied, "voodoo correlations,"[58] circular analysis,[59] the effects of the statistical "smoothing" of results and so on.[60] For example, the way that complex mental phenomena are realized in the human brain still has not been clarified. One question to ask in this context is whether the long-dominant focus on the localization of functions in the brain is fruitful or whether the research on patterns of activation is not more promising.[61] This has

Principles in Collective Decision Support Systems," *Proceedings of the Thirtieth AAAI Conference on Artificial Intelligence* (2016), 4148. It is noteworthy that the last-instance arbiter of human moral judgment in this passage is a region of the brain that is associated with emotional, deontological judgment, albeit here couched in the terms of some kind of virtue ethics. It is unclear how this can be reconciled with Greene's theses on fast and slow moral thinking.

Kahane et al., "Beyond Sacrificial Harm," convincingly argue that two elements of utilitarianism need to be distinguished: The element of impartial beneficence and the element of permissible or even required instrumental harm (i.e. harm inflicted on persons for the greater benefit of others). It is, however, also crucial to include in the analysis of moral cognition the insight highlighted here that the principles of equality at the heart of utilitarianism do not distinguish utilitarianism from deontology because they are utilitarianism's deontological base. The principles of equality together with other deontological principles like the prohibition of instrumentalization and its deeper normative foundations may also help us to understand such findings as reported in Kahane et al., "Beyond Sacrificial Harm," 152 ff., 155: While impartial beneficence is associated with greater emphatic concern, with helping with greater generosity, with greater welfare-based concern for the environment and with greater identification with the whole of humanity, these measures were either not or negatively associated with the moral acceptance of inflicting instrumental harm (the latter, however, positively associated with psychopathy, ibid. 151). These findings may be best understood as the expression of an underlying universalist, egalitarian, emphatic, other-regarding moral framework within which individuals are respected and valued for their own sake.

These problems affect other studies that build on these assumptions, too – for example, on the effects of variation in the oxytocin receptor gene on moral judgment, cf. Regan Bernhard et al., "Variation in the Oxytocin Receptor Gene (*OXTR*) Is Associated with Differences in Moral Judgement," *Social Cognitive and Affective Neuroscience* 11, no. 12 (2016). Another example is Kahnemann and Sunstein, *Cognitive Psychology of Moral Intuitions*. The study identifies morality with emotional intuitions but states that such intuitions can be transformed by conscious reasoning, ibid. 92, 103. Which moral principles are the basis of this transformation by conscious reasoning?

58 Cf. Edward Vul et al., "Puzzling High Correlations in fMRI Studies of Emotion, Personality, and Social Cognition," *Perspectives on Psychological Science* 4, no. 3 (2009).

59 Cf. Nikolaus Kriegeskorte et al., "Circular Analysis in Systems Neuroscience: The Dangers of Double Dipping," *Nature Neuroscience* 12 (2009).

60 Cf. e.g. Russell Poldrack, "The Future of fMRI in Cognitive Neuroscience," *Neuroimage* 62, no. 2 (2012), 1216 f. on some statistical problems.

61 Cf. e.g. Poldrack, "The Future of fMRI in Cognitive Neuroscience," 1216, 1217 f., on the move away from "blobology" to pattern analysis: "[T]he goal of finding blobs in a specific region can drive researchers into analytic gymnastics in order to find a significant blob to report. However,

consequences for the interpretation of patterns of neuronal activity that form the basis for the hypotheses of neuroimaging studies, because it is far from clear what a given observed neuronal activity really means. This is due not least to a classical problem of neuroimaging studies: reverse inference. One cannot conclude from the fact that a brain region is active when performing a certain task that whenever this brain region is active, this cognitive task is being performed. This is because a single brain region may perform many tasks – interacting with other areas of the brain, for instance. Reverse inference can produce research hypotheses but cannot provide conclusive evidence of how a mental function maps onto the brain.[62] The fact that a brain region – say, the DLPFC – is active when performing certain tasks involving cognitive control thus does not entail that whenever the DLPFC is active, cognitive control tasks are being performed. The same is true of the VMPFC and emotional reactions. Consequently, if they stand the test of further research, the results of neuroimaging studies such as the ones referred to are in no way proof that deontological morality is the expression of emotion. In addition, there are many competing empirical findings,[63] interestingly – if critically interpreted – also in studies

for the last few years the most interesting and novel research has focused on understanding patterns of activation rather than localized blobs. The appreciation of patterns is happening at multiple scales. At the systems (whole-brain) scale, the modelling of connectivity and its relation to behaviour continue to grow. ... I think the jury is still out on how well fMRI can ever characterize neuronal connectivity; as we outlined in Ramsey et al. (2010), there are a number of fundamental challenges in using fMRI to characterize causal interaction between brain regions." For a similar assessment (from phrenology to network theories) cf. Lutz Jäncke, *Kognitive Neurowissenschaften* (Bern: Hogrefe, 2013), 71 ff.

62 Cf. Russell Poldrack, "Can Cognitive Processes Be Inferred from Neuroimaging Data?" *Trends in Cognitive Science* 10, no. 2 (2006); Russell Poldrack, "Inferring Mental States from Neuroimaging Data: From Reverse Inference to Large-Scale Decoding," *Neuron* 72, no. 5 (2011); Poldrack, "The Future of fMRI in Cognitive Neuroscience," 1216, 1218 f., on the (difficult) task of finding "a region that is engaged *selectively*, such that activation of the region is actually predictive of the mental process" (emphasis in original), as a precondition for overcoming the problems of reverse inference; Russell Poldrack, *The New Mind Readers* (Princeton, NJ: Princeton University Press, 2018), 20 ff.

63 The insights gained through experimental work should not be overestimated. To take an example: There are studies suggesting that patients with lesions to the VMPFC are more vindictive in ultimatum games than normal subjects (cf. Michael Koenigs and Daniel Tranel, "Irrational Economic Decision-Making after Ventromedial Prefrontal Damage: Evidence from the Ultimatum Game," *The Journal of Neuroscience* 27, no. 4 (2007): 951), which seems to imply a less "utilitarian" and more "deontological," fairness-oriented outlook, while the same brain defect is used as an argument for the thesis that "deontological" judgments are emotional reactions emanating from the VMPFC; see above. This is not really convincing as "[s]uch patients exhibit both an abnormal utilitarian *and* an abnormal deontological tendency!" Kahane and Shackel, "Methodological Issues in the Neuroscience of Moral Judgment," 573 (emphasis in original). On the same problem cf. Aaron Duke and Laurent Bègue, "The Drunk Utilitarian: Blood Alcohol Concentration Predicts Utilitarian Responses in Moral Dilemmas," *Cognition* 134 (2015): 121, 124: "Alcohol intoxication is associated with increased emotional reactivity and selective attention towards emotional cues, which according to Greene's dual process conceptualisation, should lead to increased deontological (non-utilitarian) inclinations, the opposite of what was observed here." On another study with the result that "there is little

coauthored by Greene himself.[64] In light of what has been said, there is thus ample reason to reinterpret such findings and what they tell us about the workings of the mind, considering closely the analysis above of cases such as trolley problems and what they mean for plausible theories of moral judgment.

In this context, we should stress that no one doubts that emotions are a central part of moral evaluation. The question is, however, whether such emotions constitute moral (deontological) evaluation, as emotivists contend, or play a

relation between sacrificial judgements in the hypothetical dilemmas that dominate research, and a genuine utilitarian approach to ethics," Guy Kahane et al., "'Utilitarian' Judgments in Sacrificial Moral Dilemmas Do Not Reflect Impartial Concern for the Greater Good," *Cognition* 134 (2015): 193. A related debate appears in Jorge Moll and Ricardo de Oliveira-Souza, "Moral Judgments, Emotions and the Utilitarian Brain," *Trends in Cognitive Science* 11, no. 8 (2007); Joshua Greene, "Why Are VMPFC Patients More Utilitarian? A Dual Process Theory of Moral Judgement Explains," *Trends in Cognitive Science* 11, no. 8 (2007); Jorge Moll and Ricardo de Oliveira-Souza, "Response to Greene: Moral Sentiments and Reason: Friends or Foes?" *Trends in Cognitive Science* 11, no. 8 (2007); another move is to reinterpret findings on the trolley problem in the framework of "intuitive/counterintuitive judgments," cf. Guy Kahane et al., "The Neural Basis of Intuitive and Counterintuitive Moral Judgment," *Social Cognitive and Affective Neuroscience* 7, no. 4 (2011); on some reinterpretations of the role of the VMPFC in moral decision-making, Joshua Greene, "The Cognitive Neuroscience of Moral Judgement and Decision Making," in *The Cognitive Neurosciences*, eds. Michael Gazzaniga and George Mangun (Cambridge, MA: MIT Press, 2014), 1017 ff. Cf. for some more possible functions of brain regions associated with moral judgment, Joanna Demaree-Cotton and Guy Kahane, "The Neuroscience of Moral Judgement," in *The Routledge Handbook of Moral Epistemology*, eds. Aaron Zimmermann, Karen Jones and Mark Timmons (New York: Routledge, 2019), 84–104, 92 ff. One can conclude from these debates that moral and legal theory is urgently needed to create a theoretical framework in which experimental findings can be designed and interpreted more successfully, including a much more finely grained account of the structure and content of morality and the role of emotions as a precondition and consequence of moral judgment than is sometimes used in these experiment-based debates.

64 Cf. Karen Huang, Joshua Greene and Max Bazerman, "Veil-of-Ignorance Reasoning Favors the Greater Good," *Proceedings of the National Academy of Sciences* 116, no. 48 (2019). The authors investigate the effect of prior veil-of-ignorance reasoning on subsequent moral judgments about moral dilemma situations, including the footbridge case. They find that such prior veil-of-ignorance reasoning increases the number of people opting for pushing the man off the bridge to stop the trolley in the footbridge case. The study does not discuss an evidently important factor, namely that self-interest may dominate over moral considerations that still continue to influence human beings – for instance, through the indirect effects of a bad conscience. If you imagine yourself in veil-of-ignorance conditions as one of the persons on the track (a 5 in 6 chance) compared to the person pushed onto the track (1 in 6 chance), you may opt for pushing the person because of fear for your life but still find it morally problematic to do so. It is a lot to ask others to opt to endanger their own life for moral reasons. Criminal law often accounts for such cases with elements of exculpation (not justification). Interestingly, the number of participants finding it morally acceptable to push the person still remains low – 38 percent in comparison to 24 percent in control conditions. The majority, thus, even under the threat of their own death, would not opt to instrumentalize the person on the bridge to save themselves. These results confirm the importance of this principle of noninstrumentalization, which is at the heart of the footbridge case, as we have seen. The other cases imply further problems that the studies do not address – the earthquake case raises the problem of threshold deontology and the autonomous vehicle cases lead to the question of the effect that the responsibility for creating a risk (using an autonomous vehicle) has on the decision about the distribution of risk.

different role. Again, the theoretical power of imagination evident in emotivist accounts seems far too limited to explain the complexity of the human moral world.[65] One important point is these accounts' analytical failure to distinguish emotions that are the *consequences* of moral judgment from emotions that *constitute* moral judgment. Consider the case of outrage after witnessing a grave injustice. Here, the cognition of injustice is the precondition of and thus not identical to the feeling of moral outrage. The fact that moral sentiments arise is predicated upon certain preconditions, such as the indignation about an injustice upon the unequal treatment of two persons who are equal in the respects that are relevant in the situation at hand. Only if the agent thinks that these elements of an immoral act exist will the respective feeling ensue. This is why such feelings disappear when one understands that the facts actually were different – for example, that there was indeed a relevant difference between the persons being unequally treated.

For the study of the neurological basis of morality, this means that it would be very surprising if brain functions relevant for human sentiment (whatever they turn out to be) were not engaged when an agent evaluates a situation in moral terms. However, these moral sentiments do not constitute moral judgment, but are the consequence of an analysis of structural elements of the action (agency, patients of action, intentions and their kind and object, relations of equality, etc.).

In addition, as our analysis of the concept of fundamental or human rights and the history and justificatory theory of human rights have shown, the preconditions of the predication of rights are highly complex both in form and in substance. Equating such complex judgments with an emotional gut reaction does not seem a very promising approach to the matter.

All of this is nothing more than a reminder that the interpretation of empirical data is dependent upon theory: Data only have meaning within a theoretical framework. In our concrete case, the value of neuroimaging studies of the neurophysiological basis of moral judgment is dependent on the merits of the theoretical framework in which these studies are developed. If this framework is deficient, the interpretation of the data will be insufficient, too.[66]

In addition, identifying rationality with utilitarianism seems somewhat naive.[67] The question is: Why should the scope of practical reason, to use a traditional term,

[65] Cf. Matthias Mahlmann, "Ethics, Law and the Challenge of Cognitive Science," *German Law Journal* 8, no. 6 (2007): 586 ff.; Pardo and Patterson, *Minds, Brains, and the Law*, 58 on emotions accompanying moral judgments.

[66] Current debates often criticize "armchair philosophers" for their naivete, sometimes with good reason. One should, however, not overlook the deficits of some of the experimental work, which would benefit a great deal from more preliminary theoretical work (cf. n. 63).

[67] Greene, "Why Cognitive (Neuro)Science Matters for Ethics," 696, posits that slow thinking is "a general-purpose reasoning system, specialized for enabling behaviors that serve long(er) term goals." This overlooks the theory of justice's insight that equality as a normative principle is not the same as general rationality, cf. Gosepath, *Gleiche Gerechtigkeit*. Berker, "The Normative Insignificance of Neuroscience," 293 ff., underlines correctly that a normative argument is

not be wider? In the history of thought, it was the default assumption that human thought is made up not only of some kind of instrumental rationality, but that there are other, qualitatively different yardsticks, most importantly those of justice and moral goodness. This is the common denominator of much of the greatest thought on these matters. Why should this be wrong? Why are deontological principles a priori not rational, or reasonable, if you prefer? What is intrinsically better about the principle of utility (forgetting for a moment its deontological foundations) as compared to the prohibition of instrumentalization, the principle of the justice of the equal treatment of equals or the obligation to care for others?[68] A strange impoverishment of the richness of human thought is at play in such theories that fails to live up to the insights of practical philosophy and legal theory.

It is important to emphasize that the mental gizmo thesis is not a necessary consequence of the dual-process model of the mind as such. It is possible to believe that this model describes an important aspect of human cognition without finding the mental gizmo thesis convincing. Deontology could be part of slow thinking; there is no a priori reason why this could not be the case. Consequently, not being convinced by the mental gizmo thesis does not say anything about the value of the dual-process model of the mind. The mental gizmo thesis is just an implausible thesis developed within this model of the human mind.

Nor do neuroscientific or psychological approaches to ethical and legal issues as such wed us to a certain perspective on the cognitive origin of ethics and law. In particular, nothing in the theory of mind, in neuroscientific research or in psychology forces us to develop an impoverished account of human practical thought. The answer to psychological skepticism is consequently neither to ignore neuroscience and psychology, nor to escape into a normative theory where psychology, whatever it says, simply does not count. Rather, the answer is to develop a substantial concept of human moral cognition as an element of a wider theory of human rights that is more plausible than its skeptical alternatives.

6.5 RIGHTS AND BEHAVIORAL SCIENCE

One large and creative area of research concerns the analysis of law on the basis of behavioral science. Classical law and economics operating within the parameters of rational choice theory assume that human beings are rational maximizers of their expected utility in absolute terms. This assumption is not only meant to be

needed to justify the conclusion that deontological judgments use morally irrelevant criteria, whereas utilitarianism does not. These normative criteria cannot be drawn from neuroscientific research as such, ibid. 326.

68 Greene, *Moral Tribes*, 136: "Reasoning, as applied to decision making, involves the conscious application of decision rules." Why, according to this rather broad definition, is the principle of utility (or the principle of impartiality or the "Golden Rule," see n. 56) a candidate for reasoning but the categorical imperative and Rawls' principles of justice are not?

descriptive, but often forms part of a normative theory: Justified decisions must be based on such rational choices.

Behavioral law and economics take their impetus from systematic differences between the assumptions of rational choice theory and actual human decision-making.[69] One influential element is prospect theory.[70] The central thesis of prospect theory is that people make choices not on the basis of utility determined by a final state, but rather in the light of changes relative to their specific situation or reference point. Losses and gains are central elements of perceived utility. People are loss averse – the utility of gains is perceived to be smaller than the disutility of losses, even if gains and losses are equal in absolute terms. When making decisions, people use heuristics, general decision principles that may work well in many cases but may yield results that are irrational – for example, the representational heuristics that ascribe properties, sometimes falsely, to individuals because of the class to which they belong. Judgments are also influenced by biases, such as the omission bias – all things equal, people prefer not to act. Framing effects are a third example: The way a decision situation is framed – for instance, in terms of losses and not of gains – influences the decision, even though the outcome is the same in absolute terms.

Within this conception of the mind, theories of rights are developed. One such theory explores the possible effects of loss aversion on conceptions of rights. The distinction between civil and political rights on the one hand and social and economic rights on the other, or between so-called first- and second-generation rights, is of interest in this context. A key question is whether or not there are reasons to protect both kinds of rights equally or whether only the former qualify as true human rights. A possible approach to this question is not to engage in the debate about the justification of these different rights, but instead to try to explain the reasons for the widespread perception (be it justified or not) that there is such a difference.[71] One way to do so is to refer to loss aversion as a psychological mechanism. Taking this approach, "the crucial distinction is not necessarily between governmental acts and omissions, but rather between government giving and not taking."[72] Civil and political rights are perceived as being about the government not taking something, such as the unrestrained possibility of free expression. Social and economic rights, by contrast, are about giving something to the rights-holders. As losses loom larger than gains, the former kind of rights enjoys greater plausibility than the latter. Reference points are one major factor in analyzing this problem. The fact that many legal systems demand that if social or economic benefits are provided then this must be done without discrimination is based on such a reference point: Not receiving the benefit is experienced as a loss,

69 Cf. for a restatement Eyal Zamir and Doron Teichman, *Behavioral Law and Economics* (Oxford: Oxford University Press, 2018).

70 Cf. for a summary Kahneman, *Thinking, Fast and Slow*, 109 ff.

71 Zamir, *Law, Psychology and Morality*, 140.

72 Zamir, *Law, Psychology and Morality*, 143.

because those similarly situated persons who do receive the benefit serve as reference points.[73]

This view is of considerable interest when attempting to explain why civil and political rights are perceived as being different from social and economic rights, at least in modern debates. Whether this difference also exists in this form from a historical perspective is far from clear, given the prominent place of rights to material goods in older reflections.[74]

This approach leads to the following question, however: Why does loss aversion (assuming that it plays a role in this context, if only for the sake of the argument) not settle the case? Why do questions about social rights not only arise at all but do so very powerfully, and arguably since the beginnings of the discourse on rights? This seems to indicate that certain normative principles have an influence on human perceptions of the justification of human rights beyond loss aversion, including principles of justice, which are particularly relevant for social and economic rights.

This does not speak against an impact of loss aversion on such debates, but rather against assuming that this is the decisive or even only psychological influence on the perception of whether these rights are justified.

Other examples seem to confirm this kind of analysis. One such example is affirmative action, which is a controversial issue in the interpretation of equality guarantees and thus in the interpretation of an important element of human rights. Legal systems apply affirmative action to benefits that people do not yet possess.[75] Accordingly, affirmative action programs concern, for instance, access to university or employment for people who do not enjoy this access yet, but do not demand that others relinquish places at universities or jobs they already hold. This can be explained by loss aversion: The losses of losing a benefit (admission to university, employment, etc.) loom larger than the gains for those who are not enjoying this benefit yet.[76]

There are interesting questions to be asked beyond loss aversion in this context, including the legitimate protection of trust and the reliance on certain decisions for allocating the goods of students admitted to university programs. Revisiting decisions on university admission should only be possible under very restrictive conditions, such as applicants intentionally providing wrong information, because they will have based many subsequent decisions on their admission. Such considerations are mirrored in some administrative law.

But even if one disregards this for the sake of the argument, an answer still is needed to the question of why the desire for affirmative action arises in the first place. This desire is connected with the idea of justice as equality. The ultimate

73 Zamir, *Law, Psychology and Morality*, 143.

74 Thomas Aquinas' theory of strong obligations of mutual help is but one example discussed in Chapter 3.

75 Zamir, *Law, Psychology and Morality*, 148.

76 Zamir, *Law, Psychology and Morality*, 144 ff.

aim is, after all, to achieve equal access to the benefits of society independently of characteristics that are irrelevant for the allocation of such goods, as skin color is for admission to university. For this reason, minorities who were excluded previously are treated preferentially in order to overcome traditional patterns of exclusion. The question is not whether this connection between affirmative action and justice exists, but rather whether considerations of this sort can trump the principle of equal treatment for a transitional period in order to achieve this aim.[77]

It is argued that loss aversion is compatible with common-sense morality – which adheres to threshold deontology.[78] Classical distinctions in ethics between doing and allowing or between intending (in the sense of purposeful action) and foreseeing mirror loss aversion, it is argued: The duty to avoid doing harm is stricter than the duty (if it exists at all) to help others (or to not allow harm to happen to them). The two distinctions are not the same, as illustrated by cases in which one intentionally allows harm or harms somebody by an action, but only as a side effect.[79]

The problem with this account is that loss aversion may be compatible with a version of threshold deontology but clearly fails to adequately specify the relevant moral principles that are the real core of the matter. These principles are more complex than the doing/allowing or intending/foreseeing distinctions suggest.

Take the trolley problem: Mere loss aversion gives no reason to judge flipping the switch in the bystander case to be permissible but throwing the person off the bridge in the footbridge case to be impermissible. In both cases, the losses are the same – five people killed, one person not killed, or vice versa, depending on whether or not action is taken. Even loss aversion supplemented with the distinction between doing and allowing is not enough. Consider a variant of the footbridge case: The person on the bridge is a toddler, Hannah, on her tricycle who will fall on the track as the railing is damaged, stopping the train, if the other person on the bridge who is entrusted to care for the toddler does not prevent the child's fall, which the other person is easily capable of doing. It seems impermissible to let the toddler fall in order to stop the train, even though one is not doing anything, only allowing something to happen. The reason has already been pointed out: More complex principles than loss aversion or the distinction between doing/allowing determine the evaluation of such cases. What is key here is an ends–means distinction and the prohibition of using human beings (merely) as means for other ends, be it by doing or allowing.

Loss aversion consequently has limited power to explain the problems investigated here. However, studies in experimental psychology and behavioral economics deal directly with normative principles relevant for our argument, looking at intuitions about justice and benevolence – the next topic to which we will turn.

[77] This insight can be translated in the terms of prospect theory, cf. Zamir, *Law, Psychology and Morality*, 228.

[78] Zamir, *Law, Psychology and Morality*, 177 ff.

[79] Zamir, *Law, Psychology and Morality*, 182.

6.6 JUSTICE AND BENEVOLENCE

Research on justice has a substantial tradition in social psychology, encompassing research on relative deprivation, distributive justice and the fairness of outcome distributions, procedural justice and corrective justice.[80] One prominent example from the current debate is the extensive discussion of fairness or, to use another term, inequality aversion. Yet another example is altruism, which can be seen, for example, in the case of contributions to social goods or in the (related) form of altruistic punishment. Importantly, altruism is understood in the sense of strong reciprocity; that is, behavior that does not lead to individual economic benefit of the agent.[81] There is cross-cultural research on such attitudes.[82] Another aspect of this research is the development of such patterns of behavior in children.[83]

From the perspective of our inquiry, one problem of these studies is that they are predominantly concerned with patterns of behavior (e.g. distributive acts, punishments, rewards) and not with the internal mental states of the agents. In particular, they are not concerned with the reflective evaluation of actions by an agent or observer that has deontic, prescriptive consequences either from the first-person perspective of the agent or the third-person perspective of the observer. Reflective evaluation is crucially important for human morality, however, as moral judgment involving a prescriptive dimension is the core of the matter, as already indicated. Morality is not concerned simply with acting in conformity with certain (other-regarding) standards; it is concerned with a moral evaluation that yields prescriptive propositions such as "You should not bombard hospitals in civil wars" and possibly gives rise to action on the grounds of and motivated by such prescriptive propositions.

It is important to remain aware of a traditional insight of moral philosophy in this respect: There is no necessary or deterministic connection between moral evaluation and moral behavior. An agent may very well perceive the morality or immorality of an action but nevertheless fail to act accordingly due to intervening interests, weakness of moral will and so forth. Agents' failure to display altruistic or just

80 Cf. Tom Tyler et al., *Social Justice in a Diverse Society* (New York: Routledge, 1997), 11 ff., for an overview of earlier research.

81 Cf. Ernst Fehr and Urs Fischbacher, "The Nature of Human Altruism," *Nature* 425 (2003).

82 cf. e.g. Joseph Henrich et al., "'Economic Man' in Cross-Cultural Perspective: Behavioural Experiments in 15 Small-Scale Societies," *Behavioural and Brain Sciences* 28, no. 6 (2005).

83 Cf. e.g. Kristina Olson and Elizabeth Spelke, "Foundations of Cooperation in Young Children," *Cognition* 108, no. 1 (2008) (three- and five-year-olds); Marco Schmidt and Jessica Sommerville, "Fairness Expectations and Altruistic Sharing in 15-Month-Old Human Infants," *PLoS ONE* 6, no. 10 (2011); Ernst Fehr, Helen Bernhard and Bettina Rockenbach, "Egalitarianism in Young Children," *Nature* 454, no. 7208 (2008); Ernst Fehr, Daniela Glätzle-Rützler and Matthias Sutter, "The Development of Egalitarianism, Altruism, Spite and Parochialism in Childhood and Adolescence," *European Economic Review* 64 (2013). On the effect of self-reflection in the framework of identity utility, cf. Christoph Engel and Michael Kurschilgen, "The Jurisdiction of the Man within – Introspection, Identity, and Cooperation in a Public Good Experiment," *MPI Collective Goods Preprint* (2015).

behavior does not allow direct conclusions to be drawn as to the principles governing their moral judgment. They may simply not be acting on the basis of their moral judgment.

There is another problem concerning the theoretical and conceptual framework of such studies and thus the determining framework for the interpretation of data. Concepts such as "inequality aversion" or "other-regarding preferences" play a central role in some of these studies. These concepts do not fully fathom the intricacies of moral judgments, however. Aversions and preferences describe inclinations to act. An aversion to asparagus means that one has no wish to eat this vegetable if it can be avoided. Moral judgment concerns something qualitatively different, as we just have seen, namely the *reflective evaluation* of an intention or action (e.g. based on such inclinations). This evaluation has deontic, prescriptive consequences, a moral ought. This "ought" is categorically different from a mere aversion or preference. It does not *incline* – it *obligates* persons, whatever their inclinations may be. The possible conflict between prescriptions that obligate and inclinations to act, such as preferences, or not to act, such as aversions, reveals the difference between the two categories, showing that we should not mistake the one for the other. Moreover, there is the basic deontic category of permissions, which is important for the concept of rights and cannot be translated into preferences or aversions either. Whether you have an aversion or preference to do something is irrelevant for the question of whether you are permitted to do it.

These methodological and theoretical problems notwithstanding, this area of research offers important findings. There are a large number of studies that provide empirical evidence about the egalitarian intuitions of human beings, prominently in the ultimatum game, for instance, which involves the following: A player receives a sum of money and distributes it between themself and another player. If the recipient accepts the distribution, both keep the amount distributed; if not, nobody receives anything. There are many variants of this game – for instance, the dictator game. As a baseline, the results show that proposers offer an almost equal share and that responders will not accept just any distribution but reject very low shares.[84] We should note that neither an unequal proposal nor the acceptance of an unequal distribution means that the offer is considered just. Selfish impulses evidently have a strong hold on human beings (whether the proposer has a persistently good

[84] Cf. for instance Colin Camerer, *Behavioral Game Theory: Experiments in Strategic Interaction* (New York: Russell Sage Foundation, 2003), 43 ff. Results for the dictator game (the proposer sets the share unilaterally) indicate similar patterns: The average given is about 42 percent, though about 36 percent maximize their own profit from the game: "Even generous subjects thus tend to have a selfish side," Christoph Engel, "Dictator Games: A Meta Study," *Experimental Economics* 14 (2011): 583, 607 concludes. Joseph Henrich, *The Secret of Our Success: How Culture Is Driving Human Evolution, Domesticating Our Species, and Making Us Smarter* (Princeton, NJ: Princeton University Press, 2017), 193, reports different results for traditional small-scale societies.

conscience is, however, a different question), and the responder may consider receiving a smaller, unequal share to be a lesser evil than receiving nothing at all.

The most plausible interpretation of these results is that human beings are not (only) maximizers of utility, but that their evaluation of distributions is based on moral principles – for instance, of (proportional) equality.[85] If they were simple utility maximizers, they would accept any distribution that improves their situation, however small it might be. Importantly, the preservation of relations of equality seems to be a value in itself, and greater than at least some material benefits.

The results of studies on altruistic punishment point in the same direction: Human beings value certain standards and act to enforce them, even if this comes at a certain cost to themselves. Whether the reason for this kind of behavior is that they expect to benefit from the maintenance of such structures themselves at some point or that they consider defending certain normative principles to be of intrinsic value is quite another question.

There are other patterns of behavior that are discussed in connection with questions of social norms and morality. To take some examples:[86] Communication has the effect of increasing cooperative behavior. Many people are conditional cooperators – they cooperate in proportion to the cooperation of others. In finitely repeated public good games, levels of cooperation deteriorate over time, despite high initial cooperation rates. Stable group composition leads to higher cooperation rates. Framing a game as a community game has positive effects on cooperation in comparison to framing the same game as a stock market game. If the games are played sequentially, however, the effect of this framing disappears. Peer punishment leads to greater levels of cooperation, but its effects can be undermined if the punishment indicates selfish intentions. There may even be forms of punishment of cooperators. Punishment means a certain investment. Nevertheless, people prefer an environment with peer punishment. Rewarding cooperators increases cooperation. Bringing cooperative individuals together also augments cooperation.

How to explain such patterns of behavior? One way to approach the problem is to account for these patterns by the effects of social norms. This is how Ernst Fehr and Ivo Schurtenberger proceed, for instance. In their influential analysis, they supplement a direct social norm approach with the key idea of conditional cooperation and a

85 Zamir and Teichman, *Behavioural Law and Economics*, 102, sum up research on social justice: "The most influential theory in the social-psychological study of substantive fairness has been *equity theory*. It posits that people perceive that they are treated fairly when the ratio between their received outcomes (for example their salary) and their input (e.g., the effort, talent and commitment they put into their work) is equal to the ratio between the received outcomes and the inputs of other peoples" (emphasis in original). This is evidently nothing but an evaluation on the basis of proportional equality and certain criteria of distribution (effort, talent, commitment) regarded as relevant for certain spheres of distribution, cf. Chapter 5.

86 Cf. for the following list of behavioral patterns Ernst Fehr and Ivo Schurtenberger, "Normative Foundations of Human Cooperation," *Nature Human Behaviour* 2, no. 7 (2018): 458–68, 459 ff.

set of particular psychological mechanisms. The direct social norm approach calculates the utility and disutility of following a social norm. The (dis)utility depends on an intrinsic desire to comply with norms.[87] The conditional cooperation approach postulates that people will cooperate dependent on others' level of cooperation. Because of the mechanism of conditional cooperation, the mentioned patterns of behavior arise, Fehr and Schurtenberger argue, with the exception of: peer punishment; punishment of cooperators that threatens the positive effects on cooperation; and the preference for environments with peer punishment. Here, Fehr and Schurtenberger's theoretical account relies on additional psychological mechanisms, such as social preferences for fairness/equity, reciprocity, a prosocial self-image or an aversion against guilt.[88] The social preferences for fairness and equity are themselves determined by social norms.[89] From these authors' perspective, institutional structures play an important role: Punishment is necessary to maintain cooperation and institutions that guarantee norm conformity.[90]

It is true that "unconditional normative prescriptions like 'be selfless'" alone cannot account for such patterns of behavior.[91] But this does not mean that the normative principles that we have discussed in the present inquiry are irrelevant or nonexistent and that the moral world is limited to conditioned cooperation and the particular understanding of fairness and equity considered by this experimental work. This is because a moral obligation provides a sometimes-powerful motivation but is always just one of other impulses that influence human behavior. According to the view defended here, human beings are not selfless beings, but beings who have the faculty to limit their many selfish impulses because of moral judgments and the volitional consequences of these judgments. Moreover, cooperation is a complex affair and evidently not just based on moral impulses of selflessness, justice and altruism.

Therefore, the patterns of behavior recalled as examples of this strand of research come as no particular surprise: Communication can help with cooperation for many reasons – for instance, defining one's mutual advantage, clarifying common interests or strengthening the will to adhere to moral intuitions. That levels of cooperation can be influenced by the declining cooperative behavior of others is easily reconcilable with a moral orientation, too, as the latter does not imply a readiness to be exploited. Even if we feel a moral obligation to act in certain ways, our preparedness to do so may diminish if we see others pursuing egoistic goals. The sobering effects of repeatedly played games with declining levels of cooperation may have related reasons but do not say anything about the reality of more exacting standards of behavior. In the same vein, partner matching or the framing of a game as community-oriented action can

[87] Fehr and Schurtenberger, "Normative Foundations," 461 f.
[88] Fehr and Schurtenberger, "Normative Foundations," 463.
[89] Fehr and Schurtenberger, "Normative Foundations," 463.
[90] Fehr and Schurtenberger, "Normative Foundations," 464.
[91] Fehr and Schurtenberger, "Normative Foundations," 461.

help agents to adhere more faithfully to some moral standards and prudential principles that are also important for cooperation. The sequential playing of these games may have the mentioned sobering effect.

Altruistic and peer punishment has much to do with principles of justice. Distinguishing just punishment from unprincipled, potentially boundless revenge and determining the principles that make punishment just have been permanent themes of the theory of justice, dealt with in many contributions, including Aristotle's classic treatment of the matter. A preference for entrenched systems of punishment is a possible product of cool-headed assessments of the pacifying, conflict-reducing effects of such arrangements. That rewards may help to motivate people to do anything, including to cooperate, needs as little proof as the positive effects of working with like-minded cooperators.

The reference to fairness, equity and moral emotions like guilt takes us straight to the question of the structure underlying human moral cognition. Here, one has to be analytically precise and try to determine more concretely what a moral judgment is about, avoiding in particular the category error of mistaking a preference or aversion for an obligation or prohibition. We already tried to give some indications of what such an analytical theory of morality could look like, and we will proceed further on this path in the last chapter. Moreover, this body of empirical evidence does not conclusively answer the question of the origins of foundational moral intuitions; in particular, it cannot tell us whether they are culturally induced or based on the innate structure of the human mind. We will also ask, therefore, whether it is really true that ideas of fairness and equity are wholly the offspring of social norms or whether these social norms are rather in at least some part the expression of basic moral intuitions, not least in the light of child psychology.

The behavioral studies we have reviewed contain no findings that have a direct and robust bearing on the question of human rights. We identified some problems of the theoretical framework of the interpretation of the empirical findings. Nevertheless, the thrust of this important research underlines the fact that intuitions about justice such as equality and altruism are not mere theoretical chimeras, but psychological realities of substantial importance for human beings, their decision-making, the explicit norms they develop and their subsequent actions.

7

Where Did It All Come From?

Morality and the Evolution of the Mind

And this tattooing, had been the work of a departed prophet and seer of his island, who, by those hieroglyphic marks, had written out on his body a complete theory of the heavens and the earth, and a mystical treatise on the art of attaining truth; so that Queequeg in his own proper person was a riddle to unfold; a wondrous work in one volume; but whose mysteries not even himself could read, though his own life heart beat against them; and these mysteries were therefore destined in the end to moulder away with the living parchment whereon they were inscribed, and so be unsolved to the last. And this thought it must have been which suggested to Ahab that wild exclamation of his, when one morning turning away from surveying poor Queequeg – "Oh, devilish tantalization of the gods!"

Herman Melville, *Moby Dick*

7.1 MORALITY AND EVOLUTION

Human beings are part of the natural world and thus owe their makeup, including their cognitive capacities and limitations, to the same forces as any other organism. Therefore, it is natural, at least for the purposes of a scientific theory-building whose methods are not concerned with religious interpretations of human existence, to ask what the theory of evolution can tell us about the nature and content of human morality. As the law is a central element of human beings' normative world, the answer to this question potentially has important consequences for the understanding of the law as well.

Evolutionary thinking has permeated many disciplines. Theorems of evolutionary biology in particular have been put to use – not always felicitously – in many other contexts, from cultural development based on war[1] on to social theory.[2]

[1] Cf. Peter Turchin, *Ultrasociety: How 10,000 Years of War Made Humans the Greatest Cooperators on Earth* (Chaplin, CT: Beresta Books, 2015).

[2] Cf. Luhmann, *Recht der Gesellschaft*; Luhmann, *Gesellschaft der Gesellschaft*.

The key question for the concerns of our inquiry is whether there are hardwired, genetically inherited mental structures that influence or even determine human moral evaluations, intentions and concrete actions. As these moral evaluations clearly impact upon both the making and (according to the most plausible theories of interpretation) the application of law, the influence of such hardwired mental structures on the law may be substantial.

There is a huge variety of research in this area. Some investigations emphasize the importance of the biological foundations of human morality, some the evolution of culture after modern human beings started populating the Earth some 80,000 years ago. Some research challenges traditional assumptions about the content of morality, explicitly including the idea of human rights or the idea of a universalist moral outlook. One example of the former, the mental gizmo thesis, was already discussed in the Chapter 6, although we did not go into detail with respect to the underlying evolutionary theory. From this point of view, evolutionary mechanisms constrain the moralities possible in a way that rules out any natural morality consisting of generous, solely other-regarding altruism or egalitarian justice, because such a morality could not form a behavioral evolutionarily stable strategy for an organism. By contrast, other approaches confirm notions of altruism, fairness and mutual respect not limited to small groups, albeit to varying degrees, in the framework of a naturalistic theory of morality.[3]

As far as the topic of human rights is concerned, there are two dimensions to the problem. The first concerns human rights themselves, whose evolutionary origin forms the object of some such theories, including the mental gizmo thesis. The second dimension concerns the normative principles that we have identified, which underpin intuitions about individual claims and the justification of human rights, including justice, obligatory concern for the well-being of others and respect for their worth. Our review of evolutionary theories needs to deal with both of these dimensions.

[3] Cf. Buchanan and Powell, *The Evolution of Moral Progress*, arguing for evolutionary fixed plasticity that produces a small-group morality under distress cues like out-group threats, but under favorable circumstances allows for the development of inclusivist moralities like human rights; Michael E. McCullough, *The Kindness of Strangers* (London: Oneworld, 2020), arguing that human beings' three key natural endowments are an instinct for reciprocity, the "appetite for helping others in hopes of appearing virtuous" and the instinct for reasoning. These instincts were activated in history to create care for strangers by: (1) god-kings during the Agricultural Revolution generating loyalty by appearing to care for the weak; (2) the Axial Age discovery of the Golden Rule; (3) the sixteenth century discovery of the prudential advantages of helping the weak – for instance, keeping unrest under control; (4) the Enlightenment convictions about equality, dignity and natural rights; (5) nineteenth-century humanitarianism; (6) the post-World War II humanitarianism; and (7) the contemporary drive towards efficient giving, ibid. 115 ff.; quote at 264.

7.2 PUZZLING ALTRUISM

Evolutionary biology has long been concerned not just with the physical traits of organisms, but also with behavior and the mental structures and inner states that underpin behavior.[4] Evolutionary explanations form a central part of ethology. Sets of behavioral patterns include social behavior, which occurs in many different forms. Some species, like bees and ants, live in highly organized, complex communities. How do such behavioral patterns and the underlying cognitive structures arise? What is their evolutionary origin?

In this context, behavioral traits that benefit organisms other than the actor are of particular interest. Altruistic behavior is a special object of scrutiny for some approaches to evolutionary theory, because it does not seem to fit well into what is regarded as the basic mechanisms of evolution, and into natural selection in particular. How can evolution select for traits that are beneficial not for the bearer of these traits, but for others?

These questions also arise for highly cooperative organisms such as human beings. Human morality is crucial to understanding this cooperative behavior. The mental world of humans includes prescriptive moral rules that affect both the formation of intentions to act and actual action. For humans at least, the evolutionary point of altruism is not the only problem to arise: Justice is another equally puzzling issue. Its principles limit the gains people can reap for themselves. How does this constraint fit into the picture of evolutionary theory? An equivalent question can be asked of the idea of obligatory respect for others. What are the evolutionary roots of this phenomenon?

Many approaches to the issue observe that the gains an organism reaps by cooperating are a central factor in the evolutionary process. It is argued that other-regarding behavior is only an evolutionarily stable strategy if it increases the chances of reproduction by augmenting the reproductive fitness of the cooperating organism. Moreover, every behavioral trait needs to yield such reproductive benefits if it is to continue to form part of the evolutionary process. Otherwise it will be weeded out by the forces of selection.

7.3 VARIOUS FORMS OF COOPERATION AND THE PROBLEM OF WHAT MORALITY IS

Before embarking on a review of the main findings of evolutionary theory that have a bearing on the theory of human rights, it is worth mentioning a few points that are sometimes overlooked in discussions of this matter and that will inform our analysis.

[4] Cf. for instance Konrad Lorenz, *Das sogenannte Böse* (Vienna: Dr G. Borotha-Schoeler, 1963); Edward Wilson, *Sociobiology: The New Synthesis* (Cambridge, MA: Harvard University Press, 1975).

First, sociality and cooperation are not necessary Forms of existence for organisms – solitary life forms can be very successful at assuring the reproduction of a species. There is no evolutionary necessity to be social or cooperative; it is simply one of many possible ways of living. Arguments claiming that humanity's specific form of life had to develop – a kind of natural teleology in the form of evolutionary theory – are therefore untenable.

Second, cooperation comes in many shapes and sizes. This is a simple but absolutely crucial observation. A herd of animals staying together to create protection in numbers; active group defense; temporary intragroup coalitions to outcompete other group members or to kill their offspring;[5] the complex functional differentiation of ant colonies or a beehive, including the infertility of some organisms for functional purposes; the mechanisms of cooperation in a human society of hunter-gatherers in 20,000 BCE; or human society in 2023, organized through the institutions of a constitutional state based on human rights, part of the global community under international law – these are all very different forms of cooperation.

Third, human forms of cooperation face the normative standard of legitimacy – bees have no other option than their hives, but how humans should build societies is far from clear. In human history and thought, very different forms of cooperation were used for long stretches of time: A stratified slaveholder society under an authoritarian ruler cooperates, but not in terms of justice, beneficence and mutual respect. In *Politeia*, Plato envisaged a highly cooperative society, where all members devoted their best abilities to the good of the polis – a vision that 2,500 years later was denounced as the seed of totalitarianism.[6]

Fourth, the diverse forms of cooperation presuppose very different cognitive abilities on the part of the organisms cooperating. The mechanisms used by antelopes to cooperate in herds, by bees to assemble in a hive, by ants to form a colony and by human beings to form a constitutional state within the UN system are not the same. These forms of cooperation consequently also come about in very different ways. Herds of antelopes or ant colonies are not created by centuries of reflection, reform and political revolution, while human social institutions are. These developments and the often-radical reorganization of human societies are of major interest, even though humans were living in hunter-gatherer societies, not constitutional states when the survival of the human species was decided, because they may offer clues to human beings' potential, including cognitive capacities that were put to use only in later stages of their history. The fact that human beings are able to form highly complex mathematical theories about the world with explanatory power is certainly of interest for understanding the cognitive machinery of human beings, even though differential equations were (most probably) only rarely discussed in the average cave 60,000 years ago.

5 Cf. Tomasello, *A Natural History of Human Morality*, 23.

6 Karl Popper, *The Open Society and Its Enemies*.

Fifth, the mechanisms underlying cooperation are not immediately obvious and are certainly manifold. This is true for human cooperation as well. The way that human societies are integrated into something like an organized structure is a classic and highly contested sociological question. Moral precepts are only one of the mechanisms that may be relevant here. Strategic interaction based on instrumental rationality, as in trade and other tit-for-tat relations, is another. Further elements include force or the threat of violence to command obedience, or the belief in an authority's legitimacy because of its divine origin or because of the leader's particular charisma. Force and belief in the legitimacy of some sort of authority are two very significant factors assuring cooperation in human history, used, for example, to build the pyramids, to construct the Palace of Versailles and to lead millions of Germans to become agents of bloodshed during World War II, often sacrificing their own lives on the way into the moral abyss.

Sixth, it is not obvious that human morality is only or even primarily a tool for cooperation. If one is to even start considering this problem, one needs to know what kind of cooperation is at issue, as we have seen. The effects of morality are not limited to what is functionally necessary for any form of cooperation. Morality can even become a lasting impediment to particular forms of cooperation: A sense of justice is a substantial obstacle to certain highly efficient forms of cooperation that would be useful if only reproductive fitness were at issue – say, an authoritarian command structure. Morality often demands the reorganization of society, thus challenging existing forms of cooperation, not on the terms of what is functionally needed to enhance reproductive fitness, but for the sake of the intrinsic value of justice. The ensuing conflicts have often torn human societies apart. Morality thus does not serve simply any form of cooperation; rather, it *defines legitimate forms of cooperation* – for instance, a just political order. In addition, it provides the tools to make such an order a reality.

The oft-encountered references in evolutionary theory simply to "cooperation" without any further qualifications are therefore inadequate. The explanatory task at stake is much more demanding: What is needed is an explanation of human sociality's very particular forms of cooperation and – as the foundation of the specific forms of human cooperation – of the emergence of the peculiar phenomenon of human morality in the natural history of cognition.

Seventh, care must be taken when determining the *explanandum*, which in our case is human moral precepts and their workings in the human mind. The determination of the *explanandum* is particularly important in the case of morality because what this *explanandum* is is far from clear. There is not only no consensus about how to explain an *explanandum* whose properties are generally accepted (say, apples move perpendicularly to the ground), but the *explanandum* itself is controversial (say, whether humans are psychological egoists or not). Moreover, one encounters another problem in this context: The preferred evolutionary explanatory theory sometimes fallaciously determines what is assumed to be the content of morality. The following line of argument may serve as an example: Because it is assumed that the mechanisms of evolution can only produce psychological egoists, it is held that human beings must in fact be psychological egoists, because humans are ultimately the product of these evolutionary mechanisms and accordingly can only have the properties that these mechanisms can create.

It is important to avoid this fallacy, which ascertains that what cannot be explained from the point of view of some evolutionary theories cannot in fact exist. This would mean committing a fallacy analogous to the argument that gravitational force cannot exist because gravity cannot be explained within the framework of contact mechanics. The world is full of surprises, and we must remain open to the possibility that human moral cognition contains some of them. Therefore, a proper analysis of the phenomenon to be explained is the precondition of any attempt to formulate an explanatory theory of this phenomenon.

Eighth, it is important to be mindful of the fact that there are quite substantial controversies about the fundamental aspects of evolution – there is not one, let alone "The One" uncontested evolutionary theory, but a plurality of evolutionary approaches that merit serious consideration.

7.4 ANIMAL MORALITY?

A first step towards getting a grip on these matters is to ask whether there is anything species-specific about morality. This is not an easy question to answer. However, there is a substantial body of work on animal cognition that can help to formulate some plausible theses.

The starting points of this research are the great apes, particularly chimpanzees and bonobos, which are human beings' closest relatives. This does not mean that there is not considerable evolutionary distance between us and them – in fact, the evolutionary development of human beings branched off from that of the great apes some 7 million years ago. Human beings are thus separated from great apes by 14 million years of development.

Studies on great apes have produced evidence of differentiated cognitive abilities. To name just some of these abilities that are important for moral psychology:[7] There is reason to believe that great apes act with instrumental rationality, at least in some instances. Under certain circumstances, they comprehend intentional states such as the goals and desires of others, particularly in the context of competition. They are able to maintain social relationships over long periods among subordinates, dominants and friends within their group. They are able to identify such relations between familiar third parties. They have and express emotions and are emotionally empathetic. They communicate intentionally. Within this framework, they engage in prosocial behavior, including instrumental helping: "When costs are small, and

[7] Cf. on these findings Tomasello, *A Natural History of Human Morality*, 20 ff., 35.

food competition is absent, great apes help others."[8] They are able to control some of their impulses for immediate self-gratification for prudential reasons, such as avoiding conflict. They are able to inhibit the impulse to forage individually and collaborate with others to obtain resources not available without such cooperation.

As far as morality proper is concerned, some have argued that great apes have some kind of proto-morality, others have denied this and others again have proposed a middle ground.[9] There seems to be evidence that great apes exhibit signs of what is called sympathy towards their kin and friends, including acts of instrumental helping.[10] But various experiments, including adapted forms of the ultimatum game, for instance, produced no evidence that great apes have a sense of fairness.[11]

What seems clear from all of this is that the human moral world is structured on different terms. Humans certainly entertain many warm feelings towards others, from friendly concern and sympathy to love, feelings that motivate them to act in ways beneficial to others. In addition, however, human moral cognition implies principles of altruism and justice that are prescriptive in nature, implying a moral ought, and that are the product of engaging in different forms of reflection on the object of evaluation, sometimes limited to a spontaneous intuition about the justness or moral wrongness of an act, sometimes the result of painstaking soul-searching. Not only acts, but also internal mental states such as intentions form possible objects of such evaluations. These intentions come in more than one shape – direct and oblique intentions, for example. Accordingly, not only does the evaluation of these intentions presuppose an intricate cognitive machinery, but so do these mental states themselves and observers' ability to identify them.

Things become even more complex when we come to further key notions of human moral cognition, such as the concept of "ought" and moral responsibility. The moral ought cannot be conceptualized without a notion of freedom, because ought is not a determining "must," but leaves the agent the freedom to act otherwise. It is related to the notion of responsibility, another central category of the moral world of human beings, including their psychology, which presupposes that human beings can understand what is right, that they can make this insight the motivation for action and that they therefore can be held accountable for said action. All of this obviously presupposes a particular cognitive makeup, and this is true whatever one's

[8] Tomasello, *A Natural History of Human Morality*, 31.

[9] Cf. for instance Frans de Waal, *The Bonobo and the Atheist* (New York: W. W. Norton & Company, 2013), 239 f.: "Who says the bonobo can do whatever he wants? . . . Even if he lacks notions of right and wrong that transcend his personal situation, his values are not altogether different from those underlying human morality. He, too, strives to fit in, obeys social rules, empathizes with others, amends broken relationships, and objects to unfair arrangements. We may not wish to call it morality, but his behaviour isn't free of prescriptions, either"; Joan Silk et al., "Chimpanzees Are Indifferent to the Welfare of Unrelated Group Members," *Nature* 437, no. 7063 (2005), 1357; Tomasello, *A Natural History of Human Morality*, 36.

[10] Tomasello, *A Natural History of Human Morality*, 25.

[11] Tomasello, *A Natural History of Human Morality*, 32 ff., 36.

position may be on the question of free will, be it indeterminist, determinist or compatibilistic.

A further point: Morality does not equal sympathy, as illustrated by the moral obligations one has towards those people one does not sympathize with and the shame one may feel if one does not live up to these obligations, despite disliking the patient of the moral action. The same holds for empathy (if distinguished from sympathy). One may understand very well how it feels to be incarcerated and still think that it is not only the legally, but also the morally right thing to do in some cases of crime.

Finally, human moral judgment is connected to a set of particular sentiments that are the consequences of certain moral evaluations. These sentiments include shame, indignation and resentment.

The differences between the cognitive and thus moral makeup of human beings and great apes manifest themselves in the way they are treated in morally relevant contexts:

> Despite the fact that they live in cooperative social groups and behave pro-socially towards kin and friends – and are of course worthy targets of our moral concern – chimpanzees themselves are not moral agents. We do not allow them to roam freely in our midst for fear that they will attack our children, steal our food, destroy our property, and generally wreak havoc without regard for anyone else. And if they did all these antisocial things, no one would blame them or hold them responsible.[12]

This kind of differential treatment implies assumptions about the differences between chimpanzees' and human beings' structure of cognition that are the reasons why such differential treatment is justified.

Given these observations, it comes as no surprise that any nonhuman animal can be raised with humans without this animal developing the cognitive abilities of human beings, whereas every human infant develops these abilities, whatever human environment they grow up in, drastic cases of deprivation aside.

There is simply no way around the fact that human cognition and nonhuman animal cognition are different and that there is some kind of biological basis for this difference. The question is only what this biological basis is and how to account for its development in evolutionary terms. This is a first important result.

7.5 EVOLUTIONARY PSYCHOLOGY

7.5.1 *The Morality of Selfish Genes*

Evolutionary psychology represents one very influential account of the origin and nature of human moral psychology. It draws on certain well-known ultimate

[12] Tomasello, *A Natural History of Human Morality*, 39.

evolutionary mechanisms – kin selection, reciprocity and group selection – to explain the evolution of cooperation.[13]

Inclusive fitness and kin selection are seen to be the solutions to the conundrum of other-benefiting behavior. From this perspective, single "selfish" genes are the objects of the evolutionary process.[14] Their reproduction is assured not only if the individual who is acting survives, but also if other individuals who likewise carry these genes have a sufficiently high chance of reproducing. This is the case if these individuals share a sufficiently great amount of the same genetic material: The behavior that benefits other organisms and that seems to be implausibly altruistic from an evolutionary point of view is in fact a tool to increase the chance of reproduction of the gene responsible for this behavior and will therefore be selected for. The proximate psychological mechanism is other-benefiting; the ultimate evolutionary cause for this mechanism is a higher chance of reproduction for the selfish gene.

7.5.2 *Reciprocal Altruism*

Another central element of evolutionary psychology is reciprocal altruism, which consists of tit-for-tat relations: An individual does something beneficial for another organism in order to be paid back, either now or at a later point. One variant of this is indirect reciprocal altruism, which factors reputation into the equation: Actors do something to increase their good reputation in order to reap benefits from others through their standing, albeit perhaps not in the concrete relation in which they are acting, but in other contexts. A good reputation may pay off in the long run.[15]

Evolutionary psychologists argue that reciprocal altruism is both a proximate psychological mechanism and operates on an evolutionary level. As a proximate psychological mechanism, it inclines an organism to other-benefiting behavior if there is a payback, whether direct or indirect: Organisms help others because they, too, will benefit from offering help – not necessarily now, but perhaps later, when

[13] Cf. for an overview Stephen Stich, John Doris and Erica Roedder, "Altruism," in *The Moral Psychology Handbook*, ed. John Doris (Oxford: Oxford University Press, 2010). As ultimate evolutionary mechanisms, kin selection, direct reciprocity, indirect reciprocity, network reciprocity and group selection play prominent roles in current theory, cf. e.g. Martin Nowak, "Five Rules for the Evolution of Cooperation," *Science* 314, no. 5805 (2006). For an example of an attempt to explain human cooperation by evolutionary game theory, Leda Cosmides, Ricardo Andrés Guzmán and John Tooby, "The Evolution of Moral Cognition," in *The Routledge Handbook of Moral Epistemology*, eds. Aaron Zimmerman, Karen Jones and Mark Timmons (New York: Routledge, 2019), 174–228, 195 ff. Kar, "Psychological Foundations," 122 ff. understands the psychological capacities of humans to use human rights as evolutionary solutions of "social contract problems."

[14] Richard Dawkins, *The Selfish Gene* (Oxford: Oxford University Press, 2018).

[15] Cf. Richard D. Alexander, *The Biology of Moral Systems* (New York: Aldine de Gruyter, 1987), 94: compensation by improved reputation, rewards by other group members and success of the group.

they themselves are in need. On the evolutionary level, reciprocal altruism is a possible evolutionarily stable strategy because any seemingly other-benefiting act ultimately increases the reproductive fitness of the actor through the benefits it produces and thus is advantageous from an evolutionary perspective.

There is more than one possible proximate psychological mechanism to make an organism behave according to the principles of reciprocal altruism. One is conscious reciprocal altruism – the actor thinks strategically and offers the patient an advantage in order to get something in exchange. Another is – to use de Waal's terminology – not calculated, but attitudinal reciprocal altruism: The actor is not consciously acting in a strategic manner, but has developed an other-regarding emotional attitude.[16] Some forms of social relationships of primates or other mammals exemplify this – for example, the grooming of kin and friends.

Supporting mechanisms include partner control through sanctioning, partner choice and social selection: Actors choose those partners who are good collaborators, shunning cheaters. Social selection is the product of partner control and partner choice: It promotes the selection of certain individuals because of the attractiveness of having them as a partner.[17]

There is also the idea of multilevel selective processes: An individual's adaptiveness depends on the adaptiveness of the way of living of the group to which that individual belongs.[18]

7.5.3 *The Morality of Tribes*

At the same time, these mechanisms restrict the possible outcome of evolution: Only a small-group morality makes evolutionary sense because of the "environment of evolutionary adaptation" of modern humans, it is often argued. This is the core claim of what has been called "evoconservatism."[19] Only such a morality would have been selected for because concern for others must be limited to those who plausibly share a sufficiently large number of genes. Given the living conditions of early human beings, who associated in small groups and were faced by out-group competition for resources, concern for a small, limited group is the only possible product of evolution. By evolutionary necessity, there is a natural tribalism, based on an in- and out-group morality.

The logic of this argument leads to the conclusion that the idea of rights that all human beings, not just group members, enjoy, with correlative duties of all human

[16] Frans de Waal, "Attitudinal Reciprocity in Food Sharing among Brown Capuchin Monkeys," *Animal Behaviour* 60, no. 2 (2020).

[17] Tomasello, *A Natural History of Human Morality*, 18. On partner choice as an explanation for "otherwise puzzling features of human cooperation," Pascal Boyer, *Minds Make Societies: How Cognition Explains the World Human Create* (New Haven, CT: Yale University Press, 2018), 173 ff.

[18] Haidt, *The Righteous Mind*; Tomasello, *A Natural History of Human Morality*, 142.

[19] Buchanan and Powell, *The Evolution of Moral Progress*.

beings in turn, is not supported by evolutionary psychology. The same follows for the moral principles that give rise to this idea. As discussed, justice, solidarity and respect are not limited to some in-group, but apply to all human beings. Human rights and principles of justice, altruism and respect in this sense have no ally in human nature from this perspective. They are at best justified cultural artifacts created to tame human nature – or, if one takes a more critical view of their ultimate justification, not even that. Instead, they are a kind of heuristic applied only to in-group members that has a certain rhetorical effect strong enough to make them empirically important factors in human behavior, but that has no substantial legitimacy and does not extend beyond the limits of the group.[20]

Such accounts are important for the theory of human rights, even if one is as firmly committed to the is/ought distinction as the present inquiry is. Even if one rightly holds that human beings are capable of defying their natural inclinations, whatever they may be, and could and ought to do so in this area, too, by following the commands of a universalistic morality, the question of whether universal human rights are principles and institutions that are contrary to the nature of human beings requires serious consideration. The significance of this point is underlined by various voices that consider the claim that people are in fact not (and cannot be) naturally motivated to respect the rights of every human being to be an important argument against human rights.[21]

7.5.4 *Explanatory Problems*

The basic mechanisms of evolution mentioned above are of more limited explanatory power than is often assumed, however: As discussed above, there is substantial evidence that the basic assumption underlying many accounts of the evolutionary origin of morality that human beings lived in small groups of hunter-gatherers competing with other such groups is not on the right track. The respective cultures often spread over geographically huge spaces, individuals travelling large distances, creating groups that were not based on biological kinship relations in any

[20] Cf. on this argument Chapter 6.

[21] Richard Rorty, *Contingency, Irony, and Solidarity* (Cambridge: Cambridge University Press, 1989), 191: "'[B]ecause she is a human being' is a weak, unconvincing explanation of a generous action"; Michael Ignatieff, *Human Rights as Politics and Idolatry* (Princeton, NJ: Princeton University Press, 2001), 79; Michael Ignatieff, "Human Rights, Global Ethics, and the Ordinary Virtues," *Ethics & International Affairs* 31, no. 1 (2017): 3, 11. "From the perspective of ordinary virtues, the first question we ask of another human being is always: Are you one of us or one of them? From this initial question everything follows, including whether we owe this individual anything. If they are fellow citizens, we may owe them shelter, clothing, a hearing, healthcare, and other forms of assistance. If they are strangers, what we owe them ceases to be a duty and becomes instead a matter of pity, generosity, and compassion"; David Miller, *On Nationality* (New York: Oxford University Press, 1995), 80.

discernable sense, but rather on common cultural bonds.[22] The perception that anyone outside a particular group was regarded as an enemy is not tenable either, given the evidence for complex social ties beyond small groups.[23]

Moreover, kin selection is not a mechanism that could explain the emergence of the particular properties of human morality.[24] The architecture of human morality includes such complex phenomena as duties, rights, specific moral emotions and responsibilities. Humans have the ability to create, apply and enforce moral norms. Kin selection is not sufficient to explain this sophisticated cognitive structure. To serve the ends of kin selection, much simpler psychological proxy mechanisms would suffice – say, some straightforward prereflective attraction to kin, without any intricate moral machinery in place. Furthermore, the commands of morality are not limited to kin, neither as an intuition nor in reflective evaluation. Principles of justice can and often do limit the benefits that kin receive, because others can claim an equal share to kin. Morality and justice thus constitute checks on kin favoritism and are not proximate mechanisms to serve it.

Reciprocal altruism raises similar questions. In particular, first, there is the problem of first altruistic acts: What motivates the initial altruistic act, given that no tit-for-tat pattern has been established yet and thus no rational expectation exists that the beneficent of the altruistic act will reciprocate – "blind optimism or accident"?[25] The second problem is the free-rider problem, the "powerful incentive to defect."[26] What reason is there not to follow this incentive? The same problems

[22] Cf. for instance Douglas W. Bird et al., "Variability in the Organization and Size of Hunter-Gatherer Groups: Foragers Do Not Live in Small-Scale Societies," *Journal of Human Evolution* 131 (2019): 96–108, 106: "This general disconnect between traditional views of hunter-gatherer social organization and quantitative ethnographic evidence highlights an important weakness in current paleoanthropological/neurological models of the co-evolutionary relationships between human cognition, pro-sociality, and hunter-gatherer group size and organization. Most well-documented highly mobile hunter-gatherers live and work in groups that are relatively smaller, and more fluid in composition, than farming groups. But the smaller local groups of foragers are not drawn from small discrete communities, and none are dominated by close ties of genetic relationship. Variability in the size of residential and foraging groups is likely shaped in landscapes of anthropogenic construction; and their composition is drawn from expansive, trans-generational networks of relational wealth, bound together in ties of social interaction that extend well beyond a small community of individuals"; Graeber and Wengrow, *Dawn*, 122, 279 ff.

[23] Graeber and Wengrow, *Dawn*, 547 n. 4.

[24] Cf. similarly Tomasello, *A Natural History of Human Morality*, 139 arguing that kin selection cannot produce intricate mechanisms of morality such as joint collective commitments, creating and enforcing social norms, feeling resentment, self-regulating one's actions by feelings of responsibility, obligation and guilt. Richard Dawkins, *The God Delusion* (London: Bantam Press, 2006), 221, understands care for others who are unrelated and unable to reciprocate (as sexual desire without the possibility of procreation) as "misfirings, Darwinian mistakes: blessed, precious mistakes."

[25] Tomasello, *A Natural History of Human Morality*, 13.

[26] Tomasello, *A Natural History of Human Morality*, 13.

arise for indirect reciprocity, which takes reputation into account.[27] Why should there be no free-riding here?[28] What is needed to break this deadlock is either an agreement to adhere to certain norms, as has been rightly underlined,[29] which is beyond the cognitive capacities of nonhuman animals, or, it is important to add, a form of altruism that is not conditioned upon reciprocal advantages. Similarly, in the case of emotional, attitudinal reciprocal altruism one can ask: Why do individuals form friendly social relationships with nonkin in the first place? Why do they help these friends?[30]

This aside, it is decisive that human morality is limited neither to calculated nor to attitudinal reciprocal altruism in descriptive terms. As already underlined above and as will be fleshed out in greater detail below, it is a complex reflective capacity to judge corresponding principles of altruism and justice with motivational and emotional consequences, and thus it is neither a calculation of the benefits of nor simply an emotional attitude fostering tit-for-tat advantages.

The paradigmatic case of moral acting is sacrificing some of one's own goods for the benefit of others – agents perhaps even giving their life to save others. The evaluation of such an act as morally good is not restricted to saving kin and friends. On the contrary, agents who save only their kin and friends when they are able to save others as well, or saving others only because they are expecting advantages as a result of their deed, would not count as performing a particularly impressive example of moral action. Similar observations hold for justice: Distributing something justly to receive benefits oneself is not what the idea of justice is about.

It is not a good counterargument to assert that early modern humans' morality was different from what we find today. As we will see, we have only indirect clues to the cognitive abilities of early modern humans. None of them conclusively shows that moral cognition was limited to a small-group morality, speculative just-so stories aside, which are, moreover, based on the most probably wrong assumption, as discussed above, that hunter-gatherers did not live in larger cultural spaces.

Pointing to the distinction between proximate mechanisms and ultimate evolutionary causation does not help to counter this critique either: The nonreciprocal altruism of human beings and their sense of justice, among other principles, do not with sufficient probability produce paybacks for those adhering to them. The fact that being moral regularly does not pay constitutes a central conundrum of moral philosophy: For Kant, for instance, the fact that acting morally often does not lead to particular happiness and not seldom leads to the dungeon and the stake was so obvious that it served as an argument for the existence of God and eternal life, so that the scales of justice could be balanced at least in the afterlife.[31] Consequently,

27 Tomasello, A *Natural History of Human Morality*, 14.

28 It is useful to remember the results of the ultimatum and dictator games here – despite continuing selfishness, agents clearly do not exploit any chance to get a free ride, cf. Chapter 6.

29 Tomasello, A *Natural History of Human Morality*, 13.

30 Tomasello, A *Natural History of Human Morality*, 14.

31 Kant, *Kritik der reinen Vernunft* (2. Ed. 1787), 525 ff.

human morality cannot be understood merely as a proximate psychological mechanism for reciprocal altruism as an evolutionarily stable strategy. It does not deliver the advantages that reciprocal altruism presupposes.

A further point of criticism homes in on the assumption that forms the foundation of the evolutionary approach, namely that all of an organism's traits have an adaptive function. This poses overly narrow constraints on the process of evolution, as will be illustrated below.

There are, however, other accounts that paint a different picture of the evolutionary origin of morality. Arguably, the currently most sophisticated theory of the evolution of morality describes a process driven forward by mutualism and interdependence, enabled, however, by a wide-ranging and complex, inborn, species-unique cognitive endowment of human beings. Because of its paradigmatic importance for current debates, a closer look is necessary to see whether this approach by Michael Tomasello solves the riddles of the evolution of human morality.

7.6 THE POWER OF JOINT INTENTIONALITY: INTERDEPENDENCE AND COOPERATION

7.6.1 *Some Specifics of Human Cooperation*

Tomasello's theory, too, is guided by the idea of cooperation: Its central thesis is that human moral psychology is a phenomenon emerging from the increasingly sophisticated forms of collaboration of hominids and finally human beings. Cooperation is also key to moral ontogeny: Moral development does not depend on general intelligence, but on a set of inborn, species-specific cognitive capacities universally possessed by all human beings independent of cultural background, which enable human beings to develop their rich moral world through cooperative constructive interaction similarly to the way they acquire other parts of their cognitive and social world:[32] "It is precisely this biological preparation – in the form of maturationally expressed capacities – that makes uniquely human sociocultural activities and

[32] Michael Tomasello, *Becoming Human: A Theory of Ontogeny* (Cambridge, MA: Harvard University Press, 2021). The set of inborn capacities includes joint attention/common ground, cooperative/referential communication, role-reversal imitation, dual-level collaboration and basic helping, ibid. 312 f. Tomasello underlines that maturation and experience all go hand in hand in complex psychological phenomena. The theory is therefore "Neo-Vygotskian," ibid. 6, 34, 297 ff. For these five competencies, however, the maturational (that is, inborn) element predominates, ibid. 313. He identifies further species-specific inborn capacities, from pointing, iconic gestures and pretense to laughter and smiling, ibid. 54 ff., 95 ff., 106 ff. The main factors driving development are interaction with peers and adults and executive self-regulation, ibid. 36. The terminology adapted here takes for granted that the predicates "innate" or "inborn" do not exclude the influence of triggering experiences. They do not imply that the process is "impervious to experience," ibid. 83. Even acquiring the ability to walk upright is dependent on the child having the chance to move their limbs, even though the ability itself is innate.

experiences possible in the first place."[33] It is not just "general biological preparedness for learning and inference, but also specific biological preparedness for uniquely human cooperative interaction and mental coordination with others."[34] The capacity for joint intentionality is key:[35] It is the "ultimate source of human uniqueness."[36]

The main criteria for identifying capacities as innate are a lack of cultural diversity of outcome in experimental intercultural designs with small children and very similar maturational age trends across cultures.[37] All children, for example, learn the complex activity of upright walking irrespective of cultural background in a "quite predictable developmental period."[38] It is thus safe to assume that the capacity of upright walking is innate.

Cooperation between human beings extends to the rules they apply to their own cooperative activities: The "'cooperativization of self-regulation' is of the essence of normative sociality and morality."[39]

The theory (quite correctly) emphasizes how fundamental human cooperation is for the human way of living. While cooperative cultural institutions in particular create a framework for competition, competition is not the true driver of human development: "It is only if one neglects the cultural-institutional context of human behaviour that one can hallucinate the competitive cart as leading the cooperative horse."[40]

As a first very important step, this approach goes to greater effort than others properly to account for the specifics of forms of human cooperation. This includes identifying the various layers of the cognitive dimensions and preconditions of cooperation. This proves very fruitful because cooperation is a highly underdetermined concept – as illustrated above, cooperation can take very different forms and does not necessarily imply moral norms – it could be based, for instance, solely on force and power.

A battery of experiments provides some clues about the differences between the cooperative behavior of humans and that of great apes. More precisely, this research concerns the behavior of small children and thus does not even focus on the mature forms of cooperation between adults because Tomasello argues that the cognitive capacities of children are similiar to the cognitive capacities of early humans. These findings provide at least some good indications of distinctively different cognitive dimensions of forms of cooperation, spelled out in respective behavior. These include the following patterns, for instance:[41]

33 Tomasello, *Becoming Human*, 7.
34 Tomasello, *Becoming Human*, 301.
35 Tomasello, *Becoming Human*, 8, 15 ff., 27, 56, 63, 190, 304.
36 Tomasello, *Becoming Human*, 86.
37 Tomasello, *Becoming Human*, 312 f.
38 Tomasello, *Becoming Human*, 33.
39 Tomasello, *Becoming Human*, 215.
40 Tomasello, *A Natural History of Human Morality*, 158.
41 Tomasello, *A Natural History of Human Morality*, 20 ff.; Tomasello, *Becoming Human*, 45 ff., 193 ff., 219 ff.

Children cooperate with joint intentionality: They pursue joint goals with others, and with joint attention. They reverse roles in collaborative activities and communicate cooperatively to coordinate collaboration. Children divide goods in particular ways: They share goods even if these goods are readily monopolized by one partner. They display a tendency to share goods more equally if these goods are the result of collaborative efforts. They have a preference for collaboration even if the payoffs are identical to those of solo activity. In relation to their partners in the respective collaborative activity, children share less with a free rider. They help others in various forms. They modify their behavior when peers are watching. They show a particular quality of commitment to the collaborative activity: They continue to collaborate until the end, even if they have already received the advantages offered by the collaboration. Unlike great apes, children from the age of three sanction others for violating social norms, and they do so on behalf of others. This indicates that their attitude towards social norms is not just prudential.[42] They are as prepared to help when they are alone as when they are with their mother. They help persons who do not know that they are being helped. Such research bolsters the view that small children are intrinsically motivated to foster the well-being of others. None of the above examples forms part of the cognitive repertoire of great apes:[43] "[G]roup actions of apes are all about individuals achieving their individual ends in group contexts – they are using one another as social tools."[44]

This provides some hints on how different the cognitive apparatus of great apes and of human beings already is at a relatively early age. It illustrates vividly the point made above: One needs to spell out what kind of cooperation one is talking about and what the cognitive preconditions are that make it possible before one even can start thinking about an evolutionary theory of this form of cooperation.

7.6.2 *Sympathy and Fairness Develop in Small Steps*

The evolutionary theory of morality that tries to explain these findings is a theory of the incremental development of morality. This incremental development theory offers an alternative to standard accounts based on kin selection and inclusive fitness, which are regarded as insufficient.[45]

Tomasello's approach starts by identifying two forms of cooperation: altruistic concern for others and mutualistic collaboration and, correspondingly, a morality of sympathy and of fairness. The former is freely performed, while the latter is accompanied by a sense of obligation and deservingness and by punitive moral attitudes such as resentment or indignation towards others who are unfair. The

[42] Tomasello, *A Natural History of Human Morality*, 101.

[43] Tomasello, *A Natural History of Human Morality*, 76 for a summary of these findings. On the lack of joint intentionality in great apes, Tomasello, *Becoming Human*, 13.

[44] Tomasello, *Becoming Human*, 190. Cf. e.g. on chimpanzee group hunting, ibid. 193 ff.

[45] Tomasello, *A Natural History of Human Morality*, 13 ff.

former is pure cooperation, the latter the "cooperativization" of competition to find balanced solutions for conflicting demands. Morality in this sense is unique to human beings:[46]

> We proceed from the assumption that human morality is a form of cooperation, specifically, the form that has emerged as humans have adapted to new and species-unique forms of social interaction and organization. Because *Homo sapiens* is an ultracooperative primate, and presumably the only moral one, we further assume that human morality comprises the key set of species-unique proximate mechanisms – psychological processes of cognition, social interaction and self-regulation – that enable human individuals to survive and thrive in their especially cooperative social arrangements.[47]

Note that this passage raises an important problem that will occupy us in more than one context: According to this formulation, there are "new and species-unique forms of social interaction" *prior* to human morality, as morality is a means to adapt to these forms of interaction. The problem is: Do not these "new and species-unique forms of social interaction" *presuppose* the existence of the cognitive mechanisms necessary for morality? Is a certain cognitive apparatus not the *precondition* for certain forms of living, including forms of collaboration, and consequently cannot be interpreted as an *adaptation* to these forms? If the cognitive abilities are *prior* to the "new and species-unique forms of social interaction" they enable, the evolutionary theory needs to account for the emergence of these cognitive abilities independently of the way of living that was only possible *after* these cognitive abilities were acquired.[48]

How, then, did this "key set of species-unique proximate mechanisms," the "psychological processes of cognition, social interaction and self-regulation" that are the natural mental foundations of human morality, evolve?

Tomasello argues that all began far back in time, with hominid species: First, there were dyadic relations of cooperation in hominids that led via role formation to normative standards. These cooperative relations were established to aid survival by foraging together, which led to sympathy beyond kin and friends, including collaborative partners.[49] In order to enable them to collaborate, hominids evolved joint intentionality – that is, the capacity to form a common goal with a partner and to know things together.[50] At the same time, Tomasello asserts that a context of collaboration including "obligate collaborative foraging with various and robust means of partner choice and partner control" is necessary for the development of

[46] Tomasello, A *Natural History of Human Morality*, 1 f.
[47] Tomasello, A *Natural History of Human Morality*, 3.
[48] The concept of adaptation becomes meaningless if every property of a species is regarded as an adaptation to the kind of life the organism's capacities enable it to lead.
[49] Tomasello, A *Natural History of Human Morality*, 4.
[50] Tomasello, A *Natural History of Human Morality*, 4.

joint intentionality.[51] This is a concrete example of the problem just identified: According to this account, are forms of collaboration the precondition for the evolution of cognitive abilities such as joint intentionality or, vice versa, are cognitive abilities the preconditions for the possibility of certain forms of collaboration?

This collaboration shaped role models of what it meant to be a good partner, which were the first step to impartial normative prescriptions. This had a major consequence: "Recognizing the impartiality of role standards meant recognizing that self and other were of equivalent status and importance in the collaborative enterprise."[52] The self–other equivalence led to mutual respect among partners. Each could hold the other accountable for living up to this role ideal. A self-regulating "we" emerged that was considered legitimate because it derived from a joint commitment that the partners had created themselves and because both regarded the other as deserving of respect. This was the birth of an "evolutionarily novel form of psychology."[53] The ensuing behavior is motivated by genuine moral motivation, not just by the wish to avoid punishment or reputational attacks: "And so was born a normatively constituted social order in which cooperatively rational agents focused not just on how individuals do act, or on how I want them to act, but, rather, on how they *ought to* act if they are to be one of 'us'."[54] Tomasello hypothesizes that this natural, second-personal morality emerged 400,000 years ago.[55]

7.6.3 *The Path to Objective Group Morality*

A second evolutionary step was taken with the emergence of *Homo sapiens*. The reasons for this step lay in demographic development: Groups of modern human beings formed tribes that built up a culture, "one big interdependent 'we'" that secured role conformity through identification with the group and sympathy of the group members towards each other in order to ensure survival. The individual learned to use the perspective of "any rational person," based on the self–other equivalence, and thus "served as interchangeable (agent-independent) cogs in the conventional cultural practices that kept the culture going."[56] Humans become persons through social recognition.[57] In order to enable the cognitive coordination of their activities, group members evolved "new cognitive skills and motivations of *collective intentionality* – enabling the creation of cultural conventions, norms and institutions."[58] Group members knew about similarities between them and knew that

[51] Tomasello, *A Natural History of Human Morality*, 40.
[52] Tomasello, *A Natural History of Human Morality*, 4.
[53] Tomasello, *A Natural History of Human Morality*, 5.
[54] Tomasello, *A Natural History of Human Morality*, 5.
[55] Tomasello, *A Natural History of Human Morality*, 86.
[56] Tomasello, *A Natural History of Human Morality*, 96.
[57] Tomasello, *A Natural History of Human Morality*, 106.
[58] Tomasello, *A Natural History of Human Morality*, 5, 92 ff. (emphasis in original).

the others knew, too.[59] Conventional cultural practices were turned into social norms, representing the right and wrong thing to do, and substituting partner control – that is, the sanctioning of cheating – by social control with the aim of creating conformity.[60] Institutions enshrined social norms and created institutional facts.[61] New forms of *cultural agency* with respect to the group's conventions, norms and institutions emerged.[62] Humans found new forms of self-regulating *self-governance* based on collective commitments that created obligations and led to moral judgments about others' moral judgments and to specific moral emotions, such as guilt.[63]

Group identity was based on similarity; solidarity was therefore felt with in-group members who resembled the actor in behavior and appearance, not with "out-group barbarians" in the vicinity.[64] The fact that the preferential treatment of in-group members as compared to out-group members already is evident in children is taken to confirm this point: "In-group favouritism accompanied by outgroup prejudice is one of the best-documented phenomena in all of contemporary social psychology . . ., and it emerges in young children during the late preschool and especially during the school-age period."[65]

Moral norms were considered legitimate because the members of groups identified with their respective culture, formed a moral identity, regarded themselves as coauthors and felt respect towards the other group members.[66] Deviation could only be justified by recourse to the shared values of the moral community. These processes led to the second novel form of moral psychology: "It was a kind of scaled-up version of early humans' second-personal morality in that the normative standards were fully 'objective', the collective commitments were by and for all in the group, and the sense of obligation was group mindedly rational in that it flowed from one's moral identity and the felt need to justify one's moral decisions to the moral community."[67] For modern human beings, the result of this objectification of conventional norms was a "kind of cultural and group-minded 'objective' morality."[68] As a consequence, human beings harbor three kinds of morality in their breast: the "cooperative proclivities of great apes, the 'joint morality of collaboration' and an 'impersonal collective morality' of cultural norms and institutions in which all members of the cultural group are equally valuable."[69] These kinds of moralities may conflict in dilemmas such as: "Shall I steal for a friend?"

[59] Tomasello, *A Natural History of Human Morality*, 93 f.
[60] Tomasello, *A Natural History of Human Morality*, 98 f.
[61] Tomasello, *A Natural History of Human Morality*, 104.
[62] Tomasello, *A Natural History of Human Morality*, 87, 107 ff.
[63] Tomasello, *A Natural History of Human Morality*, 89, 108 ff.
[64] Tomasello, *A Natural History of Human Morality*, 89 f., 122.
[65] Tomasello, *A Natural History of Human Morality*, 91.
[66] Tomasello, *A Natural History of Human Morality*, 86 ff.
[67] Tomasello, *A Natural History of Human Morality*, 6.
[68] Tomasello, *A Natural History of Human Morality*, 6, 123.
[69] Tomasello, *A Natural History of Human Morality*, 7.

Social norms as objectified conventional norms are moral insofar as they conform with the second-personal morality of sympathy and fairness[70] – this "natural morality" forms a baseline of human morality, not only in developmental but also in normative terms. Interestingly, Tomasello's theory incorporates studies that suggest that young children regard norms frequently connected with sympathy and fairness as applicable to all humans, not just in-group members. This does not seem to be easy to reconcile with a simple in-group/out-group dichotomy and the supposedly dyadic nature of second-personal morality.

Cases giving rise to competing moral claims need to be solved on an individual basis using "creativity." Moral debates are crucially shaped by the second-personal moral principles of sympathy and fairness, what these principles mean and the answer to the question of who is part of the moral community.[71] Exclusion from the moral community was, it is argued, the reason for the justification of slavery or apartheid. The standards of inclusion and exclusion can change.[72] "Moral entrepreneurs" like Martin Luther King Jr. and Mahatma Gandhi were able to move people by putting suffering and injustice in front of people's eyes: a "second-person protest writ large."[73]

In any case, there is a genuine, not just strategic concern for morality,[74] although the ultimate evolutionary cause is to increase reproductive fitness – morality ultimately emerged because "early humans who were concerned for the welfare of others and who treated others fairly had the most offspring."[75] Moral humans simply had "more babies."[76]

Children are socialized in the moral community. Second-personal morality is culturally universal, Tomasello asserts, objective morality is not. This can be explained by reference to the ontogenesis of morality: Children first develop a second-personal morality and later the culturally relative social norms.[77] Humans in general have some "built-in responses to morally relevant situations based on intuition and emotion that have evolved to deal with evolutionarily important situations, especially those in which there is no time for a considered decision."[78]

70 Tomasello, A *Natural History of Human Morality*, 100, 122, 124, 127.

71 Tomasello, A *Natural History of Human Morality*, 127.

72 Tomasello, A *Natural History of Human Morality*, 113 ff., 126 f.

73 Tomasello, A *Natural History of Human Morality*, 134; Tomasello, *Becoming Human*, 290: "[T]he individual is always free to go beyond the culture's social norms if necessary."

74 Tomasello, A *Natural History of Human Morality*, 108: Children give to a needy person despite seeing others not doing so (not just reputation management); ibid. 111: "The proximate psychological mechanisms responsible for human moral action do not involve, essentially, prudential concerns for one's self-serving interests or strategic calculations of one's own reputation: they involve moral judgement by a moral self (with the representative authority of the moral community) that endures over time and that judges the self impartially in the same way that it judges others."

75 Tomasello, A *Natural History of Human Morality*, 7.

76 Tomasello, A *Natural History of Human Morality*, 149, quote 163.

77 Tomasello, A *Natural History of Human Morality*, 117, 155 ff.

78 Tomasello, A *Natural History of Human Morality*, 118, following Haidt.

Besides the evolution of the principles of morality that are foundational for human rights, rights as a normative category (albeit not human rights) Tomasello explicitly discusses as part of human morality.[79] In addition, the reflection about fairness and "deservingness" as other considerations seems to imply the idea of the rights of moral patients. Law in general is conceptualized as an institutionalized framework of social integration.[80] The idea of equal respect, which is foundational for human rights, is also important, albeit somewhat ambiguous: It is limited to a cultural group but can be extended by moral entrepreneurs to all human beings.

Concern for the well-being of others does not mean reciprocal altruism: More demanding principles are involved. The two problems mentioned above – how to explain the first altruistic act and the free-rider problem – indicate the explanatory limits of an account based on reciprocal altruism. The element crucial to overcoming this difficulty, especially the "undermining effect of cheating," is interdependence.[81]

Mutualism (as reciprocity) works at the level of the individual. A stakeholder model is endorsed: Mutualism provides benefits for others, depending on the stake the agent has in the survival (because of the benefits the other provides) of their partner in mutualism.[82] Group selection is not held to be a major influence, because the gene flow between different groups prevents the development of a genetic makeup that is sufficiently differentiated between groups.[83]

Tomasello argues, however, for cultural group selection: Those groups with the "conventions, norms and institutions that best promoted cooperation and group cohesion won out, by assimilating or eliminating competitors from other groups."[84] Such groups formed collective agents. With the sedentary lifestyles established by the Agricultural Revolution, intergroup competition shifted towards a reconciliation of the moralities of different subgroups.[85] Gene–culture coevolution can be a factor in this process.[86] The preconditions for cultural group selection are "species-universal skills and motivations for creating social norms and institutions in the first place,"[87] as general learning mechanisms are not sufficient to create moral mental categories.[88] The evolutionary process of moral development was initiated by the shortage of individually available food, a growing population and group competition.[89]

[79] Tomasello, *A Natural History of Human Morality*, 101.
[80] Tomasello, *A Natural History of Human Morality*, 130 ff.
[81] Tomasello, *A Natural History of Human Morality*, 147.
[82] Tomasello, *A Natural History of Human Morality*, 15.
[83] Tomasello, *A Natural History of Human Morality*, 12 ff.
[84] Tomasello, *A Natural History of Human Morality*, 119.
[85] Tomasello, *A Natural History of Human Morality*, 134.
[86] Tomasello, *A Natural History of Human Morality*, 12.
[87] Tomasello, *A Natural History of Human Morality*, 142.
[88] Tomasello, *A Natural History of Human Morality*, 154.
[89] Tomasello, *A Natural History of Human Morality*, 136.

Interestingly, Tomasello posits that similar mechanisms are involved in this phylogenetic trajectory as are at work in the ontogeny of human beings.[90]

7.6.4 *Self–Other Equivalence as a Spandrel*

Tomasello's argument contains an important pillar: Self–other equivalence is crucial to the development of morality.[91] It is argued that, at the beginning, this was a purely cognitive judgment that paved the way for the normative "deservingness" of human beings to be treated equally.[92] This is important, as there is a gap between the judgment that two agents fulfill equivalent roles and the judgment that they deserve equal respect, the former a factual, the latter a normative statement.[93]

The cognitive judgment of self–other equivalence thus forms the basis for the emergence of new normative principles. It is "moral-structural" in the sense that it is a cognitive structure that could be recruited for moral functions. It is thus, in Gould and Lewontin's famous terms, a "spandrel"[94] – an architectural element used for other purposes than the one for which it was built. This is a crucial observation – it opens the door to additional dimensions in evolutionary accounts of cognitive abilities and invites us to take a fresh look at morality.

The theory of interdependence takes the argument very seriously that the evolution of a species motivated to subordinate or equate their own interests to those of others cannot be explained by natural selection. The reference to spandrels sends this "spectre,"[95] Tomasello highlights, to its final resting place.

7.6.5 *Paradigmatic Incrementalism*

This theory is arguably currently the most detailed attempt to explain the evolution of moral cognition, relating its findings to current moral philosophy and social science. It stands for a certain research paradigm in evolutionary theory, one that

90 Cf. Tomasello, *Becoming Human*, 195 ff. (joint intentionality, second-personal agency and morality); ibid. 198 ff. (self–other equivalence and the emergence of normative claims, role ideals, role reversals); ibid. 204 ff. (self-regulation by joint commitments, second-personal protest as indicator of respect); ibid. 249 ff., 287 (collective intentionality).

91 Tomasello, *A Natural History of Human Morality*, 150 ff.

92 Tomasello, *A Natural History of Human Morality*, 150 ff.

93 Tomasello, *Becoming Human*, 201: "[T]he recognition of self–other equivalence is not by itself a moral motivation or act; it is simply the recognition of an inescapable fact that characterizes the human condition."

94 Tomasello, *A Natural History of Human Morality*, 151: "The term structural indicates that, on the evolutionary level, this dimension of human morality was not originally selected to serve this function; it came into existence in the service of other functions. Of course, this would not work if the recognition of self-other equivalence was maladaptive in the social-interactive contexts we are considering, but it could easily be a cost-neutral 'spandrel' that cognitively structured such contexts."

95 Tomasello, *A Natural History of Human Morality*, 153.

can be called functional incrementalism: Its leading hypothesis is that all cognitive capacities have evolved ultimately to increase reproductive fitness through an incremental process of small evolutionary steps. From this perspective, morality is a functional tool narrowly tailored by natural selection to enable cooperation, albeit enabled by the "spandrel" of self–other equivalence.

The questions that this account raises vividly illustrate some of the challenges encountered by an evolutionary explanation of morality. These questions are thus likewise of paradigmatic importance.

7.6.6 *The Analysis of Morality and the Evidence for Evolutionary Incrementalism*

A first problem to be discussed is the precise analysis of human morality: As already explained, in morality, there are not only sympathy and fairness, sympathy understood as an inclination to benefit others, but there is also (under qualified circumstances) an obligation to foster the well-being of others. It is not only the commands of justice that have obligatory force. Certain commands of human benevolence do as well: There is an obligation not to let somebody die in front of your porch if you can pick up the phone and call an ambulance. Such actions are evaluated as being morally good. Therefore, they possess a specific deontic status. Moreover, morality concerns not just the behavior, but also specific kinds of intentions of agents. Sympathy and fairness thus do not exhaust the content of morality.

A second problem is that there is no evidence confirming that human moral evolution did in fact take the steps described, that there were first dyadic forms of interaction in which role models emerged, that cooperative forms of foraging lead to sympathy and equal respect, to moral self-regulation and a moral ought, that hominids had a sense of legitimacy and that anything like a second-personal morality existed among them. The same holds for the second step, the development of the objective morality of groups, the exclusion of outsiders based on "similarity," the individual turning into a "cog in the cultural machine" or the group-mindedness of moral orientation. There is no evidence either that early human beings were like young children in terms of their cognitive capacities. There may be a huge, qualitative difference between the maturing cognitive capacities of the young children of modern humans and the mature capacities of hominids.

Tomasello is entirely honest about the complete lack of evidence that the described stages did in fact exist. The methodological problem of sparse evidence[96] is acknowledged, and Tomasello highlights that what is presented is not an account of human cognitive development sufficiently based on paleoanthropological evidence, but a "speculative evolutionary narrative."[97] It is an "imaginative

[96] Tomasello, *A Natural History of Human Morality*, 105.
[97] Tomasello, *A Natural History of Human Morality*, 143.

reconstruction of historical events with little in the way of artefact or paleoanthropological fact to help."[98]

This comes as no surprise: There are not many clues generally that help us to understand what kind of cognitive skills hominids possessed. Artifacts such as tools are key, as are some indications of behavioral patterns, like signs of cannibalism or burial rites (or the lack thereof). Many cognitive activities simply leave no traces behind. We know from striking pieces of art that early modern human beings evidently had the cognitive capacity to produce art. We do not know, however, whether they engaged in mathematical thinking, in whatever form, because such thinking leaves no traces in the paleoanthropological record, though some artifacts like the Ishango bone raise intriguing questions. This is also true for moral precepts. Whether group life in some hominids included ideas of "self–other equivalence" or not, whether "legitimacy" played any role or not or whether ideas of a moral "ought" structured their thought along the lines of a second-personal morality or not is anybody's guess, because there are simply no clues that would help to decide these questions. One cannot brush over this state of affairs. It is very important – not to mention an issue of fundamental scientific ethics – to be prepared to leave questions open if there is no way of answering them given the evidence available.

7.6.7 *Stumbling Blocks on the Way to Second-Personal Morality*

Further important lessons for the understanding of the evolution of morality can be drawn from the details of the "speculative evolutionary narrative." These concern in particular the conceivable argument that the lack of evidence does not matter as the evolutionary trajectory had to be as described, because this and only this trajectory makes evolutionary sense.

A key question in this respect concerns the transition from one stage of the hypothesized incremental process of cognitive development to the next. There are two dimensions to this process – the development of new skills acquired by individuals and the development of new genetically inherited skills of the species. The first must be based on some kind of learning mechanism and the cognitive ability to create cultural traditions if these skills are passed on to the next generation to learn anew. The second must be based upon genetic change – that is, mutations that inscribe certain cognitive capacities in the human genome.

According to this theory, there is in certain respects a parallel between phylogeny and ontogeny – similar mechanisms are held to drive the development of the species and of the individual forward, such as joint intentionality, role-taking or self–other equivalence.[99] According to the incremental account of evolution, some of the steps described seem to be taken by individuals, although it is not quite clear how many.

98 Tomasello, *A Natural History of Human Morality*, 154.
99 Cf. n. 90.

In any case, hominids acquire increasing cognitive capacities during the development of the species until the species-specific competencies that Tomasello identifies as the basis of modern humans' moral ontogeny have evolved.[100]

These different competencies are responses to new ecological challenges. Those individuals possessing the properties making them able to meet these challenges have an adaptive advantage that sets the stage for further developments.[101] The question is, then, whether one of the stages described leads necessarily to the next. If not, if there are other developmental options, what the evolutionary trajectory really looked like and to what ecological challenges hominids and modern humans adapted remain open questions, given that, as Tomasello underlines, no conclusive paleoanthropological evidence bearing on these questions exists. That any such evolutionary necessity exists is far from clear, however. On the contrary, the apparently continuous development from the dyadic interactions of foragers to human moral codes contains yawning gaps. Crucially, in order to bridge these gaps, certain cognitive resources are necessary that are qualitatively different from those required to engage in other forms of interaction assumed to be prior, without there being any discernible evolutionary necessity that these capacities and no others had to evolve.[102]

To illustrate what is at issue: The development starts, it is argued, in dyadic relations of cooperation. If one assumes for the sake of the argument that there are role models for cooperation (although, as explained above, no evidence is presented either for this or for the consecutive steps), these may give rise to prudential rules (how to be a good forager), but not to moral rules (help other group members in need). Role models derived from certain tasks like foraging are functionally circumscribed, moral rules are not. There is no bridge from one to the other. This problem arises in the next stage of the development as well: Cooperative foraging does not necessarily lead to sympathy for one's partner, an instrumental relation to them is also possible – and the reality is that there are many forms of human collaboration, from soccer to lawyering, where one can effectively cooperate (play the decisive pass on the field or in the courtroom) without sympathy (because one wants to win, not because one likes the striker or one's legal teammate).

This problem continues to plague this incremental account: Equal importance in cooperative foraging may not lead to equal mutual respect either. First of all, the roles in cooperative foraging need not be equal but may be very different, according to a division of labor. In modern humans, collaboration does not necessarily

[100] Tomasello, *Becoming Human*, 45 ff., 312 f.

[101] Tomasello, *Becoming Human*, 5, 11.

[102] Tomasello, *Becoming Human*, 11, refers to "environments of evolutionary adaptedness." Such environments do not necessitate specific developments, given that they merely make certain developments evolutionarily advantageous and that there are many different ways to adapt to such an environment. Moreover, it is unclear what these environments exactly looked like, given the lack of paleoanthropological evidence.

lead to equal respect between cooperators – say, the bank teller and the bank's CEO. The "impartiality of role standards" (if there are any) has the effect that there is an objective yardstick for measuring whether a role-defining task is performed well, but it does not necessarily have the effect that everyone is regarded as being of "equivalent status and importance in collaborative enterprises," as actors may fail to fulfill these role standards or may simply fulfill a functionally marginal role according to an impartial role standard, leading to a low status – as the low social respect for cleaners in human societies exemplifies (unfortunately, of course). In addition, any such notions of equality could be limited to the collaborative effort and not extend what is supposed to develop, namely equal respect for all. Self–other equivalence in role fulfillment does not help either. Role equivalence (if given) does not entail mutual respect, because the latter encompasses all of a person's characteristics, not just their ability to fulfill roles. (You can respect somebody as being as good a defender as yourself on your football team and disrespect them in other contexts.)

The assumed legitimacy of such role-derived norms of an "us" indicates another problem. It presupposes (without further argument) that legitimacy was an important concept for hominids. In addition, a kind of social contract, a "joint commitment," and the idea of the equal status of others are invoked to provide legitimacy – substantial and controversial assumptions about normative reasons. It is implied, not explained, why these reasons were necessarily valid reasons for hominids more than 400,000 years ago – and not just concepts that were alien to the cognitive capacities of hominids or, if comprehensible at all, were as unconvincing as critics of contractarian theory consider them to be today.

Moral "self-regulation" is a demanding cognitive task, including the idea of moral obligations to do or not to do something and the idea of respect for obligations that motivate the agent to perform the obligatory action. The origin of such an "ought" as a central element of self-regulation creates specific riddles. The need to fulfill a role may lead to an instrumental ought (if you want to catch this prey, you ought to approach it without making any noise), but not to a moral ought. Holding others "accountable" – with sanctions, one has to assume – can lead to strategic behavior, conforming to norms when sanctions are likely and not conforming to norms when the chance of being sanctioned is remote, but it will not necessarily lead to moral self-regulation.

How this development leads to joint intentionality is unclear, too. This is no minor point, because joint intentionality is the very precondition for certain forms of collaboration, as the research on the difference between great apes and children shows, not its consequence – another example of the problem flagged above. Again, there are explanatory gaps between the different stages of development. Thus, phylogenetically, there is no evolutionary necessity for one stage to follow the other as described – many other developmental pathways are open, including not developing any of the species-specific capacities of modern humans discussed by

Tomasello, as indeed many species, including great apes, have failed to do.[103] Ontogenetically, similar conclusions must be drawn, because the incremental steps described are, for the reasons just discussed, also not sufficient to explain how individuals ultimately develop the cognitive capacities that are the basis for their normative thinking and culture.

7.6.8 *The Objective Morality of Cogs in the Machine*

Similar problems are encountered in the second stage, the development from the natural, second-personal morality to the cultural and group-minded "objective" morality, "scaling up" sympathy and justice. To illustrate this with some examples: The perspective of "any rational person" now taken entails many things, not least a concept of rationality. Where does this concept come from? How role conformity leads to a strong idea of universalization and even rationality remains unexplained. Self–other equivalence presupposes that the other is regarded as a person. This seems irreconcilable with Tomasello's assertion that personhood depends on recognition by others, not recognition of others as equal on the prior understanding of the shared personhood of human beings.

The problems of the relevance of the concept of legitimacy and the reasons providing legitimacy are pertinent here, too. Morality is not just based on a group-minded rationality. According to some elements of the discussed theory, morality is content neutral in a certain respect: If something turns into a group morality, it is obligatory, regardless of its content. Morality, however, is not content neutral: It is about justice and what we owe to others. Accordingly, these norms are not simply obligatory because they are the norms of "us," but because of their specific content. There are some good reasons to see the set of possible moralities as being substantially constrained. According to the analysis above, this is particularly plausible if one distinguishes between a conventional morality and a reflective morality that is the product of critical scrutiny of moral precepts, ideologies and prejudices inherited from the past. The understanding of the second-personal morality of sympathy and fairness as a baseline of moral systems actually seems to point in the same direction, as it forms a critical yardstick for justified moral norms. However, second-personal morality is conceptualized in too constrained a manner, as we have seen, and its emergence is not sufficiently accounted for.

[103] At some stages of the theory, reference is made to something that resembles final cause arguments: In order to enable them to collaborate, the theory maintains, hominids evolved joint intentionality. In order to enable the cognitive coordination of their activities, *Homo sapiens* evolved new cognitive skills and became motivated by collective intentionality. Such statements do not sit well with evolutionary theory, because there is no teleology in evolution. Evolution (whatever its mechanisms may be) has no purpose, it simply has results, and human cognition, including its moral domain, may be one of these. Tomasello underlines this, too, cf. Tomasello, *Becoming Human*, 340. His arguments, however, do not seem to adhere always to this methodological stance.

Then there is the related problem of moral innovation: Many deviations from traditional morality came from individuals who relied on sources other than group morality. Socrates is a leading example of this, as are Jesus and Gautama Buddha, not to mention the many crucially important but forgotten moral innovators in human history. In the light of this, there are compelling reasons to conclude that the "objectivity" of morality is not derived from conformity with a group morality, but is a matter of critical thought and insight, often contrary to group perceptions. Moreover, the history of human morality is not one of intragroup harmony and intergroup strife: The moral battles within what may count as such a group (blurry as this concept is), which were often deadly, teach a different lesson. It is not enough to explaining this strife by referring to subgroups. What is central is a person's capacity for autonomous moral reasoning that makes them more than a "cog in the conventional cultural practices," empowering them to become the *subject of change*. The reference to the need for creative solutions to norm conflicts underlines this point but cannot easily be reconciled with the thrust of the argument emphasizing that objective morality is a group-minded system of rules. Where does moral creativity come from if morality is group based? What are the mental resources of critical moral thought?

The reflective morality that is important in this context is not just that of dyadic second-personal relations. Altruism and justice are not limited to such relations but include every moral patient. This leads us to the next point: The reference to in-group/out-group differentiations certainly captures one feature of human judgment and behavior. But it does not exhaust the principles of human moral judgment, because there are other patterns of judgment and behavior that clearly transcend and subvert this distinction. Again, the theory concedes this point – for example, by admitting that transcending the in-group/out-group distinction happens in dramatic cases such as slavery or apartheid.

It is important to ask: Why do arguments about the inclusion of human beings in the moral community work, as highlighted in the fight against slavery or apartheid? If there truly is a hardwired in-group morality, this success seems hard to understand. If "similarity" of appearance and manners counts, then how does this account for the power of arguments for including people in the group of those who deserve respect, arguments that appeal not to such conventional similarities but to the common humanity of all people? Why is it not only possible but morally compelling to look at others as more than "out-group barbarians"? The task is to explain the reasons for accepting the equal status of human beings as moral patients independently of in-group/out-group considerations and to understand what this tells us about the moral cognition of human beings.

Evolutionary mechanisms affect an individual's phenotype. Arguments for group selection therefore need to be taken with great caution. Something like cultural group selection is even less plausible. The eradication of the Maya culture by the conquistadores is not an example of cultural group selection for better cooperators, but of the victory of violence and greed using superior technological means over human beings who shared the same properties and possibilities for cooperation (on both moral and other terms) as the conquerors. The (at least temporary) influence of the human rights idea on human affairs is the product not of mechanisms discussed by adaptationist theories of cultural evolution,[104] but of dire historical experience and a normative idea with the power to convince.

A last exemplary point: As in the case of joint intentionality, collective intentionality seems to be the precondition of certain forms of culture, not their result.

7.6.9 *Is There an Alternative to Incrementalism?*

These criticisms show that the argument stalls on both the phylogenetic and the ontogenetic level: The mechanisms described by the incremental evolution theory cannot plausibly be taken to necessarily produce the cognitive structures that are taken to have developed in the species, and the ontogenetic account appears not to be sufficient to explain the emergence of the cognitive capacities acquired by individuals. The theory therefore in fact formulates a hypothesis about a successive number of mutations that lead to an incremental change in the cognitive abilities of hominids and modern humans, including the acquisition of joint intentionality, self-regulation, obligations mediated through an ought, self–other equivalence, group-mindedness, collective intentionality and so on that are the basis for human ontogeny. It implies that the proximate psychological mechanisms underlying these capabilities became biologically fixed. The ultimate mechanism underpinning the development is that hominids and later humans who cooperate in these increasingly advanced ways have "more babies" and consequently other, differently endowed individuals are "weeded out"[105] by natural selection. The fact that individuals with specific cooperative skills have more babies would not matter if certain proximate cognitive mechanisms were not fixed in the parent generation and bequeathed to their offspring. Otherwise, the next generation would have to learn these cooperative skills anew. The result would be a cultural, not a biological evolution. However, the incremental theory assumes precisely the latter. The account posits that the genetically inherited traits developed in this incremental fashion and proved to be of adaptive value (or to be at least neutral or not sufficiently maladaptive to reduce reproductive fitness), one after the other, and thus persisted in the evolutionary

[104] Such mechanisms are, for instance, that a trait is (randomly) adopted by successful and prestigious group members and then is widely adopted by others because it serves human needs, cf. e.g. Turchin, *Ultrasociety*. Such accounts do not include the decisive element of critical reflection and convictions based on reasons. Cf. for some critique Buchanan and Powell, *The Evolution of Moral Progress*, 396 ff. On the thesis of a "culture–gene coevolutionary process" as the key to understanding human cooperation, Henrich, *The Secret of Our Success*, 210, 319 f.

[105] Tomasello, *A Natural History of Human Morality*, 106.

process. Therefore, the newly acquired capabilities are passed on to the next generations. These next generations then move up the ladder, acquiring new, enhanced cognitive skills due to more mutations and passing them on to their offspring, until the level of proximate cognitive mechanisms enabling the formation of an "objective" morality of humans is reached. There is an important qualification: Some of the proximate cognitive mechanisms are understood as "spandrels," cognitive structures that evolved because of certain nonmoral functions they serve but recruited to new tasks with potentially no (immediate) adaptive value.

All of this means that the baseline of the account is the assumption of consecutive accidental mutations that lead, step by step, to the set of cognitive capacities that ultimately formed the psychological mechanisms that enable human beings to judge and act morally.[106] Some crucial aspects of these capacities are understood as "spandrels," the primary function of which was not moral. Joint intentionality, for instance, opened up a whole range of new possibilities of human life.[107]

As we have seen, the described development does not make unique evolutionary sense on the level of the evolution of the species, so the problem of lacking evidence for this particular trajectory cannot be circumvented.

Moreover, the assumption of a *gradual, incremental* evolution in small steps in hominids and *Homo sapiens* is not the only possibility. On the contrary, as we will see in greater detail when reviewing other evolutionary accounts, it is rather implausible given the evidence of the development of complex traits in various organisms and the paleoanthropological evidence about human development. It is in fact widely accepted that after very long periods of comparatively little cognitive development, as evidenced by the lack of major change in tools used, a qualitatively different kind of intelligence emerged with the cognitively modern *Homo sapiens*. Rather than incremental steps, this indicates a major evolutionary reorganization of the cognitive capacities of modern human beings. How and why this evidence fits into current evolutionary theory is something the following section will explore.

We can already learn something important from these interesting and differentiated arguments about the incremental evolutionary growth of human morality and their critique, however: The incremental succession of mutations, including the creation of spandrels, is not more probable than other accounts allowing for more far-reaching change, let alone the only evolutionary account that makes sense. This is even more so if one stays mindful of the fact that – as the theory underlines itself – there is no evidence that the described stages were those through which hominids in fact passed. It is possible that they are pure imagination.

The cognitive mechanisms enabling human morality, created by mutations that reorganized human cognitive abilities, were the *preconditions* (not the *consequences*)

[106] Tomasello, *Becoming Human*, 312 f.

[107] Tomasello, *Becoming Human*, 340, underlining that "the fact that a psychological adaptation is 'aimed at' a specific ecological challenge does not constrain its subsequent application."

of qualitatively new forms of collaboration (not of collaboration as such) and other forms of human thought and action – for example, based on joint or collective intentionality, ideas of self–other equivalence or respect and the morality of altruism and justice that have structured human ways of living ever since. Given the "sparse evidence" of what happened in the history of the human species, *the question of the evolution of these cognitive capacities underlying morality thus continues to be an open one*. Acknowledging these limits of our current understanding is of fundamental importance for any evidence-based scientific endeavor.

These sobering findings have an important consequence: *So far, there is no reason whatsoever to assert that human beings, given what we know about the evolution of human moral cognition, can only have a small-group morality irreconcilable with the ethical principles embodied in human rights.* The simple reason is: We know so little about this process that there are no sufficient grounds to come to any such far-reaching conclusions.

The summarized theory therefore does not provide a fully convincing account of the evolution of morality. But what it does do, which is of substantial interest, is help to determine important elements of the set of psychological mechanisms that allow (among other things) for the specific forms of human cooperation, in particular on moral grounds. It helps to distinguish the cognitive apparatus of the nearest relatives of human beings from humans' mental capacities. It has substantial things to say about the content of morality. There is no explicit reference to the problem of human rights, but it seems clear that rights play a role in the context of the discussion of notions such as "deservingness" or fairness. Morality's contents of sympathy, fairness and – importantly – equal respect for everybody are in line with the human rights idea. One should take this seriously, at least as showing that contemporary evolutionary theory does not necessarily mean human rights skepticism. These findings are further underlined by other approaches of contemporary evolutionary theory.[108]

The theory of the incremental growth of human morality through interdependence makes another important point that shows us which direction to pursue further, given the preliminary results of our reflection: The reference to "spandrels" opens the door to evolutionary theories that take mechanisms of evolution operating in addition to natural selection seriously, among which nonadaptive structures such as spandrels play an important role, albeit not the only one. Such approaches help to paint a much more differentiated picture of the mechanisms of evolution than those which have been reviewed by us so far. These approaches form some of the most influential thought on evolution today and therefore merit closer investigation.

[108] Cf. e.g. the biocultural theory of inclusivist morality by Buchanan and Powell, *The Evolution of Moral Progress*.

7.7 EVOLUTIONARY PLURALISM

7.7.1 *The Contested Scope of Evolutionary Theory*

The review of some influential and paradigmatic approaches to the evolution of morality (which have some direct consequences for the understanding of the law) renders it crucial to answer the following questions: How much scope do evolutionary possibilities offer for the development of human beings' cognitive capacities? Can any well-defined constraints on the mental mechanisms possible (whatever they may be) be derived from evolutionary theory?

Thus far, our discussion of attempts at an evolutionary explanation of the idea of human rights, including the normative principles that underpin these rights, has provided no reason to assume that this idea is formed contrary to humans' cognitive nature – because the cognitive faculties underlying human morality are geared to produce a narrow tribal code of proper behavior, for instance. Nor are there reasons to assume that the idea of human rights is a misleading cognitive illusion produced by a hardwired cognitive gizmo. How do these results fit into the framework of the current understanding of evolution?

Evolutionary biology has developed since Darwin, and the transformations of evolutionary thinking in the *Modern Synthesis* have become a controversial field.[109] Nevertheless, current evolutionary biology appears to provide strong support for our analysis so far. To begin with, it is worth noting that in a considerable number of accounts of the evolution of morality, a set of assumptions play a guiding role: An organism is understood as an ensemble of singular traits. These traits are designed by natural selection for a specific fitness-enhancing function. Given the obvious fact of the interaction of traits, trade-offs are allowed, which are, however, understood as the best possible solutions in the face of the different competing functional demands expressed by natural selection. These are the tenets of what Stephen J. Gould and Richard Lewontin famously called the adaptationist program or the Panglossian paradigm.[110]

However, some very good arguments suggest that this picture of evolution is too simple. Evolution involves more than just gradual, simple lineage modification through natural selection. First of all, it is not so easy to say what a "trait" actually is, because organisms are "integrated entities, not collections of discrete objects" that allow for an atomization of properties.[111] In addition, the function that a trait possesses is not necessarily obvious. Take a well-known example: "Bones serve the function of providing rigidity to the body and attachments for muscles. But they also

[109] Cf. Robert Berwick and Noam Chomsky, *Why Only Us: Language and Evolution* (Cambridge, MA: MIT Press, 2016), 15.

[110] Stephen Jay Gould and Richard Lewontin, "The Spandrels of San Marco and the Panglossian Paradigm: A Critique of the Adaptationist Programme," *Proceedings of the Royal Society of London, Series B* 205, no. 1161 (1979): 585.

[111] Gould and Lewontin, "The Spandrels of San Marco and the Panglossian Paradigm," 585.

are the sites for the storage of calcium, and the bone marrow is the tissue within which new red blood cells are produced. Depending on the causal pathway of interest, 'bones' are either macroscopic structural elements or collections of cells that secrete calcium or embryonic tissue of the circulatory system."[112] Often, there is no evidence available that would allow us to choose between the possible options.[113]

Traits that have developed themselves in turn define the conditions of evolution: Without hands that are anatomically able to make tools, tool-making remains beyond an organism's reach. In order to cultivate fire, an organism needs sufficient body mass to collect enough wood. This is also important for cognitive traits: "[T]he evolutionary questions about cognition are questions both of the evolution of cognition and the effects of cognition on evolution."[114]

Furthermore, for theory-building it is important that – as Darwin himself underlined[115] – natural selection is certainly a central, but not the only causal factor of evolution. Many other factors need to be considered, as the example of spandrels already indicates. Evolution is, for instance, a stochastic, not a deterministic process. Very different factors that are unrelated to natural selection can influence the evolutionary pathway. Evolution plays out, for example, in finite, not infinite populations. Therefore, sampling effects in small populations – genetic drift – can shape the traits of a given population. Even without the influence of natural selection, because of stochastic inheritance patterns, some traits (including adaptive ones) may become extinct while others are passed on.[116]

[112] Richard Lewontin, *The Triple Helix: Gene, Organism, and Environment* (Cambridge, MA: Harvard University Press, 2000), 79.

[113] Richard Lewontin, "The Evolution of Cognition," in *Methods, Models, and Conceptual Issues: An Invitation to Cognitive Science*, Vol. 4, eds. Don Scarborough, Saul Sternberg and Daniel Osherson (Cambridge, MA: MIT Press, 1998), 119: "The problem of origin is the problem of reconstructing the functions of traits in long-extinct environments together with their long extinct forms. While on purely mechanical grounds, we may exclude some explanations, we cannot choose among many allowable ones. Did the dinosaur stegosaurus use the large leaflike plates along its back for physical defense, for appearing deceptively large to potential predators, for sexual attraction, for thermoregulation, for all four, for some at one time and others at another, or none of the above? We will never know."

[114] Lewontin, "Evolution of Cognition," 113: "Eighteen-inch monkeys may remind us of humans and seem clever when we watch them in the zoo, but they are too short and too weak to raise a weight high enough and bring it down with enough force to break rocks, or to gather and process large chunks of fuel wood needed to maintain and control fire, and so they could never mine ore and smelt iron." On ecological niches, Buchanan and Powell, *The Evolution of Moral Progress*, 367.

[115] Cf. Darwin's well-known comment, Charles Darwin, *The Origin of Species* (London: John Murray, 1872), 421: "As my conclusions have lately been much misrepresented, and it has been stated that I attribute the modifications of species exclusively to natural selection, I may be permitted to remark that in the first edition of this work, and subsequently, I placed in a most conspicuous position – namely at the close of the Introduction – the following words: 'I am convinced that natural selection has been the main, but not the exclusive means of modification.' This has been of no avail. Great is the power of steady misrepresentation."

[116] Gould and Lewontin, "The Spandrels of San Marco and the Panglossian Paradigm," 585 ff.; Berwick and Chomsky, *Why Only Us*, 16 ff.

Furthermore, the problem of the stochastic "gravity well" has to be overcome.[117] Newly evolved adaptive traits may disappear again because there are only a small number of carriers of the trait that all become extinct before becoming sufficiently numerous to reproduce successfully – for example, because they all accidentally fall prey to some predator:

> It is, for example, of little value to be the smartest member of your species, if, in an environment crawling with predators, you are also the slowest – or even just the most unfortunate. What's more, in an indifferent world your reproductive success may not in the end have much to do with how magnificently you are adapted to any one thing. Whether or not that predator gets you, or whether or not you get the girl, may simply be a function of blind luck and circumstance.[118]

There are stochastic migration patterns that can lead to hybridization with existing organisms, with evolutionary effects.[119]

In addition, genes interact in complex ways – as epitomized by Darwin's observation that blue-eyed cats are deaf. Genetic change may therefore have effects unrelated to natural selection. Natural selection operates on the whole organism – mutations leading to the genotype with the alleles XX may have different effects on fitness if combined with the alleles YY as compared to a genotype XX, ZZ.[120] Looking at the fitness of single traits therefore possibly misses important factors of development. Other conditions of development have to be considered, too: Fitness levels, for instance, can fluctuate if the frequency of the trait increases, as in the case of overpopulation.[121]

Nonadaptive mutations can persevere in the evolutionary process because of such influences. There are also nonadaptive side effects of adaptive properties that are established by natural selection. Architectural constraints are an important limit on the acquisition of new traits – not all developmental paths are even theoretically possible: "[T]here are no animals with wheels presumably because there is no way to make an appendage that rotates on an axle and still can be supplied with blood and nerves."[122] Moreover, only a limited amount of what is theoretically possible has been explored by evolution.[123] Consequently, the traits of an organism can be determined by path-dependent phylogenetic trajectories that circumscribe the possible future development independently of natural selection and create the oft-observed "inertia" of evolution: "There appear, then, to be basic body plans that

[117] Berwick and Chomsky, *Why Only Us*, 22.

[118] Ian Tattersall, *Masters of the Planet: The Search for Our Human Origins* (New York: St. Martin's Press, 2013), XIX f.

[119] Berwick and Chomsky, *Why Only Us*, 29.

[120] Cf. Lewontin, *The Triple Helix*, 82 ff., with the example of chromosomal polymorphisms in the grasshopper *Moraba scurra*; Berwick and Chomsky, *Why Only Us*, 23.

[121] Berwick and Chomsky, *Why Only Us*, 23.

[122] Lewontin, "Evolution of Cognition," 114.

[123] Berwick and Chomsky, *Why Only Us*, 19 n. 9, 169 n. 9, 176.

are maintained through immensely long evolutionary periods despite dramatic changes in the life activity patterns of organisms and the functions of their parts."[124] There are, for instance, no vertebrates with six limbs or insects with eight, not six.[125] Or, to take another example: "[T]he contingent fact that we have five fingers and five toes may be better explained by an appeal to how toes and fingers develop than that five is optimal for their function."[126] There is substantial debate about the reasons for the uniformity of certain common structures of organisms.[127] In addition, evidently, any development can only unfold within the framework of natural laws (physics, chemistry, etc.) and the physicochemical constraints that they impose.

Some of an organism's adaptive, nonadaptive or neutral traits can be coopted for new functions – "exaptation" is another factor to be aware of in evolutionary theory.[128] This term clarifies an ambiguity of the term "adaptation," which refers either to the genesis of a trait and its reason (features developed by natural selection for their present role) or to current features with fitness-enhancing utility irrespective of how they arose.[129] Darwin himself noted the existence of traits developed because of "laws of growth" but coopted for other (adaptive) purposes.[130] Mixing both dimensions might lead to "a common flaw in much evolutionary reasoning – the inference of historical genesis from current utility."[131] One example of an exaptation that opened up striking new functional possibilities is the evolution of feathers. Finds such as gigantic feathered dinosaurs support the theory that feathers initially served thermoregulation and were only later coopted for flight. Other examples include the acquisition of limbs in a marine environment that later were used for movement on land, or the wings of insects.[132] After a trait is recruited for a new function, it may evolve further, becoming more adapted to this new function.[133] The cooptation of existing traits is of great importance for the evolutionary process:

[124] Lewontin, "Evolution of Cognition," 117.

[125] Lewontin, "Evolution of Cognition," 117.

[126] Berwick and Chomsky, *Why Only Us*, 60.

[127] Berwick and Chomsky, *Why Only Us*, 58 ff.

[128] Stephen Jay Gould and Elisabeth Vrba, "Exaptation – A Missing Term in the Science of Form," *Paleobiology* 8, no. 1 (1982): 6.

[129] Gould and Vrba, "Exaptation," 1 ff.

[130] Darwin, *Origin of Species*, 158: "The sutures in the skulls of young mammals have been advanced as a beautiful adaptation for aiding parturition, and no doubt they facilitate, or may be indispensable for this act; but as sutures occur in the skulls of young birds and reptiles, which have only to escape from a broken egg, we may infer that this structure has arisen from the laws of growth, and has been taken advantage of in the parturition of higher animals," as quoted by Gould and Vrba, "Exaptation," 5.

[131] Gould and Vrba, "Exaptation," 14.

[132] On feathered dinosaurs, cf. Xing Xu et al., "A Gigantic Feathered Dinosaur from the Lower Cretaceous of China," *Nature* 484 (2012): 94, noting the alternative possibility of feathers as a display structure, too. On the evolution of feathers and limbs, Gould and Vrba, "Exaptation," 7 ff.; Tattersall, *Masters of the Planet*, 68, 210 f. On wings of insects, Lewontin, "Evolution of Cognition," 119.

[133] Gould and Vrba, "Exaptation," 11.

"[T]he enormous pool of nonadaptations must be the wellspring and reservoir of most evolutionary flexibility. We need to recognize the central role of 'cooptability for fitness' as the primary evolutionary significance of ubiquitous nonadaptation in organisms. In this sense, and at its level of the phenotype, this nona[da]ptive pool is an analog of mutation – a source of raw material for further selection."[134]

We already encountered the idea of spandrels, which are unavoidable byproducts of architectural choices – for example, to construct a dome on rounded arches.[135] Given that they exist, they are put to good use for ornamental purposes and often are so accomplished that it seems as if they are built precisely for this decorative reason. Analogously, traits of an organism can serve a function even though they may have evolved not because of this function, but because of such architectural constraints: "One must not confuse the fact that a structure is used in some way . . . with the primary evolutionary reason for its existence and conformation."[136]

It is even less admissible to go a step further and conclude from the assumption that selection could produce only one kind of trait in an organism that this organism in fact has this and no other trait. As explained above, one also encounters this functional fallacy in accounts about the evolution of morality that maintain that human beings have a naturally tribal, small-group morality – not because there is strong evidence that human beings indeed have this kind of morality, but because only such a morality is held to make evolutionary sense.

As indicated earlier, in Tomasello's account of the evolution of morality we encountered a reference to spandrels at a crucial point of the argument: Proxy psychological mechanisms producing cognitive judgments of self–other equivalence are assumed to have been recruited for moral purposes – which only underlines the importance of these broader evolutionary perspectives.

The evolutionary processes captured by the idea of exaptation are of particular importance when considering the evolution of human beings' higher mental faculties: As Gould and Vrba note on the debate between A. R. Wallace and Darwin on the evolutionary explanation of the development of the brain, Darwin recognized

> that the brain, though undoubtedly built by selection for some complex set of functions, can, as a result of its intricate structure, work in an unlimited number of ways quite unrelated to the selective pressure that constructed it. Many of these ways might become important, if not indispensable, for future survival in later social contexts . . .. But current utility carries no automatic implication about historical origin. Most of what the brain now does to enhance our survival lies in the domain of exaptation – and does not allow us to make hypotheses about the selective paths of human history.[137]

[134] Gould and Vrba, "Exaptation," 12.
[135] Gould and Lewontin, "The Spandrels of San Marco and the Panglossian Paradigm," 581.
[136] Gould and Lewontin, "The Spandrels of San Marco and the Panglossian Paradigm," 587.
[137] Gould and Vrba, "Exaptation," 13. They conclude: "Thus, the two evolutionary phenomena that may have been most crucial to the development of complexity with consciousness on our

7.7.2 *Nature Does Not Make Leaps, Does It?*

A classic topic that already occupied early evolutionary theory is whether evolution is exclusively based on micromutations, as Darwin for instance assumed,[138] echoing the traditional metaphysical idea that nature does not make leaps (*natura non facit saltum*). There is conclusive evidence to show that this is an overly narrow conception of what is evolutionarily possible. There are examples demonstrating that rapid change is possible, leading to a very fast divergence of closely related forms, arguably based on small genetic changes – in particular in regulatory genes – that have far-reaching effects, including the classic case of the stickleback, a small fish with spines, or the evolution of the basic elements of eyes (light-sensitive cells, pigment cells), among others.[139] Thus, the possible evolutionary trajectory of a species needs to include more than just evolutionary accounts of incremental change.

Furthermore, the evolutionary theory of human cognition faces particular challenges. One such challenge we have already encountered: the lack of evidence for the existence of particular cognitive capabilities of early human beings. If certain kinds of artifacts are found, say a tool or a flute, we can be sure that the cognitive abilities necessary for making this kind of tool or this musical instrument must have been in place. So, too, must other capacities – for example, those making it possible to identify the need for tools, or the capacity for purposive functional inventions, for using tools or for producing and enjoying music. But how are we to know whether a group of modern humans sang a song while making the tools or the flute? What were their social relations like? How did they communicate? Did the members of this species tell tales while sitting at campfires? Did they use arithmetic to keep track of the quantity of their provisions? Did they possess a sense of justice that guided them when dividing up prey? Such cognitive activities do not leave any traces behind. So how are we to know?

planet (if readers will pardon some dripping anthropocentrism for the moment) – the process of creating genetic redundancy in the first place, and the myriad and inescapable consequences of building any computing device as complex as the human brain – may both represent exaptations that began as nonaptations, the concept previously missing in our evolutionary terminology."

138 Darwin, *Origin of Species*, 156: "For natural selection can act only by taking advantage of slight successive variations, she can never take a leap, but must advance by the shortest and slowest steps."

139 Cf. Tattersall, *Masters of the Planet*, 94 ff., including the example of the development of *Homo ergaster*, as shown by the Turkana Boy – another example that genetic modification involving a radical change of morphology does not need to lead to "hopeful monsters," derided in evolutionary theory: "Perhaps the Turkana Boy's radically new bodily confirmation can be attributed to a genetic event of similar kind. A minor mutation had occurred in the Boy's lineage that, through altering gene timing and expression, had radically changed its possessor's morphology – and had, entirely accidentally, opened new adaptive avenues to them. … Something routine and unremarkable on the genomic level had occurred among the Boy's precursors; and it just happened to change the course of hominid history," ibid. 98; Berwick and Chomsky, *Why Only Us*, 2, 5, 26 ff., 31 ff., 67 ff.

Giving an evolutionary description of the developmental process of human cognition is equally difficult. It is far from clear who the predecessors of modern humans are, as the paleoanthropological record contains insufficient evidence to determine the lines of relationship between species and distinguish ancestral lines from those forms that are not ancestors.[140] It is equally unclear what cognitive capabilities any of the species that may be part of the lineage of modern human beings possessed, as here, too, the problem of evidence for such capabilities rears its head. The split between Neanderthals and modern humans happened 400,000–600,000 years ago. Tool-making was typical of Neanderthals.[141] Recent research on Neanderthal artwork indicates symbolic thought on the part of this certainly cognitively gifted species, but the evidence is controversial and very sparse. And, whatever the results of future research may be on Neanderthal symbolic behavior, there is no evidence of any systematic use of symbolic thought – in contrast to modern humans.[142] We have already observed that the closest living relatives of modern humans are primates, chimpanzees and bonobos, about 14 million years of evolutionary time away from modern humans – a substantial amount of time in which to develop differently. As animals adapted in crucial aspects to life in forests, and in some cases adapted behaviorally to life in the savannah,[143] there already is a difference from early hominids, who – enabled by their new body form – moved out of forests and into other environments and modes of life.[144] The number of existing "close" relatives is sparse, which makes it difficult to determine a trait's successive changes: "The evolutionary space is too sparsely populated to be able to connect the points sensibly."[145] In addition, the paleoanthropological evidence suggests that early hominids developed cognitive skills that are not available to primates living today: "The evidence of tool use, and yet more of tool-making, tells us that the bipedal apes had graduated – perhaps as much as 3.4 million years ago, and at least before 2.6 million years ago – to a cognitive state that lay beyond anything we can infer for the apes as we know them today."[146] Tattersall argues that early hominids' "entirely new and radical way of interacting with the world around them" had its roots in an early "leap of nature" and later exaptation of cognitive

140 This is a problem that applies to the emergence of the genus *Homo*, too: "To put the situation in a nutshell, there is not one fossil among all those known in the period before two million years ago that presents itself as a compelling candidate for the position of direct progenitor of the new hominids to come," Tattersall, *Masters of the Planet*, 85. Lewontin, "Evolution of Cognition," 115, 118.

141 Tattersall, *Masters of the Planet*, 175 ff.

142 Ian Tattersall, "The Minimalist Program and the Origin of Language: A View from Paleoanthropology," *Frontiers in Psychology* 10, no. 677 (2019); Tattersall, *Masters of the Planet*, 180.

143 Tattersall, *Masters of the Planet*, 70.

144 Tattersall, *Masters of the Planet*, 57, 70.

145 Lewontin, "Evolution of Cognition," 122.

146 Tattersall, *Masters of the Planet*, 49 f. Cf. e.g. throwing with precision, understanding properties of materials or tool-making, ibid. 53 f. On the latter cf. n. 160. On vocal skills, ibid. 61.

skills. The best explanation is that "the cognitive potential to make stone tools was born in the large genetic alteration that must have been involved in the acquisition of the new and radically different bipedal body form; and that this potential lay dormant for some time before being expressed in the invention of stone tool making."[147] The fact that evolution is not a continuous, linear, incremental process creates specific problems for the understanding of the evolution of cognition, because it is possible for closely related forms to diverge very rapidly.[148] The similarity of traits can vary from trait to trait – an organism may be similar in some respects but quite different in others.[149] And there is another crucially important possibility, namely that the trait "simply does not exist in some or all related lines, that it is a novelty, and so has no observable evolutionary history."[150]

Furthermore, there is the functional change of traits – less closely related organisms may share more properties with certain organisms than with others that are more closely related, as illustrated by an evolutionarily convergent system such as vocal learning in songbirds and humans, which are separated by millions of years of evolutionary time.[151] There is a need to differentiate between homologous and analogous structures and to identify homologies, especially because homologous structures may change functionally and because of the abovementioned possibility of novelties without homologies in other species.[152] In any case, as in other organisms, it is not singular traits that determined the survival of modern humans but the human organism as a whole, with its many specific adaptive and not-so-adaptive features and their complex interactions,[153] which renders an account of the evolutionary history of any one element of this integrated organism even more difficult.

All of this arguably leads to the conclusion that there is simply not enough evidence to ever decisively settle the question of how exactly modern humans' cognitive capacities came into being over the course of evolution.[154]

It goes without saying that any evolutionary theory of the development of human cognition has to take into account the existing evidence of human cognitive development. There is widespread consent, given the current stage of knowledge, that around 200,000 years ago anatomically modern humans were living in Africa.[155] About 80,000 years before the present day, there is uncontested evidence of symbolic behavior such as beads, shell ornaments and geometric engravings, though there are some earlier artifacts.[156] This indicates that at least from this time onwards, modern

[147] Tattersall, *Masters of the Planet*, 67 f.
[148] Lewontin, "Evolution of Cognition," 116 with some examples of such rapid change.
[149] Lewontin, "Evolution of Cognition," 117.
[150] Lewontin, "Evolution of Cognition," 118.
[151] Berwick and Chomsky, *Why Only Us*, 12 ff., 140 ff.
[152] Lewontin, "Evolution of Cognition," 124 ff.
[153] For some examples cf. Tattersall, *Masters of the Planet*, 212.
[154] This is the famous conclusion in Lewontin, "Evolution of Cognition," 108.
[155] Tattersall, *Masters of the Planet*, 184 ff.
[156] Tattersall, *Masters of the Planet*, 142, on earlier objects of a contested nature, including the "Venus" of Berekhat Ram, concluding that there is "nothing in the material record to suggest

humans had the cognitive capacity for symbolic thought and used it systematically. Other early indicators for new cognitive abilities are bladelets (stone flakes sunk into handles), making tools from artificially hardened materials, pressure flaking, barbed harpoons and, on the social level, the functional division of living spaces.[157]

The capacity for symbolic thought is plausibly taken as an indicator that cognitively modern humans had arrived on the scene: With modern humans, an unprecedented and rapid development set in, with cultural and technological innovations that transformed the world – and by now are threatening the continued existence of this simultaneously creative and destructive species. This development is dramatic proof that these beings possessed some revolutionary new creative abilities in both thought and action. Before that, over the millions of years of development there had been many striking innovations like tool-making, the use of fire, spears, composite tools, "prepared core" implements and blades.[158] However, there was a disconnect between technological innovation and the development of a new species of the *Homo* genus.[159] Technological innovations persisted unchanged for hundreds of thousands of years and were of very limited scope in comparison to what happened later, although they were very remarkable innovations in themselves, beyond the cognitive capacities and other abilities of great apes:[160] Mode 1/Oldowan tools (sharp stone flakes) were invented 2.5 million years before the present and mode 2/ Acheulean hand axes 1.5 million years before the present, although they were widely applied only hundreds of thousands of years later. These tools continued to be used even though new species like *Homo ergaster* developed during this time.[161] There is consequently no necessary connection between the appearance of a new kind of hominid and technological innovation, nor is there evidence of any gradualism in the appearance of technologies for long stretches of time.

The cognitive abilities evident in Acheulean hand axes are already remarkable – foresight and the planning of complex sequences of actions, the knowledge of materials, anticipating need by keeping stocks of suitable stone, among others. Hand axes even indicate economic and social specialization.[162] Later developments furnish further examples of the advanced cognitive skills of the various branches of hominids. But with *Homo sapiens*, change starts to take place at breathtaking speed. In just 80,000 years the species traveled from hand axes that had already been used

that the symbolic manipulation of information was in any way a regular part of the cognitive repertoire of *Homo heidelbergensis*. Had it been, we would surely expect to see more material evidence of it."

157 Tattersall, *Masters of the Planet*, 200 ff.

158 Tattersall, *Masters of the Planet*, 112, 138 ff.

159 Tattersall, *Masters of the Planet*, 62.

160 Cf. e.g. on chimpanzees' inability to produce such hand axes, arguably not only because of their cognitive abilities, but also because of the form of their hands, which are ill formed for this purpose, although chimps are able to learn to use existing hand axes and to produce other tools, Tattersall, *Masters of the Planet*, 43 ff., 49 ff. (on the spear-making of chimpanzees).

161 Tattersall, *Masters of the Planet*, 42 ff., 103, 116 f., 124 ff., 138, 187.

162 Tattersall, *Masters of the Planet*, 126 ff.

in different forms for over 2 million years to the technical civilization of today. This change cannot but be based on cognitive abilities of modern human beings that are qualitatively new in comparison to those of their predecessors, abilities that have increasingly been put to use.[163] Symbolic thinking and action is one such ability, in itself of far-reaching importance for culture-building and science. Technical skills also point clearly to certain abilities – for example, the analysis of complex causal chains as a precondition for developing new technologies in the making of tools and weapons. The existence of art is an indicator not only of symbolic thought, but also of a very rich inner life of early humans, including the search for meaning and beauty – and this tells us a lot about the species' cognitive capacities. In the case of other cognitive abilities, there is only little evidence until much later in history. Theory-building therefore turns to the second-best option: interpreting the emergence of symbolic thought and action as a proxy for the existence of other cognitive abilities that are crucial to being human but leave no material evidence behind.

Language is at the forefront of many debates, as an instrument of complex thought and communication,[164] but any other aspect of the human mental world qualifies as well, of course. One example is human moral understanding and judgment. There are some indications of forms of care for others in hominid history: One example is a 1.8-million-year-old skull of an elderly male who already lost his teeth during his lifetime but survived nevertheless. This seems to indicate help from members of the group to which he belonged, although other possible explanations also exist. If help was indeed provided, the skull "furnishes us with the first putative instance of social concern in the hominid record."[165] Other traces are (different forms of) cannibalism or burial practices that indicate concern (or lack thereof) for species members.[166]

Beyond this, as for other possible mental abilities, there is no direct evidence of the exact kind of cognitive capacities existing in hominid history that constituted the foundation for the moral world in which modern humans lived, answering the question of which concepts and principles they applied, what moral feelings they entertained and how these were spelled out in social practices and institutions. Did modern humans have a sense of fairness? Did they experience shame? Did they feel bound by obligations?

If one accepts symbolic thought as a proxy for a fully developed modern human cognition because of the reasons outlined, one has to conclude that early modern humans possessed the same cognitive abilities to form moral ideas as contemporary

[163] Tattersall, *Masters of the Planet*, 205.

[164] Cf. Tattersall, *Masters of the Planet*, 183 (Neanderthals: no language), 214 ff.; Berwick and Chomsky, *Why Only Us*, 1 ff.

[165] Tattersall, *Masters of the Planet*, 124. He asks whether such attitudes may have their roots in forms of empathic behavior in chimpanzees towards wounded or oppressed group mates, despite the chimpanzees lacking the technical abilities to provide help. For the example of a disabled aged male Neanderthal, ibid. 171.

[166] Cf. Tattersall, *Masters of the Planet*, 152 f. (*Homo antecessor*), 172 ff. (Neanderthal "survival cannibalism" and burial).

humans (whatever these abilities may turn out to be and to whatever use they may have been put).

When considering these problems, it is useful to distinguish between the evolution of cognitive capacities (human beings have the cognitive capacity to produce symbolic artifacts, primates do not) and the development of skills and insights within the framework of these evolved cognitive abilities. This is particularly important when considering the human species. Evidently, the great historical change that gave rise to the transformative creative innovations highlighted above is a central element of the history of modern humans. There is, however, no evidence of any evolution of modern humans' cognitive capacities themselves that underpins this striking history of change and innovation. Therefore, it comes as no surprise that one could transfer a child born in a contemporary tribal society whose way of life is similar to a Stone Age culture to Zürich, New York or Beijing and know that it will develop in the same way as any other kid in the world, becoming unhealthily attached to its smartphone at far too early an age.

It is consequently reasonable to conclude that modern humans' basic abilities in the cognitive domain have stayed unchanged since their appearance at least 80,000 years ago. If this is indeed the case, we can project backwards whatever we know about the structure of the mind of humans living today: If human beings today are distinguished by a general learning ability, then it is plausible to assume that this formed the basis of their early development as well. If they possess the ability for shared intentionality, then plausibly early modern humans had this capacity, too. If there is evidence for other additional or alternative cognitive abilities – say, a language faculty – then most probably language was among the cognitive tools with which modern humans started their journey. Accordingly, the current cognitive capacities of modern humans can be taken as a clue to the mental parameters of life in the remote past.

One should note that making this assumption is justified because it is the most plausible interpretation of what we know at present. Nevertheless, within this general framework, much is unclear. Regarding language, for instance, one prominent account in fact speculates about an evolutionary pathway along these lines: First the semantic–conceptual system of language evolved, then the systems of the externalization of language through speech and other means such as signs.[167] This is relevant for the assessment of the cognitive abilities of all hominids, including Neanderthals, for instance: "It is merely assertion that complex stone working, fire control, clothing, ochre, and the like require language. We may have them all, but that does not mean Neanderthals had to have all the features that co-occur in us just because they had some of them."[168] This cautionary observation underlines that confident assertions about the precise path of the evolution of human cognition are simply not possible.

[167] Berwick and Chomsky, *Why Only Us*, 80, 87. For comments e.g. Tattersall, "The Minimalist Program and the Origin of Language."

[168] Berwick and Chomsky, *Why Only Us*, 153.

There is another problem: For many such cognitive traits, we do not know what kind of heritable variations existed, and it is difficult to determine their reproductive function for the first individuals possessing the trait within a species, which is decisive for these traits to become established.[169] Nor do we know whether and how these cognitive traits led to the replacement of other species. Take language, a central topic of evolutionary research. Despite the large number of contributions to the theory of the evolution of language, the function of language is less clear than it may appear.[170] A cofounder of evolutionary theory, Wallace, famously wondered what function human language may serve, because he saw no biological function that could not be met by other, simpler means than human language[171] – a problem still relevant today (although Wallace's proposed solution, divine intervention, may now be less accepted).[172] The proposals entertained today range widely, including language as a tool of successful cheating, of sexual selection, of communication for the purpose of cooperation or of structured thought, in the latter case a tool that evidently is still very useful.[173] Moreover, it is impossible to determine whether the function of such cognitive traits had any substantial effect on reproductive success: "[W]e cannot measure the survival advantage, if any, in our remote ancestors of the ability to do arithmetic."[174] Thus, one cannot determine whether any cognitive trait that might have had an effect on reproductive rates *did in fact* have an effect on reproductive rates.[175]

Such problems need to be considered for morality, too. Experiencing altruistic obligations in a group with members devoid of such inclinations may simply make the respective individual easy prey. The functional value of morality for collaboration is not obvious either, as, for instance, it precludes effective forms of

[169] Lewontin, "Evolution of Cognition," 112: "Evolution by natural selection occurs when individuals within a species possess a trait that gives them a reproductive or survival advantage over others within the species that lack the trait. It is an explanation of how a new trait spreads *within* a species, not how the species may replace other species once the trait has been incorporated. ... Thus a species that possesses linguistic competence may indeed take over the earth as a consequence of the technological and managerial capabilities that are the result of language, but in a species lacking linguistic competence, the rudimentary ability to form linguistic elements by a few individuals may be taken as a sign of difference that causes them to be expelled or even killed" (emphasis in original).

[170] Berwick and Chomsky, *Why Only Us*, 65 ff.

[171] Berwick and Chomsky, *Why Only Us*, 3.

[172] Berwick and Chomsky, *Why Only Us*, 80 ff. with a review of the debate including comments from Nobel Laureate Salvador Luria and François Jacob.

[173] Berwick and Chomsky, *Why Only Us*, 80 ff.; Tecumseh Fitch, *The Evolution of Language* (Cambridge: Cambridge University Press, 2010), 297 ff.; Szabolcs Számado and Eörs Szathmáry, "Selective Scenarios for the Emergence of Natural Language," *Trends in Ecology & Evolution* 21, no. 10 (2006): 555 ff.

[174] Lewontin, "Evolution of Cognition," 111.

[175] Lewontin, "Evolution of Cognition," 120. To ascertain this, one needs to find: first, contrasting groups, one that possesses the trait and one that does not; second, the differences in reproductive rates need to be substantial enough to be measured; and third, there must be evidence that a trait is genetically inherited, ibid.

collaboration such as anthill- or beehive-like human societies. Collaboration for survival is not only possible on moral terms.

In this context, too, we should stay mindful of the observation that just because a trait is used in certain ways does not mean that it evolved because of this function. The fact that morality makes possible certain sophisticated forms of collaboration based on solidarity and respect does not mean that it evolved because of this function. The mental abilities creating the possibility of moral thought might have any of the evolutionary origins mentioned and form, for instance, a side effect of an (overall) adaptive cognitive reorganization or an example of exaptation, a spandrel perhaps, which turned out to be a major influence on the modern human life form.

There is no reason to assume that any account of human moral cognition has to satisfy the constraints of the adaptationist paradigm, namely to be favored by natural selection as an isolated trait within the framework of functional trade-offs between different traits. It is entirely possible from the point of view of evolutionary theory that various elements of human cognition are structures that evolved without any clear adaptive advantage but still define the kind of creatures we are.

On all accounts, the paleoanthropological timeline quite clearly indicates a case of rapid evolutionary development that led to a fundamental cognitive reorganization of human beings – albeit perhaps caused by minor genetic change, probably of regulatory genes, which had far-reaching consequences. In comparison to the 1 million years that passed between the invention of Oldowan stone tools and the designing of Acheulean hand axes as a major technological innovation, the development of our current civilization in a mere 80,000 years has been fast indeed. As this rapid change *did* happen, there is a pretty clear answer to the question of whether it *could* have happened.[176] With modern human beings, nature simply *did* make a leap.[177]

[176] Tattersall, *Masters of the Planet*, 63: "The extraordinary human cognitive style is the product of a long biological history. From a non-symbolic, non-linguistic ancestor (itself the outcome of an enormously extended and eventful evolutionary process), there emerged our own unprecedented symbolic and linguistic species, an entity possessing a fully-fledged and entirely individuated consciousness of itself. This emergence was a singular event, one that involved bridging a profound cognitive discontinuity. For there is a *qualitative* difference here; and, based on any reasonable prediction from what preceded us, the only reason for believing that this gulf *could* be ever have been bridged, is that it was" (emphasis in original). The Pleistocene offered arguably favorable conditions for "the local fixation of genetic novelties and for speciation. Both of these are processes that in creatures such as hominids depend on physical isolation, and small population sizes," both features of the living conditions of hominids of that era, ibid. 149. On genetic evidence about a small founding African population, ibid. 194. Cf. Berwick and Chomsky, *Why Only Us*, 37. The current situation may have created reverse conditions: "Modern human populations have simply become too large and dense to witness the fixation of any significant genetic novelties that might in theory make us smarter and more protective of our own long-term interests," Tattersall, *Masters of the Planet*, 231.

[177] Tattersall, *Masters of the Planet*, 207: "[W]e evidently came by our unusual anatomical structure and capacities very recently: there is certainly no evidence to support the notion that we gradually became who we inherently are over an extended period, in either the physical or

The conclusion to be drawn regarding the evolution of whatever psychological capacities enable human morality is, then: As things stand, there are good reasons to believe that these cognitive capacities were part of the set of faculties with which modern humans embarked on their journey at least 80,000 years ago – faculties that define modern humans and have made their journey since then *human* history.

7.8 THE EVOLUTIONARY POSSIBILITY OF HUMAN GOODNESS

This leads to the crucial lesson for the cognitive interests of this inquiry: Evolutionary theory provides no discernible argument as to why the cognitive faculties yielding both the idea of human rights and the identified justificatory principles of this idea could *not* be the products of evolutionary processes. It may have a "wonderful reductionist appeal" to think that the cognitive abilities of modern humans are determined by the living conditions of early modern humans[178] – for example, yielding a "small-group morality." But this reductionism does not do justice to an evolutionary theory aware of the complexity of the human mind. Striking things evolved, such as the faculty to create a phenomenon as breathtaking as art,[179] and there is no reason to think that the ability for moral reasoning, motivation and emotion may not be a further example of an equally striking quality. There are no compelling grounds to restrict what is evolutionarily possible to such a "small-group morality" or any other form of psychological mechanisms that make the idea of human rights alien to human cognition.[180] Nothing in what we know about the history of the evolution of cognition, nor anything in evolutionary theory speaks against the possibility that human beings possess a sense of justice, evaluate genuine care and respect for others as morally good, regard just and morally good acts as obligatory and embed moral judgments in a rich, sometimes painful, sometimes ravishing world of moral emotions.

the intellectual sense. . . . [T]his suggests that the physical origin of our species lay in a short-term event of major developmental reorganization, even if that event was likely driven by a rather minor structural innovation on the DNA level."

178 Tattersall, *Masters of the Planet*, 228.

179 "Decorating the dank and dangerous depth of caves with fabulous animal images and a whole vocabulary of geometrical symbols is, to put it mildly, a rather unusual pursuit," Tattersall, *Masters of the Planet*, 205.

180 Buchanan and Powell's thesis, Buchanan and Powell, *The Evolution of Moral Progress*, that under out-group pressure an evolutionarily fixed, exclusivist, in-group morality thrives is thus not convincing. The supplementary thesis that (only) under favorable conditions without out-group threats and with an abundance of resources can the "luxury good" of inclusivist morality develop is not convincing either. There is a clear disconnect in social history between inclusivist morality and such socioeconomic circumstance. The human rights idea has convinced people under very dire conditions and motivated them, among others, to transform societies accordingly. One should not mistake favorable conditions for the social institutionalization of a normative idea for conditions necessary for individual humans to develop this idea.

The answer to our initial question on the origin of the cognitive capacities enabling the moral world of human beings is thus: There are many riddles hidden under the human skin, as Ahab despairingly realizes, and the attempt to hunt down the elusive essence of human existence can even lead to a self-destructive chase. But this much is clear: The scope of evolution is certainly wide enough to include cognitive mechanisms (whatever they turn out to be) that enable human beings to form notions of justice, concern and respect for others and, after a long development, ultimately articulate the remarkable idea of human rights.

8

The Mentalist Theory of Ethics and Law

When a man denominates another his enemy, his rival, his antagonist, his adversary, he is understood to speak the language of self-love, and to express sentiments, peculiar to himself, and arising from his particular circumstances and situation. But when he bestows on any man the epithets of vicious or odious or depraved, he then speaks another language, and expresses sentiments, in which he expects all his audience are to concur with him. He must here, therefore, depart from his private and particular situation, and must choose a point of view, common to him with others; he must move some universal principle of the human frame, and touch a string to which all mankind have an accord and symphony.

David Hume, *An Enquiry Concerning the Principles of Morals*

No doubt wickedness hath its rewards to distribute; but whoso wins in this devil's game must needs be baser, more cruel, more brutal than the order of this planet will allow for the multitude born of woman, the most of these carrying a form of conscience – a fear which is the shadow of justice, a pity which is the shadow of love – that hindereth from the prize of serene wickedness, itself difficult of maintenance in our composite flesh.

George Eliot, *Daniel Deronda*

8.1 A FRESH LOOK AT FRAMEWORKS OF MORALITY

Our discussion thus far has shown that a solid analytical theory of morality is crucial as a starting point for further theory-building about the nature and origin of moral cognition. Once this analytical theory of morality has been achieved, we can attempt to reconstruct the psychological mechanisms underpinning human moral judgment and investigate how they are acquired. There are no a priori constraints on the ways that human morality *could* be structured, and in particular no constraints that can be derived from the theory of evolution. What plausibly can be taken as constitutive of human morality is simply a matter of the evidence given. Therefore, any account of morality's constitutive elements is well-advised to take seriously the rich debates of moral philosophy, whose insights must inform plausible theories of morality.

In order to develop an analytical theory of morality, one needs to identify the building blocks of the human moral world. Such a theory must be based on an analysis of the practice and phenomenology of moral judgment. It needs to tell us what humans actually do when they exercise their moral understanding. One complication of such a study – and a major one at that – is the fact that moral judgments are intrinsically contested. Which moral judgments form the basis of theory-building? The views of a misogynist racist or those of a female Black Lives Matter activist?

One plausible way of proceeding is to look at qualified moral judgments. These judgments have to be "considered judgments," to borrow a useful term, in the sense that they are reflective, dispassionate judgments that are not skewed by interest, passion, errors of fact and so forth.[1] This methodological move has as its background the distinction between competence and performance, the faculty to perform a certain cognitive task and the actual performance of this task.[2] Humans have the competence to construct an image of the external world using the specific structures of their visual cognition. This does not mean that the effects of imbibing a certain amount of alcohol may not affect the functioning of this competence and make what is perceived appear strangely blurred. As this example shows, only indirect conclusions about an agent's competence can be drawn from their performance, because the performance is influenced by many other factors than just the structure of their competence. There is no doubt that the loud sound of techno music will influence the mathematical problem-solving capacity of people exposed to it. However, nobody would ever entertain the idea that techno music is of great relevance to studying the cognitive apparatus enabling humans to do math. The capacity for moral evaluation is another such competence usually possessed by human beings. Nevertheless, the performance of this capacity, the final evaluation of an action can be biased – for example, by the interests of the evaluating person. Consequently, such influences need to be factored out of the analysis if we are to properly study the cognitive competence in question, which is not an easy thing, particularly in empirical work.

1 Cf. on this matter John Rawls, A *Theory of Justice*, revised edition (Cambridge, MA: Harvard University Press, 1999), 42: "Thus in deciding which of our judgments to take into account we may reasonably select some and exclude others. For example, we can discard those judgments made with hesitation, or in which we have little confidence. Similarly, those given when we are upset or frightened, or when we stand to gain one way or the other can be left aside. All these judgments are likely to be erroneous or to be influenced by an excessive attention to our own interests. Considered judgments are simply those rendered under conditions favorable to the exercise of the sense of justice, and therefore in circumstances where the more common excuses and explanations for making a mistake do not obtain"; Mikhail, *Elements*, 51 ff.

2 Cf. for the (crucial) competence/performance distinction Noam Chomsky, *Aspects of the Theory of Syntax* (Cambridge, MA: MIT Press, 1965), 3 ff.; Mahlmann, *Rationalismus*, 73 f.; Mikhail, *Elements*, 51 ff.

This crucial issue is sometimes overlooked in recent moral psychology studies, which claim to be studying human moral competence, but in fact to a surprisingly large degree are concerned with performance problems, such as the skewing of moral judgment by nonmoral factors, from smells[3] to the feeling of being controlled.[4] Another methodological approach to dealing with the contested nature of moral judgment is to look at highly idealized and often artificial cases that appear to be as little politically and culturally loaded as possible.[5] By contrast, studying the human moral faculty by looking at opinions about issues as contested and ideologically charged as abortion, for example, is a methodological nonstarter.

One preliminary result of our discussions so far has been the observation that some concepts of morality in contemporary debates are too narrow, both as to the substantive material principles of morality and as to the subjects of moral concern. In particular, morality is neither an ultimately selfish enterprise seeking to reap the profits of in-group cooperation, nor is it simply a set of preferences or aversions. The analysis below will flesh this out in more detail.

One theoretical approach that explains how these findings may fit into a theory of moral cognition is the so-called mentalist approach to ethics and law. A mentalist model of moral cognition investigates the question of whether it is possible to identify generative principles of moral judgment specific to human moral cognition that are universal and uniform across the species – a universal moral grammar, if you will, to use a metaphor sometimes employed to capture the basic intuition of this approach.[6] The mentalist model has been a very influential research paradigm in

3 Simone Schnall et al., "Disgust as Embodied Moral Judgement," *Personality and Social Psychology Bulletin* 34, no. 8 (2008): 1096 ff. Cf. Haidt for further examples, Haidt, *Righteous Mind*, 35 ff.

4 Cf. Kevin J. Haley and Daniel M. T. Fessler, "Nobody's Watching? Subtle Cues Affect Generosity in an Anonymous Economic Game," *Evolution and Human Behaviour* 26 (2005): 245 ff.

5 Cf. Mikhail, *Elements*, 56 ff.; Mahlmann, *Rationalismus*, 107.

6 Cf. e.g. Noam Chomsky, *Language and Problems of Knowledge* (Cambridge, MA: MIT Press, 1988), 152; Matthias Mahlmann and John Mikhail, "Cognitive Science, Ethics and Law," in *Epistemology and Ontology*, ed. Zenon Bankowski (Stuttgart: Franz Steiner Verlag, 2005), 95 ff.; John Mikhail, "Rawls' Linguistic Analogy: A Study of the 'Generative Grammar' Model of Moral Theory Described by John Rawls in *A Theory of Justice*," PhD dissertation, Cornell University, 2000; Mikhail, *Elements*; John Mikhail, "Chomsky and Moral Philosophy," in *The Cambridge Companion to Chomsky*, 2nd edition, ed. James McGilvray (Cambridge: Cambridge University Press, 2017); Mahlmann, *Rationalismus*; Mahlmann, "Ethics," 577 ff.; Gilbert Harman, "Using a Linguistic Analogy to Study Morality," in *Moral Psychology, Vol. 1: The Evolution of Morality*, ed. Walter Sinnott-Armstrong (Cambridge, MA: MIT Press, 2008), 345 ff.; Erica Roedder and Gilbert Harman, "Linguistics and Moral Theory," in *The Moral Psychology Handbook*, ed. John M. Doris (Oxford: Oxford University Press, 2010), 273 ff.; Ray Jackendoff, *Language, Consciousness, Culture: Essays on Mental Structure* (Cambridge, MA: MIT Press, 2007), 277 ff.; Susan Dwyer, "Moral Competence," in *Philosophy and Linguistics*, eds. Kumiko Murusagi and Robert Stainton (New York: Routledge, 1999), 169 ff.; Marc Hauser, *Moral Minds* (New York: Harper Collins, 2006). For a critique, cf. Pardo and Patterson, *Minds, Brains, and the Law*, 12 ff., 63 ff., especially because of the (externalist)

other domains of the theory of mind – for example, in the study of language – stirring many intense controversies and debates.[7] The thrust of the mentalist argument echoes a long tradition of thought on moral understanding – after all, the belief that human beings are endowed with a particular faculty of moral evaluation has been one of the thoughts guiding moral philosophy ever since antiquity.

8.2 SOME PROPERTIES OF MORAL COGNITION

8.2.1 *The Cognitive Space of Morality*

A close and careful look at the phenomenology of morality gives rise to some important observations.[8] One is that something like a moral experience exists at all. Humans operate naturally within a mental space that has a normative dimension. There is a specific mental domain of morality, a qualitatively distinguished element of conscious thought, an introspectively accessible, distinctive, intuited, subjectively experienced aspect of our mental life, a *qualia*, as it is often said, or – to use standard understandings of this term – a certain phenomenal character of certain forms of experience. The availability of such a cognitive domain is not self-evident; rather, this domain represents an empirical property of the human mind that not all organisms share. Human beings do not perceive ultrasound, but bats do. Human beings see the world in the distinct colors of morality, but bats do not. This cognitive domain does not concern a side issue but defines nothing less than an element central to the identity of the human species: the moral dimension of human lives. Its existence consequently merits close attention.

A further interesting observation concerns the fact that there is a highly and intricately qualified limited set of possible objects of moral evaluation. This set already restricts the kinds of morality that are possible. The dropping of an apple from a tree into the hands of a hungry person is not a virtuous action on the tree's part. Or, as Hume observed: "A young tree, which over-tops and destroys its parent, stands in all the same relations with Nero, when he murdered Agrippina," but does not commit matricide.[9] This is because agency is a precondition for the moral evaluation of certain events in the world. If these events cannot be attributed to agents, questions of moral evaluation do not arise.[10]

thesis that there can be (on conceptual grounds) no unconscious rule-following. On Wittgenstein's concept of the rules underlying this argument and its critique, Mahlmann, *Rationalismus*, 121 ff.

7 Cf. Chomsky, *Aspects of a Theory of Syntax*; Noam Chomsky, *The Minimalist Program* (Cambridge, MA: MIT Press, 1995); Noam Chomsky, *New Horizons in the Study of Language and Mind* (Cambridge: Cambridge University Press, 2000).

8 Cf. Mahlmann, *Rechtsphilosophie und Rechtstheorie*, 374 ff.

9 Hume, "Enquiry Concerning the Principles of Morals," 293.

10 This does not mean that inanimate things have not been taken as agents – cf. Xerxes' whipping of the sea to punish the sea for destroying his bridges, Herodotus, *Histories*, 7.35.

Moreover, placing your pen gracefully on your desk cannot be the possible object of moral evaluation either (except under very particular circumstances), even though an agent performs this act. However, this act is a possible object of aesthetic evaluation – another distinctive element of human experience.[11] Kicking a ball so as to feel like Dzsenifer Marozsán for a few precious seconds is morally very different from kicking a defender or a dog that is in your way. A precondition of moral evaluation is thus – to put it very roughly – something like volitionally controlled or controllable bodily actions or omissions of agents with consequences for the well-being of sentient beings and other qualified objects of moral concern; intentions concerning such actions or omissions; states of affairs resulting from such intentions, actions and omissions; or qualified emotions directed at the well-being of others.[12]

8.2.2 *Principles of Morality*

As we already have seen, in analyses of morality it is particularly important to distinguish *behavior* and motivational *inclinations* to behavior from the *moral evaluation* of this behavior and the intentions underlying it. Concrete behavior, including what is called prosocial behavior, and the inclination or preference for such behavior are one thing, the reflexive appraisal of this behavior, inclination or preference with deontic dimensions quite another. Only the latter falls within the proper realm of morality and ethics.[13]

If we turn to the content of morality and carefully analyze some qualified (only seemingly simply structured) considered judgments of the kind described above, we see that these judgments seem to be guided by principles of egalitarian justice and altruism across a wide range of cases. That it is just to distribute party favors equally to the young guests of a child's birthday party seems as uncontroversial as that it is a morally good deed to help prevent starvation in Yemen.[14] Respect for others is a further important principle. This state of affairs is not particularly surprising, as all of these principles run through the history of ideas, too, as the core of morality, across cultures and millennia, albeit accompanied throughout by influential skeptical voices from Thrasymachus to Nietzsche and beyond, who have argued (with greater

[11] On the classical distinction between the distinct and potentially contradictory moral and aesthetical evaluation, Kant, *Kritik der praktischen Vernunft*, 204 f.

[12] Intricate problems arise in this area. Actions that have an effect for objects of art or the environment represent a matter of complex debate, for example. The latter in particular are of great practical concern. In both areas, ethical principles matter. Another problem is posed by virtues that are not other-regarding. A fuller statement of the possible objects of moral evaluation would need to take account of these special cases, refining the basic principles stated here.

[13] This point is relevant, for example, to the question of "animal morality," cf. Chapter 7. Prosocial behavior of nonhuman animals does not in itself constitute morality in the sense understood here. On the question of a possible continuum and differences between humans and (nonhuman) animals, e.g. John Mikhail, "Any Animal Whatever? Harmful Battery and Its Elements as Building Blocks of Moral Cognition," *Ethics* 124 (2014): 750 ff.

[14] Cf. for some remarks Mahlmann, *Rechtsphilosophie und Rechtstheorie*, 374 ff.

or lesser philosophical sophistication) that morality has no content that lends itself to rational reconstruction and that apparently core normative concepts do not mean anything at all.[15]

Substantial empirical work carried out in recent years points in the same direction, supporting the observation that certain identifiable elements – more precisely, egalitarian and altruistic principles – seem to play an important role in the evaluation of the justness and goodness of actions, despite some theoretical limits of parts of this research that already have been reviewed above.[16] Other frontiers of research include the prohibition of the instrumentalization of human beings that plausibly lies at the heart of a proper analysis of the extensively empirically researched trolley problems and distinctions between different subjective cognitive and volitional attitudes towards potential actions, including direct and oblique intentions and their relevance for human moral evaluation.[17]

If we analyze the empirical work on justice and basic uncontroversial judgments about the justice and injustice of intentions, actions and states of affairs and do not forget what the struggles of social history seem to suggest about ideas of justice, then differentiated principles of equality as already discussed above[18] seem to have considerable explanatory power to account for many patterns of moral evaluation. We have said that a just distribution demands proportional equality between the value of the specific criterion of distribution reasonably related to a particular sphere of distribution on the one hand and the amount of the good distributed on the other. Other normative demands concern the equal treatment of persons, restitution and respect for the equal worth of each human being – as indicated, the ultimate yardstick of just treatment and a just state of affairs. Such egalitarian principles match the empirically identified patterns of moral evaluation recalled in this study, including standard examples such as the ultimatum or dictator game, the many debates about the proper interpretation of these findings notwithstanding.[19] The same also holds for other clues to the moral world in which human beings live beyond experimental data, not least social history and its many egalitarian struggles, some of which we have recalled. It should be noted that a main bone of contention in these political struggles was not the

[15] Cf. for just two more recent examples Kelsen's attempt to show the emptiness of concepts of justice, Hans Kelsen, "Das Problem der Gerechtigkeit," in Hans Kelsen, *Reine Rechtslehre* (Vienna: Deuticke, 1960), 357 ff., or Luhmann's idea that justice is a "contingency formula" (*Kontingenzformel*) whose function is to hide that law is not based on a notion of material legitimacy because no such legitimacy exists, Luhmann, *Recht der Gesellschaft*, 235.

[16] Cf. Chapter 6.

[17] Cf. for instance Edmond Awad et al., "Universals and Variations in Moral Decisions Made in 42 Countries by 70 000 Participants," Proceedings of the National Academy of Sciences 117, no. 5 (2020): 2332–7, concluding that the observed patterns (bystander: permissible; footbridge: impermissible) are "best explained by basic cognitive processes rather than cultural norms," 2332. Cf. Chapter 6.

[18] Cf. Chapter 5. Note again that the principles of justice also are foundational for notions of substantial equality.

[19] These results indicate, uncontroversially, egalitarian intuitions and an interest in maintaining principles of just distribution for their own sake. On this and other examples, cf. Chapter 6.

principle that equals ought to be treated equally, but the criteria of distribution and who and what actually fulfill these criteria. Regarding rights, for instance, an important question in history was whether fundamental rights are distributed in a society on the basis of the bearer's humanity or some other criterion (say, aristocratic birth) and who fulfills this criterion (for instance, whether women are fully human or some kind of deficient being and thus not entitled to a full set of fundamental rights). If we pay due attention to such factors, the core of the human quest for justice becomes considerably more transparent.

To achieve sufficient explanatory depth, however, the analysis of these empirical observations needs to remain aware of the distinction between a moral competence and its actual use, the plurality of motivational factors influencing human action, including nonmoral interests and the complex structure of moral judgments, with their cognitive, volitional and emotional components (to be discussed in more detail below), which are not reducible, for example, to preferences or aversions.

Whether there is such a thing as genuinely other-regarding altruistic behavior or whether any action beneficial to others is ultimately motivated by some (albeit perhaps refined and hidden) self-interest of the agent is one of the traditional questions of practical philosophy.[20] As in the case of justice, this is a huge debate that today is enriched by interesting empirical work.[21] In this context, it is important, too, to rely on a sufficiently complex theory of morality, in particular to distinguish between actual behavior and considered evaluation and thus distinguish the question of whether people are *in fact acting* because of a genuinely altruistic motivation from the question of whether genuine altruism is the precondition for *evaluating* something as morally good. There is not much reason to believe that people generally excel in altruistic behavior. However, this observation tells us nothing about the principles that guide moral judgment – for example, when evaluating the selfish behavior prevalent around us (including our own).[22] Concerning these

[20] Hume, "Enquiry Concerning the Principles of Morals," 212 ff., went to considerable length to refute the selfishness hypothesis, clearly influenced by the arguments of Joseph Butler, "Fifteen Sermons," in *The Works of Joseph Butler*, Vol. II, ed. William Ewart Gladstone (Oxford: Clarendon Press, 1896), 35 ff., 185 ff., or Francis Hutchinson, *An Inquiry into the Original of Our Ideas of Beauty and Virtue*, ed. Wolfgang Leidhold (New York: Garland Publishing, 1971), 125 ff.

[21] Cf. the empirical research on genuinely altruistic motivation and action, summarized in C. Daniel Batson, *Altruism in Humans* (Oxford: Oxford University Press: 2011); C. Daniel Batson, *A Scientific Search for Altruism: Do We Care Only About Ourselves?* (Oxford: Oxford University Press, 2019).

[22] The incongruence of justified moral principles and behavior is not a new observation, cf. Thomas Nagel, *The Possibility of Altruism* (Oxford: Clarendon Press, 1970), 146: "To say that altruism and morality are possible in virtue of something basic to human nature is not to say that men are basically good. Men are basically complicated; how good they are depends on whether certain conceptions and ways of thinking have achieved dominance, a dominance which is precarious in any case. The manner in which human beings have conducted themselves so far does not encourage optimism about the moral future of the species."

principles of evaluation, there are reasons to think that such a genuinely altruistic motivation is in fact a core element of moral evaluation. More precisely, it seems plausible to assume that an action is morally good if it is performed with the direct intention (or purpose), not only the oblique intention (or knowledge), to foster the well-being of the patient. If this is so, it is irrelevant for the moral evaluation whether or not the fostering of the interests of the agent is – at the same time – a directly intended or foreseen (obliquely intended) consequence of the action and forms a second reason for action in a bundle of motives. The direct intention to foster the well-being of the patient of the action appears to be a necessary condition of morally good action.[23]

To illustrate the meaning of this principle, it is useful to look at one of the most refined versions of ethical egoism. This form of egoism holds that altruistic behavior is ultimately motivated by the desire to experience the satisfaction of having acted in a morally appropriate manner. This argument makes an important point, namely that moral action does indeed provide some particular form of satisfaction for the agent and that agents are certainly often aware of this. In addition, acting immorally can have unpleasant effects, too, such as feelings of shame. These observations do not settle the issue, however. Consider the following case: Pawel helps Mio, thinking: "I do not care for this person and her well-being at all (what a silly person she is, in fact!), it just happens (unfortunately) that I have to do something for her in order to reap the sweet fruit I really desire, namely to feel the satisfaction of being a truly nice person!" Is this really a morally laudable deed? If doubts arise about the moral praiseworthiness of an action with such an intention, it seems to confirm the analysis above. This is because the Pawel has only an oblique intention to help the other person and not the direct intention to be beneficial to her: His direct intention is to satisfy one of his own personal desires, and helping the other person is only a (perhaps even unwelcome) means to achieve that end.[24]

[23] Cf. Mahlmann, *Rechtsphilosophie und Rechtstheorie*, 375 ff. It is assumed that the evaluation of the action is dependent on the nature of the underlying intention. Cf. for the same criteria to provide a *definition of altruism*, Batson, *A Scientific Search for Altruism*, 22 ff. This definition provides an important clarification. The thesis pursued here is that one can take one step further: These criteria are understood as key to evaluating an intention or action as morally good, and thus to ascribe a deontic status to them, not only to identify them as altruistic.

[24] This analysis can be buttressed by the observable asymmetry between responsibility for a foreseen bad side effect and the praiseworthiness of a foreseen good side effect: Only action with the purpose of bringing about a good side effect is morally praiseworthy, not an action with a merely foreseen but not intended good side effect. This asymmetry is traditionally framed in terms of intentions: Bad side effects are taken as intentional, good side effects as unintentional, cf. Joshua Knobe, "Intentional Action and Side Effects in Ordinary Language," *Analysis* 63, no. 3 (2003): 190 ff. Cf. Batson, *A Scientific Search for Altruism*, 41 ff., on sets of experiments that exclude other intentions than empathy-based altruism as motivation for certain other-regarding behaviors. These alternative motivations include the egoistic desire to remove emphatic concern, avoiding guilt, the desire for esteem-enhancing reward, sadness relief, the pleasure of emphatic joy and self–other merging. This is an important result. However, these experiments concern motivation not evaluation and do not include motivations to act because

Another point is perhaps worth noting: Justice seems to be something like a limiting condition of morally good action. There are reasons to believe that there is no morally good intention that violates principles of justice. If Pawel, for instance, helps three out of four people in need, not because he cannot help them all, but just because he feels like excluding one person on a whim, this is not a morally good action, despite his direct intention to help the other three, because it violates principles of equal treatment.

A third principle is respect for human beings. Respect in a moral sense must be distinguished from admiration for achievements of other kinds – for instance, for a skillful free kick right into the corner of the goal. Unlike admiration of this kind, respect in a moral sense has prescriptive consequences: One ought to behave towards other human beings in certain ways. One important element is to treat them as ends-in-themselves and not only as means to achieve other purposes, to once again use the Kantian version of an ancient idea. Evidently, reducing somebody to a means of some ulterior purpose degrades this person. As we saw when discussing the trolley problem, substantial empirical data suggest that people do in fact apply this principle when evaluating certain morally salient situations: The recorded moral evaluations of the footbridge scenario and its most promising analysis show that these evaluations are best explained by an operative principle demanding that people not be instrumentalized based on a structural means/ends distinction.[25]

Furthermore, there are other forms of disrespect for human beings that do not instrumentalize them: Regularly flooding a prison cell with feces, not to torture the inmate but simply due to negligence concerning the sanitary conditions of inmates, is an illuminating example of this from constitutional case law.[26]

The importance of recognition as a being of equal worth has rightly been flagged as a key element of social struggles:[27] These struggles are not only about bread-and-butter issues, but also about exploited and degraded groups of people's demand to be respected as human beings. This is a central ethical and political dimension in the fight against slavery, old and new, and in the fight against the subjugation and exploitation of women. The same holds for struggles for the emancipation of the working classes, which likewise were not only about material concerns like decent wages, but also about respect for the humanity of workers, who demanded (and indeed still demand) that they not be reduced to beasts of burden.

of a perceived moral obligation. A full analysis of morality has to account for these elements of human moral judgment, too.

[25] Cf. Chapter 7.

[26] BVerfG: Verfassungsgebot menschenwürdiger Haftbedingungen (March 16, 1993), *Neue Juristische Wochenschrift* 1993, 3190.

[27] Bloch, *Naturrecht und menschliche Würde*; Axel Honneth, *Der Kampf um Anerkennung* (Frankfurt am Main: Suhrkamp, 1992).

These findings help us to tackle some of the problems that the supervenience of moral judgments over facts poses.[28] They help us to identify the principles that determine, first, the moral evaluation and normative consequences of moral judgments that are triggered by certain facts (e.g. by the fact of a direct intention to harm somebody) and thus to determine *how* moral judgments supervene over facts (not just that they do) and, second, which facts are morally relevant in the first place (e.g. that the agents' intentions to act matter morally but not their haircuts). These tentatively outlined principles, which are obviously in need of much refinement, are abstract but not without meaningful content, as can be exemplified by the justification of human rights, as we have seen.[29] To recall: The principles underlying the attribution of rights to persons have to be equal for all potential rights-bearers. It would, for example, be unjust to let some people enjoy fundamental rights because of their personhood and deny these rights to others because for them the color of their skin (and not their personhood) is taken to be relevant. In addition, the reasonable – more precisely, the only reasonable – criterion for the attribution of rights is a person's humanity. As a just system of rights has to preserve a relation of equality between the value of this criterion and the distribution of rights, and as all humans are equal in their humanity, only a system of equal rights is consequently a just system of rights. The theories of human rights that imply a diminishing humanity of older people and, correspondingly, a diminishing set of protected rights, which may seem to be at odds with this principle, actually confirm it: These theories simply entertain the (implausible) idea that the humanity of elderly people diminishes, even though the elderly, of course, enjoy the same humanity and consequently the same rights as every other human being – no minor point, as the Covid-19 pandemic has reminded us.

Moreover, fostering the enjoyment of rights is morally good. Accordingly, as has been said before, given the importance of the goods that rights protect and the significance of the rights themselves, the promotion of rights is a prima facie obligation of human solidarity. The theory of the justification of human rights has shown, too, that one of its building blocks is respect for human beings, today widely understood as grounded on their dignity. In sum, justice, the altruism of solidarity and respect for the worth of others take us a long way when trying to identify the normative principles that are key to the justification of human rights.

28 Cf. e.g. Henry Sidgwick, *The Methods of Ethics*, reprint of the 7th edition, 1907 (Indianapolis, IN: Hackett, 1981), 208; Richard Mervyn Hare, *The Language of Morals* (Oxford: Clarendon Press, 1952), 80 ff.

29 Another example showing that these principles are not meaningless is that, for example, Rawls' principles of justice can be derived from them: The first principle of universal freedom and the principle of equal access to office are principles of equally distributed goods, namely freedom and offices. The difference principle is a prudential modification of an egalitarian distribution of material goods in a society.

8.2.3 *Basic Harms, Human Rights and the "Seeds of a Collective Conscience"*

Human rights play an important role in John Mikhail's pioneering work on the mentalist framework of ethics and law.[30] His reconstruction of a set of principles of a "universal jurisprudence" based on common moral precepts that are "the seeds of a collective conscience"[31] includes reflections on human rights that constitute some of the most advanced thought on the topic of our inquiry. His main thesis is that the prohibition of basic wrongs that is an element of the inborn structures of human moral cognition is mirrored in fundamental human rights norms.[32] The universal moral grammar "implies that human beings possess tacit or implicit knowledge of specific, human rights-related norms."[33] The small set of principles that guide human moral judgments include the prohibition of intentional battery, the prohibition of intentional homicide, the rescue principle and the principle of double effect.[34] Of particular importance for human rights are the prohibitions of intentional battery and homicide, which are "lesser included offenses of a wide range of human rights abuses, including murder, extermination, deportation, torture, rape, genocide, and other crimes against humanity."[35] Human rights protect against a set of "core human wrongs" like battery and other torts, "although they by no means exhaust these violations."[36] A "clear conceptual and empirical bridge between moral grammar and human rights can be built" because "[t]hese basic wrongs and, in particular, the tort of harmful battery likewise supply the basic perceptual and cognitive tasks of many influential research programs in the cognitive science of morality."[37] Mikhail's work on the trolley problems is itself an outstanding example of this.[38]

These remarks lead to three questions that can be addressed fruitfully in the light of the results of our analysis.

The first is the question of foundational principles. Our analysis suggests that the principles of justice, altruism and respect that are the normative core of our normative theory of human rights are consistent with Mikhail's analysis but seem to have additional explanatory power. As indicated, the obligation to foster the well-being of others is the flipside of the coin of the prohibition to inflict harm – the minimum you can do for others is not to harm them, we said. It is the normative core of demands for mutual support and solidarity as well. Moreover, human rights are not just about the prohibition of specific wrongs, but also about the allocation of

30 Mikhail, *Moral Grammar and Human Rights*, 161 ff.
31 Mikhail, *Moral Grammar and Human Rights*, 170.
32 Mikhail, *Moral Grammar and Human Rights*, 173 ff.
33 Mikhail, *Moral Grammar and Human Rights*, 173.
34 Mikhail, *Moral Grammar and Human Rights*, 180.
35 Mikhail, *Moral Grammar and Human Rights*, 184.
36 Mikhail, *Moral Grammar and Human Rights*, 196.
37 Mikhail, *Moral Grammar and Human Rights*, 196.
38 Mikhail, *Elements*.

goods, such as normatively protected spheres of liberty. Such an order of freedom presupposes yardsticks for the justified allocation of such goods – in our analysis, for instance, principles of justice. This is important not least for ascertaining the justified limitations of human rights – for instance, when rights of different persons collide. Moreover, human rights only make sense, as we have seen, if there are reasons to believe that the beings who enjoy them have some kind of worth that justifies protecting these beings' goods. Principles of human worth, today spelled out in human rights ethics and law as human dignity, are therefore likewise key to the understanding of human rights. These principles and their normative consequences, such as the principle of noninstrumentalization, are arguably also key to the solution of the trolley problems.

The second question asks why goods are guaranteed by rights and not some other means in the first place. If normative means to protect human goods are employed (and not just sheer force), why are duties and prohibitions not enough? After all, influential theories argue for the importance of systems of duty and their superiority at least in some respects to systems of rights.[39] Our analysis has suggested (apart from the analytical connection of duties and rights) that normative principles like justice and altruism provide the answer, as these principles give rise to the normative phenomenon of rights that have the important function of normatively empowering people, turning them from patients of others' obligations to subjects of justified claims.

The third issue is the question of construction. Our analysis has suggested that a process of complex construction is necessary to transform concrete, principled moral judgments about moral claims into explicit, critically reflected human rights in ethics and law, a process that spanned thousands of years. This process includes only seemingly straightforward tasks like the generalization, universalization and objectification of the abstract core content of particular moral judgments. Moreover, human rights systems are highly selective. To account for this selectivity and its justification, among other things, a theory of human goods is essential. The importance of a political theory of human rights has been underlined in our inquiry as well. It is essential to include these complex issues in a theoretical account of the link between human moral cognition and the idea of explicit human rights in ethics and law.[40]

8.2.4 *Volitional Consequences of Moral Judgment*

A further important element of an analysis of morality is that human moral judgment has volitional consequences: A moral evaluation does not yield information

[39] Cf. Chapter 1.

[40] A mentalist theory of ethics of law is, thus, not about the mechanical application of unchangeable rules of fully explicit moralities, as Hanno Sauer, *Moral Judgements as Educated Intuitions* (Cambridge, MA: MIT Press, 2017), 41 ff. assumes. It is about clarifying the cognitive resources necessary to form concrete sets of moral principles.

about a fact of the world like a descriptive proposition, but has prescriptive content.[41] Saying "X is just" is different from saying "X is a table," and an important element of this difference is that a moral judgment tells us how we ought to act. This can have direct volitional consequences: An ought creates a motive for action for agents who are evaluating their options for acting.[42] Their will is *bound* to form certain intentions to act, to use a metaphor for a common introspectively accessible internal state of an agent. Everybody knows how it feels when you come to the conclusion that you *ought* to hand in the smartphone you have found lying on the ground.

If an observer evaluates not his own options for action but the intention or action of another agent, moral judgments still provide information on how one ought to act. For example, they tell the observer how the observed agent ought to act if the observed agent is in a position to act as a person is obligated to act in the particular situation in question – for instance, to hand in the smartphone found, even though the observer himself is not in this position.

A moral judgment can also remain abstract in the sense that there is nobody currently in a position to act accordingly. "One should hand in the valuables of others one has found" is a meaningful statement even if all valuables on the planet are safely in their owners' pockets. Moral judgment then tells us what one ought to do if the conditions for this obligation obtain.

The fact that a normative statement is about an obligation, a permission or a prescription – in short, about a moral ought that provides a motivation to act – does not mean that the obligation necessarily forms the predominant, decisive, let alone only motivation to act. To be sure, human motivation encompasses many other inclinations that have great power and have nothing to do with moral considerations. Human history is to a large extent the history of greed and the pursuit of power, not the history of moral niceties. The claim is thus that only an element – and perhaps a precious element – of human moral motivation derives from moral insight.[43]

The prescriptive content of a moral judgment can – and this is important for our particular topic – constitute a *right*.[44] If an act is just, the agent has an obligation to

[41] Mahlmann, "Ethics," 599 ff.

[42] Cf. for a concise statement Richard Price, *A Review of the Principal Questions in Morals*, ed. David Daiches Raphael (Oxford: Clarendon Press, 1948), 186: "When we are conscious that an action is *fit* to be done, or that it *ought* to be done, it is not conceivable that we can remain *uninfluenced*, or want a *motive* to action" (emphasis in original). On the background debate of motivational externalists and internalists, e.g. Hare, *The Language of Morals*, 20, 30, 169, 197; Richard Mervyn Hare, *Moral Thinking: Its Levels, Methods and Point* (Oxford: Clarendon Press, 1982), 23; David Owen Brink, *Moral Realism and the Foundations of Ethics* (Cambridge: Cambridge University Press, 1989), 39; Gilbert Harman, *Explaining Value: And Other Essays in Moral Philosophy* (Oxford: Oxford University Press, 2000), 30; Philippa Foot, *Virtues and Vices and Other Essays in Moral Philosophy* (Oxford: Oxford University Press, 1978), 148; John Leslie Mackie, *Ethics: Inventing Right and Wrong* (London: Penguin Books, 1977), 40.

[43] Cf. Mahlmann, *Rationalismus*, 158 ff.; Mikhail, *Moral Grammar and Human Rights*, 169 ff.

[44] Cf. above the analysis of rights and the connection of duties and (claim-)rights. On the relation of moral judgment and rights, cf. Mikhail, *Elements*, 295 ff.; Mikhail, *Moral Grammar and*

act justly and the patient has a right to that action: In the limited time available to comment and set things in intellectual order after an abysmal lecture on the foundation of human rights by a legal theoretician from Zürich, every discussant has the right to the same amount of time because this is a just distribution of this scarce good. The chair of the discussion has the obligation to ensure this fair distribution of time – for example, by restraining the loquacious Swiss theoretician's vacuous responses. The connection between obligation and right holds for an obligation stemming from a duty to benefit somebody, too, unless it is a supererogatory action: Not only is there an obligation to pick up your phone to call an ambulance if somebody in front of you collapses, but the person who has collapsed has a right that you do (at least) this. The obligation to respect others is the correlative of others' right to be respected: Respect is not an act of grace, but means acting in a way to which others have a claim.

8.2.5 *Questions of Metaethics and the World of Moral Emotions*

The principles of justice and altruism that guide reflexive evaluation have cognitive content. Whether or not there is (for example) a relation of equality between patients of actions or between a criterion of distribution and the good distributed in the sense explained above is not felt physically in the same way that cold or heat are, for example, but stems from a complex structural analysis[45] of the evaluated act that eventually predicates a relation of equality or its absence and thus constitutes a judgment with cognitive content. The same is true for other structural elements of the action that play a role for moral evaluation, such as agency, the properties of patients of the action (e.g. whether they are sentient or not) and intentions and their kind (direct or oblique) and object. The presence of these elements is not physically felt either, but is ascertained by a judgment with cognitive content – the obtaining of a direct intention to benefit somebody, for instance.

As we already have seen, this does not mean that the relevance of moral sentiments is diminished. They are evidently crucial to the impact of morality on a human life. There may even be emotions that are "geological upheavals" of moral thought.[46] Nor is the importance denied that certain emotions have for the design of law, not least for the skeptical project of constitutionalism.[47] However, insofar as they are moral emotions, these emotions are not simply emotions relevant for ethics

Human Rights, 160 ff.; Matthias Mahlmann, "The Cognitive Foundations of Law," in *Foundations of Law*, ed. Hubert Rottleuthner (Dordrecht: Springer, 2005), 75 ff.; Mahlmann, *Grundrechtstheorie*, 517 ff.

45 Cf. the discussion of the trolley cases in Mikhail, *Elements*, 77 ff. for an example of how complex such analysis is.

46 To use the Proust metaphor of Martha Nussbaum, *Upheavals of Thought* (Cambridge: Cambridge University Press, 2001), 1.

47 Cf. András Sajó, *Constitutional Sentiments* (New Haven, CT: Yale University Press, 2011), not least on fear. Mortimer Sellers, "Law, Reason, Emotion," in *Law, Reason, Emotion*, ed.

(like the fear of tyrants) but are the *consequence* of moral judgment with the cognitive content just identified, and thus do not *constitute* moral judgment. The moral evaluation based on the obtaining of the necessary elements of a good or just intention or action is the precondition for the experience of moral emotions – for instance, the unequal treatment of a person who is equal in the relevant respects in question is the precondition for the feeling of indignation about injustice. If there is no unequal treatment of equals, we will not feel moral indignation because of an injustice.

In light of this observation, traditional arguments about the constitutive role played by human moral sentiment in moral evaluation fail to convince because they are not precise enough. Hume wrote:

> If any material circumstance be yet unknown or doubtful, we must first employ our inquiry or intellectual faculties to assure us of it; and must suspend for a time all moral decision or sentiment. While we are ignorant whether a man were aggressor or not, how can we determine whether the person who killed him be criminal or innocent? But after every circumstance, every relation is known, the understanding has no further room to operate, nor any object on which it could employ itself. The approbation or blame, which then ensues, cannot be the work of the judgement, but of the heart; and is not a speculative proposition or affirmation, but an active feeling or sentiment.[48]

Our argument so far indicates that two elements of the structure of moral evaluation are missing from Hume's account. Hume rightly emphasizes the importance of ascertaining the facts of a case to be evaluated. What he does not address, however, is the structural analysis of the intention or action that determines the outcome of the evaluation – for example, the analysis of whether Norbert killed another person with the direct intention to do so for personal gain or whether he did so to defend himself against an aggressor. We have already clarified that this analysis is not a sentiment, but a judgment with cognitive content. The second missing element is the evaluation that ensues on the basis of this analysis – for example, that killing a person for personal gain is (deeply) immoral. This evaluation assigns a deontic status (good/bad, just/unjust) to an intention or action. This is the propositional content of statements such as "Murder is a heinous crime." The moral judgment causes and is accompanied by a sentiment – for instance, the feeling of abhorrence towards murder for gain. The feeling of abhorrence does not constitute the entirety of the evaluation of murder for gain, however.

Interestingly, Hume rightly draws our attention to agency as a structural precondition of evaluating something as morally right or wrong. In Hume's example of the young tree outstripping and eventually overwhelming and killing its parent, the

Mortimer Sellers (Cambridge: Cambridge University Press, 2007), 11 ff. for some general comments.

48 Hume, "Enquiry Concerning the Principles of Morals," 290.

tree's growth does not elicit any moral feeling because a precondition of moral evaluation, agency, is not fulfilled.[49] Once again, whether or not a tree is an agent is not felt in the same way as our skin feels a cold breeze. Rather, any such conclusion is a statement about a complex state of affairs constituting agency (responsible, spontaneous beginning of new chains of causation, authorship of intentions to act and of actions, etc.). This cannot be reconciled with simply identifying moral judgment with sentiment. There certainly are moral sentiments, but they depend on such a prior structural analysis of the eliciting situations, including of criteria such as agency, and a consequent moral evaluation.

A central concern for Hume and the many thinkers following in his footsteps is to explain moral motivation. How could a judgment of reason cause a motivation to act? A proposition stating a matter of fact has no motivational impact. "There is a table" is, even if true, motivationally neutral, as we clarified in the preceding section. Only sentiment, it thus seems, can cause people to act. There is, however, a third path beyond the traditional but not exhaustive dichotomy of moral judgment as an act of reason and as sentiment. This third path offers the key to the problem: The motivational effects of moral judgments we highlighted above are crucial in this respect. Moral evaluation has a direct motivational effect, we said, because of its *prescriptive* content. Moral evaluation is not limited to stating the deontic status of an intention or action. It does not merely inform us about this status like a proposition about a fact of the world. Agents do not react to moral judgments in the same way they react to factual propositions. They do not say after a moral judgment, "Oh, this is unjust, how interesting!" in the same way they may observe, following some scrutiny, "Oh, this stone is in fact blue, how interesting!" Moral evaluation gives rises to a moral *ought*, and this ought alone can motivate people to act: It binds the human will, to use this basic metaphor. This is very much an everyday experience. Take the lost object example: You see a wallet that somebody has lost lying in the street. You ask yourself whether you should pocket the money in it. You look around – nobody is watching you. Do you do it? Perhaps you do not, because you have come to the conclusion that taking the money would harm the owner and thus would constitute an immoral act. This moral evaluation does not leave you untouched, because it creates an obligation not to do what is immoral that affects your will and may ultimately make you hand in the wallet. Perhaps you overcome this moral impulse by thinking of something nice you want to buy with the money, but even in this case the moral impulse is not nothing. It was simply not strong enough to outweigh the attraction of the thing you want to buy. Unsurprisingly, the direct motivational force of the moral ought has not escaped the attention of important contributions to moral philosophy.

In discussions about the nature of morality, we sometimes find the idea that a cognitivist approach to moral judgment is wedded to conscious, explicit reasoning

[49] Hume, "Enquiry Concerning the Principles of Morals," 293.

based on deontological moral rules. As there is ample evidence for spontaneous moral judgments, such intuitions are understood as showing that moral emotivism is correct: These intuitions are emotions, not acts of reason-based cognition. This assumption, too, fails to fathom the nature of morality. Evidently, a structural analysis of the kind discussed – for example, as regards agency – is a quick, largely unconscious process that is not necessarily transparent to the agents themselves. However, this does not mean that the structural analysis is based on a sentiment – it clearly is not, as we just have seen. One thus has to broaden the analysis of moral judgment and include these structural analysis mechanisms, which, while they are largely intuitive, are not simply emotive. Such mechanisms can be made explicit, as Hume did in the case of agency, a process very important for the understanding and practice of morality.

Thus, it turns out that the simple dichotomy between moral judgments as cognitive acts of reason or as expressions of sentiment does not adequately capture the intricacies and rich content of moral judgments, their cognitive, volitional and emotional dimensions that need to be differentiated and accounted for in a theory of human moral cognition.

To repeat: None of this doubts the importance of moral feeling. It is no less than one of the most important elements of human identity. It makes morality the powerful force that it sometimes is in human life. The rich colors of moral emotions are sources of both the beauty and the profound sorrows of human life. These remarks simply intend to clarify what the role of these emotions in moral thought actually is.

A further central function of emotion in moral judgment is to fathom what an action means for the patient of the action. It is a piece of moral heuristics: Without empathy for the experience of victims of racial discrimination, for instance, without the emotional understanding of how it feels to be degraded and humiliated, nobody will be able properly to evaluate the significance of this injustice. If one thinks that being relegated to the back of a bus is a minor issue, the issue that the *Freedom Riders* in the USA were fighting for will remain inexplicable.

8.3 EXPLANATORY LIMITS OF EMOTIVISM

8.3.1 *Ruled by Moral Taste Buds?*

Contemporary contributions to moral philosophy and psychology with a – broadly understood – emotivist background do not call these findings into question. We have already investigated the explanatory power of the mental gizmo thesis. A further influential perspective, the *social intuitionist model* or *moral foundations theory* by Jonathan Haidt, does not change this perception either. This theory argues along emotivist lines that emotional intuitions form the basis for moral judgments. Arguments that appear to be rational are used to justify such emotion-based moral attitudes post hoc. Moral reasoning is not engaged in to critically improve one's own moral point of view.[50] Rather, moral argument is directed at manipulating others – in fact, reason is a "public relation firm" of emotional intuitions for "strategic purposes such as managing reputation, building alliances, and recruiting bystanders to support your side."[51] At the same time, however, rational argument is supposed to have an influence on these emotional reactions, although the theory does not clarify exactly how this influence is to be understood, in particular whether reasoning causes and changes moral judgments or overrides moral judgment.[52]

Jonathan Haidt claims that there are six "moral taste buds of the righteous mind."[53] Haidt intends to expand the ethics of autonomy of WEIRD (Western, educated, industrial, rich and democratic) people (who form the sample of many psychological studies) to include moral systems that are "hierarchical, punitive, and religious" because they include ideas of loyalty, authority and sanctity.[54] The six foundations of morality are the pairs care/harm, fairness/cheating, loyalty/betrayal, authority/subversion, sanctity/degradation and liberty/oppression.[55] Fairness is about the allocation of goods proportionally to merit; demands for equality are matters of nondomination and therefore are based on the liberty taste bud.[56] These pairs are moral modules that form the basis and common ground upon which all of the different human moralities develop. They define the possible contents of any given moral code. It is a misconception, Haidt argues, to focus on just some of these foundations as Western individualism does – for example, overlooking other moralities where loyalty and sanctity are of great importance.

The thrust of the argument is illustrated well by the following example:

> [W]ithin any given culture many moral controversies turn out to involve competing ways to link a behavior to a moral module. Should parents and teachers be allowed to spank children for disobedience? On the left side of the political spectrum, spanking typically triggers judgments of cruelty and oppression. On the right, it is sometimes linked to judgments about proper enforcement of rules, particularly rules about respect for parents and teachers. So even if we all share the same small set of cognitive modules, we can hook actions up to modules in so many ways that we can build conflicting moral matrices on the same small set of foundations.[57]

50 Haidt, *Righteous Mind*, 50.
51 Haidt, *Righteous Mind*, 46, 74.
52 Haidt, *Righteous Mind*, 67 f., admitting that there are good arguments in moral disputes, although he does not explain their nature, content or origin.
53 Haidt, *Righteous Mind*, 113.
54 Haidt, *Righteous Mind*, 110, 166.
55 Haidt, *Righteous Mind*, 125, 155 ff.
56 Haidt, *Righteous Mind*, 170 ff., 176 ff.
57 Haidt, *Righteous Mind*, 124.

This, then, explains why "good people" can disagree about right and wrong (for instance, the right and wrong of spanking) – they are simply operating in different moral matrices.[58]

Haidt uses these moral matrices to explain US politics. If care, fairness and liberty are dominant, one becomes a liberal, if loyalty, authority and sanctity are guiding, a conservative.[59] The dominant influence of these taste buds is genetically fixed.[60] These moral taste buds are explained by their evolutionary functions. The moral foundations have evolved, it is argued, in response to the adaptive challenges of "caring for vulnerable children" (care/harm); of "reaping the rewards of cooperation without getting exploited" (fairness/cheating); of "forming and maintaining coalitions" (loyalty/betrayal); of "forging relationships that will benefit us within social hierarchies" (authority/subversion); and of "the omnivore's dilemma, and then to the broader challenge of living in a world of pathogens and parasites" (sanctity/degradation).[61] There is no clear account of why the liberty/oppression foundation evolved.

Group selection and gene–culture coevolution may have played a role in this evolutionary development, it is argued.[62] The point of morality is to enable cooperation, albeit limited to the groups of which the agent is a member. Parochial altruism is the ultimate frontier of ethics. Oxytocin is important for explaining this within the framework of the theory of group selection: "Oxytocin should bond us to our partners and our groups, so that we can more effectively compete with other groups. It should not bond us to humanity in general. Several studies have validated this prediction."[63] The benefits of cooperation also are why groups evolved that entertain religious beliefs: These beliefs make people better cooperators.[64]

Human rights are explained in this framework: They are post-hoc rationalizations of the intuitions of people with particularly receptive liberty taste buds.[65] The different moral matrices complement each other – liberals are, for instance, right about the necessity of some regulation, while conservatives are right that markets are "miraculous."[66]

[58] Haidt, *Righteous Mind*, 181 ff.

[59] Haidt, *Righteous Mind*, 181, 294 ff.

[60] Haidt, *Righteous Mind*, 312: "People whose genes gave them brains that get a special pleasure from novelty, variety, and diversity, while simultaneously being less sensitive to signs of threat, are predisposed (but not predestined) to become liberals. … People whose genes give them brains with the opposite settings are predisposed, for the same reasons, to resonate with the grand narrative of the right (such as the Reagan narrative)."

[61] Haidt, *Righteous Mind*, 153 f., assuming also an ongoing evolution of the cognitive faculties of modern humans, for which there is no evidence at all.

[62] Haidt, *Righteous Mind*, 189 ff.

[63] Haidt, *Righteous Mind*, 234.

[64] Haidt, *Righteous Mind*, 246 ff.

[65] Haidt, *Righteous Mind*, 175.

[66] Haidt, *Righteous Mind*, 294 ff.

This psychological theory is descriptive, it is underlined. Haidt notes that if taken as a normative definition of morality, the simple acceptance of loyalty and authority could lead to a defense of political orders such as fascism, which would be given "high marks" as long as they produced high levels of cooperation.[67] For questions of normative theory, therefore, other arguments are necessary – more precisely, what is needed is rule utilitarianism, which should be decisive and guide public policy decisions that take into account the importance of loyalty, authority and sanctity.[68] For the individual, virtue ethics is tentatively endorsed.[69]

The overall vision of morality presented is a narrow one: "Parochial love – love within groups – amplified by similarity, a sense of shared fate, and the suppression of free riders, may be the most we can accomplish."[70]

8.3.2 *A Testing Case: Corporal Punishment – A Question of Taste?*

Spanking is an interesting example for assessing moral foundations theory in the context of human rights, because the corporal punishment of children is a standard human rights issue and in a leading decision of the ECtHR, for instance, was declared to violate Art. 3 ECHR on inhuman or degrading treatment or punishment.[71]

Was this decision just an emotional gut reaction on the part of the majority of judges of the ECtHR, who were led by their particular moral taste buds in their interpretation of Art. 3 ECHR, while the dissenting judge arguing for the permissibility of this kind of sanction simply used other taste buds?

This example reveals a major shortcoming of moral foundations theory quite clearly: It does not distinguish between factual, traditional morality and critically reflected ethics. One major point of moral philosophy is to critically investigate certain moral issues that may turn out not to stand the test of such critical scrutiny, such as the morality of loyalty to fellow slaveholders or respect for the sanctity of moral rules subjugating women – or the fairness of the physical punishment of children. The effects of this critical scrutiny can make history – as the abolition of slavery and the women's liberation movement illustrate. Only critical reflection on morality, based on considered judgments, will tell us what human morality ultimately is about, while factual, traditional morality, by contrast, will tell us about precisely those influences that skew moral judgment – say, racist ideas, misogyny or an authoritarian tradition of child-rearing. Studying a traditional morality that sanctions violence against children as a good starting point for understanding moral cognition is comparable (with a dose of exaggeration) to studying mathematical cognition by looking at the belief that 79 + 86 = 164. Such studies may tell us a lot

67 Haidt, *Righteous Mind*, 271 f.
68 Haidt, *Righteous Mind*, 272.
69 Haidt, *Righteous Mind*, 272 n. 68.
70 Haidt, *Righteous Mind*, 245.
71 ECtHR, Tyrer v UK, Judgement of March 15, 1978, appl. no. 5856/72.

about the factors influencing counting, such as a lack of attention, but they are not key to the psychological foundations of mathematics.

Let us take a closer look at the example of corporal punishment to better understand what the further problems of the moral foundations theory may be. There is much to be said about this example, particularly in relation to children. Thinking about the effects of such punishment on children, its educational merit, brutalizing consequences and so on, is an important exercise if one wants to do justice to children. None of this means simply to rationalize emotional intuitive reactions. Rather, this exercise clarifies the issues – in particular, whether corporal punishment does any good or simply harms children, as very many people (rightly) assume today, and whether it should come with corresponding legal consequences. Beyond these important arguments, the ultimate moral evaluation relies on the elements of the action identified above – for instance, the kind of intentions of the agent of corporal punishment. If the intention is to gratify the cruel instincts of the punishing adult, the evaluation will differ from the evaluation of the ill-advised but well-meaning intention of a loving parent who uses corporal punishment as means of education, even though in the latter case, too, it is ultimately an unjustified harm done to children.

This search for moral understanding is the daily business of any responsible human being. It is thus analytically unconvincing to regard morality simply as a manipulation device to strategically influence others, not as a guide to one's own actions. One distinguishing feature of moral judgment is that is aspires to correctness based on reasons – and there are certainly good reasons for certain forms of action. This is what motivates the painstaking efforts of many human beings who honestly want to get it right. Interestingly, the social intuitionist model underlines this itself because it includes reflection in its reconstruction of morality, albeit ambivalently and without clarifying its precise role. The fact that it refers to rule utilitarianism as the ultimate yardstick for the evaluation of social policy and as a bar to "high marks" being awarded to fascism bears witness to this. By trying to limit the harmful conclusions that may be drawn from its arguments by reference to the principles of an ethical maxim such as rule utilitarianism, moral foundations theory denies intuitions generated by moral taste buds the ultimate rule that it appears to defend. In this context, we can note once again that utilitarianism itself is based on notions of equality that are not the consequence, but the normative precondition of utilitarian evaluation. Utilitarianism takes us right back to moral principles of justice and offers no escape route from them, as we have seen. Moral foundations theory's inconsistent impression is only deepened by making virtue ethics a yardstick for individual action. Virtue ethics is, like all ethical systems, contested. However, it does not endorse the rule of emotional intuitions as the core of ethics.[72]

[72] Cf. for a concise statement, Rosalind Hursthouse, *On Virtue Ethics* (Oxford: Oxford University Press, 1999).

These observations are important for assessing the merits of the six foundations of morality. They point to further deficiencies in the analysis of morality: Care and harm, fairness and betrayal point to notions of justice and altruism, albeit not very precisely, as betrayal, for instance, is simply one form of unfairness. The relationship of proportionality and equality is analytically misunderstood, too: If the criterion of distribution is equally fulfilled in two agents, equal treatment is the consequence of principles of proportional equality, as we have seen. Therefore, for example, the equality of rights is a consequence of proportional equality: The humanity of humans as a criterion for the enjoyment of rights is simply the same for each person.

Liberty is a central good for human beings, to be sure. Moral foundations theory, however, does not discuss the normative principles that are relevant in balancing the liberty of one with the liberty of all and that may even create rights. The reference to a "liberty taste bud" can be seen as a metaphor that can be reconciled with (but is no substitute for) the theory of liberty as a human good sketched above. However, this reference does not answer the problem faced by any normative theory of liberty that has been at the heart of many debates since antiquity, namely the question of who justifiably enjoys which liberty and to which degree in relation to others.

Another example: Loyalty, authority and sanctity are only secondary virtues. Loyalty and respect for authority are morally justifiable if they serve the good of people; loyalty to dictators and reference of their authority is not a virtue but a vice, as Haidt himself admits, realizing that its content may cause "high marks" to be awarded to fascism if it manages to achieve social cooperation. Sanctity is a difficult concept, too. Respect for the sanctity of a certain conception of marriage may be bad news for gay couples. Here, too, other moral principles, such as respect for the autonomy of other human beings and their dignity, need to be considered.

Moreover, the theory does not engage in any detail with what basic notions of justice or altruism actually entail – for example, as to the intentions of the agents, the effects of actions, means/ends distinctions and so forth, as roughly outlined above.[73]

[73] Cf. for experiments providing empirical evidence that such distinctions and relations are part of the mental representations that underlie moral judgments, Sydney Levine, Alan M. Leslie and John Mikhail, "The Mental Representation of Human Action," *Cognitive Science* 42, no. 4 (2018): 1229 ff. The tools chosen to clarify the structure of these representations are action trees, Mikhail, *Elements*, 125 ff. The authors rightly underline that these findings pose a "challenge to those researchers who either ignore the problem of how moral intuitions arise from eliciting situations ... or who uncritically assume that the mental representations of human action underlying moral judgement are exceedingly simple and can be adequately described in terms of heuristics and biases," ibid. 1259, referring to Jonathan Haidt, "The Emotional Dog and Its Rational Tail: A Socialist Intuitionist Approach to Moral Judgement," *Psychological Review* 108, no. 4 (2001): 814 ff. and Sunstein, "Moral Heuristics," 531–41. Hugo Mercier and Dan Sperber, *The Enigma of Reason* (Cambridge, MA: Harvard University Press, 2017), 299 ff., endorse Haidt's model but highlight the effects of deliberation in the case of abolitionism and other cases of moral evaluation without, however, analyzing the structure of moral argument and without specifying the normative principles that have the power to convince.

Finally, as a last point: The examples of political differences explained by the different operation of the moral taste buds are loaded with prudential arguments, such as arguments about the question of when regulation actually works or whether and under which conditions markets deliver good results. Regulatory choices or the design of markets evidently have ethical implications. But discussing such prudential arguments as part of the core normative machinery of morality does not help to clarify what morality is about.

This notwithstanding, these analytical shortcomings teach us a constructive lesson: They show that the six categories of moral foundations theory do not adequately capture the normative principles that are central for ethical systems. In light of its critical discussion, the principles of justice, altruism and respect continue to seem valuable candidates for the foundational elements of ethics that a psychological theory needs to account for.

The evolutionary framework of moral foundations theory suffers from a failure to present any evidence whatsoever that the evolutionary story it recounts is actually true. It remains one of those "just-so" stories that are falsely taken as valid evolutionary theory-building.[74] Moreover, as indicated above, the first step for any convincing evolutionary theory of morality is to construct a theory of morality that possesses sufficient analytical precision. As this is lacking, Haidt's evolutionary theory is unable to get off the ground.

Moreover, as we have seen, the idea of human rights has highly complex roots in history and human normative reflection. To reduce it to the effects of a liberty taste bud and the post-hoc rationalization of its operations seems not to do full justice to these findings.

The social intuitionist model illustrates a danger already identified previously: When the idea that corporal punishment is admissible, for instance, is interpreted as the expression of certain moral taste buds that simply are different from the taste buds used to criticize this form of punishment, the criticism of corporal punishment loses its ground because there is no reason to prefer the one taste over the other. The theory tries to deal with this problem by introducing rule utilitarianism as a normative yardstick for public policy and virtue ethics for individual acting, contradicting its emotivist message in doing so. Nevertheless, ideas of loyalty to in-groups, respect for authority without questioning its legitimacy and reverence for sanctity without inquiring into its origin and content are understood as expressions of moral judgment on par with any other moral code, in particular one based on human autonomy. In this way, psychological theory may serve to shield unjustified moral precepts against criticism by presenting them as products of a genetically fixed and thus unchangeable natural morality.

In line with various theorists of morality, moral foundations theory argues that only a morality of "love within groups," a "parochial altruism" is the horizon of

[74] Cf. above on evolutionary theory. Interestingly, Haidt criticizes just-so stories – only to then develop one himself, cf. Haidt, *Righteous Mind*, 122 f.

human moral possibilities. Concern for all humanity is simply too much for human beings. The human rights project, which is a real practice, not an ephemeral dream, indicates that these theses do not fathom what morality is really about.

8.3.3 *Sentimental Rules*

In another very interesting approach, Shaun Nichols argues for a sentimentalist picture of morality. It takes as its starting point the body of data suggesting that children from an early age distinguish between conventional and nonconventional moral rules.[75] The former can be changed by authorities, the latter not. The former deal with prudential arrangements, the latter are centered on the avoidance of harm. The latter are more serious than the former. The latter can be generalized over situations and contexts, the former less so.[76] Moreover, moral objectivism is the psychological default position, Nichols argues.[77]

Nichols claims that moral rules are based on moral judgment, which he argues has two components: information about normative violations and a noncognitive response. The former is provided by rules proscribing certain behavior, while the latter consists of specific emotions. Only those rules relating to behavior that triggers reactive concern and distress cues are nonconventional moral rules.[78] It is the particular emotional engagement of the evaluating person that turns them into moral rules. These emotions are also the reason why these rules are able to survive historical change and development.[79]

As we saw above, the mental gizmo theory already claimed that emotions explain moral judgment such as that reached in the footbridge case, namely that it is impermissible to kill the bystander to save five lives. The sentimental rules approach goes further than the mental gizmo theory, however, in claiming that this is not only because of the emotionally salient features of the act. Rules on the prohibition to perform this act are also important. However, these rules need to be backed by emotions in order to yield the impermissibility judgments observed in the footbridge case.[80] A third factor influencing moral judgment consists of cost–benefit

75 Shaun Nichols, *Sentimental Rules: On the Natural Foundations of Moral Judgement* (Oxford: Oxford University Press, 2004), 6.

76 Larry P. Nucci, Elliot Turiel and Gloria Encarnacion-Gawrych, "Children's Social Interaction and Social Concepts," *Journal of Cross-Cultural Psychology* 14, no. 4 (1983): 469 ff.; Judith G. Smetana and Judith L. Braeges, "The Development of Toddlers' Moral and Conventional Judgement," *Merril-Palmer Quarterly* 36, no. 3 (1990): 329 ff.

77 Nichols, *Sentimental Rules*, 166 ff.

78 Nichols, *Sentimental Rules*, 187. Norms on what is disgusting (e.g. spitting in a glass one drinks from) are also nonconventional because of emotional reactions to the disgusting action.

79 Shaun Nichols, "On the Genealogy of Norms: A Case for the Rule of Emotion in Cultural Evolution," *Philosophy of Science* 69, no. 2 (2002): 234 ff.; Nichols, *Sentimental Rules*, 16 ff.

80 Shaun Nichols and Ron Mallon, "Moral Dilemmas and Moral Rules," *Cognition* 100, no. 3 (2006): 530 ff., 540.

assessments along utilitarian lines.[81] These factors interact in a complex way, without there being a unified normative theory that captures all moral intuitions.

Metaethically, morality therefore is not objective, but bound to feelings relative to particular groups of people. There is no argument why one should prefer one set of emotions to another. It is not possible to evaluate the emotions determining the content of morality with these very emotions.[82] The illusion of objectivity hides the respondent-dependent relativity of emotionally based sentimental rules. This notwithstanding, the objectivist intuition persists and guides human lives.[83]

This theory faces the same problems already identified as decisive for emotivist accounts of moral judgment: The emotional reaction to some harm is not all there is to moral judgment. A harm may cause considerable unease without it being immoral – to use Nichols' own example, a medically justified operation, for instance. It is only immoral if the intention and the action have certain properties – for instance, the intention to torture the patient and not to heal them. These properties need to be determined based on an analysis of the intention and action, as outlined above in some detail. This analysis then elicits the moral evaluation. This, in turn, gives rise to moral feelings, which are different and need to be distinguished from feelings such as unease at witnessing an operation. Feeling nauseous at the sight of blood during such an operation is not already a moral feeling, while feeling abhorrence because of the wrongness of an attempt to torture a person is. The evaluation of an action as morally wrong is, however, the precondition and cause of these moral feelings. Like an Escher cube, the same action can change its moral nature, depending on what evaluation the analysis of the action's intentions and effects yields.

Nichols developed a theory of moral learning that adds a further qualification, underlining another influence that reason has on moral judgment. It is best considered in the framework of the discussion in Section 8.5 on the acquisition of moral knowledge.

8.4 EXPLAINING MORAL DISAGREEMENT

Given the great variety of moral opinions visible both today and in history, any theory of moral cognition will need to formulate a theory of moral disagreement as part of its explanatory enterprise. Moral disagreement is yet another traditional and vast topic of practical philosophy, and empirical work has been carried out in this field, too.[84] It is sometimes argued that the mere existence of moral disagreement

[81] Nichols and Mallon, "Moral Dilemmas," 530 ff., 540.

[82] Nichols, *Sentimental Rules*, 188.

[83] Nichols, *Sentimental Rules*, 197 f.

[84] Cf. the attempts to explain different reactions, for example, to insults and other issues through different "cultures of honor" in the north and south of the USA, Richard E. Nisbett and Dov Cohen, *Culture of Honor: The Psychology of Violence in the South* (Boulder, CO: Westview

already proves moral relativism.[85] In this respect, however, conclusions should not be drawn too rashly: "Establishing the best explanation of stubborn ethical disagreement requires understanding all the possible origins of these conflicting beliefs and all the possible resources that might resolve the conflict – no quick or easy job."[86] There may be ways to account for moral disagreement, even radical disagreement, with substantial explanatory power without any implications about irreconcilable foundational moral principles.

A first task, thus, is to determine precisely what kinds of moral disagreement actually exist. This is far from obvious. Some studies on the supposedly different moral orientations of different cultures, for instance, under critical scrutiny turn out to have overlooked important communalities.[87] The second task is to see what the causal factors for apparently different moral beliefs are and what they teach us about the structure of moral judgment. Not just law, but morality, too, is often based on express moral rules. These rules can embody conceptions of what is good and just that do not withstand critical scrutiny. It is therefore necessary to distinguish between traditional, prereflective social moralities and a critical, reflective ethics in the context of analytical theories of moral disagreement, too. The conditions for the successful criticism of traditional moral practices are key to understanding the principles underlying human moral deliberation and judgment that may in the end lead to the abandonment of such practices.

One factor of considerable importance in explaining the existence of moral disagreement is disagreement about the nonmoral preconditions of moral judgment. This includes understanding what an action, practice or institution means for other persons. These assumptions may even lead to denying certain persons moral status: As we have seen, a central question during the conquest of the Americas in the sixteenth century was whether the indigenous people of the Americas were actually fully human or some other kind of creature. The identification of the proper objects of evaluation likewise shows the relevance that these factual questions hold for moral judgment: For instance, the institutions of the state have to be regarded as products of human volition and action and not as unchangeable elements of the makeup of the world to be evaluated on the basis of principles of justice.

Other factors that rightly play a prominent role in this debate are the influence of interests and the impact of ideological constructions, both the source of extremely

Press, 1996); Richard E. Nisbett, *The Geography of Thought: How Asians and Westerns Think Differently … and Why* (New York: Free Press, 2003); Haidt, *Righteous Mind*, 11 ff. The disagreement can encompass the domain of morality as such, ibid. 14 ff.

85 Mackie, *Ethics: Inventing Right and Wrong*, 36.

86 Griffin, *On Human Rights*, 129 ff.

87 Cf. for instance, for some comparative research, John Mikhail, "Is the Prohibition of Homicide Universal? Evidence from Comparative Criminal Law," *Brooklyn Law Review* 75, no. 2 (2009): 497 ff.

powerful emotions and motives of action. An entirely fantastic ideology like National Socialism, for instance, was capable to motivate people to commit mass murder before leading them to their own deaths and the destruction of their country. Taking these factors into account may already reduce the cases of real moral disagreement about basic principles of morality considerably. Take the (important) example of the rights of women: The denial of equal rights of women was (and is) partly based on wrong factual anthropological assumptions, such as the idea that women lack the capacity for autonomous self-determination and rationality and therefore have to be guided by men.[88] The suffering of women who were denied an equal part in social life because of these assumptions about their interests and capabilities needed to be understood. This required massive cultural and political efforts, sustained over generations and still ongoing today. The interests of men in comfortable structures of domination were an evident further factor: "When, however, we ask why the existence of one-half the species should be merely ancillary to that of the other – why each woman should be a mere appendage to a man, allowed to have no interest of her own, that there may be nothing to compete in her mind with his interests and his pleasure; the only reason which can be given is, that men like it."[89] Ideological constructs, partly in religious garb, about the place of women in the world buttressed these social structures, too. Such factors continue to play an important political role today, despite the progress made. If these false assumptions about the nature of women, their experience of repressive patriarchic structures and the power of interests and ideologies lose their influence, apparently irreconcilable moral disagreements can disappear quickly and the equal rights of women appear as an evident truism even across cultural boundaries (as indeed they should).

Another important issue is the process of clarifying ethical concepts – for instance, that responsibility for actions depends on the internal state of the agent, an intention to act, an insight of major importance for the development of criminal law. Some forms of human behavior may be wrongly moralized or wrongly demoralized, often as a consequence of false factual assumptions, interests and ideologies. Take the example of LGBTIQ* rights: If one understands that the only consequence of preventing consensual intimate relations between same-sex partners is to cause suffering while not promoting any discernable good enjoyed by human beings, traditional moralities about the wickedness of same-sex partnerships quickly crumble, as we have witnessed in the last thirty years or so. If one understands that

[88] For another example, Griffin, *On Human Rights*, 244, on the exclusion of some people from democracy: "These exclusions were supported by largely factual beliefs: that certain races were of lower intelligence, that they were child-like, that women were not interested in politics, that they were already adequately represented by their husbands, and so on. Once the falsity or irrelevance of these beliefs was recognized, these excluded groups had to be admitted into the class of 'people' referred to in the defining formula 'the people rule'."

[89] Taylor Mill, "Enfranchisement of Women," 62.

harassing people because of their sexual orientation means doing an unjustified harm to them, then refraining from mistreating them in this way becomes a moral imperative and may even lead to a prohibition by law of certain qualified forms of this kind of behavior. Reflective ethics helps us to achieve consistency – if autonomy, for instance, is a key value, autonomous decisions about the persons one loves should be protected robustly. Ethical reflection of this kind can expand the circle of persons included in moral deliberation: If all persons count equally, the interests of future generations of human beings and thus questions of intergenerational justice should be factored into our debates about the appropriate measures to combat climate change, as courts around the world have now started to do explicitly.[90] If sentient beings are objects of moral concern, then ethical and legal protections for nonhuman animals are required. Moral values and standards of virtuous acting may not stand the test of critical thought – that it is imperative to fight a duel with somebody who has insulted one has ceased to be a convincing interpretation of proper, self-respecting behavior. A further example illustrating the importance of critical normative thinking is the scrutiny of theories of morality themselves: The critique, for instance, of the (as we have seen) false idea that human rights are products of the post-hoc rationalization of emotional reactions to certain stimuli will prevent the conclusion that human rights should be made irrelevant.

Finally, there are real moral dilemmas to which no easy solution is available – for instance, in the case of conflicting duties, say, the duty to save lives in a pandemic and the duty to prevent the domestic violence increased by lockdowns. In sum, there are a plethora of factors helping to explain different moral points of view without taking recourse to substantially and unchangeably different underlying moral conceptions.[91] There is thus reason to believe that under the surface of apparently insurmountable moral disagreement, there may be a deep, shared structure of common moral principles.[92]

[90] Cf. for example BVerfG, Order of the First Senate of March 24, 2021, 1 BvR 2656/18. The challenges for human rights caused by climate change include, first, the consequences that are related to climate change for the protection of classical human rights positions – for instance, state repression of climate activists or climate migration. Moreover, the question arises as to how to "climatize" human rights, by developing new doctrinal tools as to the bearer of rights (rights of nature?), the addressee or causality and responsibility, cf. for more details César Rodríguez-Garavito, "Human Rights 2030: Existential Challenges and a New Paradigm for the Human Rights Field," in *The Struggle for Human Rights: Essays in Honour of Philip Alston*, eds. Nehal Bhuta et al. (Oxford: Oxford University Press, 2021), 328 ff., 342 ff.; César Rodríguez-Garavito (ed.), *Litigating the Climate Emergency. How Human Rights, Courts, and Legal Mobilization Can Bolster Climate Action* (Cambridge: Cambridge University Press, 2022).

[91] Buchanan and Powell, *The Evolution of Moral Progress*, 54 ff., present a very helpful theory of moral progress that considers comparable factors (better compliance with moral norms; better moral concepts; better understanding of virtues; better moral motivation; better moral reasoning; proper demoralization and moralization; better understanding of moral standing and moral statuses; improvements in the understanding of the nature of morality; better understanding of justice).

[92] Cf. Mahlmann, "Ethics," 593 ff.; Mikhail, *Moral Grammar and Human Rights*, 170 ff.

8.5 THE DEVELOPMENT OF MORAL COGNITION

8.5.1 *How Do We Learn to Be Moral?*

One question that remains to be explored is the ontogenetic origin of moral cognition. The development of moral cognition forms the subject of landmark debates in moral psychology.[93] Our analysis thus far suggests that central issues here include – among other factors – the acquisition of the cognitive domain of morality, the restrictive principles that determine the possible objects of evaluation, the material principles of morality discussed, the prescriptive, volitional effects of moral judgments, the moral ought, including necessary connections between duties and rights, and the emotional consequences of moral experience. Such phenomena could be constructed and acquired by secondary learning processes (instruction, repetition, role-taking, peer pressure, sanctioning, etc.), as many normative principles are (e.g. the intricacies of Swiss law on unjust enrichment), or alternatively they could be at least in part the product of the unfolding of innate cognitive structures triggered by experience. The latter is the way a mentalist approach to ethics would approach the issue.

It is important to emphasize that the importance of social and cultural influences on ethics and law is not denied in the latter case: As noted, the freedom of the press, for instance, as a legal norm and the underlying principles of political morality presuppose the cultural achievement (a late achievement with plenty of preconditions) of the press and, in addition, the experience of its suppression even by democratic governments, among many other things. "The freedom of the press is protected" is certainly not an inborn principle of human moral cognition. As we saw in our survey of the history and the theory of justification of human rights, fundamental moral judgments about the wrongness and justice of certain intentions and actions are the seeds of the idea of human rights. The real question is therefore: What kind of mind do you need to possess in order to develop such an idea? What is so special about the human mind that only humans and no other organism developed a concept like human rights? What are the cognitive preconditions for starting the long cultural process leading, after many thousands of years of human cultural and social development, to the idea that one can not only wish for or have an interest in, but in fact enjoy a *right* to a free press? None? Is simply being smart enough? Or does one need to have certain specific conceptual tools with which to build a system of rights?

[93] E.g. of the work of Jean Piaget, *Le jugement moral chez l'enfant: perspectives piagétiennes* (Paris: F. Alcan, 1932) or Lawrence Kohlberg, *Essays on Moral Development, Vol. I: The Philosophy of Moral Development: Moral Stages and the Idea of Justice* (San Francisco, CA: Harper & Row, 1981) and Lawrence Kohlberg, *Essays on Moral Development, Vol. II: The Psychology of Moral Development: The Nature and Validity of Moral Stages* (San Francisco, CA: Harper & Row, 1984).

The simple observation already recalled above that any child acquires a differentiated set of moral concepts and categories whereas no nonhuman animal acquires any of the same, even if it is raised in the same environment, seems to indicate strongly that very different cognitive abilities are in place. Some of the empirical work on this difference between humans and nonhuman animals has been discussed in Chapter 7. To repeat: The question therefore is not whether there are species-specific inborn cognitive structures enabling the formation of moral precepts, but what exactly these cognitive structures are.

8.5.2 *The Moral World of Infants and Toddlers*

Jean Piaget pioneered the idea that children apply complex moral ideas and concepts, not least when they play, as illustrated by his fascinating analysis of children playing with marbles.[94] Recent years have produced many more highly creative studies on the moral psychology of children, increasingly focusing on young children. We have already encountered some important examples in our inquiry. As we have seen, these studies operate with different theoretical background assumptions and sometimes yield contradictory results. Some research is constrained by theoretical and conceptual problems, limits of the design of experiments and contestable interpretations of their results. One important problem is the lack of a sufficiently fine-grained analytical theory of moral judgment that does not commit, for instance, the category error of conflating moral judgment with simple preferences and aversions. The thrust of this research is, however, that children operate in a richly textured moral world from very early on. This fits well with research into other cognitive domains that also indicates that human beings are not born blank slates.[95]

A classical set of experiments concerns the moral–conventional distinction, for instance: As mentioned above, children distinguish between conventional norms and moral, nonconventional norms.[96] Other experiments suggest that toddlers by the age of eighteen months and even earlier exhibit spontaneous helping behavior towards others.[97] They engage in so-called paternalistic helping: Children want to accommodate the well-being of others, not just their wishes.[98]

Children act with an intrinsic moral motivation: They also help when nobody is watching or when others do not know that they are being helped.[99] External rewards

[94] Piaget, *Jugement moral.*
[95] Cf. Stephen Pinker, *The Blank Slate* (London: Allen Lane, 2002).
[96] Nucci, Turiel and Encarnacion-Gawrych, "Children's Social Interaction," 469 ff.; Smetana and Braeges, "Development of Toddlers'," 329 ff.
[97] Felix Warneken and Michael Tomasello, "Altruistic Helping in Human Infants and Young Chimpanzees," *Science* 311, no. 5765 (2006): 1301–3; Felix Warneken and Michael Tomasello, "Helping and Cooperation at 14 Months of Age," *Infancy* 11, no. 3 (2007): 271 ff.
[98] Tomasello, *Becoming Human*, 226 ff.
[99] Tomasello, *Becoming Human*, 226.

even seem to undermine their intrinsic motivation.[100] Helping somebody themselves and seeing somebody being helped render them equally content.[101] There are studies on extended sympathy – for instance, for the victims of some harmful action after the deed.[102]

Studies indicate that – unlike great apes – small children act according to principles of distributive egalitarian justice, particularly in collaborative contexts.[103] While there are studies suggesting that children limit fairness to in-group members,[104] there is also substantial evidence that three-year-olds apply egalitarian principles universally.[105] Such intuitions extend to procedures of distribution.[106] Three- to five-year-olds take need or merit as criteria of distributive justice. They protect the entitlements of others, create social norms, employ normative categories and engage in third-party punishment.[107] Intentions are a central factor in this punishment.[108] There are studies on the specific moral feelings of guilt and shame – for instance, arguing that three-year-old children feel guilt over the harm they inflict, not just sympathy for the victims of this harm.[109]

According to various studies, it is plausible to assume that infants already operate with at least some kind of proto-morality. Twelve-month-olds categorize actions on the basis of their social valency.[110] Studies on social evaluation indicate that six- to ten-month-old infants base their evaluation of another individual as appealing or aversive on this individual's actions towards others: For instance, they like individuals better who help others and who act more cooperatively to facilitate the achievement of these others' aims than those who hinder the achievement of others' goals. They also like helpers better than neutral individuals, and the latter better than hinderers.[111] These experiments concern actors who are unknown to the infants

[100] Tomasello, *Becoming Human*, 226.
[101] Tomasello, *Becoming Human*, 226.
[102] Tomasello, *Becoming Human*, 227.
[103] Cf. Tomasello, *Becoming Human*, 229 ff., 245: Children have an aversion to disadvantageous and advantageous inequity and an equality bias.
[104] Ernst Fehr, Helen Bernhard and Bettina Rockenbach, "Egalitarianism in Young Children," *Nature* 454 (2008): 1079 ff.
[105] Tomasello, *Becoming Human*, 252, 258.
[106] Tomasello, *Becoming Human*, 240.
[107] Tomasello, *Becoming Human*, 257, 259, 264.
[108] Tomasello, *Becoming Human*, 264.
[109] Tomasello, *Becoming Human*, 282.
[110] David Premack and Ann James Premack, "Infants Attribute Value to the Goal Directed Actions of Self-Propelled Objects," *Journal of Cognitive Neuroscience* 9, no. 6 (1997): 848 ff.
[111] J. Kiley Hamlin, Karen Wynn and Paul Bloom, "Social Evaluation by Preverbal Infants," *Nature* 450 (2007): 557 ff.; J. Kiley Hamlin and Karen Wynn, "Young Infants Prefer Prosocial to Antisocial Others," *Cognitive Development* 26, no. 1 (2011): 30 ff.; Julia W. Van de Vondervoort and J. Kiley Hamlin, "Evidence for Intuitive Morality: Preverbal Infants Make Sociomoral Evaluations," *Child Development Perspectives* 10, no. 3 (2016): 143 ff.; Valerie Kuhlmeier, Karen Wynn and Paul Bloom, "Attribution of Dispositional States by 12-Month-Olds," *Psychological Science* 14, no. 5 (2003): 402 ff. The experiments rule out any influence of superficial perceptual factors on judgment.

and actions that have no effect on them as observers. This rightly has been identified as an important element of moral judgment: It is not personal experience with the agent that causes the agent to be evaluated a certain way, but the latter's action affecting unrelated others. Eight-month-olds showed a preference for individuals with good intentions, basing their evaluation on mental states of the agent, not outcome.[112] Other research indicates that actions towards inanimate entities do not enter into infants' evaluation of intentional agents.[113] Knowledge of an agent's goals is relevant for ten-month-olds' evaluations: Only an agent who knowingly helps another is preferred to other agents. It is not far-fetched to draw the conclusion from this research on infants that the capacity to evaluate others based on their behavior towards third parties is universal and unlearned, given their early age. It should be noted once again, however, that a social preference is not the same as a moral evaluation of an intention or action. The former is at best indirect evidence for the latter.

Many of these studies understand these mental capacities as biological adaptations for cooperation and interpret them as tools to identify free riders, cooperators and reciprocators. As we have seen already, this biological interpretation is too narrow and overlooks the many forms of cooperation that are both possible and entirely reconcilable with the constraints of a plausible evolutionary trajectory.

8.6 POVERTY OF STIMULUS AND THE DEVELOPMENT OF A MORAL POINT OF VIEW

These studies on child psychology tell us something interesting about the early cognitive stages of human mental development. The younger the children are for whom plausible evidence shows that they operate within a moral cognitive domain, the less plausible it becomes that these children were born as blank slates in moral terms. There are some studies on the lack of cultural variation in crucial areas of the development of moral cognition that point in the same direction.[114] This kind of evidence supports the hypothesis that foundational elements of morality are part of the natural cognitive endowment of human beings that matures during childhood, just like other cognitive faculties. But even if clear traces of a mature system of morality were not in place at an early age, the possibility of such a natural endowment could not be excluded, for it is entirely conceivable that a specific mental faculty matures only later in childhood. The fact that puberty (including its cognitive components) occurs in the second decade of human beings' lives does not speak against it being based on inborn properties of the human species.

[112] J. Kiley Hamlin, "Failed Attempt to Help and Harm: Intention versus Outcome in Preverbal Infants' Social Evaluations," *Cognition* 128, no. 3 (2013): 451 ff.

[113] Amanda L. Woodward, "Infants Selectively Encode the Goal of an Actor's Reach," *Cognition* 69, no. 1 (1998): 1 ff.

[114] Cf. for a review Tomasello, *Becoming Human*, 232 (helping), 241 (sharing), 268 (justice).

The decisive argument is therefore the *poverty of stimulus argument*: If the input of an organism's experience is not sufficient to generate a certain cognitive ability, at least some of the cognitive structures underlying this ability must be inborn.[115] This argument holds for any cognitive ability of any organism. To take a fascinating example that illustrates the structure of this argument:[116] Honeybees communicate the location of food through their dance in the hive. They determine the position of food by the position of the sun relative to a known terrain. They can do this even if the sky is overcast, because their circadian clock and their orientation systems enable them to determine the solar ephemeris – that is, the position of the sun relative to the time of the day. Their dance can thus refer to this position even if they were unable to see the sun itself. How do bees acquire this striking faculty? The following experiment gives the answer: Bees were raised in an incubator and foraged only in the late afternoon and had thus no direct experience of the sun's morning position. One day, they were let out to forage in the morning under an overcast sky. They still were able to determine and communicate the position of food relative to the position of the sun they had never observed: They had determined the solar ephemeris and with it the position of the food. As they had no experience of the sun's morning position but were still able to determine it, this ability cannot be learned. The only explanation for bees' acquisition of this ability is an innate cognitive mechanism of orientation operating in conjunction with the circadian clock.

This example illustrates the point of the poverty of stimulus argument and shows what intricate cognitive mechanisms are in place in organisms like bees. It may encourage us to ask seriously what structures the vastly more complex apparatus of human cognition may contain.

If the poverty of stimulus argument is considered in detail in the context of morality, many questions arise. Given the sheer scope of the issue, some hints at the gist of the argument must suffice here. Hume's implicit use of it *avant la lettre* provides a good illustration of its structure:

> This principle, indeed, of precept and education, must so far be owned to have a powerful influence, that it may frequently increase or diminish, beyond their natural standard, the sentiments of approbation or dislike; and may even, in particular instances, create, without any natural principle, a new sentiment of this kind; as is evident in all superstitious practices and observance: But that *all* moral affection or dislike arises from this origin, will never surely be allowed by any judicious enquirer. Had nature made no such distinction, founded on the original constitution of the mind, the words, *honourable* and *shameful*, *lovely* and *odious*,

[115] Cf. Stephen Laurence and Eric Margolis, "The Poverty of the Stimulus Argument," *The British Journal for the Philosophy of Science* 52, no. 2 (2001): 217 ff.; Mahlmann, *Rationalismus*, 74 ff.; Mikhail, *Elements*, 70 ff.

[116] Cf. Charles R. Gallistel, "Learning Organs," in *Chomsky Notebook*, eds. Jean Bricmont and Julie Franck (New York: Columbia University Press, 2007), 193, 197 ff.

> *noble* and *despicable*, had never had any place in any language; nor could politicians, had they invented these terms, ever have been able to render them intelligible, or make them convey any idea to the audience.[117]

Hume's point is that basic moral concepts are not learned from scratch, they are the *precondition* for moral learning. If one takes as examples a constitutive element of human morality like the moral cognitive space, some aspects of the principles governing moral judgment, the concept of ought and moral emotions like guilt or shame, the argument can be fleshed out somewhat more: As to the moral cognitive space, the poverty of stimulus argument asks whether a child can acquire this particular dimension of its perception of the world *de novo*, through the example of peers, instruction, imitation and so forth. In order to answer this question, one has to imagine a child who has no idea whatsoever of the qualitative content of the moral perspective: It sees the world only as a world of facts and events, including actions of other persons, but not in the very different colors of moral evaluation. How could a child possibly step from this perception of the world into the very different kind of world possessing a moral dimension? Quite aside from the fact that there is no such thing as instruction about this matter in real educational settings, even direct instruction would not help: How could a child understand what is meant by explanations of the moral dimension of human actions if it did not have access to this category of thinking? It would be like explaining the scent of chocolate to somebody who cannot smell.

The same is true for the concept of ought or moral emotions. What is a child to do with the explanation that an ought binds the will? How can the child be enlightened about what is meant by this if it has no access to this experience? Moreover, how is such a verbal definition to be turned into the actual subjective experience of being under an obligation?

Other mechanisms often used to explain the development of a moral orientation do not help either. Sanctions as such do not create the experience of an inner ought, only the experience of outward compulsion. A child with no access to the experience of moral obligation will feel a sanction as a harm inflicted upon it and a prudential reason not to show certain behaviors in order to avoid this harm, but will not feel any inner obligation not to do certain things. Sanctions enforce obligations but cannot trigger the subjective experience of a moral obligation.

Another example is role-taking. Sometimes it is argued that learning to take the perspective of another person leads to the understanding of the idea of a moral ought.[118] Role-taking, however, informs us about the perspective of another person only in a qualified sense: We understand how *we with our capacities* would perceive the world if we were in the other person's place. A person who cannot smell cannot

[117] Hume, "Enquiry Concerning the Principles of Morals," 214 (emphasis in original).

[118] Cf. for instance Tomasello, *Becoming Human*, 281, who argues that role reversal is the origin of conscience.

understand what scent is just by taking the role of somebody who can smell. The same is true for moral concepts: If, as imagined, a child is a moral blank slate, nothing about this state of affairs will change by taking the role of another person. The child will only imagine what a world without access to the idea of moral obligation looks like from the point of view of the other person.[119]

The case of moral emotions seems even more obvious. How are we to teach a child what the feeling of guilt or shame is like if this child is assumed to have no access to this emotion? Note that this is not about teaching the reasons for feeling guilty or ashamed, but about the emotion itself and its quality. Invoking internalization does not help either. One cannot internalize something to which one has no cognitive access. What the hypothesis of internalization tries to capture in these contexts is in fact the process of some experience triggering the maturation of cognitive capacities that make some cognitive or emotional phenomena accessible to the person in question.[120]

Finally, it is not particularly plausible that a child is ever instructed about the differentiation between direct and oblique intentions for the moral evaluations of seemingly altruistic acts. The same seems true for the prohibition of instrumentalization or the intricacies of proportional justice.

The same kinds of question need to be asked about other elements of an analytical theory of morality, in particular the dependency of moral judgment on agency, the limited class of possible objects of moral evaluation and the foundational relation between rights and the principles of justice and altruism. The concept and normative category of "right" is itself of great interest in this respect, as is what this category entails, namely the intricate web of normative positions sketched above, the necessary connections between claims and duties, privileges and negations of duties, the intentional content of these deontic categories, the

[119] The point is related to the discussion of irreducible subjective experience in the theory of consciousness, cf. Thomas Nagel, "What Is It Like to Be a Bat?" in Thomas Nagel, *Mortal Questions* (Cambridge: Cambridge University Press, 2020), 165–81. The problem illustrated by the thought experiment is how to teach a "moral bat" the subjective experience of morality – a problem that is comparable to the question of how to teach a child the experience of orienting oneself via a sonar system.

[120] Tomasello, *Becoming Human*, 214 posits: "[T]he sense of obligation is basically the internalization of an interpersonal commitment (given an agent who already has a sense of instrumental pressure to do what is needed to attain goals), and guilt is likewise the internalization of an interpersonal process of second-personal protest (given an agent who already engages in executive regulation)." This passage is useful to illustrate the problem: An interpersonal commitment is a normative phenomenon and presupposes that an obligation is a cognitively accessible phenomenon. There is no bridge from "instrumental pressure" to a normative obligation because the two are categorically different. Second-person protest can elicit all kinds of reactions – for instance, sarcasm, contempt, boredom, counterprotest, etc. Second-person protest does not necessarily give birth to feelings of guilt in others. Guilt is simply another primordial category of the moral life of human beings. However, it can be and often is triggered by the recriminations of others, because the agents realize that they have done something morally wrong.

semantics of obligation, permission and prohibition and the necessary volitional and emotional consequences of moral judgment's implications for rights. In all these cases, one needs to consider carefully what the poverty of stimulus argument may teach us about the acquisition of this complex set of normative positions.

8.7 SENTIMENTAL RULES, RATIONAL RULES?

8.7.1 *The Power of Statistical Learning*

It is instructive to look at an account of moral learning developed by Shaun Nichols that takes seriously the argument made thus far, namely that there is no direct input from parents and peers that explains the development of moral cognition.[121] He underlines that there is a consensus that for some capacities an empiricist account and for other capacities a nativist account is more plausible.[122] His account, already referred to briefly above, complements his moral sentimentalism with a rationalist element[123] and presents an alternative to assuming that concrete moral rules are based on certain inborn structures, claiming that statistical Bayesian learning abilities suffice to infer the content of the existing rules of a community from the given evidence of identified violations of rules.[124] This is how deontological rules arise: "Our hypothesis is that non-utilitarian judgement derives from learning narrow-scope rules, i.e. rules that prohibit intentionally producing an outcome, in a way that approximates Bayesian learning."[125] Nevertheless, there is a nativist element in his theory, or his theory is at least consistent with a nativist approach: Learners have an aptitude for concepts like agent, intention and cause, and the capacity for acquiring rules.[126]

More concretely, Nichols' argument takes its start from the observation that a distinct evaluation of doing on the one hand and allowing on the other is a reality of human moral psychology. This distinction presupposes that humans apply act-based rules, not consequence-based rules. Moral rules are about prohibitions of or prescriptions for action and not about minimizing unwelcome outcomes or maximizing welcome consequences.

Nichols goes on to ask how children can learn that the moral rules that they apply are act-based, not consequence-based.[127] His argument is that they are exposed to act-based input by adults, such as "Don't do X!" or "Do Y!" Through mechanisms of

[121] Shaun Nichols et al., "Rational Learners and Moral Rules," *Mind and Language* 31, no. 5 (2016): 530 ff.; Nichols, *Rational Rules*, 49 f.

[122] Nichols, *Rational Rules*, 20.

[123] Nichols, *Rational Rules*, 10, on rationalism as evidentialism.

[124] Nichols, *Rational Rules*, 57 ff.; for background cf. Fei Xu and Joshua B. Tenenbaum, "Word Learning as Bayesian Inference," *Psychological Review*, 114, no. 2 (2007): 245–72.

[125] Nichols et al., "Rational Learners," 549.

[126] Nichols, *Rational Rules*, 22.

[127] Nichols, *Rational Rules*, 50 ff.

statistical learning, the children acquire act-based rules, rather than consequence-based rules, as experimental evidence confirms in his view. The core statistical mechanism is the size principle: When a learner has to choose between two hypotheses, one of which is a nested subset in the other, it is rational on probabilistic grounds to choose the hypothesis with the smaller scope if all of the evidence available is consistent with this smaller hypothesis. This is because there is a higher likelihood that the smaller hypothesis is in fact correct. It would form a "suspicious coincidence" if all of the evidence falls in the smaller hypothesis while the larger hypothesis is true.[128] Humans are able to perform this statistical operation because they possess substantial statistical learning abilities, Nichols holds.[129]

As the input that learners are exposed to is based on the application of act-based rules (for instance, the command "Don't do X!"), this evidence is consistent with both the hypothesis that act-based rules are applied and the hypothesis that consequence-based rules are applied, the latter hypothesis also including act-based rules. As the first hypothesis is a nested subset of the latter and the evidence that the learners is exposed to is act-based, it is rational to conclude that act-based rules are applied. Act-based rules are thus acquired by the learners. Nichols concludes, albeit somewhat hesitatingly, that this learning process could explain why people apply the principle of double effect – for instance, in the trolley cases.[130] It can also account for the acquisition of parochial moral codes.[131]

Furthermore, there is evidence that humans expect new rules to be act-based, showing a "pronounced prior" in this respect.[132] The reasons for this are over-hypotheses in the sense defined by Nelson Goodman – because the experience of rules consists of act-based rules, an overhypothesis is formed that rules tend to be act-based.[133]

Normative systems need a default principle of the normative status of those intentions and acts that are not explicitly prohibited or permitted. *Everything that is not prohibited is allowed* or *everything that is not permitted is prohibited* are such closure principles, for instance.

Nichols argues that learners acquire the one or the other depending on the input received: If they encounter permissions, they conclude that what is not permitted is prohibited. If, however, they encounter prohibitions, they conclude that what is not prohibited is permitted. This conclusion is based on pedagogical sampling: Learners assume that their teacher is using methods of rational and efficient instruction. Based on this principle, it is rational for learners to conclude that if they are only

[128] Nichols, *Rational Rules*, 57 ff., 134.
[129] Nichols, *Rational Rules*, 16 ff.
[130] Nichols, *Rational Rules*, 64 ff., 73.
[131] Nichols, *Rational Rules*, 74 ff.
[132] Nichols, *Rational Rules*, 82 ff., 135.
[133] Nichols, *Rational Rules*, 84 ff.

presented with prohibitions of certain acts by the instructor, then other acts are permitted, and vice versa.[134]

Nichols also explains perceptions about the universal or relative validity of norms along these lines. If learners encounter widespread consensus, they acquire the idea that the respective norms are universally valid, while if they encounter disagreement, they conclude that these rules are of relative validity. The statistical principle at play is the trade-off between fit and flexibility: The hypothesis has to fit the data but must remain flexible so as to accommodate other factors producing consensus or variety of opinion (for instance, unreliability of the persons evaluating the topic), without becoming too flexible and thus empty, accommodating any data.[135] These mechanisms also explain the distinction between moral and conventional rules. If people (on statistical grounds) judge an action as universally right or wrong, they should regard it as a wrong in itself, independent of authority, too.[136]

8.7.2 *The Limits of Statistical Learning*

Importantly, this approach rightly underlines the significance of a descriptively adequate account of morality. It acknowledges the necessity for theory-building to determine properly the "acquirendum," the mental structure that human beings actually acquire in the moral domain.[137] It convincingly refutes various theories that identify morality as the expression of a small set of primitive emotions, seeking to deny that the operations of moral cognition are based on a rich systems of structures, rules, principles and representations.[138] It applies the poverty of stimulus test but arrives at the result that there is in fact no such poverty: The input available to children and statistical principles suffice to acquire the basic elements of the moral world of human beings it investigates. The theory is, therefore, an important constructive contribution to the understanding of human moral ontogeny.

However, several problems arise with regard to the reach of statistical learning. As just discussed, cognitive access to basic elements of the moral world is the precondition for understanding what moral judgment and explicit norms are about in the first place. You need to know what *ought* means, for instance, before you can grasp what you ought to do, as Hume already argued. Statistical learning is unable to bridge this gap. No quantity of references to ought by others will tell you what ought means from a first-person perspective, just as no quantity of references by others to the pleasant smell of coffee in the morning can teach you the nature of this odor

[134] Nichols, *Rational Rules*, 95 ff., 135 f.

[135] Nichols, *Rational Rules*, 109 ff., 132 f.

[136] Nichols, *Rational Rules*, 199 ff., argues that "default universalism" is functional – for instance, because it facilitates cooperation.

[137] Nichols, *Rational Rules*, 22.

[138] Nichols, *Rational Rules*, 8 ff., 150 f.

from a first-person perspective if you cannot smell. The same holds for the other elements of human beings' moral world, including moral emotions like shame.

Another problem stemming from an insufficient determination of the acquirendum consists in the following: The moral principles human beings acquire are not captured with sufficient precision if one looks only at the doing/allowing distinction. The distinction between (intentionally) *doing something and allowing* X *to happen when you have a duty to act to prevent* X *from happening* on the one hand and (intentionally) *allowing* X *to happen when there is no such duty* on the other comes closer to a central element of human moral cognition.[139] The prohibition against a girl hitting her brother as punishment for taking her ball is morally equivalent to the prohibition against the child not preventing her younger brother from falling from a swing as punishment for taking her ball when she is playing with her sibling at a playground and has a duty to see that her younger brother does not hurt himself. In contrast, there is no equivalent moral duty to prevent all possible harm to all other children on the playground. Unsurprisingly, the relevance of this distinction is mirrored in basic provisions on criminal omissions in penal law around the world.

Moreover, children do not just learn that rules are act-based. They acquire the principle that internal states like direct intention (purpose) or oblique intention (knowing) matter when evaluating an action. Moreover, these internal states are relevant in complex ways for moral assessment: If one commits armed robbery of a bank with the purpose of getting money and knowingly creates a risk that a guard will be killed, and this indeed happens, in many legal systems this will count as intentional (knowing) homicide. The foreseen but not intended negative side effect of a purposive morally wrong act only makes it worse. In other constellations, for instance, when one intentionally acts to prevent harm but foresees harm to third parties as a side effect of the benevolent action, the act may be justified, as in the standard trolley bystander case. Thus, the acquirendum seems to be of a different and much more complex nature than is allowed for in the doing/allowing distinction that Nichols addresses. That any of these acquired complex structures can be learned through the statistical operations Nichols employs is far from clear, given our findings thus far. Take his example of intentional act-based rules. The evidence he considers ("Do not do X!" etc.) allows for the conclusion that somebody wants the agent to refrain from doing X, perhaps backing the prohibition to do X with the threat of sanctions. It does not allow for the conclusion that one is to refrain from acting with a specific internal state – for instance, an intention – or that one is to see intentions and actions causing harmful foreseen consequences as sometimes prohibited, sometimes justified, let alone that one is to acquire the capabilities to

[139] The question of whether the agent has a duty to act is crucial to evaluating such cases as "Footbridge-Allow," Nichols, *Rational Rules*, 4. It is also relevant for possible constraints on possible moral allow-based rules, Nichols, *Rational Rules*, 159 ff. Cf. n. 147.

experience in oneself a moral ought and the other cognitive, volitional and emotional elements of the subjective world of morality already discussed above.[140]

The discussion of closure principles is also of interest. It tells us something relevant about the reactions to explicit instruction by prohibitions or permissions concerning the specific type of action (in Nichols' study, for instance, mice entering a barn).[141] For moral theory-building, however, the problem that closure principles deal with is a different one. It concerns the question of how people assess the permissibility of action even *without* explicit permissions or prohibitions concerning a specific type of action: Do you need an explicit prohibition to take an action as prohibited or do you need an explicit permission to regard it as permitted? What is the default principle (if there is indeed one) if there are no such explicit prohibitions or permissions? Nichols does not investigate this question because he is concerned with reactions after explicit instruction, though he indicates that there may indeed be a default principle of liberty. Only if one addresses this question, however, can one reasonably discuss the problem of how such a principle – for instance, of residual liberty – becomes part of the moral and (in liberal orders) legal world of human beings.[142]

As to the discussion of universalism and relativism, it is important that the validity of a norm is not dependent on the quantity of assent it finds, but on material validity conditions. Thus, the norm that Jews are just as entitled to life as other human beings was valid even in German extermination camps. Statistical learning thus allows for the hypothesis that many people agree about the validity of a certain norm, not that it is (in fact) valid. So-called authority independence is not related to consensus either. The point is rather that such universally valid, authority-independent norms are the basis to challenge even majority opinions. The phenomenon of critical reflection creates the possibility of changing a consensus using reasons – a process in which the universality of some norms is a possible argument. In Nichols' account, any norm could be understood as universal and authority-independent, as its universality depends solely on factually existing consent patterns. If the input that a child is exposed to consists of a consensus that it is justified to kill Jews, this norm enjoys universal validity, for instance. Nichols is not very clear on when and under which conditions the acquired rules change, but it seems that this change is dependent merely on new experiences of consensus or varieties of opinion. This account appears to miss the point that

140 Nichols argues that the moral relevance of internal states like intentions can be explained by our general interest as humans in intentions, Nichols, *Rational Rules*, 159. The phenomenon to be explained is, however, not a general interest in intentions, but the origin of the constitutive and complex role of internal states for moral evaluation, which is already found at an early age, as we have seen.

141 Nichols, *Rational Rules*, 101 ff.

142 Cf. for such a discussion Mikhail, *Elements*, 132 ff. Nichols, *Rational Rules*, 107, reports the interesting result that the residual permission principle seems to be limited by prohibitions of harm.

content matters for the question of universality, and that only certain content is a serious candidate for universally valid norms – for instance, norms prohibiting harm, but not norms prescribing gratuitous cruelty. This is also observed in the child psychology studies on the moral/conventional divide that Nichols accepts – not just any norms are at issue, but in particular prohibitions of harm.[143] That any of these norms constantly change with the shifting of opinions is hard to reconcile both with experience and with evidence.

As to some concrete rules that we discussed, it is not clear what kind of statistical evidence there is, for instance, for the prohibition of the instrumentalization of people. Do children observe a lot of this? How come human beings are able to critique and transcend norms that were robustly enforced in their environment – for example, on the permissible instrumentalization of women in patriarchal societies?

Nichols rightly underlines the difference between possible learning processes and actual learning and emphasizes that his account is only concerned with the former, not the latter.[144] The reviewed literature on the ontogeny of moral cognition seems to underline the relevance of the identified problems of his account. Moral development in fact seems to take not the course that statistical learning foresees, but a rather different one, including differentiated moral concepts in young children, cross-cultural equal age trends of developments of moral cognition, intention-based moral evaluation and so forth.

An interesting point that Nichols raises is the origin of the limited hypothesis space with which child learners operate. The theory offers no explanation (as it underlines itself) of how learners arrive at the hypothesis space. This hypothesis space is thus understood as possibly innate,[145] though there is some counterevidence against even such constraints, it is argued.[146]

The problem of constraints on hypotheses of possible morality is very important: What if children were exposed to the punishment of unintended actions? Some kind of strict liability morality? Would they then acquire a morality in which intention does not count in the moral evaluation of actions? Is there any evidence of this happening? Or is rather the opposite indicated not only by experimental work, but also by the passionate protests of children around the world when they are punished for something that they did not intend to do? The answer must be based on the poverty of stimulus argument: If the learning child does not receive sufficient

[143] The experimental evidence Nichols adduces uses nonmoral norms with unknown content. It seems to be not about the statistical learning of norms regarded as universal or relative, but rather about something different, namely how subjects use information in vignettes to assess the universality of norms whose content is unknown. They seem to regard consensus as a proxy.

[144] Nichols, *Rational Rules*, 152 ff.

[145] Nichols et al., "Rational Learners," 549; Nichols, *Rational Rules*, 154 ff.

[146] Tyler Millhouse, Alisabeth Ayars and Shaun Nichols, "Learnability and Moral Nativism: Exploring Wilde Rules," in *Methodology and Moral Philosophy*, eds. Jussi Suikkane and Antti Kauppinen (New York: Routledge, 2019), 64 ff.

input to form the hypothesis space – including the constraint that intentions count in a morality, for instance – then the constraints must be innate.[147]

In sum, the reference to statistical learning thus does not seem sufficient to account for the acquisition of the basic elements of morality.[148] Exploring the problem of the origin of the initial conception of morality that frames the acquisition of moral knowledge, the hypothesis space and its possible nativist explanation is an important point of the theory and highlights the need for open-minded research in this area. In any case, nothing in this research rules out that the Bayesian learning mechanism would lead to the acquisition of a morality incompatible with the content of human rights – on the contrary, this theory argues that human beings can learn any rule.[149] They are in no way naturally limited to narrow parochial tribalism. Statistical learning is open to acquiring inclusive norms,[150] such as – one may add – human rights.

8.8 THEORIES OF MIND AND HUMAN MORAL PROGRESS

There is thus a prima facie case for seriously considering the possibility that the moral space of human cognition, the concept of ought, moral emotions or certain elements of the principles of morals such as altruism, justice and respect for others form part of human beings' natural cognitive endowment that matures throughout childhood.

As illustrated by the mental gizmo thesis, the moral foundations theory, various approaches of evolutionary psychology, behavioral economics and the joint intentionality theory of cognitive development among others, the time has passed when studying the structures of the mind was considered unimportant because only one kind of theory of mind was believed to be plausible, namely a theory that assumed that the only inborn property of the human mind is that it is an unspecified learning

147 The counterevidence adduced against this is not conclusive. The studies in Millhouse, Ayars and Nichols, "Learnability," 64 ff., investigate the doing/allowing distinction in moral rules to check whether a rule that only prohibits allowing something but not doing it violates possible innate constraints. This overlooks the fact that the crucial distinction is (as explained) not between doing and allowing, but between (for instance) intention (and its various forms) and negligence – one can intentionally do or allow something or negligently do or allow something. If there is a duty to act, allowing something to happen is morally relevant. The test case, therefore, is whether there is a norm not violating such constraints that prohibits the negligent killing of human beings but not their intentional killing, or that prohibits negligently allowing the death of human beings but not intentionally allowing them to die when there is a duty to act – a duty that will often exist in the case of danger to the life of others if one is in a position to help.

148 Cf. for similar criticisms, with additional examples of the problems of underdetermination by statistical learning of children's moral knowledge, John Mikhail, "Review of Shaun Nichols, Rational Rules: Towards a Theory of Moral Learning," *The Philosophical Review* (2022) 131 (3): 399–403.

149 Millhouse, Ayars and Nichols, "Learnability," 77.

150 Nichols, *Rational Rules*, 189.

device.[151] The mental gizmo thesis and moral foundations theory, for instance, are substantial empirical theses about the structure of the human mind, as is any assumption about the importance of shared intentionality, heuristics, framing effects and biases. Some of these theories have triggered a vast amount of research across the globe. Their claims may be right or wrong, but they certainly are serious scientific efforts that need to be evaluated based on their explanatory merits, and the same is true of the mentalist approach to ethics and law.

These remarks show that it is possible to frame an empirically minded theory of moral psychology that understands deontological principles not as cognitive illusions, but as part of the makeup of the human mind that may be the precondition enabling the cultural development of moral systems and the law.

Substantial empirical evidence suggests that there is a faculty of language with highly restrictive principles in which natural languages unfold, and there are many theoretical reasons for assuming its existence. This is a highly contested area of research, but even if this hypothesis is true, the theory of a faculty of language is still a long way from explaining the origin of the verses of *King Lear*. However, the language faculty is a precondition for humans' ability to produce and enjoy something like *King Lear*, whatever the hidden secrets of human creativity ultimately may turn out to be that put the language faculty to such thrilling use. Similarly, what has been said about the history, justification and psychological theory of human rights perhaps renders plausible the idea that a theoretical account of the human moral faculty is a long way from an understanding of the sources and justification of the *Universal Declaration* or other concrete, historically shaped catalogues of rights in constitutions and international bills of rights. But this moral faculty could – in the same way as the faculty of language for the verses of *King Lear* – turn out to be the cognitive precondition for the possibility of ultimately producing something like the *Universal Declaration* and the aspirations it implies.

8.9 CRITIQUE AND CONSTRUCTION: EXPLANATORY THEORY AND NORMATIVE ARGUMENTS

Let us assume that a mentalist account of morality and law has some merits and is preferable, for example, to the mental gizmo thesis or the moral foundations theory. This would be a very substantial insight for an explanatory theory of human moral cognition and for the theory of mind in general. But what normative significance

[151] Cf. the remarks in Chomsky, *Aspects*, 47 ff. For an overview of research on language acquisition, cf. Charles Yang et al., "The Growth of Language: Universal Grammar, Experience, and Principles of Computation," *Neuroscience and Biobehavioral Reviews* 81, no. B (2017): 103 ff. Note that these findings have epistemological consequences (e.g. for the problem of induction, Nelson Goodman, *Facts, Fiction, and Forecast* [Cambridge, MA: Harvard University Press, 1983], 64 ff.), as they help us to clarify the origin of the core conceptual space of human beings.

would this have if one wanted to avoid a naturalistic fallacy? This is the next question our inquiry will address.

The discussion thus far has already made clear a first function of the analysis of the relation between mind and rights: *identifying unwarranted human rights criticism based on unconvincing theories of the mind* – for instance, on unsatisfactory neuroscientific studies or insufficient evolutionary theory. This obviously already is a very important function.

Our findings so far refute, for instance, the idea that deontology is no more than a cognitive or moral illusion from a hard-headed, non-armchair, scientific point of view. Deontological arguments are not discredited in any way by the theory of mind, psychology or neuroscience. Of course, critiquing implausible theories of moral cognition does not in itself justify the normative principles that enter into a theory of justification of human rights. But defending cognitive principles outlined as reasonable is quite a different matter from defending the normative value of principles that are products of the post-hoc rationalization of hardwired emotional gut reactions. Moral psychology cannot substitute normative theory-building in ethics and law. But it is indispensable to show that normative theory is not just the illusionary offspring of hidden mechanisms of the mind and thus can be reconciled with what is known about the mind's structure and workings.

The same holds for forms of evolutionary tribalism: Our discussion showed that a kind of universalist ethics is at least not an evolutionary impossibility. While this does not make the normative case for such an ethics, it is a different justificatory task to argue the legitimacy of rights that are contrary to human beings' cognitive nature, assuming, for instance, that "parochial love – love within groups . . . may be the most we can accomplish,"[152] and where it remains a complete riddle as to how the cognitive machinery that produced them could have evolved, than to argue for a set of rights that is entirely reconcilable with cognitive mechanisms that easily fit into a plausible theory of the evolution of the human mind.

This critique, is, if you will, preparatory work that lays the ground for normative arguments by showing what kind of counterarguments are insufficient to discredit a justificatory theory of human rights.

This critical function of an inquiry into mind and rights already justifies the efforts made thus far. It is quite clear from our review of current thinking about moral psychology that the is/ought distinction does not prevent the theories scrutinized from influencing how human rights are conceptualized. They are among the influential sources that feed into human rights skepticism today.

But can such a theory of human moral cognition provide more than this crucial criticism? Can it perhaps even provide some kind of additional normative justification of human rights?

[152] Haidt, *Righteous Mind*, 295.

Of particular interest in this respect is the question of whether a universalist justification of human rights exists or whether human rights are culturally relative. In our survey of human rights history and normative theories of human rights, we encountered no compelling evidence for the latter.

The question of universalism is of substantial interest because it concerns a central claim of human rights – to be valid for everybody, everywhere. This question is important in both practical and political terms: The answer decides, for instance, whether Uighurs have a claim to religious freedom and nondiscrimination against China, or whether the cultural difference between Zürich and Beijing acts as a bar to such claims.

Our discussion of the justification of human rights has helped us to clarify the issue. As we have seen, a theory of the justification of human rights contains three elements: first, a theory of goods and, as part of it, anthropological assumptions; second, a political theory of the role of rights in society; and third, normative principles of justice, solidarity and respect. Anthropological assumptions are a matter of empirical knowledge about human beings and have no direct connection to moral cognition. The political theory of rights has normative elements but concerns other questions, too, such as the factual effects of a political order of rights on people's well-being. The question of universalism thus mainly concerns the normative element of the justificatory theory of human rights. Are the guiding principles and the normative tenets of such a theory universally valid? This is the core question at issue in debates about the universalism of human rights.

What do our findings so far tell us about the justification of normative universalism? Is the idea of a universal and uniform human moral faculty, a universal moral grammar, perhaps the high road to universalism? Is this the claim made and the ultimate point of the argument? If one takes the is/ought distinction seriously, however, it seems that this cannot be true. Whatever the factual makeup of the human mind may be, it has no bearing on the question of normative justification because no ought follows from it.

On the other hand, there are theories that doubt the relevance of the is/ought distinction.[153] Does the discussion thus far offer new support for these theories?

Two steps are necessary to answer this question. First, we will clarify in greater detail what normative universalism is about and what its justification might be. In light of this, we will then ask what kinds of consequences a plausible account of human moral cognition has for the understanding of the universalism of human rights.

8.10 THE EPISTEMOLOGY OF HUMAN RIGHTS UNIVERSALISM

Are human rights only legitimate for some groups of human beings – say, Europeans, North Americans, Christians and whites? Is the global appeal of human

[153] Cf. for example John R. Searle, "How to Derive 'Ought' from 'Is'," *Philosophical Review* 73, no. 1 (1964): 43 ff.

rights based on an epistemological error, namely on the flawed idea that the core normative ideas of human rights can be justified across the borders of different communities? Or are these principles potentially of universal validity, and thus the project of human rights enjoys universal validity, too?

These are standard questions of any discourse on human rights, and ones that we hope to answer, if we are able, to clarify the content of universalism and determine at least the rough contours of its epistemological merits.

Universalism in the sense relevant for ethics and law is an epistemological stance.[154] It holds that the truth conditions of normative claims are the same for all human beings. These truth conditions are thus not relative to certain contingent properties of human beings, such as the groups that they belong to or their social, cultural, religious or other background. This epistemological doctrine applies to any normative propositions, including those concerning the moral rightness and justness of intentions, actions and states of affairs brought about by such intentions and actions. It also applies to the obligations people have, to what they are forbidden and permitted to do and to what rights they enjoy. Such universal standards are valid even if a given subject thinks otherwise. From such a point of view, a man is obligated to respect a girl's right to education, even if he thinks that this is contrary to important norms of his patriarchal customary morality.

A defense of universalism may be based on two lines of argument: The first is an indirect argument for the plausibility of universalism derived from the implausibility of the opposite of universalism, which is relativism.[155] One argument commonly cited in support of relativism that we have already encountered is moral disagreement. The great diversity of moral opinions is taken to be an argument for the relativity of moral propositions. This is a fallacious argument, however, and for the following reasons.

To start with, universalism is a theory about the justification of normative propositions. It does not imply that universally valid principles are in fact universally accepted. The existence of even deep moral disagreement does not contradict universalist perspectives. Parallel observations are possible in the realm of science. For example, there are quite good reasons to assume that the Earth is not flat. These reasons are in no discernible sense relative to the contingent properties of a thinking subject making this proposition about the shape of the Earth. This does not mean,

[154] For some other uses of the term "universalism," cf. e.g. Seyla Benhabib, "Another Universalism: On the Unity and Diversity of Human Rights," *Proceedings and Addresses of the American Philosophical Association* 81, no. 2 (2007): 7, 11.

[155] Cf. e.g. Gilbert Harman and Judith Thompson, *Moral Relativism and Moral Objectivity* (Oxford and Malden, MA: Blackwell Publishing, 1996), 3–64; Philippa Foot, "Moral Relativism," in Philippa Foot, *Moral Dilemmas and Other Topics in Moral Philosophy* (Oxford: Clarendon Press 2002), 20–36; Richard Rorty, *Objectivity, Relativism, and Truth: Philosophical Papers* (Cambridge: Cambridge University Press, 1991); Bernhard Williams, "The Truth in Relativism," in Bernhard Williams, *Moral Luck* (Cambridge: Cambridge University Press, 1982), 132–43; Dworkin, *Justice for Hedgehogs*, 23 ff.

however, that there were not times in history when the very opposite of this insight was the common wisdom of the age. And even today, flat-earthers courageously try to make their case. However, their disagreement does not imply that there is no justification for assuming that the Earth is round.

Moreover, as we have already seen, there are factors entirely reconcilable with universalism that account for this – evident – diversity, such as nonmoral preconditions of moral evaluation, competing interests and passions or problems of ethical reflection – for instance, concerning the proper conceptualization of morality and its content or the consistency and coherence of normative reasoning.

Another important point is that relativism suffers from an insufficient determination of the factors to which moral principles are supposed to be relative. The reference to cultures or religions is a good example of this. Cultures and religions are not monolithic wholes but encompass a whole variety of ideas. Western culture (whatever the exact boundaries of this entity may be) was characterized for centuries by religious intolerance leading to bloody wars, authoritarian regimes and dogmatic systems of thought, contempt for human beings, various forms of racism, slavery, colonialism and imperialism, to name just some features that may spring to mind. At the same time, great ideas of human benevolence, freedom, autonomy and justice were outlined in forms of which some made history. Who is the true European – Kant or Friedrich Wilhelm III? Or – more precisely – the Kant of the principle of humanity and dignity,[156] the Kant of the disenfranchisement of women[157] or his Prussian king?

Another problem is the following: How do background factors such as culture or religion determine moral perceptions *exactly*? Cultural determinism is a highly implausible theory given the fact of constant change in the normative sphere. How can normative principles be determined by the cultures that these principles ultimately transform?

This points to the central problem of relativism that we already encountered in our survey of human rights history: It overlooks the importance of *human subjectivity and autonomous reasoning* for the development of ethics and the legitimation of law. Any cultural influence is mediated by human reflective subjectivity and reasoning. There are many cultural influences on human beings, but no person's ethical identity is necessarily merely the product of the lullabies sung by the hand that rocked the cradle. On the contrary: Human reasoning is the ultimate source of ethical beliefs. Critical reflection can transcend the given parameters of culture and history and ultimately change their course. This does not mean that such autonomous thinking is what always or even predominantly determines the actual moral and political path of the human species. The reality is that ethics and law often fall prey to outlived customs, the self-righteous perpetuation of principles without

[156] Kant, *Grundlegung zur Metaphysik der Sitten*, 429.
[157] Kant, *Grundlegung zur Metaphysik der Sitten*, 313 ff.

thought, reverence to social authorities, powerful and harmful political emotions such as the hatred of minorities, fear and other such influences. But these need not be the last word. People are not just the malleable victims of such factors. As thinking subjects, they are in a position where they are responsible for reducing the importance of such driving forces for the course of history, and sometimes do so successfully – as the many steps taken towards a more humane world indicate, from the partial vindications of the rights of women to the defenses of democracy and human rights.

The second way of arguing for the plausibility of universalism is to defend certain normative propositions as universally justifiable. But is this possible? Is this not epistemologically naive? To answer this question, some remarks on the epistemology and ontology of morals are necessary.

8.11 THE EPISTEMOLOGY AND ONTOLOGY OF MORALS

The justification of moral judgments is crucial.[158] There is no a priori metacriterion that does not require scrutiny and defense. While ethical reflection is not about the revelation of higher truths, it is not about whimsical skepticism either. One needs reasons to justify any normative proposition, but one also needs reasons to doubt it. Simply maintaining that a certain normative position still could be doubted is not good enough. One can doubt any proposition, including the idea that the Earth is not flat, as flat-earthers happily do. No bolt of lightning will punish such a doubt, no voice from heaven will confirm that the Earth is in fact not flat. Nothing renders doubt about anything impossible. Nothing in the best argument imaginable compels a thinking subject to get its point. Demanding that a good argument be literally indubitable is a flawed demand because it is too exacting. Not even the best argument about the shape of the Earth irresistibly commands assent. This is a necessary consequence of the fact that the assessment of the truth value of any proposition is an act of human mental cognition. There is no epistemic authority over and beyond such acts of cognition. There is no more stable ground of human insight. Such acts of human cognition are the stuff of which the perception of truth is made.

This analysis is confirmed by a plausible ontological theory of morality: The problem of whether moral judgments refer to objective, mind-independent moral facts in the world (as moral realists assert) or not is a classic epistemological question. In the former case, a truth condition of moral propositions consists in correspondence with moral facts, in the latter case other truth conditions are key. As far as the ontology of morality is concerned, it is plausible to take moral cognition as being

[158] As convincingly emphasized by Forst, *Recht auf Rechtfertigung*, irrespective of whether one is convinced by this approach's discourse on ethical foundations.

nonreferential: There are no objective moral facts in the world, the correspondence with which is the truth condition of moral predicates, as moral realists maintain.[159] Nevertheless, moral judgments are not merely subjective in the sense of them being idiosyncratic and relative to the outlook of a specific agent.[160] This is because their truth is authenticated by internal mental yardsticks for justified propositions, as in other areas of thought.[161]

It is useful to note that not only from the point of view of a nonreferential moral ontology, but also from a moral realist point of view, there is no escaping from acts of cognition that rely on internal standards of human understanding for their truth. This is because even a moral realist ontology ultimately is based on the assumed truth of such nonreferential statements: The correspondence of a moral proposition with a moral fact can only be ascertained by such an act of cognition. Moreover, the moral realist thesis that a truth condition of moral judgments is that moral predicates correspond to objective moral facts in the world does not itself correspond to an

159 On this cf. Mikhail, *Elements*, 317; Mahlmann, "Ethics," 580 ff. For a defense of the view that there are, to the contrary, objective, irreducibly normative facts, cf. e.g. Russ Shafer-Landau, *Moral Realism: A Defence* (Oxford: Oxford University Press, 2003); David Enoch, *Taking Morality Seriously: A Defense of Robust Realism* (Oxford: Oxford University Press, 2011). A nonreferential theory of ethics does not commit one to noncognitivism, desire-based ethics, expressivism and the like, as explained in the text. The debate between moral realists and antirealists – as it stands today – does not exhaust the theoretical possibilities.

160 On a standard view on this and its critique, Griffin, *On Human Rights*, 111 ff.: Factual judgments are objective, value judgments are "subjective – subjective in both the most common senses. They are, first of all, merely expressions of taste or attitude. And, second, values are not part of the furniture of the world; the world contains physical objects, properties, events, minds, but it does not also contain values."

161 That there are genuine normative reasons whose truth does not depend on correspondence with entities that are part of the nonmental fabric of the world is defended from different points of view. Cf. Christine Korsgaard, *The Sources of Normativity* (Cambridge: Cambridge University Press, 1996), 108, 122 ff., 165 arguing for a "reflective endorsement theory" that bases normativity on the self-endorsement of the humanity of the autonomous self; Dworkin, *Justice for Hedgehogs*, outlining an interpretative theory "all the way down"; Derek Parfit, *On What Matters*, Vol. 2 (Oxford: Oxford University Press, 2011), arguing that there are "some irreducibly normative reason-involving truths," which are "not about entities or properties that exist in some ontological sense," ibid. 618; Thomas Michael Scanlon, *Being Realistic about Reasons* (Oxford: Oxford University Press, 2014), developing a realistic "reasons fundamentalism." On the question of the authentication of truth ultimately through foundational intuitions of truth, Ray Jackendoff, *A User's Guide to Thought and Meaning* (Oxford: Oxford University Press, 2012), 213 ff., taking this as evidence that (in the terminology of the dual-process model of the mind) System 2 (slow thinking) rides on top of System 1 (fast thinking) with the means of language, without, however, making thinking irrational or emotional, because "it behoves us to show intuitive thinking more respect," ibid. 215. On a view that bases arguments on a specific language game and lifeworld, Griffin, *On Human Rights*, 113: "Certain values are part of the necessary conditions for our language, which sets for us the bounds of intelligibility" (on Wittgenstein and Davidson). Bernhard Williams has defended a related view on thin and thick ethical concepts, ultimately basing moral judgment on particular "languages" in the specific sense of particular comprehensive systems of belief, cf. Bernhard Williams, "Truth in Ethics," *Ratio* 8, no. 3 (1995): 227–42. In his view, an alternative is to try to identify a deep structure of moral judgment – this is what is attempted in the argument of this book.

objective epistemic fact in the world. Its truth thus depends on other sources of epistemic justification.[162]

Given this epistemic state of affairs, it is always possible to ask: Is this right? The possibility of doubt is the necessary consequence of the human capacity for unfettered, free thought. It is a fallacy, however, to mistake this possibility of doubting any proposition for the proof that no proposition is better justified than any other. It is necessary to have arguments for doubt that are more convincing than the arguments that (for the time being) confirm a certain normative position, at least if the argument is supposed to be more than a superfluous game.

Let us take the example of the principles important for the project of human rights, the idea that every human being has the right to protected dignity, autonomy and equality. There are many thoughtful and rich theories of human rights, as we have seen. And there are rather good reasons to assume that these rights are legitimate not only in Zürich, but also in Laos, Bogotá and Beijing, because the goods they protect, if ever enjoyed, turn out to be of extremely high value. This is shown, for example, by the longing for equal dignity and freedom of the victims of the Tiananmen Square protests, a powerful example of important "Asian values," as is the struggle for freedom in Hong Kong, the fight against the military dictatorship in Myanmar or the rebellion driven by Iranian women against the regime, although in all these cases expressed from below, not through government announcements.[163]

[162] Cf. on this argument recently, Dworkin, *Justice for Hedgehogs*, 76; Scanlon, *Being Realistic*, 16 n. 1. For a critique of such theories, arguing in particular with the impossibility of distinguishing on internal grounds true reasons and false moral propositions, rendering all argument indistinguishable from fictions, Enoch, *Taking Morality Seriously*, 121 ff. The central point to counter this concern is that internal truth conditions of moral propositions are not matters of the agents' whim. Moreover, the argument is self-defeating: the moral-realist claim about objective moral facts, the correspondence with which is the truth condition for moral propositions, is necessarily itself based on a nonreferential theory of human epistemology, as just explained in the main text.

[163] There is an interesting debate about such "Asian values," which is paradigmatic for some important features of the debate about relativism, not the least its political side, more precisely on the political instrumentalization of relativism for authoritarian purposes. Cf. e.g. Zakaria, "Culture is Destiny," 109 and the rejoinder: Kim Dae Jung, "Is Culture Destiny? The Myth of Asia's Anti-democratic Values," *Foreign Affairs* 73, no. 6 (1994): 189. These discussions sometimes revolve around whether there is a particular tradition that predominantly endorses human rights or other such values, or rather an authoritarian tradition. This is an interesting question, but it misses the most important problem, however: The crucial point is not whether or not there is a given tradition (e.g. of authoritarianism), but whether such a practice is justified. An authoritarian tradition certainly is manifest in much of European history. One central achievement of dawning constitutionalism, for instance, was to break with this tradition to vindicate some of the most important rights of human beings, step by step. The same holds for any other tradition as well (if it is more than an ideological construct): "The so-called Asian values that are invoked to justify authoritarianism are not especially Asian in any significant sense. . . . The case for liberty and political rights turns ultimately on their basic importance and on their instrumental role. This case is as strong in Asia as it is elsewhere." Amartya Sen, "Human Rights and Asian Values," in *Ethics & International Affairs*, ed. Joel H. Rosenthal (Washington, DC: Georgetown University Press, 1999), 170 ff., 190.

That there is a political case for human rights to protect such goods has been argued extensively above. That this basic good should be distributed equally among human beings, that it is not justifiable for some groups – say, party functionaries and their partners in the economy – to be entitled to such freedoms while peasants are not, seems equally plausible in light of the basic principles of equal treatment that are constitutive of justice. If these arguments and their foundations are doubted, reasons need to be given for this – for example, that serfdom is in fact good for some people (say, people of color) and that justice can as plausibly mean unequal treatment as it does equal treatment, at least for some (e.g. in the Global South). While the preceding remarks on the justification of rights surely have many flaws, they at least indicate that shouldering this burden is not an easy task.

8.12 EPISTEMOLOGICAL RESILIENCE

There has been a long debate about foundational theories in ethics and law.[164] What are the ultimate principles of justification of normative precepts and what is their status? How can one argue for these principles without becoming entangled in infinite regress, dogmatism or tautology?[165] The line of the argument seems to point in the following direction: The normative justification of human rights is ultimately based on a fallible account of certain foundational moral principles that have proven to be resilient to systematic, conscious theoretical doubt. This account is informed by critical thinking that is committed to the decisiveness of reasons and open to the possibility that sometimes such reasons are good enough to rest a case. This stance implies a certain amount of trust that human understanding does not lead us entirely astray, and that consequently what seems well justified to us may, all things considered, in fact be true – an epistemological stance that can be defended against skeptical challenges.

This reflexive resilience of fallible normative principles when scrutinized by critical, in principle reliable human thinking that is respectful of reasons is the epistemological alternative to the trilemma of infinite regress, the dogmatic termination of the justificatory argument and tautology. The principles of justice, altruism and respect play an important role because there is good reason to believe that they (or some variant of them) are foundational not only for human rights, but for morality as such. They are not self-authenticating truths, but improvable, preliminary approximations to those principles that constitute morality.[166] Other principles may play an important role, too, such as the principle of the noninstrumentalization

[164] Cf. for a survey Mahlmann, *Rechtsphilosophie und Rechtstheorie*.

[165] Cf. on this trilemma Hans Albert, *Traktat über kritische Vernunft* (Tübingen: Mohr Siebeck, 1991), 14.

[166] Cf. on these matters Mahlmann, "Ethics," 593 ff.; Mahlmann, *Rechtsphilosophie und Rechtstheorie*, 510 ff. For some comments on why such judgments should be taken as foundational, cf. Mahlmann, "Cognitive Foundations," 75 ff.

of human persons as a concretization of obligatory respect for others or those specifying the permissibility of otherwise-prohibited acts.[167]

On this basis, further, more concrete questions can be asked – for example, whether the ethical thought formulated in the principle of humanity and the idea of human dignity can be put to ethical and legal use to guide the evaluation of specific problems, from assisted suicide to abortion to "dwarf-tossing".[168] In this way, we may be able to approach a more comprehensive theory of human rights at a much-needed level of detail.

8.13 UNIVERSALISM WITHOUT DOGMATISM AND HUMAN RIGHTS PLURALISM

There is thus a case for the universal justification of human rights. There is, however, another problem: The ethical ideas about human rights and the legal systems enshrining them differ, and sometimes more than just in detail. How are we to deal with this fact of ethical and legal human rights pluralism?

Can human rights pluralism in the real world be reconciled with normative universalism? This may seem implausible if the assumption is that universalism must demand normative uniformity around the world. But this is by no means a necessary conclusion, and for various reasons.

The normative questions human rights are concerned with are difficult and complex. Even if we assume that normative universalism makes good sense as an epistemological theory, this does not imply that it is reasonable to expect everybody to agree on all normative matters after a little deliberation. Moral and legal problems are more complicated than that. There is no reason to believe that the tortuous path of cognition is easier to walk in practical reflection than in other fields of human knowledge, including natural science. Modern theory of science is very varied, and the historicization of scientific paradigms is an important element of this reflection on the nature of science.[169] However, these qualifications do not change the epistemic claim of science that whatever seems to be the best theory available at a given moment enjoys this status universally. Higgs particles are supposed to make as much sense at CERN in Geneva as in Saigon. Science's history of getting where it has got so far has not been a smooth ride to insight. On the contrary, its path is so fascinating and rich precisely because of the many difficulties encountered, dead-end roads pursued and breakthroughs achieved. The expectation that it might be any easier to gain normative insight through practical, ethical and legal thought seems somewhat outlandish.

[167] The latter is the argument advanced in Mikhail, *Elements*. On the common law concept of "battery" and its possible role in a mentalist ethics, Mikhail, "Any Animal Whatever?" 750 ff.

[168] On this question, cf. Mahlmann, "Good Sense of Dignity," 593 ff.

[169] Cf. e.g. Kuhn, *Structure of Scientific Revolutions*; Paul Feyerabend, *Against Method* (London and New York: Verso, 2010).

Universalism as an epistemological stance gives no reason whatsoever for anybody to be sure that one has in fact reached normative insights that hold universal validity. This is because human thought, not least practical thought, is irredeemably fallible. It is important both for individuals and their sense of epistemic modesty and for collectives to remain conscious of this fact, so as to avoid unwarranted self-righteousness about the justification of the respective realizations of certain basic values that they (at the given historical moment) deem to be right. Any normative claim is at best a better or worse approximation of principles that are perhaps really universally justified.

The internal pluralism of interpretations of given norms within ethical reflection or legal systems therefore comes as no surprise. The origins of such diverse opinions are manifold. Legal norms, in particular, pose many problems and are often ambiguous and vague. The difficulty of identifying the content of such norms and the underlying normative principles is one reason for the diversity of legal opinions, even about the content of very fundamental norms. In addition, there are political agendas, interest-based legal interpretations and the like at play.[170]

This consciousness of the fallibility of human practical thought has a pragmatic side: It implies the necessity of freedom for experimental ways of living,[171] of attempts to explore different ways of realizing certain important normative principles.

This is also true for fundamental rights. How to best protect rights is not always obvious, and it makes good sense to see how certain approaches work in practice. There will be limits to such experiments,[172] but universalism certainly does not categorically exclude the possibility of such searches for normatively justified solutions – to the contrary, the awareness that any normative conclusion will be tentative in fact demands scope for such searches.[173]

The plurality of attempts to approximate a set of well-justified norms is therefore one of the practical consequences of this uneven path of practical cognition.

[170] "There is nothing that interpretation just is," Cass R. Sunstein, *A Constitution of Many Minds: Why the Founding Document Doesn't Mean What It Meant Before* (Princeton, NJ: Princeton University Press 2009), 19 ff.

[171] Mill, "On Liberty," 281.

[172] From this perspective, the importance of the "Western" systems of rights protection can be relativized. Cf. Heiner Bielefeld, "'Western' versus 'Islamic' Human Rights Conceptions?: A Critique of Cultural Essentialism in the Discussion on Human Rights," *Political Theory* 28, no. 1 (2000): 90, 101 f., on the "Western model" being an example, not a normative paradigm for the struggle for human rights.

[173] J. Donnelly argues, for example, for a "relative universalism," a variation of universal concepts derived from alternative conceptions and implementations of rights on the basis of an overlapping consensus on universalism, taken as a Rawlsian political approach. In his view, freedom of religion can be reconciled with the prohibition of apostasy, albeit with the crucial qualification that sanctions of the prohibition should not violate human rights. With this qualification, the argument becomes tautological. Whether human rights allow for such qualification is the question at stake. Cf. Jack Donnelly, "The Relative Universality of Human Rights," *Human Rights Quarterly* 29, no. 2 (2007): 281, 298 and more generally Jack Donnelly, *Human Rights in Theory and Practice* (Ithaca, NY: Cornell University Press, 2003).

Human rights pluralism is a necessary tribute to the difficulties of the problems posed for practical reflection on human affairs and to the fallibility of human thought.

Another reason why normative universalism is reconcilable with human rights pluralism is very straightforward, namely *respect for personal autonomy and democratic choices*, another source of the legitimacy of experiments in different ways of living. If autonomy means anything, it means the ability to make such choices, without any control of their content as long as they do not violate basic normative principles, most importantly the rights of others. Any legitimate order must leave scope for such acts of self-determination. This includes acts that may (and with good reason) appear less than wise, acts that are the product of partisan political interests or passing political passions. Human rights orders are not just products deduced from the textbook of normative insights. They are embedded in societies' political processes, with all of the political upheavals and untidy decision-making that make democracies a living, admirable and demanding form of political life. Such political processes have effects on human rights law, sometimes becoming law, sometimes coloring the interpretation of norms, adding to and modifying the meaning of the pluralism of human rights.

Defending the kind of universalism outlined here therefore does not fall prey to dogmatism, Eurocentrism or moral imperialism. The epistemic status of a proposition is one thing, the practical consequences drawn from the status of such propositions quite another. One may think that certain normative principles have universal validity, such as the equality of women, without implying that this provides sufficient reason to invade other countries to spread this gospel by force in communities that think otherwise. Universalism with humility is a very helpful starting point.[174] The parallel to science may once again be illuminating here: Scientists may have compelling reasons to assume the existence of black holes. This does not mean, however, that they are entitled to muster an army to subdue all those astronomers who think otherwise. The reasons for this are the very rights that universalism defends, prominently including the autonomy of free human thought and decision-making. As this is so, the pluralism of normative orientations is the welcome companion of universalist normative theory. Pluralism, including human rights pluralism, thus not only is reconcilable with universalism, but is in fact its necessary consequence.[175]

[174] Cf. András Sajó, "Introduction: Universalism with Humility," in *Human Rights with Modesty: The Problem of Universalism*, ed. András Sajó (Leiden: Martinus Nijhoff, 2004), 26: "Overreaching application of norms should really only be grounds for criticism of what they in fact are: the erroneously extended application of universalism, and not for criticism of the underlying concept of universalism itself."

[175] This does not imply that all factually held positions are equally justified. It just means that there are reasons derived from human autonomy to respect normative positions despite the fact that they may not be fully justified. For a different view, arguing for the idea of the possibility of diverging positions that are equally justified, Rawls, *Political Liberalism*, 144. Rawls, however, assumes the shared norm that human beings are free and equal, which seems not to be open for reasonable disagreement from his point of view: The idea of reasonable disagreement does not reach all the way down to the core principles.

A further point needs mentioning: Values are not just intellectual positions. A certain view on freedom of expression or religion, equality or human dignity is not the same in nature as a position on the question of whether or not Higgs particles exist. In contrast to descriptive propositions, value statements have emotional dimensions in at least two senses. First, certain emotions are the consequences of moral judgments – say, moral outrage at the sight of gross injustices. As we have seen, the moral judgment is the precondition of such emotions; the emotions do not constitute the moral judgment, as emotivists maintain.[176] Second, emotions have a heuristic function, as we underlined above: They are necessary to fully understand what certain acts mean for human beings. One needs to have fathomed the importance of the goods protected by human rights to give them their proper weight: One will not fully understand what freedom of expression means if one has not experienced the preciousness of the possibility of free speech. Freedom of religion will only be appreciated appropriately if one has a conception of the existential importance that religion holds for many people, irrespective of one's own religious, atheist or agnostic views. The meaning of prohibitions of discrimination can only be understood if one has a sense of the emotional harm inflicted through degradation by the many forms of discrimination – for example, by racism. Human equality will only acquire its full importance if one has a sense of what respect and disrespect for humans as equals feel like.

This consciousness of the existential meaning of human rights, of how they and their violations are spelled out in concrete human lives, is of central importance not only for ethics, but also for law. It is a key to the weight of rights. The appreciation of the importance of certain rights guides decisions about the inclusion or exclusion of rights in a given human rights catalogue. This appreciation is of great importance in the specifying of rights and rendering them concrete, in particular with regard to weighing and balancing rights in the framework of a proportionality analysis. One's answer to the question of whether a limitation on religious expression – for instance, a ban on headscarves, kippahs, monks' or nuns' habits or turbans – is legitimate or not depends very much on how important one considers freedom of religion to be.

Such sensitivities need time to develop, and they will do so unequally in different societies. They may fade away because certain experiences become remote – for example, the experience of what religious strife may mean for a society or what life in societies without freedom feels like. In addition, powerful political passions influence the course of history, including constitutional history, which in the best case are channeled and put to good use to foster the core ideas of human rights, which is not an easy task: "We are not passion's slave, but we have to apply cunning for reason's success."[177] However, the taming of such passions may not succeed, with potentially severe consequences for certain elements or even for the general

[176] Cf. Mahlmann, "Ethics," 585 ff.

[177] Sajó, *Constitutional Sentiments*, 2.

architecture of law. Accordingly, normative views will shift, adding, reinforcing, altering the variety of normative positions held on certain issues. All of this can be expressed in human rights norms and interpretations. Given today's internationally interwoven legal systems, such a variety of approaches will include a transnational dimension of norms with a human rights function. Human rights in legal reality are thus inevitably of a protean nature – heterogeneity and variety will continue to be their mode of existence as law.

These observations lead us to a final point: There can be no teleology in any universalist theory worth considering. Universalism does not imply that universally valid norms will necessarily become the law of humankind. There is nothing in history or theory to support this thought. Human beings have moral insights, but they are driven by many motives, and some of the most powerful such motives are the most destructive. The possibility of human societies at least approximately ruled by universally justified norms, although these norms are always only tentatively identified, is a hope, not a certainty, and is entertained to a large degree despite, not because of human history.

The pluralism of human rights orders may therefore violate universally valid norms of equality, liberty and autonomy, and the equal worth of human beings. It did so in the past, and there is no guarantee that it will not do so in the future. But this may not necessarily be the case. Pluralist orders can be something else, namely the fertile attempts of human beings to come a few steps closer to the ideas of justice, solidarity and respect that are the core attractions of the human rights project.

8.14 A NEW CASE FOR UNIVERSALISM?

In sum: Universalism as an epistemological position does not demand a necessary uniformity of the moral judgment of all human beings in the real world with its profound complexities and many influences on moral opinions. Nor does it rule out human rights pluralism. What is, then – to return to the important question asked above – the normative importance of a theory of moral cognition? Does it add something to the justification of the validity of those core moral principles that seem to be sufficiently resilient against doubt to form the heart of the normative argument for human rights? In particular, would a theory of a universal and uniform human moral faculty strengthen the case for a universalism of the kind outlined?

The answer is: A theory of the structure of moral cognition has no normative consequences as such, because normative arguments are required to justify any normative point. This also is true for universalist claims with the qualified content outlined. Even if there is indeed something like a universal moral grammar with justice, altruism and respect as its core principles that specify how moral judgements supervene over facts, this would not add anything to the justificatory argument. One would still need to make the case that these principles ought to guide ethical reasoning and legal norms and institutions and need not be corrected, say, by utility calculations or adherence to the principle of "might is right." One way to make this case involves the arguments developed above, including the absence of any discernible reasons to doubt the validity of these central principles. There is no good case for assuming that it is morally right to intend to harm others, that it is just to treat equals unequally or that one should disrespect other human beings.[178]

John Mikhail has explored the "weak normativity" of empirically given structures of moral thought. He argues that properly describing these structures of moral thought already is a meaningful step towards justifying their validity. This argument draws on Goodman's theory of induction and its use in Rawls's theory of justice. Goodman argues concerning the problem of induction:

> We no longer demand an explanation for guarantees that we do not have, or seek keys to knowledge that we cannot obtain. It dawns upon us that the traditional smug insistence upon a hard-and-fast line between justifying induction and describing ordinary inductive practice distorts the problem. And we owe belated apologies to Hume. For in dealing with the question how normally accepted inductive judgements are made, he was in fact dealing with the question of inductive validity. The validity of a prediction consisted for him in its arising from habit, and thus in its exemplifying some past regularity. His answer was incomplete and perhaps not entirely correct; but it was not beside the point. The problem of induction is not a problem of demonstration but a problem of defining the difference between valid and invalid predictions.[179]

Rawls' use of the reflective equilibrium can be interpreted along these lines. From this perspective, Rawls provides a descriptively adequate account of the sense of justice, as shown by considered judgments. A descriptively adequate account of the sense of justice is an account that captures correctly the main properties of the sense of justice. Considered judgments are judgments that are not skewed by interest, bias and so on, as explained above. The argument advanced on the basis of this interpretation of Rawls is not to follow directly in Goodman's footsteps and hold that a descriptively adequate account of the sense of justice already serves as the key to the justification of the principles of justice – the practice of justice in itself is not enough to justify the principles of justice.[180] This is because the principles of justice have to pass the test of rationality. The argument is, rather, that a descriptively adequate account of moral judgment provides presumptive, defeasible reasons for

[178] These findings are important for the project of "computational ethics," Awad et al., "Computational Ethics." Ultimately, not descriptive accounts of moral intuitions but normative arguments are decisive for answering normative questions, including the evaluation of the use and functions of AI designed to assist or substitute for human decision-making.

[179] Nelson Goodman, *Facts, Fiction, and Forecast* (Cambridge, MA: Harvard University Press, 1983), 64 f.

[180] Mikhail, *Elements*, 208.

the justifiedness of the principles of justice identified as underlying considered judgments of human beings.[181]

For the problem of the normative relevance of the findings of moral psychology, the most important point regarding Mikhail's profound idea is that it also seems to point to the view that, ultimately, it is normative arguments that count for the validity of a moral principle: In the end, such normative arguments are the decisive resource for refuting the defeasible reason for the justifiedness of moral principles that descriptively adequately account for considered judgments. In this sense, it confirms the argument presented here that there is no getting away from normative reasoning.

A very interesting problem looms in the background here: If it is true that human beings have certain mental faculties, the properties of which enable their thought but necessarily at the same time also limit the scope of their thinking, then any normative argument ultimately draws on these given mental resources. In this case, the principles that in fact determine moral judgment ultimately are the principles used to evaluate these very principles that in fact determine moral judgment: The justness of the principles of justice that in fact direct human moral judgment is then based on principles of justice that in fact direct human moral judgment – an obviously circular argument.[182]

This can be formulated more generally as a structural problem of human thought: If it is true that human beings have certain mental faculties, the properties of which enable their thought but necessarily at the same time limit the scope of their thinking, any argument for the truth of a proposition ultimately draws on these very same mental resources. The principles that in fact determine human thought ultimately are used to determine the truth of these very principles that in fact determine human thought – a circular argument, as in the case of morality.

How to escape from this circle?

Referring to a hierarchy of principles does not help. The metaprinciples themselves would need to be evaluated with the resources of human thought whose validity is to be justified, begging the question just asked.

The conclusion to be drawn is a familiar one from human epistemology: There is no way of escaping the limits of human thought. But this does not mean that we have to embrace skepticism and abandon any hope of human insight. One important lesson from the history of skepticism is, after all, that there is no valid skeptical argument proving that what seems to be true to human beings is *not* really true. Any such assertion would lead skepticism into self-contradiction – the familiar self-contradiction of asserting that the proposition that there is no true proposition is

[181] Mikhail, *Elements*, 221 ff. Cf. also Mikhail, *Moral Grammar and Human Rights*, 164, 173, 197, on the relation between a universally shared structure of moral cognition and arguments for the universalism of human rights.

[182] For a sentimentalist version of this problem, Nichols, *Sentimental Rules*, 188.

itself a true proposition. Given this situation, there is no alternative but to assume that human thought, in theory and morals, does not lead us astray, but reveals something meaningful about the world. This argument is based on trust in human beings' faculties of thought and understanding, which form the ultimate foundation of any serious effort to wrest some kind of insight from the vast swathes of what has not and perhaps never will be understood. This trust seems to be warranted by its results: Both science and practical life show that human thought does have a productive relation to the facts of the world – airplanes fly; vaccines offer protection; computers help us in our tasks. In the moral sphere, a world of justice, solidarity and respect is a rather attractive vision. There is thus no particular reason to mistrust human thought in principle. The specter of Descartes' evil demon having become flesh in the cognitive structures of human beings and frustrating our search for insight should now find its final resting place.[183] The task is, then, to engage in constructive scientific work, while remaining aware of the limits of human understanding, of the fallibility of any theory and of any theoretical stance's permanent need for critical revision.

For the normative force of psychological facts, these arguments lead to the following conclusion: Even if the properties of human cognitive abilities, including ethical cognitive abilities, ultimately set limits to human understanding, no normative proposition is valid or invalid simply because it is based on empirically operative principles rooted in the nature of human cognition. It is not such psychological facts that are decisive for the validity of normative propositions: Rather, a normative proposition convinces as a piece of normative argumentation against which no valid normative doubts can be mustered. Normative arguments ultimately count only insofar as they formulate compelling normative reasons, not because they are rooted in the psychological makeup of human beings, even if these normative arguments themselves ultimately are the offspring of certain empirical properties of human cognition.

If one accepts this conclusion, the need for normative theory-building in the defense of human rights needs to be reasserted. Psychological theory is no substitute for it, nor can psychological theories ultimately challenge the normative case for (or against) human rights.

This result does not render a theory of moral cognition superfluous: As we have seen, important points of a theory of human moral cognition are, first, to provide a rich explanatory theory of human moral judgment and, second, to perform the critical function of dispelling doubts stemming from theories of the mind and its evolution about whether an ethics of human rights is possible. Moreover, this theory

[183] This argument is the secular version of Descartes' argument that there is no *genius malignus*, no evil demon that betrays us, which we discussed in the introduction, cf. introduction Fn 59, 60 and René Descartes, *Meditationes de prima philosophia*, in *Œuvres de Descartes*, Vol. VII, eds. Charles Adam and Paul Tannery (Paris: Léopold Cerf, 1904), I, 16; IV, 6 – a methodological stance to which there is no alternative in science.

serves a third and rather intriguing function, one that can be identified as the ultimate perspective of this inquiry: A theory of human moral cognition can show that there may, perhaps surprisingly, be at least a partial convergence between what normative theory tells us is right and just and what humans in actual fact empirically regard to be morally right and just. This is not self-evident: Human beings could, for instance, be the selfish utility maximizers that some theories both past and present imagine them to be, creating a mismatch between the world of moral principle and the facts of human moral cognition. *In a profound sense, then, human beings in the realm of human ethical understanding are what they morally ought to be: beings committed to justice, respect and concern for others.* Given humanity's track record of self-inflicted suffering, this is perhaps a precious source of hope, although certainly limited in scope.

Epilogue

The Tilted Scales of Justice

This inquiry, with all its limits and flaws, has drawn a partly familiar, partly surprising picture about the place of human rights in human life and the human makeup.

Our conceptual and analytical clarifications have indicated that human rights are best understood as a subcategory of a particular normative position in which human beings find themselves: the position of having a subjective right. This position consists of complex normative relations including a rights-holder's claims to do or not to do X, a necessarily correlated duty of the addressee of the right to do or not to do Y, a privilege to do or not to do X on the part of the rights-holder and a necessarily correlated no-right of the addressee that the rights-holder does or does not do X. Powers and immunities are often part of the normative content of such a right.

Human rights are those subjective rights that protect specific goods of human beings, in particular dignity, life, certain liberties, equality and the material means for pursuing a dignified life. They are part of ethics and legally enshrined in (national) constitutions and supranational and international law. To limit human rights to human rights guaranteed in international law is a fundamental misunderstanding both of the current global legal architecture of human rights and of the explicit intentions of those constructing it.

The history of the development of the human rights idea and ultimately of the institutions embodying it reveals quite clearly that this idea has deep roots in humans' social form of life. This does not mean that we can expect to discover a universal declaration of human rights written by a prehistoric cave dweller. The lessons taught by the history of human rights are much more complex than this. This history is not about every aspect of ethics, but it is not just the history of the explicit concept of human rights either. There are various normative phenomena that are *not* human rights but still are important for the history of human rights, because they contributed to the formation of those building blocks that ultimately became the material for the explicit concept of human rights.

The most plausible account of this trajectory is that the raw material of the human rights idea includes specific, concretely situated not arbitrary, but principled moral judgments about the justness and moral rightness of particular intentions, actions and states of affairs – archetypically exemplified by Creusa's rebellion against the permissibility of her rape in which she invokes the rights she enjoys, even towards a god. During a long historical process, these specific judgments were slowly objectified as to the goods protected, framed in abstract terms, generalized across cases, universalized across people, purged of persistent patterns of exclusion, ultimately made explicit in political and ethical thought and very recently turned into working institutions of positive law. This process was not a smooth ride but – as always in the history of ideas and social change – a tale of progress and regression, during which generations who lived under new and treacherous ideological stars consigned to oblivion the hard-won insights of their forbears, a history of struggle and of the successful suppression of ideas by force. A good example of this, with little consequence for the author but not entirely insignificant consequences for the history of human rights, is the banning of some of Las Casas' works by the Spanish Inquisition and the effects that this ban had on Europeans' self-perception of their role in the world, among many other such cases involving the consignment of unpleasant historical truths to the "memory hole" that Orwell so clear-sightedly described.[1]

Some examples have illustrated this conclusion – from the political rights of Athenian noninclusive democracy to Enlightenment theories of rights. The discussion did not seek to provide a full account of the complex social, political, economic, religious and cultural contexts of these examples. Moreover, and importantly, no assumptions were implied about a linear, continuous, triumphant historical process, coherent ideas about rights over millennia or simple causal connections between the thoughts about rights of different epochs. The historical review served limited expository purposes: It pursued merely the modest aim of highlighting some important findings for the specific cognitive interests of our inquiry.

Importantly, our study has made the case that intellectual elitism and cultural myopia, which sometimes even smack of racist bias, must be avoided. If we are to steer clear of such prejudice, investigating indigenous cultures, including oral and acephalous civilizations, is of crucial interest. This book has argued that it is entirely implausible to deny human beings living in such societies and cultures the basic, principled moral intuitions that form the raw material of human rights. The voices of the victims of colonialism or slavery, as far as we know anything about them, speak rather strongly against the assumption that the human beings living in these cultures were just moral blank slates, who might have felt the pain of, say, dying in the desert like the Herero in the German genocidal campaign of 1904, but not its injustice.

[1] Orwell, *Nineteen Eighty-Four.*

There is thus substantial historical evidence to show that these moral intuitions are not limited to white, male Europeans (or any other subgroup of the human species), but form part of the common ethical heritage of human beings. The journey from such intuitions to an explicit concept of human rights is a long one. There is, however, no reason to assume that only one group of people can make this journey. No one group has privileged access to the idea of human rights. It should be noted that Europeans, the "West" or the "Global North" did not travel smoothly down this road either. The idea of human rights met with fierce resistance in Europe as elsewhere, and whatever sway it has over human affairs was wrested from the hands of the leading social and political powers.

The more recent history of the explicit idea of human rights only confirms these findings. The human rights project has been promoted by people from very different cultural, political and religious backgrounds, but with a common idea – the idea that governmental and social power has to be limited, that human beings and their well-being count equally, that humans owe each other concern and respect and that liberty is no minor affair for a human life.

Importantly, the history of human rights illustrates a further point. The problem of the inclusion of all human beings in the sphere of protection afforded by human rights is one of the core issues of human rights history. It lies at the root of major historical tragedies, including racism, slavery and the subjugation of women. This problem has two dimensions: first, the formulation of a proper concept of what makes a human being human and thus entitled to rights; and second, the proper application of this concept to all members of the human species. The former does not necessarily entail the latter. Various theories throughout history had a plausible idea of what human beings were but did not apply it to subsets of the human species, such as indigenous Americans because of racist prejudice or women because of misogynist ideas about women's inferior capacity. This problem is far from solved – today, for instance, problems of bioethics or the rights of elderly people (which have become matters of life and death during the Covid-19 pandemic) show that the question of who is to be regarded as a (full) human being and bearer of rights is still open to intense debate in many aspects. Moreover, the question of the rights of nonhuman animals indicates yet another frontier of the theory of rights. The question of whether human beings have human rights is, however, independent of the question of whether and in which sense nonhuman animals have rights, too. One can assert the former without precluding the latter.

Our reflection on the justification of human rights has suggested that any justificatory account of human rights needs to formulate a theory of goods essential for human beings that are important enough to be protected by human rights, a political theory of the role of human rights in society that contributes to the enjoyment of these goods and a theory of the normative principles of justice, solidarity and respect for the intrinsic worth of human beings, the principles that are the ultimate sources of the normative position of rights.

In light of what we can reasonably assume about human beings, the protection of dignity, life, liberty, equality and the means to lead a dignified life is well justified by an anthropologically informed theory of human goods. Political theory offers no compelling case against human rights as ethical and political principles and legal institutions. Human rights promise not a perennially blissful Elysium, but something that nevertheless is very precious: an order in which certain basic demands stemming from the principles of justice, solidarity and respect are satisfied to such a degree that human beings can pursue meaningfully whatever their aim in life may turn out to be. Given the experience of the mass appeal and destructive power of totalitarian ideologies propagating the worthlessness of human life and existence as such, doubts about the need to protect basic goods of human beings by means of human rights are politically naive and a slap in the face for the victims of these regimes, who perished because of the mass support for the contempt of their rights.

A theory of human rights cannot rest its case here. Recent research on moral cognition and evolution has put the question of whether human rights are justifiably regarded as universally obligatory normative principles squarely on the table. Perhaps, this research implies, human rights are something quite different, nothing but a cognitive illusion necessarily produced by the structure of the human mind but without any claim to normative justification. Moreover, some evolutionary accounts of morality have asked whether a morality of human rights and correspondingly the institutions of the law are in fact irreconcilable with the kinds of proximate cognitive mechanism that natural selection could have produced in humans and that empirically determine moral judgment – that is, whether human rights do not ultimately demand the impossible of human beings as they really are.

Our survey of current neuroscientific theories of moral cognition and the evolution of the human mind has given ample reason to conclude, however, that nothing in this theoretical field undermines the legitimacy of human rights. There is no compelling empirical evidence or theoretical argument proving that human rights are cognitive illusions or anything of the sort. A sufficiently complex theory of evolution confirms the possibility of human cognitive faculties (whatever they may turn out to be) that do not merely produce the illusion of being directed by altruism, justice and respect, but are in fact determined by these principles.

A promising theory to account for the structure and content of human morality is the mentalist theory of moral cognition, assuming a common framework of human moral judgment, thought and sentiment, generated by a shared faculty of moral cognition – a moral competence with well-defined principles that enables human moral judgment with its rich volitional and emotional consequences. By means of a differentiated account of human cognition, this theory thus reconstructs an assumption that has guided the history of ideas since antiquity, namely that humans are endowed with a moral understanding that is one of the defining features of their human identity.

An empirical theory of the human moral mind provides no normative arguments for the justification of human rights as such. This is also true in the weak Goodmanian sense of taking an epistemic practice as an element of justification. Understanding a descriptively adequate account of human moral cognition as a presumptive, defeasible reason for the justification of the principles identified as empirically determining human moral judgment leads to the same conclusion: Ultimately, arguments for the normative validity of normative propositions must be derived from normative theory, not from psychological facts.

The theory of moral cognition nevertheless fulfills three important constructive functions. First, it helps to form nothing less than a rich, empirically grounded explanatory theory of the cognitive basis of human moral judgment and legal thought, which, if correct, would be a major scientific achievement. Second, it is a tool to assess critically theories that aim to delegitimize ethical precepts such as human rights with the means of moral psychology, neuroscience or evolutionary theory. Third, as a rather intriguing perspective, it provides reason to think that there is at least a partial congruence between normative ideas justified by normative theory and the empirical structures of human moral thought: In certain respects, human beings may turn out to be the creatures they ought to strive to be.

Any argument for the validity of human rights is fallible and open to criticism. But this does not mean that the propositions "It is justified to enslave black people" or "It is justified to rape women" enjoy the same epistemic status as "It is not justified to enslave any human being" or "It is a severe crime to rape women." The history of skepticism has taught us that there is no argument proving beyond possible doubt that what seems true or right to human beings is in fact true or right. However, it also has long been clarified that there is no argument showing that what seems true or right to human beings is in fact *not* true or right – the latter being the well-known self-contradiction of a skepticism asserting the truth of the proposition that no proposition is true.

If it thus is possible that human beings do in fact understand something true and right about the object of their reflection when they think that they understand something true and right about an object, there is only one epistemological way forward: to seize this precious epistemic chance and to engage in the constructive, fallible pursuit of insight, based on whatever argument can be mustered in favor of a given proposition. That human beings are bound by the necessarily existing limits of their (moral and legal) understanding forms no reason not to travel as far as these boundaries permit. Looking at concrete arguments may provide some epistemological encouragement to pursue this course: For instance, it seems rather hard to maintain that there are not better arguments for the prohibition of slavery and rape (and the implied rights of people) than for the permissibility of such actions.

In this fallible, albeit meaningful sense, universal human rights are justified. However, the universalism that they imply is open for concrete human rights pluralism. One reason for this is epistemic modesty, which does not confuse the possibility of universally valid insight with the assumption that one oneself (as an individual or as a community) has actually gained this universally valid insight. Abstract principles of human rights can, moreover, be realized in more than one form – there is not just one concrete way to a meaningful protection of human rights. Furthermore, human rights spelled out in concrete terms are about important choices of individuals and communities. Given human autonomy, both individuals and the communities they form retain the right to experiment with new ways of living, including varying ways of rendering human rights concrete that must be respected as long as they do not betray the core promises of human rights. Human rights universalism is therefore not wedded to a rigid system of indubitable content revealed by solitary master thinkers, but is a living aspiration, a quest to critically reappropriate the idea of human rights in endeavors that in the best case are collective and democratic, excluding nobody.

In sum, the argument leads to this encouraging conclusion: Principles of egalitarian justice, of human solidarity, care and respect for human dignity, together with a sufficiently rich concept of human existence and a political theory of the means for human flourishing embedded in a plausible theory of mind and its place in natural history provide good reasons to believe that the idea of human rights is as well-justified as anything ever has been in the history of fallible human thinking about morality and law.

Such a theory of human rights, which has answers to the theoretical challenges formulated by the many kinds of skeptics encountered in this inquiry, constitutes an essential element of the intellectual defense of human rights. This would be no small achievement.

The Greek poet Giorgos Seferis wrote in his poem *Santorini*:

> Naked we found ourselves on the pumice-stone
> watching the rising islands
> watching the red islands sink
> into their sleep, into our sleep.
> Here naked we found ourselves, holding
> the scales that tilted towards
> injustice.[2]

[2] Giorgos Seferis, *Poiimata* (Athens: Ikaros, 1998), 75 line 7–13, Gymnopaidia: A΄. Santorini:

> Βρεθήκαμε γυμνοὶ πάνω στὴν ἀλαφρόπετρα
> κοιτάζοντας τ᾿ ἀναδυόμενα νησιὰ
> κοιτάζοντας τὰ κόκκινα νησιὰ νὰ βυθίζουν
> στὸν ὕπνο τους, στὸν ὕπνο μας.
> Ἐδῶ βρεθήκαμε γυμνοὶ κρατῶντας
> τὴ ζυγαριὰ ποὺ βάραινε κατὰ τὸ μέρος
> τῆς ἀδικίας.

Translation: George Seferis, *Complete Poems*, trans. Edmund Keely and Philip Sherrard (Vancouver: Anvil Press, 1993), 31.

This is how things are, after about 100,000 years of human civilization, ingenuity, foolhardiness, petty sordidness, enchanting and even sublime nobility, after much longing for and the intermittent reality of justice. We stand naked on the rough pumice-stone of our epoch and the scales are still tilted towards injustice. Human rights represent one attempt to balance these scales, never completely, never forever, never on all accounts, but for long enough to show sufficient respect to what humans owe to the better parts of their own humanity.

Human rights therefore are not trivial. They are more than playthings to satisfy one's intellectual ludic drive. Human rights are not the means of solving all of the world's problems. But there is a lot that depends on rights, most importantly the well-being of individuals and sometimes even their dignity and lives.

Moreover, respect for human rights is of great significance not only for those who suffer from human rights violations. It also is of some consequence for those people lucky enough to have their human rights sufficiently respected. At least this is so if they belong to the perhaps not insignificant number of people who, despite their own favorable circumstances, are still not able to breathe freely when they have to witness the ongoing tragedy of folly and pain, of repression and contempt for the equal worth of human beings that already have marked too much of human history because they sense the force of some probably quite common elements of human experience: To feel the spark of generous, liberating magnanimity that adds considerable beauty to humans' inner life and that makes it natural to care for our fellow mortals, whoever they are, wherever and under whatever stars they spend their short and precious time on Earth; to be enlivened by the unpretentious daily work of justice and human goodness; and thus to long for the profound relief of some fresh air bestowed by any modest steps towards a culture and law of human decency.

Bibliography

Ackerly, Brooke A. *Universal Human Rights in a World of Difference*. Cambridge: Cambridge University Press, 2008.

Adorno, Theodor W. "Minima Moralia." In *Theodor W. Adorno: Gesammelte Schriften*, Vol. 4, edited by Rolf Tiedemann. Darmstadt: Wissenschaftliche Buchgesellschaft, 1998.

"Negative Dialektik." In *Theodor W. Adorno: Gesammelte Schriften*, Vol. 6, edited by Rolf Tiedemann, 7–412. Darmstadt: Wissenschaftliche Buchgesellschaft, 1998.

Agamben, Giorgio. *Homo Sacer: Sovereign Power and Bare Life*. Translated by Daniel Heller-Roazen. Stanford: Stanford University Press, 1998.

Agi, Mare. *René Cassin (1887–1976), Prix Nobel de la Paix: Père de la Déclaration universelle des Droits de l'homme*. Paris: Perrin, 1998.

Albert, Hans. *Traktat über kritische Vernunft*. Tübingen: Mohr Siebeck, 1991.

Alexander, Richard D. *The Biology of Moral Systems*. New York: Aldine de Gruyter, 1987.

Alexy, Robert. *Theorie der Grundrechte*. Baden-Baden: Nomos, 1985.

A Theory of Constitutional Rights. Oxford: Oxford University Press, 2010.

Alonso, José Louis. "Fault, Strict Liability, and Risk in the Law of the Papyri." In *Culpa: Facets of Liability in Ancient Legal Theory and Practice*, edited by Jakub Urbanik, 19–81. Warsaw: The Raphael Taubenschlag Foundation, 2012.

Alston, Philip. "Does the Past Matter? On the Origins of Human Rights." *Harvard Law Review* 126 (2013): 2043–81.

Appiah, Kwame Anthony. *Experiments in Ethics*. Cambridge, MA: Harvard University Press, 2008.

Aquinas, Thomas. *The Summa Theologica*. Translated by Fathers of the English Dominican Province. Notre Dame, IN: Christian Classics, 1981.

Arendt, Hannah. *The Human Condition*. Chicago, IL: University of Chicago Press, 1958.

Elemente und Ursprünge totaler Herrschaft. Munich: Piper, 2005.

Eichmann in Jerusalem: A Report on the Banality of Evil. New York: Penguin Books, 2006.

The Origins of Totalitarianism. London: Penguin Books, 2017.

Aristophanes. "Assemblywomen." In *Frogs, Assemblywomen, Wealth*, edited and translated by Jeffrey Henderson, 238–411. Loeb Classical Library 180. Cambridge, MA: Harvard University Press, 2002.

"Frogs." In *Frogs, Assemblywomen, Wealth*, edited and translated by Jeffrey Henderson, 3–236. Loeb Classical Library 180. Cambridge, MA: Harvard University Press, 2002.

Aristotle. *The "Art" of Rhetoric, Aristotle Vol. XXII*. Translated by John Henry Freese. Loeb Classical Library 193. Cambridge, MA: Harvard University Press, 1926.

Politics. Translated by Harris Rackham. Loeb Classical Library 264. Cambridge, MA: Harvard University Press, 1932.

"Metaphysics." In *Metaphysics, X–XIV, Oeconomica, Magna Moralia*, edited by George Patrick Goold, 2–319. Loeb Classical Library 287. Cambridge, MA: Harvard University Press, 1990.

Nicomachean Ethics. Translated by Harris Rackham. Loeb Classical Library 73. Cambridge, MA: Harvard University Press, 2003.

Augustinus. "In Joannis Evangelium." In *Patrologia cursus completus, series latina*, Vol. 35. Paris: Jacques-Paul Migne, 1845.

Aulard, Alphonse and Boris Mirkine-Guetzévitch. *Les déclarations des droits de l'homme: Textes constitutionnels concernant les droits de l'homme et les garanties des libertés individuelles dans tous les pays*. Paris: Payot, 1929.

Aust, Helmut Philipp. "From Diplomat to Academic Activist: André Mandelstam and the History of Human Rights." *The European Journal of International Law* 25 (2015): 1105–21.

Awad, Edmond, Sohan Dsouza, Azim Shariff, Iyad Rahwan and Jean-Francois Bonnefon. "Universals and Variations in Moral Decisions Made in 42 Countries by 70 000 Participants." *Proceedings of the National Academy of Sciences* 117, no. 5 (2020): 2332–7.

Awad, Edmond, Sydney Levine, Michael Anderson, et al. "Computational Ethics," *Trends in Cognitive Sciences* 26, no. 5 (2022): 388–405.

Bacon, Francis. *Novum Organum*, edited by Wolfgang Krohn. Hamburg: Felix Meiner Verlag, 1999.

Baer, Susanne. "Who Cares? A Defence of Judicial Review." *Journal of the British Academy* 8 (2020): 75–104.

Barak, Aharon. *Human Dignity: The Constitutional Value and the Constitutional Right*. Cambridge: Cambridge University Press, 2015.

Barbeyrac, Jean. "Preface." In *Gerard Noodt, Du pouvoir des souverains et de la liberté de conscience*, 2nd edition, 28–47. Amsterdam: Pierre Humbert, 1714.

Bashō, Matsuo. In: *The Penguin Book of Japanese Verse*, edited by Geoffrey Bownas and Anthony Thwaite, 105–107. London: Penguin Books, 2009.

Batson, C. Daniel. *Altruism in Humans*. Oxford: Oxford University Press, 2011.

A Scientific Search for Altruism: Do We Care Only about Ourselves? Oxford: Oxford University Press, 2019.

BBC News. "German Family's Namibia Apology." Accessed November 29, 2021. http://news.bbc.co.uk/2/hi/africa/7033042.stm

Beitz, Charles R. *The Idea of Human Rights*. Oxford: Oxford University Press, 2011.

"Human Dignity in the Theory of Human Rights: Nothing but a Phrase?" *Philosophy & Public Affairs* 41, no. 3 (2013): 259–90.

Bellagamba, Alice. ""Being a slave, I was afraid…": Excerpt from a Case of Slave-Dealing in the Colony of the Gambia." In *African Voices on Slavery and the Slave Trade*, edited by Alice Bellagamba, Sandre E. Green and Martin A. Klein, 343–59. Cambridge: Cambridge University Press, 2013.

Benhabib, Seyla. "Another Universalism: On the Unity and Diversity of Human Rights." *Proceedings and Addresses of the American Philosophical Association* 81, no. 2 (2007): 7–32.

Benjamin, Walter. "Das Passagen-Werk." In *Gesammelte Schriften*, Vol. V-1, edited by Rolf Tiedemann. Frankfurt am Main: Suhrkamp, 1982.

"Zum Bilde Prousts." In *Gesammelte Schriften*, Vol. II-1, edited by Rolf Tiedemann and Hermann Schweppenhäuser, 310–24. Frankfurt am Main: Suhrkamp, 1991.

The Arcades Project. Translated by Howard Eiland and Kevin McLaughlin. Cambridge, MA: Harvard University Press, 2002. Accessed September 28, 2022. https://monoskop.org/images/e/e4/Benjamin_Walter_The_Arcades_Project.pdf

Bennett, Matthew R. and Peter Michael Stephan Hacker. *The Philosophical Foundations of Neuroscience*. Oxford and Malden, MA: Blackwell Publishing, 2003.

Bentham, Jeremy. "An Introduction to the Principles of Morals and Legislation." in *The Collected Works of Jeremy Bentham*, edited by James Henderson Burns and Herbert Lionel Adolphus Hart. Oxford: Oxford University Press, 1996.

"Nonsense upon Stilts." In *The Collected Works of Jeremy Bentham: Rights, Representation and Reform: Nonsense upon Stilts and Other Writings on the French Revolution*, edited by Philip Schofield, Catherine Pease-Watkin and Cyprian Blamires, 317–401. Oxford: Clarendon Press, 2002.

Berker, Selim. "The Normative Insignificance of Neuroscience." *Philosophy & Public Affairs* 37, no. 4 (2009): 293–329.

Bernhard, Regan, Jonathan Chaponis, Richie Siburian, et al. "Variation in the Oxytocin Receptor Gene (*OXTR*) Is Associated with Differences in Moral Judgement." *Social Cognitive and Affective Neuroscience* 11, no. 12 (2016): 1872–81.

Berwick, Robert and Noam Chomsky. *Why Only Us: Language and Evolution*. Cambridge, MA: MIT Press, 2016.

Besson, Samantha. "Justifications." In *International Human Rights Law*, 3rd edition, edited by Daniel Moeckli, Sangeeta Shah and Sandesh Sivakumaran, 22–40. Oxford: Oxford University Press, 2018.

"The Human Right to Democracy in International Law: Coming to Moral Terms with an Equivocal Legal Practice." In *The Cambridge Handbook of New Human Rights: Recognition, Novelty, Rhetoric*, edited by Andreas von Arnauld, Kerstin von der Decken and Mart Susi, 481–90. Cambridge: Cambridge University Press, 2020.

Bielefeld, Heiner. ""Western" versus "Islamic" Human Rights Conceptions?: A Critique of Cultural Essentialism in the Discussion on Human Rights," *Political Theory* 28, no. 1 (2000): 90–121.

Bird, Douglas W., Rebecca Bliege Bird, Brian F. Codding and David W. Zeanah. "Variability in the Organization and Size of Hunter-Gatherer Groups: Foragers Do Not Live in Small-Scale Societies." *Journal of Human Evolution* 131 (2019): 96–108.

Blackstone, William. *Commentaries of the Law of England, Vol. 1: Of the Rights of Persons*, edited by David Lemmings. Oxford: Oxford University Press, 2016.

Bleicken, Jochen. *Die athenische Demokratie*. Stuttgart: UTB, 1995.

Blickle, Peter. *Die Revolution von 1525*, 4th edition. Munich: Oldenbourg, 2004.

Bloch, Ernst. *Naturrecht und menschliche Würde*. Frankfurt am Main: Suhrkamp, 1961.

Bluntschli, Johann Caspar. *Das moderne Völkerrecht der civilisirten Staaten als Rechtsbuch dargestellt*, 2nd edition. Nördlingen: Beck, 1872.

Bogdandy, Armin von and Ingo Venzke. *In Whose Name? A Public Law Theory of International Adjudication*. Oxford: Oxford University Press, 2014.

Bollig, Michael and Jan-Bart Gewald. "People, Cattle, Land – Transformations of Pastoral Society." In *People, Cattle and Land: Transformations of a Pastoral Society in Southwestern Africa*, edited by Michael Bollig and Jan-Bart Gewald, 3–54. Cologne: Rüdiger Köppe Verlag, 2000.

Boyer, Pascal. *Minds Make Societies: How Cognition Explains the World Human Create*. New Haven, CT: Yale University Press, 2018.

Boysen, Sigrid. "Remnants of a Constitutional Moment: The Right to Democracy in International Law." In *The Cambridge Handbook of New Human Rights: Recognition, Novelty, Rhetoric*, edited by Andreas von Arnauld, Kerstin von der Decken and Mart Susi, 465–80. Cambridge: Cambridge University Press, 2020.

Brandom, Robert B. *Making It Explicit*. Cambridge, MA: Harvard University Press, 1994.

Brandt, Richard B. *A Theory of the Good and the Right*. Oxford: Clarendon Press, 1979.

Brink, David Owen. *Moral Realism and the Foundations of Ethics*. Cambridge: Cambridge University Press, 1989.

Brożek, Bartosz, Jaap Hage and Nicole Vincent, eds. *Law and Mind: A Survey of Law and the Cognitive Sciences*. Cambridge: Cambridge University Press, 2021.

Buchanan, Allen. *The Heart of Human Rights*. Oxford: Oxford University Press, 2013.

Buchanan, Allen and Russell Powell. *The Evolution of Moral Progress*. New York: Oxford University Press, 2018.

Büchner, Georg. "Der Hessische Landbote." In *Georg Büchner, Werke und Briefe, Münchner Ausgabe*, edited by Karl Pörnbacher, Gerhard Schaub, Hans-Joachimg Simm and Edda Ziegler, 39–65. Munich: Deutscher Taschenbuch Verlag, 2001.

Burckhardt, Jacob. *Die Kultur der Renaissance in Italien*. Stuttgart: Alfred Kröner Verlag, 2009.

Burgers, Jan Herman. "The Road to San Francisco: The Revival of the Human Rights Idea in the Twentieth Century." *Human Rights Quarterly* 14, no. 4 (1992): 447–77.

Burke, Edmund. *Reflections on the Revolution in France*. London: Penguin Books, 1968.

Burke, Roland. *Decolonization and the Evolution of International Human Rights*. Philadelphia: University of Pennsylvania Press, 2010.

Burlamaqui, Jean-Jacques. *Principes du droit naturel*. Geneva: Barrilot & File, 1747.

Butler, Joseph. "Fifteen Sermons." In *The Works of Joseph Butler*, Vol. II, edited by William Ewart Gladstone, 31–274. Oxford: Clarendon Press, 1896.

Butler, Judith. *Gender Trouble*. London and New York: Routledge, 1990.

Undoing Gender. London and New York: Routledge, 2004.

Camerer, Colin. *Behavioral Game Theory: Experiments in Strategic Interaction*. New York: Russell Sage Foundation, 2003.

Camus, Albert. "19 Novembre 1946: La siècle de la peur." In *Cahiers Albert Camus Vol. 8: Camus à Combat – éditoriaux et articles d'Albert Camus (1944–1947)*, edited by Jacqueline Lévi-Valensi, 608–13. Paris: Gallimard, 2002.

"Le Mythe de Sisyphe." In *Œuvres complètes Vol. I: 1931–1944*, edited by Jaqueline Lévi-Valensi, 217–315. Paris: Gallimard, 2006.

"L'homme révolté." In *Albert Camus, Œuvres complètes Vol. III: 1949–1956*, edited by Raymond Gay-Crosier, 61–324. Paris: Gallimard, 2008.

"Le Premier Homme." In *Albert Camus, Œuvres complètes Vol. IV: 1957–1959*, edited by Raymond Gay-Crosier, 741–915. Paris: Gallimard, 2008.

Carozza, Paolo G. "From Conquest to Constitution, Retrieving a Latin American Tradition of the Idea of Human Rights." *Human Rights Quarterly* 25, no. 2 (2003): 281–313.

Chomsky, Noam. *Aspects of the Theory of Syntax*. Cambridge, MA: MIT Press, 1965.

America and the New Mandarins. New York: Vintage Books, 1969.

Language and Problems of Knowledge. Cambridge, MA: MIT Press, 1988.

Language and Thought. Wakefield and London: Moyer Bell, 1993.

Year 501: The Conquest Continues. Boston, MA: South End Press, 1993.

The Minimalist Program. Cambridge, MA: MIT Press, 1995.

New Horizons in the Study of Language and Mind. Cambridge: Cambridge University Press, 2000.

For Reasons of State. New York: The New Press, 2003.

Chryssipus. "Chrysippi fragmenta moralia." In *Stoicum Veterum Fragmenta*, Vol. III, edited by Hans von Arnim, 3–205. Munich and Leipzig: K. G. Saur Verlag, 2004.

Cicero, Marcus Tullius. *De legibus, Paradoxa stoicorum: Über die Gesetze, Stoische Paradoxien*. Latin–German. Translated and edited by Rainer Nickel. Düsseldorf: Artemis & Winkler, 2008.

De Officiis: Vom pflichtgemässen Handeln. Latin–German. Translated and edited by Rainer Nickel. Düsseldorf: Artemis & Winkler, 2008.

De re publica, Der Staat. Latin–German. Translated and edited by Karl Büchner. Düsseldorf: Artemis & Winkler, 2008.

On Invention, The Best Kind of Orator, Topics. Translated by H. M. Hubbell, 1-146. Loeb Classical Library 386. Cambridge, MA: Harvard University, 1949.

Clapham, Andrew. *Human Rights Obligations of Non-state Actors*. Oxford: Oxford University Press, 2006.

Cohen, Gerald Allan. *Rescuing Justice and Equality*. Cambridge, MA: Harvard University Press, 2008.

Cohn, Haim. *Human Rights in the Bible and the Talmud*. Tel Aviv: MOD Books, 1989.

Cole, David. "Must Counterterrorism Cancel Democracy?" *The New York Review of Books* no. 1 (2015): 26–8.

Coleman, Jules L. *The Practice of Principle: In Defence of a Pragmatist Approach to Legal Theory*. Oxford: Oxford University Press, 2001.

Columbus, Christopher. *The Diario of Christopher Columbus's first voyage to America: 1492–1493*. Abstracted by Fray Bartolomé de Las Casas. Translated by Oliver Dunn and James E. Kelley. Norman: Oklahoma Press, 1991.

Conrad, Joseph. "Typhoon." In *Typhoon and other Stories*, edited by Paul Kirschner, 53–131. London: Penguin Books, 1992.

Heart of Darkness. London: Penguin Books, 2000.

Corpus Iuris Civilis, Vol. I, text and translation, 2nd edition, translated by Okko Behrends, Rolf Knütel, Berthold Kupisch and Hans Hermaann Seiler. Heidelberg: C. F. Müller Verlag, 1997.

Vol. II, translated by Okko Behrends, Rolf Knütel, Berthold Kupisch and Hans Hermaann Seiler. Heidelberg: C. F. Müller Verlag, 1995.

Cosmides, Leda, Ricardo Andrés Guzmán and John Tooby. "The Evolution of Moral Cognition." In *The Routledge Handbook of Moral Epistemology*, edited by Aaron Zimmerman, Karen Jones and Mark Timmons, 174–228. New York: Routledge, 2019.

Crenshaw, Kimberlé. "Demarginalizing the Intersection of Race and Sex: A Black Feminist Critique of Antidiscrimination Doctrine, Feminist Theory and Antiracist Politics." *The University of Chicago Legal Forum* 1989, no. 1 (1989): 139–67.

Darwall, Stephen. *The Second-Person Standpoint: Morality, Respect, and Accountability*. Cambridge, MA: Harvard University Press, 2009.

Darwin, Charles. *The Origin of Species*. London: John Murray, 1872.

Dawkins, Richard. *The God Delusion*. London: Bentam Press, 2006.

The Selfish Gene. Oxford: Oxford University Press, 2018.

De Waal, Frans. "Attitudinal Reciprocity in Food Sharing among Brown Capuchin Monkeys." *Animal Behaviour* 60, no. 2 (2020): 253–61.

The Bonobo and the Atheist. New York: W. W. Norton & Company, 2013.

Demaree-Cotton, Joanna and Guy Kahane. "The Neuroscience of Moral Judgement." In *The Routledge Handbook of Moral Epistemology*, edited by Aaron Zimmermann, Karen Jones and Mark Timmons, 84–104. New York: Routledge, 2019.

Demosthenes. "Second Olynthiac." In Demosthenes, *Orations 1–17 and 20, Olynthiacs, Philippics, Minor Public Orations*. Translated by James Herbert Vince, 22–41. Loeb Classical Library 238. Cambridge, MA: Harvard University Press, 1930.

"The Third Philippic." In Demosthenes, *Orations 1–17 and 20, Olynthiacs, Philippics, Minor Public Orations*. Translated by James Herbert Vince, 222–66. Loeb Classical Library 238. Cambridge, MA: Harvard University Press, 1930.

Derrida, Jacques. "Force of Law: The 'Mystical Foundation of Authority'." In *Deconstruction and the Possibility of Justice*, edited by Drucilla Cornell, Michel Rosenfeld and David Gray Carlson, 3–67. London and New York: Routledge, 1992.

Descartes, René. "Meditationes de prima philosophia." In *Œuvres de Descartes*, Vol. VII, edited by Charles Adam and Paul Tannery. Paris: Léopold Cerf, 1904.

"Principia Philosophiae." In *Œuvres de Descartes*, Vol. VIII, edited by Charles Adam and Paul Tannery. Paris: Léopold Cerf, 1905.

"Les Passions de l'Ame." In *Œuvres de Descartes*, Vol. XI, edited by Charles Adam and Paul Tannery, 293–502. Paris: Léopold Cerf, 1909.

Diels, Hermann and Walter Kranz. *Die Fragmente der Vorsokratiker*, Vol. 2. Zürich: Weidmann, 2005.

Diggelmann, Oliver. "The Creation of the United Nations: Break with the Past or Continuation of Wartime Power Politics?" *Journal for International Peace and Organization* 93 (2020): 371–89.

Donnelly, Jack. *Human Rights in Theory and Practice*. Ithaca, NY: Cornell University Press, 2003.

"The Relative Universality of Human Rights." *Human Rights Quarterly* 29, no. 2 (2007): 281–306.

"Draft Convention on Rights and Duties of Neutral States in Naval and Aerial War." *The American Journal of International Law* 33 (1939): 175–203.

Du Bois, William Edward Burghardt. *The Souls of Black Folk*. New York: W. W. Norton, 1999.

Duke, Aaron and Laurent Bègue. "The Drunk Utilitarian: Blood Alcohol Concentration Predicts Utilitarian Responses in Moral Dilemmas." *Cognition* 134 (2015): 121–7.

Dupré, Catherine. *The Age of Dignity: Human Rights and Constitutionalism in Europe*. Oxford: Hart, 2015.

Durkheim, Émile. *De la division du travail social*. Paris: PUF, 2007.

Dworkin, Ronald. *Taking Rights Seriously*. London: Duckworth, 1991.

Sovereign Virtue. Cambridge, MA: Harvard University Press, 2002.

Justice for Hedgehogs. Cambridge, MA: Harvard University Press, 2011.

Dwyer, Susan. "Moral Competence." In *Philosophy and Linguistics*, edited by Kumiko Murusagi and Robert Stainton, 169–90. New York: Routledge, 1999.

Ehrlich, Eugen. *Grundlegung der Soziologie des Rechts*. Berlin: Duncker & Humblot, 1989.

Elias, Norbert. *Über den Prozess der Zivilisation*. Frankfurt am Main: Suhrkamp, 1976.

Eliot, George. *Daniel Deronda*. Oxford: Oxford University Press, 2014.

Engel, Christoph. "Dictator Games: A Meta Study." *Experimental Economics* 14 (2011): 583–610.

Engel, Christoph and Michael Kurschilgen. "The Jurisdiction of the Man within – Introspection, Identity, and Cooperation in a Public Good Experiment." *MPI Collective Goods Preprint* (2015).

Engels, Friedrich. *Socialism: Utopian and Scientific*. Translated by Edward Aveling. London: Swan Sonnenschein & Co., 1892.

"Die Entwicklung des Sozialismus von der Utopie zur Wissenschaft." In *Marx-Engels-Werke*, Vol. 19, edited by Ludwig Arnold, 189–201. Berlin: Dietz Verlag, 1987.

Enoch, David. *Taking Morality Seriously: A Defense of Robust Realism*. Oxford: Oxford University Press, 2011.

Euripides. "Suppliant Women." In *Suppliant Women, Electra, Heracles*, edited and translated by David Kovacs, 1–139. Loeb Classical Library 9. Cambridge, MA: Harvard University Press, 1998.

"Trojan Women." In *Trojan Women, Iphigenia among the Taurians, Ion, Euripides Vol. IV*. Translated by David Kovacs, 1–143. Loeb Classical Library 10. Cambridge, MA: Harvard University Press, 1999.

"Ion." In *Trojan Women, Iphigenia among the Taurians, Ion, Euripides Vol. IV*. Translated by David Kovacs, 313–511. Loeb Classical Library 10. Cambridge, MA: Harvard University Press, 1999.

"Helen." In *Helen, Phoenician Women, Orestes, Euripides Vol. V*, edited and translated by David Kovacs, 2–199. Loeb Classical Library 11. Cambridge, MA: Harvard University Press, 2002.

Euripides, "Phoenician Women." In *Helen, Phoenician Women, Orestes, Euripides Vol. V*, edited and translated by David Kovacs, 203–397. Loeb Classical Library 11. Cambridge, MA: Harvard University Press, 2002.

Fragments, Euripides Vol. VII, edited and translated by Christopher Collard and Martin Cropp. Loeb Classical Library 504. Cambridge, MA: Harvard University Press, 2008.

"Phrixus A or B." In Euripides, *Fragments: Oedipus-Chrysippus, Other Fragments, Euripides Vol. VIII*, edited and translated by Christopher Collard and Martin Cropp, 444–57. Loeb Classical Library 506. Cambridge, MA: Harvard University Press, 2008.

Evans, Tony. *The Politics of Human Rights: A Global Perspective*. London: Pluto Press, 2005.

Fehr, Ernst and Urs Fischbacher. "The Nature of Human Altruism." *Nature* 425 (2003): 785–91.

Fehr, Ernst, Helen Bernhard and Bettina Rockenbach. "Egalitarianism in Young Children." *Nature* 454, no. 7208 (2008): 1079–83.

Fehr, Ernst, Daniela Glätzle-Rützler and Matthias Sutter. "The Development of Egalitarianism, Altruism, Spite and Parochialism in Childhood and Adolescence." *European Economic Review* 64 (2013): 369–83.

Fehr, Ernst and Ivo Schurtenberger. "Normative Foundations of Human Cooperation." *Nature Human Behaviour* 2, no. 7 (2018): 458–68.

Feinberg, Joel and Jan Narveson. "The Nature and Value of Rights." *The Journal of Value Inquiry* 4 (1970): 243–60.

Ferrone, Vincenzo. *The Enlightenment and the Rights of Man*. Liverpool: Liverpool University Press, 2019.

Feyerabend, Paul. *Against Method*. London and New York: Verso, 2010.

Finch, George A. "The International Rights of Man." *The American Journal of International Law* 35, no. 4 (1941): 662–5.

Fiore, Pasquale. *Le droit international codifié et sa sanction juridique*. Paris: Librarie Marescq Ainé, 1890.

Fitch, Tecumseh. *The Evolution of Language*. Cambridge: Cambridge University Press, 2010.

Foot, Philippa. "The Problem of Abortion and the Doctrine of the Double Effect." *Oxford Review* 5 (1967): 5–15.

Virtues and Vices and Other Essays in Moral Philosophy. Oxford: Oxford University Press, 1978.

"Moral Relativism." In *Moral Dilemmas and Other Topics in Moral Philosophy*, 20–36. Oxford: Clarendon Press, 2002.

Forst, Rainer. *Das Recht auf Rechtfertigung*. Frankfurt am Main: Suhrkamp, 2007.

Foucault, Michel. *Les mots et les choses: Une archéologie des sciences humaines*. Paris: Gallimard, 1966.

Surveiller et punir. Paris: Gallimard, 1975.

Qu'est-ce que la critique? Suivi de La culture de soi. Paris: Librairie Philosophique Vrin, 2015.

France, Anatole. *Le lys rouge*. Paris: Calmann-Lévy, 1894.

Frank, Thomas. "Archeological Evidence from the Early Pastoral Period." In *People, Cattle and Land: Transformations of a Pastoral Society in Southwestern Africa*, edited by Michael Bollig and Jan-Bart Gewald, 77–94. Cologne: Rüdiger Köppe Verlag, 2000.

Fredman, Sandra. *Discrimination Law*, 2nd ed. Oxford: Oxford University Press 2011.

Frisch, Max. *Tagebuch 1946–1949*. Frankfurt am Main: Suhrkamp, 1985.

Gallistel, Charles R. "Learning Organs." In *Chomsky Notebook*, edited by Jean Bricmont and Julie Franck, 193–202. New York: Columbia University Press, 2007.

Gargarella, Roberto. *Latin American Constitutionalism, 1810–2010: The Engine Room of the Constitution*. Oxford: Oxford University Press, 2013.

Gazzaniga, Michael S. *The Ethical Brain*. Chicago, IL: University of Chicago Press, 2005.

Gehlen, Arnold. *Der Mensch, seine Natur und seine Stellung in der Welt*. Berlin: Junker und Dünnhaupt, 1940.

Getachew, Adom. *Worldmaking after Empire: The Rise and Fall of Self-Determination*. Princeton, NJ: Princeton University Press, 2019.

Gewald, Jan-Bart. "Colonization, Genocide and Resurgence: The Herero of Namibia 1890 – 1933." In *People, Cattle and Land: Transformations of a Pastoral Society in Southwestern Africa*, edited by Michael Bollig and Jan-Bart Gewald, 187–226. Cologne: Rüdiger Köppe Verlag, 2000.

Gewirth, Alan. *The Community of Rights*. Chicago, IL: University of Chicago Press, 1996.

Gilligan, Carol. *In a Different Voice: Psychological Theory and Women's Development*. Cambridge, MA: Harvard University Press, 1982.

Glendon, Mary Ann. *A World Made Anew: Eleanor Roosevelt and the Universal Declaration*. New York: Random House Publishing Group, 2001.

Glover, Jonathan. *Humanity: A Moral History of the Twentieth Century*. London: Jonathan Cape, 1999.

Goldsmith, Jack Landman and Eric Andrew Posner. *The Limits of International Law*. Oxford: Oxford University Press, 2005.

Goodale, Mark. *Anthropology and the Law: A Critical Introduction*. New York: New York University Press, 2017.

Goodman, Nelson. *Facts, Fiction, and Forecast*. Cambridge, MA: Harvard University Press, 1983.

Gosepath, Stefan. *Gleiche Gerechtigkeit: Grundlagen eines liberalen Egalitarismus*. Frankfurt am Main: Suhrkamp, 2004.

Gouges, Olympe de. *Déclaration des droits de la femme et de la citoyenne: Suivi de eligio pour les Dames ou le portrait des femmes*. Paris: Mille et une nuits, 2003.

Gould, Stephen Jay and Richard Lewontin. "The Spandrels of San Marco and the Panglossian Paradigm: A Critique of the Adaptationist Programme." *Proceedings of the Royal Society of London, Series B* 205, no. 1161 (1979): 581–98.

Gould, Stephen Jay and Elisabeth Vrba. "Exaptation – A Missing Term in the Science of Form." *Paleobiology* 8, no. 1 (1982): 4–15.

Graeber, David and David Wengrow. *The Dawn of Everything*. London: Penguin Books, 2021.

Greene, Joshua. "Why Are VMPFC Patients More Utilitarian? A Dual Process Theory of Moral Judgement Explains." *Trends in Cognitive Science* 11, no. 8 (2007): 322–3.

Moral Tribes: Emotion, Reason and the Gap between Us and Them. New York: Penguin Press, 2013.

"Beyond Point-and-Shoot Morality: Why Cognitive (Neuro)Science Matters for Ethics." *Ethics* 124, no. 4 (2014): 695–726.

"The Cognitive Neuroscience of Moral Judgement and Decision Making." In *The Cognitive Neurosciences*, edited by Michael Gazzaniga and George Mangun, 1013–23. Cambridge, MA: MIT Press, 2014.

Greene, Joshua, Brian Sommerville, Leigh Nystrom, John Darley and Jonathan Cohen. "An fMRI Investigation of Emotional Engagement in Moral Judgement." *Science* 293, no. 5537 (2001): 2105–8.

Greene, Joshua, Francesca Rossi, John Tasioulas, Kristen Venable, Brian Williams. "Embedding Ethical Principles in Collective Decision Support Systems." *Proceedings of the Thirtieth AAAI Conference on Artificial Intelligence* (2016): 4147–51.

Griffin, James. *On Human Rights*. Oxford: Oxford University Press, 2008.

Grossman, Vasily. "The Hell of Treblinka." In *The Road: Stories, Journalism, and Essays*, edited by Robert Chandler, 116–162. New York: New York Review of Books, 2010.

Grotius, Hugo. *Mare Liberum: Sive – De iure quod Batavis competit ad Indicana commercia – Dissertatio*. Amsterdam: Elzevir, 1618.

De jure praedae commentarius. The Hague: Martinus Nijhoff, 1868.

De Iure Belli ac Pacis Libri Tres, Editio Nova, Vol. I, Reproduction of the Edition of 1646 by James Brown Scott. Washington, DC: Carnegie Institution of Washington, 1913.

Grunert, Frank. "The 'Iura Connata' in the Natural Law of Christian Wolff." In *Philosophy, Rights and Natural Law, Essays in Honour of Knud Haadkonssen*, edited by Ian Hunter and Richard Whatmore, 196–215. Edinburgh: Edinburgh University Press, 2019.

Günther, Klaus. "Anerkennung, Verantwortung, Gerechtigkeit." In *Sozialphilosophie und Kritik*, edited by Rainer Forst, Martin Hartmann, Rahel Jaeggi and Martin Saar, 269–87. Frankfurt am Main: Suhrkamp, 2009.

"Geteilte Souveränität, Nation und Rechtsgemeinschaft." *Kritische Justiz* 3 (2016): 321–37.

Guthrie, William Keith Chambers. *The Sophists*. Cambridge: Cambridge University Press, 2005.

Haakonsson, Knut. "Hugo Grotius and the History of Political Thought." *Political Theory* 13, no. 2 (1985): 239–65.

Habermas, Jürgen. *Strukturwandel der Öffentlichkeit: Untersuchungen zu einer Kategorie der bürgerlichen Gesellschaft*. Darmstadt: Luchterhand, 1979.

Theorie des kommunikativen Handelns, Frankfurt am Main: Suhrkamp, 1981.

Moralbewusstsein und Kommunikatives Handeln. Frankfurt am Main: Suhrkamp, 1983.

Erläuterungen zur Diskursethik. Frankfurt am Main: Suhrkamp, 1991.

Faktizität und Geltung. Frankfurt am Main: Suhrkamp, 1992.

Auch eine Geschichte der Philosophie, Vol. I: Die okzidentale Konstellation von Glauben und Wissen. Berlin: Suhrkamp, 2019.

Häfelin, Ulrich, Georg Müller and Felix Uhlmann. *Allgemeines Verwaltungsrecht*, 8th edition. Zürich: Dike, 2020.

Hafner-Burton, Emilie M. and Kiyoteru Tsutsui. "Justice Lost! The Failure of International Human Rights Law to Matter Where Needed Most." *Journal of Peace Research* 44 (2007): 407–25.

Haidt, Jonathan. "The Emotional Dog and Its Rational Tail: A Socialist Intuitionist Approach to Moral Judgement." *Psychological Review* 108, no. 4 (2001): 814–34.

The Righteous Mind: Why Good People are Divided by Politics and Religion. New York: Pantheon Books, 2012.

Haley, Kevin J. and Daniel M. T. Fessler. "Nobody's Watching? Subtle Cues Affect Generosity in an Anonymous Economic Game." *Evolution and Human Behaviour* 26 (2005): 245–56.

Hamlin, J. Kiley, Karen Wynn and Paul Bloom. "Social Evaluation by Preverbal Infants." *Nature* 450 (2007): 557–9.

Hamlin, J. Kiley and Karen Wynn. "Young Infants Prefer Prosocial to Antisocial Others." *Cognitive Development* 26, no. 1 (2011): 30–9.

Hare, Richard Mervyn. *The Language of Morals*. Oxford: Clarendon Press, 1952.

Moral Thinking: Its Levels, Methods and Point. Oxford: Clarendon Press, 1982.

Harman, Gilbert and Judith Thompson. *Moral Relativism and Moral Objectivity*. Oxford and Malden, MA: Blackwell Publishing, 1996.

Harman, Gilbert. *Explaining Value: And Other Essays in Moral Philosophy*. Oxford: Oxford University Press, 2000.

"Using a Linguistic Analogy to Study Morality." In *Moral Psychology, Vol. 1: The Evolution of Morality*, edited by Walter Sinnott-Armstrong, 345–51. Cambridge, MA: MIT Press, 2008.

Hart, Herbert Lionel Adolphus. "Are There Any Natural Rights?" *The Philosophical Review* 64, no. 2 (1955): 175–91.

"Between Utility and Rights." *Columbia Law Review* 79, no. 5 (1979): 828–46.

Essays on Bentham. Oxford: Oxford University Press, 1982.

The Concept of Law. Oxford: Oxford University Press, 2012.

Hauser, Marc. *Moral Minds*. New York: Harper Collins, 2006.

Hegel, Georg Wilhelm Friedrich. "Vorlesungen über die Philosophie der Geschichte." In *Werke*, Vol. 12, edited by Eva Moldenhauer and Karl Markus Michel. Frankfurt am Main: Suhrkamp, 1970.

"Grundlinien der Philosophie des Rechts." In *Werke*, Vol. 7, edited by Eva Moldenhauer and Karl Markus Michel. Frankfurt am Main: Suhrkamp, 1986.

"Phänomenologie des Geistes." In *Werke*, Vol. 3, edited by Eva Moldenhauer and Karl Markus Michel. Frankfurt am Main: Suhrkamp, 1986.

"Vorlesungen über die Geschichte der Philosophie I." In *Werke*, Vol. 18, edited by Eva Moldenhauer and Karl Markus Michel. Frankfurt am Main: Suhrkamp, 1986.

Heidegger, Martin. *Sein und Zeit*. Tübingen: Max Niemeyer Verlag, 1984.

Heine, Heinrich. "Vorrede zum ersten Band des 'Salon'." In *Sämtliche Schriften, Vol. 4: Schriften zu Literatur und Politik II, Vermischtes*, 522–30. Darmstadt: Wissenschaftliche Buchgesellschaft, 2022.

Henrich, Joseph. *The Secret of Our Success: How Culture Is Driving Human Evolution, Domesticating Our Species, and Making Us Smarter*. Princeton, NJ: Princeton University Press, 2017.

Henrich, Joseph, Robert Boyd, Samuel Bowles, et al. "'Economic Man' in Cross-Cultural Perspective: Behavioural Experiments in 15 Small-Scale Societies." *Behavioural and Brain Sciences* 28, no. 6 (2005): 795–815.

Henrichsen, Dag. "Ozongambe, Omavita, and Ozondjembo – The Process of (Re-) Pastoralization amongst Herero in Pre-colonial 19th Century Central Namibia." In *People, Cattle and Land: Transformations of a Pastoral Society in Southwestern Africa*, edited by Michael Bollig and Jan-Bart Gewald, 149–86. Cologne: Rüdiger Köppe Verlag, 2000.

Herder, Johann Gottfried. "Ideen zur Philosophie der Geschichte der Menschheit." In *Johann Gottfried Herder: Werke*, Vol. 6, edited by Martin Bollacher. Frankfurt am Main: Deutscher Klassiker Verlag, 1989.

Herodotus. *The Landmark Herodotus: The Histories*. Translated by Andrea L. Purvis, edited by Robert B. Strassler. New York: Anchor Books, 2009.

Hoebel, Edward Adamson. *The Law of Primitive Man: A Study in Comparative Legal Dynamics*. Cambridge, MA: Harvard University Press, 1954.

Hohfeld, Wesley Newcomb. *Fundamental Legal Conceptions as Applied in Judicial Reasoning*, edited by David Campbell and Philip Thomas. London and New York: Routledge, 2001.
Hölderlin, Friedrich. *Hyperion oder der Eremit in Griechenland*. In: Sämtliche Werke und Briefe, edited by Jochen Schmidt and Katharina Grätz, 9–176. Frankfurt am Main: Deutscher Klassiker Verlag, 1994.
Hyperion, or the Hermit in Greece. Translated by Howard Gaskill. Cambridge: Open Book Publishers, 2019.
Holt, James Clarke. *Magna Carta*, 3rd edition. Cambridge: Cambridge University Press, 2015.
Holzleithner, Elisabeth. "Feminisische Menschenrechtskritik." *Zeitschrift für Menschenrechte* 1 (2016): 110–20.
Homer. *Odyssey, Vol. I: Books 1–12*. Translated by Augustus T. Murray. Revised by George E. Dimock. Loeb Classical Library 104. Cambridge, MA: Harvard University Press, 1919.
Odyssey, Vol. II: Books 13–24. Translated by Augustus T. Murray. Revised by George E. Dimock. Loeb Classical Library 105. Cambridge, MA: Harvard University Press, 1919.
Honneth, Axel. *Der Kampf um Anerkennung*. Frankfurt am Main: Suhrkamp, 1992.
Honoré, Tony. *Ulpian: Pioneer of Human Rights*. 2nd edition. Oxford: Oxford University Press, 2002.
Horkheimer, Max and Theodor W. Adorno. "Die Dialektik der Aufklärung." In *Theodor W. Adorno: Gesammelte Schriften, Vol. 3*, edited by Rolf Tiedemann. Darmstadt: Wissenschaftliche Buchgesellschaft, 1998.
Huang, Karen, Joshua Greene and Max Bazerman. "Veil-of-Ignorance Reasoning Favors the Greater Good." *Proceedings of the National Academy of Sciences* 116, no. 48 (2019): 23989–95.
Humboldt, Wilhelm von. "Ideen zu einem Versuch, die Gränzen der Wirksamkeit des Staates zu bestimmen." In *Wilhelm von Humboldt, Werke, Vol. I: Schriften zur Sprachphilosophie*, edited by Andreas Filtner and Klaus Giel, 56–233. Darmstadt: Wissenschaftliche Buchgesellschaft, 2002.
"Über die Verschiedenheiten des menschlichen Sprachbaues." In *Wilhelm von Humboldt, Werke, Vol. III: Schriften zur Sprachphilosophie*, edited by Andreas Filtner and Klaus Giel, 144–367. Darmstadt: Wissenschaftliche Buchgesellschaft, 2002.
Hume, David. "An Enquiry Concerning the Principles of Morals." In *David Hume: Enquiries Concerning Human Understanding and Concerning the Principles of Morals*, 3rd edition, edited by Peter Harold Nidditch, 169–282. Oxford: Oxford University Press, 1975.
"An Enquiry Concerning Human Understanding." In *David Hume: Enquiries Concerning Human Understanding and Concerning the Principles of Morals*, 3rd edition, edited by Peter Harold Nidditch, 6–166. Oxford: Oxford University Press, 1975.
Humphrey, John P. *Human Rights & the United Nations: A Great Adventure*. New York: Transnational Publishers, 1984.
Hunt, Lynn. *Inventing Human Rights: A History*. New York: W. W. Norton & Company, 2007.
Hunter, James Davison and Paul Nedelsky. *Science and the Good: The Tragic Quest for the Foundations of Morality*. New Haven, CT: Yale University Press, 2018.
Hursthouse, Rosalind. *On Virtue Ethics*. Oxford: Oxford University Press, 1999.
Hutchinson, Francis. *An Inquiry into the Original of Our Ideas of Beauty and Virtue*, edited by Wolfgang Leidhold. New York: Garland Publishing, 1971.
Ignatieff, Michael. *Human Rights as Politics and Idolatry*. Princeton, NJ: Princeton University Press, 2001.
"Human Rights, Global Ethics, and the Ordinary Virtues." *Ethics & International Affairs* 31, no. 1 (2017): 3–16.
Irwin, Terence. *The Development of Ethics: A Historical and Critical Study, Vol. II: From Suarez to Rousseau*. Oxford: Oxford University Press, 2008.

Jackendoff, Ray. *Language, Consciousness, Culture: Essays on Mental Structure*. Cambridge, MA: MIT Press, 2007.

A User's Guide to Thought and Meaning. Oxford: Oxford University Press, 2012.

Jäncke, Lutz. *Kognitive Neurowissenschaften*. Bern: Hogrefe, 2013.

Jellinek, Georg. *Die Erklärung der Menschen- und Bürgerrechte*. Berlin: Duncker & Humblot, 1895.

Jensen, Steven L. B. *The Making of International Human Rights: The 1960s, Decolonization, and the Reconstruction of Global Values*. Cambridge: Cambridge University Press, 2017.

Jhering, Rudolph von. *Geist des römischen Rechts auf den verschiedenen Stufen seiner Entwicklung, Teil III*. Leipzig: Breitskopf und Härtel, 1924.

Joas, Hans. *Die Sakralität der Person: Eine neue Genealogie der Menschenrechte*. Frankfurt am Main: Suhrkamp, 2011.

Johnson, Uwe. *Jahrestage 1–4*. Berlin: Suhrkamp, 2013.

Jones, Owen D., Jeffrey D. Schall and Francis X. Shen. *Law and Neuroscience*. New York: Wolters Kluwer, 2020.

Jung, Kim Dae. "Is Culture Destiny? The Myth of Asia's Anti-democratic Values." *Foreign Affairs* 73, no. 6 (1994): 189–94.

Kafka, Franz. *Das Schloss*. Frankfurt am Main: Fischer Taschenbuch Verlag, 2018.

The Castle. Translated by J. A. Underwood. London: Penguin Books, 2019.

Kahane, Guy and Nicholas Shackel. "Methodological Issues in the Neuroscience of Moral Judgment." *Mind & Language* 25, no. 5 (2010): 561–82.

Kahane, Guy, Katja Wiech, Nicholas Shackel, Miguel Farias, Julian Savulescu and Irene Tracey. "The Neural Basis of Intuitive and Counterintuitive Moral Judgment." *Social Cognitive and Affective Neuroscience* 7, no. 4 (2011): 393–402.

Kahane, Guy. "Sidetracked by Trolleys: Why Sacrificial Moral Dilemmas Tell Us Little (or Nothing) about Utilitarian Judgment." *Social Neuroscience* 10, no. 5 (2015): 551–60.

Kahane, Guy, Jim Everett, Brian Earp, Miguel Farias and Julian Savulescu. "'Utilitarian' Judgments in Sacrificial Moral Dilemmas Do Not Reflect Impartial Concern for the Greater Good." *Cognition* 134 (2015): 193–209.

Kahane, Guy, Jim A. C. Everett, Brian D. Earp, et al. "Beyond Sacrificial Harm: A Two-Dimensional Model of Utilitarian Psychology." *Psychological Review* 125, no. 2 (2018): 131–64.

Kahneman, Daniel and Cass R. Sunstein. "Cognitive Psychology of Moral Intuitions." In *Neurobiology of Human Values*, edited by Jean-Pierre Changeux, Antonio Damasio, Wolf Singer and Yves Christen, 91–105. Berlin: Springer, 2005.

Kahneman, Daniel. *Thinking, Fast and Slow*. New York: Farrar, Straus, and Giroux, 2011.

Kant, Immanuel. "Grundlegung zur Metaphysik der Sitten." In *Kants gesammelte Schriften*, Vol. IV, Akademieausgabe, 385–464. Berlin: Georg Reimer, 1911.

"Kritik der reinen Vernunft. 1st ed. 1781." In *Kants gesammelte Schriften*, Vol. IV, Akademieausgabe, 1–252. Berlin: Georg Reimer, 1911.

"Kritik der reinen Vernunft. 2nd ed. 1787." In *Kants gesammelte Schriften*, Vol. III, Akademieausgabe. Berlin: Georg Reimer, 1911.

"Kritik der praktischen Vernunft " In *Kants gesammelte Schriften*, Vol. V, Akademieausgabe, 1–164. Berlin: Georg Reimer, 1913.

"Metaphysik der Sitten." In *Kants gesammelte Schriften*, Vol. VI, Akademieausgabe, 203–494. Berlin: Georg Reimer, 1914.

"Zum Ewigen Frieden." In *Kants gesammelte Schriften*, Vol. VIII, Akademieausgabe, 341–86. Berlin and Leipzig: Walter de Gruyter, 1923.

"Perpetual Peace." Translated by Mary J. Gregor. In *Practical Philosophy (The Cambridge Edition of the Works of Immanuel Kant)*, edited by Mary J. Gregor, 311–52. Cambridge: Cambridge University Press, 1996.

Critique of Pure Reason (The Cambridge Edition of the Works of Immanuel Kant). Translated by Paul Guyer and Allen W. Wood. Cambridge: Cambridge University Press, 1999.

Kar, Robin Bradley. "The Psychological Foundations of Human Rights." In *The Oxford Handbook of International Human Rights Law*, edited by Dinah Shelton, 104–43. Oxford: Oxford University Press, 2013.

Kaser, Max and Rolf Knütel. *Römisches Privatrecht*, 20th edition. Munich: C. H. Beck, 2014.

Kateb, George. *Human Dignity*. Cambridge, MA: Harvard University Press, 2011.

Kelsen, Hans. *Das Problem der Souveränität und die Theorie des Völkerrechts*. Tübingen: Scientia Verlag, 1928.

"Das Problem der Gerechtigkeit." In *Reine Rechtslehre*, 357–444. Vienna: Deuticke, 1960.

Reine Rechtslehre, 2nd edition. Vienna: Deuticke, 1960.

Kennedy, David. *The Dark Side of Virtue: Reassessing International Humanitarianism*. Princeton, NJ: Princeton University Press, 2004.

Kiener, Regina. "Grundrechte in der Bundesverfassung." In *Verfassungsrecht der Schweiz/ Droit constitutionell Suisse*, edited by Oliver Diggelmann, Maya Hertig Randall and Benjamin Schindler, 1193–221. Zürich: Schulthess, 2020.

Kieran, Ben. *Blood and Soil: A World History of Genocide and Extermination from Sparta to Darfur*. New Haven, CT: Yale University Press, 2007.

Klose, Fabian. *Human Rights in the Shadow of Colonial Violence*. Philadelphia: University of Pennsylvania Press, 2013.

Knobe, Joshua. "Intentional Action and Side Effects in Ordinary Language." *Analysis* 63, no. 3 (2003): 190–4.

Koenigs, Michael and Daniel Tranel. "Irrational Economic Decision-Making after Ventromedial Prefrontal Damage: Evidence from the Ultimatum Game." *The Journal of Neuroscience* 27, no. 4 (2007): 951–6.

Koestler, Arthur. *Darkness at Noon*. London: Vintage Classics, 2020.

Kohlberg, Lawrence. *Essays on Moral Development, Vol. I: The Philosophy of Moral Development: Moral Stages and the Idea of Justice*. San Francisco, CA: Harper & Row, 1981.

Essays on Moral Development, Vol. II: The Psychology of Moral Development: The Nature and Validity of Moral Stages. San Francisco, CA: Harper & Row, 1984.

Korsgaard, Christine. *The Sources of Normativity*. Cambridge: Cambridge University Press, 1996.

Fellow Creatures: Our Obligations to the Other Animals. Oxford: Oxford University Press, 2018.

Koskenniemi, Marti. *The Gentle Civilizer of Nations: The Rise and Fall of International Law 1870 – 1960*. Cambridge: Cambridge University Press, 2001.

From Apology to Utopia: The Structure of International Legal Argument. Reissue with a new epilogue. Cambridge: Cambridge University Press, 2005.

Kotsidu, Haritini. *ΤΙΜΗ ΚΑΙ ΔΟΞΑ: Ehrungen für hellenistische Herrscher im griechischen Mutterland und in Kleinasien unter besonderer Berücksichtigung der archäologischen Denkmäler*. Berlin: Akademie Verlag, 2000.

Kriegeskorte, Nikolaus, Kyle Simmons, Patrick Bellgowan and Chris Baker. "Circular Analysis in Systems Neuroscience: The Dangers of Double Dipping." *Nature Neuroscience* 12 (2009): 535–40.

Kuhlmeier, Valerie, Karen Wynn and Paul Bloom. "Attribution of Dispositional States by 12-Month-Olds." *Psychological Science* 14, no. 5 (2003), 402–8.

Kuhn, Thomas. *The Structure of Scientific Revolutions*. Chicago, IL: University of Chicago Press, 2012.

Kymlicka, Will. *Multicultural Citizenship*. Oxford: Oxford University Press, 1995.

Las Casas, Bartolomé de. *Obras Completas Vol. 7: Apologética Historia Sumaria II*. Madrid: Alianza Editorial, 1988.

Obras Completas Vol. 10: Tratados de 1552, Impresos por Las Casas en Sevilla. Madrid: Alianza Editorial, 1992.

Obras Completas Vol. 11.2, Doce Dudas. Madrid: Alianza Editorial, 1992.

Obras Completas Vol. 12: De regia potestate, Questio Theologalis. Madrid: Alianza Editorial, 1992.

Lauren, Paul Gordon. *The Evolution of International Human Rights: Visions Seen*. 3rd edition. Philadelphia: University of Pennsylvania Press, 2011.

"The Foundations of Justice and Human Rights in Early Legal Texts and Thought." In *The Oxford Handbook of International Human Rights Law*, edited by Dinah Shelton, 164–92. Oxford: Oxford University Press, 2013.

Laurence, Stephen, and Eric Margolis. "The Poverty of the Stimulus Argument." *The British Journal for the Philosophy of Science* 52, no. 2 (2001): 217–76.

Lauterpacht, Hersch. *An International Bill of Rights of Man*. New York: Columbia University Press, 1945.

International Law and Human Rights. London: Stevens & Sons, 1950.

Lee, Robert Warden. "Hugo Grotius." *Proceedings of the British Academy* 16 (1930): 219–79.

Leibniz, Gottfried Wilhelm. "Initium institutionum juris perpetui." In *Rechtsphilosophisches aus Leibnizens ungedruckten Schriften*, edited by Georg Mollat, 1–7. Leipzig: J. H. Robolsky, 1885.

"Vorrede zum Codex Juris Gentium Diplomaticus." In *Die philosophischen Schriften von G. W. F. Leibniz*, edited by C. I. Gerhardt, 388–93. Berlin: Weidmann, 1887.

"Nouveaux Essais." In *Gottfried Wilhelm Leibniz, Sämtliche Schriften und Briefe: Philosophische Schriften*, Series VI, Vol. 6. Akademieausgabe. Berlin: Akademie-Verlag, 1990.

"Aus der Neuen Methode, Jurisprudenz zu lernen und zu lehren (1667)." In *Frühe Schriften zum Naturrecht*, Latin–German, translated by Hubertus Busche, 26–87. Hamburg: Felix Meiner Verlag, 2003.

"Entwürfe zu den Elementen des Naturrechts." In *Frühe Schriften zum Naturrecht*, Latin–German, translated by Hubertus Busche, 91–322. Hamburg: Felix Meiner Verlag, 2003.

"Monadologie." In *Monadologie und andere metaphysische Schriften*, translated by Ulrich Johannes Schneider, 110–51. Hamburg: Felix Meiner Verlag, 2003.

"Universale Gerechtigkeit als klug verteilte Liebe zu allen." In *Frühe Schriften zum Naturrecht*, Latin–German, translated by Hubertus Busche, 215–43. Hamburg: Felix Meiner Verlag, 2003.

"Letter to Thomas Burnett of Kemney, 2 February 1700." In *Sämtliche Schriften und Briefe*, Series I, Vol. 18, Akademieausgabe, 367–88. Berlin: Akademie-Verlag, 2005.

"Letter to Thomas Burnett of Kemney, 18 July 1701." In *Sämtliche Schriften und Briefe*, Series I, Vol. 20, Akademieausgabe, 278–87. Berlin: Akademie-Verlag, 2006.

"Sur la nature de la bonté et de la justice." In *Das Recht kann nicht ungerecht sein...: Beiträge zu Leibniz' Philosophie der Gerechtigkeit*, edited by Wenchao Li, 143–63. Stuttgart: Franz Steiner Verlag, 2015.

"Sur la notion commune de la justice." In *Das Recht kann nicht ungerecht sein...: Beiträge zu Leibniz' Philosophie der Gerechtigkeit*, edited by Wenchao Li, 164–80. Stuttgart: Franz Steiner Verlag, 2015.

Lemkin, Raphael. *Axis Rule in Occupied Europe: Laws of Occupation, Analysis of Government, Proposals for Redress (Foundations of the Laws of War)*. Clark, NJ: Lawbook Exchange Ltd, 2008.

Lenski, Noel. "The Significance of the Edict of Milan." In *Constantine: Religious Faith and Imperial Policy*, edited by Edward Siecienski, 27–56. London and New York: Routledge, 2017.

Letsas, George. "Proportionality as Fittingness: The Moral Dimension of Proportionality." *Current Legal Problems* 71, no. 1 (2018): 53–86.

Levi, Primo. *Is This a Man?* Abacus: London, 1987.

Levine, Sydney, Alan M. Leslie and John Mikhail. "The Mental Representation of Human Action." *Cognitive Science* 42, no. 4 (2018): 1229–64.

Lewontin, Richard. "The Evolution of Cognition." In *Methods, Models, and Conceptual Issues: An Invitation to Cognitive Science*, Vol. 4, edited by Don Scarborough, Saul Sternberg and Daniel Osherson, 106–32. Cambridge, MA: MIT Press, 1998.

The Triple Helix: Gene, Organism, and Environment. Cambridge, MA: Harvard University Press, 2000.

Liao, S. Matthew. *The Right to Be Loved*. Oxford: Oxford University Press, 2015.

Lloyd, Lorna. "'A Most Auspicious Beginning': The 1946 United Nations General Assembly and the Question of the Treatment of Indians in South Africa." *Review of International Studies* 16, no. 2 (1990): 131–53.

Locke, John. *A Letter Concerning Toleration*, edited by James Tully. Indianapolis, IN: Hackett, 1983.

Two Treatises of Government, edited by Peter Laslett. Cambridge: Cambridge University Press, 1988.

An Essay Concerning Human Understanding. Harmondsworth: Penguin Books, 1997.

Lorenz, Konrad. *Das sogenannte Böse*. Vienna: Dr G. Borotha-Schoeler, 1963.

Luhmann, Niklas. *Soziale Systeme*. Frankfurt am Main: Suhrkamp, 1987.

Das Recht der Gesellschaft. Frankfurt am Main: Suhrkamp, 1995.

Die Gesellschaft der Gesellschaft Vol. 1 and 2. Frankfurt am Main: Suhrkamp, 1998.

Grundrechte als Institution. Berlin: Duncker & Humblot, 2009.

Mackie, John Leslie. *Ethics: Inventing Right and Wrong*. London: Penguin Books, 1977.

MacKinnon, Catharine. *Toward a Feminist Theory of the State*. Cambridge, MA: Harvard University Press, 1989.

Madley, Benjamin. *An American Genocide: The United States and the California Indian Catastrophe, 1846–1873*. New Haven, CT, and London: Yale University Press, 2016.

Mahlmann, Matthias. "Katastrophen der Rechtsgeschichte und die autopoietische Evolution des Rechts." *Zeitschrift für Rechtssoziologie* 21, no. 1 (2000): 247–77.

"Law and Force: 20th Century Radical Legal Philosophy, Post-modernism and the Foundations of Law." *Res Publica* 9, no. 1 (2003): 19–37.

"1789 Renewed? Prospects of the Protection of Human Rights in Europe." *Cardozo Journal of International and Comparative Law* 11, no. 3 (2004): 903–38.

"The Cognitive Foundations of Law." In *Foundations of Law*, edited by Hubert Rottleuthner, 75–100. Dordrecht: Springer, 2005.

"Ethics, Law and the Challenge of Cognitive Science." *German Law Journal* 8, no. 6 (2007): 577–615.

Elemente einer ethischen Grundrechtstheorie. Baden-Baden: Nomos Verlag, 2008.

Rationalismus in der praktischen Theorie, 2nd edition. Baden-Baden: Nomos Verlag, 2009.

"The Basic Law at 60 – Human Dignity and the Culture of Republicanism." *German Law Journal* 11, no. 1 (2010): 9–31.

"The Dictatorship of the Obscure? Values and the Secular Adjudication of Fundamental Rights." In *Constitutional Topography: Values and Constitutions*, edited by András Sajó and Renáta Uitz, 343–65. The Hague: Eleven International Publishing, 2010.

"Human Dignity and Autonomy in Modern Constitutional Orders." In *The Oxford Handbook of Comparative Constitutional Law*, edited by Michel Rosenfeld and András Sajó, 370–96. Oxford: Oxford University Press, 2012.

"Le Chariot – Bemerkungen zu den Grundlagen des Rechts." *Zeitschrift für Schweizerisches Recht* 131 (2012): 123–44.

"Die Garantie der Menschenwürde in der Schweizerischen Bundesverfassung." *Aktuelle Juristische Praxis* 22, no. 9 (2013): 1307–20.

"The Good Sense of Dignity: Six Antidotes to Dignity Fatigue in Ethics and Law." In *Understanding Human Dignity*, edited by Cristopher McCrudden, 593–614. Oxford: Oxford University Press, 2013.

"Menschenwürde in Politik, Ethik und Recht – universelle Fassade, kulturelle Relativität?" In *Rechtsstaatliches Strafrecht: Festschrift für Ulfrid Neumann zum 70. Geburtstag*, edited by Frank Saliger, 267–81. Heidelberg: C.F. Müller, 2017.

"Die geistige Wurzel der Gerechtigkeit – Rationalismus und Epistemologie in Leibniz' praktischer Philosophie." In *Rechts- und Staatsphilosophie bei G. W. Leibniz*, edited by Tilmann Altwicker, Francis Cheneval and Matthias Mahlmann, 89–104. Tübingen: Mohr Siebeck, 2020.

"Autonomie, Gleichheit und Eigentum." *Zeitschrift für Schweizerisches Recht* 140, no. 4 (2021): 377–402.

"On the Foundations of a Democratic Culture of Freedom: Law and the Normative Resources of Art." In *The Quest for Core Values in the Application of Legal Norms: Essays in Honor of Mordechai Kremnitzer*, edited by Khalid Ghanayim and Yuval Shany, 15–35. Berlin: Springer, 2021.

Rechtsphilosophie und Rechtstheorie, 7th edition. Baden-Baden: Nomos, 2023.

"Dignity and the Philosophy of the Republic." In *The Oxford Handbook of Republicanism*. Forthcoming.

Mahlmann, Matthias and John Mikhail. "Cognitive Science, Ethics and Law." In Epistemology and Ontology, edited by Zenon Bankowski, 95–102. Stuttgart: Franz Steiner Verlag, 2005.

Maloney, Tim Ryan, India Ella Dilkes-Hall, Melandri Vlok, et al. "Surgical Amputation of a Limb 31,000 Years Ago in Borneo." *Nature* 609 (2022): 547–51.

Mandelstam, André. *La Protection Internationale des Droits de l'Homme*. The Hague: Academie de droit international de La Haye, Recueil des cours, 1931.

Marino, Katherine M. *Feminism for the Americas: The Making of an International Human Rights Movement*. Chapel Hill: University of North Carolina Press, 2019.

Maritain, Jacques. *Les Droits de l'Homme et la Loi Naturelle*. New York: Édition de la Maison Française, 1942.

Marks, Susan. *A False Tree of Liberty: Human Rights in Radical Thought*. Oxford: Oxford University Press, 2019.

Marx, Karl. "Thesen über Feuerbach." In *Marx-Engels-Werke*, Vol. 3, 5–7. Berlin: Dietz Verlag, 1975.

"Kritik des Gothaer Programms." In *Marx-Engels-Werke*, Vol. 19, edited by Ludwig Arnold, 13–32. Berlin: Dietz Verlag, 1987.

Mauer, Hartmut and Christian Waldhoff. *Allgemeines Verwaltungsrecht*, 8th edition. Munich: C.H. Beck, 2020.

Mayenburg, David von. *Gemeiner Mann und Gemeines Recht. Die Zwölf Artikel und das Recht des ländlichen Raums im Zeitalter des Bauernkriegs*. Frankfurt am Main: Vittorio Klostermann, 2018.

Mazower, Mark. "The Strange Triumph of Human Rights 1933 – 1950." *The Historic Journal* 47, no. 2 (2004): 379–98.

No Enchanted Palace: The End of Empire and the Ideological Origins of the United Nations. Princeton, NJ: Princeton University Press, 2009.

Governing the World: The History of an Idea. London: Penguin Press, 2012.

McCrudden, Christopher. "Human Dignity and the Judicial Interpretation of Human Rights." *European Journal of International Law* 19, no. 4 (2008): 655–724.

"Human Rights and Traditional Values." In *Law's Ethical, Global and Theoretical Contexts*, edited by Upendra Baxi, Christophier McCrudden and Abdul Paliwala, 38–72. Cambridge: Cambridge University Press, 2015.

"Human Rights Histories." *Oxford Journal of Legal Studies* 35, no. 1 (2015): 179–212.

"On Portraying Human Dignity." In *Human Dignity in Context*, edited by Dieter Grimm, Alexandra Kemmerer and Christoph Möllers, 23–54. Baden-Baden: Nomos, 2018.

"Where Did 'Human Dignity' Come from? Drafting the Preamble to the Irish Constitution." *American Journal of Legal History* 60 (2020): 485–535.

McCrudden, Christopher and Jeff King. "The Dark Side of Nudging: The Ethics, Political Economy, and Law of Libertarian Paternalism." In *Choice Architecture in Democracies: Exploring the Legitimacy of Nudging*, edited by Alexandra Kemmerer, Christoph Möllers, Maximilian Steinbeis and Gerhard Wagner, 75–140. Oxford and Baden-Baden: Hart and Nomos, 2015.

McCullough, Michael E. *The Kindness of Strangers*. London: Oneworld, 2020.

Mendelssohn, Moses. "Jerusalem oder über religiöse Macht und Judentum." In *Gesammelte Schriften: Jubiläumsausgabe, Vol. 8: Schriften zum Judentum II*, edited by Alexander Altmann, 99–204. Stuttgart and Bad Cannstatt: Frommann-Holzboog, 1983.

Melville, Herman. *Moby-Dick or, The Whale*. Harmondsworth: Penguin Books, 1986.

Mercier, Hugo and Dan Sperber. *The Enigma of Reason*. Cambridge, MA: Harvard University Press, 2017.

Meyers, Diana Tietjens. "Feminist Philosophy of Human Rights." In *The Oxford Handbook of Feminist Philosophy*, edited by Kim Q. Hall and Ásta, 462–83. Oxford: Oxford University Press, 2021.

Mikhail, John. "Rawls' Linguistic Analogy: A Study of the "Generative Grammar" Model of Moral Theory Described by John Rawls in a Theory of Justice." PhD dissertation, Cornell University, 2000.

"Moral Heuristics or Moral Competence? Reflections on Sunstein." *Behavioural and Brain Sciences* 28, no. 4 (2005): 557–8.

"Universal Moral Grammar: Theory, Evidence and the Future." *Trends in Cognitive Sciences* 11 no. 4 (2007): 143–52.

"Is the Prohibition of Homicide Universal? Evidence from Comparative Criminal Law." *Brooklyn Law Review* 75, no. 2 (2009): 497–515.

Elements of Moral Cognition: Rawls' Linguistic Analogy and the Cognitive Science of Moral and Legal Judgment. Cambridge: Cambridge University Press, 2011.

"Moral Grammar and Human Rights: Some Reflections on Cognitive Science and Enlightenment Rationalism." In *Understanding Social Action, Promoting Human Rights*, edited by Ryan Goodman, Derek Jinks and Andrew Woods, 160–98. Oxford: Oxford University Press, 2012.

"Any Animal Whatever? Harmful Battery and Its Elements as Building Blocks of Moral Cognition." *Ethics* 124 (2014): 750–86.

"Chomsky and Moral Philosophy." In *The Cambridge Companion to Chomsky*, 2nd edition, edited by James McGilvray, 235–54. Cambridge: Cambridge University Press, 2017.
"Review of Shaun Nichols, Rational Rules: Towards a Theory of Moral Learning." *The Philosophical Review* (2022) 131 (3): 399–403.
Mill, John Stuart. "Utilitarianism." In *The Collected Works of John Stuart Mill, Vol. X – Essays on Ethics, Religion, and Society*, edited by John M. Robson, 203–60. Toronto: University of Toronto Press, London and New York: Routledge, 1985.
"On Liberty" In *The Collected Works of John Stuart Mill, Vol. XVIII – Essays on Politics and Society Part I*, edited by John M. Robson, 213–310. Toronto: University of Toronto Press, London and New York: Routledge, 2008.
Miller, David Hunter. *The Drafting of the Covenant*, Vol. 2. New York: G.P. Putnam's Sons, 1928.
Miller, David. *On Nationality*. New York: Oxford University Press, 1995.
"Grounding Human Rights." *Critical Review of International Social and Political Philosophy* 15, no. 4 (2012): 407–27.
Millhouse, Tyler, Alisabeth Ayars and Shaun Nichols, "Learnability and Moral Nativism: Exploring Wilde Rules." In *Methodology and Moral Philosophy*, edited by Jussi Suikkane and Antti Kauppinen, 64–78. New York: Routledge, 2019.
Moeckli, Daniel. "Equality and Non-discrimination." In *International Human Rights Law*, 3rd edition, edited by Daniel Moeckli, Sangeeta Shah and Sandesh Sivakumaran, 148–64. Oxford: Oxford University Press, 2018.
Moll, Jorge and Ricardo de Oliveira-Souza. "Moral Judgments, Emotions and the Utilitarian Brain." *Trends in Cognitive Science* 11, no. 8 (2007): 319–21.
"Response to Greene: Moral Sentiments and Reason: Friends or Foes?" *Trends in Cognitive Science* 11, no. 8 (2007): 323–4.
Morrison, Toni. "The Nobel Lecture in Literature." In *The Source of Self-Regard: Selected Essays, Speeches, and Meditations*, 102–9. New York: Vintage Books, 2020.
Morse, Stephen J. and Adina L. Roskies, eds. *A Primer on Criminal Law and Neuroscience: A Contribution of the Law and Neuroscience Project, Supported by the MacArthur Foundation*. Oxford: Oxford University Press, 2013.
Morse, Stephen J. "Law, Responsibility, and the Sciences of the Brain/Mind." In *The Oxford Handbook of Law, Regulation and Technology*, edited by Roger Brownsword, Eloise Scotford and Karen Yeung, 154–73. Oxford: Oxford University Press, 2017.
Morsink, Johannes. *The Universal Declaration of Human Rights: Origins, Drafting and Intent*. Philadelphia: University of Pennsylvania Press, 1999.
The Universal Declaration of Human Rights and the Holocaust: An Endangered Connection. Washington, DC: Georgetown University Press, 2019.
Moyn, Samuel. *The Last Utopia: Human Rights in History*. Cambridge, MA: Harvard University Press, 2010.
"Personalism, Community, and the Origins of Human Rights." In *Human Rights in the Twentieth Century*, edited by Stefan-Ludwig Hoffmann, 85–106. Cambridge: Cambridge University Press, 2011.
"The Continuing Perplexities of Human Rights." *Qui Parle* 22, no. 1 (2013): 95–115.
"The Secret History of Constitutional Dignity." In *Understanding Human Dignity*, edited by Christopher McCrudden, 95–111. Oxford: Oxford University Press, 2013.
Human Rights and the Uses of History. London and New York: Verso Books, 2014.
Christian Human Rights. Philadelphia: University of Pennsylvania Press, 2015.
Not Enough: Human Rights in an Unequal World. Cambridge, MA: Harvard University Press, 2018.

Müller, Angela. *States, Human Rights, and Distant Strangers: The Normative Justification of Extraterritorial Obligations in Human Rights Law*. Abingdon/New York: Routledge, 2023.
Münch, Ingo von, and Kunig, Philip, *Grundgesetz-Kommentar*, Band 1, 7th edition. Edited by Jörn-Axel Kämmerer and Markus Kotzur. Munich: C. H. Beck, 2021.
Mutua, Makau. *Human Rights: A Political and Cultural Critique*. Philadelphia: University of Pennsylvania Press, 2002.
Nagel, Thomas. *The Possibility of Altruism*. Oxford: Clarendon Press, 1970.
"What Is It Like to Be a Bat?" In *Mortal Questions*, 165–81. Cambridge: Cambridge University Press, 2020.
Nichols, Shaun. "On the Genealogy of Norms: A Case for the Rule of Emotion in Cultural Evolution." *Philosophy of Science* 69, no. 2 (2002): 234–55.
Sentimental Rules: On the Natural Foundations of Moral Judgement. Oxford: Oxford University Press, 2004.
Rational Rules: Towards a Theory of Moral Learning. Oxford: Oxford University Press, 2021.
Nichols, Shaun and Ron Mallon. "Moral Dilemmas and Moral Rules." *Cognition* 100, no. 3 (2006): 530–42.
Nichols, Shaun, Shikhar Kumar, Theresa Lopez, Alisabeth Ayars and Hoi Yee Chan. "Rational Learners and Moral Rules." *Mind and Language* 31, no. 5 (2016): 530–54.
Nickel, James W. *Making Sense of Human Rights*, 2nd edition. Malden, MA: Blackwell, 2007.
Nietzsche, Friedrich. "Jenseits von Gut und Böse." In *Friedrich Nietzsche: Sämtliche Werke, Vol. 5: Jenseits von Gut und Böse, Zur Genealogie der Moral, Kritische Studienausgabe*, edited by Giorgio Colli and Mazzino Montinari, 9–243. Munich: Deutscher Taschenbuch Verlag, 1999.
Beyond Good and Evil. Translated by Reginald John Hollingdale. London: Penguin Books, 2003.
Nisbett, Richard E. and Dov Cohen. *Culture of Honor: The Psychology of Violence in the South*. Boulder, CO: Westview Press, 1996.
Nisbett, Richard E. *The Geography of Thought: How Asians and Westerns Think Differently ... and Why*. New York: Free Press, 2003.
Nowak, Martin. "Five Rules for the Evolution of Cooperation." *Science* 314, no. 5805 (2006): 1560–3.
Nozick, Robert. *Anarchy, State, and Utopia*. Oxford and Malden, MA: Blackwell Publishing, 2008.
Nucci, Larry P., Elliot Turiel and Gloria Encarnacion-Gawrych. "Children's Social Interaction and Social Concepts." *Journal of Cross-Cultural Psychology* 14, no. 4 (1983): 469–87.
Nussbaum, Martha C. "Capabilities and Human Rights." *Fordham Law Review* 66, no. 2 (1997): 273–300.
Upheavals of Thought. Cambridge: Cambridge University Press, 2001.
Women and Human Development. Cambridge: Cambridge University Press, 2001.
O'Neill, Onora. "Children's Rights and Children's Lives." *Ethics* 98, no. 3 (1988): 445–63.
"The Dark Side of Human Rights." *International Affairs* 81, no. 2 (2005): 427–39.
Oberdiek, John F. K. "Specifying Rights Out of Necessity." *Oxford Journal of Legal Studies* 28, no. 1 (2008): 127–46.
Okin, Susan Moller. *Women in Western Political Thought*. Princeton, NJ: Princeton University Press, 1979.
Olson, Kristina and Elizabeth Spelke. "Foundations of Cooperation in Young Children." *Cognition* 108, no. 1 (2008): 222–31.

Orford, Anne. *International Law and the Politics of History*. Cambridge: Cambridge University Press, 2021.

Orwell, George. *Animal Farm*. London: Vintage Classics, 2021.

Homage to Catalonia. London: Vintage Classics 2021.

Nineteen Eighty-Four. London: Vintage Classics, 2021.

Ossipow, William and Dominik Gerber. "The Reception of Vattel's Law of Nations in the American Colonies: From James Otis and John Adams to the Declaration of Independence." *American Journal of Legal History* 57, no. 4 (2017): 521–55.

Paine, Thomas. *Common Sense and Other Writings*. New York: Barnes & Noble Classics, 2005.

Pardo, Michael S. and Dennis Patterson. *Minds, Brains and Law: The Conceptual Foundations of Law and Neuroscience*. Oxford: Oxford University Press, 2013.

Parfit, Derek. *On What Matters*, Vols. 1 and 2. Oxford: Oxford University Press, 2011.

On What Matters, Vol. 3. Oxford: Oxford University Press, 2017.

Peters, Anne. *Beyond Human Rights: The Legal Status of the Individual in International Law*. Translated by Jonathan Huston. Cambridge: Cambridge University Press, 2016.

Piaget, Jean. *Le jugement moral chez l'enfant : perspectives piagétiennes*. Paris: F. Alcan, 1932.

Pinker, Steven. *The Language Instinct: How the Mind Creates Language*. New York: William Morrow and Company, 1994.

The Blank Slate: The Modern Denial of Human Nature. London: Penguin Books, 2002.

"The Stupidity of Dignity." *New Republic*, May 28, 2008.

The Better Angels of our Nature: A History of Violence and Humanity. London: Penguin Books, 2012.

Plato. "Timaeus." In *Timaeus, Critias, Cleitophon, Menexenus, Epistles*. Translated by Robert Gregg Bury, 1–253. Loeb Classical Library 234. Cambridge, MA: Harvard University Press, 1929.

"Euthyphron." In *Platon: Werke, Vol. 1*. Greek-German. Translated by Friedrich Schleiermacher, 351–198. Darmstadt: Wissenschaftliche Buchgesellschaft, 2005.

"Apologia Sokratous." In *Platon: Werke, Vol. 2*. Greek-German. Translated by Friedrich Schleiermacher, 1–70. Darmstadt: Wissenschaftliche Buchgesellschaft, 2005.

"Gorgias." In Werke, Vol. 2. Greek-German. Translated by Friedrich Schleiermacher, 269–504. Darmstadt: Wissenschaftliche Buchgesellschaft, 2005.

"Politeia." In *Platon: Werke, Vol. 4*. Greek-German. Translated by Friedrich Schleiermacher. Darmstadt: Wissenschaftliche Buchgesellschaft, 2005.

"Nomoi, Tomoi I–VI." In *Platon: Werke, Vol. 8 1*. Translated by Klaus Schöpsdau. Darmstdadt: Wissenschaftliche Buchgesellschaft, 2005.

"Nomoi, Tomoi VII–XII." In *Platon: Werke, Vol. 8 2*. Translated by Klaus Schöpsdau. Darmstdadt: Wissenschaftliche Buchgesellschaft, 2005.

Republic, Volume I: Books 1–5, edited and translated by Christopher Emlyn-Jones and William Preddy. Loeb Classical Library 237. Cambridge, MA: Harvard University Press, 2013.

Republic, Volume II: Book 6-10, edited and translated by Christopher Emlyn-Jones and William Preddy. Loeb Classical Library 276. Cambridge, MA: Harvard University Press, 2013.

Pohlenz, Max. *Die Stoa*. Göttingen: Vandenhoeck & Ruprecht, 1992.

Poldrack, Russell. "Can Cognitive Processes Be Inferred from Neuroimaging Data?" *Trends in Cognitive Science* 10, no. 2 (2006): 59–63.

"Inferring Mental States from Neuroimaging Data: From Reverse Inference to Large-Scale Decoding." *Neuron* 72, no. 5 (2011): 692–7.

"The Future of fMRI in Cognitive Neuroscience." *Neuroimage* 62, no. 2 (2012): 1216–20.

The New Mind Readers. Princeton, NJ: Princeton University Press, 2018.
Popper, Karl. *The Open Society and Its Enemies, Vol. I: The Spell of Plato*. London and New York: Routledge, 2009.
The Open Society and Its Enemies, Vol. II: Hegel and Marx. London and New York: Routledge, 2009.
Posner, Eric Andrew. *The Twilight of Human Rights Law*. Oxford: Oxford University Press, 2014.
Posner, Richard A. *Economic Analysis of Law*. New York: Wolters Kluwer, 2014.
Power, Samantha. *"A Problem from Hell": America and the Age of Genocide*. New York: Harper Collins, 2007.
Premack, David and Ann James Premack. "Infants Attribute Value to the Goal Directed Actions of Self-Propelled Objects." *Journal of Cognitive Neuroscience* 9, no. 6 (1997): 848–56.
Price, Richard. *A Review of the Principal Questions in Morals*, edited by David Daiches Raphael. Oxford: Clarendon Press, 1948.
Pufendorf, Samuel. *De Jure Naturae et Gentium*. Lund: Junghans, 1672.
De Officio Hominis et civis juxta legem naturalem. Lund: Junghans, 1673.
Putnam, Hilary. *Pragmatism: An Open Question*. Oxford and Malden, MA: Blackwell Publishing, 1995.
Rawls, John. *A Theory of Justice*. Cambridge, MA: Harvard University Press, 1971.
Political Liberalism. New York: Columbia University Press, 1996.
A Theory of Justice, revised edition. Cambridge, MA: Harvard University Press, 1999.
The Law of Peoples. Cambridge, MA: Harvard University Press, 1999.
Lectures on the History of Moral Philosophy. Cambridge, MA: Harvard University Press, 2000.
Raz, Joseph. *The Authority of Law: Essays on Law and Morality*. Oxford: Clarendon Press, 1979.
The Morality of Freedom. Oxford: Oxford University Press, 1986.
"Human Rights in the Emerging World Order." In *Philosophical Foundations of Human Rights*, edited by Rowan Cruft, S. Matthew Liao and Massimo Renzo, 217–231. Oxford: Oxford University Press, 2015.
Repgow, Eike von. *Der Sachsenspiegel*. Translated by Paul Kaller. Munich: Beck, 2002.
The Saxon Mirror. Translated by Maria Dobozy. Philadelphia: University of Pennsylvania Press, 1999.
Rodríguez-Garavito, César. "Human Rights 2030: Existential Challenges and a New Paradigm for the Human Rights Field." In *The Struggle for Human Rights: Essays in Honour of Philip Alston*, edited by Nehal Bhuta, Florian Hoffmann, Sarah Knuckey, Frédéric Mégret and Margaret Satterthwaite, 328–47. Oxford: Oxford University Press, 2021.
ed. *Litigating the Climate Emergency. How Human Rights, Courts, and Legal Mobilization Can Bolster Climate Action*. Cambridge: Cambridge University Press, 2022.
Roedder, Erica and Gilbert Harman. "Linguistics and Moral Theory." In *The Moral Psychology Handbook*, edited by John M. Doris, 273–96. Oxford: Oxford University Press, 2010.
Rómulo, Carlos Peña. *The Meaning of Bandung*. Chapel Hill: University of North Carolina Press, 1956.
Rorty, Richard. *Contingency, Irony, and Solidarity*. Cambridge: Cambridge University Press, 1989.
Objectivity, Relativism, and Truth: Philosophical Papers. Cambridge: Cambridge University Press, 1991.
"Human Rights, Rationality and Sentimentality." In *On Human Rights: The Oxford Amnesty Lectures*, edited by Stephen Shute and Susan Hurley, 111–34. New York: Basic Books, 1993.
Rosen, Michael. *Dignity*. Cambridge, MA: Harvard University Press, 2012.

Rosenmann, Samuel L., ed. *The Public Papers and Addresses of Franklin D. Roosevelt: Vol. IX: War and Aid to Democracies 1940*. New York: Harper & Brothers, 1950.
Roth, Hans Ingwar. *P. C. Chang and the Universal Declaration of Human Rights*. Philadelphia: University of Pennsylvania Press, 2018.
Roth, Martha Tobi. *Law Collections from Mesopotamia and Asia Minor*. Atlanta, GA: Scholars Press, 1997.
Rottleuthner, Hubert. *Foundations of Law*. Dordrecht: Springer, 2005.
Roy, Arundhati. *The God of Small Things*. London: Flamingo, 1997.
Rudolf, Beate. "Menschenrechte und Geschlecht – eine Diskursgeschichte." In *Menschenrechte und Geschlecht*, edited by Ulrike Lembke, 24–50. Baden-Baden: Nomos, 2014.
Russell, Bertrand. *The Practice and Theory of Bolshevism*. London: Allen and Unwin, 1962.
Sajó, András. "Introduction: Universalism with Humility." In *Human Rights with Modesty: The Problem of Universalism*, edited by András Sajó, 1–32. Leiden: Martinus Nijhoff, 2004.
Constitutional Sentiments. New Haven, CT: Yale University Press, 2011.
Sajó, András and Renáta Uitz. *The Constitution of Freedom: An Introduction to Legal Constitutionalism*. Oxford: Oxford University Press, 2017.
Sandel, Michael J. *Justice: What's the Right Thing to Do?* New York: Farrar, Straus and Giroux, 2009.
Sands, Phillippe. "Introduction." In *An International Bill of the Rights of Man*, edited by Hersch Lauterpacht, vii–xxv. Oxford: Oxford University Press, 2013.
Santos, Boaventura de Sousa. *Epistemologies of the South: Justice Against Epistemicide*. Boulder, CO: Paradigm Publishers, 2014.
Sartre, Jean-Paul. *L'existentialisme est un humanisme*. Paris: Nagel, 1946.
Sauer, Hanno. *Moral Judgements as Educated Intuitions*. Cambridge, MA: MIT Press, 2017.
Savigny, Friedrich Carl von. *System des heutigen Römischen Rechts*, Vol. 1. Berlin: Veit, 1840.
Scanlon, Thomas M. *What We Owe to Each Other*. Cambridge, MA: Harvard University Press, 2000.
Being Realistic about Reasons. Oxford: Oxford University Press, 2014.
Schabas, William Anthony, ed. *The Universal Declaration of Human Rights: The Travaux Préparatoires*, Vol. I–III. Cambridge: Cambridge University Press, 2013.
Schiller, Friedrich. *Über die ästhetische Erziehung des Menschen in einer Reihe von Briefen*. Ditzingen: Reclam, 2000.
On the Aesthetic Education of Man. Translated by Keith Tribe. London: Penguin Books, 2016.
Schmidt, Marco and Jessica Sommerville, "Fairness Expectations and Altruistic Sharing in 15-Month-Old Human Infants." *PLoS ONE* 6, no. 10 (2011): e23223.
Schmitt, Carl. *Die Diktatur*. Berlin: Duncker & Humblot, 1928.
Verfassungslehre. Berlin: Duncker & Humblot, 1928.
Politische Theologie. Berlin: Duncker & Humblot, 1934.
Schnall, Simone, Jonathan Haidt, Gerald L. Clore and Alexander H. Jordan. "Disgust as Embodied Moral Judgement." *Personality and Social Psychology Bulletin* 34, no. 8 (2008): 1096–109.
Schopenhauer, Arthur. *Preisschrift über das Fundament der Moral*. Hamburg: Felix Meiner Verlag, 1979.
"Die Welt als Wille und Vorstellung, Vol. 1." In *Sämtliche Werke*, Vol. 1, edited by Wolfgang von Löhneysen. Frankfurt am Main: Suhrkamp, 1986.
"Die Welt als Wille und Vorstellung, Vol. 2." In *Sämtliche Werke*, Vol. 2, edited by Wolfgang von Löhneysen. Frankfurt am Main: Suhrkamp, 1986.

Searle, John R. "How to Derive 'Ought' From 'Is'." *Philosophical Review* 73, no. 1 (1964): 43–58.
Seferis, George. *Complete Poems*. Translated by Edmund Keely and Philip Sherrard. Vancouver: Anvil Press, 1993.
Poiimata. Athens: Ikaros, 1998.
Sellers, Mortimer. "Law, Reason, Emotion." In *Law, Reason, Emotion*, edited by Mortimer Sellers, 11–31. Cambridge: Cambridge University Press, 2007.
Sen, Amartya. "Human Rights and Asian Values." In *Ethics & International Affairs*, edited by Joel H. Rosenthal, 170–93. Washington, DC: Georgetown University Press, 1999.
"Elements of a Theory of Human Rights." *Philosophy and Public Affairs* 32, no. 4 (2004): 315–56.
The Idea of Justice. London: Penguin Books, 2009.
Senn, Marcel. "Rassistische und antisemitische Elemente im Rechtsdenken von Johann Caspar Bluntschli." *Zeitschrift der Savigny-Stiftung für Rechtsgeschichte* 110 (1993): 376–405.
Shafer-Landau, Russ. *Moral Realism: A Defence*. Oxford: Oxford University Press, 2003.
Shakespeare, William. *The Merchant of Venice. The Arden Shakespeare*. Edited by John Drakakis. London: Bloomsbury, 2010.
Sidgwick, Henry. *The Methods of Ethics*, reprint of the 7th edition, 1907. Indianapolis, IN: Hackett, 1981.
Siedentop, Larry. *Inventing the Individual: The Origins of Western Liberalism*. Cambridge, MA: Harvard University Press, 2017.
Sikkink, Kathryn. *Evidence for Hope: Making Human Rights Work in the 21st Century*. Princeton, NJ: Princeton University Press, 2017.
Silk, Joan, Sarah Brosnan, Jennifer Vonk, et al. "Chimpanzees Are Indifferent to the Welfare of Unrelated Group Members." *Nature* 437, no. 7063 (2005): 1357–9.
Simmons, Beth. *Mobilizing for Human Rights: International Law in Domestic Politics*. Cambridge: Cambridge University Press, 2009.
Simpson, Alfred William Brian. *Human Rights and the End of Empire: Britain and the Genesis of the European Convention*. Oxford: Oxford University Press, 2001.
Singer, Peter. "Ethics and Intuitions." *The Journal of Ethics* 9, no. 3/4 (2005): 331–52.
Skard, Torild. "Getting Our History Right: How Were the Equal Rights of Women and Men Included in the Charter of the United Nations?" *Forum for Developmental Studies* 35, no. 1 (2008): 37–60.
Smetana, Judith G. and Judith L. Braeges. "The Development of Toddlers' Moral and Conventional Judgement." *Merril-Palmer Quarterly* 36, no. 3 (1990): 329–46.
Smith, Adam. *The Theory of Moral Sentiments*. New York: Prometheus Books, 2000.
Smith, Andrew B. "The Origins of Pastoralism in Namibia." In *People, Cattle and Land: Transformations of a Pastoral Society in Southwestern Africa*, edited by Michael Bollig and Jan-Bart Gewald, 55–76. Cologne: Rüdiger Köppe Verlag, 2000.
Snyder, Timothy. *Bloodlands*. New York: Basic Books, 2010.
Sophocles. "Antigone." In *Antigone, The Women of Trachis, Philoctetes, Oedipus at Colonus*, edited and translated by Hugh Llyod-Jones, 1–127. Loeb Classical Library 21. Cambridge, MA: Harvard University Press, 1994.
Stich, Stephen, John Doris and Erica Roedder. "Altruism." In *The Moral Psychology Handbook*, edited by John Doris, 147–205. Oxford: Oxford University Press, 2010.
Suárez, Francisco. *Defensio fidei catholica et apostolica, Pars Prima*. Naples: Ex Typis Fibrenianis, 1872.
De Legibus ac deo legislatore, Liber III, Teil 1, edited and translated by Oliver Bach, Norbert Brieskorn and Gideon Stiening. Stuttgart and Bad Cannstatt: Frommann-Holzboog, 2014.

De Legibus ac deo legislatore, Liber II, edited and translated by Oliver Bach, Norbert Brieskorn and Gideon Stiening. Stuttgart and Bad Cannstatt: Frommann-Holzboog, 2016.

Sunstein, Cass R. "Moral Heuristics." *Behavioural and Brain Sciences* 28, no. 4 (2005): 531–73.

A Constitution of Many Minds: Why the Founding Document Doesn't Mean What It Meant before. Princeton, NJ: Princeton University Press, 2009.

Számado, Szabolcs and Eörs Szathmáry. "Selective Scenarios for the Emergence of Natural Language." *Trends in Ecology & Evolution* 21, no. 10 (2006): 555–61.

Tasioulas, John. "Human Dignity and the Foundations of Human Rights." In *Understanding Human Dignity*, edited by Christopher McCrudden, 291–312. Oxford: Oxford University Press, 2013.

"Justice, Equality, and Rights." In *The Oxford Handbook of the History of Ethics*, edited by Roger Crisp, 768–92. Oxford: Oxford University Press, 2013.

"On the Foundations of Human Rights." In *Philosophical Foundations of Human Rights*, edited by Rowan Cruft, S. Matthew Liao and Massimo Renzo, 45–70. Oxford: Oxford University Press, 2015.

"Saving Human Rights from Human Rights Law." *Vanderbilt Journal of Transnational Law* 52, no. 5 (2019): 1167–1207.

Tattersall, Ian. *Masters of the Planet: The Search for Our Human Origins*. New York: St. Martin's Press, 2013.

"The Minimalist Program and the Origin of Language: A View from Paleoanthropology." *Frontiers in Psychology* 10, no. 677 (2019): 1–5.

Taylor Mill, Harriet. "Enfranchisement of Women." In *The Complete Works of Harriet Taylor Mill*, edited by Jo Ellen Jacobs and Paula Harms Payne, 27–73. Bloomington, IN and Indianapolis, IN: Indiana University Press, 1998.

Thaler, Richard H. and Cass R. Sunstein, *Nudge*. London: Penguin Books, 2008.

Thomasius, Christian. *Fundamenta juris naturae et gentium*. Halle: Salfeld, 1718.

Thomson, Judith Jarvis. "The Trolley Problem." *Yale Law Journal* 94 (1985): 1395–415.

"Killing, Letting Die, and the Trolley Problem," *The Monist* 59, no. 2 (1976): 204–17.

The Realm of Rights. Cambridge, MA: Harvard University Press, 1990.

Thucydides. *History of the Peloponnesian War, Vol. I: Books 1–2*. Translated by Charles Forster Smith. Loeb Classical Library 108. Cambridge, MA: Harvard University Press, 1928.

History of the Peloponnesian War, Vol. II: Books 3–4. Translated by Charles Forster Smith. Loeb Classical Library 109. Cambridge, MA: Harvard University Press, 1930.

History of the Peloponnesian War, Vol. III: Books 5–6. Translated by Charles Forster Smith. Loeb Classical Library 110. Cambridge, MA: Harvard University Press, 1931.

History of the Peloponnesian War, Vol. IV: Books 7–8. Translated by Charles Forster Smith. Loeb Classical Library 169. Cambridge, MA: Harvard University Press, 1935.

Tierney, Brian. *The Idea of Natural Rights*. Grand Rapids, MI: Wm. B. Eerdmans Publishing Co., 1997.

Todorov, Tzvetan. *Face à l'Extrême*. Paris: Seuil, 1991.

Tomasello, Michael. *A Natural History of Human Morality*. Cambridge, MA: Harvard University Press, 2016.

Becoming Human: A Theory of Ontogeny. Cambridge, MA: Harvard University Press, 2021.

Torres, Nelson Maldonado. "On the Coloniality of Human Rights." In *The Pluriverse of Human Rights: The Diversity of Struggles for Dignity*, edited by Boaventura de Sousa Santos and Bruno Sena Martins. London and New York: Routledge, 2021.

Tuck, Richard. *The Rights of War and Peace*. Oxford: Clarendon Press, 1999.

Natural Rights Theories. Cambridge: Cambridge University Press, 2002.

Turchin, Peter. *Ultrasociety: How 10,000 Years of War Made Humans the Greatest Cooperators on Earth*. Chaplin, CT: Beresta Books, 2015.

Tyler, Tom, Robert Boeckmann, Heather Smith and Yuen Huo. *Social Justice in a Diverse Society*. New York: Routledge, 1997.

Vattel, Emer de. *Le droit des gens ou Principes de la loi naturelle appliqués à la conduite et aux affaires des nations et des souverains. Tome 1*. London: s.n., 1758.

Villey, Michel. "Suum Jus Cuique Tribuens." In *Studi in onore di Pietro de Francisi*, Vol. 2, 361–71. Milan: Giuffrè, 1956.

Vitoria, Francisco de. "On Law: Lectures on St. Thomas Aquinas." In *Vitoria: Political Writings*, edited by Anthony Pagden and Jeremy Lawrence, 153–204. Cambridge: Cambridge University Press, 1991.

Political Writings, edited by Anthony Pagden and Jeremy Lawrence. Cambridge: Cambridge University Press, 1991.

"De Indis." In *Vorlesungen (Relectiones) Vol. II: Völkerrecht, Politik, Kirche*, edited by Ulrich Horst, Heinz-Gerhard Justenhoven and Joachim Stüben, 370–541. Stuttgart: Kohlhammer, 1997.

De Iustitia: Über die Gerechtigkeit, Teil 2, edited by Joachim Stüben. Stuttgart and Bad Cannstatt: Frommann-Holzboog, 2017.

Vlastos, Gregory. "Isonomia." *The American Journal of Philology* 74, no. 4 (1953): 337–66.

"Justice and Happiness in the Republic." In *Platonic Studies*, 111–39. Princeton, NJ: Princeton University Press, 1981.

Socrates: Ironist and Moral Philosopher. Cambridge: Cambridge University Press, 1991.

"The Rights of Persons in Plato's Conception of the Foundation of Justice." In *Studies in Greek Philosophy, Vol. 2: Socrates, Plato, and Their Tradition*, edited by Daniel W. Graham, 104–25. Princeton, NJ: Princeton University Press, 1995.

"The Theory of Social Justice in the Polis in Plato's Republic." In *Studies in Greek Philosophy, Vol. 2: Socrates, Plato, and Their Tradition*, edited by Daniel W. Graham, 69–103. Princeton, NJ: Princeton University Press, 1996.

Vondervoort, Julia W. van de and J. Kiley Hamlin. "Evidence for Intuitive Morality: Preverbal Infants Make Sociomoral Evaluations." *Child Development Perspectives* 10, no. 3 (2016): 143–8.

Vul, Edward, Christine Harris, Piotr Winkielman and Harold Pashler. "Puzzling High Correlations in fMRI Studies of Emotion, Personality, and Social Cognition." *Perspectives on Psychological Science* 4, no. 3 (2009): 274–90.

Waldron, Jeremy. *Dignity, Ranks, and Rights*. Oxford: Oxford University Press, 2012.

"Is Human Dignity the Foundation of Human Rights?" NYU School of Law, Public Law & Legal Theory Research Paper Series, Working Paper No. 12-73 (2013).

"It's All for Your Own Good." *The New York Review of Books* no. 15 (2014). Accessed September 28, 2022. www.nybooks.com/articles/2014/10/09/cass-sunstein-its-all-your-own-good/

One Another's Equals: The Basis of Human Equality. Cambridge, MA: Harvard University Press, 2017.

Waluchow, Wilfrid J. *Inclusive Legal Positivism*. Oxford: Clarendon Press, 1994.

Walzer, Michael. *Spheres of Justice*. New York: Basic Books, 1983.

Warneken, Felix and Michael Tomasello. "Altruistic Helping in Human Infants and Young Chimpanzees," *Science* 311, no. 5765 (2006): 1301–3.

"Helping and Cooperation at 14 Months of Age." *Infancy* 11, no. 3 (2007): 271–94.

Weber, Max. "Wirtschaft und Gesellschaft – Herrschaft." *In Max Weber Gesamtausgabe* Vol. I/22-4, edited by Edith Hanke and Thomas Kroll. Tübingen: Mohr Siebeck, 2005.

Weinar, Leif. "The Nature of Rights." *Philosophy & Public Affairs* 33, no. 3 (2005): 223–52.

Weitz, Eric. A *Century of Genocide*. Princeton, NJ: Princeton University Press, 2003.
Wells, Herbert George. "War Aims: The Rights of Man." *The Times*, October 25, 1939. The Times Digital Archive. Accessed September 28, 2022. link.gale.com/apps/doc/CS100873561/GDCS?u=unizur&sid=book mark-GDCS&xid=31252630.
The Rights of Man; or, What Are We Fighting for? Harmondsworth: Penguin Books, 1940.
Welzel, Hans. "Zum Notstandsproblem." *Zeitschrift für die gesamte Strafrechtswissenschaft* 63 (1951): 47–56.
Whorf, Benjamin Lee. *Language, Thought and Reality: Selected Writings of Benjamin Lee Whorf*. Cambridge: Technology Press of Massachusetts Institute of Technology, 1956.
Williams, Bernhard. "The Truth in Relativism." In *Moral Luck*, 132–43. Cambridge: Cambridge University Press, 1982.
"Truth in Ethics." *Ratio* 8, no. 3 (1995): 227–42.
Shame and Necessity, 2nd edition. Berkeley, University of California Press, 2008.
Williams, Roger. "The Bloudy Tenent of Persecution." In *The Complete Writings of Roger Williams*, Vol. 3, edited by Samuel L. Caldwell. Paris, AR: The Baptist Standard Bearer, 2005.
Wilson, Edward. *Sociobiology: The New Synthesis*. Cambridge, MA: Harvard University Press, 1975.
Windscheid, Bernhard. *Lehrbuch des Pandektenrechts*, Vol. 1. Aalen: Scientia Verlag, 1906.
Wingert, Lutz. *Gemeinsinn und Moral*. Frankfurt am Main: Suhrkamp, 1993.
"Türöffner zu geschlossenen Gesellschaften: Bemerkungen zum Begriff der Menschenrechte." In *Ethik, Politik, Kulturen im Globalisierungsprozess: Eine interdisziplinäre Zusammenführung*, edited by Ralf Elm, 392–407. Bochum: Projektverlag, 2003.
Wittgenstein, Ludwig. "Philosophische Untersuchungen." In *Werkausgabe Vol. 1: Tractatus logico-philosophicus, Tagebücher 1914–1916, Philosophische Untersuchungen*, 225–579. Frankfurt am Main: Suhrkamp, 1984.
Zettel. Berkeley and Los Angeles: University of California Press, 2007.
Wolff, Christian. *Institutiones Naturae et Gentium*. Halae Magdeburgicae: Renger, 1750.
The Law of Nations Treated according to the Scientific Method. Translated by Joseph H. Drake. Revised by Thomas Ahnert. Carmel, IN: Liberty Fund, 2017.
Wollstonecraft, Mary. A *Vindication of the Rights of Woman*. London: Penguin Books, 1983.
Woodward, Amanda L. "Infants Selectively Encode the Goal of an Actor's Reach," *Cognition* 69, no. 1 (1998): 1–34.
Xu, Xing, Kebai Wang, Ke Zhang, et al. "A Gigantic Feathered Dinosaur from the Lower Cretaceous of China." *Nature* 484 (2012): 92–5.
Yang, Charles, Stephen Crain, Robert C. Berwick, Noam Chomsky and Johan J. Bolhuis. "The Growth of Language: Universal Grammar, Experience, and Principles of Computation." *Neuroscience and Biobehavioral Reviews* 81, no. B (2017): 103–19.
Zakaria, Fareed. "Culture Is Destiny. A Conversation with Lee Kuan Yew." *Foreign Affairs* 73, no. 2 (1994): 109–26.
Zamir, Eyal. *Law, Psychology and Morality: The Role of Loss Aversion*. Oxford: Oxford University Press, 2015.
Zamir, Eyal and Barak Medina. *Law, Economics and Morality*. Oxford: Oxford University Press, 2010.
Zamir, Eyal and Doron Teichman. *Behavioral Law and Economics*. Oxford: Oxford University Press, 2018.

Index

For EU product safety concerns, contact us at Calle de José Abascal, 56–1°, 28003 Madrid, Spain or eugpsr@cambridge.org.

www.ingramcontent.com/pod-product-compliance
Lightning Source LLC
LaVergne TN
LVHW011655200926
848484LV00004B/951
9781107184220